LIONEL H. PRIES

ARCHITECT, ARTIST, EDUCATOR

LIONEL H. PRIES, ARCHITECT, ARTIST, EDUCATOR

From

Arts and Crafts

to

Modern Architecture

JEFFREY KARL OCHSNER

UNIVERSITY OF WASHINGTON PRESS *Seattle and London*

Publication of *Lionel H. Pries, Architect, Artist, Educator* was made possible in part by a grant from the Graham Foundation for Advanced Study in the Visual Arts.

Additional support was provided by the Johnston-Hastings Endowment of the College of Architecture & Urban Planning and the Architecture Publications Fund, University of Washington; the Max and Helen Gurvich Advised Fund at The Seattle Foundation; and by Nanhee and William Hahn, Alan Liddle, Jon A. Oien, Victoria Reed, and other individuals. A full list of donors can be found on page 391.

© 2007 by the University of Washington Press
Designed by Veronica Seyd
Printed in Singapore
12 11 10 09 08 07   5 4 3 2 1

University of Washington Press
P.O. Box 50096, Seattle, WA 98145
www.washington.edu/uwpress

Library of Congress Cataloging-in-Publication Data
Ochsner, Jeffrey Karl.
Lionel H. Pries, architect, artist, educator : from arts and crafts to modern architecture / Jeffrey Karl Ochsner. — 1st ed.
 p. cm.
 Includes bibliographical references and index.
 ISBN-13: 978-0-295-98698-2 (hardback : alk. paper)
 ISBN-10: 0-295-98698-0 (hardback : alk. paper)
1. Pries, Lionel H., 1897–1968. 2. Architects United States—Biography. 3. Artists—United States—Biography. 4. Gay men—United States—Biography. 5. College teachers— United States—Biography. 6. University of Washington—Faculty—Biography. 7. Architecture—United States—20th century. I. Title.
NA737.P687O28 2007
720.92—dc22   2007008276
[B]

The paper used in this publication meets the minimum requirements of American National Standard for Information Sciences—Permanence of Paper for Printed Library Materials, ANSI Z39.48-1984.

Frontispiece: Lionel Henry ("Spike") Pries, 1952. Photo by Dorothy Conway. Pries collection, Special Collections Division, University of Washington Libraries. UW2219.

In memory of Gordon B. Varey
(1931–1994), who introduced me
to the importance of Lionel Pries

CONTENTS

Lionel Pries at
Legend Room,
ca. 1951. Photo
courtesy of DLR
Group.

PREFACE

In mid-May 1958, University of Washington architecture graduates from all over the country returned to campus to participate in the three-day inauguration of the newly created College of Architecture and Urban Planning. Founded in 1914, the Washington architecture department had grown from two faculty members to more than twenty, and from a handful of students to more than 250. In the 1940s, the school had expanded its offerings to include planning, and the new college would shortly add landscape architecture as well. The architecture program had produced a body of distinguished graduates, many of them successful architects who submitted work for display; those who could afford the time came to Seattle to join in the celebration. At the banquet the evening of 16 May, Arthur Herrman, the new dean of the college, introduced the faculty members. When he came to Professor Lionel Pries, the audience rose as one and the applause and cheers seemed to go on forever. For a few minutes all shared their respect and gratitude with the extraordinary teacher who had given so much to them and to the school.

Six months later, Lionel Pries was unemployed. For reasons never stated, the university administration forced Pries to resign from the faculty. After three decades of distinguished service—including almost two decades at the center of the architecture school—Pries left the campus on a Friday evening at the end of October, never to return. For the next forty years, his departure remained a mystery.

These two events, a few months apart, suggest the complexity of Pries's life and personality. Former students were often surprised to discover how little they actually knew of the man. In 1978 Kenneth Anderson, a UW graduate of 1934, wrote to Victor Steinbrueck, "As you know he [Pries] was the greatest single influence on my life—my appreciation knows no limit," then added, "it comes as a shock to me that I know so little about this man's antecedents as I do—and it wasn't until your letter brought me up short that I realized my lack of information about him."[1]

Lionel Pries died in April 1968, nearly ten years after he left the university. Seattle newspapers published obituaries, but there was no mention of Pries in University of Washington publications. In fact, it was close to twenty years after Pries stopped teaching and ten years after his death before his reputation began to grow beyond his clients, colleagues, friends and former students. In 1978, Victor Steinbrueck contacted graduates and colleagues to gather materials and recollections to help prepare a lecture about Pries for the UW Alumni Association.[2] Most of the letters Steinbrueck received focused on Pries's career as a teacher, and secondarily on his architectural practice.[3] The lecture sparked new interest in Pries, and in 1981 the College of Architecture and Urban Planning established the Lionel Pries Endowed Fund to honor Pries through an annual lecture. The same year, Grant Hildebrand, then serving as architecture critic for the *Seattle Times,* wrote a column addressing Pries's influence on his students and, through them, his influence on design in the Pacific Northwest.[4] Hildebrand spoke of his appreciation of the "rich quality" of Seattle's small scale architecture and argued that this was likely the result of Pries's teaching. In 1984, architecture student Andrew (Drew) Rocker published an essay on Pries in the regional design journal *Arcade,* and two years later the *Times* Sunday magazine featured Pries's home.[5] About the same time, students in the College of Architecture and Urban Planning established the "Lionel Pries Teaching Award," a student-selected award to recognize teaching excellence.[6] When the College established a "Roll of Honor" in 1987–88, "Pries" was one of the first eight names inscribed on the frieze in the Architecture Hall Auditorium.[7] In the early 1990s, Drew Rocker wrote an essay on Pries for *Shaping Seattle Architecture: A Historical Guide to the Architects.*[8] By the mid-1990s, Pries's status as a legendary teacher was well established, at least in the Northwest, but available information about his life and career remained surprisingly limited.[9]

I have spent more than a dozen years pursuing the elusive Lionel Pries, trying to piece together the puzzle he presents. This book is the result. It tells the story of Pries, not just as an educator but also as a practicing architect in California and Seattle; an exhibiting artist and one-time director of Seattle's Art Institute; a collector of important pre-Columbian, Native American, and Asian artifacts; and a member of the West Coast gay cultural community.

I became interested in Pries in the early 1990s when I was editing essays for *Shaping Seattle Architecture.* I viewed the collection of Pries materials held at the University of Washington Libraries and was impressed by the beautiful pencil and watercolor renderings. A series of blueline prints of measured drawings of Spanish Colonial buildings in Mexico especially piqued my curiosity. The draw-

ings were by the Mexican architect Juan O'Gorman, who is today studied for his contributions to the development of Modern architecture and painting in Mexico. Each print bore his original ink signature. Exploring this link between Pries and O'Gorman, I learned that Pries had visited Mexico regularly from the 1920s to the 1940s. Looking at the images of Pries buildings, particularly the Willcox residence on Hood Canal and Pries's own house in Seattle, I realized that Pries's interaction with avant-garde artists, architects, and collectors in Mexico—not just O'Gorman but also William Spratling, Fred Davis, Diego Rivera, Miguel Covarrubias, and others—had deeply influenced his approach to design. It seemed that here was a hidden story, a possible key to Pries's design sensibility and an unrecognized influence within the development of regional architecture in the Northwest.

Once I began my research, I learned of other experiences that had shaped Lionel Pries—the Asian antiquities he saw at the Gump's store where his father worked in San Francisco, the Arts and Crafts ethos that was so powerful in the Bay Area, the academic eclecticism taught at Berkeley and Penn, as well as the personalities of his teachers John Galen Howard and Paul Cret. Along with his Mexican sojourns, these early experiences contributed to Pries's personal sensibility as described by Steinbrueck: "His concept of architectural design has a special romantic quality which combined a love of the best of the past with the ability to culturally and technically relate to the present."[10]

But uncovering Pries's life, career, ideas, and influence presented unexpected difficulties. It is challenging to trace precisely the thinking of any architectural educator. The "structures" an educator builds are most often found in the minds of his or her students. We depend on the recollections of architecture graduates, now sixty, seventy, eighty or even ninety years old. But memories may fade, and while the emotional power Pries exuded comes through in conversations with graduates, details are not always available. Part of education is always a mystery: a good teacher usually seeks to draw his students out and will not always reveal the thinking behind his methods. An architectural instructor typically does not expect his students to design a project as he would do it himself. A teacher's design thinking may develop for a long time before he modifies his classroom approach. In addition, an architecture teacher does not teach alone. Pries was always part of a larger faculty within a shared curriculum. Students' projects and graduates' design work cannot be traced to the influence of any single individual. Fortunately, throughout his life, even after he began teaching full time, Pries continued to practice as an architect. Before 1928 and after 1932, his practice was as a sole proprietor, so his buildings serve as an indicator of emerging directions in his thinking, and through his buildings the evolution of his ideas can be discerned.

Pries was a designer and an artist, not a keeper of records. His European sojourn in 1922–23 is revealing. A friend gave him a diary in which to record his travels. Pries made his first entry the day he left New York but made only ten more entries over the next thirteen months, and some of these are quite brief. Instead, Pries recorded his impressions by drawing and painting—more than ninety drawings and watercolors from that trip make it possible to trace his route and identify what he found of most interest. Even this account is incomplete; if Pries did a drawing or a watercolor that did not meet his high standards, he destroyed it.

The most complete record of Pries's design teaching is found in the archives of the Department of Architecture at the University of Washington. There one can see a remarkable collection of student design work (though, over the years, the school retained only a small fraction of student projects). Many of the final studio projects from the 1920s onward reflect Pries's teaching. The quality of the presentations is outstanding, but it is from the changing subjects of the projects, the varying approaches to delineation, and the evolving character of the designs that we can infer changes in teaching and the influence of the larger world.

The best records of Pries's design thinking are his architectural projects. Here we can discover his evolution as a designer and his personal response to modernism. But, Pries never compiled a complete list of all the buildings he designed; there are no surviving financial records of any kind. (The catalogue of buildings included here is no doubt incomplete.) For his career as an artist we depend primarily on his paintings, drawings, prints, and similar works. There are few written materials and only a few surviving letters, and the locations of many art works remain unknown.

The lack of written records reflects Pries's priorities and may also reflect his personal circumstances

and the compartmentalization of his life. In the university setting, Pries was a deeply closeted gay man in a period when homosexuality was neither accepted nor understood. He masked this part of his life so well that some of his students of the 1930s, upon learning of his homosexuality in the 1990s, refused to believe it. Yet, Pries's homosexuality was one of the sources of his vibrant creativity and many friendships, and it was also central to his forced resignation from the university in 1958. He had given three decades of his life to the school but was forced out four years short of retirement. Although he had planned to leave his books, drawings, and collections to the university, he subsequently chose not to do so. Many of these materials were dispersed during the last years of his life, and, while others were given to the university in the 1990s by his heir, Robert Winskill, the full collection will never be reassembled.

To capture the breadth of Pries's life and achievements, I have depended on a wide range of source materials but, more important, I have been helped by Pries's friends, colleagues, and students. Among my many informants two stand out: Keith R. Kolb and Robert W. Winskill.

Keith Kolb was a student in the Department of Architecture from 1940 to 1943 and 1946 to 1947; he was Pries's colleague as a faculty member after 1952; and he stayed in contact with Pries after 1958. Throughout his career, Kolb kept detailed records and gathered information on the history of the UW school of architecture. We initially discussed my Pries research in 1994, I taped a lengthy interview with him in 1995, and we have remained in regular contact since that time. Kolb answered questions, shared his notes and other records, reviewed draft texts, and allowed me to borrow freely from his collection of materials relating to Pries and the history of the school.

Equally important was Robert W. Winskill, who first met Pries in 1948–49 and remained his close friend through the last two decades of Pries's life. Winskill was Pries's heir and after Pries's death he saved most of Pries's collections, moving them to his own Pries-designed house in Mill Valley, California. In 1994, I visited Winskill, saw the collections, and taped a lengthy interview. Over the next three years he generously donated to the University of Washington most of Pries's drawings, photographs, books and other materials, and in subsequent years he continued to donate materials. He also gave some materials directly to me with the understanding that I would add them to the UW collections once this book was complete. Like Kolb, Winskill regularly responded to questions, allowed me to copy letters and other personal materials, and reviewed draft texts. He also allowed me to borrow Pries artworks that he had retained. Both Kolb and Winskill gave substantial time to this project and provided many insights to Pries's complex personality. Without their contributions it would have been impossible to write this book.

Others who graciously agreed to be interviewed were Sue Harris Alden, Fred Bassetti, Kelly Foss, Seth M. Fulcher, George A. Graham, Douglas Haner, George W. Hazen, L. Jane Hastings, James Klontz, Palmer D. Koon, Alan Liddle, Wendell Lovett, Gerald Pomeroy, John Rohrer, Duane Shipman, Daniel Streissguth, William Svensson, Roland Terry, and T. C. Warren. Anne Gould Hauberg, Julie Vance Ivarsson, W. Richard Frahm, Robert Hugh Ross, and Joseph Vance participated in more informal conversations. Others who provided recollections or information through letters and e-mail included Ronald R. Burke, Robert J. Burman, Sidney Cohn, Jack M. Crabs, Edward Duthweiler, Ross Edman, Theodore N. Foss, Donald L. Johnson, Elaine S. Jones, Bryant Milliman, Robert Mosher, Jon Anders Oien, Bjarne Olsen, Gerhard Olving, William Paddock, Robert Patton, Don Paulson, Paul W. Pelland, William A. Phipps, Richard M. Proctor, William G. (Gary) Jr., and Victoria Reed, Robert Shomler, William Trogdon, and Barry Upson.

I also made extensive use of the written recollections of Pries gathered in 1978 by Victor Steinbrueck (made available to me by Keith Kolb) from Ken Anderson, Fred Bassetti, Flora Allen Casey, Robert Dietz, Perry Johanson, Wendell Lovett, Keith Kolb, Lloyd Lovegren, Ivan Meyer, Robert Ross, Charles Schiff, Roland Terry, Gerald Williams, George ("Pete") Wimberly, Robert Winskill, and Minoru Yamasaki. In addition, Jon Anders Oien provided pages from his father's memoirs. Janet Wimberly and Scott Cheever allowed me access to Pete Wimberly's letters from Mexico. William Matchett provided access to Anne Gayler's autobiographical manuscript. Alan Liddle provided a copy of John Davis Hatch's typescript of recollections of the Art Institute of Seattle. William G. Reed, Jr., provided pages from his father's memoirs. Seth Fulcher allowed me the use of his unpublished

novel based on his experiences in architecture school. For the early history of the UW Department of Architecture, I depended on Norman J. Johnston's account, *The College of Architecture and Urban Planning, Seventy-five Years at the University of Washington: A Personal View.*

Property owners who gave me access to buildings included Tucker and Melody Barksdale, Susan Barnes, H. Lynn and Nanette Cadwell, Sonya and Thomas Campion, Blake Clark, James L. Eland, William and Sandra Evenson, John ("Jack") Fay, Jeffrey and Sally Fiorini, Rochelle and Henry Ford, Max and Helen Gurvich, Craig and Marion Hopkins, Charles and Laurie Lyford, Cecilia and Phillip Hughes, Stephen Jr. and Judee Lea, William and Judy Matchett, Scott and Kathryn Missall, William and Sally Neukom, Carol E. and K. Carolyn Ramamurti, Hope and Richard Stroble, Susan Thorbrogger and Philip Hardin, Melinda Tyrell, Joseph Vance, Ed and Ann Zamojski, and Puget Sound Association DKE. Others who provided information or assistance relative to individual properties included Sumpter Carmichael, Richard Hobbs, Jeanette Lea, Darle Maveety, Anne G. Miller, and Susan Morris.

Ink drawings of plans of Pries's houses were drawn by University of Washington student Byung Keun Choi through the support of the Department of Architecture as approved by Department Chair Vikramaditya Prakash. (In many cases these drawings were based on old sets of prints retained by the current owners of the properties.)

David Martin, partner in the Seattle gallery Martin-Zambito Fine Art, and an authority on the history of art in Seattle, assisted in the effort to find missing Pries artworks. He gave generously of his time in evaluating and interpreting Pries's paintings and discussing the Northwest art community of the 1920s and 1930s. William Zimmerman also gave advice and assistance in regard to Pries watercolors. Digital restoration of severely faded, discolored and damaged watercolors was carried out Stephen Rock of Rock's Studio, Seattle.

In tracing Pries's architectural practice in California, I received indefatigable assistance from Gary Goss. The completeness of my discussion of Pries's California career is due in large part to his knowledge of architectural works in the Bay Area.

Several individuals provided assistance in understanding the Mexican context for Pries's travels.

James Oles aided my understanding of the interaction between American and Mexican artists and intellectuals in the 1920s and 1930s and provided other assistance with regard to recent scholarship. Edward R. Burian offered many insights into architecture in Mexico, especially with regard to the career of Juan O'Gorman. He also pointed to new scholarship addressing architecture and art in Mexico from the 1920s to the 1950s. Penny C. Morrill gave information about William Spratling and Fred Davis. Sergio Palleroni helped identify locations in Mexico and explained aspects of the evolution of Mexican arts and culture. Keith Eggener assisted with the history of architecture in Mexico. W. Jackson Rushing provided information regarding René d'Harnoncourt and exhibition of Native American art in the 1930s and 1940s. Thomas Goddard provided images of Spratling silver.

In regard to the radical shift in architectural education from the 1930s to the 1950s, I benefited especially from discussions with Anthony Alofsin, whose publications have described the development of the program at Harvard that served as a model for American architectural pedagogy in the 1940s and 1950s.

Gary L. Atkins, author of a pioneering history of Seattle's gay community, introduced me to the wide range of scholarly work in gay and lesbian studies and helped me to understand the historical importance of male-male friendships and mentor-mentee relationships.

Richard Mellott, former curator at the San Francisco Asian Art Museum, provided information and insights regarding Pries's collections.

The University of Washington Libraries, Special Collections Division, supported my research in innumerable ways, most importantly by allowing access to the entire collection of Pries materials, including items not yet catalogued. At various times specific assistance was received from Carla Rickerson, Sandra Kroupa, Kris Kinsey, Nicolette Bromberg, John Bolcer, Gary Lundell, Karyl Winn, and Gary Menges.

Additional Seattle research assistance was received from: David Goldberg, DLR Group (Shannon Soady); NBBJ (William J. Bain, Jr., Rick Buckley, Midge Hunnicutt); Seattle Art Museum (Yukiko Shirahara, Jill Walek, Sarah Berman, Patricia Junker, Paul Macapia); Seattle Public Library (Jodee Fenton); State of Washington Archives, Puget Sound Regional Branch (Phil Stairs, Greg Lange).

Additional Bay Area research assistance was received from: Michael Corbett, Abby Bridge, Inge Horton, and Tim Kelly. Los Angeles research assistance was received from Anna Smorodinsky. Other assistance in California came from University of California, Berkeley, College of Environmental Design Archives (Waverly Lowell and Carrie McDade) and Bancroft Library (William Roberts); University of California, Santa Barbara, University Art Museum (Kurt Helfrich) and Special Collections Department, Davidson Library; Berkeley Architectural Heritage Association (Anthony Bruce); California Academy of Sciences (Russell Hartman); California Historical Society, North Baker Research Library; Gump's (James K. Kjorvestad); Lick-Wilmerding High School (Lissa Crider); Mills College Art Museum (Stephen Jost); Oakland Public Library, Oakland History Room; San Francisco Public Library, San Francisco History Center (Susan Goldstein, Thomas Carey, Tami Suzuki); Santa Barbara Historical Museum, Gledhill Library (Michael Redmon); Telegraph Hill Neighborhood Association (Denise McCarthy).

Assistance relative to Pries's Philadelphia career was received from Adam E. Levine and Sandra Tatman, and from William Whitaker (University of Pennsylvania Architectural Archives). Ann P. Rowe (The Textile Museum, Washington, D.C.); Melissa Smith (Tulane University Libraries, Special Collections); Heather Wagner (Hoover Institution Archives, Stanford University); Dann Sears (Aberdeen [Washington] Museum); Museum of Modern Art, New York; Thunderbird Foundation for the Arts, Salt Lake City; and Faith Lutheran Church, Bellingham provided additional assistance.

Nancy Hines and Christina Burtner at University of Washington Photography scanned items from the Pries collections and assisted with photography of other artworks. John Stamets gave advice relative to photographing Pries buildings. Grant Hildebrand and Tori Williamson photographed selected buildings. Kelly R. Schiff in Alabama and Ivey Imaging in Seattle provided photographic assistance. Michael McFaul, John Galt Productions, Seattle, helped significantly in achieving accurate color rendition of Pries paintings.

Others who helped in various ways include Patricia Aitken, Lincoln Bartley, T. William Booth,

Michael Boyle, Christine Carr, Scott Cheever, Gail Cleere, Sheryl Conkelton, Jerry Finrow, Lyn Firkins, Lachlan Pries Foss, Seth Kelly Fulcher, David Gebhard, Marta Gutman, Art and Rita Hupy, Larry Johnson, Norman J. Johnston, Georgia Jones, Victoria Kastner, Martha Kingsbury, Toddi Morneau, Charles R. Pearson, Vikramaditya Prakash, Drew Rocker, Janet Lynn Roseman, Heather Seneff, Jeffrey Tilman, Kaz Tsuruta, Gordon Varey, Kelly Walker, Carolyn Wennblom, Ed Winskill, Monica Wooten, and Fikret Yegul.

While the research was under way, I presented papers at conferences and wrote articles that appeared in *Column 5* (journal of the University of Washington Department of Architecture) and in *Pacific Northwest Quarterly*. Those papers and articles and the parts of this book that grew from them benefited from the input of session chairs, editors, and reviewers including Gail Fenske, Nezar AlSayyad, Marie Frank, Leslie Humm Cormier, Jennifer Dee, and Kim McKaig, as well as University of Washington architecture students Charles Choo, Christina Eichbaum Merkelbach, Michael Garceau, and Justin Kliewer.

I also benefited from those individuals who read my text in manuscript form. Edward R. Burian, Seth M. Fulcher, David Martin, John Anders Oien, John Rohrer, Robert H. Ross, and William Svensson reviewed selected chapters. Dennis Andersen, Gary Atkins, Marie Frank, Alan Liddle, and David Rash commented on the complete text in draft form. Grant Hildebrand read an early draft and did a mark-up of several chapters, providing many suggestions for improvements. Keith Kolb and Robert Winskill reviewed and commented on multiple drafts.

Early in my research I received a grant from the Graduate School Research Fund of the University of Washington that supported initial research activities, including my first trip to California in pursuit of Pries.

I am especially grateful to those whose generous financial support helped make this publication possible: N. Sue Alden, Dennis Andersen, Fred Bassetti, Ronald R. Burke, Ronald D. Childers and Richard M. Proctor, Edward Duthweiler, the C. R. Foss Living Trust, Nanhee and Bill Hahn, Norman Johnston and Jane Hastings, Keith R. Kolb, Alan Liddle, Bryant Milliman, Margaret Morrison, Robert Mosher, Jon A. Oien, Victoria Reed, and Barry and Louise Upson.

Significant funding for this publication also came in the form of grants from the following sources: the Graham Foundation for Advanced Studies in the Fine Arts, the Max and Helen Gurvich Advised Fund at the Seattle Foundation, the University of Washington Architecture Publications Fund, and the Johnston-Hastings Endowment of the College of Architecture and Urban Planning, University of Washington.

The book exists in its present form because of the encouragement and expertise of many individuals at the University of Washington Press.

During the past decade of research and writing I several times thought I had fully encompassed Pries's achievements, only to have new evidence indicate that there were aspects I had missed. I believe that I have now addressed the important facets of Pries's life and career, although I recognize that there may be sides to Pries that have not yet been uncovered. Any errors or omissions of fact or interpretation in the text are mine alone.

JEFFREY KARL OCHSNER
July 2007

LIONEL H. PRIES

ARCHITECT, ARTIST, EDUCATOR

I

INTRODUCTION

"Do You Want to Be

an Architect?"

On a Friday afternoon in fall 1941, the sophomore architecture students at the University of Washington were hunched over their drafting boards, working feverishly. Most were running watercolor washes on their presentation drawings. The tension in the room was palpable. The project, a design for a stair hall in the lobby of an art museum, was due at 1:00 p.m. the following day. It was early in the year, but the students had already learned that their instructor, Professor Lionel H. ("Spike") Pries, was a perfectionist. He expected far more from them than they had ever thought they were capable of producing. As he did every afternoon, Professor Pries went from desk to desk, offering critiques, making suggestions. Though just six feet tall, he was physically as well as personally imposing. That afternoon, he carried a bundle of watercolor brushes, and he sometimes sat down at a student's drafting board, pulled out a big sable brush with which he could get a very fine point, and began to draw on the student's project; or he might lay down a large area of wash. Because the students were relative beginners, they were often timid in their use of watercolor, but Pries used richer browns and darker grays and blues to develop deeper shades and shadows and stronger effects. His hand moved quickly, and the students saw their work come alive.

Keith Kolb looked up nervously, checked his watch, and smiled to himself. He was ahead of schedule and was well along in his watercolor drawing of the stair hall. There was a dance on campus that evening, and he had a date. He knew he could work until just after 6:00, then get cleaned up, have dinner, pick up his date, and get to the dance on time. He planned to stay out late, but he knew he had time to finish his presentation before 1:00 the next day.

Kolb's reverie did not last. Pries, who had been looking over Kolb's shoulder at the project, interrupted: "Boy, you got a sponge?"

Kolb's "yes" was hesitant. Pries picked up a big sponge, dipped it in Kolb's water bowl, and washed out the entire center of the drawing. Faint pencil lines remained, but the watercolor had disappeared. Then Pries took his sable brush and started drawing; he drew only a small part, then he stopped and said, "Now, that is the way it's supposed to be." He looked at Kolb and said, "You understand?"

Kolb was ashen.

Pries asked, "What's the matter?"

"I was just wondering how I was going to get it done." Kolb knew it had to be done on time—late work was not accepted, and neither were excuses.

3

"Oh, you have lots of time," Pries replied. "It's only 3:30 Friday and this is not due until 1:00 tomorrow. What's the problem?"

Kolb answered, "I was thinking I would go to the dance tonight."

There was a brief pause as Pries stared at Kolb, dumbfounded.

"Dance?" Pries's voice rose; the studio grew quiet, and everyone could hear what he was saying. "Dance? I thought you wanted to be an architect! Do you want to be an architect, or do you want to go to the dance?"[1]

More than sixty years later, in spring 2002, Keith Kolb, by then retired from a successful career as an architect and educator, related this story, as part of a retrospective presentation of his life and work, to a roomful of fellows of the Seattle chapter of the American Institute of Architects. He added emphatically, "It was wonderful!" That afternoon had been a turning point in his career. Kolb did not remember much about the dance, though he added, "My poor date must have had a miserable time, because all I could think about was that drawing." But he did remember that after the dance he had gone back to the architecture studio, worked all night, and got the drawing done on time. From this experience he drew the lesson that architecture demands devotion that cannot be short-changed.[2]

Although this might seem a harsh beginning, Kolb developed an abiding affection and respect for Professor Lionel Pries, as any motivated student will for a truly great teacher. In the late 1940s, after graduating from Washington, Kolb went on to Harvard to study under Walter Gropius, and he subsequently worked for Gropius's firm, The Architects Collaborative. Kolb now credits most of his architectural education to just these two men, Lionel Pries and Walter Gropius, but adds that Pries was "by far the greatest teacher I have ever known."[3]

Kolb was not alone in his assessment of Pries's influence. When many of Pries's students of the years from 1928 through the mid-1940s emerged in the 1950s and 1960s as leaders in American architecture, they invariably credited Pries with making the difference in their careers. Among them was Minoru Yamasaki, best known today for his design of the World Trade Center, who cited Pries among all the teachers he had.[4] A. Quincy Jones, who became a leading Modern architect in southern California, spoke often of Pries's influence.[5] And the leaders of the regional Modernism that emerged

in the 1950s in the Pacific Northwest—architects such as Paul Kirk, Roland Terry, and others—cited Pries as the teacher who had awakened them to spatial sequences, materials and forms, colors and textures: to what have been called the experiential dimensions of design.[6] Yet there was never a "school of Lionel Pries"; instead, each of his students found his or her own direction in architecture.

ARCHITECT AND EDUCATOR

Pries was an elitist, at a time when that term was not a pejorative one. He believed it was his job to push his students and to set the highest possible standards. He would cajole, criticize, goad, needle, praise, use every available technique to push his students beyond their own expectations. Most of his students of the 1920s to the 1940s did not resent his demands. In part this was because Pries could also show them what was possible. He was facile with a pencil or pen and a wizard with those watercolor brushes. He was also extraordinarily knowledgeable; he frequently sent students to the library to look up precedents from Europe or Asia or Latin America, or he might talk about buildings he knew from his travels in Europe or Mexico. The students had never met anyone like him. Many of them came from small towns, and few had much experience of big cities other than Seattle. Pries introduced them not only to architecture but also to art, music, and the artifacts of cultures from around the world. He was inspiring because he believed that they could learn and could achieve great things, and he expected them to dedicate themselves completely to the pursuit of excellence in the career they had chosen.

Pries was at the peak of his influence in 1941. Born and raised in the San Francisco Bay Area, educated at the Universities of California and Pennsylvania, Pries had come to Seattle in early 1928 with few connections and little knowledge of the city. He joined the University of Washington architecture faculty later that year and quickly enlivened the whole school. In less than a decade, he rose to prominence as the inspirational leader of the architecture program, as a notable designer, and as an exhibiting artist.

Pries was a romantic. Although he taught within the traditional pedagogy derived from the Ecole des Beaux-Arts, he saw this approach as a means to develop students' creativity. Like others of his generation, he understood the Beaux-Arts system as teaching a problem-solving method, not a particular style. Pries taught that history offered lessons, but that precedents should never be slavishly copied; instead, every project should be addressed on its own terms and in its own time and place. Pries was therefore accepting of emerging design vocabularies, including those of Modernism, as long as these were appropriate to a particular problem. His own design work had evolved from historical eclecticism to creative intermingling of the Modern and the traditional, the universal and the particular, but always with an emphasis on the specifics of client and site. His mature architectural designs were characterized by close attention to the integration of architecture and landscape. Usually his projects were richly colorful and many were artistically embellished, as Pries believed that no work was complete until complemented by art. In the early 1930s, Pries had served as director of the Art Institute of Seattle (predecessor to today's Seattle Art Museum), and from the 1920s to the 1940s he frequently exhibited his watercolors and oils. Pries's activities as an artist were an added dimension of his influence on students—for many, Pries exemplified the ideal of the architect as a cultured individual with wide-ranging knowledge and skill in the fine and decorative arts.

From the 1920s to the mid-1940s, students flocked around Pries. He was the center of the school. The breadth of his knowledge and the range of his skills gave him a level of confidence, sometimes bordering on imperiousness, that led others naturally to defer. Other faculty members were married, with families, but Pries was single and could devote himself completely to the architectural program and to the students. Pries lived in a large house near campus, and the frequent soirees he offered at his home were legendary—the talk would be about architecture, art, and culture, and Pries would show students his collections of Mexican and Asian artifacts, Peruvian textiles, and other objects he had gathered in his travels. He even took in selected architecture students as boarders—providing them with inexpensive lodgings, sharing with them his books and collections, and showing them how one's life might embrace architecture and the arts.

After the Second World War, Pries continued to produce notable designs, his work reflecting the richness of an architectural vision different from the technological Modernism that dominated that era. Nevertheless, his influence at the university diminished. The architecture school grew rapidly as a tidal wave of new students sought realistic and pragmatic professional education. Most of the new faculty embraced the architectural pedagogy of the Bauhaus and emphasized a technological approach to Modern architecture. Pries became an exceptional figure, regarded by many as "old school" but treasured by a few because his romantic approach incorporated a richer array of possibilities—colors, textures, materials, and the like—that contrasted with the austere functionalism of most of his younger colleagues.[7]

Many of the students Pries taught from the 1920s to the 1950s went on to notable careers, but not because they emulated Pries's work—they did not. Rather, each found his or her own way in architecture, and their work over the decades after 1945 varied widely. When they recalled their architectural education years later, these graduates seldom mentioned the vocabularies of their projects. Instead, they remembered the method of design and the many lessons Pries had imparted.

LIONEL PRIES AND NARRATIVES OF ARCHITECTURE AND DESIGN

Pries was an extraordinary teacher, but exploring the breadth of his life and career is important not only because he was so important to his students but also because his personal odyssey helps illuminate many of the forces that shaped American architecture in the twentieth century.

The familiar narrative of American architectural history presents a sequential story in which the major tendencies in American architecture played themselves out by the 1930s or 1940s. The Arts and Crafts movement, based on the writings of John Ruskin and the example of William Morris, rose at the turn of the century but disappeared as a coherent direction by World War I.[8] Academic eclecticism, in which new designs were derived from scholarly study of historical precedents, began earlier (in the 1890s) and remained powerful until the 1930s, but it, too, waned during the Depression.[9] Art Deco emerged in the 1920s but was already fading by 1940.[10] Although there were progressive tendencies and a nascent American Modernism in the 1930s, these were supplanted after 1945 by the Modern architecture that developed in Europe—an architecture that was first presented in the United

States as the "International Style" by the Museum of Modern Art in 1932.[11] It was International Style Modernism that emerged triumphant in the persons of the immigrant architect-educators, especially Walter Gropius and Ludwig Mies van der Rohe, who came to the United States in the late 1930s and were hailed as leaders of the American profession until the late 1960s.[12] Mies, Gropius, and other European Modernists were celebrated in their lifetimes as heroic figures who pointed the way to a new architecture appropriate to the twentieth century. Their influence was so strong, and the shadows they cast were so large, that others who contributed to architectural development in America and elsewhere in the period are often ignored or forgotten.

Since the 1980s, as historians have begun to reassess the breadth of Modern architecture, it has become increasingly clear that Modernism was never a singular or even a unified movement.[13] Although the architecture we know as Modernism generally coalesced in the 1920s in Europe, by the end of the 1930s widely varying interpretations of the Modern Movement could be found in Brazil, Japan, Mexico, and other places, and the transplantation of Modernism after World War II produced diverse responses to individual conditions and cultures.[14] Similarly, some American architects were already engaged in the search for an "American Modernism" before the arrival of Gropius and Mies, and the Modernism that emerged in the United States after 1945 actually incorporated a diversity of approaches, from the International Style to the remnants of the progressive tendencies of the 1930s, encompassing the various regionalisms of the West and the South as well as such idiosyncratic figures as Frank Lloyd Wright.[15] Indeed, using the general term "Modernism" can sometimes lead us to forget the tensions and conflicts among the various strains of Modern architecture and among the different individuals who created them. Exploring the architectural career of Lionel Pries will add to our understanding of the search for an American Modernism and to our recognition of the breadth of Modern architecture in America in the middle years of the twentieth century.

The familiar linear narrative of American architectural history has also shaped the narrative of architectural education, which has focused almost exclusively on the transforming influence of immigrant architects on American schools—Gropius at Harvard, Mies at Illinois Institute of Technology—and on the broad influence of the Bauhaus. But this narrative completely ignores almost all other architects and architectural educators—individuals like Pries—who were already in the United States, and whose careers as teachers spanned from the 1920s through the 1950s. How they responded to changes in society, to new developments in architecture, and to the changing contexts of their own institutions is rarely if ever discussed. Yet most of the architectural education that took place in the United States was carried out by these individuals. If we are to understand the broad currents of continuity and change that shaped American architecture and American architectural education in the mid-twentieth century, the focus cannot be just on a few heroic personalities but must encompass a much wider range of influential educators. To write the broad history of architectural education, we need to rediscover many more influential teachers. Pries is one such figure.

Recovering Pries's life and career also illuminates other currents in American architecture and the arts. An example is the later influence of the Arts and Crafts movement. Traditional narratives of the Arts and Crafts trace its rise in England in the mid-nineteenth century, its subsequent spread to North America, its post-1900 maturity, particularly in the Midwest and Far West, and its precipitous decline at the time of the World War I. The later influence of the Arts and Crafts is seldom addressed in any detail. Yet there was a generation of artisans and architects who were educated in the Arts and Crafts but did not begin their own design careers until the 1920s; apart from a few architects in California, their story is not well known, and the influence the movement had in their lives and careers remains largely unexplored.[16] Pries offers one beginning to such an exploration. Raised and educated in the Bay Area in the years before World War I, he felt the full force of the Arts and Crafts, yet his professional career did not begin until 1923. By that date, the movement was no longer ascendant, but its attitudes shaped Pries's work throughout his life, especially his responses to particular sites and landscapes and his incorporation of a wide range of art objects in the best of his architectural designs.

Pries's contributions as teacher and architect are central to the story of architecture and the arts in Seattle and the Northwest. Pries's own work is part of this story; the post-World War II work of his students is another. In this regard, Pries helps us to understand the phenomenon of regionalism within

Modern architecture.[17] Pries himself would probably not be considered a regionalist architect, but his experiences in Mexico, where he encountered avant-garde artists and architects seeking to create art and architecture that was both Modern and distinctively Mexican, clearly influenced his own work as well as the lessons he passed on to his students. Exploring Pries's career reminds us of the diversity within Modernism by the 1930s and helps both to illuminate the sources of regional interpretations of Modernism and to identify the specific role that Pries may have played in the creation of a Modern Northwest architecture. Similarly, most studies of art in the Northwest have focused on the region's artistic production after 1945 or, occasionally, on the earlier careers of the artists who later became the leaders of the "Northwest School."[18] Recovering Pries's largely unknown artistic career can help expand awareness of the diversity of the region's artistic activity before 1950.

There is one more side to Pries's life, and one more story that this biography illuminates: Pries was gay. In some circles, this was well known; in others, it was completely hidden. At the university, if students or colleagues knew Pries was gay, it was never mentioned, and many simply did not know. Yet within Seattle's artistic community, it was always understood—indeed, homosexuality was not uncommon among Seattle artists. The history of Seattle's gay community has only begun to be written, and few narratives have yet appeared that address the place of homosexuality in Seattle's cultural development.[19] Obviously, this biographical monograph cannot fill that void, but recounting Pries's life will begin to reveal a small part of this dimension of regional history. Further, if the power of Pries's teaching is to be fully understood, it must be through recognition of the way in which mentoring young architects was central to Pries's own emotional life.

Lionel Pries was an extraordinary individual. As an educator, architect, artist, and collector, he touched many lives. His life and career spanned almost seven decades of the twentieth century. In this period, Seattle grew from a provincial outpost to a major metropolitan center, the University of Washington became one of the nation's major research universities, and the university's architecture school achieved wide recognition. It was also an extraordinary period in architectural history, with the rise and fall of academic eclecticism and the Arts and Crafts movement, the coming of International Style Modernism, and the emergence of regionalism. By reconstructing Pries's story, this book also addresses these larger histories, offering new perspectives and suggesting ways in which their narratives might be broadened or reconceived. Although the lack of some written records means that certain details of Pries's life may never be known, it is important to record what we do know because it speaks to a time and a place, to a great teacher and his students, and to someone who believed not just that architecture and the arts could offer shelter and functional accommodation but that they could truly shape a life of feeling.

2

ORIGINS

Lionel Pries was a child of a particular time and place—the time was the beginning of the twentieth century, the place was California. It was a time of economic stability and optimism: the financial stringency of the Panic of 1893 was in the past; the nation would not suffer a larger economic debacle until 1929. But if the time was a special one, the place was even more so. California, at the beginning of the twentieth century, was a place of dreams and aspirations, seemingly filled with opportunity—an American Eden. The reality of California was a paradox: perceived as a mythical paradise of promise where one could begin anew and live close to nature, in contrast to the materialistic culture "back East," California was becoming part of the very world it appeared to reject. Yet, as shown by the cultural historian Kevin Starr, the myth was powerful enough to endure in the face of the emerging reality.[1] For most, California in the early twentieth century was still a place of romantic conceptions of the past and of belief in a future abounding in possibilities.

As the historian Robert Winter has noted, "The idea that California was a retreat from the excesses of progress made it deeply vulnerable to the message of William Morris, the father of the English Arts and Crafts movement."[2] The message of the Arts and Crafts, drawn from Morris and from John Ruskin, was transformed in California to focus on the simple life, in buildings made of local materials and in keeping with climate and tradition. As elsewhere in America, the revolutionary aspects of Ruskin's and Morris's writings were often ignored; one could focus on a life lived in harmony with nature, surrounded by objects of grace and beauty. The machine was accepted as long as it was kept in its place.

The dream of California always embodied a complex mix of ideas and influences. The climate and landscape frequently reminded visitors of the Mediterranean, and many Californians embraced the idea of a new Mediterranean culture; some linked this idea to California's romanticized Hispanic past, while others suggested a new Italy or a new Greece —indeed, the development of the University of California was sometimes characterized as having created the "Athens of the West."[3] At the same time, the dream embraced the influence of Asia: California was the center of Pacific trade, and awareness of China and Japan shaped almost every aspect of art and culture.[4] Nowhere is the mix of influences reflected more than in California's garden traditions—the landscape and benign climate led many to believe that a new arcadian society could be created. This belief led in turn, as shown by the landscape historian David Streatfield, to extraordinary achievement in garden design, which often blended influences from Europe and Asia.[5]

The romance of California's past, its climate and landscape, and the sense of opportunity and promise all shaped Lionel Pries.

EARLY LIFE: OAKLAND AND SAN FRANCISCO

Lionel Henry Pries was born in San Francisco on 2 June 1897, the only surviving child of Rathje Pries (1856–1917) and Magdalena Koepke Pries (1859–1919).[6] His father had been born in New York to German immigrants; his mother was born and raised in Holstein, Germany, and emigrated to the United States in 1880. The Pries family was German Lutheran, and Pries grew up bilingual in English and German.[7]

The Pries family lived in the northern part of Oakland, at 894 61st Street, in a symmetrical one-story house with a raised basement[8] (fig. 2.1). The Oakland where Pries spent his childhood was largely a city of free-standing single-family homes, a marked contrast with high-density San Francisco. After the opening, in the late 1870s, of a railroad line from Berkeley to a ferry terminal on the bay,

lots in the north Oakland area had been promoted heavily to San Franciscans who wished to build country villas or cottages. The streets were laid out in a grid pattern, and the lots—40 to 50 feet wide and often more than 100 feet deep—accommodated a variety of one- and two-story houses in simplified vernacular versions of the American late-Victorian architectural modes.[9] The house the Pries family acquired in 1896 was similar to many other small houses in the neighborhood.

Lionel was a relatively late child; his parents had married in July 1882[10] (fig. 2.2). As a result, he was indulged as a child—he later told friends he had been spoiled.[11] He also later said he was close to his mother but distant from his father.[12] His distance from his father may have been partly due to the forty-one-year difference in their ages but more likely reflects the fact that Rathje Pries worked in San Francisco his entire life and so, with a long commute, left home early and returned late.[13] It was Lionel's mother who sent him off to school in the morning and welcomed him home each afternoon. Lionel walked to the nearby Bay School, a large wooden Queen Anne-style building dating from 1892.[14] Photographs show him in a class of about forty-five pupils, with some ethnic diversity, but otherwise little is known of his elementary school education—no one can recall his ever mentioning it.

Pries told few stories of his childhood to his friends and colleagues of later life. However, when

Fig. 2.1
Pries residence, Oakland, California, ca. 1900–1905; Magdelena Koepke Pries and Lionel Pries in a carriage in front of the family house; Pries collection, University of Washington Libraries, Special Collections Division, UW23792z.

Fig. 2.2
Lionel Pries with
his parents, 15
September 1907
(tintype). Pries
collection, Univer-
sity of Washington
Libraries, Special
Collections Divi-
sion.

asked by University of Washington students in the 1950s how he had developed his extraordinary powers of visual recall, Pries said his father would take him on long walks and upon their return insist that he give a detailed account of everything he'd seen.[15]

One of Pries's strongest memories from childhood was of the San Francisco earthquake and fire.[16] The quake struck San Francisco at 5:19 A.M. on 18 April 1906, less than two months before Lionel's ninth birthday. Although the quake lasted less than a minute, it set off a conflagration that was not brought under control for three days. Oakland received only minor damage, but residents could easily see San Francisco burning just across the bay. Pries later recalled going to the Oakland waterfront to watch the fire. When the smoke finally cleared, on 22 April, downtown San Francisco was in ruins—4.7 square miles had been leveled; streets and property lines were indistinguishable in the rubble.[17] Jack London compared the destroyed area to the "the crater of a volcano."[18]

The disaster was more than just a curiosity for the Pries family. Rathje Pries worked downtown for S. & G. Gump Company, a San Francisco firm importing and retailing mirrors, picture frames, cornices and mantels, paintings, engravings and other works of art.[19] By the turn of the century, European artworks had become a primary focus of the business. The Gump's store on Geary Street was completely destroyed by the earthquake, yet Gump's reopened shortly afterward, in temporary space, and

by 1908 had moved into an expanded store on Post Street, near Union Square. Gump's now turned to Asia as well as Europe for works of art, and the company was soon the leading importer of Chinese and Japanese artifacts, a development that led in turn to a major remodeling of the store. Artisans were brought from Japan and China to construct a series of "Oriental rooms" as appropriate settings to display Asian arts and crafts. These rooms—the Tansu Room, the Jade Room, the Lotus Room—were the basis of Gump's growing fame in the next several decades (fig. 2.3).

The extraordinary impact of Gump's in this period is nowhere more evident than in an account written by Emily Post when she visited the Panama-Pacific International Exposition, hosted by San Francisco from 20 February to 4 December 1915, the official world's fair for that year.[20] Post wrote that, once in San Francisco, she hurried each morning to the exposition, only to have people repeatedly inquire whether she had been to Gump's. Finally she agreed to visit the store, expecting that it would be no different from stores she knew in New York, but she was overwhelmed:

It was as though we had been transported, not only across the Pacific, but across centuries of time. Through the apartments of an ancient Chinese palace, we walked into a Japanese temple, and again into a room in a modern Japanese house. You do not need more than a first glance to appre-

& G. Gump Company
230-268 Post Street
San Francisco.

Fig. 2.3
S. & G. Gump
Company
("Gump's") store,
250 Post Street,
San Francisco;
interior of "Black
and Gold Room,"
Oriental depart-
ment, ca. 1915.
Photo courtesy
of Gump's.

ciate why they lead visitors to a shop with the unpromising name of Gump. . . .

In this museum-shop each room has been assembled as a setting for the things that are shown in it. Old Chinese porcelains, blue and white sang-de-boeuf, white, apple-green, cucumber-green and peacock blue, are shown in a room of the Ming Period in ebony and gold lacquer.

The windows of all the rooms, whether in the walls or ceiling, are of translucent porcelain in the Chinese, or paper in the Japanese; which produces an indescribable illusion of having left the streets of San Francisco thousands of miles, instead of merely a few feet, behind you.[21]

The store that overwhelmed the sophisticated Emily Post completely enthralled the young Lionel Pries. His romantic streak was cultivated by his exposure to the exotic artworks and settings at Gump's. Throughout his life, Pries would be a collector of art and artifacts. His interests would be broad, and the focus of his collecting would change across the course of his life, but Asian art would always be a

part of his collections. Pries's home would even come to embody the experience of Gump's—it was filled with items he collected, and when he enter-tained, he would show items from his collection one by one, just as the Gump's salesclerks had done in displaying the fine art objects of Asia to potential purchasers.

Lionel also began to play the violin at an early age; he later described himself as a "prodigy"[22] (fig. 2.4). But his interest in the violin waned, and he increasingly focused on the visual arts, although he did retain a lifelong interest in the symphony.

In 1912, Pries gained admission to the Wilmer-ding School of Industrial Arts, in San Francisco.[23] It was allied with the nearby California School of Mechanical Arts (also known as the Lick School); the two would merge in 1915.[24] Until the merger, Lick focused on the mechanical arts, and Wilmer-ding focused on the building arts, but academic classes were often shared. Both schools were tuition-free. A majority of the students came from San Francisco, but some from outlying areas enrolled as well.[25]

Fig. 2.4
Lionel Pries
with violin,
date unknown.
Pries collection,
University of
Washington
Libraries, Special
Collections
Division.

Fig. 2.5
Lionel Pries,
"Literary"
drawing. From
Wilmerding Life
11/4 (June 1914);
Lick-Wilmerding
High School, San
Francisco.

The Wilmerding academic curriculum included English, mathematics, science, history, civics, and similar courses. In addition, all students took freehand and mechanical drawing for two years, and they were exposed to a series of fundamental courses in the mechanical or building trades before selecting an area of specialization. Those who demonstrated aptitude in drawing, English, and mathematics could pursue the architecture curriculum, beginning in their second year.[26] The students in architecture worked in the drafting room each afternoon, and over the course of several years they carried out a series of drawing exercises that included copying of plates (probably from standard texts), drawing details of steel construction, drawing the orders, and producing analytical and measured drawings. Once these exercises were completed, architecture students undertook several simple design problems, such as a small office building and a residence.[27] Graduates who did not go to college could become drafters in architectural offices; those who went on to higher education could consider entering a university architecture program.

The Wilmerding quarterly student publication, the *Wilmerding Life,* regularly included a section

titled "Shop Notes," and glimpses of Pries's activities are revealed in the subsection "Architecture."[28] Thus, in March 1914, Pries was working on his drawings of the orders; three months later, he had started on his "measurements" (a term probably meaning measured drawings of some kind). Over the next two years, Pries also did exercises in "shades and shadows" and designed a "class 'C' office building" and a "suburban residence."

Pries served on the *Wilmerding Life* art staff from the beginning of his sophomore year until he graduated. He shared in the overall design of the publication, but, more important, produced partial or full-page drawings that served as headers or division pages for each section of the journal. His first published drawing headed the "Shop Notes" section in December 1913, and others appeared occasionally thereafter.[29] Some of these were clearly student efforts, but others seem unusually sophisticated[30] (fig. 2.5).

The Panama-Pacific Exposition fascinated students at the Lick and Wilmerding schools.[31] Occupying 635 acres of land along the water's edge at the north end of San Francisco, the exposition celebrated the opening of the Panama Canal while

Fig. 2.6
Avenue of Palms,
Panama Pacific
International
Exposition, San
Francisco, 1915.
From *The Great
Exposition: The
Panama-Pacific
International
Exposition* (San
Francisco: Robert
A. Reid, 1915).

also demonstrating to visitors that San Francisco had fully recovered from the 1906 disaster. The exposition was planned on Beaux-Arts principles, with eight major buildings enclosing several "courts" along a primary axis that terminated at one end in the Machinery Hall and at the other in the Fine Arts Pavilion. The architecture of the primary buildings looked back to California's Spanish heritage—they have been variously described as Beaux-Arts and Mediterranean (fig. 2.6). Additional coherence was achieved because consistent colors, selected by the well-known architectural delineator Jules Guerin, were used on all major buildings.[32] The focus of the exposition was the "Tower of Jewels" at the gateway to the central cross axis. It featured thousands of crystalline ribbons of iridescent glass "jewels" that reflected light and swayed in the breeze. The buildings were constructed of "staff," a plaster material finished to imitate travertine, and were intended to last only for the year of the fair. The June 1915 issue of *Wilmerding Life* was devoted to the exposition and included a two-page essay by Pries; surprisingly, his essay

focused not on the architecture but on the color scheme:

> When wandering along the avenues and through the courts of the Panama-Pacific International Exposition, one is struck by the aged appearance of the buildings. This is due in no small degree to Jules Guerin's color-scheme.
>
> To Guerin, one of the world's greatest colorists, was entrusted the execution of a new exhibition feature, namely: a definite and harmonious color-scheme. The Exposition as one sees it to-day is a Guerin picture brought into real existence: a picture reflecting the personality of Guerin himself. Once a man while gazing at a canvas, asked his artist friend if he had ever seen such colors in nature. The artist answered, "No, but wouldn't you *like* them to exist?" Guerin actually has *created* an artist's ideal in nature, and the result is certainly a happy one.[33]

Pries's lifelong romantic attitude is presaged in the rhetorical question "Wouldn't you *like* them to exist?"

His essay went on to discuss the relationship of the color selection to the landscape, the character of the surfaces, and the location of each color (even the colors of garbage cans and uniforms). He also discussed the murals that adorned the primary buildings. His last paragraph was nearly as romantic as his opening:

> If one could picture a beautiful Persian rug, with soft and mingled tints, accented by brilliant splashes of color, over a square mile in area, resting among verdure-colored hills and sparkling waters, one would have only a faint idea of the charm of the Exposition. The pen is powerless to describe what must be seen to be appreciated, at the Panama-Pacific International Exposition—the Exposition whose memory will remain long after the "Rainbow City" has perished in the dust.

Over twenty years later, Pries, talking with the parents of a student who wished to visit the 1939 San Francisco fair, recalled how much he had enjoyed the 1915 exposition.[34]

During Pries's years at Wilmerding, he started his lifelong close friendships with Carlos Maas and Theodore Maas, who, like Pries, were Wilmerding students specializing in architecture.[35] Carlos J. Maas (1897–1972), although nearly the same age as Pries, was a year ahead of him in school. He served on the *Wilmerding Life* staff and was editor in 1913–14. His younger brother, Theodore A. Maas (1899–1971), a year behind Pries, also served on the journal staff and, like Pries, continued on the staff of *LWL Life* after the Lick-Wilmerding consolidation. The Maas brothers were the sons of a German immigrant, Theodore J. Maas, and of Ida Sutter Maas, a descendant of the well-known Sutter family of California.[36] When school activities ran late, Pries often stayed overnight at the Maas home in San Francisco. Indeed, Pries became so close to the Maas family that he would, in later years, sometimes describe his personal background in terms of the Maas family history rather than his own.[37] The Maas family would play a critical role in Pries's professional success when he opened his San Francisco office in 1923.

Pries graduated from the Lick-Wilmerding School on 2 June 1916 "with honor" in "an apprenticeship in architectural drawing."[38] The following September, he entered the University of California, Berkeley.

THE BAY AREA ARCHITECTURAL MILIEU, 1900–1920

Although Lionel Pries's formal education in design did not fully begin until he enrolled at Berkeley, the milieu of Oakland and San Francisco no doubt played a role in shaping his lifelong attitudes toward architecture. The wide range of designs that Bay Area architects were developing—from monumental classical institutional buildings to rustic shingled cottages—today seems almost incomprehensible, but within the architectural ethos of the time there was a widespread acceptance of this diversity, as the architects' philosophy recognized that radically different design solutions were appropriate to different programs and sites.

The architectural development of the Bay Area in the early twentieth century was shaped by the generation of architects who arrived in San Francisco in the 1890s, including A. Page Brown, Willis Polk, A. C. Schweinfurth, Ernest Coxhead, and Bernard Maybeck.[39] They were joined, after 1900, by others who shared their attitudes, including John Galen Howard, Louis Christian Mullgardt, and Julia Morgan.[40] In contrast to the freely inventive nineteenth-century Victorian architects and builders, these new leaders of Bay Area architectural practice depended on scholarly knowledge of the past, and they believed that the flexible adaptation of principles derived from historical examples could serve contemporary needs. All had been educated in the design approach now described as "academic eclecticism": the eclectic designer was to choose, from a wide range of precedents, an appropriate approach to each design problem.[41] Making such choices was considered a creative act for which scholarly knowledge of the widest array of precedents was necessary, since only with broad knowledge was it possible to transcend the limits of an individual precedent. The past was also a source of inspiration and a basis for understanding the principles of good design.

The diversity of the academic eclectic approach was enhanced by its acceptance of regional expression. Regionalism had appeared early in the academic movement, when architects began to study New England's older shingled buildings, an exploration that led in turn to what is now called the Shingle Style.[42] Some at the time described this architecture as "modernized colonial," and it was not seen as limited to New England but could be applied in other places by drawing on local versions of shingled vernacular.[43] By the 1890s, recognition of regional differences was generating considerable diversity in design. The key was not directly reproducing local architecture but rather selecting and combining wide-ranging and even foreign references, to create an architecture evocative of a region even if there was no local precedent. In 1891, Chicago architect Daniel Burnham, chief of construction for the World's Columbian Exposition held in 1893, confirmed the appropriateness of such an approach when he specifically requested regionally expressive designs for the exposition buildings that would represent the various states.[44]

When academic eclectic architects began to practice in the Bay Area, they developed a varied architecture appropriate to the region and to each individual design problem. The younger architects who had arrived in the 1890s created what architectural historians now call the Bay Area Tradition.[45] This tradition, appropriate to domestic architecture and similar small buildings, often constructed on rural or suburban sites, drew upon sources such as the Shingle Style, the chalet mode, and California's Mission Revival. This tradition was suffused with romanticism and the ethos of the Arts and Crafts movement and was shaped in the first decades of the twentieth century by Charles Keeler's 1904

book *The Simple Home* (dedicated to the architect Bernard Maybeck) and by Gustav Stickley's *Craftsman* magazine.[46] Most buildings of the Bay Area Tradition displayed spatial complexity as well as sensitive use of wood, tile, natural stone, and earth colors—these materials and colors seemed integral to their sites and appropriate to the California landscape. While Pries's north Oakland neighborhood was not directly affected by this work, buildings representing the Bay Area Tradition were found nearby in Oakland and Berkeley (fig. 2.7).

California regional design was also embodied in the Mission Revival. By the end of the nineteenth century, Californians had begun to take an interest in the restoration of surviving mission buildings, which were seen as uniquely representative of the region (fig. 2.8). This interest continued to grow in the first decades of the twentieth century, even reaching Pries's generation. When a "California" issue of *LWL Life* was published in December 1915, the frontispiece was Pries's imaginative drawing of a mission.[47] The missions were seen as an indigenous architectural precedent, especially after the 1893 exposition in Chicago, where A. Page Brown's California building, which drew from several of the surviving examples, showed the creative possibilities of the new mode. A year later, the Mission Revival was predominant at the 1894 Midwinter Fair in San Francisco, and by the turn of the century it had spread across the state.[48] Although southern

Fig. 2.7
A. C. Schweinfurth, First Unitarian Church, Berkeley, 1898. North Baker Research Library, California Historical Society, San Francisco.

Fig. 2.8
Santa Barbara
Mission, Santa
Barbara, 1812–20.
Photo ca. 1920;
Santa Barbara
Historical
Museum.

California was most strongly affected, buildings with overhanging tile roofs, mission gables and arches, and Moorish towers were constructed in the Bay Area as well. With their crafted wood interiors and built-in wood furniture, Mission Revival buildings were understood as one direction within Arts and Crafts, and elements of the mode were readily accepted within the architecture of the Bay Area Tradition. The Mission Revival also provided an initial basis for the Spanish Colonial Revival that would dominate California architecture during Pries's early years in practice.

Yet, at the same time, buildings in the urban centers of San Francisco and Oakland were shaped by the classical styles that have been generally characterized as the American Renaissance. Downtown San Francisco was radically transformed after the 1906 earthquake; the new business blocks, reflecting the city's wealth and ambitions, were executed in the educated design vocabularies of the new generation of architects.[49] Pries would have been familiar with these buildings; he would also have witnessed the creation of the San Francisco Civic Center, one of the few realized examples of the American City Beautiful movement. The focus of the complex, Bakewell and Brown's City Hall, was completed in 1915, when Pries was in high school in San Francisco—and the Public Library and Civic Auditorium were also built in those years (fig. 2.9). The Arts and Crafts and City Beautiful movements were not really contradictory; both were concerned about order and use, but in different kinds of places: the shingled architecture found along the winding roads of the Oakland and Berkeley hills was simply not appropriate for the civic and commercial sections of San Francisco.

The range of possibilities in the period may best be represented by the career of the architect Bernard Maybeck.[50] Although he is most often remembered for his role in fashioning the development patterns and rustic residential buildings of north Berkeley, Maybeck was also a key instigator of the design competition for the University of California campus plan—a competition won by a monumental classical scheme—and he designed the romantic classical Palace of Fine Arts at the Panama-Pacific International Exposition. A leading architect in the Bay Area Tradition, he was nonetheless willing to work with new materials—his Andrew Lawson residence (1906–7) was of reinforced concrete—and to mix new and old, as at the First Church of Christ, Scientist, in Berkeley (1910), with its structure of concrete and wood, its cement-asbestos sheathing and industrial windows, its Gothic tracery and its trellises covered with wisteria. Maybeck's Berkeley work exemplified the possibility of total integration of architecture with landscape. Maybeck was highly active in the years when Pries was in high school and college. He was occasionally a design critic at the University of California when Pries was a student, and his work in the Berkeley hills was easily accessible from the California campus. Indeed, from the late 1930s to the 1950s, Pries's recollections of Maybeck's work would prove a significant influence on Pries's personal search for a Modern architectural vocabulary.

PRIES AT THE UNIVERSITY OF CALIFORNIA, 1916–1920

When Lionel Pries matriculated at the University of California, in fall 1916, he already had some ideas about what he could expect; he lived little more than a mile away and was familiar with the school. (In May 1916, he had been among the first to sign the visitors' log for the tenth annual exhibi-

Fig. 2.9
Lionel H. Pries's
view of Bakewell
and Brown's
City Hall, San
Francisco, 1912–15;
untitled watercolor
(ca. 1923–27),
14 x 10½ inches.
Pries collection,
University of
Washington
Libraries, Special
Collections Division, UW23235z.

tion of the Student Architecture Association.[51]) But with what, exactly, would he have been familiar?

There was then a consistency in American architectural education that is difficult to imagine today. Although the Berkeley program was just thirteen years old when Pries began, its approach to architectural education was based on the much older Ecole des Beaux-Arts in Paris, which had become, by the late nineteenth century, the most famous school of architecture in the world.[52] John Galen Howard (1864–1931), the first professor of architecture at Berkeley and head of the school from 1903 to 1927, had studied at the Ecole from 1891 to 1893. Following the example of almost all other American collegiate programs in architecture, he adopted the Ecole approach for California's curriculum. Thus, when Pries entered the California program, he was initiated into a tradition of architectural education that was shared by schools across the United States for several decades after 1890.[53] As applied in American schools, the Ecole system provided a consistent approach to design lodged in academic eclecticism, focusing on scholarly knowledge of historical sources and a search for fundamental design principles. However, different schools could focus on different aspects of the Ecole pedagogy. The program at Berkeley emphasized the Ecole method—its approach to problem solving—not slavish copying of historical styles.

Central to the pedagogy of the Ecole de Beaux-Arts was the "atelier," or teaching studio.[54] All but three of the Ecole's approximately twenty ateliers were sponsored by *patrons,* leading architects in Paris who served as design professors and accepted paying students into their ateliers. Each atelier was separate from the architect's office and was approved by the Ecole but was otherwise largely self-regulating, following traditions passed along by each generation of students. Admittance to an atelier meant having not just a place to work and a *patron* but, most important, a group of peers at different stages of their education. A key feature of Ecole education was the tradition of older students aiding the younger through critiques, and of younger students helping the older to complete their presentations for the more advanced competitions. This tradition of working together created a strong spirit of camaraderie. Many ateliers had long histories; some ateliers were even passed down from one *patron* to another.

The Ecole exercised control through its entrance exams, the problems issued for design competitions (or *concours*), the jurying of students' submissions, and the awarding of points by which students, accumulating these points by entering the *concours,* could progress from one level to the next. (New students began at the Second Class; with enough points they could progress to the First Class.) Although the Ecole did offer lecture courses in architectural history and in construction, these were not required and generally were not well attended. The school also provided a library, a gallery of prints, and a vast collection of plaster casts of architectural features and details as well as significant works of sculpture.

In the atelier, students could come and go as they wished; to maintain enrollment, one was required only to enter a minimum number of *concours* each year. These were of two types: the esquisse (or sketch) and the *projet rendu* (the longer and more complex problem—literally, a "rendered project"). Sketch problems were issued in alternate months. A sketch problem was usually a small building, such as a pavilion or a gatehouse, and it was prepared in a short time—usually no more than twelve hours. Students did these problems in complete isolation—*en loge*—in cubicles provided for this purpose. (When American schools of architecture adopted the Ecole system, they identified these short sketch problems with the term "esquisse-esquisse.") The longer *projets rendus* were also issued every two months. These were larger, more complex projects—for example, a railroad station or a courthouse. The *projet rendu* began with an esquisse done *en loge,* completed in no more than twelve hours, typically showing a plan, a section, an elevation. At the end of the timed period, the student turned in the esquisse but retained a copy, which was brought back to the atelier to serve as the basis for the next two months of development and refinement under the supervision of the *patron* and with the advice of the student's peers. The student presented the final project at large scale, in the form of beautifully rendered drawings. If the final *projet rendu* strayed too far from the initial esquisse, it was marked *hors de concours* ("H.C."—literally, "outside the competition"), which meant that it was disqualified, and the student received no points at all for the work.

As summarized by Professor John Harbeson of the University of Pennsylvania, the purpose of Ecole training was "to impart to each student *a method of attacking and studying any problem in architectural design which may be presented.*"[55] The Ecole method taught students to organize their designs rapidly and clearly, and to develop the elements and details through a focused process of refinement. The impact of the Ecole system is evident in the work of its American graduates. H. H. Richardson, for example, became known for his ability to quickly capture his idea for a building in a sketch plan and an elevation; he then depended on his office staff for the development of the design under his criticism, but only occasionally did the plan change significantly from his initial sketch. Louis Sullivan, although he later denigrated eclecticism, drew from the Ecole a belief in an architecture based on fundamental principles. Richard Morris Hunt (in the late 1840s) and Richardson (in the early 1860s) were the first Americans to attend the Ecole. Their success inspired others, and the number of Americans attending the Ecole grew from fewer than 10 in the 1860s to more than 110 in the 1890s. In the same period, the first architecture schools were founded in the United States, at the Massachusetts Institute of Technology (1865), the University of Illinois (1869), Cornell University (1871), the University of Pennsylvania (1874), and Columbia College (1881). By 1910, there were nineteen American collegiate architecture schools, and most adopted the Ecole model for their curricula.[56]

By 1893, New York had become the center of the American Beaux-Arts movement; in that year, the city's architects founded the Society of Beaux-Arts Architects to promote the influence of the Ecole. After 1893, the society's Education Committee started making standardized design problems ("programmes") available to American architecture schools and independent ateliers (which offered training to draftsmen already working in offices); schools and ateliers that chose to use these programmes could send their students' projects to New York to be reviewed and graded in competition with projects from other participating schools. This structure was parallel to that of the Ecole and the various ateliers in Paris. It offered a means to raise standards and provide consistent evaluations among all those participating. Most projects were simply passed or received the grade "mention"; a few outstanding projects were awarded "medals." By 1916, the society had delegated these activities to the Beaux-Arts Institute of Design (BAID), an organization created for the sole purpose of supporting Beaux-Arts education in American architectural schools.[57]

Fig. 2.10 John Galen Howard, date unknown. College of Environmental Design Archives, University of California.

John Galen Howard, as head of the architecture program at Berkeley, was one of the key mentors who shaped Lionel Pries's development[58] (fig. 2.10). Although somewhat reserved and aloof, Howard was directly involved in teaching and could empathize with his students because of his own early efforts to find his way in the profession. Howard had enrolled at the Massachusetts Institute of Technology (MIT) in architecture in 1882, but, unhappy with the technical focus of the program at that time, he left to work in the office of H. H. Richardson. Richardson had structured his office on the atelier model, to the extent feasible within the financial imperatives of practice. After Richardson's death, in 1886, Howard worked for about a year in Los Angeles and then made his first trip to Europe; on his return, in 1889, he went to work for McKim, Mead and White, in New York. The influence of the Ecole permeated that office. With the financial assistance of Charles McKim, himself an Ecole man, Howard returned to Europe in 1891 to complete his education by enrolling at the Paris school.

By his second year at the Ecole, Howard had risen to the First Class, but he left after only two years—the Ecole experience was much more important than the diploma, and, at twenty-nine, he felt ready to practice on his own. For the next eight years, he was the design partner in the New York firm of Howard and Cauldwell. Although the firm's success lay in large houses and small institutional buildings, in September 1899 the University of California announced that Howard and Cauldwell's design had placed fourth (out of 104 entries) in the competition for the new campus plan. In 1901, when the winning architect, Emile Bénard of Paris, declined to move to California to supervise the development of the campus, President Benjamin Wheeler appointed Howard as supervising architect. In 1903, Wheeler made Howard the university's first professor of architecture and charged him with developing a new architecture program.[59]

The challenge Howard faced was similar to that facing other American educators: how to fit the Ecole system into the university's academic structure. As at other American schools, design studio was central to the curriculum; other classes, while separate, supported studio. At Berkeley, however, students generally did not take architectural design studio until the junior year.[60] First- and second-year students took an array of liberal arts and science courses and coursework in drawing, including pen and ink, shades and shadows, descriptive geometry, perspective, and freehand sketching. In the student's third year, studio focused on elements of architecture (doors, windows, columns, moldings, and so forth), addressed in simple design problems—for example, an entrance to a museum or a loggia at the end of a garden. As at all schools following the Ecole model, the student at this level presented the final project in the form of a drawing called an "analytique," a carefully composed monochromatic sheet including a partial plan, an elevation, and fragments of the architectural elements at larger scale.[61] In the fourth year, the design studio addressed complete architectural design problems for smaller or simpler structures, similar to the problems undertaken in the Second Class at the Ecole. Design problems in the graduate years were more complex, approaching

the level of those undertaken in the Ecole's First Class. Occasionally students in the fourth year and graduate years of Berkeley's program undertook the same problems. Problems undertaken in the junior, senior, and graduate years corresponded to the levels of the BAID programmes, but these were only occasionally used in the Berkeley studios.[62]

By 1916, when Pries enrolled, Howard had been joined by two other permanent design faculty: William Charles Hays, a graduate of the University of Pennsylvania who had attended the Ecole and joined Howard as an assistant in 1906; and Warren C. Perry, an early student of Howard's who later attended the Ecole. The school also recruited local practicing architects as part-time design instructors and critics; in the years around 1920, these part-time faculty included Bernard Maybeck, Ernest Coxhead, John Bakewell Jr., John Donovan, and Raymond Yelland.[63]

On the California campus, Pries encountered an environment largely shaped by John Galen Howard.[64] Most of the campus buildings were permanent structures in classical styles, including the Hearst Mining Building (1902–7), Doe Library (1907–18), and Sather Tower (1902–14). Howard also designed several "temporary" wood buildings, including one for the architecture school, on the north edge of campus, adjacent to Hearst Avenue. Completed in 1906 and expanded in 1908 and 1912, this shingled structure reflected Howard's knowledge of similar buildings by Richardson and by McKim, Mead and White as well as those of the Bay Area Tradition (fig. 2.11). Known as the Ark, this building's informal composition and wood construction served as

Fig. 2.11 John Galen Howard, Architecture Building ("The Ark"), University of California, Berkeley, 1906, 1912. College of Environmental Design Archives, University of California.

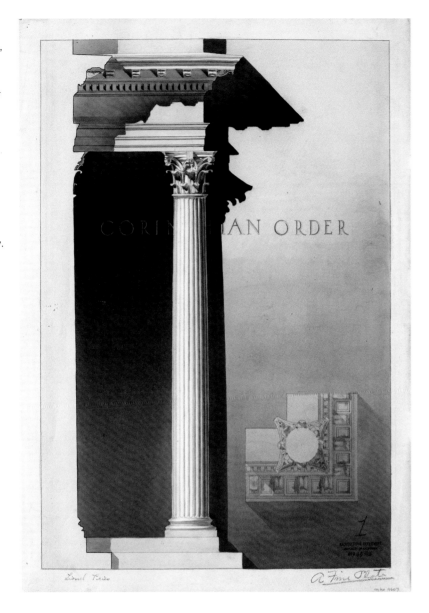

reminders of the wide range of possibilities in architecture.[65] In 1964, William W. Wurster, then dean of the College of Environmental Design, who had been one year ahead of Pries at Berkeley, wrote of the Ark, "Generations of students have come under the spell of this timeless simple structure."[66]

The unconventionality of the Ark suggests that Howard recognized that he could not simply duplicate the program of one of the eastern schools but must respond both to the West Coast location and to the experience of the students. In 1914, answering an inquiry from Carl F. Gould, who was then determining the program at the University of Washington, Howard noted the unique aspects of his approach as well as the difficulties he was encountering:

Our schedule does not permit of working on Beaux-Arts Society problems always, but we are still part of a great movement. I must say, however, that the long distance discourages, or that the personal touch is necessary. Of course our conditions on this coast are very different from the east and everything has to be adjusted more or less to the point of view and lack of background.[67]

Pries left no written records of his years at Berkeley.[68] A few of his drawings survive, and "scrapbooks" with small blueline reproductions of the best student work from the period include nine Pries projects from his junior and senior years; a list of the problems Pries was assigned as a senior is also available.[69] Several studies of the orders, executed in spring of Pries's sophomore year, show his early mastery of architectural delineation (fig. 2.12).

A MEMORIAL HALL

From his third year, the scrapbooks include two Pries analytiques; the words "placed first" are marked on his courtyard façade of a library.

In Pries's senior year (1919–20), the studios included projects, such as "A War Memorial" and "A Memorial Hall," that were clearly intended to be monumental classical designs, and Pries did well on these—both placed first, as did his "Ticket Office," also developed with a classical vocabulary (fig. 2.13). His projects for "The Physical Education Division of a High School Group" and "A Village Inn," which invited regional solutions, also received high marks but were not premiated.

In April 1920, Pries won the school's Alumni Prize competition with his design for a tile manufactory. The program statement, which opened with a discussion of the importance of the "ancient art of ceramics" through human history, fully engaged Pries's romantic imagination.[70] The project required a two-part building—one part to include a museum, library and administrative spaces, the other housing eight studios for individual craftsmen. The program also required "that flat colored tiles enter extensively into the decorative scheme of the principal façade of the group." Located on a rural site, the building complex offered the opportunity to draw on the architectural heritage of California. Pries's scheme, although suggesting the influence of Spanish precedents, was freely composed and not overtly

historical. The reproduction of Pries's elevation suggests that his original drawing must have been richly polychromatic (fig. 2.14).

When, in April 1917, the United States entered what was then called the Great War, Pries was at first not directly affected. In May, Congress passed the Selective Service Act, but initially only those between the ages of twenty-one and thirty-one were eligible for the draft. Pries, who only turned twenty in June 1917, was not included. By 5 June 1918, however, when the next cohort was called, Pries was eligible; he was accepted into the Enlisted Specialists Preparatory School at the beginning of August, pending his induction into the service, but his induction was delayed until 15 October. Thereafter, Pries served in the Coastal Artillery Corps; he was based at Fort Winfield Scott but commuted from home and maintained his enrollment at Berkeley. The war ended less than a month after Pries's induction, and he was honorably discharged in mid-December 1918.[71]

Although his service was minimal, Pries created a lasting memorial to those lost in the war when he won the competition for the Class of 1920 Memorial Bench. The clarity of Pries's thought is evident in the two distinct parts of his composition (fig. 2.15). The broad back and narrow end panels, standing 4 feet tall, are crisply rectilinear. In contrast, the seat has molded edges and is supported by curved

Fig. 2.13
Lionel H. Pries, "A Memorial Hall," senior project, 14 February 1920, University of California; ink and watercolor on stiff paper, 19 x 36½ inches. Pries collection, University of Washington Libraries, Special Collections Division.

brackets. The inscription on the front face states that the Class of 1920 provided the bench "to Commemorate the Heroism of the Sons of this University who died in the Great War"; the back side is inscribed "Lionel H. Pries '20 Designer." Each end panel is surmounted by a mourning bear, sculpted by Joseph Jacinto ("Jo") Mora (1876–1947), a San Francisco artist. The travertine bench, fabricated and installed in 1921, was Pries's first executed design.[72]

Pries's later years in college were personally difficult. In December 1917, his father died of prostate cancer after an illness of several months; he was only sixty-one.[73] Although Lionel Pries was still in school, he now had to provide for his mother. Over the next two years, he supported her and himself by drawing women's fashions in his spare time.[74] Magdalena Pries lived only seventeen months longer; she died of pneumonia in May 1919.[75]

Sometime in that period, Pries found work in the

Fig. 2.16
Tau Sigma Delta
honorees for 1920
with Architecture
faculty; *front row*:
Warren C. Perry,
John Galen
Howard,
W. C. Hays;
back row:
G. J. Fitzgerald,
Lionel H. Pries,
G. T. Spencer,
D. A. Lovell,
M. Gunzendorfer.
College of Envi-
ronmental Design
Archives, Univer-
sity of California,
Berkeley.

office of Charles K. Sumner as well as in the office of John Galen Howard.[76] It is not known exactly when Sumner employed Pries, and what work Pries did for him, but Pries was definitely working in Howard's office in 1920. Pries was an outstanding student, but Howard may also have been motivated by Pries's personal losses: Howard's father had died while he was at MIT, and his mother had died when he was at the Ecole. The one project in Howard's office on which Pries is known to have worked was the Stephens Memorial Union (1920–23), on the University of California campus.[77]

Pries was successful as a student, but he was not what in later years would be called a "grind."[78] He mixed easily with his classmates. It was at Berkeley that his friends gave him the nickname "Spike" because he was so thin.[79] He and his friends occasionally went hiking or on other outings together.[80] Pries was an active member of the Architecture Student Association from 1918 to 1920, and in December 1919, after his parents had died and he may have needed financial assistance, he was elected "storekeeper" for the following term—the person who ran the school's architectural supply store was traditionally allowed to retain half the profits[81] Pries also joined the Abracadabra Club, a men's residential club, one of several such clubs at the university. Abracadabra provided Pries a non-

architecture peer group; it also had several faculty advisors, including Professor Robert G. Sproul.[82] During these years, Pries developed an enduring friendship with Helen Sutherland, who was in the class behind him in the architecture program.[83] Although the precise nature of their relationship is unknown, the friendship was deep enough that it continued through frequent correspondence after Pries left California.[84]

Pries graduated from the university in June 1920 at the top of his architecture class.[85] He received the degree of A.B. (bachelor of arts) in architecture, with honors. He was a member of two honor societies, Tau Sigma Delta (in architecture) and Tau Beta Pi (in engineering) (fig. 2.16). The deaths of his parents had cut his ties to the Bay Area, and he may have sought a psychological separation from the place of his losses; at any rate, he had been admitted for graduate study at the University of Pennsylvania, and he moved to Philadelphia in time for the fall term.[86]

PRIES IN PHILADELPHIA, 1920–1922

Pries was drawn to the University of Pennsylvania because of the reputation of the architecture school. Under Professor Warren Laird, its head, and Paul Cret, its atelier director and inspirational leader (fig. 2.17), the Pennsylvania program had risen to

Fig. 2.17
Paul Philippe
Cret, 1925. Paul
Philippe Cret
Collection, Archi-
tectural Archives
of the University
of Pennsylvania.

prominence among American architecture schools
and was the first to achieve international stature.
The program was larger than the one at Berkeley
and offered a more diverse faculty, but the presence
of Paul Cret was the key factor in Pries's decision
to seek admission.[87]

In 1920, when Pries arrived, all design studios
at the University of Pennsylvania were taught in a
single room, nearly 200 feet long, on the second
floor of Hayden Hall. Students began at one end of
the room as freshmen and progressed year by year
toward the other end. The shared space fostered a
high level of interaction among the students and
reinforced the tradition of advanced students
advising younger ones, and of lower-level students
helping the more senior. Different instructors were
responsible for the students of each year, and Cret
was directly responsible only for the senior students,
but in his role as atelier director, or *patron*, Cret
shaped the character and tone of the whole school.
Because Pries entered as a graduate student, he
worked directly under Cret's supervision for his
full year at Penn.

Paul Philippe Cret (1876–1945) was born into a
working class family in Lyon, France. In 1893, with
the assistance of his in-laws, he entered the Ecole
des Beaux-Arts in Lyon, where talent and hard work
propelled him to the head of his class. He won the
Lyon school's Paris Prize, which provided a three-
year stipend to study at the Ecole des Beaux-Arts
in Paris. Cret joined the atelier of Jean-Louis Pascal.
As noted by Elizabeth Grossman, Pascal's teaching
approach emphasized helping students develop
their own ideas about a project: "Pascal contributed
to formalizing the method of intervention of the
professor on the project of the student. He was the

principal contriver of a pedagogy specific to the
project: this idea by which the professor, adopting
the project of the student, must help him pull if
off."[88] Pascal's approach depended on creative use
of knowledge about the past to address the specifics
of a project in the present, not on replication of past
solutions or past architecture. By late 1900, Cret
had progressed to the First Class at the Ecole; by
1902, it seemed likely that he would soon compete
for the Rome Prize, but decided instead, when he
received his Ecole diploma in June 1903, to accept
a position at the University of Pennsylvania. Cret
began as atelier director at Penn in the fall. Only 5
feet 3 inches tall, he led by force of personality and
through his extraordinary teaching and design
abilities. Cret's teaching at Pennsylvania mirrored
his experience in Pascal's atelier.

By 1908, Penn students had become so successful in Society of Beaux-Arts Architects competitions
that *American Architect* requested articles from Cret
on his approach to architectural education.[89] Cret
also began to compile a notable record in national
design competitions by winning the competition for
the Pan American Union Building in 1907. In his
professional career, he won four such competitions
and placed second or third in seven others.[90]

Although Cret practiced professionally throughout his career at Penn, he spent every weekday after
2:00 P.M. in the studio. As the due dates for the
upper level approached, he often spent Sunday afternoons there as well. Theo White, a graduate of Penn,
described Cret's teaching:

> Cret's criticism was made largely on rolls of tracing
> paper spread over the student's problem, drawing
> with a soft pencil and with a minimum of talk
> (quite different from the modern critic). . . . Cret
> would move from table to table unhurriedly, drop-
> ping here and there a word of commendation and
> encouragement. Sometimes, when the student's
> work had not shown sufficient diligence or thought-
> fulness, Cret would quietly and sarcastically remark,
> "Did you leave your brain home on the bureau?"
> or make his famous statement "You do not know
> what you are doing." Such remarks were made
> without rancor and the import of them never
> carried into the criticism of the next day. It was
> wonderful training. It was the match held deli-
> cately to dry kindling.[91]

Pries later recalled that Cret would rifle through

each student's pile of sketches; if the pile was not thick enough, the student would receive no crit, and Cret would ask, "What have you been doing?"[92]

Cret was firmly committed to the Beaux-Arts pedagogy, especially the method of the esquisse at the beginning of each problem. He believed that the preliminary sketch not only taught students to come to a solution quickly but also established that the primary aim of studio was not to experiment with different schemes but to learn how to study a single scheme. Cret argued that the method of the esquisse also produced the widest possible variety of design solutions, since each student developed his or her esquisse without knowing what the others were doing. This benefited every student, since each could see how different schemes might address the same program.[93] The historian George Thomas observes, "An Ecole saying, 'The esquisse is the student's one safeguard against his critic,' meaning that neither the student nor patron could alter the original scheme, reiterates the importance of this part of the Ecole method."[94]

Cret's belief in the esquisse reflects his understanding that the instructor is to assist the student in resolving the student's project, not in transforming it into what the instructor might prefer. But Cret was never a passive observer. As White has noted, Cret's criticism usually took the form of drawing—that is, showing the students possible means of developing or refining their schemes. Further, in a time when students routinely helped with the completion of each other's final drawings, the instructor might intervene as well to demonstrate how to achieve the most effective presentation:

> Frequently a half-dozen students would gather around a table while [Cret] was criticising another student's work, hoping to gather a tidbit that they might apply to their own problem. Then came the time when the problems were ready for rendering in watercolor. The paint boxes were brought out, with a small pail of water and the inevitable sponge for washing out mistakes in the washes. Then students would cluster around a table not theirs and watch the Master as he would put on a wash or delicately pick out an architecture motive in color. Once he called for a tube of Prussian blue and the student protested that that color faded in time. Cret remarked acidly, "Are you painting for posterity?"[95]

Cret, who remained a French citizen until 1927,

routinely vacationed in France in the summer. He was in France in August 1914; he enlisted in the French army and served until 1919. He experienced the horrors of war in the trenches and returned to Philadelphia partially deaf from the impact of shell explosions. Cret characterized the war as utter "waste" and added, "There are but two remedies for the ravages of the war—love and work."[96] He threw himself back into his work as an architect and teacher.

Cret and Pries developed a closer relationship than was typical between teacher and student; Pries, after all, had gone to Penn specifically to study with Cret. Like Cret, Pries had not been born to wealth, but through his abilities had excelled in the study of architecture. Although Pries studied at Penn for only one year, it was decisive for the course of his career.

The few surviving examples of Pries's student work under Cret include a large pen-and-watercolor rendering of a classical interior, a pencil rendering of a warehouse, and a published esquisse-esquisse for a gate lodge[97] (figs. 2.18, 2.19). The only other surviving projects by Pries are his entries in the 1921 Rome Prize competition. His design for "A Country School for Boys," submitted for the preliminary Rome competition, showed a group of buildings of varying scale and program—the main building (with classrooms, library, assembly hall, dining hall, offices, and reception rooms), a gymnasium, a chapel, two cottages, and a headmaster's residence—disciplined by selective use of symmetry, an overall U-shaped plan, and a continuous brick arcade that framed the formal lawn and drive, suggesting the influence of Jefferson's University of Virginia (fig. 2.20). Pries's design for "A University Group," submitted for the final competition, offered somewhat more monumental classical structures, appropriate to an institution of higher learning (fig. 2.21). Pries later called the competition one of the disappointments of his life. He was told that he had "tied for first" so was asked to wait a year because there were already two Penn graduates ("Cret men") at the American Academy in Rome. Either he felt that this was unfair or he was unwilling to wait; ultimately, he placed second in the Rome competition.[98]

Pries graduated from the University of Pennsylvania in 1921 with the degree of M.A. (master of arts) in architecture. During his year at Penn, he won three BAID medals—one first, one second,

Fig. 2.18
Lionel H. Pries, "A Staircase Hall, Class A - II Projet," 1920–21, University of Pennsylvania; ink and watercolor on stiff paper, 58½ x 39¼ inches. Pries collection, University of Washington Libraries, Special Collections Division.

LIONEL H. PRIES
UNIV. OF PENNSYLVANIA
CLASS "A" — II PROJET
"A STAIRCASE HALL"

Fig. 2.19
Lionel H. Pries,
"A Storage Ware-
house, Class A - III
Projet," 1920–21,
University of Penn-
sylvania; pencil
on stiff paper, 26
x 38 inches. Pries
collection, Univer-
sity of Washington
Libraries, Special
Collections
Division.

Fig. 2.20
Lionel H. Pries, "A
Country School for
Boys," preliminary
competition for
the Rome Prize,
spring 1921; pencil
on illustration
board, 40 x 30
inches. Pries
collection, Univer-
sity of Washington
Libraries, Special
Collections
Division.

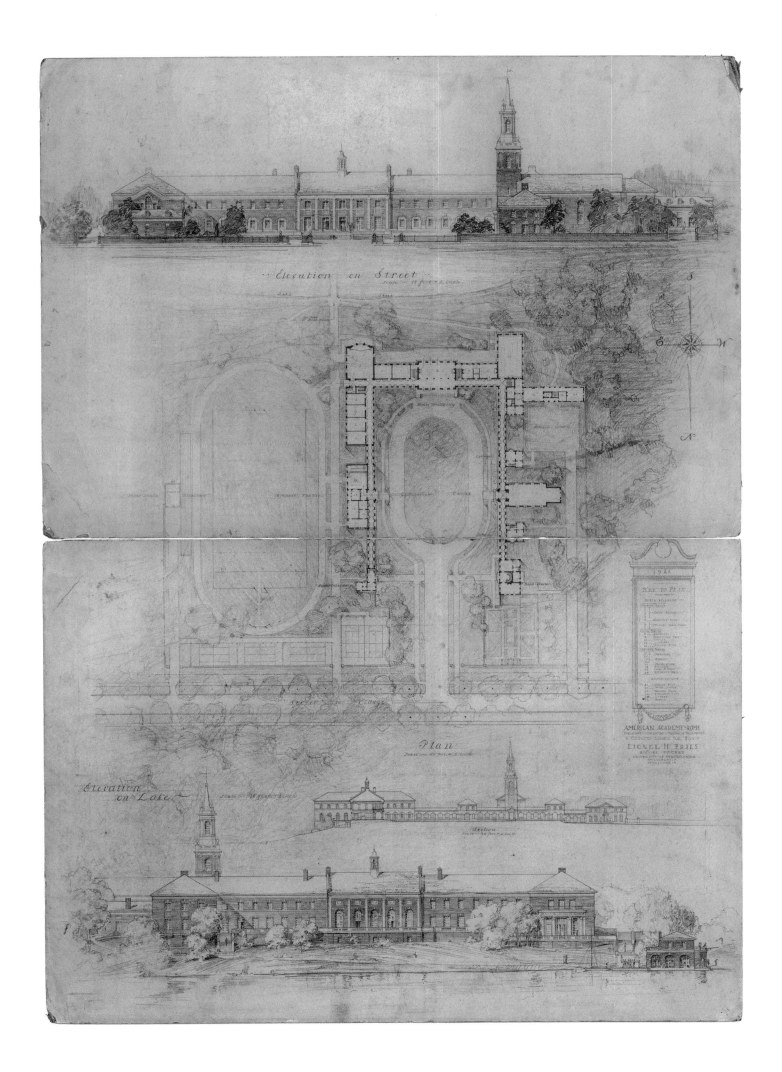

Elevation on Street

Plan

Elevation on Lake

Section

AMERICAN ACADEMY ROME

LIONEL H. PRIES

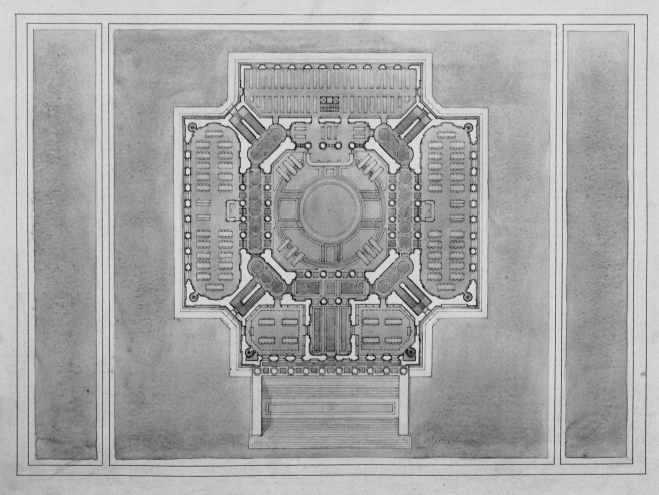

and one third. He also won the Arthur Spayd Brooke Gold Medal for merit in design.[99]

Pries served for a year after graduation as Cret's teaching assistant in the T-Square Club of Philadelphia. The club, sometimes called the T-Square Atelier, had been initiated as a draftsmen's sketch club, but by the twentieth century it was operating as an independent atelier, with a different *patron* at each level and with students undertaking the Beaux-Arts Society (later BAID) programmes and submitting work to be judged in competition with projects from collegiate architecture schools.[100] Since draftsmen worked in firms during the day, the club met in the evenings and on weekends. Cret, whose days were already full with his professional practice and his directing duties at the Penn studio, nonetheless also served as one of the T-Square *patrons*.[101] Pries was then working for professional firms in Philadelphia, and he no doubt welcomed the invitation to assist Cret in his T-Square Club teaching

Cret, more than any of Pries's other teachers, shaped his design teaching. Many features that Pries brought to Washington's studio culture echoed those he had encountered in Philadelphia. Some commonalities were no doubt simply the result of the Beaux-Arts system, but Pries's use of drawing in his critiques, his occasional sarcastic comments, and his watercoloring on students' presentations all derive, at least in part, from his own experiences

with Cret. Pries also emulated Cret's dedication—for example, visiting the studio in the evening and on weekends.[102]

Sometime in 1921, perhaps even before his graduation, Pries began working for the firm DeArmond, Ashmead and Bickley, preparing drawings for their scheme for Philadelphia's Sesqui-Centennial Exhibition.[103] Although the firm's proposal was not successful, Pries's drawing of the central feature of their scheme, the "Proposed Aurora Towers and Court of Pageantry," was published in the *1922 Year Book* of the Philadelphia AIA and the T-Square Club.

From July 1921 through February 1922, Pries worked in the office of the city architect of Philadelphia, John P. B. Sinkler.[104] Sinkler put him "in charge of the Dept. of Sewage Engineering," handling the architectural design work and approving architectural drafting.[105] During his nine months in this position, Pries designed several buildings. Among them was the pumping station of the southwest sewage treatment plant, the first building of what would become the Southwest Sewage Treatment Works[106] (fig. 2.22). The *Philadelphia Evening Bulletin* of 29 September 1929 reported: "The southwest sewage disposal pumping station is a typical example of the uniformly good architectural design adopted for all these disposal plants."[107]

In November 1921, Pries won an award in the first Birch Burdette Long Sketch Competition, sponsored by the draftsmen's journal *Pencil Points*. The

Fig. 2.23
Lionel H. Pries,
*Pencil Sketch
of a Bit of Old
Philadelphia*,
Burch Burdette
Long Sketch
Competition 1921.
From *Pencil Points*
3/1 (Jan. 1922).

jury described Pries's work as "five sketches of great charm that showed an appreciation of architecture as understood by the architect," and added, "While in some cases they were ambitious in character, these sketches were, nevertheless, admirably drawn as to values." One sketch appeared in *Pencil Points* and another in *American Architect*[108] (fig. 2.23).

Although Paul Cret was the dominant figure in Pries's life during his two years in Philadelphia, Pries also gained exposure to the city's broader professional community. Philadelphia was the site of a distinctive "regional school" of architecture from the 1880s to the early 1930s.[109] The city's designers were particularly interested in English architecture, both historical Tudor and progressive Arts and Crafts examples, and in the vernacular architecture of rural Pennsylvania and Delaware, as models for new suburban and rural residential buildings. These precedents fostered the creation of picturesque residences that fit their natural settings. The firms for which Pries worked were not involved in residential design, but he became familiar with these projects through the city's close-knit architectural community and the annual exhibitions of the AIA and the T-Square Club.[110] The full impact of Pries's exposure to the domestic designs of Philadelphia professionals would become apparent after his move to Seattle.

TRAVEL IN EUROPE, 1922–1923

The 1921 Rome Prize had eluded Pries, but there were others for which he could try. The (American) Paris Prize provided a stipend for three years of study at the Ecole. Two traveling scholarships— the Stewardson sponsored by the Philadelphia AIA, and the LeBrun, by the New York AIA—provided substantial sums for travel and study abroad.[111] Pries entered the 1922 LeBrun competition. The project was a "Municipal Bath Building," sited in a city park. Pries's design was a courtyard building of Mediterranean character, with relatively simple classical detail and a tile roof.[112] (Fig. 2.24a,b)

On 1 March 1922 Pries went to work as the "head draughtsman" in the office of Philadelphia architect Edgar V. Seeler.[113] Shortly after he started, however, Pries received notification from the New York Chapter AIA that he had won the LeBrun Traveling Scholarship; he resigned his position to spend the next year traveling in Europe. The scholarship provided roughly $1400 and required a minimum of six months travel in Europe. Pries stretched the money to travel for almost thirteen months from April 1922 to May 1923.[114]

Although a friend gave him a travel diary, Pries rarely wrote in it.[115] But more than 90 drawings and

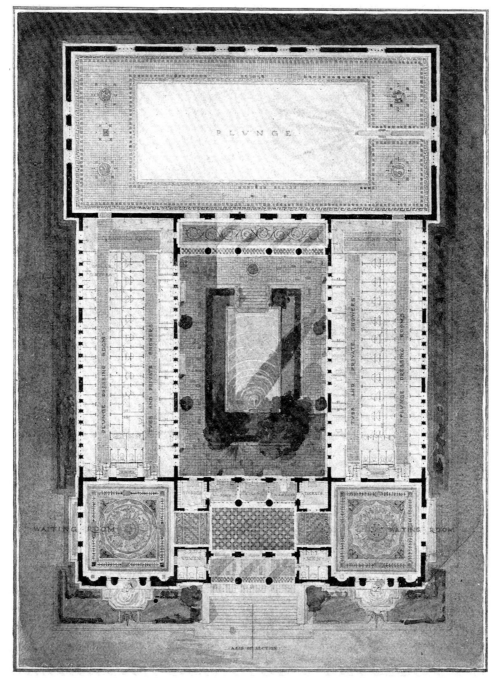

Fig. 2.24 a, b
Lionel H. Pries,
"Municipal Bath
Building," LeBrun
Traveling Scholar-
ship Competition,
1922. From
*American Architect-
Architectural
Review* 121
(10 May 1922).

Fig. 2.25
Lionel H. Pries,
Garden of Linda-raxa, Granada, Alhambra, May 1922; pencil on paper, 12¾ x 9¾ inches. Pries drawing collection, University of Washington Libraries, Special Collections Division, UW24136z.

watercolors survive from his trip; these, together with the few entries in Pries's diary, record of what he saw.[116] Pries visited Mr. and Mrs. Pierre LeBrun in New York on 26 April 1922, then sailed the next day for France on the *Rochambeau*. His note in the diary reads, "Just before sailing—how I hate to leave." By early May he was in Paris. He stayed a week to ten days, then left for Spain. His train trip to Madrid, stretching over several days, was the occasion for one of his rare diary entries:

> seemed very French until leaving Poitiers when the familiar interlocking tile roofs began to be replaced by Spanish tile. The colorings became

increasingly warmer and masses & groupings more interesting as Bordeaux approached. The *culmination* was Angoulême. Angoulême is worth a long stay. Several beautiful spired chateaux lie within a 1/2 hour beyond.

And later he commented on the colors:

> Pyrenees are very grand. Surprising Swiss chalets with tile roofs. Many peaks crowned with castles. The churches are all marvelously picturesque. Then there are the handsome peasants in the fields with their fine oxen. Houses are well built— of ochre-rock, cut stone-work appears. Roofs are

Fig. 2.26
Lionel H. Pries,
*Ronda—Vermillion
Bridge* [May 1922];
pencil on paper,
12¾ x 10 inches.
Pries drawing
collection, University of Washington
Libraries, Special
Collections Division, UW24135z.

brilliantly colored (pinks and reds thus far). The
masses are harmonious rather than our modern
jumbling. Picturesqueness is still achieved. Flowers
are wonderful—wild hyacinths—flowering haw-
thorns. . . . O the color of it all. The blues of the
mountains and the ochres & blacks & oranges
of the buildings—and above all the wonderful
greenness of everything (there are earth colors
as well!). This certainly must be the proper time
to come! Spain has its hilltowns too!

Pries remained in Spain for a month. Previously,
he had produced only three drawings, but in Spain
he began to draw and paint much more frequently.

He visited Seville, Ronda, Toledo, Segovia, and
Salamanca but was most taken by Granada and its
Alhambra; in just a week, at the end of May, he
produced a half-dozen finished drawings and one
watercolor (figs. 2.25, 2.26). Several of these drawings
record familiar monuments; others capture small
garden spaces or building details. His drawings and
watercolors were more than quick sketches: on the
back of his watercolor of the interior of the cathedral
at Salamanca, Pries noted, "2 sittings, 5 1/2 hours
total," and other drawings and paintings clearly
required similar effort (fig. 2.27).

In late June, Pries passed through southern
France, stopping briefly in Narbonne, Albi, and

SALAMANCA JUNE·17·1922

Carcassonne on his way to Italy. In July and August, he was in Venice. Of nearby cities, only Verona is represented in a drawing. Again Pries's drawings included the familiar monuments—for example, San Marco and the Bridge of Sighs—but he also drew some docks as well as a narrow canal. From Venice he sent at least one drawing back to the United States: in November, his oblique perspective of a café adjacent to the Doge's Palace placed second, in a field of several hundred drawings from five countries, in the 1922 Birch Burdette Long Sketch Competition, and it appeared in *Pencil Points* the next month[117] (fig. 2.28). By September, Pries had moved on to Florence, Fiesoli, Siena, and Perugia. His drawings tended to focus on the vernacular (for example, old houses in Florence) or details (the door of a church in Perugia; figs. 2.29, 2.30). He concluded this portion of his travels with a few days in Assisi.

After five and a half months of continuous travel, Pries arrived in Rome on 6 October. Later that day, he made his first tour of the Capitoline Hill, the Forum, and the Victor Emmanuel Monument. The next day he found a *pensione* at no. 5 via Gregoriana "with a room on a terrace overlooking all of Rome & S. Peters, besides being sunny." Via Gregoriana is on the ridge of the Pincian Hill, above the Spanish Steps, and Pries's room must have looked over the whole of the Campo Marzio to the south, and west across the Tiber, toward St. Peter's Basilica.[118] This was his home for the next four months. That afternoon, he visited the American Academy, where he would have gone had he received the 1921 Rome Prize. He described it as "very nice" but commented that there was "a dreadfully forgotten atmosphere" and added, "Thank God that I command my own destiny!"

Pries's first days in Rome were spent exploring. There is a sense in his diary entries that Pries saw this sojourn as the high point of his travels—he made entries on six succeeding days, the only time on his trip he wrote with this frequency. On 8 October he made his first visit to St. Peter's, noting in his diary:

> Off early to St. Peters! O the *glorious* thrill of the Piazza! Façade not the least disappointing, except for the attic! Interior wonderful! Of course, hardly religious, but still wonderful. Took all morning to casually inspect *only* the main level. . . .

That afternoon, he walked to the Pantheon by way of the Trevi Fountain, Santa Maria della Pace, Piazza Navona, the Cancelleria, and the Palazzo Massimo. On Monday, 9 October, he began with the Church of St. John Lateran and its "marvelous cloisters!"; later that day, he first saw the Colosseum:

> The noble mass was teeming with the crys [sic] & shouts of thousands. I really shivered—the place is dreadfully awe-inspiring, not even guides could interfere with the immense emotion called forth by the structure. The size is astounding.

No pencil drawings that Pries produced in Rome are known. Perhaps he made only a few. He was more settled and apparently felt he had the time to do watercolors. Still, the nine watercolors in the Pries collection seem a small output for his stay in the city (figs. 2.31, 2.32). Keith Kolb recalls that Pries talked of making measured drawings at the Pantheon— and experiencing vertigo when standing on the roof adjacent to the oculus.[119]

Pries's interests focused on architecture and art; he paid no attention to politics. The Fascist "March on Rome" took place on 27 October 1922, and Mussolini formed his first cabinet of Fascists and Nationalists four days later. On 25 November, the king and parliament granted Mussolini dictatorial powers (originally to last only through 1923) to restore order and introduce reforms, and thereafter the Fascists began to penetrate every level of government. Although Pries was present for the Fascists' initial ascension to power, his diary contains no comments on these events.

In the second half of January 1923, Pries was in Sicily, at Palermo, Agrigento, and Taormina, where he produced several haunting watercolors (figs. 2.33, 2.34). No records indicate where he was during February. His departure from Italy, at end of that month, prompted some melancholy reflections. Waiting in Milan for the train north, he wrote of his weariness (possibly due, at least in part, to his recognition that his European tour was now more than two-thirds complete), and he commented in his diary:

> I leave behind me a world of the past and its achievements as well as a people who live very much in the future—an ambitious and passionate people. . . . I leave Italy far less boisterously enthusiastic than on entering it—probably because of a really intimate acquaintance with it, which well supplements the statement that in the world all places are beautiful provided they are removed from the commonplace.

His comment about the Italian people living "in the future" may have been a reference to Fascism; if so, it is the only such reference in his writing. Pries described Italy as "a land of remarkable churches" but "*no religious* buildings" except "the intensely ritualistic Byzantine churches" and Milan Cathedral, which he characterized as "deeply religious, particularly in the deep, gloomy light of a winter day." Pries's comments suggest a premonition of his life in architecture. Rome was regarded as the pinnacle by Beaux-Arts education; but in five months in Italy, Pries discovered that he was not, at heart, a classi-

Fig. 2.29
Lionel H. Pries,
Lugarno, Florence
[September 1922];
pencil on paper, 9
x 10 inches. Pries
collection, University of Washington
Libraries, Special
Collections Division, UW 24138z.

Fig. 2.30 (*opposite*)
Lionel H. Pries,
*Door of the Church
of the Company of
the Dead* [Perugia,
September 1922];
watercolor, 9¾ x
7 inches. Pries
collection, Univer-
sity of Washington
Libraries, Special
Collections Divi-
sion, UW24133z.

Fig. 2.31 (*right*)
Lionel H. Pries,
untitled [façade of
St. Peter's, Rome,
fall/winter 1922–
23]; watercolor,
15 x 10 inches.
Pries drawing
collection, Univer-
sity of Washington
Libraries, Special
Collections Divi-
sion, UW12128z.

Fig. 2.32 (*left*) Lionel H. Pries, *On Monte Mario, Rome* [fall/winter 1922-23]; watercolor, 8¾ x 6 inches. Pries collection, University of Washington Libraries, Special Collections Division, UW24132z.

Fig. 2.33 (*opposite, top*) Lionel H. Pries, *Palermo, Monte Pellegrini,* 20 January 1923; watercolor, 8½ x 14½ inches. Pries drawing collection, University of Washington Libraries, Special Collections Division, UW24127z.

Fig. 2.34 (*opposite, bottom*) Lionel H. Pries, *Girgenti, Temples of Concord and Juno,* 24 January 1923; watercolor, 7 x 10 inches. Pries drawing collection, University of Washington Libraries, Special Collections Division, UW 24126z.

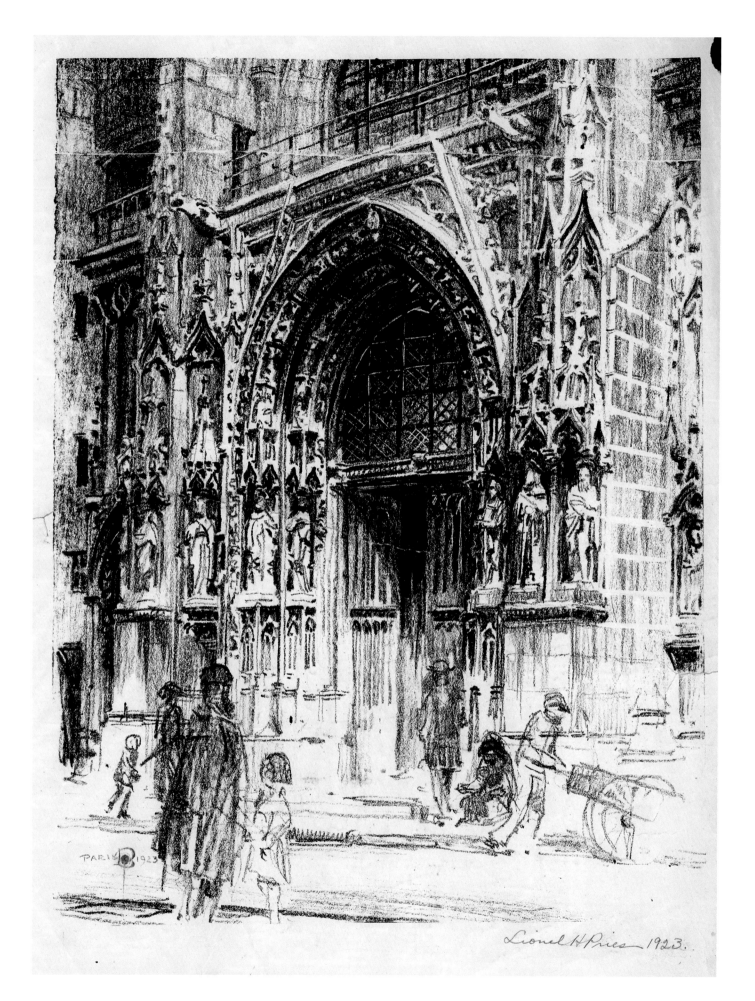

PARIS 1923

Lionel H Pries 1923.

cist. Throughout his career, Pries would appreciate classical design, but he would deeply feel that a truly living architecture had to appeal to the senses and the emotions, characteristics he seldom found in the achievements of ancient Rome or the Renaissance.

By 3 March, Pries's enthusiasm had returned as he wrote of his journey through the Alps, describing it as a "sojourn in fairyland," but he saved his highest praise for Strasbourg:

Strasbourg!! What glory—small wonder so fought over! At present a most thoroughly German city—will it ever be French? A cathedral in brownstone, and successful *because* of it!! Certainly the Gothic is baroque, yet as with all conventionally restrained baroque it has a great appeal to me. S. is the first town of multiplied peep-hole dormers and exaggerated roofs—a treatment which lends charm with even ugly walls, but those in S. are *not* ugly. Hundreds and hundreds of examples exist that have glorious half-timber and bulls-eye glass. . . . In all Strasbourg is worth returning to.

Although Pries arrived in Paris in early March and probably spent the first weeks exploring, his paintings and drawings were all produced in the second half of the month (fig. 2.35). He also visited some smaller towns, and at Longpont he made his one drawing of damage from the war. In early April he was in Rouen, and from there he went to England. His last diary entry, written at Waterloo Station on 12 May 1923, noted that his train was about to leave for Southampton, where he would board a ship back to the States.

Pries's "grand tour" took thirteen months. He focused on the Mediterranean countries, with a month in Spain, almost seven months in Italy, and a month in Paris. His itinerary reflects the Beaux-Arts celebration of classical tradition—but Pries's drawings and paintings do not focus solely on classical buildings. Many address vernacular structures, and even those that do address great monuments do so in unique ways that often emphasize these landmarks' picturesque character. His diary entries especially praise the picturesque landscape and architecture of the Pyrenees and the Alps and the German-French architecture of Strasbourg. Pries had been schooled in the Beaux-Arts, but his childhood had also been shaped by the romance of the California landscape and its regional Arts and

Crafts-influenced architecture. His artistic sensibility would remain broadly encompassing throughout his life.

On his return to the United States, Pries exhibited some drawings from his trip at the Architectural League of New York and, later, at the Bohemian Club of San Francisco. He produced a portfolio, primarily for friends, of small reproductions of nine of the pencil drawings; five were from Spain, two from France, and two from Italy; these were also published in *Architect and Engineer* for July 1926.[120]

Pries never returned to Italy or Spain. In 1933, he made his only other trip to Europe, and his itinerary included northeastern France, Belgium, Germany, Austria, and Scandinavia. Once he began teaching at the University of Washington, Pries frequently offered advice to students and graduates planning to travel in Europe.[121] The basis of his knowledge was primarily his 1922–23 trip, but he had come to know the places he visited so well that those he advised found his counsel invaluable.

Within a month after Pries's return, he was in California. On his passport he had given San Francisco as his permanent address; apparently he had always intended to return there.

REGIONAL VARIATIONS ON A BEAUX-ARTS THEME

Pries's training was similar, in general terms, to that received by hundreds of other architects of his generation who attended American schools with programs modeled on the Ecole des Beaux-Arts. John Galen Howard had called the Beaux-Arts a "great movement," and Pries's education had prepared him to join that movement. However, at Berkeley and at Penn, Pries encountered faculty who primarily emphasized the problem-solving character of the Ecole method; and in California and Philadelphia, he encountered two of the strongest "regional schools" within the broad design framework of academic eclecticism.[122] Although skilled in classical design, he never became a committed classicist.[123] Pries's romanticism, his educational and emotional ties to the regional architectures of California and Philadelphia, and his early experience of the arts of Asia, the landscape of California, and the Arts and Crafts ethos of the Bay Area decisively shaped his life in architecture and the arts.

3

FINDING
HIS WAY

SAN FRANCISCO AND

SANTA BARBARA, 1923–1928

THE SAN FRANCISCO TO WHICH PRIES RETURNED in the summer of 1923, just after his twenty-sixth birthday, had long since recovered from the 1906 earthquake and fire. As the financial capital of the West, the city experienced rapid growth throughout the 1920s. New office blocks and institutional structures were built in the academic modes, following the pattern that had developed at the turn of the century, but suburban residential design had changed markedly as the Arts and Crafts movement waned after 1914, and the lingering Bay Area Tradition of freely composed wood and shingle buildings was dealt a severe blow by the September 1923 fire that destroyed more than five hundred structures in the Berkeley hills.[1] Afterward, Bay Area residential clients usually preferred houses with walls of stucco, or occasionally of brick or stone, and tile roofs. While a few clients still pursued adventurous designs with architects like Bernard Maybeck, the cultural uncertainty of the interwar years led many to prefer historical vocabularies including Tudor, French, and Italian but especially Spanish Colonial Revival or Mediterranean.

As a talented young architect, Pries must have been ambitious to open his own office; but, realistically, he was not quite ready to start out on his own.[2] He had been away from the Bay Area for nearly three years and had not engaged in practice for almost fourteen months.

The San Francisco architectural profession had matured since the turn of the century, and the offices that received the larger architectural commissions in the 1920s were led by the generation of designers who had come of age before 1910. Many had attended the Ecole des Beaux-Arts; others were graduates of American architectural schools.[3] With his education and abilities, Pries had no difficulty finding employment. He initially worked as a draftsman for the firm of George Kelham, associated at the time with William G. Merchant; it may have been Merchant, a graduate of the Wilmerding School, who offered Pries the position.[4] Pries worked on the Medico-Dental Building (1923–25), a fifteen-story office structure at the corner of Post and Mason in downtown San Francisco. It was considered a model medical office building, featuring straightforward design and limited embellishment. Pries evidently worked on design development and construction drawings and may have detailed the travertine walls and metal screens in the lobby.[5]

Architectural Practice, 1923–1925

In 1923–24, Pries began to accept independent design commissions. His first projects came from close friends, particularly the Maas family. Although they had both been in the architectural curriculum at (Lick-)Wilmerding, neither Carlos nor Theodore Maas had gone on to a career in the profession. Instead, both joined the business and philanthropic ventures of their great uncle Henry E. Bothin. Bothin's only son had died many years before, so Carlos and Theodore Maas (and their older brother, Donald) were groomed to take over various Bothin enterprises.[6]

Henry Ernest Bothin (1853–1923) was born and raised in Ohio but went west as a young man. He was successful as an importer, and he invested in real estate, manufacturing, insurance, utilities, and other ventures.[7] By the early twentieth century, he owned more than seventy buildings in San Francisco. After 1905, he began to take an interest in philanthropy. He provided 122 acres in Marin County to serve as a summer camp for children from San Francisco's Telegraph Hill Neighborhood Association (Settlement House) and subsequently funded construction of the Bothin Convalescent Home on the same property. He later gave additional acreage for the Arequipa Tuberculosis Sanitorium for Working Women, and in 1917 he established a charitable foundation, the Bothin Helping Fund.[8] Not long after the San Francisco earthquake, Bothin began to winter in Santa Barbara, and he invested in that community as well. In 1914–17, he built a winter home, called Piranhurst, in nearby Montecito.[9]

Carlos Maas initially worked for the Bothin Real Estate Company, but about 1920 he joined the Bothin-controlled Judson Manufacturing Company, a leading steel manufacturer based in Oakland.[10] After Henry Bothin's death, in 1923, Maas was elected president of that company. At the same time, Bothin's second wife, Ellen Chabot Bothin, succeeded to the presidency of the Bothin Real Estate Company, and Theodore Maas became its vice president.[11] Ellen Bothin and Theodore Maas also served as trustees of the Bothin Helping Fund, to which Henry Bothin had bequeathed his Santa Barbara properties.

In 1923–24, Pries developed several residential designs for Ida Sutter Maas, mother of the Maas brothers. The first pages of his scrapbook include sketches, dated January 1924, for a San Francisco townhouse remodeling for "Mrs. Maas" at Van Ness Avenue and Chestnut Street.[12] But, two months later, Ida Maas went forward with an entirely new townhouse of Pries's design, described in the March 1923 permit as a three-floor building with "two flats."[13] As constructed, the stucco-faced building at 1242 Francisco Street was divided into a symmetrical block to the left and a slightly recessed subsidiary block to the right; this design gave primacy to the main entrance below a bay window at the center of the primary block, and it reduced the visual impact of the garage door (fig. 3.1). The San Francisco city directory for 1925 listed Ida, Donald, Theodore, and Henry Maas and Lionel Pries all at the 1242 Francisco address.[14] Ida Maas owned the building and had a large apartment with space for her sons. Pries had an apartment of his own, but it was interconnected to the Maas apartment, as he was almost like another son. Both apartments were of his design[15] (fig. 3.2).

Pries's scrapbook includes numerous sketches of unidentified projects from this period.[16] The many sketches suggest a prolific imagination ready for any willing client. That so many of these projects went unrealized also indicates the difficulty Pries faced: finding clients who would give him commissions in the competitive professional environment of the Bay Area.

The 1923 Berkeley Hills fire destroyed the Abracadabra House in which Pries had lived as a student. Members turned to Pries for design of a replacement. His sketches of the project show a composition of simple forms suggesting Mission or Spanish precedents, although the almost complete absence of ornament gave a surprisingly abstract character. Completed in time for the 1925 fall term, the new seventeen-room Abracadabra House (1924–25; destroyed) was built of untinted concrete block (called "thermotite construction" on the permit), perhaps to reduce the cost[17] (figs. 3.3, 3.4). The appearance was startlingly severe, with only one ornamental touch: a small tile panel above the entrance. A humorous commentary on the project suggests its unexpected character: "Taking unquestioned rank as the eighth wonder of the world, the new Abracadabracadabracadabracad [sic] house, is rapidly nearing completion. Everyone who views it, with the exception of the loyal brothers, has asked the same question, 'What is it?'"[18] The unusual design suggests that Pries, even at this early date, was willing to experiment with utilitarian materials, and that he did not feel a need to follow historical

Fig. 3.1
Lionel H. Pries,
Ida Sutter Maas
two-flat apartment
building, San
Francisco, 1924
(altered); colored
pencil on paper,
4¾ x 3¾ inches.
Pries scrapbook,
1r; Pries collection,
University of
Washington
Libraries, Special
Collections Division,
UW23685z.

precedent. But the stark appearance of the building was not likely to attract new clients; in fact, 1924 brought no more new commissions.[19]

In the first half of 1925, Pries fared little better. He sketched several alternatives for a residence at a Palo Alto site, but when the client, J. M. Johnson, decided to proceed, he turned to another architect[20] (fig. 3.5). Pries's proposed two-story building for the Sausalito Land and Ferry Company (a Bothin enterprise headed by Theodore Maas) received a building permit in July, but construction never began.[21]

Thus, in his first two years after returning to San Francisco, Pries realized only two buildings.[22] Even with his early struggles, Pries might gradually have attracted more clients and slowly built up his practice, but the Santa Barbara earthquake of June 1925 gave him the opportunity to take on larger commissions. Three weeks after the quake, the *Santa Barbara Morning Press* reported that the Bothin Helping Fund would spend $300,000 to reconstruct twelve large buildings in the city.[23] The article named a San Francisco company, Mattock and Feasey, as the contractor for these projects and said that plans for reconstruction were being "rushed," although no

architect was mentioned. A few weeks later, Pries relocated to Santa Barbara as the architect for the Bothin Helping Fund.

REBUILDING SANTA BARBARA, 1925–1926

Santa Barbara had developed as a unique California community. Located on the only section of the California coast facing south, with mountains to the north and east and islands to the southwest, the city has a benign climate, an attractive feature for wealthy winter residents. With limited harbor facilities and no railroad link until 1887, Santa Barbara became a city of fine homes and resorts. In the 1890s, it was compared to the French Riviera. Most wealthy residents came from New York and Chicago, with a few exceptions, such as the Bothins of San Francisco. Nearby Montecito, an unincorporated portion of Santa Barbara County, was the site of many large estates.

Although its late-nineteenth-century buildings reflected national trends, Santa Barbara remained the most Spanish city in California. The survival

Fig. 3.3
Lionel H. Pries,
Abracadabra
House, Berkeley,
1924–25
(destroyed). Pries
collection, University of Washington
Libraries, Special
Collections Division, UW23761z.

Fig. 3.4
Lionel H. Pries,
Abracadabra
House, interior
(destroyed). Pries
collection, University of Washington
Libraries, Special
Collections Division, UW23762z.

SKETCH for PALO ALTO RESIDENCE for MR. J + M. JOHNSON

ARCHITECT LIONEL H. PRIES

Fig. 3.5
Lionel H. Pries,
J. M. Johnson
residence project,
Palo Alto, ca.
1924–25 (unbuilt);
pencil and water-
color on paper, 9¼
x 12¼ inches. Pries
scrapbook, 39r;
Pries collection
University of
Washington
Libraries, Special
Collections Divi-
sion, UW23676z.

of the Mission church (its Mission remained in the hands of the Franciscans), a large number of adobe structures from the Spanish-Mexican period, and several Spanish-Mexican ranches, as well as the impact of the Mission Revival after 1890, provided the basis for a consistent architectural character for the community.[24]

The desire to refashion Santa Barbara as a completely Spanish community predated the 1925 earthquake. After the turn of the century, the city's upper middle class had begun to show a preference for sophisticated Mediterranean or Spanish Colonial Revival design. About 1919, Bertram Goodhue suggested redeveloping older blocks in central Santa Barbara in Spanish Colonial Revival, and others followed with similar proposals. The Santa Barbara Community Arts Association, formed in 1920, began to build support for planning and architectural con-

trols. Three years later, the city created a planning commission and adopted zoning and building ordinances. A board of architectural review was proposed in 1924 but was not yet in place at the time of the earthquake.

The earthquake of 29 June 1925 struck at 6:43 A.M. The initial intense shock lasted fifteen seconds and was followed two minutes later by another shock lasting ten to twelve seconds.[25] The two tremors damaged many downtown buildings. Older brick façades proved particularly vulnerable, but later buildings experienced much less damage. Nineteenth-century Victorian architecture suffered the most destruction, providing the opportunity to remake Santa Barbara with a consistent Spanish/ Mediterranean character. The city approved the creation of the Board of Architectural Review, and in the next nine months it processed over two thou-

sand designs. When the *Santa Barbara Morning Press* reported that the Bothin Helping Fund would rebuild twelve Santa Barbara structures, it noted that all would "conform or harmonize with the Spanish architecture adopted by the city."[26]

The Spanish Colonial Revival adopted by Santa Barbara was a flexible mode that included a range of Mediterranean precedents:

> Spanish Colonial Revival is really a catalog of styles, unified by the use of arches, courtyards, form as mass, plain wall surfaces, and tile roofs, all derived from the Mediterranean world. Designers were inspired by a number of sources: the adobe and colonial buildings of Monterey, California; late forms of Moorish architecture; medieval Spanish and Italian church architecture; Ultra-Baroque design of colonial Spain and Portugal; rural forms from Andalusia; Italian Romanesque and Renaissance revival elements; and southwestern Hopi and Pueblo Indian adobes. This broad source base made it relatively easy to create a convincing harmony between the exterior image, interior space, decorative elements, and the building's function.[27]

Although Santa Barbara had numerous architects skilled in the Spanish Colonial Revival, including Pries's Berkeley friend Lutah Riggs (then working with the leading Santa Barbara architect George Washington Smith), the Bothin Helping Fund trustees turned instead to Pries. He was probably in Santa Barbara by late July.[28]

The flexibility of Spanish Colonial Revival design proved well suited to Pries. His projects drew on a wide range of precedents, displaying a sensitivity to overall composition and spatial development as well as to the design of individual decorative elements. Three of Pries's early buildings, on the fringe of the downtown core, addressed the burgeoning automobile industry. The first was the one-story Blake Motor Building (1925; destroyed), on State Street at Sola. The *Santa Barbara Morning Press* described it as "reconstructed to a unique design in harmony with the new architectural program"[29] (fig. 3.6). Although it was a modest one-story structure, the architect Winsor Soule featured it in his article on Santa Barbara in the July 1926 *American Architect*, describing it as a design where "limiting conditions were paramount in importance," adding, "Here Mr. Pries has retained every opening as it existed before the quake, but by careful attention to color, texture and proportion has attained a building notable for its simplicity and charm."[30] Pries must have appreciated such praise, which highlighted just those elements—color, texture, and proportion—that were the focus of so many of his later designs as well as of his teaching. Pries's next project was the Hollingsworth-Overland Agency building (1925–26; altered), in the 400 block of State Street. A one-story structure with a tile roof, completed in January, this building showed Pries's first use of pointed (Moorish) arches—here, with notably broad proportions[31] (fig. 3.7). He repeated the use of Moorish arches at the El Camino Real Garage (1925–26; altered), in the 300 block of State.[32] This utilitarian structure,

Fig. 3.6
Lionel H. Pries, Blake Motor Building, Santa Barbara, 1925 (destroyed). Santa Barbara Historical Museum, Santa Barbara.

Fig. 3.7
Lionel H. Pries,
Hollingsworth-
Overland Agency
Building, Santa
Barbara, 1925–26
(altered). Special
Collections,
Davidson Library,
University of
California, Santa
Barbara.

Fig. 3.8
Lionel H. Pries,
El Camino Real
Garage (Auto
Showrooms and
Seaside Oil Com-
pany Building),
Santa Barbara,
1925–26 (altered).
Special Collec-
tions, Davidson
Library, Univer-
sity of California,
Santa Barbara.

constructed at a cost of $35,000, featured a roman-
tic streetfront arcade detailed in patterned brick-
work and stucco[33] (fig. 3.8).

Pries's primary contributions to the reconstruction of the downtown core were the Bothin and
McKay Buildings. Pries displayed drawings for the
Bothin Building, in the 900 block of State, in late
September (fig. 3.9). The original structure, completed in 1902, had been a three-story brick building in a vaguely classical mode; the reconstruction
is a steel-framed two-story structure. Pries's design
features arches at the first floor and a recessed balcony at the second; he intended the wood timbers
of the balcony roof to be stenciled with bright colors.
Soule, commenting in *American Architect,* especially
praised the balcony: "The delightful open loggia of

the second floor gives a distinct air of Southern
Spain—the balconies of Seville or the loggias of
Cadiz—and is cleverly lighted at night from pots set
in the balcony rail"[34] (fig. 3.10). In their guide to the
city's historic core, Rebecca Conrad and Christopher
H. Nelson describe the Bothin Building as "one of
the really distinguished examples of Spanish Colonial Revival in Santa Barbara."[35]

The McKay or LaPlacita Building (1925–26)
was the last large building that Pries designed in
the city. The *Santa Barbara Morning Press* heralded
the replacement of the pre-earthquake McKay Building (dating from 1904) in July 1925, noting, "The
McKay Building facing De la Guerra Plaza and State
Street is one of the most important buildings in the
[Bothin] group, as its completion will remove the

Fig. 3.9
Lionel H. Pries,
Bothin Building,
Santa Barbara,
1925–26, pre-
liminary scheme;
watercolor, 8½ x
14½ inches. Pries
collection, Univer-
sity of Washington
Libraries, Special
Collections Divi-
sion, UW24231z.

Fig. 3.10
Lionel H. Pries,
Bothin Building.
Special Collec-
tions, Davidson
Library, Univer-
sity of California,
Santa Barbara.

Fig. 3.11
Lionel H. Pries,
McKay Build-
ing (La Placita
Building), Santa
Barbara, 1925–26,
De la Guerra Plaza
elevation. Special
Collections,
Davidson Library,
University of
California, Santa
Barbara.

Fig. 3.12
Lionel H. Pries,
McKay Building
(La Placita Build-
ing), State Street
elevation. Photo
by author, 2004.

last vestige of 'Main Street' architecture from City Hall plaza."[36] Yet, as a result of the complexity of the project, construction did not begin until April 1926.[37] The building fronts both State Street and the plaza, and an appropriate treatment was necessary for each side.[38] Designed to house three stores on the first floor and offices on the floors above, the McKay Building is rectilinear facing State and turning into De la Guerra; but, facing the plaza, it is picturesquely composed with an outside stair, a projecting wood balcony, and a three-story tower[39] (figs. 3.11, 3.12).

Fig. 3.13
Lionel H. Pries,
A. B. Watkins
real estate office
project, Santa
Barbara, 1925–26
(unbuilt); water-
color, 9¼ x 6¾
inches. Pries
scrapbook, 47r;
Pries collection,
University of
Washington
Libraries, Special
Collections
Division,
UW23671z.

At least one Pries commission in downtown Santa Barbara did not go forward. The *Santa Barbara Morning Press* reported in October 1925 that A. B. Watkins, the realtor who represented the Bothin interests, would build a new office of "Moorish architecture harmonizing with other types prevalent in the business district."[40] Pries was fascinated by this project and produced numerous sketches and a beautiful watercolor of the interior (fig. 3.13). But Watkins entered a partnership, and Pries's design was never built.

Pries was also involved in the design of the Bothin family's Montecito estate, Piranhurst. The residence was a Mediterranean design dating from 1917. Pries, who had familiarity with the design of country estates from his time in Philadelphia, was responsible for a new landscape plan that included a redesigned drive and motor court. He lined the drive with palm trees to create an impressive formal approach to the house.[41] Though Pries never claimed to be a landscape architect, this was just the first of his landscape designs; throughout his career he would address landscape, most often in connection with his own building designs, typically creating seamless relationships between indoor and outdoor spaces.

It seems that Pries, during his time in Santa Barbara, did not try to expand his practice beyond the Bothin Helping Fund, likely because Santa Barbara was a small, closed community, both socially and professionally.[42] Nevertheless, one of Pries's most important Santa Barbara projects came from a non-Bothin client, another newcomer, Frank Morley Fletcher (1866–1949). Fletcher was a painter and printmaker who, in 1923, gave up his position as director of Edinburgh College of Art to become director of the newly created Santa Barbara School of the Arts.[43] Fletcher selected Pries to design his Santa Barbara home. The project began while Pries was in Santa Barbara, but the drawings were finished in May 1926, after Pries returned to San Francisco.[44]

A one-story house of only four major rooms, the Frank Morley Fletcher residence (1926–27) was the first of Pries's notable houses (figs. 3.14, 3.15). The two primary blocks of the Spanish design—a large studio (with a small attached kitchen) and a bedroom wing (with two bedrooms, a bathroom, and a sleeping porch)—formed an L linked only by a 7–foot-wide gallery. The front door opened into the gallery, offering access both to the studio and,

through its glazed north wall, directly to the outdoor terrace and landscaped private yard (fig. 3.16). The large room labeled "studio" on Pries's plan was used by the Fletcher family as their living-dining room; the ceiling, at a height of 14 feet, featured wood paneling and a stencil pattern of Pries's design. Many of the elements seen first in the Fletcher residence—a relatively opaque front, a layered sequence of spaces from the entry to an outside view, a tall living room with crafted wood ceiling, and the integrated design of house and site—were to recur often in Pries's later work. Thus, by 1926, Pries was beginning to find his métier and was developing design ideas that would serve him through much of his life. The quality of the project was recognized locally; during the 1927 Santa Barbara Better Homes Week, the Fletcher residence won a special award in the five-room small house competition.[45]

RETURN TO SAN FRANCISCO, 1926–1928

When Pries returned to San Francisco, he received a series of commissions that allowed him to demonstrate his increasing capabilities as a residential designer.[46] These projects show his flexible use of precedent and his increasing ability to respond to varying contexts, sites, and clients.

Before the end of 1925, Pries began collaborating with the contractor Mattock and Feasey on a residential development scheme in San Francisco.[47] In December of that year, Mattock and Feasey acquired a group of lots on the west side of Miraloma Drive, in the city's St. Francis Wood neighborhood. They planned to sell lots to buyers who would commission designs by Pries, which Mattock and Feasey would then construct. The architectural challenge was to design individual yet compatible houses, each tailored to client and site.

Several Pries sketches suggest that he hoped the Miraloma houses would be commissioned simultaneously and could be designed as a group. However, only three houses were realized: the Theodore Maas residence (1925–26; destroyed), the Norris K. Davis residence (1926), and the Alfred H. and Clarence Feasey residence (1926). The houses are notable for their consistent palette of primary materials—stucco walls and tile roofs—and for the free treatment of their individual designs.

Maas acquired two lots, a decision that allowed a two-story L-shaped design, with the longer side

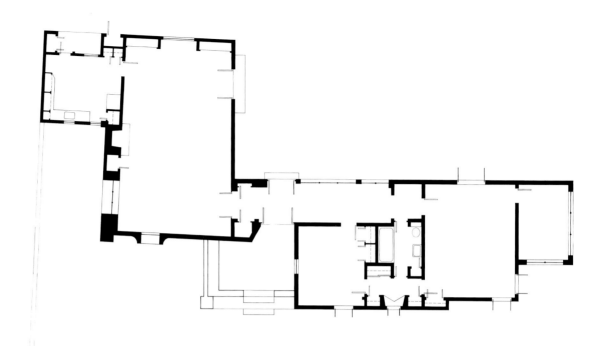

Fig. 3.14
Lionel H. Pries,
Frank Morley
Fletcher residence,
Santa Barbara,
1926–27 (altered);
floor plan. Draw-
ing by Byung Keun
Choi (based on
blueprint held
by University Art
Museum, Univer-
sity of California,
Santa Barbara).

Fig. 3.15
Lionel H. Pries,
Frank Morley
Fletcher residence,
front elevation.
Photo by author,
2004.

Fig. 3.16
Lionel H. Pries,
Frank Morley
Fletcher residence,
landscaped court-
yard and rear
elevation. Photo
by author, 2004.

Fig. 3.17
Lionel H. Pries,
Frank Morley
Fletcher residence,
hall at entry.
Special Collections,
Davidson Library,
University of
California, Santa
Barbara.

parallel to the street.[48] In addition to stucco and tile, Pries used wood siding on a portion of the second floor; the design is notable for its relative simplicity, plain surfaces, and astylar character (fig. 3.18). Davis also acquired two lots.[49] His house was planned as a 20–foot-wide rectangle with a slight L at one end. The plainness of the stucco walls is relieved by the rectangular window openings, an arched door, a corner balcony on the second floor, and a few other decorative details that activate the surface (fig. 3.19). The Feasey residence, the least expensive of the three, is on a single lot.[50] The plan is L-shaped but perpendicular to the street; the most unusual feature is the thick wall, with Moorish arches, for the garage doors (fig. 3.20). Like the Maas and Davis residences, this is a two-story house, but one of the living floors is a level below the street. The entrance, on an intermediate level, is reached through a gate and at the bottom of some steps to one side of the garage. Only a small decorative detail at the balcony breaks the planar wall surface.

Pries considered two more houses along Miraloma Drive. He developed a design for Mrs. Edward W. (Helen Thompson) Hopkins after she bought a lot in January 1927, but she never built.[51] Sketches show a rectilinear block of relatively plain design. In the same month, Pries acquired a lot on Miraloma Drive for himself, but no design for his site has been discovered.[52]

Pries's next project was the Fred B. and Cleo A. Kerrick residence (1926–27), in the Lakeshore Highlands district of Oakland, permitted in September 1926.[53] Constructed at a reported cost of $7,500, the house is a rectangle in plan, with a cylindrical volume at the east end, facing the street[54] (fig. 3.21). The primary first-floor spaces are the octagonal dining room (within the cylinder) and the large living room. The front door opens directly into a broad hall that links these two rooms and connects to a small office and to the stair to two second-floor bedrooms. Pries's hand is evident in the well-detailed stucco exterior and tile roof, Moorish arched openings, and wood-beam ceiling of the living room.[55]

Two residential buildings in Berkeley for Dr. Clair H. Denman were permitted in October.[56] These are just a few blocks north of the University of California campus, on a parcel about 50 feet wide and more than 400 feet long (two lots joined end to end), extending from Euclid Avenue to Hawthorne Terrace. The Denman residence (1926–27), 1521 Hawthorne Terrace, is built into the steeply sloped west end of the lot. The garage is at the level of Hawthorne, and the house rises up the slope. Pries's sketch placed his design in an imaginary context of similar structures, although the house is actually quite distinct in its context, which is less romantic than he suggested (figs. 3.22, 3.23). From the top-floor balcony there are views to San Francisco Bay to

Fig. 3.18 Lionel H. Pries, Theodore Maas residence, San Francisco, 1925–26 (destroyed). Pries collection, University of Washington Libraries, Special Collections Division, UW23784z.

Fig. 3.19 (*opposite, top*) Lionel H. Pries, Norris K. Davis residence, San Francisco, 1926. Pries collection, University of Washington Libraries, Special Collections Division, UW23783z.

Fig. 3.20 (*opposite, bottom*) Lionel H. Pries, Alfred H. and Clarence Feasey residence, San Francisco, 1926. Pries collection, University of Washington Libraries, Special Collections Division, UW23782z.

the west. As in Pries's other structures from this period, the materials are stucco and tile, and the detailing is abstracted from the Spanish Colonial Revival. The Denman studio (1926–27), originally 1519 Hawthorne Terrace, a more conventional one-floor residential structure with a gable roof, is on the flat portion of the site, east of the house.[57]

Pries's most unusual project of 1926 was an early scheme for the San Francisco-Oakland Bay Bridge. How Pries came to be involved remains a mystery, but a surviving perspective, titled "San Francisco Abutment, Telegraph Hill-Goat Island Bridge," identifies R. S. Crew as the engineer and Pries as the architect for the project[58] (fig. 3.24).

The eighteen months from the spring of 1926 to the fall of 1927 were a time of increasing professional success for Pries. His workload was such that he briefly took on an employee—Norman K. Blanchard, a Berkeley graduate of 1922.[59] Pries's work also attracted the attention of the architectural press. His portfolio of drawings from Europe had already appeared in *Architect and Engineer* in July

1926, and several Santa Barbara projects had been illustrated in Winsor Soule's article in *American Architect* the same month. The February 1927 issue of *Pacific Coast Architect* featured Pries's drawing of the proposed Bay Bridge abutment on the cover and devoted eleven pages to drawings of Pries designs, including the Johnson residence project, the A. B. Watkins office project, the Abracadabra House, the Feasey residence, the Kerrick residence, and several unidentified projects.[60] Drawings by Pries would also be featured on the covers of six of the twelve issues of *Pacific Coast Architect* in 1928, although these were drawings from his LeBrun Traveling Scholarship trip, not current work.[61]

In late 1926, Pries began designing a house in Palo Alto for Dr. Emma K. Willits (1869–1965), a pioneering woman surgeon who was chair of the Department of General Surgery at San Francisco's Children's Hospital.[62] This commission proved to be one of the more important of his career. Willits and her partner, Elizabeth Ristine, became Pries's lifelong friends. Willits acknowledged that she

Fig. 3.21
Lionel H. Pries, Fred B. and Cleo A. Kerrick residence, Oakland, 1926–27. Pries collection, University of Washington Libraries, Special Collections Division, UW23785z.

Fig. 3.22
Lionel H. Pries,
Dr. Clair H.
Denman residence,
Berkeley, 1926–27;
pencil on paper, 6
x 7¼ inches. Pries
scrapbook, 52r,
Pries collection,
University of
Washington
Libraries, Special
Collections
Division,
UW23667z.

Fig. 3.23
Lionel H. Pries,
Dr. Clair H.
Denman residence.
Pries scrapbook,
48v, Pries collec-
tion, University
of Washington
Libraries, Special
Collections Divi-
sion, UW23669z.

SAN FRANCISCO ABUTMENT
TELEGRAPH·HILL – GOAT ISLAND BRIDGE
R.S. CHEW · · · · · · ENGINEER
LIONEL·H·PRIES·ARCHITECT

PRIES
1926

Fig. 3.24
R. S. Crew, engineer; Lionel H. Pries, architect, preliminary scheme for San Francisco abutment, San Francisco-Oakland Bay Bridge, 1926; charcoal pencil on paper, 13 x 10 inches. Pries collection, University of Washington Libraries, Special Collections Division, UW24370z.

knew little about design and gave Pries a relatively free hand, although she did exercise some control over costs.[63] When the building permit was issued, in mid-April 1927, the project was described as a two-floor residence costing $17,000.[64] Pries not only designed the house but was also largely responsible for the interior furnishings. Thus the Emma K. Willits residence (1926–27; altered) was the most complete realization of Pries's early design ideas.

The site for the Willits residence is a relatively flat southwest-facing midblock lot measuring 85 by 111 feet. Pries placed the primary two-story block of the house about 10 feet from the back (northeast) lot line; the living room and the garage extend from the main block toward the street, forming an L-plan surrounding two sides of the outdoor courtyard. Low walls create a series of zones of increasing privacy as one approaches the house; the low wall opposite the living room curves to incorporate a built-in bench. Both the dining room and the living room open to the courtyard through large Moorish arched doors (fig. 3.25). The front entrance hall, at the corner of the L-plan, connects the living room, the dining room, the stair, and the kitchen. The first floor also includes a guest bedroom and maid's rooms. Two bedrooms, dressing rooms, and bathrooms are on the second floor.

Pries attended to every detail. Notable exterior features that show his hand include the chimney and the wrought iron grille at the guest bedroom window, both derived from Mediterranean vernacular precedents. The large, high-ceilinged living room features a coffered and stenciled wood ceiling, two chandeliers, and a cast-stone fireplace, all of Pries's design. Pries also selected the tapestry, the window coverings, and most of the furniture. Some of the pieces—for example, the sofa—may have been of his own design (figs. 3.26, 3.27). The dining room was more simply treated—the arched ceiling with stenciled beams was its most notable feature (fig. 3.28). The second-floor hall and bedrooms also have beamed ceilings; here, Pries was responsible for the selection of the textiles, including the many Native American rugs (fig. 3.29).

Fig. 3.25
Lionel H. Pries, Dr. Emma K. Willits residence, Palo Alto, 1926–27 (altered). Pries collection, University of Washington Libraries, Special Collections Division, UW23775z.

Fig. 3.26
Lionel H. Pries,
Dr. Emma K.
Willits residence,
living room as seen

from hall, water-
color, 10¼ x 7¾
inches. Courtesy
of Ed Winskill.

Fig. 3.27
Lionel H. Pries,
Dr. Emma K.
Willits residence,
living room. Pries

collection, University of Washington
Libraries, Special
Collections Division, UW23777z.

Fig. 3.28
Lionel H. Pries,
Dr. Emma K.
Willits residence,
dining room. Pries
collection, University of Washington
Libraries, Special
Collections Division, UW23778z.

Fig. 3.29
Lionel H. Pries,
Dr. Emma K.
Willits residence,
bedroom. Pries
collection, University of Washington
Libraries, Special
Collections Division, UW23780z.

Fig. 3.30
Lionel H. Pries,
Telegraph Hill
Neighborhood
Association Build-
ing remodeling
and addition,
1927–28 (altered),
courtyard. San
Francisco History
Collection, San
Francisco Public
Library.

With its stucco walls, tile roof, and Moorish arches, the Willits residence can be easily identified as a Spanish Colonial Revival design. But this label may be too simple if it fails to recognize the continuing influence of the Arts and Crafts tradition on Pries's work. Pries's incorporation of well-crafted woodwork, his design of many of the fixtures, and his selection of furnishings and textiles are all indicative of the spirit of Arts and Crafts that he had absorbed in his youth and that was now transformed as his design vocabulary reflected the more overtly historical tendencies of the 1920s.

In 1927, Pries designed the enlargement of San Francisco's Telegraph Hill Neighborhood Association building (1927–28; altered). Founded in 1902, the Telegraph Hill Neighborhood Association was part of the settlement house movement that swept across the country in the late nineteenth and early twentieth centuries.[65] In 1907, the Telegraph Hill Association built a chalet-style building, designed by Bernard Maybeck, on Stockton Street, to provide meeting rooms, a dispensary, and flats for nurses and settlement workers. Maybeck designed addi-

tions in 1909 and 1913, adding a library, clinical space, a small operating room, and a small gymnasium.[66] In her 1920 report to the association board, Director Elizabeth Ashe commented that the building had done "yeoman's service."[67] By 1923, there were discussions of another addition, and in 1927, with funding in hand (possibly including contributions from the Bothin Helping Fund), the association turned to Pries.

Pries's building reconstructed the oldest Maybeck structure (on the north side of the site) and reconfigured the courtyard. He moved the gymnasium and added spaces that included an office, a game room, a sewing room, a club meeting room, and a music and dancing room.[68] Pries told the association that his intention was to make the building "like 'Old Italy,'" with balconies and stairways surrounding a sunny courtyard[69] (fig. 3.30). Pries's additions clearly achieve this effect, and they fit so seamlessly into the earlier portions of the building that they have frequently been credited to Maybeck rather than to Pries.[70]

PROPOSED RESIDENCE
FOR
MR: A GERSKE
BURLINGAME HILLS·CALIF.

Lionel H. Pries, ARCHITECT.

LEAVING CALIFORNIA, 1927–1928

Pries no doubt had mixed feelings about his practice in 1926 and 1927. He had seen more of his buildings constructed, and he had developed some new friendships, but he still remained dependent on the Maas brothers for most of his commissions. Although Pries had been busy in 1926 and early 1927, it seems that by late that year his volume of work was declining. He may also have felt frustrated about the opportunities that were open to him.

Through his work in Santa Barbara and his Bay Area residential clients, Pries had become identified as a Spanish Colonial Revival designer.[71] His built work attracted those who wanted more of the same. But Pries increasingly wished to engage in a wider range of design vocabularies. Only his remodelings and additions, which were not well known, showed his capabilities in other modes. And he was exhausted—in California, Pries was a sole proprietor and, apart from a brief period in 1926 and early 1927, had no employees.[72] He was responsible for all aspects of practice—seeking projects, developing designs, preparing construction documents, and overseeing construction. In Santa Barbara, he had

handled at least eight projects in little more than ten months, and he frequently traveled back to San Francisco. From mid 1926 to mid 1927, he was responsible for buildings scattered from Marin County to Oakland and Berkeley to Palo Alto as well as for numerous designs that did not proceed.[73] Renderings of several unbuilt residential projects suggest that the geographical reach of Pries's practice was expanding; locations included San Mateo, Burlingame, Hillsborough, and even Beverly Hills[74] (fig. 3.31). Even projects that did not proceed beyond design still required travel as Pries pursued clients and presented preliminary schemes.

Pries had enjoyed growing success as an architect, but, after four years, he was also aware of his limitations. His most successful projects were those for close friends like Carlos and Theodore Maas, or for clients who became close friends, such as Emma Willits. He had been less successful in expanding his clientele significantly beyond this circle. He may well have been uncomfortable with the need to "sell" his services. After four years, he was likely growing disenchanted with pursuing clients and administering projects during construction. His strengths were in design and delineation.

Fig. 3.31
Lionel H. Pries, Gerske residence project, Burlingame Hills, ca. 1927 (unbuilt); pencil and watercolor on paper, 5½ x 10¼ inches. Pries scrapbook, 49r, Pries collection, University of Washington Libraries, Special Collections Division, UW23670z.

Sometime in late 1927, Pries entertained William and Mildred ("Billee") Bain when they visited San Francisco from Seattle. William Bain was a classmate from Penn who had a growing practice in the Pacific Northwest. During the visit, he invited Pries to become his partner.[75] Pries probably had not anticipated receiving an offer outside California. Acceptance would mean moving to a city he did not know, where he had few personal contacts. It would also mean leaving friends and the only place he had ever called home. However, there was no certainty that he would find a similar opportunity in the Bay Area. Pries did not hesitate; by mid to late February 1928, he was on his way to Seattle. In March 1928, *Architect and Engineer* carried the following notice: "Lionel H. Pries, architect, has terminated his San Francisco practice to join William J. Bain in partnership. All future professional communications should be addressed to Messrs. Bain & Pries, Liggett building, Seattle, Washington."[76]

Later on, Pries sometimes thought of returning to California, but he lived in Seattle for the rest of his life. Lutah Riggs, who had known Pries both at Berkeley and in Santa Barbara, told the architectural historian David Gebhard, "Lionel Pries is the best architect California ever lost."[77]

4

TO THE NORTHWEST

Bain and Pries, 1928–1931

WILLIAM·J·BAIN·&·LIONEL·H·PRIES·ARCHITECTS

On 6 August 1928, the City of Seattle issued a building permit for the Richard L. Frayn residence, a single-family house in the Washington Park neighborhood, just off Madison Street. The design was the work of Bain and Pries, and the permit listing in Seattle's business newspaper was the first confirmed publication of a project by the five-month-old Seattle partnership.[1] Over the next several years, the Bain and Pries partnership was responsible for more than five dozen such projects.[2] Most of the partnership's works were residential, including single-family houses, multifamily apartment buildings, and several sorority and fraternity houses, but Bain and Pries also received occasional institutional and small industrial commissions. Although Lionel Pries began teaching at the University of Washington in the fall of 1928, he continued as a full participant in the firm through 1931. Bain and Pries was initially quite successful, but ultimately the firm could not survive the Depression.

When Pries joined William Bain's growing practice, he gained the support staff he had never had in California. Pries had never lived in Seattle before and had few personal contacts in the city, so Bain could not expect him to play a significant role in attracting clients, at least not initially. Pries now enjoyed a level of freedom he had never experienced in California; he could focus on design, and he could draw on a much wider array of architectural vocabularies. More than anything else, this opportunity had probably induced him to join Bain's firm.[3] The designs he produced in the four years of the Bain and Pries partnership show Pries's virtuosity and the underlying romanticism of his approach to design.

In Practice with William J. Bain

Pries had met his partner, William James Bain (1896–1985), when the two were students at the University of Pennsylvania[4] (fig. 4.1). Bain had been born and raised in British Columbia but arrived in Seattle when he was eight. His father was a contractor, so Bain grew up familiar with design and construction. While in high school, he found a job with the Seattle architects W. R. B. Willcox and William J. Sayward.[5] The Willcox and Sayward office focused primarily on residential commissions but also handled a variety of other work. It was an ideal place to learn about architecture, especially as Willcox, the senior partner, took an interest in young Bain and

taught him the rudiments of architectural drafting and other aspects of practice.[6] After high school, Bain worked briefly for architects in Los Angeles and Seattle and then entered military service during World War I. In the fall of 1919, he enrolled at the University of Pennsylvania, in an accelerated program for ex-servicemen with prior experience in architecture.[7] Thus, in 1920–1921, Bain was in Penn's upper-level design studio under the direction of Paul Cret—the same year Pries was earning his graduate degree under Cret's guidance. Pries and Bain had very different backgrounds, but both had come from the West Coast. Bain, moreover, had worked in Los Angeles and was interested in California. Their shared background likely provided the beginning to their friendship.

After graduation and a tour of Europe, Bain again worked for architects in Seattle, including Arthur Loveless, B. Marcus Priteca, and Willcox. From 1921 to 1923, he worked for the Los Angeles firm Johnson, Kaufman and Coate, but by 1924 he had returned to Seattle, married Mildred ("Billee") Clark, and opened his own office.[8] Because Bain's experience and interest were primarily in residential architecture, that was the initial focus of his practice.[9]

Residential design was a highly competitive field in Seattle in the 1920s. When Bain opened his own office, the leading residential designers in the city were the Columbia University-educated Arthur Loveless (1873–1971) and Pennsylvania graduates Edwin Ivey (1883–1940) and J. Lister Holmes (1891–1986).[10] Several partnerships with diverse

practices—notably Schack, Young and Myers—also routinely accepted residential commissions, and even firms usually identified with institutional work, such as Bebb and Gould, occasionally took on residential projects.[11] The work that these firms produced reflected the eclecticism of the period, with designs in classical, Tudor, French, colonial, and Mediterranean vocabularies.[12]

In Bain's first year in practice, he had few projects, and his one large commission, a lodge building for the Masons, was not constructed.[13] His office was just 20 feet square. Recalling his first year, Bain later wrote that "money was not nearly so plentiful as it would become by 1927 and 1928."[14] But within a year he began to attract clients, and thereafter growth was gradual but steady.

In his first few years, Bain's single-family residential projects rarely exceeded a cost of $10,000, as larger projects went to more established firms. Still, Bain developed a reputation for client service, good design, and attention to all phases of a project, and he began to win larger commissions. By 1927, the success of the firm seemed assured: the number of projects continued to grow, and new projects included several very large residences as well as retail and commercial commissions.[15] Bain's designs also won professional recognition: the Shoremont Apartments and the Joseph Carman Jr. residence, both in Seattle, received Washington State chapter AIA awards in 1927.[16] With this success, the Bains were able to take some time to vacation in California, and it was during their 1927 trip that they visited Pries, and William Bain tendered the invitation to join his practice.

The exact date of Pries's move to Seattle cannot be determined, but he was in the city by mid February 1928.[17] The résumé he prepared just a few months later, when he negotiated his teaching position with the University of Washington, stated, "Entered into partnership with William J. Bain, at Seattle, March 17, 1928"[18] (fig. 4.2).

In reminiscences written in 1978, Ivan W. Meyer, who had worked as a draftsman in Bain's office a half-century before, recalled how Pries first entered the firm:

> It must have been about early 1927, I was Bill's drafting force, Waldo McKinney was Lister Holmes' and Galen Bentley and Norm Fox shuttled in between as the needs required. Spike appeared and Bill introduced him as head designer—a big

deal for Spike. After a short period they formed the Bain & Pries business. We started getting those lovely presentation drawings—in color yet—that only Spike could do . . . .[19]

Although Meyer's recollection of the date was off by one year, his statement makes clear that Bain brought Pries into the firm for his design talents.

The kinds of buildings that Bain and Pries designed between 1928 and 1931 were similar to those that Bain had done before Pries arrived. Over the course of the partnership, they designed at least forty-five residences, of which approximately thirty were built. They also designed a half-dozen apartment buildings and a few commercial and industrial structures. Pries's University of Washington connection likely helped secure several fraternity and sorority house projects, as Bain had not previously received such commissions. And Pries's previous experience on the Hill Farm/Bothin Convalescent Home in Marin County would have added to the firm's qualifications, helping to secure the commission for Seattle's Convalescent Home for Crippled Children.

Pries's primary role was design critic. Lloyd Lovegren, who worked for Bain and Pries in 1930–32, recalled: "The most productive period in my contact with Spike came out of my employment in the office of 'Bain & Pries.' In the drafting of working drawings I was subject to daily crits from him on a number of residence jobs in Broadmoor and outlying areas."[20] As head designer, Pries offered regular critiques and produced design drawings but rarely if ever did

any drafting. Meyer noted, "Of course we all envied that brush and pencil. I doubt that he knew how to use a triangle and T-square; if he did, it surely was reluctantly."[21] Construction documents from Pries's later independent practice show that he was a fine draftsman, but at Bain and Pries, production of construction documents was not his role.

Pries contributed most to the firm's larger residential projects. Other projects—particularly several small apartment buildings and a few industrial structures, where economics were, of necessity, the paramount concern—provided fewer creative opportunities.[22] Still, it would be a mistake to imagine that Pries was unaware of the practicalities of building. Lovegren noted, "While Spike's designs were always highly imaginative, they were never difficult to detail and construct. His concepts were based on a sincere use of materials and an awareness of the structural integrity of the building."[23] Pries was also apparently not limited by routinely accepted conventions. Meyer wrote:

> I suppose he was responsible, though I was not aware of it, for my philosophy of considering each job on its own requirements and not trying to become famous by latching on to some cute cliché. I think he made me realize how important it is to see—remember—and adapt. . . .
>
> I think he taught the old hang-loose-system; if necessary to hell with the system and what we were taught was correct, and rather, do it as it should be done and for God's sake try and make it beautiful and a pleasure to live with.
>
> And last, he made me aware of the necessity of detailing things nicely, so a blind man could find pleasure.[24]

Pries's wish to design in different modes was met at Bain and Pries. The firm's skill with different styles is reflected in two early speculative residences designed for new developments facing Puget Sound. For the advertising brochure for Woodway Park, north of Seattle, Bain and Pries produced a large residence showing Tudor and English Arts and Crafts influence[25] (fig. 4.3). Although this particular design was not constructed, the steep roof, the tall chimney, and the small-paned windows all reappeared in later projects. When the Normandy Park subdivision, south of Seattle, was announced in August 1928, the *Seattle Post-Intelligencer* carried a sketch of a Bain and Pries residence showing "pro-

Fig. 4.3
Bain and Pries,
speculative project
for Woodway Park
development,
north of Seattle,
ca. 1928; ink
on stiff paper,
14½ x 23 inches.
Pries collection,
University of
Washington
Libraries, Special
Collections Division,
UW14404.

verbial French characteristics" and capable of being constructed "in a variety of interesting materials— stucco, white-washed brick or cedar shingles."[26] The L-shape plan, the tall roof, and the French details of this project were similar to features of Pries's unbuilt Palo Alto house for J. M. Johnson; these reappeared in the firm's Peter and Edyth Andrae residence (1928–29; altered), in the developing Broadmoor subdivision, a project that was permitted in December 1928 (fig. 4.4). The firm was skilled in other modes as well: the Ralph and Evelyn Stewart residence (1930–31), southwest of Seattle, was a Spanish Colonial design; the Walter and Edith Johnson residence (1930), in Magnolia, was a French Norman design (fig. 4.5). For some clients, the firm offered multiple schemes in different styles: a watercolor of the William and Winnie St. Clair residence (1929), in Broadmoor, showed a Spanish Colonial proposal; the constructed house was a Tudor design[27] (fig. 4.6).

While their architectural vocabularies ranged from English to French to Spanish, the plans of many of the larger Bain and Pries residences displayed a high degree of consistency (fig. 4.7). For the firm's larger houses, the front door typically led to an entry hall that was the circulation center of the

house. To one side was a large living room, usually with a higher ceiling (and sometimes down several steps). The living room typically opened through pairs of double doors to a terrace, often with a view: at the Andrae residence, to the Broadmoor golf course; at the Stewart residence, to Puget Sound; at the St. Clair residence, to the private back yard. The entry hall also usually connected to the dining room, and there may have been a reception room or a parlor or other rooms on the ground floor as well. These other rooms depended on the owners' requirements: at the St. Clair residence, there was a small office; at the Stewart residence, the master suite was on the first floor.

When the opportunity presented itself, Bain and Pries extended the order of their houses into the landscape. Creating a seamless transition from the house to the landscape was a common aim of residential design in the first decades of the twentieth century—the design of the house and the landscape together was a typical practice of Philadelphia and California architects.[28] Bain and Pries not only provided terraces adjoining their houses but also, where possible, added walls to enclose courtyards or garden "rooms" as extensions of the houses. Such features were shown in their speculative designs for

Fig. 4.4
Bain and Pries,
Peter and Edyth
Andrae residence,
Seattle, 1928–29
(altered). Photo by
author, 2005.

Fig. 4.5
Bain and Pries,
Walter E. and
Edith Johnson
residence, Seattle,
1930. Photo by
author, 2005.

Fig. 4.6
Bain and Pries,
William and
Winnie St. Clair
residence, Seattle,
1929 (altered).
Photo by author,
2005.

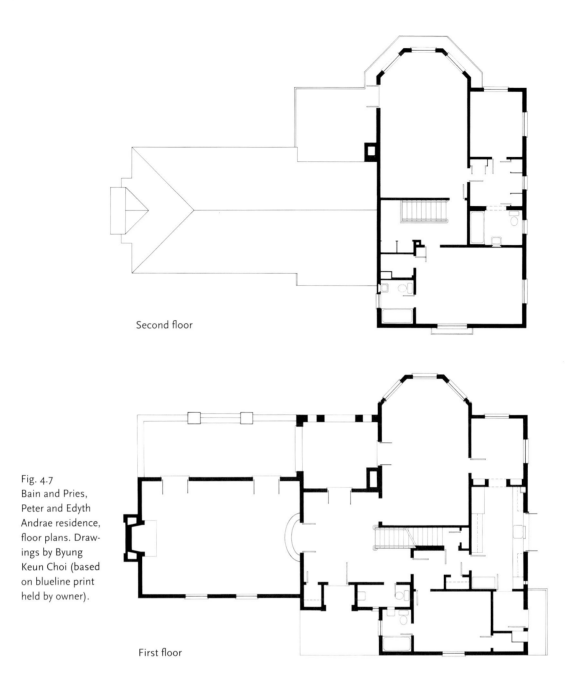

Second floor

Fig. 4.7
Bain and Pries,
Peter and Edyth
Andrae residence,
floor plans. Draw-
ings by Byung
Keun Choi (based
on blueline print
held by owner).

First floor

Woodway Park and Normandy Park; but in many suburban locations, expansive landscape development was often not possible. An exception was the Stewart residence, where the landscape at both the front and the back of the house was developed with walkways and plantings (fig. 4.8).

Many Bain and Pries houses show Pries's hand in the details. The firm's Spanish Colonial houses often feature a wood ceiling in the living room and sometimes in several other rooms. Hard-surface materials are always used for the floor of the entry hall; in the Stewart residence, Batchelder tile from southern California, including a pattern of art tiles, recalls Pries's links to California's Arts and Crafts

movement[29] (fig. 4.9). Entries of several houses are framed by unusual elements: Baroque columns and pediment at the Robert and Nellie Moody residence (1929–30), on Seattle's Queen Anne Hill; an Art Deco cast-stone lintel at the Horace and Anne Peyton residence (1930–31), in Broadmoor, a building described as "of the modern and Spanish type of architecture"[30] (fig. 4.10).

Not all Bain and Pries houses were large mansions. Although the firm was often identified with large, custom-designed homes, it took on a variety of smaller projects. A speculative residence in Magnolia, designed for the Seattle Trust Company in 1930, had a compact plan but still included familiar

Fig. 4.8
Bain and Pries,
Ralph and Evelyn
Stewart residence,
Seattle, 1930–31,
rear elevation
with landscape
extending from
the house. Private
collection.

Fig. 4.9
Bain and Pries,
Ralph and Evelyn
Stewart residence,
entry hall with
Batchelder tile
floor. Private
collection.

Fig. 4.10
Bain and Pries,
Horace and Anne
Peyton residence,
Seattle, 1930–31
(altered). State
of Washington
Archives, Puget
Sound Regional
Branch.

Fig. 4.11
Bain and Pries,
Lyman Bunting
residence, Yakima,
1929–30 (altered).
From *Architect
and Engineer* 137/3
(June 1939).

features, such as a high living room ceiling. The lower fees on these smaller projects likely meant that Pries's participation was limited. In fact, in June 1930, when *Pacific Builder and Engineer* reported on the firm's "Prudence Penny Budget Home," in Normandy Park—a small house in "early Cape Cod style"—the designer was identified as Bain.[31]

The reputation of Bain and Pries extended well beyond Seattle. During their four years in partnership, the firm received commissions in Yakima, Washington; Portland, Oregon; and Vancouver, British Columbia. One of the firm's more unusual projects was the Lyman Bunting residence in Yakima; it was featured in *Architect and Engineer* in June 1939 because the exterior was entirely of unfinished cedar[32] (fig. 4.11). Not all these projects were built, however: Bain and Pries proposed a large Spanish Colonial residence for an estate looking down to the Fraser River in Vancouver, but the client, George Reifel, built a local architect's design.[33]

Residential projects by Bain and Pries included several fraternity and sorority houses. Pries was deeply involved in the design of the Alpha Tau Omega fraternity house (1929–30; now the Delta

Kappa Epsilon house, altered), at the northeast corner of 18th Avenue and 47th Street (fig. 4.12). The L-shaped design responds to the corner site by creating a large southwest-facing lawn enclosed by a wall. The longer west wing rises to two stories, and the south wing is three stories, but the overall scale is reduced because each top floor is an attic story under a steeply sloping roof. The brick exterior reflects Tudor precedents; a notable feature is the cast-stone entrance. The first floor is devoted to the living and dining rooms, the kitchen, and support space; the second and third floors are sleeping and study rooms. The relatively open entry foyer features a vaulted plaster ceiling supported by round arches resting on massive columns with exaggerated entasis, as shown in Pries's watercolor (fig. 4.13). Pries's charcoal sketch of the living room, showing the wood paneling and beamed ceiling, indicates his involvement in every aspect of the design (fig. 4.14). Double doors from the living and dining rooms open to the exterior courtyard, creating an indoor-outdoor space for entertaining. Wendell Lovett, a member of Alpha Tau Omega in the 1940s, and later a professor in the Department of Architecture, recalls being intrigued by the building:

It was a fascinating, romantic house—only Spike could do something like that. The entry, the unsymmetrical qualities of it, I think, had a not classical origin—it was Gothic. It was quirky and strange. It had wonderful stairs and spaces and level changes and differences of ceilings. . . . it was quite a fascinating place . . . full of little weird things. . . .[34]

Lovett believes that Pries even had a hand in designing the furniture:

Most of the furniture was either designed by Pries or certainly selected by him—in the living room and in the study. . . . I think he must have designed the sofas. They looked a little like church pews but they were upholstered and relatively comfortable.[35]

Another major project of 1929 was the Convalescent Home for Crippled Children (1929–30; destroyed), a facility for children recuperating after treatment at Seattle's Children's Orthopedic Hospital.[36] Although Bain was the primary contact with the client, Lovegren recalled that Pries gave daily critiques on the project.[37] For the large site on Seattle's Magnolia bluff, Bain and Pries designed a long,

Fig. 4.12
Bain and Pries, Alpha Tau Omega Fraternity House (now Delta Kappa Epsilon Fraternity House), Seattle, 1929–30 (altered); photograph of Pries perspective. Pries collection, University of Washington Libraries, Special Collections Division, UW23774z.

Fig. 4.13
Bain and Pries,
Alpha Tau Omega
Fraternity House
lobby; Pries
watercolor, 6¼ x
9¼ inches. Pries
collection, Univer-
sity of Washington
Libraries, Special
Collections Divi-
sion; UW24233z.

Fig. 4.14
Bain and Pries,
Alpha Tau Omega
Fraternity House,
living room; Pries
drawing, charcoal
on illustration
board, 13 x 18
inches. Pries col-
lection, University
of Washington
Libraries, Special
Collections Divi-
sion, UW 24230z.

Fig. 4.15
Bain and Pries,
Convalescent
Home for
Crippled Children,
Seattle, 1929–30
(destroyed). From
*Architect and
Engineer* (August
1941).

Fig. 4.16
Bain and Pries,
Convalescent
Home for Crippled
Children, porte-
cochere at entrance
(destroyed). From
*Architect and
Engineer* (August
1941).

low building that had the feeling of a large house rather an institutional structure (figs. 4.15, 4.16). Throughout the building were small details likely of Pries's design—for example, small cutout silhouettes of children incorporated into the entry. The *Seattle Times* described the building as "a low, rambling story-book house with figures of funny, friendly little animals scurrying over the fireplace and down the corridors and carved in the porch-ways."[38] The architectural character of the Convalescent Home is captured in a comment

by the critic Peter Staten: "There is evidence that Bain and Pries knew something of the work of Edwin Lutyens in England, who distilled the steep shingle roof, stucco walls, and small paned windows of English country houses into bold abstractions of shape and pattern that are strikingly modern in feeling."[39]

Bain and Pries apartment buildings were generally straightforward two-, three-, or four-story designs that responded directly to the size and shape of each site. The most interesting is the

Fig. 4.17
Bain and Pries,
Bel-Roy Apart-
ments, Seattle,
1930–31. Photo
by author, 2005.

Bel-Roy Apartments (1930–31), on the west side of Seattle's Capitol Hill. The building was constructed for a partnership involving the Bain family, so Bain no doubt took the lead in the project. Still, unusual features of the building, such as the zigzag wall and the large bay windows on the south side, suggest Pries's involvement (fig. 4.17). The detailing is simple, reflecting the impact of the Depression, yet the building has been described as "one of the best examples of Art Deco design in Seattle."[40]

Although all projects of Bain and Pries involved input from both partners, Meyer identified two projects as "strictly Spike": the Karl A. and Emita Krueger residence (1928–29, 1930; altered), and the John and Fannie Hamrick residence (1929–30; altered).[41] Karl Krueger was the conductor of the Seattle Symphony Orchestra. John Hamrick was the operator of several leading Seattle movie theaters (and was the first in Seattle to show "talking pictures"). The Kruegers and the Hamricks—involved in the arts and culture, with adequate means, and willing to follow his lead in matters of design—were the kind of clients Pries preferred.

Krueger, a relatively young man who had studied in Paris and Vienna and lived in Los Angeles, arrived in Seattle as conductor of the symphony.[42]

After he received a permanent appointment, the Kruegers went forward, in the fall of 1928, with the construction of their new house; in the summer of 1930, they added a new wing for a master suite. Meyer did not distinguish between the two phases of construction:

It was a fairy-tale house with a stair tower and third floor studio. It also had a lovely gazzabo-like-gizmo [sic] as a part of the 1st floor owners' suite. While I worked on the drawings I don't remember much except that it was nicely detailed under Spike's supervision. At the time I felt that it was lovely and different, it probably still is. . . . Lovely place and pure Spike.[43]

The Krueger site is a large wooded tract, so the residence is approached by a long drive. The building is positioned at the top of a slope and oriented to Puget Sound, to the southwest. The side the visitor approaches is relatively closed, with small openings. The house appears volumetrically additive, building up to the three-story central block (fig. 4.18). The first floor includes the primary living and entertainment spaces—a "great hall" with tall ceiling to one side of the foyer, and the dining room, the kitchen, a

library, and support spaces to the other side. Living quarters were originally only on the second floor, and the third-floor "tower room" served as Karl Krueger's personal studio. In 1930, when an accident permanently confined Emita Krueger to a wheelchair, Pries designed a first-floor addition to the master suite, including a bedroom and a sitting room.[44] This new wing projects at an angle from the west side of the house (figs. 4.19, 4.20). Its corner bay window with roof dome is the "gazebo" to which Meyer referred. Pries designed several stained-glass windows, and he may even have helped paint the decoration that once graced the panels of the living room ceiling. Unfortunately,

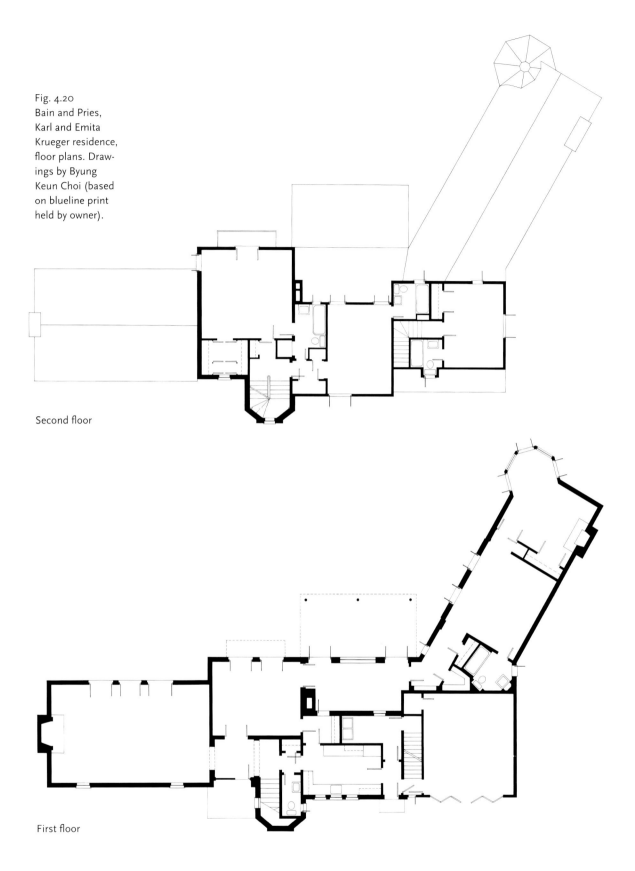

Fig. 4.20
Bain and Pries,
Karl and Emita
Krueger residence,
floor plans. Draw-
ings by Byung
Keun Choi (based
on blueline print
held by owner).

Second floor

First floor

the Kruegers lived in the house only a short time. The Seattle symphony encountered severe financial difficulties that were due to the Depression; Krueger resigned his position in 1931, and the Kruegers soon left Seattle, but they remained Pries's lifelong friends.

While the Krueger residence was rather fanciful, the white-painted brick, the tile roof, the pointed Moorish arches, and the wrought iron grillwork of the Hamrick residence reflect the creative freedom with which Pries used Spanish and other Mediter-ranean precedents (fig. 4.21). Meyer remembered

Pries's deep involvement in every detail of this project:

> The John Hamrick House in Broadmoor, Santa Barbara Spanish with a lot of Spike mixed in. I did yards of F.S.D. [full size details] of wrought iron grilles—gates—etc. under Spike's close direction and old Mike Olendoefer (?) did the work. 1st class and beautiful and that's how I became a W.I. [wrought iron] expert. My recollection is there was some nice—gutty [sic] common type—of tile work and no doubt some woodcarving.[45]

The plan of the Hamrick residence is a compact T, with an arched vehicle entrance to an auto court and garage (fig. 4.22). The "public" entrance is reached through a gate to a loggia along one side of the stem of the T, facing the private yard. The large living room features a high beamed ceiling supported on carved wood trusses; Pries's romantic sensibility is reflected in the "atmospheric" interiors of the other rooms as well (figs. 4.23, 4.24). Here, as at the Willits residence in California, Pries's participation extended well beyond architecture to include the selection of furnishings. The precedents here may even include residential interiors that Pries had known in the East—those by Wilson Eyre, for

example, on Philadelphia's Main Line.[46] The *Seattle Times* featured the Hamrick residence in a photo essay titled "A Spanish Villa in a Charmed Landscape," describing the house as a "$150,000 Mission-type dwelling"; no doubt this price included the site and the furnishings as well as the building.[47] But, with the onset of the Depression, opportunities of this scale diminished and would become increasingly rare in the years ahead.

THE CHRISTOPHER COLUMBUS MEMORIAL LIGHTHOUSE COMPETITION

During his four years in partnership with Bain, Pries undertook only a single project apart from the firm. In 1928–29, he entered the Christopher Columbus Memorial Lighthouse Competition, sponsored by the Pan American Union. As announced in early 1928, this was an international design competition for a 600-foot-tall lighthouse to be constructed in Santo Domingo, in the Dominican Republic, as a monument to Christopher Columbus. The competition drew nearly seven hundred registrants, three hundred of them from the United States.[48]

Pries received the competition's rules and program in the fall of 1928.[49] The project was unusual—to design a "beacon to guide navigation

Fig. 4.21
Bain and Pries, John and Fannie Hamrick residence, Seattle, 1929–30, (altered); photo ca. 1930. Private collection.

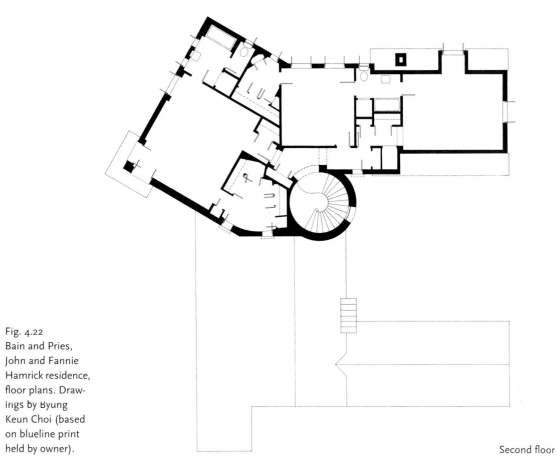

Fig. 4.22
Bain and Pries,
John and Fannie
Hamrick residence,
floor plans. Draw-
ings by Byung
Keun Choi (based
on blueline print
held by owner).

Second floor

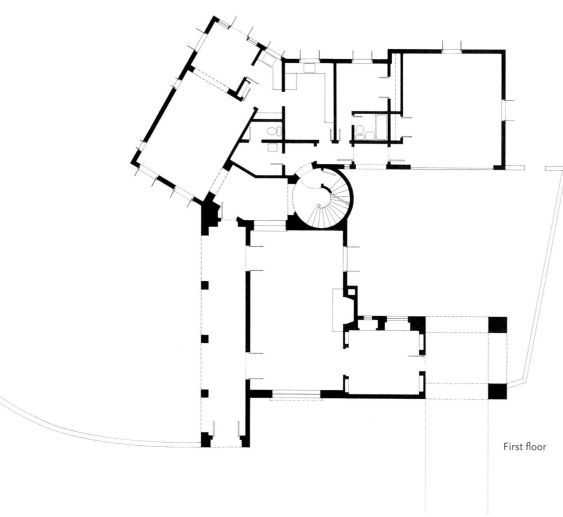

First floor

Fig. 4.23
Bain and Pries,
John and Fannie
Hamrick residence,
living room; photo
ca. 1930. Private
collection.

Fig. 4.24
Bain and Pries,
John and Fannie
Hamrick residence,
hall looking
toward stair;
photo ca. 1930.
Private collection.

by sea and air" that would also serve as a commemorative monument and house a chapel for Christopher Columbus's tomb, which was to be moved from the Santo Domingo cathedral. Although competitors were to plan the 2,500–acre site—providing a new airport as well as a new governmental center and adjoining residential quarters—the focus was clearly on the lighthouse, as four of the six specified drawings were to address its design.

Pries's romantic imagination fully embraced the project, and he submitted six beautifully colored boards by the deadline of 1 April 1929 (figs. 4.25, 4.26, 4.27). Pries attempted a complex symbolism in his design, stating, "The competitor has endeavored to express in his monument the soaring adventurous spirit . . . the courageous ego that makes possible the material and spiritual advancement of civilization."[50] Details at the base suggest Pries's awakening interest in pre-Columbian art and architecture, reflecting his visits to Mexico, which began in the late 1920s. His memorial tower rises above a pictorial pavement. Pries saw its shape as expressive of the rise of civilization, writing that "the plan begins at the earth in the form of the cross of sacrifice and trial, at a higher level changes to signify the triumph of conviction and the solidarity of purpose, at mid-point again changes to a cross of besetment and persecution, and finally emerges at the top as a single unassailable idea . . . the proven word . . . the 'light of the world.'"

The jury—Eliel Saarinen, Raymond Hood, and Horacio Acosta y Lara—met in Madrid in mid-April, reviewed the 455 submissions, and selected ten finalists and ten honorable mentions.[51] Pries was not among them. The competition book, however, included Pries's scheme; both his plan and his elevation were shown. The text praised his treatment of the beacon ("The metallic lantern and

Fig. 4.25 Lionel H. Pries, Christopher Columbus Memorial Lighthouse Competition project, Santo Domingo, Dominican Republic, 1928–29 (unbuilt), elevation; pencil, ink, watercolor on stiff paper, 64½ x 32 inches. Pries collection, University of Washington Libraries, Special Collections Division, UW25615z.

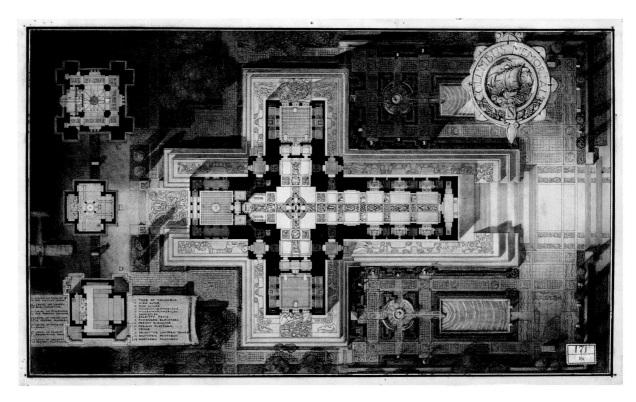

Fig. 4.26
Lionel H. Pries,
Columbus Memo-
rial Lighthouse
Competition proj-
ect, plan; pencil,
ink, watercolor
on board, 16 x 27
inches. Pries col-
lection, University
of Washington
Libraries, Special
Collections Divi-
sion, UW23903z.

Fig. 4.27
Lionel H. Pries,
Columbus Memo-
rial Lighthouse
Competition
project, details
of base, entrance,
lantern; pencil,
ink, watercolor
on board, 16 x 27
inches. Pries col-
lection, University
of Washington
Libraries, Special
Collections Divi-
sion, UW23904z.

PROPOSED CHAPTER·HOUSE · THETA · CHI ·
WILLIAM·J·BAIN AND LIONEL·H·PRIES ARCHITECTS · UNIVERSITY OF WASHINGTON

balcony is distinct and separate from the monument and yet crowns it with a lightness and niceness that is in perfect harmony with the whole") and commented on "the spirit of the details that animate this design."[52] Pries's site plan was published as an example for competitors who advanced to the second stage.

Pries's Columbus Memorial suggests the imagination that Pries could bring to a monumental project. Unfortunately, however, throughout his career, he never had the opportunity to work at such a large scale.[53]

THE BAIN AND PRIES FIRM DISSOLVES

Bain and Pries prospered from 1928 through 1930, even after the October 1929 stock market crash. In fact, more of the firm's projects began construction in 1930 than in either of the previous two years. But in 1931, the firm secured few new commissions. Three Bain and Pries projects were reported in the *Daily Journal of Commerce* in 1931—the Sigma Phi Epsilon fraternity house; a hotel in Chelan, Washington; and a house for Pries himself—but none went forward.[54] Bain and Pries also proposed a design for the Theta Chi fraternity house, but the project built in 1931–32 was by another architect (fig. 4.28).[55] Administration of construction that was already under way brought some fees in 1931, but, with little new work, the office faced severe difficulties. Describing the impact of the Depression, Mildred Bain wrote:

Architecture practice collapsed (many other businesses had collapsed before this). . . . Our crew of fine residential architects had to go elsewhere to

Fig. 4.28
Bain and Pries, Theta Chi Fraternity House project, Seattle, 1931–32 (unbuilt); pencil and colored pencil on illustration board. 14¾ x 18¾ inches. Pries collection, University of Washington Libraries, Special Collections Division, UW23901z.

try to find work. . . . We kept one draftsman, Ivan Meyer, and made him a deal. He would get one-half of the yearly gross. One year that was $850.[56]

The Bain and Pries firm was not alone in facing serious hardship. The total value of building permits in Seattle had been about $34 million in 1928, $29 million in 1929, and $30 million in 1930, but their value collapsed in the next three years, totaling less than $2 million in 1933. Under these circumstances, it is no surprise that Bain and Pries had dissolved by early 1932. Pries briefly served as director of the Art Institute of Seattle, in 1931–32, but, more important, he held a full-time teaching position at the University of Washington.[57] He had been appointed as an instructor in 1928; in the fall of 1932, he became an assistant professor and began his ascent up the academic ladder.

Bain's practice gradually recovered over the course of the 1930s, although several years passed before the number of projects approached the level of 1929–30. By 1932, Pries was already acquiring a reputation as an extraordinary teacher; he stepped away from practice and devoted himself to the Department of Architecture at the university. Although he occasionally took on design projects through the 1930s, the primary focus of his career would henceforth be architectural education.

5

SEEKING
A NEW
SYNTHESIS

PRIES IN MEXICO, 1928–1942

IN HIS FOUR YEARS IN PARTNERSHIP WITH
William J. Bain, Pries appears as an imaginative
yet still conventional eclectic designer. But it was
sometime in those years that Pries first traveled to
Mexico and began his design odyssey toward a personal approach to Modern architecture.

In the 1930s and 1940s, a highlight of an evening
at Pries's home was a viewing of his collections of
Mexican textiles, carvings, and other artifacts. While
showing his collections, Pries regaled his visitors
with stories of his Mexican travels, frequently
mentioning towns like Taxco and Guanajuato, and
individuals like Bill Spratling, Fred Davis, and René
d'Harnoncourt. Pries's focus was primarily the
objects, and then his stories; he seldom talked
directly about how these experiences were influ-
encing his design thinking. This now seems unfortunate because Pries's ideas about architecture and
art were shaped by his Mexican experience. It was
in Mexico that Pries encountered the idea that
indigenous and folk arts and crafts could be a
component of a new approach to design.

Pries was deeply aware that the architectural traditions in which he had been educated were facing
unprecedented challenges. The 1920s had seen
the rise of Art Deco, an attempt to create a new
vocabulary of design.[1] The economic hardships of
the Depression pushed architects toward simplification and minimization of expensive detail. Pries's
mentor, Paul Cret, rethought the conventions of
classicism and moved toward a "stripped down"
approach, even for public buildings.[2] But both Art
Deco and abstracted classicism preserved many of
the formal principles of the Beaux-Arts (such as
axiality, symmetry, balance, and proportion). In
contrast, the new International Style architecture
from Europe challenged even these basic principles,
and from the early 1930s this new approach was the
subject of heated discussion and debate.

Pries developed an early familiarity with emerging directions in design. The new architecture of
the Modern Movement that had evolved in Europe
began to receive attention in the United States in
the late 1920s. The May 1930 national convention
of the American Institute of Architects, held in
Washington, D.C., featured a debate about the new
European Modernism. Included among the speakers
was the influential (and formerly traditional) Philadelphia architect George Howe, who had embraced
the new direction and taken the young Swiss Modernist William Lescaze into full partnership in his

firm. Pries was not an AIA member and had not attended this event, but parts of Howe's statement were included in the March 1931 *T-Square Club Journal of Philadelphia*, which Pries received; this issue also featured Howe and Lescaze's PSFS (Philadelphia Savings Fund Society) building (1931–32), described as the first American office building conceived within the principles of the new International Style.[3] European Modernism was the focus of several other issues of the *T Square Journal* in 1930–31, with articles on both sides of the issue; illustrations of the new architecture included LeCorbusier's Villa de Monzie at Garches and Centrosoyous office building project in Moscow, as well as Brinckman and van der Vlugt's Van Nelle Factory in Rotterdam. In 1932, the Museum of Modern Art (MOMA), in New York, brought the new movement even more forcefully before American architects and the public with its exhibit "Modern Architecture: International Exhibition," curated by Henry-Russell Hitchcock Jr. and Philip Johnson.[4] Pries, then serving as director of the Art Institute of Seattle, was briefly involved in the failed effort to bring this exhibit to the West Coast.[5] From this time forward, International Style Modernism received increased attention in the American architectural press.

While Pries was aware of the new work in Europe, his personal path to an understanding of Modern architecture was informed primarily by his travels in Mexico, where new directions in art and architecture were emerging in the 1920s and 1930s. Pries's career thus calls to mind the historian William J. R. Curtis's discussion of the "complexity of a dissemi-

nation [of Modern architecture] that gained momentum in the 1930s."[6] As Curtis has argued, Latin American Modernism has been a "casualty" of the dominant narrative of American architectural history that traces Modernism from Europe to the northeastern seaboard of the United States and then across the continent; however, the recognition that Modernism had become a multinodal phenomenon by the 1930s is essential to understanding how the experience of Mexico shaped Pries's thinking.[7] Modern architecture in Mexico emerged in the aftermath of the Mexican Revolution of 1910–1917, in the context of avant-garde movements in arts and politics that rejected "imposed" cultural traditions and sought linkages to the pre-Columbian period. As summarized by Curtis, "The gradual and almost unconscious absorption of deep-rooted continuities in the minds of ensuing generations of Mexican Modern architects may be understood in the light of an 'inclusive' national mythology, binding together city and country, new and old, international and indigenous."[8] Pries's design work after 1935 shows how he absorbed these ideas in Mexico and transformed them in the Northwest.[9]

THE ATTRACTION OF MEXICO

Beginning about 1928, Pries spent his summers in Mexico.[10] Because he drove his LaSalle automobile from Seattle most years, he was free to explore as widely as he wished, and over the decade of the 1930s he traveled extensively in the country (fig. 5.1). The map in his copy of *Terry's Guide to Mexico* shows

Fig. 5.1
Lionel Pries on the road in Mexico, ca. 1930–40. Pries photo album, Pries collection, University of Washington Libraries, Special Collections Division, UW24472z.

that Pries visited cities and towns including León, Guanajuato, Querétaro, Puebla, Cholula, Taxco, Toluca, Morelia, Guadalajara, Monterrey, Pachuca, Colima, and Mexico City.[11] The places he returned to year after year were Guanajuato, Taxco, Cholula, and Puebla.[12] Occasionally he was accompanied by another faculty member or by a student, but usually he was on his own.[13] Although he kept no written records of these trips, Pries's stories (as remembered by those who heard them), as well as available paintings, photographs, drawings, and other evidence, provide the basis for a summary of his Mexican odysseys.[14]

Pries likely made his first visit to Mexico to learn more about the architecture, particularly Spanish Colonial buildings. California architects frequently traveled to Mexico in the 1910s and 1920s to become better prepared to produce more sophisticated work in the Spanish Colonial Revival.[15] Had this remained Pries's only interest, he would not have returned summer after summer. Instead, he became fascinated by emerging directions in the art, architecture, and culture of Mexico.

Pries's fascination parallels the broad interest in Mexico among American artists and intellectuals of the period. In fact, Mexico enjoyed an extraordinary cultural "vogue" from the early 1920s to the late 1930s.[16] The art historians Mary Ann Miller and James Oles have suggested some characteristics that drew Americans:

> By the 1920s, as Mexico entered a period of post-revolutionary reconstruction, Americans began to travel south in greater numbers, attracted not only by a burgeoning cultural renaissance but by untouched colonial towns, an exciting traditional culture, and an ancient capital of interlaced canals and tree-lined avenues with air so clear that the distant volcanoes were a vision of constant wonder.[17]

The cultural historian Helen Delpar has summarized other attractions of Mexico:

> The cultural and political life of Mexico after 1920 exhibited many qualities bound to enhance its appeal to American artists and intellectuals. Not only was it the Latin American nation closest to the United States, but its ancient monuments and artifacts offered eloquent testimony to the grandeur of the aboriginal civilizations of the hemisphere, which could be claimed as part of the

heritage of the United States. Moreover, those in search of premodern communities still relatively unscathed by the industrial revolution might find them throughout rural Mexico.[18]

With the fading of the American Arts and Crafts movement during World War I, American artists and intellectuals in Mexico sought, and to some extent "constructed," a refuge from industrialization and from the loss of the culture of handicraft that they experienced in the United States. The attraction of Mexico was especially strong, according to Miller and Oles, for those seeking "essential American values, colors, traditions, and histories, an alternative to the cultural dominance of Europe and especially Paris."[19] Those who went to Mexico included photographers such as Edward Weston and Tina Modotti, painters such as George Biddle, and writers such as Katherine Anne Porter and Hart Crane.[20] The Seattle artists Mark Tobey, Kenneth Callahan, Guy Anderson, and Ambrose and Viola Patterson all spent time in Mexico in the early 1930s.[21]

Artists were also attracted to Mexico's extraordinary visual richness, "marked by vivid color and brilliant sunlight."[22] Accounts of the period repeatedly use the term "picturesque," a characteristic that strongly appealed to Pries's romantic sensibility.[23] He returned year after year and, from the early 1930s to the mid-1940s, he produced a remarkable series of oils and watercolors.[24] Many of his paintings emphasize the relationship of the buildings to the landscape, and almost all suggest Pries's romanticization of Mexico.

Pries's frequent subject was Guanajuato, a mining town at an elevation of 7,000 feet, noted for its extraordinary setting and arresting beauty. *Terry's Guide* described it as "one of the richest, oldest and most picturesque towns in the Republic" and compared it to the hill towns of Italy and Sicily.[25] The American artist Everett Gee Jackson called it "a place of magic . . . surrounded by hills, up the sides of which were beautiful little houses of many colors winding along narrow cobblestone streets. And, on top of each hill was either a beautiful colonial church or a chapel."[26] Pries's watercolor *Plazuela de San Francisco* captures the spirit and color of the town; Jackson wrote of "hearing Chopin's music with your eyes"[27] (fig. 5.2). Other watercolors convey Pries's enchantment with individual buildings (fig. 5.3; also see chapter 8, this volume). Pries made sev-

Fig. 5.2
Lionel H. Pries,
*Plazuela de San Francisco—
Guanajuato*,
1942; watercolor,
21½ x 17¼ inches.
Courtesy of
Robert Winskill.

Fig. 5.3
Lionel H. Pries,
*La Parroquia—
Guanajuato*, 1942;
watercolor, 17¼ x
21½. Courtesy of
Robert Winskill.

Fig. 5.4
Lionel H. Pries,
*Corn in the River—
Guanajuato*, ca.
1946; watercolor/
tempera, 27 x 38
inches. Color
digitally restored
by Stephen Rock.
Courtesy of Robert
Winskill.

Fig. 5.5
Lionel H. Pries,
untitled view of
Taxco roofs, mid-
1930s; watercolor,
17¼ x 21½ inches.
Courtesy of Robert
Winskill.

Fig. 5.6
Lionel H. Pries,
*San Francisco in
Tlaxcalazingo*,
1938; watercolor,
20 x 17½ inches.
Courtesy of Robert
Winskill.

Fig. 5.7
Lionel H. Pries,
San Andreas—
Cholula, 1932;
oil on canvas,
24 x 20 inches.
Private collection.

eral paintings at the site of the Hacienda da Rocca, largely in ruins, in the hills about two miles from the town, near the abandoned Valencia mine. In the early 1930s, Pries produced two oils at the Hacienda, and later he did drypoint prints of the same views (discussed in chapter 8, this volume). *Corn in the River—Guanajuato*—painted in watercolor and tempera, probably dating from 1946, and likely based on an earlier oil—was one of his favorite paintings; for many years, it hung in his Seattle bedroom[28] (fig. 5.4).

Pries also stayed in Taxco, a town of fewer than five thousand residents that the writer Witter Bynner called "beautiful beyond description, with cobblestoned lanes leading always up and up into a hundred little heavens, all strange angles, and the huge ornate church standing in the center like the giant parent of eight other churches."[29] Pries's undated view, showing the roofs of Taxco, is a remarkable composition that captures the complex geometry of the town (fig. 5.5). During his travels with Pries in 1938, George ("Pete") Wimberly compared Taxco and Guanajuato: "Guanajuato is a very picturesque place, something like Taxco, but in reverse: Taxco being built on a ridge and the streets following the arms of the hills, and Guanajuato being built in a canyon and the streets following the various arroyos."[30]

And Pries visited Cholula, a town known for its many churches—it was said that there was one for each day of the year. Pries painted several of these, among them *San Francisco in Tlaxcalazingo*, a watercolor, in 1938, and *San Andreas—Cholula*, an oil, in 1932 (figs. 5.6, 5.7).

LIONEL PRIES AND WILLIAM SPRATLING

As Pries learned more about Mexico's history and culture, he, like many others in the period, came to believe that the architecture of the colonial period derived from the intermingling of the Old and New Worlds—that the Spanish conquest did not simply erase the culture of the indigenous people. Later scholarship has challenged this idea, but in the 1920s and 1930s, as Mexico's contemporary culture was being transformed by an emphasis on continuities with the pre-Columbian past, it was argued that early colonial architecture was a hybrid that often embodied elements reflecting the design contributions of the indigenous people.[31]

Fig. 5.8
William Spratling, ca. 1927–30. Photo by Tina Modotti. Natalie Scott Papers, Manuscripts Collection 123, Special Collections, Tulane University.

Pries no doubt would have encountered these ideas on his own, but he became more deeply aware of them through his friendship with William Spratling, an American architect, artist, and craftsman, who moved permanently to Mexico in 1928–29 (fig. 5.8). Spratling is remembered today primarily for his role in the development of the silver crafts of Taxco, but his early career was in architectural education.[32]

William P. Spratling (1900–1967) had been born in New York but was raised in the South. He studied architecture at Auburn University and started teaching before finishing the program. In 1921, he was appointed to the faculty of Tulane University, where he became known as a gifted instructor of architectural graphics, freehand drawing, and similar classes, as well as a writer and illustrator.[33] Spratling's years at Tulane coincided with the "renaissance" of the French Quarter, and he mixed easily with a circle of writers and artists; for a time, he shared an apartment with William Faulkner.[34]

Spratling first visited Mexico in 1926.[35] His 1927 *Architectural Forum* article reflects the period's emphasis on the contributions of Mexico's indigenous peoples:

> These remains of Spanish Colonial work in old Mexico are likely to more closely reflect the nature of the Indian builders and their own feeling in their handiwork than they are the European importations of Castilian and Iberian structural ideas. . . . As a people the Indians reveal a most amazingly fertile sense of form and color and show a vigorous impulse in all their forms of art expression. . . . [36]

Two years later, Spratling's article in *Architecture,* "Indo-Hispanic Mexico," subtitled "Some Notes on the Manner in Which Indian Form and Impulse Has Persisted and Continued through an Imposed Culture," emphasized the "surface and decorative characteristics which clearly reveal the hand of the Indian and his feeling for good form."[37] Pries later talked in much the same way about Mexican design, stating that a key aspect was the influence of the indigenous craftsmen who had transformed architectural influences received from Spain.[38]

During his early visits to Mexico, Spratling lectured for the National University Summer School and for the Committee on Cultural Relations, which had launched a series of Latin America seminars to foster "interchange of culture and ideas" between Mexico and the United States.[39] Spratling was drawn into the group that included the artists Diego Rivera, Rufino Tamayo, and David Alfaro Siqueiros as well as the Americans Fred Davis, René d'Harnoncourt, Frances Toor, and others.[40] His fascination with developments in Mexico is evident in his 1929 *Scribner's* article, "Figures in a Mexican Renaissance," in which he briefly profiled seven members of the "Intelligentsia Mexicana" and wrote of Mexico's new "cultural growth being staged against a background of real primitivism."[41] Spratling returned to Mexico in 1927 and 1928 and then moved there permanently. He settled in Taxco, a town of fewer than 5000 residents, then almost unknown to outsiders.[42] His presence drew visitors, and soon "Spratling's house became a magnet for American visitors to Mexico."[43]

Spratling and Pries were about the same age, had somewhat similar backgrounds in architecture, and were interested in collecting fine objects. Both were homosexual. Pries traveled with Spratling during one of Pries's earliest visits to Mexico and they became lifelong friends.[44] After Spratling settled permanently in Taxco, Pries began to spend part of each summer there. In 1938 Pries brought his students, Bliss Moore and Pete Wimberly, and they all stayed in Spratling's apartment (and met Ginger Rogers and Dolores del Rio who were also visiting).[45]

Like Spratling, Pries was interested in the ways in which Mexico's native people had transformed the architecture received from Spain. Pries assembled two albums of 3–by-5–inch documentary photographs, all carefully labeled, of buildings from a wide variety of Mexican cities and towns[46] (figs. 5.9, 5.10). Many of these were buildings from the first

century of colonization—structures that sometimes show complex hybridization, including elements of Spanish Renaissance, the lingering influence of the Spanish Gothic, and even techniques and decorative motifs that reflect Islamic influence from the Moorish occupation of the Iberian peninsula. Puebla, one of the cities well represented in Pries's photographs, is widely recognized as one of several places where cultures merged—pre-Columbian, Spanish Baroque, and late Moorish/Islamic. Pries made detailed measurements and drew freehand dimensioned drawings of elements of numerous Mexican buildings (fig. 5.11). He hoped to write and illustrate a book on Mexican architecture, but this project never came to fruition[47] (fig. 5.12).

Throughout his life, Pries collected paintings, books, and art objects. Books were inexpensive during the Depression, and Pries built up his library on Spanish and Latin American architecture and both folk and indigenous artistic traditions. During his Mexican travels, he acquired collections of pre-Columbian artifacts and, later, folk art. Because he drove from Seattle to Mexico and back each year,

Fig. 5.9
"Santa Magdalena, Contreras," photograph by Lionel Pries, 1930s. Pries photo album, Pries collection, University of Washington Libraries, Special Collections Division, UW24481z.

Fig. 5.10 "Ruinas Santa Cruz de la Flores, Tlajomulco, Jalisco," photograph by Lionel Pries, 1930s. Pries photo album, Pries collection, University of Washington Libraries, Special Collections Division, UW24476z.

send us through. Anyway, when we got to the border, Spike had about $200 in pesos in his pocket and he asked the border guard where they could be changed. The border guard sent him over to his brother's shack at the side of the road and Spike allowed himself to be gypped out of about $50. There were no questions asked.[49]

Pries faced similar challenges in building his own collections. Lloyd Lovegren recalled that Pries gave "hilarious and disastrous accounts of his many encounters with border guards and customs inspectors."[50]

THE "PRIMITIVE" AND THE MODERN

Spratling and Pries were not just fascinated by Mexico's past; they were also interested in how that past related to the present, particularly the relationship between indigenous traditions and Modern design.[51] Spratling was directly addressing this question in his designs in silver. The small mountain community of Taxco had once been the center of a thriving silver industry but had primarily been an exporter of raw silver rather than a producer of silver objects.[52] But eighteenth-century prosperity was short lived, and by the 1920s Taxco was an impoverished community. In the early 1930s, Spratling took on the challenge of developing the silver crafts of Taxco; this became his life's work.[53] He began by bringing in a few talented goldsmiths from a nearby town and established a silver workshop and showroom, named Taller de las Delicias, in June 1932. Spratling personally engaged in the tasks of design and promotion; he relied on others to fabricate the designs he drew. His workshop provided training to young Mexican craftsmen and offered an example that others could follow in establishing their own silver workshops. His project was a success: by the 1950s, there were over seventy-five silver workshops in Taxco.

he could carry objects back with him. Spratling and Pries shared an interest in collecting and often traded with each other.[48] Pries also occasionally couriered objects to the United States, as Wimberly recalled:

> Spike was a great friend of [Spratling] and when I went to Mexico with him, we brought out about 25 very important Precolumbian pieces. . . . It was, of course, all very illegal and we had to smuggle them out. Bliss Moore and I died a thousand deaths when Spike got too impatient to wait for the customs inspector Spratling had bribed to

For design inspiration, Spratling turned to pre-Columbian objects and contemporary folk art. A key aspect of his approach was working indigenous motifs into Modern designs. He achieved an elegant synthesis reflecting the vitality of the pre-Columbian and folk traditions, new developments in the arts, and his personal design sensibility[54] (figs. 5.13, 5.14). Spratling's approach reflected the influence of leading Mexican painters, who, in the aftermath of the Mexican Revolution, had rediscovered Mexico's

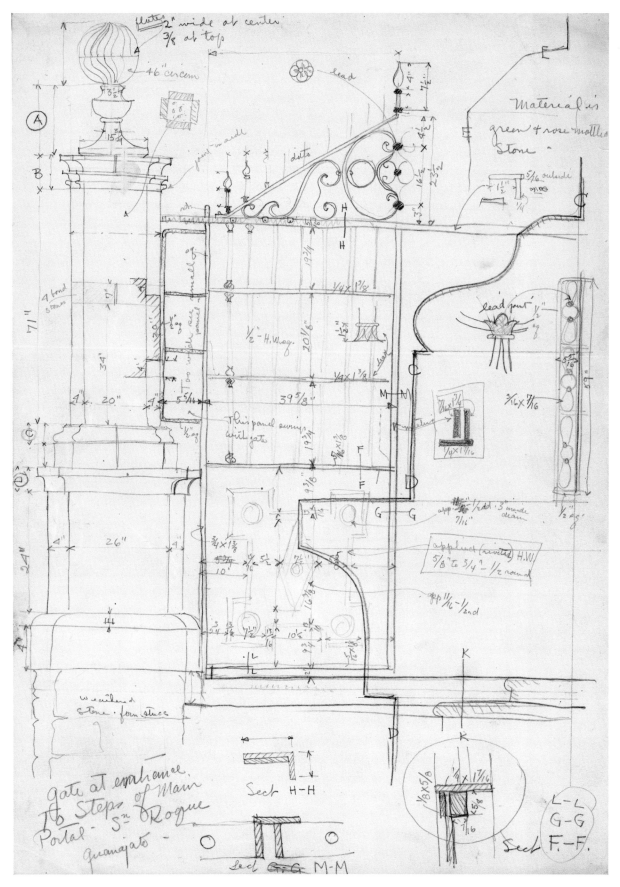

The drawing contains numerous handwritten measurements and annotations, including:

"2" wide at center 3/8 at top"

"46" circum"

"15½"

"Material is green & rose mottled Stone —"

"lead"

"71""

"4 bond stone"

"34""

"4" x 20""

"26""

"24""

"44""

"Weathered stone form stucco"

"½" H.W. o.g."

"20⅛""

"39⅝""

"This panel swings with gate"

"19¾""

"Gate at entrance to Steps of Main Portal — Sn Roque Guanajato —"

"Sect H-H"

"Sect G-G M-M"

"L-L
G-G
F.-F."

"Sect F-F"

"applied (riveted) H.W.
5/8" to 3/4" - ½ round"

Fig. 5.11
Lionel H. Pries, *Gate at entrance to Steps of Main Portal, Sn Roque—Guanajuato*, measured drawing, ca. 1930s; pencil, colored pencil on construction paper, 12½ x 11 inches. Pries collection, University of Washington Libraries, Special Collections Division, UW24467z.

Fig. 5.12 (*opposite*)
Lionel H. Pries, *Guanajuato, Stair Rail, 62 Plaza de la Paz*, measured presentation drawing; ink, pencil on stiff paper, 18 x 14 inches. Pries collection, University of Washington Libraries, Special Collections Division, UW23906z.

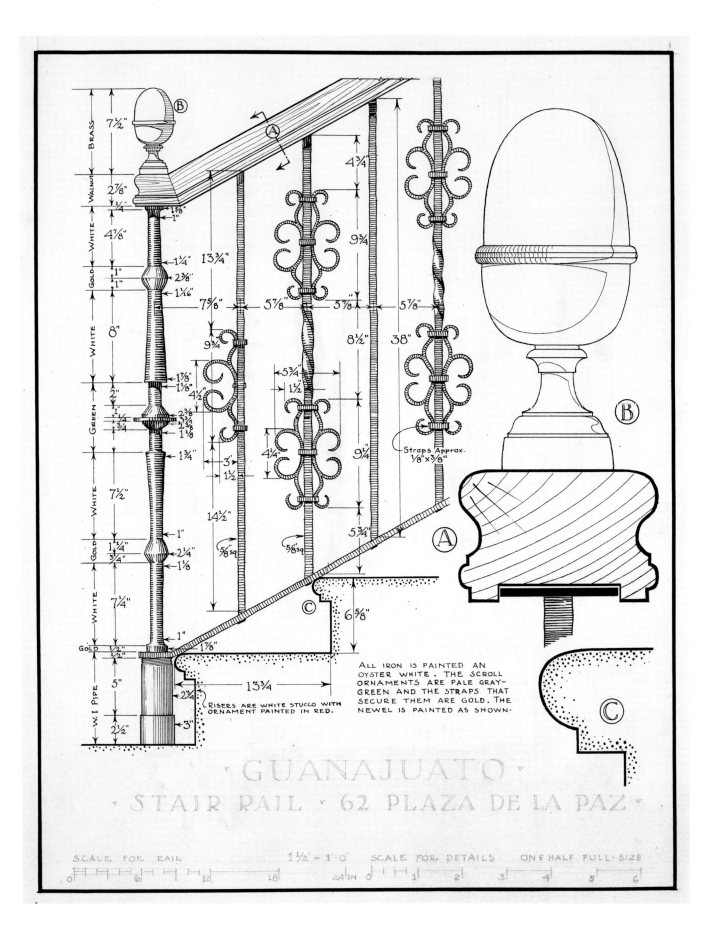

· GUANAJUATO ·
· STAIR RAIL · 62 PLAZA DE LA PAZ ·

ALL IRON IS PAINTED AN
OYSTER WHITE. THE SCROLL
ORNAMENTS ARE PALE GRAY-
GREEN AND THE STRAPS THAT
SECURE THEM ARE GOLD. THE
NEWEL IS PAINTED AS SHOWN.

RISERS ARE WHITE STUCCO WITH
ORNAMENT PAINTED IN RED.

Straps Approx.
1/8" x 3/8"

SCALE FOR RAIL   1½" = 1'-0"   SCALE FOR DETAILS   ONE HALF FULL·SIZE indigenous heritage. As the artist Jean Charlot later explained, pre-Columbian works and historical and contemporary folk art were among the most important sources of Modern Mexican art.[55] The fascination with Mexico's pre-Colonial past and its relationship to the making of a Modern Mexico emerged in multiple works; best known are the mural paintings of Rivera, José Clemente Orozco, Siqueiros, and others.[56]

Through Spratling, Pries met key members of the Mexican art and architectural communities. Of particular significance was Frederick W. Davis (ca. 1880–1961), who operated an antiquities and folk art shop in Mexico City.[57] Davis had gone to Mexico in 1910 and had been a pioneer in his attention to Mexican handicrafts. He assembled a collection that included some of the best examples of contemporary folk art as well as older popular crafts that had deteriorated or even disappeared. Because the emerging artists of the "Mexican school" were interested in both historical and contemporary folk art, they gravitated to Davis's shop, which became a gathering place for the group, "the artists' headquarters."[58] In turn, Davis was among the first to collect, display, and sell the work of these artists; he exhibited work by Rivera, Orozco, and Tamayo in 1927. Others who frequented the shop included Miguel Covarrubias and Jean Charlot.[59] Davis also displayed work by Americans, including George Biddle, Caroline Durieux, and Spratling.[60] In 1927, Davis hired René d'Harnoncourt (1901–1968), who had gone to Mexico in 1926 and quickly acquired a reputation for his knowledgeable advice to American antique collectors.[61] D'Harnoncourt, who worked with Davis until 1933, assisted in buying and selling antiques and contemporary works and also organized displays and exhibits in the showroom. Given both Pries's interest in collecting objects of fine art and his friendship with Spratling, he had an entrée into the circle around Davis and d'Harnoncourt. Davis, moreover, like Pries and Spratling, was gay.

Once he became part of the circle around Davis, d'Harnoncourt, and Spratling, Pries was exposed to the idea of Mexican artists and intellectuals that pre-Columbian art and indigenous arts and crafts could become the basis for a contemporary artistic renaissance. Further, as Mexican artists were conversant with contemporary Modern art in Europe, they fervently believed that a new Mexican art must respond both to specifically Mexican traditions and

Fig. 5.13 William Spratling, bracelet with design derived from pre-Columbian sources, 1930s. From Phyllis M. Goddard, *Spratling Silver: A Field Guide.*

Fig. 5.14 William Spratling, jaguar pin with design derived from pre-Columbian sources, 1930s–1940s. Phyllis M. Goddard, *Spratling Silver: A Field Guide.*

to international Modern art.[62] In this context, it is no surprise that Pries began to consider the marriage of the indigenous and the Modern as a possible response to the crisis in American architecture. There was, of course, a political agenda in the work of Rivera, Siqueiros, and many other Mexican artists, but this was of little interest to Pries.[63] With his romantic and artistic temperament, he was interested in the visual power of the work of Mexican artists, not its political content.

Pries's thinking was also shaped by the architect and artist Juan O'Gorman, whom he most likely met through the circle around Davis's shop.[64] Juan O'Gorman (1905–1982) was among the most influential, but also one of the most complex, of the Mexican Modern architects who began to practice in the 1920s and 1930s. Unfortunately, O'Gorman's work rarely appears in standard histories of Modern architecture. As the architect and critic Edward Burian has speculated, this omission may be due to the wide-ranging nature of his career—he was both a painter and an architect—and because "his work is not a simple progression over a career and thus is not easily digested."[65] Instead, Burian suggests, O'Gorman attempted to address multiple dichotomies, among them the "international" and the

Fig. 5.15
Juan O'Gorman,
Diego Rivera and
Frida Kahlo studios
and residences,
Mexico City, 1931.
Courtesy of Keith
Eggener.

"nativist," by seeking an architecture that was both Modern and Mexican.[66]

O'Gorman was a native of Coyoacán, a suburb of Mexico City. His early architectural education, gained at the Academy of San Carlos, was traditional, but he became interested in European Modernism in the mid-1920s, when he read LeCorbusier's *Towards a New Architecture* and encountered the Modernist teaching of José Villagrán García.[67] As Burian notes, the architects who experienced the Mexican Revolution read LeCorbusier selectively, embracing aspects such as "engineering, social programs, workers' housing, and the political nature of architecture" that fit the post-Revolutionary period.[68]

LeCorbusian ideas were evident in the schools that O'Gorman designed in the early 1930s, when he served as architect for the Department of School Construction in the Ministry of Education, but his residential designs of the same period were shaped by the desire to integrate international Modernism with local Mexican culture—a desire paralleling the work of the Mexican muralists, and of much more interest to Pries. According to Burian, O'Gorman's residences often use vernacular siting strategies and colors, functional program elements, and interior treatments as expressive devices to link the universalism of Modern architecture to specific local conditions.

O'Gorman's studios for Diego Rivera and Frida Kahlo, dating from 1929, show such a design approach.[69] The site is enclosed by a wall of cactus forming an outdoor room, and the exterior wall colors—a deep matte blue and a red similar to volcanic stone—were drawn from vernacular examples (fig. 5.15). Embedded in the floor of Rivera's studio are colored stone chips, unlike anything in LeCorbusier's work of the period. In each studio, Kahlo and Rivera displayed their own collections of historical and contemporary folk art; thus Mexican popular art was framed by an International Style enclosure, tempered by vernacular colors. O'Gorman's Francis Toor residence and studio, dating from 1934, was similar, featuring a planted wall at the street, vivid colors from Mexican vernacular architecture, and the traditional use of the roof during warm weather.[70] The interior, filled with Toor's collection of folk art, most strongly interwove international Modernism and specifically Mexican design. As Burian explains, "The juxtaposition of abstract, gridded, universalized structural slab and industrialized steel windows with anthropomorphic folk art was surreal and was an essential way to Mexicanize the house."[71]

If Pries had never met O'Gorman, he would have known these buildings through his connection to the circles around Davis, Spratling, d'Harnoncourt,

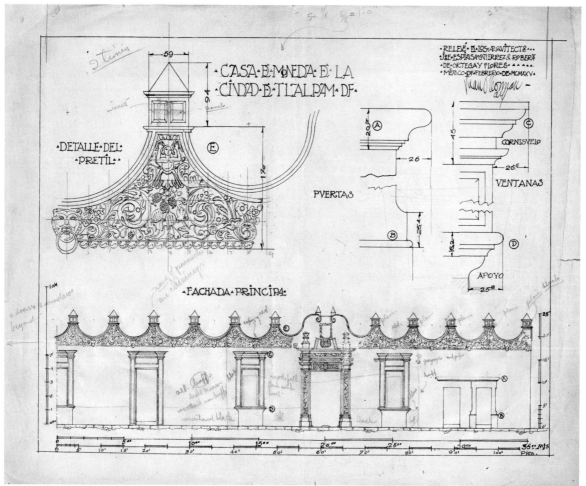

Fig. 5.16
Juan O'Gorman,
*Casa de Moneda
de la Ciudad de
Tlalpan, D.F.*,
blueline print of
measured draw-
ing, with original
ink signature, 16¾
x 13½ inches. Pries
collection, Univer-
sity of Washington
Libraries, Special
Collections
Division.

and Covarrubias, but Pries and O'Gorman had more than a passing acquaintance. Pries obtained a set of blueline prints of measured drawings, produced by O'Gorman, of historical (Spanish Colonial) Mexican buildings (fig. 5.16). The drawings were probably done when O'Gorman was a student; when he gave prints to Pries, probably for Pries's proposed book, he signed each one in ink to indicate his authorship.[72] Further, the fact that O'Gorman, like Pries, was an artist as well as an architect (he gave up the practice of architecture for painting in the mid-1930s, returning to architecture about 1950) provided an additional basis for their friendship.[73]

One more link between Pries and Mexico's Modern architects was his friendship with Federico Sánchez Fogarty of Cementos Tolteca (Tolteca Cement Company).[74] Tolteca was Mexico's leading producer of cement, and the company actively promoted the use of concrete through the promotion of Modern architecture. Indeed, the company's influence was so strong that a contemporary guidebook called Tolteca a key to the spread of Modern architecture in Mexico:

Modern architecture, almost non-existent five years ago, is now more at home in Mexico City than in almost any other city in the world. This development can be traced to six factors: one a group of restless, brilliant young architects and engineers; two, the clever propaganda of the Tolteca Cement Company, teaching the use of clean lines and clean materials (chiefly concrete of course). . . . [75]

The guidebook also cited the role played by Tolteca's "indefatigable and sophisticated advertising manager, Federico Sánchez Fogarty."[76] Whether Pries met Fogarty through O'Gorman, or O'Gorman through Fogarty, is not particularly important. What is critical is that through such friendships Pries came face to face with the new Modern architecture in a way that would have been possible nowhere else in North America in the early to mid-1930s.[77]

The subsequent development of Pries's ideas may be best illuminated through a brief consideration of the parallel path taken by d'Harnoncourt. In 1929–30, d'Harnoncourt organized an exhibit of

Fig. 5.17
Installation view, "Indian Art of the United States," Museum of Modern Art, New York, 22 January– 27 April 1941, René d'Harnoncourt, curator. Copyright Museum of Modern Art, New York.

Mexican fine and applied arts that was shown at the Metropolitan Museum in New York and then traveled to other American cities.[78] Although d'Harnoncourt left Davis's shop in 1933 and subsequently resided in the United States, he continued to summer in Mexico and stayed in touch with the circle of Mexican artists. In 1936, d'Harnoncourt became the general manager of the Indian Arts and Crafts Board (IACB), a New Deal agency created to revive Native American arts and crafts as part of an effort to seek the "human and economic rehabilitation of Native American peoples."[79] Spratling's success in Taxco was one model for IACB activities. To promote Native American craftwork, d'Harnoncourt developed an exhibit of Native American arts and crafts for the 1939 Golden Gate International Exposition, in San Francisco. Its success led to an even larger show at MOMA: the extraordinarily influential

"Indian Art of the United States" exhibition that opened in January 1941.[80]

According to the art historian W. Jackson Rushing, one of the aims of these exhibits, particularly the one at MOMA, was to demonstrate the "affinity of the primitive and the modern."[81] D'Harnoncourt's notes indicate his specific intent to show the appropriateness of Native American arts and crafts in Modern interiors. In some parts of the 1941 exhibit, the work was "contextualized"—that is, placed within groupings by tribal origin—but elsewhere the works were displayed primarily in accord with visual or functional criteria relative to fitting with abstract Modern architectural settings.[82] To advertise the exhibit—and to demonstrate this affinity— d'Harnoncourt placed a 30–foot-tall totem pole against the front elevation of the International Style museum building[83] (fig. 5.17).

What few if any who attended the MOMA show realized was that Pries, four years earlier, had achieved a similar juxtaposition in his architectural work in Washington State. As discussed in detail in the next chapter, Native American elements appeared in Pries's design for the Willcox residence, on Hood Canal, dating from 1936–37. Totem poles are key elements of the design; they appeared juxtaposed with Modern forms and materials on the exterior as well as in the interior of the Willcox project[84] (fig. 5.18).

Pries's interests, like those of d'Harnoncourt and MOMA, were primarily in aesthetics—in formal and visual relationships, and in similarities of Modern art to human traditions that had existed for centuries. One of Pries's favorite books was Ludwig Goldscheider's *Art Without Epoch*, published around 1937, which showed links between indigenous and historical works and "modern taste."[85] In 1950, d'Harnoncourt would be responsible for a Museum of Modern Art "teaching portfolio" titled *Modern Art Old and New*, which would explicitly match works of twentieth-century art with works of cultures from all times and places to "show that a kinship often exists between works of art from different epochs" and to demonstrate "that such 'modern' means of expression as abstraction, distortion, and exaggeration have been used by artists from the beginning."[86]

The point is not to suggest that d'Harnoncourt copied Pries but rather to show that a belief in the linkage of indigenous heritage (and contemporary production by folk cultures) to modernity in art and architecture permeated the thinking of those whose paths had crossed in Mexico, and that by the mid 1930s this belief was becoming influential in some segments of the art and architecture communities in the United States. In Pries's case, his personal interest in arts and crafts as elements of architecture was transformed within the emerging school of thought that linked modernity in art and architecture to indigenous traditions whose origins predated European settlement in the Western hemisphere—a school of thought that Pries first encountered in Mexico.

6

IN PRACTICE

Design Evolution, 1932–1942

Pries's primary focus after 1932 was his teaching career, but he never entirely withdrew from practice. By the mid-1930s, he had a drafting table in his bedroom and often had drawings in development. The projects he produced in this period make it possible to trace changes in his design thinking.[1] Like other architects of his generation, he had to come to terms with Modernism. Pries believed that change in architecture came about through evolution, not revolution. Thus his designs of the 1930s reflect gradual, not cataclysmic, change. The impact of his experience in Mexico is evident, especially in the work of the mid to late 1930s. However, this was not his only firsthand exposure to new architectural vocabularies, as he also visited Europe and Chicago.

In the summer of 1933, Pries traveled for three months in northern and central Europe, visiting countries he had missed a decade before (fig. 6.1). After brief stops in Bremen, Hamburg, and Lubeck in July, he spent several weeks in Sweden and then traveled through Denmark to Germany. In August he was in Berlin, Dresden, Prague, and Vienna, and then he returned north via Regensburg, Nuremburg, Stuttgart, Frankfurt, Cologne, and Aachen. He passed through Amsterdam before his return to the United States in late September.[2]

Pries produced no drawings or paintings on this trip; he was traveling too fast. Instead, he took numerous snapshots and purchased books on architecture and design. His interests continued to be wide-ranging—his photos include historical buildings and contemporary architecture. Very few photographs show the radically new architecture of the International Style in Germany. Instead, Pries was most interested in buildings that merged the traditional and the new, such as P. V. Jensen-Klint's Grundtvig Church, Copenhagen (1913, 1921–26); Ragnar Östberg's Stockholm Town Hall (1909–23); Josef Olbrich's Secession Building (art gallery), Vienna (1897–98); and the Amsterdam housing estates by Michel de Klerk and Piet Kramer. These buildings reflect Pries's search for an architecture that could move into the present but still draw upon tradition.[3]

On his way home, Pries stopped in Chicago to see the Century of Progress Exposition.[4] This world's fair focused primarily on science, engineering, and technology. Spread over more than four hundred acres along the shore of Lake Michigan were buildings in a Modernistic architectural vocabulary—

Fig. 6.1
Lionel H. Pries,
passport photo-
graph, 1933. Pries
collection, Univer-
sity of Washington
Libraries, Special
Collections Divi-
sion, UW22192z.

what is now called Art Deco or sometimes Art Moderne.[5] Bold, bright colors were used throughout the exposition—primarily white, blue, orange, and black, and lesser amounts of yellow, red, gray, and green. The fair's buildings, lightly framed and clad in metal, asbestos, gypsum board, or plywood, had few windows, and so exhibit designers were able to maximize artificial lighting effects. Everywhere the emphasis was on "the new." The Seattle architect Paul Thiry recalled attending the fair:

> I went to the Chicago Fair, "Century of Progress," in 1933, and that, of course, was the first time that I was kind of pleased with the idea that times have changed . . . a lot of it was Art Moderne, but just the same it was a complete change. . . . [6]

Pries, too, must have sensed that change. He took snapshots of Century of Progress buildings, among them the Hall of Science, by Paul Cret, and the Travel and Transportation Building, by Edward T. Bennett, Hubert Burnham, and John A. Holabird. By the end of September he was back in Seattle.

RESIDENTIAL DESIGNS FROM THE 1930S

None of Pries's designs of the early 1930s reached fruition.[7] His proposed residence for the surgeon and general practitioner Dr. Trygve W. Buschmann and his wife, Katherine, for a site facing Lake Washington was similar to the large houses by Bain and Pries, and so it likely dates from the period between 1932 and 1934. Pries envisioned a grand house in stone; the overall dimensions were roughly 90 by

65 feet (fig. 6.2). The plan was nicely resolved, with a large library intended to serve as the primary living room. This room opened on the west to a bowling green and on the east to a stepped terrace down to the water. The detailing suggests a free treatment of English precedent.[8]

A residence for Dr. Glenn Borgendale, a dentist, and his wife, Helen, intended for a site in the Broadmoor subdivision, was presented in a Pries watercolor dated 1936[9] (fig. 6.3). This two-story house shows Pries's experimentation with asymmetrical composition and with a more contemporary architectural language.[10] The white stucco walls, the streamlined fenestration, and the porthole window all derive from Art Deco. The trellis with wisteria, a feature that Pries would repeat in several later projects, may reflect Pries's recollection of Maybeck's use of similar elements.

Pries designed a Los Angeles residence for Karl and Emita Krueger in 1936–37.[11] The Kruegers' site, a large parcel in the Westwood area, provided space for a grand house. Pries planned a U-shaped residence, on one side framing a broad lawn designed for outdoor music performances and, on the other side, looking out to the view (fig. 6.4). The simple volumes, horizontal lines, overhanging roofs, and corner windows show Pries's pursuit of a new architectural idiom.[12] The project may have been too expensive; Pries developed a smaller, more affordable version, but the Kruegers did not remain long in Los Angeles, so the project was not realized.

Beginning in 1936, Pries's luck changed as he saw three of his residences constructed. Each is quite distinct: the Willcox residence reflected Pries's experience in Mexico, the Gayler residence suggested Pries's awareness of the new regional architecture in California and Oregon, and the Hoggson residence was a contemporary rendition based on historical precedent.

The Colonel Julian and Constance Willcox residence (1936–37; altered), on Hood Canal in western Washington, was the largest house of Pries's career. It was his one opportunity to create a residence in the tradition of the grand country house, yet the design also reflected emerging directions in art and architecture.

Julian Parsons Willcox had retired in June 1935 as a lieutenant colonel after thirty years of service in the U.S. Marines.[13] His wife, Constance Britt Willcox, came from a wealthy family in San Diego.[14] When Julian Willcox retired, the family decided to

BROADMOOR RESIDENCE FOR DR. GLENN BORGENDALE

Fig. 6.2 (*top*) Lionel H. Pries, Trygve and Katherine Buschmann residence project, Seattle, ca. 1932–34 (unbuilt), view from water;

pencil on illustration board, 8¼ x 13½ inches. Pries collection, University of Washington Libraries, Special Collections Division, UW23234z.

Fig. 6.3 (*above*) Lionel H. Pries, Glenn and Helen Borgendale residence project, Seattle, 1936 (unbuilt), elevation;

watercolor, 4½ x 8¼ inches. Pries collection, University of Washington Libraries, Special Collections Division, UW24230z.

Fig. 6.4
Lionel H. Pries,
Karl and Emita
Krueger residence
project, Los
Angeles, 1936–37
(unbuilt), plan;
pencil and water-
color on illustration
board, 22 x 16
inches. Pries col-
lection, University
of Washington
Libraries, Special
Collections Divi-
sion, UW24236z.

build a house in western Washington. Friends in San Francisco recommended Pries. He proved well matched to the project: he had familiarity with the country house traditions of California and Philadelphia, he shared Mrs. Willcox's experience of European culture (including the ability to speak German), and he was knowledgeable about the arts and culture of Asia.

The Willcoxes sought a large house in which they could entertain. They wanted a house that was Modern and that also reflected their love of the Orient and of the Northwest. Their site, a large parcel, with over 1,500 feet of frontage along Hood Canal, had once been logged but was now covered with second-growth forest. A level area, or "bench," close to the shore but roughly 60 feet above the water, became the site of the house. This placement required a steep drive, over half a mile in length, through dense woods, and this drive added to the sense of the house as a special place apart from the outside world.

The design was resolved by August 1936; that month, Pries produced the first contract drawings and specifications.[15] Construction proceeded thereafter, although it was slowed by winter rain. Pries was deeply involved in every aspect of the house, drafting multiple sheets of interior details—many at full size—through March 1937.[16] The house was finished by the end of summer 1937, although some landscape features were not completed until the following spring.[17]

The Willcox residence is an L-shaped structure, totaling 7,800 square feet on the two living floors.[18] The core of the house is the living room, 36 by 18 feet, and 13 feet in height; it links to the entry hall and the dining room, and to the bar and game room a half-level below. The dining room occupies the outside corner of the L-plan, with views to Hood Canal and the Olympic Mountains. From the entry hall a stair leads to a midlevel library (above the game room and bar), and then to the second-floor bedrooms for Constance, Julian, and Julian Jr. as well as to a suite for Agnes, Constance's sister.

The house is of frame construction, with the exterior clad in red hexagonal cement-asbestos shingles (fig. 6.5). The steel windows and doors and wood trim were all painted pale green. The corner windows on both floors, and the slight outward slope of the windows at the second floor, are conspicuously Modern features (fig. 6.6). The living

and dining rooms are both finished in walnut-veneer plywood with flush details (fig. 6.7). The entry hall is finished with simulated marble—Constance Willcox insisted on simulating marble rather than using real stone.[19] In other rooms finished in wood—for example, in the two men's bedrooms and in the game room and bar—cabinets and drawers were all detailed to "disappear" into the continuous wood surfaces.

Although most of the land owned by the Willcoxes was left in its natural state, the areas nearby were developed as an extension of the building (fig. 6.8). Outside the dining room is a terrace with a trellis that became overgrown with wisteria. The double doors of the living room led to walks on either side of two pools—first a lily pool with goldfish, and then a saltwater swimming pool.[20] When Pries laid out these features, he subtly angled the walkways, creating a forced perspective that made the yard seem larger when viewed from the house.

The Willcox design lacks overt historical references. In Pries's use of industrial materials, and in the trellises that soon were overgrown with wisteria, one might discern the influence of Maybeck's work (such as Maybeck's 1910 First Church of Christ, Scientist, in Berkeley), but the reference is subtle. More overt were references to Asia in the red-green color scheme, the lily pool, and a "moon gate," where the service drive passed through the wall between the house and the greenhouse (now removed). The few porthole windows and a streamline detail at the main stair are the only obvious Art Moderne features, although the interiors of the powder room and Constance Willcox's oval dressing room feature built-in Art Deco light fixtures and details; these give a feeling of gracious elegance.

The keynote of the design was the juxtaposition of elements of Northwest Native American art and Modern materials and detailing. Two totem poles rose to a height of nearly 24 feet in front of the southwest-facing primary elevation of the house. These poles were each 12 to 14 feet in height but were raised on steel supports above trellises overgrown with wisteria[21] (fig. 6.9). This juxtaposition of Native American artifacts against industrial products—cement-asbestos shingles and steel windows—was a translation of Pries's experiences in Mexico, where he had encountered Modern architecture as a setting for indigenous works of art. A similar juxtaposition was created in the living room,

Fig. 6.5
Lionel H. Pries,
Julian and
Constance Willcox
residence, Tekiu
Point (on Hood
Canal), near Sea-
beck, Washington,
1936–37 (altered),
primary elevation.
Dearborn-Massar
Collection, Univer-
sity of Washington
Libraries, Special
Collections Divi-
sion, DM-3818.

Fig. 6.6
Lionel H. Pries,
Julian and
Constance Willcox
residence, primary
elevation and
library wing.
Dearborn-Massar
Collection, Univer-
sity of Washington
Libraries, Special
Collections Divi-
sion, DM-3820.

Fig. 6.7
Lionel H. Pries,
Julian and
Constance Willcox
residence, living
room, ca. 1967.
From real estate
brochure, Willcox
House collection.

Fig. 6.8
Lionel H. Pries,
Julian and
Constance Willcox
residence, land-
scape plan. Draw-
ing by Byung Keun
Choi (based on
blueline print held
by owner).

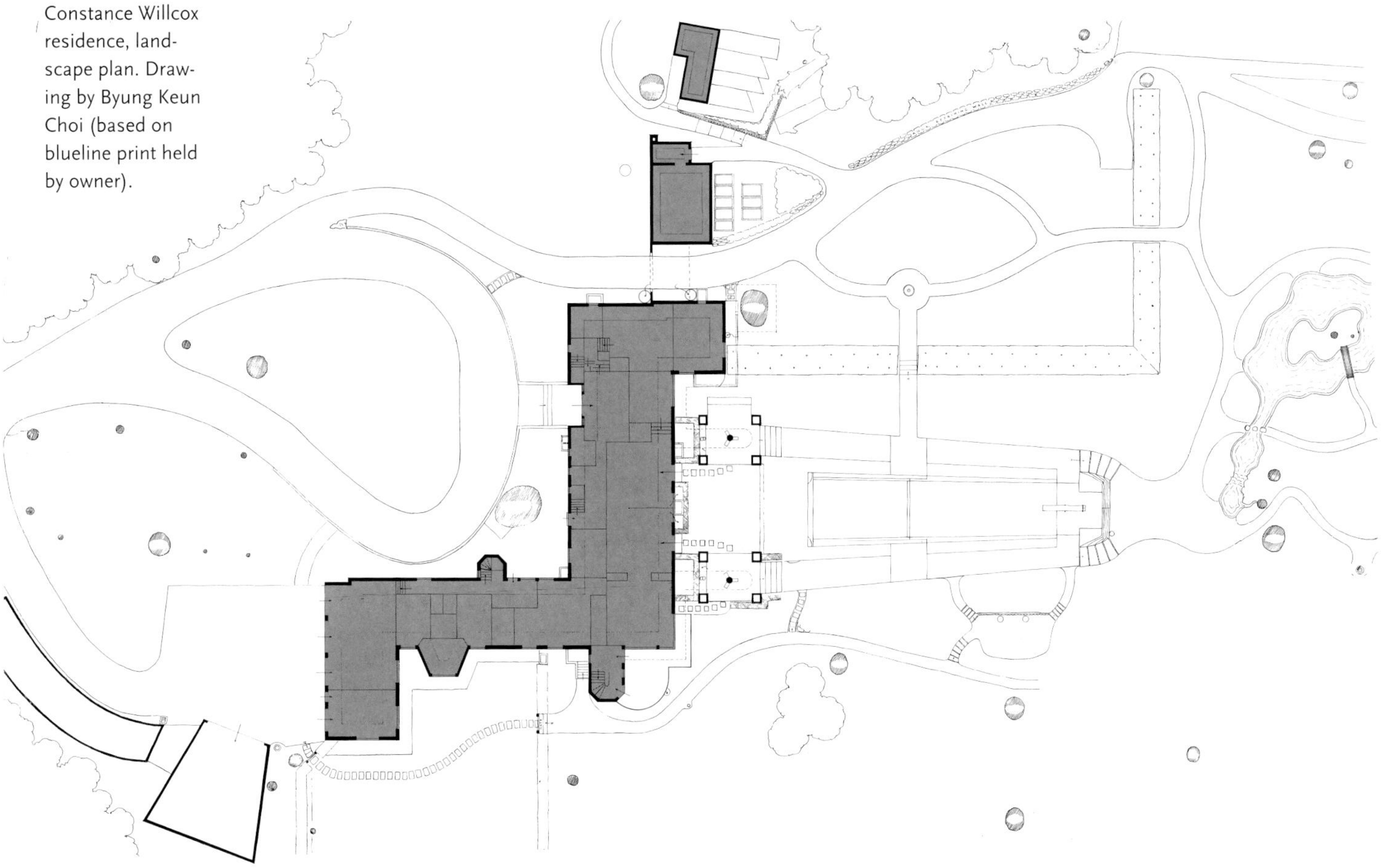

Fig. 6.9
Lionel H. Pries,
Julian and
Constance Willcox
residence, totem
pole above trellis.

Pries collection,
University of
Washington
Libraries, Special
Collections Divi-
sion, UW23767z.

where two totem poles, each about 10 feet in height, were placed on either side of the fireplace[22] (fig. 6.10). The ceiling of the living room was hand-painted, by Pries's students Bliss Moore and Pete Wimberly, in a repeating pattern based on Northwest Native American motifs; its primary colors—red, blue, black, and white—echoed those of the totem poles at the fireplace.[23]

In the Willcox residence, Pries achieved one of the most extraordinary syntheses of his career (fig. 6.11). The design is forward-looking in its modernity and highly original in its incorporation of Native American artifacts. The uniqueness of Pries's achievement is best understood in terms of the challenge that architects faced when they tried to blend the country house tradition and the new Modern architecture. As the architectural historian Mark Hewitt has discussed, the 1930s produced a series of attempts by American architects to recon-cile Modernism and the traditional country house.[24] *Architectural Forum,* in 1933, offered a rational anal-ysis of the country house, complete with adjacency

diagrams and discussions of the functionality of the various rooms. F. R. S. Yorke's *The Modern House,* published in 1934, was the first book in English to address domestic architecture in a Modern idiom.[25] But by 1936, only a few Modern American country houses had been published. The house that Edward Durrell Stone designed, in the International Style, for Richard Mandel (Mt. Kisco, New York) had appeared in *Architectural Forum* in 1934, but its style was not convincing to Pries, especially for a house in the Northwest and particularly for one sited along the rainy shore of Hood Canal.[26] More suggestive was George Howe's "Square Shadows," the William Wasserman house in Whitemarsh, Pennsylvania, published in *Fortune* as well as in *Architectural Forum* in 1935.[27] Howe was an architect whose work Pries would have known personally from his time in Philadelphia. The Wasserman house was con-structed of traditional stone and brick as well as concrete, steel pipe columns, and steel windows. In the *Fortune* article, Wasserman stated that a Modern vocabulary provided an "apt setting" for his collec-

Fig. 6.10
Lionel H. Pries,
Julian and
Constance Willcox
residence, totem
poles in living
room adjacent to
fireplace, ca. 1967.
From real estate
brochure, Willcox
House collection.

Fig. 6.11
Lionel H. Pries,
Julian and
Constance Willcox
residence, with
alterations,
ca. 1990. Photo
courtesy of Willcox
House.

tion of "very old Chinese primitives"—a statement that would have resonated with Pries.[28] Pries's Willcox residence, a synthesis of modernity and tradition, is equal in many ways to "Square Shadows." Pries's design, in its mixing of Modern architecture and Native American artifacts, was unique in the context of the American architecture of the period. This structure clearly shows Pries's personal search for a Northwest Modern architecture that would be the equivalent to what he had seen in Mexico.

The house served the Willcoxes very well. It was a center of social life on this section of Hood Canal for the next two decades and was famous locally because of the many visitors from Hollywood (said to have included Clark Gable, Errol Flynn, and Ernest Hemingway).[29] Pries was proud of the Willcox project. As already described, he involved two of his students in the decoration of the living room, and he took many others to visit in the late 1930s.[30] The Willcox residence was a unique achievement, but it remained largely unknown outside the Northwest.[31]

In 1939, the Willcoxes returned to Pries for the design of a gatehouse.[32] This was a small structure, primarily intended to provide residential spaces for a caretaker for the property.[33] Sited more than 200 feet from the house, in an area that remained otherwise undeveloped, the gatehouse is constructed of unfinished cedar, to blend with the surrounding woods. One wing of the L-shaped building spans the drive on an arch of cedar logs.[34] The entire structure has a fairy-tale appearance, no doubt a romantic folly drawn from Pries's imagination (figs. 6.12, 6.13).

The Ernest and Anne Gayler residence (1937–41, 1945–46; altered) is also on Hood Canal, just a few miles from the Willcox residence. Ernest Gayler, a career naval officer with a background in civil engineering, retired from active duty in 1937.[35] His wife, Anne Roberts Gayler, was born in South Carolina and raised in the South and in Germany, where she trained as a singer.[36] In 1936, the Gaylers acquired a site not far from where their friends, the Willcoxes, were already building their home.

Fig. 6.12
Lionel H. Pries,
Gatehouse, Julian
and Constance
Willcox residence,
1939 (altered).
Dearborn-Massar
Collection, Univer-
sity of Washington
Libraries, Special
Collections Divi-
sion, DM-3823.

Fig. 6.13
Lionel H. Pries,
Gatehouse, Julian
and Constance
Willcox residence,
1939 (altered).
Dearborn-Massar
Collection, Univer-
sity of Washington
Libraries, Special
Collections Divi-
sion, DM-3819.

The Gaylers followed the Willcoxes' example
in selecting Pries, but they had in mind a rather
different house.[37] The Gayler residence is a one-story
rustic wood structure with a partial basement. Pries
initially proposed a house around four sides of a
central patio, but the Gaylers rejected this layout
(which they thought reflected Pries's experience in
Mexico), as they feared it would create a dark and
cold outdoor space and a dark interior; the final
design was U-shaped and open to the south.[38] An
existing one-room cabin was incorporated as the
living-dining room; the service and bedroom wing
was set at an angle, an arrangement that allowed
the patio to be open to sunlight for more hours of
the day (figs. 6.14, 6.15). The partial basement,
including the garage, was located under the new
wing. The entire house was clad in vertical cedar
board-and-batten siding. Exterior detailing was
kept simple—the windows were crisply cut into
the siding with minimal trim).

Fig. 6.14
Lionel H. Pries,
Ernest and Anne
Gayler residence,
Nellita Point

(on Hood Canal),
near Seabeck,
Washington,
1937–41, 1945–46

(altered); overall
view, ca. 1970.
Photo by William
Matchett.

Fig. 6.15
Lionel H. Pries,
Ernest and Anne
Gayler residence,
patio, ca. 1970–80.
Photo by William
Matchett.

When the existing cabin was completely transformed to become the living-dining room, the floor was lowered 3 feet, to gain more height; the flat ceiling was removed, to produce a "cathedral" effect.[39] A large round window at the end of the living room provided a view to the lawn, to Hood Canal, and to the distant mountains (fig. 6.16). Finishes in most rooms were plaster or painted wood. The hall to the bedrooms and the circular stair to the basement and garage were finished in stained slash-grain cedar.

The family lived in a shack on the site during construction.[40] Because Ernest Gayler served as his own general contractor and the family did much of the work (at least the carpentry), the house took several years to complete. The Gaylers made changes to Pries's design, but features like the circular stair's ceiling, painted a rich blue, indicate Pries's continuing involvement.[41] Pries's exterior landscape design, including a formally arranged section in the garden, was not completed until after World War II[42] (figs. 6.17, 6.18).

In his design for the Gayler house, Pries may well have been influenced by work in California and Oregon. The round window at the end of the living room suggests the First Unitarian Church in Berkeley, a building of the Bay Area Tradition. The Gayler living room does not have the broad proportions of the Berkeley structure, although a wing wall with a "moon gate" as a small touch of Asia, was added later.[43] The board-and-batten exterior, which was allowed to weather naturally, suggests the influence of West Coast regional Modernism—specifically, the wood residential architecture by William W. Wurster and Harwell Hamilton Harris, in California, and by John Yeon and Pietro Belluschi, in Oregon.

Pries's Gayler residence went largely unnoticed by the broader professional community. Hood Canal was distant from the city; Seattle, in turn, was distant from the centers of architectural publishing. Construction progressed slowly, and it was almost a decade before the landscape was completed. By the postwar years, however, Pries's career, and the profession in general, were moving in new directions.

Unlike Pries's two other projects of the period, the Noble and Janet Hoggson residence (1937–38; altered) in The Highlands (the exclusive residential community on Puget Sound) looked both backward

Fig. 6.16
Lionel H. Pries, Ernest and Anne Gayler residence, living room, ca. 1980. Photo by William Matchett.

Fig. 6.17
Lionel H. Pries,
Ernest and Anne
Gayler residence,
view from north,
ca. 1940–42. Photo
courtesy of Anne
Gayler Miller.

Fig. 6.18
Lionel H. Pries,
Ernest and Anne
Gayler residence,
landscape plan,
1940. Courtesy
of Anne Gayler
Miller.

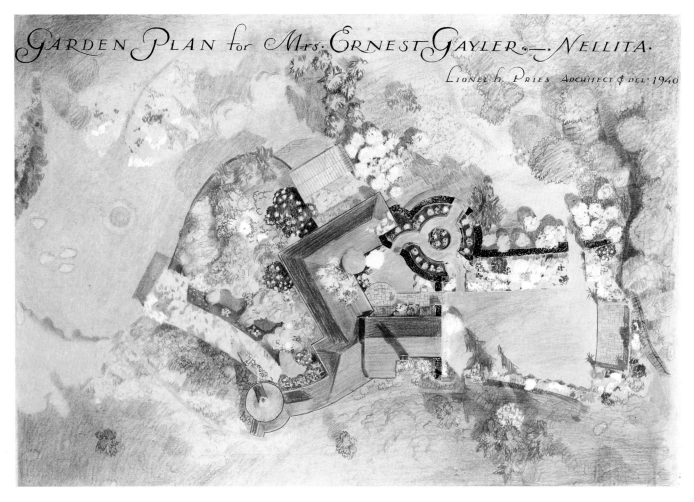

Fig. 6.19
(*opposite, top*)
Lionel H. Pries,
Noble and Janet
Hoggson
residence, The
Highlands, Wash-
ington, 1937–38
(altered), entry
court. Photo by
author, 2005.

Fig. 6.20
(*opposite, bottom*)
Lionel H. Pries,
Noble and Janet
Hoggson
residence, west
elevation. Photo
by author, 2004.

and forward—it was his last historically eclectic design. Noble Hoggson, a Harvard-trained landscape architect, had arrived in Seattle in 1930. In 1934 he married Janet A. Henry, granddaughter of Horace C. Henry, whose house had served as gallery space for the Art Institute of Seattle when Pries was director.[44] The Hoggsons had known Pries for several years before they commissioned this project. Janet Hoggson specifically requested a "French" house; once the residence was completed, Noble Hoggson created its formal landscaped setting, and so he, too, may have preferred a traditional design.[45]

The Hoggson residence is located on a lot measuring 500 by 140 feet. Pries positioned the house on the level eastern portion of the site, about 180 feet from the street, creating privacy and taking advantage of the view to the west. A surviving small sketch plan, possibly Pries's initial proposal, shows a first floor with resemblances to several of the larger residences by Bain and Pries. The Hoggsons, however, wanted a more compact house. The two-story L-shaped house bounds two sides of a square cobblestone entry court (fig. 6.19). The living and dining rooms are along the west (back) side, with double doors opening to a terrace and a lawn and, beyond, to the view of Puget Sound (fig. 6.20).

The French sources are evident in the concave mansard roof, the arched dormers, and the quoins. However, the relatively horizontal character and the asymmetry of the front elevation indicate Pries's rethinking of the historical vocabulary. At the front entrance, Pries transformed the quoins into curved walls with grooves—an Art Moderne feature. The round windows are a similar Moderne element.

The breadth of Pries's design capabilities was never more evident than in the years from 1936 to 1939. In that brief span, he designed the Willcox residence, the Gayler residence, the Hoggson residence, and the Willcox gatehouse—four notable buildings, each in a different mode, yet each showing skill and imagination. But, given the times, Pries remained quite circumspect in seeking publicity. He was aware that some local architects were unhappy that he was receiving his University of Washington salary and also competing with them for scarce commissions. None of Pries's projects of the 1930s appeared in the professional press, and Pries's reputation as a designer did not spread significantly beyond the circle of his clients, friends, colleagues, and students.

INTERLUDE: THE EARLY 1940S

For approximately nine months in 1941, William Bain and Lionel Pries reestablished their partnership. After the economic calamity of the early 1930s, Bain's practice had gradually recovered, and by the late 1930s he was one of Seattle's leading residential designers. In October 1939, Bain's office entered a joint venture with four other Seattle firms to carry out the design of Yesler Terrace, the city's first federally funded public housing project.[46] Bain, like each of his joint-venture partners, maintained his separate practice, but Yesler Terrace drew heavily on his staff. Thus, in 1940, Bain turned to Pries for help.

The collaboration developed gradually. Initially, Pries was only a consultant who did occasional drawings for Bain's firm; a notable example is the presentation perspective of the Pi Beta Phi sorority house (1940–41)[47] (fig. 6.21). The collaboration was successful enough that, in January 1941, Bain and Pries again became partners.[48] Construction drawings produced from mid-February through September were typically labeled "William J. Bain and Lionel H. Pries, Architects."[49] During this period, their practice was extraordinarily busy—they brought roughly two dozen commissions from design to construction, and there were additional projects that did not break ground.[50] Pries's role was likely that of offering design criticism and preparing presentation drawings. However, because Bain's staff was now larger and had a well-developed method of working, Pries's impact was much more muted than in their earlier partnership. Most of the 1941 Bain and Pries commissions were single-family houses with designs similar to those that Bain's office had already been producing[51] (fig. 6.22). They ranged in size from the one-story, two-bedroom Harold and Evelyn Wasson residence in Magnolia to larger structures, such as the Frank and Alice Hogue residence in Laurelhurst. These houses were well planned and comfortable but generally conventional in character.[52] Pries probably drew perspectives of many of the firm's projects, but only a few survive[53] (fig. 6.23).

The Raymond and Martha Gardner residence (1941–42), in the new Windermere development on Lake Washington, differs from the other projects and was largely Pries's design.[54] A two-story house with an L-plan, the Gardner residence presents a horizontal appearance that is due to the continuous

Pi Beta Phi
UNIVERSITY OF WASHINGTON

William J. Bain
ARCHITECT

Fig. 6.21 (*above*)
William J. Bain, Pi
Beta Phi Sorority
House, Seattle,
1940–41 (altered);

slide of drawing
by Lionel Pries.
Visual Resources
Collection, College
of Architecture &

Urban Planning,
University of
Washington.

Fig. 6.22 (*below*)
William J. Bain
and Lionel H. Pries,
Otto B. and Myrtle

Gufler residence,
Seattle, 1941
(altered); photo,
June 1942. State

of Washington
Archives, Puget
Sound Regional
Branch.

Fig. 6.23
William J. Bain
and Lionel H. Pries,
Harry W. and
Lenore Gilbert
residence project,

Mercer Island,
1941 (unbuilt);
pencil and water-
color on board,
6½ x 8¾ inches,
March 1941. Pries

collection, Univer-
sity of Washington
Libraries, Special
Collections Divi-
sion, UW24232z.

horizontal line of the eaves and to the change from the flush finish of the first floor to the horizontal siding at the second. Pries designed the house as a "threshold" to the view. The west wall, facing the drive, has relatively few openings; the entry hall leads to the living and dining rooms, which open, through a nearly continuous series of large steel windows and doors, to the terrace and, beyond, to the view to Lake Washington, prefiguring Pries's postwar designs. The corner windows at the second floor clearly recall those at the Willcox residence.[55] The oval stair adjoining the entry hall recalls a similar stair at the Hoggson residence, although the Gardner stair has an especially gracious feeling, given its increasing radius as it rises to the second floor.[56] The Gardner residence is striking for its siting, its spatial sequence, and its modernity; it is a link between Pries's projects of the late 1930s and those he designed after the war (fig. 6.24).

Bain and Pries dissolved their partnership in mid-September 1941. It seems that the pace of new commissions was slowing, although it may also be that Pries could not maintain his commitment once the new academic year began.[57] That summer and fall, Pries was evidently engaged in the independent design of houses outside Seattle, including several in Arizona. Pries's résumé of the early 1950s lists "three houses in Phoenix, Arizona," but these remain unidentified.[58] Unlabeled photographs that appear to show one of these houses during construction are dated "Dec. 10, 1941"[59] (fig. 6.25).

Ordinary architectural practice ended in 1942. During the war, construction materials were rationed; only projects with war "priorities" could move ahead. Custom single-family residential commissions disappeared; Pries's practice became inactive. Seattle faced a housing crisis as immigrants flooded the city to work in shipbuilding, airplane

Fig. 6.24
William J. Bain and Lionel H. Pries, Raymond and Martha Gardner residence, Seattle, 1941–42 (altered), east elevation. Photo by author 2005.

production, and other war industries. Many architectural firms combined in joint ventures to design
large housing projects and other facilities for the
war effort, but Pries did not participate in these
efforts. Pries did design and teach camouflage
under the direction of William J. Bain, who was
in charge of the state's camouflage program.[60] By
1943, the university had changed to a year-round
academic calendar, and Pries taught U.S. Navy V-12
students in addition to regular architecture students,
so he had little free time. Nevertheless, he did find
time to read and reflect—his projects after 1945
would show the results of his personal rethinking
of design during the four years of war.

Fig. 6.25
Lionel H. Pries,
unidentified
residence under
construction,

possibly in
Phoenix, Arizona,
1941–42; photo,
10 December 1941.
Pries collection,

University of
Washington
Libraries, Special
Collections Divi-
sion, UW22236z.

7

EDUCATOR
OF ARCHITECTS

THE UNIVERSITY OF WASHINGTON,

1928–1945

IN FALL QUARTER OF 1928, CLASSES AT THE
University of Washington began on Monday,
1 October. That afternoon, the sophomore and senior
architecture students met their studio critics for the
first time. One of those critics, Lancelot Gowen, was
well known, as he had taught at the school since
1924. The other, Lionel Pries, was so new that he
had not even been included in the 1928–29 university catalogue. The student newspaper, *The Daily*,
reported the names and departments of new faculty
in the issue of 1 October; any more than that,
however, the students would have to find out for
themselves.[1]

Whether Pries had anticipated a position in the
Department of Architecture when he moved to Seattle
in 1928 is not known. Harlan Thomas, head of the
department, had written to David Thomson, dean
of faculties, on 22 June 1928, recommending Pries's
appointment; Thomson offered the position to Pries
just two days later.[2] Negotiations had taken place
prior to this time, because Thomas's letter noted,
"We were unable to secure Mr. Pries for less than
$2500, full time." When the discussions with Pries
began is unknown, but it would not have been
surprising if Pries had had contact with the department before he left California. He had been offered
a position at the University of Washington once
before—by Carl Gould, in 1923.[3] But it was only in
1928 that he began his teaching career.

Pries joined the department at a critical time. In
the years from the late 1920s to the early 1940s, the
emergence of Modernism began to challenge architectural educators. Most American architectural programs continued to follow the model of the Ecole des
Beaux-Arts; by the end of the 1930s, however, some
leading schools, such as Columbia and Harvard,
would turn to the new pedagogy of the Bauhaus that
was then being embraced by the architectural avant-
garde.[4] Other schools, notably the University of
California at Berkeley, saw attempts to preserve the
traditional approach challenged by student revolt.[5]
Yet such contentiousness did not develop at the
University of Washington, where the Beaux-Arts
pedagogy remained in place until 1946–47.

Pries played a central role in keeping the older
pedagogy alive, for two primary reasons. First,
Pries focused on the Ecole method, but not on any
particular historical style. Pries saw the Beaux-Arts
approach as one that addressed problem solving and
allowed for wide-ranging adaptation and variety.
After 1932, Pries's own design work showed his

flexibility and adaptability as well as his personal search for an appropriate contemporary architecture. From the late 1920s to the 1940s, students' attitudes toward emerging architectural directions gradually evolved, and Pries and the other faculty did not resist the students' changing interests. As a result, the students found that they could experiment with new design vocabularies, as long as they did so within the step-by-step method derived from the Ecole. The second reason for the centrality of Pries's role in keeping the Ecole pedagogy vital was that Pries himself truly made architecture come alive. He was an exemplary teacher who transparently embodied what he believed, and he was devoted to the school of architecture. His dedication to the students and to architecture extended far beyond the limits of the classroom or the design studio. Within a very short time after he arrived, Pries emerged as the inspirational leader of the school. As Anders Oien remembered more than seventy years later, "In 1928, my second year, Lionel Pries came to teach, and he certainly woke things up."[6]

ARCHITECTURE AT THE UNIVERSITY OF WASHINGTON, 1914–1928

In 1928, the Department of Architecture was just beginning its fourteenth year. Although led by Harlan Thomas, the department reflected the personality and approach of its founder, Carl Frelinghuysen Gould (1873–1939). Gould, born and raised in New York, was a product of Harvard and the Ecole who had experience at leading offices in the East and had arrived in Seattle in 1908.[7] With his cultured background, artistic interests, and patrician bearing, he soon became a leader in the local promotion of architecture, fine arts, city planning, and architectural education. When, in January 1913, the University of Washington regents approved the formation of the College of Fine Arts, with departments of art, music, drama, and architecture, they turned to Gould, appointed him a lecturer in architecture, and directed him to plan the new program.[8]

Gould shaped the curriculum within the framework of the Ecole des Beaux-Arts as transformed for American universities.[9] On the occasion of the department's tenth anniversary, in May 1925, Gould explained this basis of the program:

> Our school is a professional school with a carefully devised and balanced educational ration

worked out. The system we follow was evolved from one begun in the time of Louis XIV, taken over by the Society of Beaux-Arts Architects in New York City, and variously adapted by the major schools of architecture in this country. Our student pursues for a period of four years the study of one of the chief elements of human culture, and does his work under a discipline in which we strive to develop his faculties of both perception and creation. The programme and esquisse as a base for our design problems are the foundations for the development of our course. Freehand drawing to train the hand and eye. Descriptive geometry to facilitate visualization. Mathematics and mechanics of materials to attain a structural understanding. History and theory to give background and a thoughtful attitude.[10]

By 1915–16, the school had affiliated with the Beaux-Arts Institute of Design, although Gould frequently supplemented the BAID programmes with locally based studio projects.[11] The method of the esquisse was applied in all design problems. Local practicing architects served on juries and as visiting critics. And, to the extent feasible with a small student body, the older students began to advise the younger ones, and the younger to help the older.

The University of Washington program grew slowly; from eleven or twelve students in 1914, enrollment climbed to thirty-eight in 1922 and forty-seven in 1923.[12] Facilities presented a constant challenge, and the department moved three times in a dozen years. From 1916 to 1921, the Department of Architecture occupied a "temporary" one-story wood-frame building that students called "the Shack." In 1922, the department relocated to the attic of Education Hall, and four years later it moved again, to another "temporary" building—the two-story wood-frame and stucco Administration Building left over from the Alaska-Yukon-Pacific Exposition (held on the University of Washington campus in 1909); it too was called "the Shack."[13] This structure was home to the department when Pries arrived in 1928 (fig. 7.1).

During his twelve years at the University of Washington, Gould held only a half-time appointment, as he remained deeply involved in practice.[14] Gould hired Harold O. Sexsmith, a graduate of the Armour Institute in Chicago, as the department's first instructor in 1915, and in 1917 he added Robert F. McClelland, a graduate of MIT.[15] He also drew

Fig. 7.1
"The Shack," former Alaska-Yukon-Pacific Administration Building, University of Washington, 1907–9 (destroyed 1937). This structure served as the home of the Department of Architecture beginning in Fall 1926. It was actually the third space occupied by architecture students to have the nickname "The Shack." University of Washington Libraries, Special Collections Division, UW24471z.

on the local professional community for design instructors and depended on other departments for such courses as drawing, watercolor, structures, and construction.[16]

In 1923, Sexsmith and McClelland both left for better opportunities. Gould was in touch with administrators across the country, and it may have been Warren Laird at Penn who suggested that Gould contact Pries, who had just returned from his trip made possible by the LeBrun Traveling Scholarship and might be available. In his letter to Pries dated 2 August, Gould wrote, "I am glad that you will be associated with us in our work in the Department of Architecture as Assistant Professor."[17] Gould proposed that Pries be made responsible for the freshman year, assist in the sophomore studio, and teach a course in building construction. Essentially, Gould assigned Sexsmith's responsibilities to Pries, perhaps because Gould had already promised the more advanced courses to his other new appointee, Ralph W. Hammett, who had degrees from Minnesota and Harvard and two years of teaching experience.[18] But Pries chose not to accept. He may have been undecided between teaching and practice and uncertain about Seattle, where he had few personal contacts. The deciding factor may

have been that he believed he should work with more advanced students, not teach basic skills to beginners.

By fall 1923, the position that Pries rejected had been filled by Arthur P. Herrman (1898–1992), who had a B.A. in architecture from Carnegie Institute of Technology.[19] Herrman took on courses in drawing, architectural history, construction documents, and design[20] (fig. 7.2). Herrman was the first faculty member recruited by Gould who made his career at the university; he would spend the next forty-five years as a member of the faculty, becoming head of the school in the 1940s and the first dean of the College of Architecture and Urban Planning in 1958.

When Ralph Hammett left, after just one year, Gould had the good fortune to attract Lancelot ("Lance") E. Gowen (1894–1958) to the department[21] (fig. 7.3). Gowen was from Seattle; his father, the Rev. Herbert H. Gowen, was a professorial lecturer in Oriental history, literature, and languages at the university. Gowen had received his B.A. in architecture from the University of California in 1916, and, after serving in World War I, he returned to Berkeley for graduate education. In 1921, Gowen won California's Alumni Prize competition, as Pries had done the previous year. Gowen also worked for John Galen Howard. From 1922 to 1924, Gowen was a

Fig. 7.2
Arthur Herrman, giving a critique to architecture student A. Baldwin Shay, 1937. Photo courtesy of George Hazen.

student at the Ecole. Carl Gould had reservations about Gowen's shyness, but Howard wrote a strong recommendation:

> Lancelot Gowen is a fine man in both character and ability. I have had no experience with him as a teacher but I should think he would be well fitted for such work. It is true Lancelot is shy and sensitive but he has a great fund of enthusiasm and devotion to his work and a passionate loyalty to his ideals which I think would more than make up for his shyness. . . . I think you would be very fortunate if you can induce Gowen to join your staff.[22]

Gowen joined the department in the fall of 1924. He took over the sophomore and senior design studios as well as courses in architectural history. Gould, in his report in the spring of 1925, described Gowen's early success:

> Mr. Gowen, who has been with us these two quarters[,] is a man of high character, much liked by the students, and he is developing into an excellent instructor in advanced design. With more experience in teaching and an understanding of the detail work of the Department, he will in my estimation become a very valuable man.[23]

Like Arthur Herrman, Gowen made his career at the University of Washington, where he remained

Fig. 7.3
Lancelot ("Lance") E. Gowen, ca. 1930s. Photo courtesy of Patricia Aitken.

on the faculty until his death, in 1958. Herrman and Gowen were Pries's colleagues throughout his teaching career. Gowen became Pries's closest friend on the faculty.

Political conflict between Henry Suzzallo, president of the university, and Washington's governor, Roland Hartley, led to Gould's resignation as head of the program in the fall of 1926.[24] Gould's successor was Harlan Thomas (1870–1953), who had received a B.S degree in mathematics and mechanics from Colorado State College in 1895 and then studied architecture in Paris and practiced in Denver before arriving in Seattle in 1906.[25] Over the course of his career, Thomas headed his own office and participated in a series of successful partnerships. Like Gould, he accepted a half-time appointment so he could continue to practice. Thomas built on the foundation that had already been created, and so his personal imprint on the school was never as strong as Gould's. Still, the school under Thomas began to achieve national recognition, and it weathered the Great Depression. In early 1928, Thomas secured funds to expand the faculty and extend the curriculum to five years. That fall, Pries joined the department.

LIONEL PRIES AND THE TEACHING OF ARCHITECTURE, 1928–1942

From 1928 to 1942, the department enjoyed a notable period of stability. In the fall of 1928, Richard Pearce joined the faculty along with Pries.[26] When Pearce was killed in a skiing accident in the winter of 1932, Henry J. Olschewsky took his place.[27] That was the only significant change in personnel for more than a decade. With four full-time design faculty, it was possible to structure the studio teaching in two teams: Gowen and Pries taught sophomores and seniors; Herrman and Pearce—and, after 1932, Herrman and Olschewsky—taught freshmen and juniors. Harlan Thomas, in his half-time role, oversaw the department, taught some history classes, and served as an occasional critic in studio but was generally remembered as a benign "father figure" by graduates of the period.[28] In 1939, as the number of students grew, additional faculty provided needed assistance, but to the students of the 1930s, "the department" was Herrman and Olschewsky, Gowen and Pries (fig. 7.4).

As at all architecture schools, the core of the curriculum was design studio, and coursework was coordinated to support the teaching of design.[29] The department followed the Beaux-Arts model until the late 1940s, but between 1931 and 1932, perhaps to save money in the depths of the Depression, the department ended its affiliation with the BAID. Although the catalogues continued to list the BAID level equivalent to each studio, the department no longer used BAID programmes and no longer sent work to New York to be reviewed. After 1932, the faculty wrote all the studio problems and did all the evaluations of student achievement.

Pries and Gowen taught together, in the sophomore year, a course called "Architectural Design Grade I." Pries, in contrast to the offer that Gould had made him in 1923, was never asked to teach basic skills in drawing and rendering. He and Gowen knew that the students in their studio already had those skills, so they could immediately focus on design problems. Pries and Gowen were also responsible for "Architectural Design Grade III," which offered the most advanced studio problems to fourth- and fifth-year seniors. Although Pries was co-teaching with Gowen, his dominant personality allowed him to play a role not unlike that played by Paul Cret at Penn.[30]

The Depression made it difficult for many students to finance their education, but enrollment in the Department of Architecture did not fall markedly after 1929. Entering classes increased gradually over the 1930s, from twenty to twenty-five at the beginning of the decade to as many as thirty-five by the end. Attrition was severe in the first year as students came to recognize the demands of the

Fig. 7.4
Architecture faculty at Tau Sigma Delta Banquet, 12 May 1939, caricatured by Robert Dietz; (*left to right*) Harlan Thomas, Lance Gowen, Guy Ardilouze (visiting faculty), Lionel Pries, Arthur Herrman, Henry Olschewsky. From *Architecture Annual*, 1939.

curriculum and the challenges of their courses. Most who survived the first year went on to complete the program. Some took time off, typically in the junior or senior year, to earn needed funds, but almost all returned to finish the degree.[31] Most students were from the state of Washington, a few came from other states in the Northwest, and occasionally one or two might enroll from farther away.

The program began in the first year with "Graphical Representation" and "Elements of Architecture," together offering an intense introduction to drawing because design work in studio could not really begin until the students had command of basic drafting skills, the conventions for representing three-dimensional objects and spaces in two dimensions, and presentation techniques.[32] "Graphical Representation" focused on the logic of drawing; taught by Pearce and then Olschewsky, the course included orthographic projection, shades and shadows, and perspective, and it also required several freehand sketches each week. Simultaneously, under Herrman's direction, students began to master the artistic aspects of presentation drawings, rendering, and delineation. The first step was learning how to run washes. Students learned to grind Chinese ink, to mix it with water in varying proportions, and to control its application to paper in order to produce the subtle gradations from dark to light that they would soon use in presentations of their own projects. Before they could practice these washes, they had to learn how to make "stretches"—wetting thick sheets of German watercolor paper in the studio sink, applying glue to the undersides of the edges, transferring the paper to a prepared board, and sometimes paper-taping the edges. A good stretch would produce a sheet of paper of "drumhead tightness" to which successive washes could be applied without the slightest wrinkle.[33] In the first year, stretches were small, often 16 by 24 inches and rarely more than 20 by 30 inches; but in the sophomore and junior years, students routinely presented their projects on sheets that were 30 by 40 inches, and in the senior years (four and five), sheets as large as 40 by 60 inches were not uncommon. After the freshman exercises, students tended to avoid ink washes: ink stained the paper fibers and errors were not easily corrected, whereas watercolor was a surface treatment that could be sponged out and reapplied—a procedure that often proved necessary.

Coursework in drafting and rendering continued through the first year. By the end of fall quarter, however, students began to focus on what, as opposed to how, they were drawing.[34] Then Herrman and Olschewsky assigned problems that directly addressed the "elements of architecture," which meant small pieces of buildings: doors, windows, walls, cornices, balustrades, balconies, stairs, and similar features. The work progressed rapidly from individual elements, such as moldings or column capitals (usually derived from plates in standard texts) to more complex combinations of elements. These were presented in the form of small analytiques—the time-honored Beaux-Arts drawing format. The typical first-year project asked the student to design a portion of a building, such as a classical window, niche, entrance, or loggia—an exercise that allowed limited individual expression. For these early projects, the student spent hours in the library looking at plates of historical examples in well-thumbed folios, such as Hector d'Espouy's *Fragments d'architecture antique,* G. Gromort's *L'architecture classique—parallèle d'ordres grecs et romains,* Paul Marie Letarouilly's *Édifices de Rome moderne,* or César Daly's *Motifs historiques—décorations extérieures* and *Motifs historiques—décorations intérieures.* Each student developed a design and then composed his or her presentation in the form of an analytique, with elevation, partial plan, and required elements. The analytique was an exercise in both composition and rendering, as students began to use the techniques of watercolor wash and detail that they had only recently mastered (fig. 7.5). About the middle of spring quarter, the next element of the Beaux-Arts system was introduced: students received a design assignment at 2 P.M. and were required to prepare the esquisse, due at 10 P.M., which then became the basis for the design work that they would carry out for the next several weeks.[35]

By the end of the first year, students had mastered basic drafting and presentation techniques. They had gained experience with small problems of their own design, and they had acquired some knowledge of architectural history from Herrman's year-long introduction, "Appreciation of Architecture."[36] But architectural education has always been about more than just training. In the Beaux-Arts period (as is still to some extent true today), the school was like a small college, with its own distinct culture that was separate from the larger university. As soon as first-year students demonstrated any command of lettering or rendering, they might seek out opportunities

Fig. 7.5
J. M. Fitzgerald,
classical window,
freshman analy-
tique; December
1929, University
of Washington;
pencil, watercolor
on stiff paper,

22 x 16 inches.
Department of
Architecture
Archives, Univer-
sity of Washington
Libraries, Special
Collections Divi-
sion.

to help upper-level students—or, more often, upper-level students, facing the pressure of presentation deadlines, would seek out lower-level students, even freshmen, to help them by running washes, darkening walls, adding lettering, and doing similar tasks. Working on an upperclassman's project was considered a privilege and an opportunity—the lower-level student became familiar with the work that he or she would be doing in the future and gained access to one or more mentors who could answer questions or give advice or criticism when faculty were unavailable or assignments seemed unclear.[37] The sharing of work by students at different levels benefited everyone and fostered a sense of esprit de corps.

The sense of a school culture was also enhanced by various rituals that took place during the year. Although all students were automatically part of Atelier, the architecture student organization (its

officers, elected each year, had the titles *massier* and *sous-massier*), in most years there was an induction ceremony for freshmen early in winter quarter.[38] After 1932, the primary task of this organization was the production of a yearly publication of student work, known as the *Department of Architecture Annual*, or simply the *Annual*; it usually appeared in June, and selection of one's project for inclusion was considered a significant honor.[39] Another ritual was the Beaux-Arts Ball, usually held in the spring and attended by faculty, recent graduates, friends, and even parents as well as current students. Not held from 1931 to 1934, the ball was renewed in February 1935 and was a highlight of each year thereafter, until 1942. The ball had grown out of the pageantry and theatricality that were part of Beaux-Arts education, and the decorations were always organized around a particular theme—for example, "The Wizard of Oz" in 1936, "Zombies" in 1937, and "Sultan's

Fig. 7.6
Students painting
mural for Beaux-
Arts Ball in senior
drafting room,
Architecture Hall,
spring 1939
(*left to right*):
Austin Grant,
Don Edwards,
Roland Terry,
Vladimir Barmuda.
Pries collection,
University of Wash-
ington Libraries,
Special Collections
Division. Caption
information pro-
vided by George
Hazen. UW23764z

Night Out" in 1938.[40] This theme was usually represented on a large wall mural on sized muslin (sometimes as long as 20 feet), which was prepared by a small group of talented students (fig. 7.6). Such murals were saved and reused as decorations in subsequent years.[41] Students, recent graduates, and faculty all attended in elaborate costumes—prizes were awarded for the most creative (fig. 7.7). Also occurring annually was the induction of high-performing juniors and seniors into the architecture honorary society, Tau Sigma Delta. This semiformal-dress event, usually held at a private house or club of notable design quality, drew student members, faculty, and graduates who had been Tau Sigma Delta honorees themselves.[42]

As freshmen, the students had little interaction with either Pries or Gowen. Neither taught in the first-year studios or the first-year lecture classes. Nevertheless, most architecture students already

held Pries in awe, and more than a few were intimidated by his reputation not just for erudition but for the demands he made on the students in his classes. Students arrived in the second-year studio knowing that they would need to make an extraordinary commitment, well beyond the fifteen scheduled hours of studio each week.[43]

Problems in "Architectural Design Grade I" (the second-year studio described in the university catalogue as "order problems and simple problems of buildings"), which focused initially on portions of buildings or smaller freestanding structures, grew more complex over the course of the year. All projects began with esquisses produced by students working alone ("en loge," as at the Ecole). At the beginning of each new problem, Pries and Gowen arrived in studio at 2 P.M., passed out the assignment—in the days before inexpensive copiers, the assignments were on thin (onionskin paper) carbon copies of

typewritten sheets—and noted that the esquisses were due eight hours later. Because space was tight in "the Shack," work was done in the studio room, usually with proctoring by an upperclassman. Students were expected to work independently, in silence; they could not visit the library. In the fall of 1937, after the school moved to larger quarters, a room with individual carrels was available for doing esquisses.

Many graduates of the period believe that Pries was the author of most of the studio programs; whether or not this is correct, many programs had the romantic flair that students associated with Pries. Sophomore problems in 1932–33 included "a wall sundial—desired by the owner of an estate as a memorial to one of his children who was particularly fond of playing about his formal flower garden"; "a tomb—in the face of a cliff overlooking a large city in honor of the architect responsible for the city's plan and many of its monuments"; and "a court for a residence, designed to be used as a background for architectural fragments collected during world tours" (fig. 7.8). Some sophomore problems in the 1930s were fairly explicit about the anticipated vocabulary; problems like "a loggia surmounting a bridge in an Italian garden" or "a memorial tablet on a wall and a rostrum below it to be used for pres-

idential inaugurations and similar functions" clearly required Renaissance or Neoclassical character (fig. 7.9). Other problems were open: "a private chapel in a modern Episcopal residence" or "the entrance to grottoes where a large grocery corporation cures Roquefort cheese" allowed more choice as to architectural vocabulary.[44]

For students with little experience outside the Northwest, such problems could be mystifying, and sometimes they involved a significant cultural stretch. A sophomore design problem in early 1942 was "a tomb, including a sarcophagus, located on an island in a lake, for an American general killed in the south Pacific." Keith Kolb recalled how difficult it was to conceive a design: "None of us knew what a sarcophagus was, or at least I didn't." And he had other worries: "I kept thinking: I have to do something to get it known that this general is out there. And so I committed myself to a vertical sarcophagus! The first crit Spike gave was, 'Did you ever think what it is like to live in eternity standing up?'"[45] But, once a student had turned in the esquisse, he or she was committed to it thereafter. This was where design training really began—the student's learning how to make something good from any esquisse he or she had submitted. Kolb remembered, "You learned by doing terrible things. Getting the wrong

Fig. 7.8
Barney Grevstad,
"A Court for a Res-
idence, designed
to be used as a
background for
architectural frag-
ments collected
during world
tours," sopho-
more analytique,
fall 1932 or winter
1933, University
of Washington;
pencil, watercolor
on stiff paper,
30 x 40 inches.
Department of
Architecture
Archives, Univer-
sity of Washington
Libraries, Special
Collections
Division.

Fig. 7.9
Erling H. Bugge,
"A Loggia in a
wall overlooking
a garden," sopho-
more analytique,
January–February
1932, University
of Washington;
pencil, watercolor
on stiff paper,
30 x 40 inches.
Department of
Architecture
Archives, Univer-
sity of Washington
Libraries, Special
Collections
Division.

ideas, and then you discovered what [the faculty] really were thinking about."[46]

The next few weeks of studio were spent in individual critiques. Each afternoon began with the arrival of Pries and Gowen in studio, looking for students ready to talk about their projects. Robert Dietz, a student in the late 1930s, who later served as dean of the college, recalled witnessing Pries's arrival:

> It was shortly after lunch . . . when, as if carried by some magic surge, a tall, erect, spritely [sic], meticulously dressed gentleman, followed by a honey-colored Cocker Spaniel, arrived at the top of the stairs, and with a swagger, inimitable to Pries alone, swished through the studio, looking about to see who was ready for a crit. . . . he [quickly] planted himself at one of the drafting boards, and immediately began questioning and sketching.[47]

Students soon learned to have a large roll of tracing paper (called "flimsy") ready because Pries and Gowen both drew as they talked—Gowen's drawings tended to be diagrammatic; Pries's often included multiple two- and three-dimensional sketches. According to Roland Terry, a sophomore in 1936–37, Pries "taught by means of many sketch demonstrations. He taught that there could be a thousand solutions to each problem. . . . He was a master with a pencil in sketching, not only beautiful ideas in plan, but also in perspective."[48] Fred Bassetti explained how he experienced this process two years later:

> When I was a sophomore (1938–39), I was first exposed to [Pries's] facile drawings. He would sharpen an Eagle draughting pencil and, with an ever-so-light touch, illustrate some point which had simply never entered my mind before. . . . I think it was an entrance to a library building or something. He drew, in plan, a series of columns which, instead of being square in plan, were rectangular, elongated in the direction of travel, rather than being just left over pieces of wall or round or just 'blah.' Then he drew a little vignette in perspective which immediately made it clear and illustrated for me for all time that a building should have "character."[49]

The students learned not just from direct critique but also by listening to critiques of others. Kolb

recalled, "You learned by watching Spike sketch as he would go around talking to the different students, and you would catch on fairly rapidly that it was a good idea to wander around listening to Spike as he gave crits at the different tables because you never knew what he was going to come up with."[50]

Because Pries and Gowen were also teaching fourth- and fifth-year seniors, they did not give individual desk crits to each student every afternoon, but they did see each student for detailed crits two or three times during the week. The students quickly learned that Pries would spend time with them only if they had work worthy of his attention. But not all students received the same level of criticism or even the same amount of time. As he got to know the students, Pries tried to figure out how to motivate each to produce the best work. Minoru Yamasaki recalled that Pries initially left him alone, and that he became frustrated:

> I was doing extremely well in structural engineering and, consequently, at a point in time during my sophomore year, I more or less made up my mind that I should switch to structural engineering. I went to Professor Pries and told him of my thinking, and he said that by all means I should stay in architecture. . . . He said he wanted to find out what my capabilities were, and had left me on my own. I had presumed this was because he was not interested in what I was doing, but he said he would give me criticisms from then on. . . .[51]

Pries's critiques frequently were very directive. At Penn, he had witnessed Cret and the other faculty sketching solutions for students, with the expectation that the students would refine what the faculty had drawn; now Pries often followed their example.[52] Whereas Gowen usually made a few marks and left it to the student to figure out which way to go, Pries typically considered his sketches more than just suggestions (fig. 7.10). Flora Allen Casey later recalled that Pries "was quite opinionated in his 'crits' and didn't take kindly to rejection of his ideas or even much questioning."[53]

Drawing was always central to the design process, since it was understood to be a method of discovery, not just representation. Pries and the other faculty believed that design depended on drawing and seeing; it could not simply be reasoned out. This was one reason why the program included an emphasis on art as well as architecture. The belief

Fig. 7.10
Lionel Pries,
sketch made
for architecture
student John
Rohrer during
studio critique,
1936. Courtesy
of John Rohrer.

PROF. PRIES   CRIT FOR ROHRER 1936

in artistic synthesis achieved through drawing, common to architects of Pries's generation, was clearly expressed by the architect Julia Morgan in a letter to a draftsman ("your hand rather than your mind will lead you").[54] Pries was never willing to answer questions about *why* a design ought to be a particular way: one simply had to see it; some students found this terribly frustrating. And Pries had little patience with students who, he believed, were not making the necessary effort. They could become a target of his caustic wit. As a result, some found him intimidating, and some grew to dislike him.

Through the first half of the sophomore year, projects were presented in analytiques, now raised to a high art. Sophomore problems lasted four to six weeks. The last two weeks were spent on the analytique. The problem statement specified the required views and their scales—for example, the fall 1938 "Memorial Tablet and Rostrum" project required a plan, section, and elevation at ¼ inch = 1 foot, 0 inches, and at least four details at not less than 1½ inch = 1 foot, 0 inches. Sheet size was set at 30 by 40 inches. By the beginning of the last two weeks, each student would have prepared pencil drawings at the correct scales of the required plans, sections, elevations and details; the next four to five days were spent on sheet composition. Each student made a full-size drawing, usually in charcoal, with each element placed and with values for shades and

shadows represented. These drawings were hung around the studio room, and Gowen and Pries, using a pointer, critiqued each one so that the whole class could benefit. Then everyone did a new version, and the process repeated itself until, after several attempts, each of the drawings was ready to be produced in final form.

The last week was spent on delineating and rendering the analytique. This process began with transferring the entire composition onto a previously prepared stretch, followed by watercolor rendering—building up tones with successive washes (usually sepia or a mixture of ultramarine blue and burnt sienna, but occasionally gray or even green) to achieve the values previously worked out. Most washes were flat, added in layers to get darker values; graded washes might be needed for curved surfaces or specific details. Although mistakes could be sponged out—properly stretched paper could take an amazing amount of reworking without the slightest wrinkle—students were often hesitant to try really dark washes or detail. At this point, Pries gave his most virtuoso studio performances, as Roland Terry described:

During the final phases of a design problem, particularly in our sophomore year when the problem was often presented in a very pictorial fashion, he would dazzle the whole establishment by moving about the room from desk to desk to his favorite problems and favorite students, painting delectable delineations of their designs for the whole class to admire, usually only on those designs by the strong students. The weak students were infuriated because they thought they were really the ones who needed help.[55]

The perception that Pries only worked on favored students' projects was not universally shared, however. Robert Hugh Ross, a sophomore in 1936–37, described Pries's involvement and then suggested another reason why Pries might paint on some projects but not others:

> Pries was a genius with watercolor. Near the end of our projects, he would make one of his commanding entrances into the drafting room. Carefully he unrolled his brushes from a bamboo mat. Next he squeezed the colors into the fine metal palette he had acquired in France. Then he went the rounds of the students. We watched enthralled as he transformed mediocre problems into exquisite paintings. He could create the lushest banana palms, gnarled oak trees, and all manner of exotic plant species to best complement anybody's architecture. Most of us practically revered his ability. Spike sensed how I yearned to see this magical performance happen to a project of mine, and as a result would seldom perform for me. But I'm sure it was because he sensed that I needed to be forced to get in and do the job on my own.[56]

Robert Dietz stated simply, "Spike was there to help, provide guidance. He took up one's pencil or watercolor brush in times of defeat, [and] turned a less than great concept into something rich and delightful."[57] Sometimes, however, students regarded Pries's interventions with trepidation. William Svensson, a sophomore in 1936–37, remembered that Pries could load up his brush with "about a quart of dark brown gook," adding that "he would never ruin anybody's drawing, but he raised a heartbeat now and then."[58]

Pries not only painted but also used his painting as the basis for more lessons. Wendell Lovett, who was a sophomore in 1941–42, recalled:

> I remember Spike talking about edges, how we recognize the essential characteristics of things by their silhouettes rather than their surfaces. He

would demonstrate with his watercolor brush so skillfully and with such assurance that his point became immediately clear.[59]

For all the emphasis on presentation, Pries warned, "Don't let your designs become exercises in painted architecture."[60]

As the final deadline approached, the hours got longer, and students often stayed up all night before the project was due. This process, working long hours in the days leading up to the due date, was called the "charrette"; students engaged in producing these drawings were described as being "en charrette."[61] Penn faculty member John Harbeson had compared the charrette to the sprint at the end of a race.[62] At Washington in the 1930s, projects were typically due on Saturday at noon, and, although the architecture building was nominally closed late in the evening, students could make arrangements to work all night.[63]

Once the projects were turned in, they were hung in the jury room and judged by all five faculty behind closed doors. Students were not present. The only records were final grades. Perhaps the students' critics—in this case, Pries and Gowen—provided some insight about each project. Projects were evaluated relative to the esquisse: those that had strayed too far were given the mark of *hors de concours* and received no credit. Otherwise, projects were ranked from highest to lowest, following typical Beaux-Arts practice: "First Mention Placed," "First Mention," "Mention," "Half Mention," and "X" (called "ding")—meaning half credit or even no credit. Most projects received Mention or Half Mention. Usually only one project, occasionally two, received First Mention Placed or First Mention. Once in a while, usually not until the senior year, a project might receive a "First Medal" or a "Second Medal," but these marks were comparatively rare. The grade was marked in a corner of the project, usually with a red grease pencil. Especially meritorious projects were stamped "retained," which meant that the school would keep the project in its archives.[64] Once the faculty departed, the jury room was opened, and the students could see how they had done. Some were elated; others were discouraged. The projects might hang for several days so that other students could see the work. The first studio meeting after the review was usually in the jury room, and Pries and Gowen discussed the projects in response to students' questions, giving insights and, in general terms, summarizing how the work had been reviewed.[65] When studio met again, there was an entirely new project—beginning with an esquisse—and the whole process was repeated.

As a drawing type, the analytique taught many lessons. It was especially challenging because of the rigor involved. California architect Joseph Esherick's summary of his experience of the analytique at Penn could equally apply to Washington:

> The entire process was demanding and time-consuming—quite uncompromising in all respects. There was no way to be suggestive or speculative. Hard and precise commitment was called for and one was continuously pushed to set forth exactly what was intended; and if what one intended was crude or awkward, the methods of presentation exaggerated rather than covered up this crudeness.[66]

It was hard work, but students did grow and improve, and those who initially received low marks often did better over time. Kolb's comment—that it "was great training, but very frustrating"—captures the experience of many.[67]

Not every day in studio was spent on large projects. In "Architecture Design Grade I," students first faced the esquisse-esquisse, or sketch problem. Pries and Gowen usually assigned an esquisse-esquisse on Tuesday or Wednesday of the second week of class, and new sketch problems were assigned about every seven to fourteen days thereafter. Students were notified a day or two ahead so that they could plan their schedules, but they had no idea as to subject until the problem statement was handed out. The first problems were fairly simple, but they grew in complexity over the course of the year, and through the junior and senior years as well. The sophomore sketch problems for 1938–39 included, in fall quarter, "a mail box," "a grade crossing," "a pavilion at the termination of a garden," "a wall fountain," and "a finial" (for a community Christmas tree); in the winter, the projects included "a belfry," "an exedra at the end of a terrace," "a shelter for a spring," "an automobile shelter," and "a child's play house"; and in the spring, they included "a water tower," "an aqueduct," "a pair of bronze doors," and "a tiller handle" (for a sailboat).[68] Each problem statement offered a brief descriptive text and an indication of the expected drawing. The problems were done en loge—students worked alone, with no access to reference materials (figs. 7.11, 7.12).

As with the longer studio projects, each esquisse-esquisse was judged behind closed doors. Students were required to accumulate "sketch points"—an average of four points each year was necessary in order to graduate on schedule. A "Mention" was worth one point; a "Half Mention" was worth half a point. Many sketch problems, especially at the beginning, were simply marked "X" ("ding") and received no points.

Students gradually learned that the key to winning sketch points was to find an idea quickly—usually in the first two hours—and then spend the rest of the time presenting the scheme. It was not necessary to have a solution complete in every detail;

Fig. 7.11 Edward J. Baar, "A Tiller Handle of Carved Oak," sophomore esquisse-esquisse, 1933–34, University of Washington; ink on paper, matted, 9½ x 12½ inches. Department of Architecture Archives, University of Washington Libraries, Special Collections Division.

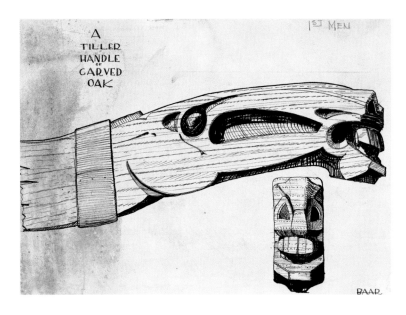

Fig. 7.12 Harvey Warren, "A Garden Sundial," sophomore esquisse-esquisse, 1935–36; watercolor on illustration board, 22 x 15 inches. Department of Architecture Archives, University of Washington Libraries, Special Collections Division.

it was necessary to have an idea that, if developed further, would address the problem. And it was necessary to have a good presentation. John Rohrer, a sophomore in 1933–34, said that one needed to learn the "sketch attitude." He explained: "It didn't have to be worked out. If you got the sense of the thing, and some romance with it, you were off and running."[69] Some students caught on quickly; others, who had a difficult time making decisions, struggled to get these points. A few students had such difficulty with sketch problems that, even though their other coursework was completed, their graduation was delayed until they compiled enough sketch points. In 1935–36, students in the junior class had fallen so far behind that Paul Kirk and John Rohrer, both of whom had extraordinary delineation skills, decided to help them out. Rohrer explained:

> When we were first-year seniors, the juniors, so many of them, were in such bad shape for sketch points (I don't know the reason why that was) that Paul Kirk and I decided to do their sketch problems for them, but they had to stay there and watch us. So I did about five and Paul did about three, and they all got points for them, until somebody snitched.[70]

Those students did not get any sketch points that time, but watching Kirk and Rohrer helped them catch on to the proper attitude, and they all did better after that. (And Kirk and Rohrer were much chastened by a short lecture from A. P. Herrman.)

In spring quarter, Pries and Gowen began assigning small buildings as design problems. Students still prepared esquisses as a basis for their designs, and they still did watercolor presentations, but the analytique was no longer required. In the mid-1930s, problems included "a garage and guest house on a garden" (spring 1934), "a sculptor's studio and residence in the Cascades" (spring 1935) (fig. 7.14), and "a kennel and residence for a commercial dog breeder" (spring 1936). Other problems had a more romantic cast: "a carillon tower" (spring 1933) (fig. 7.13), "a mortuary chapel for an Alpine community" (spring 1937)[71]. Many projects were on rural or suburban sites and encouraged "regional" solutions. The problem statements were longer, usually with a brief description of the project, a summary of site features, and a program, followed by lists of drawings required for the "commitment" (the esquisse) and for the final presentation.

At this point, Pries's critiques sometimes were aimed at helping students learn to see the opportunities in their own work. As Fred Bassetti recalled, Pries

> took my "esquisse" for a cabin in the woods, the least imaginative thing possible, just what I had seen somewhere made out of poles, and transformed it into a great stone mountain hut, full of angles and romantic spirit. When I rendered it, I remember that I got the stone masonry off straight courses and I thought I had ruined the perspective—but that was just the part he praised— the irregularity. It was serendipity, but I had not heard of that then.[72]

Fig. 7.13
Bjarne Olsen,
"Carillon Tower
on an Island in
a Lake, Erected
as a Memorial to
a Former Mayor,"

sophomore
project, 6 May
1933, University
of Washington;
pencil, watercolor
on stiff paper,
40 x 30 inches.

Department of
Architecture
Archives, Univer-
sity of Washington
Libraries, Special
Collections
Division.

Fig. 7.14
Donald W.
Hamilton,
"Sculptor's studio
and residence in
the Cascades,"
sophomore

project, 11 May
1935, University
of Washington;
pencil, watercolor
on stiff paper,
40 x 30 inches.
Department of

Architecture
Archives, Univer-
sity of Washington
Libraries, Special
Collections
Division.

And Robert Ross recalled:

One time when I had been laboring over an eleva-
tional study, he said to me in a serious vein: "Why
don't you try a different approach?" I said: "I did,
but it didn't look right." "Let me see it anyway,"
he said. Fishing it out of the wastebasket, I placed
the discarded sketch in front of him. "Very good!"
he said. "Why did you throw that away? It's sensi-
tively done. It has something the other one doesn't
have, character." Then he analyzed and contrasted
the rather light free flowing relaxed lines of the
"discard" with the more heavy-handed example.
He had really gotten through to me and I could
see exactly what he meant.[73]

Occasionally Pries, rather than drawing, sent the
student to the library, usually to look up a specific
precedent. Alan Liddle, a sophomore in 1941–42,
recalled that he was doing a memorial incorporating
sculpture, and Pries's critique was just two words:
"Research Archipenko." Because Liddle had never
before heard the name, Pries wrote it out. Liddle
then went to the library and looked up the work
of the Ukrainian sculptor Alexander Archipenko:
"I saw exactly what he was talking about—some
very smooth sophisticated shapes. So I didn't copy
an Archipenko, but I got the message very clearly."[74]
Dan Streissguth, a sophomore in 1942–43, recalled
that Pries went with him to the library so he could
look at a volume of lithographs by the Scottish

Fig. 7.15
Fred Herman, "A Ferry Wharf, Combining the Terminus of a Railroad and Bus System," junior project, 11 February 1933, University of Washington; pencil, watercolor on stiff paper, 30 x 40 inches. Department of Architecture Archives, University of Washington Libraries, Special Collections Division.

Fig. 7.16
Victor Steinbrueck, "Protestant Church and Sunday School Group in Suburb of a Large City," junior project, 6 May 1935, University of Washington; pencil, watercolor on stiff paper, 30 x 40 inches. Department of Architecture Archives, University of Washington Libraries, Special Collections Division.

engraver David Roberts and see how to render rocks.[75]

In the junior year, students entered "Architectural Design Grade II." Herrman was the primary critic, assisted by Olschewsky or occasionally a temporary instructor.[76] Grade II assignments often had a pragmatic character and usually emphasized the development of a workable plan. Some focused on resolving complex circulation problems: a ferry wharf (1932–33), a suburban railroad station (1933–34), or an airport building (1935–36) (fig. 7.15). Institutional buildings of various types were frequent assignments: a small-town post office (1933–34), a church and Sunday school (1934–35), a small museum (1936–37), or a county courthouse (1938–39) (fig. 7.16). Other projects addressed a wider range of building types: a country residence for the former director of the American Academy in Rome (1932–33), a children's convalescent home (1935–36), a winter sports lodge in the mountains (1936–37).[77] The traditional pedagogy of esquisse and rendered presentation remained, but the vocabulary of most projects reflected contemporary tendencies. Because most of the projects were public and/or institutional, their planning often showed axiality, balance, and symmetry, but their three-dimensional design

featured the planar surfaces of the Art Deco or Moderne. Although Pries did not teach in the junior year, he may nonetheless have occasionally influenced the projects; the Northwest Native American museum in spring quarter 1937 likely reflected his growing interest in indigenous art and culture (fig. 7.17). As in Grade I, Grade II students also did sketch problems. And they took a year-long course in watercolor, usually taught by the noted watercolorist Raymond Hill of the Department of Art.[78]

Because Architectural Design Grade II continued into the first (and sometimes the second) quarter of the next year, fourth-year seniors continued to do studio problems under Herrman's supervision. However, they did not escape Pries's influence, because they were also required to take two quarters of his "History of Architectural Ornament," and the third quarter, though optional, was strongly recommended.[79] The course soon became legendary. Students eagerly looked forward to it; graduates of the period still speak about the enjoyment they received from "taking ornament."

Although Pries's course in ornament was unique, it grew from the Beaux-Arts belief that decoration is an essential part of architectural design. Harbeson, in his 1926 text on the Beaux-Arts method, devoted

Fig. 7.18
Bjarne Olsen,
Bishop's chair
project for "History of Architectural Ornament"
class, ca. 1934–36,
University of
Washington;
pencil, watercolor
on stiff paper,
40 x 30 inches.
Department of
Architecture
Archives, University of Washington
Libraries, Special
Collections Division.

a full chapter, titled "The Decorative Problem," to the topic, arguing that "'stage scenery' and the interesting little details" on buildings were one key to architectural success. Harbeson advocated decorative problems, including studies of ornament, but noted that they should not be undertaken until students had a strong foundation in the basic elements of architecture and broad knowledge of the architecture of the past. Harbeson stated that the proper approach to the decorative problem was first to study historical examples and then to develop one's own personally expressive designs. The decorative problem, he argued, offered the opportunity "to develop one's own style" and "to develop the imagination."[80]

Pries was thoroughly familiar with these ideas, but he could also call on experiences at Gump's and his exposure to the Arts and Crafts culture of California. Pries was no doubt familiar with the work of artisans like Charles Connick, whose stained glass graced churches by Ralph Adams Cram, and with such companies as Tiffany Studios, whose produc-

tion included complete church interiors with stained glass, mosaics, and even liturgical vestments. Pries's course, therefore, became a series of illustrated lectures on ornament in relation to the architecture and culture of its historical period. The course emphasized the Roman, early Christian, Byzantine, medieval, and Renaissance periods. His assignments were design problems and usually included a Pompeiian wall, an arabesque, a ceremonial plate or bowl, a stained-glass window, and a bishop's throne (figs. 7.18, 7.19, 7.20). Robert Dietz's recollections capture the spirit of the class:

His course . . . made the buildings of the period live. He gave them purpose and flavor. The stone work, the windows, . . . the detail, the interrelation of these, the composition created was something for all to enjoy. One sensed a richness, it was fun to work with him, whether it was doing a bishop's chair, bedecked with jewels, inlays, and draped in sumptuous fabrics, or a stained glass window,

that took on life with its translucent iridescent glow, incorporating symbolism and historical reference. Arabesques provided subtlety of design and texture, a play of light and shade. A sarcophagus gave something respected and dear to a time in history and provided an appreciation of that period.[81]

Although the course was only two credits per quarter, students took voluminous notes and worked long hours on the assignments.[82] Pries gave desk crits on these projects, and, as in studio, frequently took up pencil or brush to enhance the quality of the presentation. At least one time he got carried away. John Rohrer told the story:

Spike Pries had assigned [James Fitzgerald] a bishop's chair to design and illustrate. Maybe you've seen the drawing—it's in the archives somewhere—

a big drawing. Spike Pries started working on that and he worked all evening; somebody came around the school around 6:00 in the morning, and Spike was already there, working on the drawing. Fitzgerald dropped in from time to time. This was Fitzgerald's project, but Spike got so wrapped up in it . . . it was a masterpiece, it really was.[83]

Rohrer added: "Fitzgerald was nearly equal in ability to Spike. . . . He could have done it himself and would have done it just as well." (Fitzgerald's ability was widely recognized: he joined the faculty of the Department of Art in 1940.) That incident was unique—Pries apparently thought better of it and never again spent so much time on a single student's project, although in 1932 he produced his own solution to a "History of Architectural Ornament" assignment (fig. 7.21).

"Design Grade III" under Pries and Gowen was the culmination of the architecture program.[84] The school did not require a terminal project or thesis in the 1930s, but problems assigned to fourth- and fifth-year seniors were large and complex. Some were pragmatic; others, as one would expect from Pries, were imaginative or romantic. The 1932–33 Grade III problems included "a railroad station in a large city, serving through transcontinental trains and local bus and interurban lines," "a national research center for 2000 advanced students, comprising physics, chemistry and electrical laboratories, museum, living quarters and administration," and "an American Academy in Florence, for students of architecture, sculpture, and painting, to be built adjoining the existing Pandolfini Palace."[85] Those for 1935–36 included both "a ferry terminal for a city of 1,000,000" and "a new Italian capitol in Rome with a monument dedicated to 'Fascismo'"[86] (fig. 7.22).

The range of project scales and sites was extraordinary; in 1939–40, Grade III problems included not only "a community playhouse," "a school of fine arts and crafts," and "a residence for three bachelors on a site near Puget Sound" but also "a national Roman Catholic shrine and retreat on a high mountain overlooking Death Valley"[87] (fig. 7.23). The first Grade III problem in fall quarter 1941 was "a memorial to Johann Sebastian Bach" that included "a monumental festival auditorium that will serve as a perpetual inspiration to keep alive the tradition of adequate performance of his works and those of a

similar nature by other master composers." No one doubts it was Pries who conceived such problems. Other Grade III problems in 1941–42 included "a student union" (at a university in the American Southwest), "a sculptor's studio" (on a triangular site bounded by steep cliffs on two sides), and "a school for shipyard workers" (no doubt a response to America's entry into World War II).[88]

The process was familiar: an eight-hour esquisse on the first day, several weeks of development, and an intense charrette at the end to complete the final presentation. The size and complexity of the drawings meant that seniors relied heavily on underclassmen to help complete the presentations, especially as the drawings sometimes measured 40 by 60 inches. The results were stunning—drawings such as those by fifth-year senior Ken Anderson in 1934–35 for "an archaeological institute in a mountain valley in Syria, including a museum, spa and research center shared by six universities," or fifth year senior Paul Kirk in 1936–37 for "a national shrine erected by a convert to Buddhism to contain a colossal stone seated Buddha removed from a Chinese cave temple," were legendary in their time and are still remembered today by graduates of the period (figs. 7.24, 7.25, 7.26).

As in all years of the program, Pries and Gowen also assigned sketch problems to Grade III students (fig. 7.27). These were still to be completed in only eight hours, but the assignments were more complex, often complete buildings. In 1941–42, the senior sketch problems included "an astronomical observatory," "an open air pulpit," "a synagogue" (a new design for a five-week problem just completed), "a weekend beach lodge," "an aquarium," and, in mid-February 1942, "a naval pantheon" (a memorial to the dead from a future naval victory in the war).[89]

A question sometimes asked is whether students of the period resisted the unrealistic or romantic projects, regarding them as not relevant, given the times. Robert Ross recalled that Pries, who was "very good at dialect" and could perform "merciless imitations of character types," deflected such challenges with an imitation of a theoretical student's "mother":

"Mr. Pries, why does my boy have to learn all about those silly shrines, or retreats, or whatever they are on top of a high mountain above Death Valley?" Then Spike would say with great and

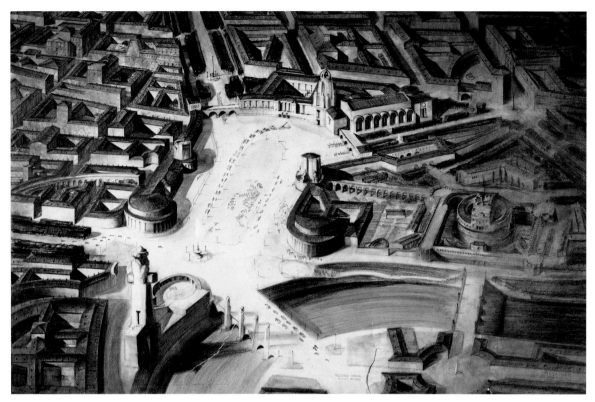

Fig. 7.22
Robert Durham,
"New Italian
capitol in Rome
and a Monument
Dedicated to
'Facismo,'"
senior/fifth-year
project, 1935–36,
University of
Washington;
colored pencil on
stiff paper, 40 x
60 inches (sheet 1
of 2). Department
of Architecture
Archives, Univer-
sity of Washington
Libraries, Special
Collections
Division.

Fig. 7.23
Robert Shields,
"A National Roman
Catholic Shrine
and Retreat on a
High Mountain
overlooking Death
Valley," senior/
fifth-year project,
1940, University
of Washington;
pencil, watercolor
on stiff paper,
40 x 60 inches.
Department of
Architecture
Archives, Univer-
sity of Washington
Libraries, Special
Collections
Division.

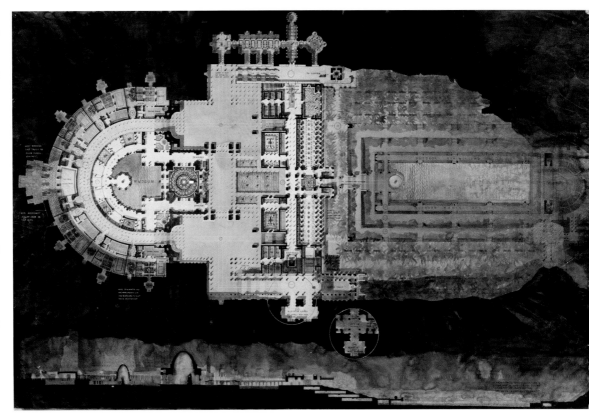

Fig. 7.24
Kenneth Anderson, "An Archaeological Institute in a Mountain Valley in Syria, including a museum, spa and research center shared by six universities," senior/fifth-year project, 17 February 1934, University of Washington; pencil, watercolor on stiff paper, 40¾ x 60¼ inches (sheet 1 of two sheets). Department of Architecture Archives, University of Washington Libraries, Special Collections Division.

Fig. 7.25
Paul Kirk, "A National Shrine Erected by a Convert to Buddhism to Contain a Colossal Stone Seated Buddha Removed from a Chinese Cave Temple," senior/fifth-year project, 12 December 1936, University of Washington; pencil, watercolor on stiff paper, 40½ x 61 inches (sheet 2 of two sheets). Department of Architecture Archives, University of Washington Libraries, Special Collections Division.

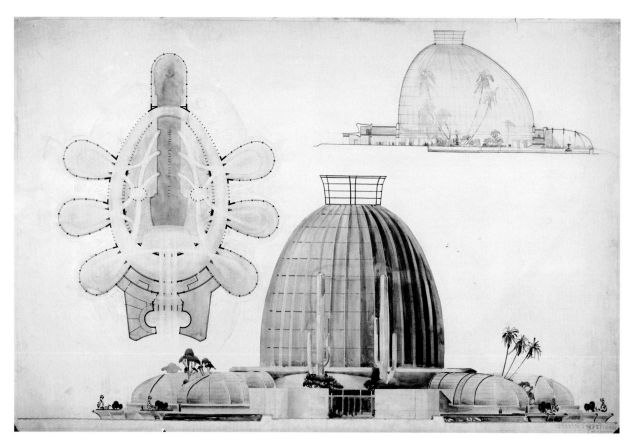

Fig. 7.26
John Whitney, "A Horticulture Building, Sited on an Island, Intended to Dominate the Grounds of a World's Fair," senior/fifth-year project, 30 January 1937, University of Washington; pencil, watercolor on stiff paper, 39¾ x 59¾ inches. Department of Architecture Archives, University of Washington Libraries, Special Collections Division.

Fig. 7.27
J. M. Fitzgerald, bus and ferry terminal, senior/ fifth-year esquisse-esquisse, 1933–35, University of Washington; pencil, watercolor on paper, matted, 17½ x 15 inches. Department of Architecture Archives, University of Washington Libraries, Special Collections Division.

serious emphasis to us: "The reason you have to do it is that if you can master the complex, large scale project, you will do the smallest project more perfectly, something you will never learn to do otherwise."[90]

Another Pries response to similar questions was "You don't learn architecture by knowing the number of nails in a keg."[91] Although Pries was a romantic, he was not impressed by the frivolous or the clichéd. Robert Ross remembered, "Architecture to him was inspirational, but he would tolerate no nonsense about it. One of his best acts was quoting someone gushing, 'Oh, Mr. Pries, don't you think that architecture is frozen music?!' He always followed this with a few growled profane exclamations."[92]

Ecole Methods, New Vocabularies

Over the course of the 1930s, students' attitudes toward architectural vocabularies continually evolved, reflecting an awareness of contemporary trends in design. Like other cities in the United States, Seattle by the late 1920s had seen a move away from historical eclecticism to Art Deco for institutional and commercial buildings.[93] The new Seattle Art Museum by Bebb and Gould, completed in 1933, was a particularly notable example of the new tendency, and it was only a mile from campus. In 1934, on its twentieth anniversary, the Department of Architecture presented an exhibit of student work titled "The City of the Future." Students emphasized that the "city of the future" would be a city of steel, concrete, and glass, but they rejected the new architecture from Europe, which they called "the much debated factory-type international style."[94] Instead, their projects clearly reflected the Art Deco/Moderne. One student, Perry Johanson, on his return from the Century of Progress Exposition in Chicago in 1933, told *The Daily* that the steel-and-glass houses on exhibit were "coldly efficient" but "far-fetched," and he argued that new technologies were likely to be applied within more traditional designs.[95]

The evolution of students' attitudes was quite rapid, however. Students were aware of the work of Frank Lloyd Wright, who had spoken in Seattle in March 1931. Wright's Kaufman House ("Fallingwater") in Pennsylvania and his Johnson Wax Building in Wisconsin, both of 1936, brought him again into the vanguard of American designers. George Hazen, who graduated from the Department of Architecture in 1939, recalls that he and a classmate, Delmar Mitchell, visited Wright's Hanna House in 1936 while it was under construction at Stanford, California.[96] By the mid- to late 1930s, students were clearly interested in the International Style, which they knew from publications. They were excited by the California work of Richard Neutra and by such buildings as Philadelphia's PSFS (Philadelphia Saving Fund Society) Building (1931–32) and the Museum of Modern Art, New York (1939). The school subscribed to a variety of American and European architectural journals, and some graduates of the period recalled that *Architectural Review* covered such buildings as Alvar Aalto's Viipuri Library, Viipuri, Finland (1935).[97] The Henry Art

Gallery, on the University of Washington campus, fostered an awareness of the new architecture through exhibits: in April 1936, there was a show of LeCorbusier's work, including photographs, drawings, and at least one model; in May 1940, the gallery presented a traveling exhibit of Aalto's work.[98] By the late 1930s, the Art Deco/Moderne influence was waning rapidly, and many student projects were conspicuously Modern, with an emphasis on planar surfaces and asymmetrical composition, reflecting the influence of the International Style (fig. 7.28).

Pries, Gowen, and the other faculty were well aware of the new directions in architecture. Pries's own design work shows his personal response to contemporary directions, and he shared his work with the students. In 1936–37, when his Willcox residence, on Hood Canal, was nearly complete, he invited his studio classes to visit.[99] He also took students to visit Pietro Belluschi's H. M. Myers residence, in the Magnolia neighborhood of Seattle, when it was under construction in 1940–41; Pries thought the house was worth seeing because of its unusual courtyard design and because it was an example of Belluschi's regional Modernist approach.[100]

Pries and Gowen used the analytique in their teaching into the 1940s, but the work of later years shows freer approaches to composition as well as a growing acceptance of Modern architectural vocabularies. The analytique, as originally developed, was intended for delineation of buildings with classical elements.[101] At Washington in the 1930s, the small analytiques done in the second and third quarters of the freshman year continued to conform to this approach, but sophomore (Grade I) problems were more varied. Each year, there was usually at least one problem in the classical language: "a two-story building surrounding a courtyard with superimposed order based on the Renaissance" (1934–35), "a roofed outside stair adjacent to a Renaissance city hall" (1935–36), or "a rostrum and memorial tablet for presidential inaugurations in Washington, D.C." (1938–39) (fig. 7.29). But other problems invited a wider array of responses, and some included the word "modern": "a stone lantern on a great modern building" (1936–37), or "a private chapel in a modern Episcopal residence" (1938–39). Further, when the problems invited a more elemental response, analytiques became bolder and simpler. Edward

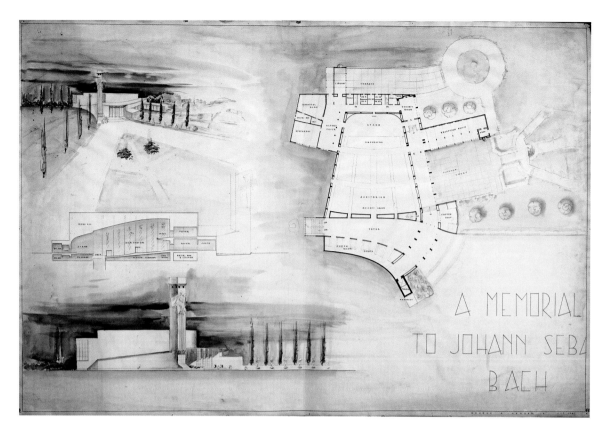

Fig. 7.28 George Graham, "A Memorial to Johann Sebastian Bach, including a monumental festival auditorium that will serve as a perpetual inspiration to keep alive the tradition of adequate performance of his works and those of a similar nature by other master composers," senior/ fifth-year project, September-October 1941, University of Washington; pencil, watercolor on stiff paper, 39¾ x 59¾ inches; Department of Architecture Archives.

Baar's design for a "family mausoleum" (1934) was reduced to a few simple volumes; his analytique is almost abstract (fig. 7.30). By the late 1930s and early 1940s, many of the traditional aspects of the analytique, such as the enclosing border, had almost disappeared. Robert Shields's entrance to a marine museum (1937–38) retained a few vestiges of classicism but was increasingly planar in character; in turn, the analytique no longer had the enclosing border (fig. 7.31). Virginia Miller's analytique for the end wing of an art museum (1938–39) showed similar reduction to just a few elements (fig. 7.32). By the early 1940s, the analytiques produced under Pries and Gowen still included plan, elevation, and details, but there was considerable freedom in composition, as shown by Douglas Mason's analytique of a Roman Catholic or High Episcopal Church

sanctuary (1940–41) (fig. 7.33). Audrey Gerth's March 1942 presentation of the west entrance to the Bremerton Navy Yard shows how far the faculty were willing to go: the architectural language was Modern, yet the drawing was still an analytique (fig. 7.34). The changing character of these projects shows how Pries and Gowen were trying to accommodate Modernism without abandoning the traditional teaching technique.

Graduates also recall that Pries and Gowen were usually supportive of any direction in which a student might take his or her project, as long as it was appropriate to the assignment. In response to a spring 1937 second-year problem to design a "major new lighthouse facility on a rocky headland, 500 feet above the sea at Cape Mendocino (northern California)," William Svensson and Roland Terry each presented asymmetrical Modern designs (figs. 7.35, 7.36). These designs would have been at home in a studio in 1957 or even 1997. Both projects were highly regarded and were retained for the archives. By 1937–38, student projects occasionally showed hints of the International Style, and by 1939–40, there was a decided turn in that direction. A comparison of two sketch problems makes the shift clear: Carl Forssen's "hermitage" sophomore sketch

Fig. 7.29 Donald W. Hamilton "Courtyard of a Two-Story Building, featuring a superimposed French or Italian order," sophomore analytique, 8 February 1935, University of Washington; pencil, watercolor on stiff paper, 39¾ x 30¾. Department of Architecture Archives, University of Washington Libraries, Special Collections Division.

Fig. 7.30 Edward J. Baar, "Family Mausoleum," sophomore analytique, 5 February 1934, University of Washington; pencil, watercolor on stiff paper, 40 x 31 inches. Department of Architecture Archives, University of Washington Libraries, Special Collections Division.

problem of 1930–31 is rustic and almost old-fashioned; Marvin Damman's "hermitage" senior sketch problem of 1938–39 shows the linearity, crispness, and asymmetry of Modernism (figs. 7.37, 7.38). When asked if there was resistance to the students' growing interest in the new architecture, William Svensson, who entered the program in fall quarter 1935, recalled that the faculty were actually quite receptive: "The faculty went right along with us. It was just assumed by everybody that we are in another age now." Svensson added that Pries, particularly, encouraged creativity: "In the sophomore

year, it was kind of a good thing that we had him, because that was the year you kind of experimented and fooled around a little bit."[102]

Describing Pries's teaching, Dan Streissguth, a graduate of the program and later a professor in the department, noted, "If you didn't know where you were going, then he gave you a nudge," but if you already had a direction, then Pries was typically very supportive. Streissguth remembered doing a project for a library and tea shop on Whidbey Island (in Puget Sound) during his sophomore year (late in winter quarter 1943), in which his scheme reflected

Fig. 7.31
Robert Shields, "Entrance to the Beebe Marine Museum, facing a waterfront boulevard," sophomore analytique, 5 February 1938, University of Washington; pencil, watercolor on stiff paper, 30¾ x 39¾. Department of Architecture Archives, University of Washington Libraries, Special Collections Division.

Fig. 7.32
Virginia Miller, "End [wing] of an Art Museum," sophomore analytique, fall 1938 or winter 1939, University of Washington; pencil, watercolor on stiff paper, 31 x 40 inches. Department of Architecture Archives, University of Washington Libraries, Special Collections Division.

Fig. 7.33
Douglas Mason,
"Sanctuary of a
Roman Catholic
or High Episcopal
Church," sopho-
more analytique,
fall 1940 or winter
1941, University
of Washington;
pencil, watercolor
on stiff paper,
39½ x 31 inches.
Department of
Architecture
Archives, Univer-
sity of Washington
Libraries, Special
Collections
Division.

Fig. 7.34
Audry Gerth,
"West Entrance
to the Bremerton
Navy Yard," soph-
omore analytique,
February–March
1942, University
of Washington;
pencil, watercolor
on stiff paper,
30¾ x 39½.
Department of
Architecture
Archives, Univer-
sity of Washington
Libraries, Special
Collections
Division.

Fig. 7.35 William Svensson, "Major New Lighthouse Facility on a Rocky Headland, 500 feet above the sea at Cape Mendocino (northern California)," sophomore project, spring 1937, University of Washington; pencil, watercolor on stiff paper, 30¾ x 39½. Department of Architecture Archives, University of Washington Libraries, Special Collections Division.

Fig. 7.36 Roland Terry, "Major New Lighthouse Facility on a Rocky Headland, 500 feet above the sea at Cape Mendocino (northern California)," sophomore project, spring 1937, University of Washington; pencil, watercolor on stiff paper, 40 x 30¾ inches. Department of Architecture Archives, University of Washington Libraries, Special Collections Division.

Fig. 7.37
Carl Forssen,
"A Hermitage,"
sophomore
esquisse-esquisse,
1930–31, University
of Washington;
pencil, watercolor
on paper, matted,
13¼ x 21 inches.
Department of
Architecture
Archives, Univer-
sity of Washington
Libraries, Special
Collections
Division.

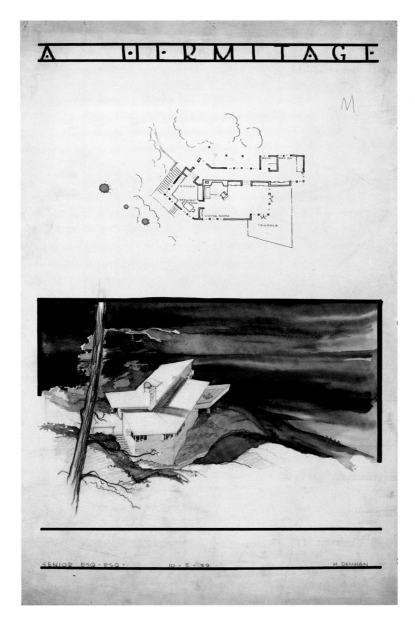

Fig. 7.38
Marvin Damman,
"A Hermitage,"
senior esquisse-
esquisse,
5 October 1939,
University of
Washington; pen-
cil, watercolor on
illustration board,
30 x 20 inches.
Department of
Architecture
Archives, Univer-
sity of Washington
Libraries, Special
Collections
Division.

PERSPECTIVE FROM GARDEN

the California regional work of William W. Wurster. Pries recognized the antecedents, made a comment about Wurster's ability to "make things so expensive, but make them look so simple," then helped Streissguth pull off the scheme. Streissguth recalled, "Pries was very supportive. I don't remember if he put the shadows in under the exposed rafters or not, but he was very supportive of it"[103] (fig. 7.39).

Pries, Gowen, and the other faculty were therefore not averse to students' attempts to respond to emerging vocabularies of architecture, as long as they did so within the framework of the traditional method of education, and following the foundation of the first two years of the program. The preamble to the school's 1937 *Annual* was clear in this regard: "While the first two years develop an appreciation of Classic Architecture and Composition, the remaining three years offer advancements to individual and creative expression."[104] Although it may seem that the first two years of the program might have generated resistance among students increasingly interested in Modernism, many had initially been attracted by the romantic quality of the student projects. Fred Bassetti, who was strongly inclined to the Modern Movement while he was a student, remembered:

> I suppose [Pries] was also the one who really
> hooked me into architecture at second-hand and

without knowing it. It was when I accidentally visited the "shack" once in 1936 and saw a display of watercolor renderings of restaurants in the San Juans [San Juan Islands, Puget Sound] and monasteries in the Himalayas, probably by Ed Baar, or Kirk or Terry or Shields, all in the manner of Pries. I was so taken with the wonder and glory of it all that, even though Herrman and Olschewsky both tried to dissuade me, I switched majors in the middle of the year.[105]

Pries believed that each student should address each problem on its own terms. Just as the idea of academic eclecticism was not to copy a single historical source, but rather to study a broad range of historical sources before creating one's own design, Pries and the other faculty strongly believed that students should not copy or follow any single contemporary architect or movement but should always be aware of the widest possible range of alternatives.[106] At the University of Washington, contemporary architectural vocabularies were acceptable—if they were responsive to the assigned problem (fig. 7.40). With his acerbic wit, Pries displayed a healthy skepticism about every new fashion and was always ready to challenge any hint of orthodoxy.[107]

Fig. 7.39
Daniel Streissguth, "Library and Tea Shop on Whidbey Island," sophomore project, winter 1943, University of Washington; pencil, watercolor on stiff paper, perspective (portion of full sheet measuring 30¾ x 39¾ inches). Department of Architecture Archives, University of Washington Libraries, Special Collections Division.

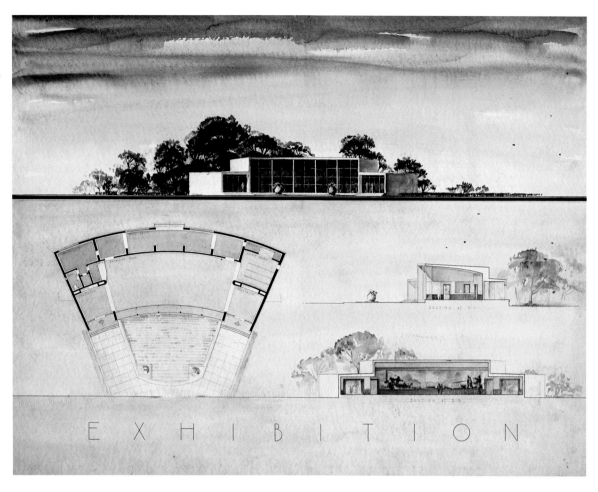

EXHIBITION

Lionel Pries as Mentor, 1928–1945

As Pries was unmarried and had no close relatives in Seattle, the school was the center of his life. For his first two years in Seattle, he lived near downtown, but by 1930 he had moved to an apartment at 4002 Brooklyn, just a five-minute walk from the school. Two years later, he leased a house at 4546 Fifteenth Avenue N.E., about a block north of the campus[108] (fig. 7.41). Pries could easily stop by the school in the evenings and on weekends, to observe students' progress, give impromptu crits, offer words of encouragement, or just raise an eyebrow. Usually he was accompanied by Hamlet, his cocker spaniel. Occasionally, on his way to a social or artistic event, he would make his appearance in semiformal dress. Some evenings he came, as Flora Allen Casey recalled, "just to talk of his experiences," and "occasionally he would decide to do a watercolor which he would take home."[109] Minoru Yamasaki explained, "Professor Pries spent many extracurricular hours giving criticism and doing beautiful watercolors in the evenings with the students and, consequently, for those of us who stayed

Fig. 7.41
Residence at 4546
Fifteenth Avenue
N.E. (destroyed),
leased by Lionel
Pries from 1932
to 1948. Photo
courtesy of Keith
Kolb.

to watch him, he was truly a great inspiration."[110]

If a student obtained a special book on art or architecture, Pries was happy to do a sketch on the endpaper or flyleaf and letter the student's name (fig. 7.42). Perry Johanson remembered, "I recall how often he would stay after hours to make a sketch in the flyleaf of an art book one of the students had acquired (I was never able to afford one to sketch in) while a group would watch."[111] Robert Ross told a similar story:

> Spike had told us Burckhardt's *Civilization of the Renaissance in Italy* was the best book ever written on the Italian Renaissance. Finally, I saved up a little money, bought it, and studied it one summer, away from school. He was pleased when I told him about it that fall at the start of school. He asked, "Would you like me to do a book plate in it for you?" Would I?! He took the book from me and went to work inside the cover. To my astonishment he started at the top, very carefully progressing down the page, all the while unfolding a beautiful garden pavilion with sculptures, classic balustrades, monumental stairways, fountains and the like. He added the ex libris, a couple of light washes, a gold dot, and it was complete. To me it is a great treasure.[112]

Pries worried about the pressures that students encountered from the demands of architectural education, although he sometimes showed his concern in an idiosyncratic manner. Believing that popular music was unduly stressful, especially during a charrette, he refused to allow radios to be played in studio. Architecture students knew of Pries's views, but interiors students, who took architecture studio to acquire drawing skills, apparently did not. Keith Kolb recalled one evening in 1941:

> This interior[s] girl had her radio set up, and she was innocently working away. She was there because she probably thought some of the architects might come help her. And we were all there working, and Spike shows up, and he has his watercolor brushes. He looks in there, with this radio raising hell, and he just goes over and picks the radio up and yanks it out of the wall and goes over to the window, and he puts the window up and, wham!—he throws it down two floors. He just doesn't toss it out the window, he throws it. Wham! That girl was startled.[113]

Pries also thought that the soft drink Coca-Cola was injurious to students' health. If he found Coke bottles in studio, he would immediately throw them out, empty or full.

Pries's assistance to students could go far beyond extra hours in studio. He was always interested in anything that would enhance design education, even extracurricular activities that involved design. Alan Liddle recalled that when he served on the staff of the 1947 *Tyee*, the university yearbook, as designer of the cover and frontispiece, and did the drawings in studio, Pries became quite interested and helped with the selection of letter forms. But Pries disliked involvement in sports, which he felt was time wasted.[114]

Pries helped Robert Ross convince his parents to let him to go to the 1939 Golden Gate International Exposition in San Francisco: "He told my parents what a great event the 1915 San Francisco exposition had been in his life and urged them to let me go to the one in 1939. He was quite effective with them." As Pries was heading to California himself, he gave Ross a ride and then showed him sites in San Francisco.[115] About 1931, when Ken Anderson and Perry Johanson received scholarships for travel in Europe (among the last such scholarships awarded, given the Depression), Pries spent an evening a week with them for about five months, reviewing the art and architecture of England, France, Germany, Spain, and Italy to help them prepare for the trip. Johanson noted, "When we eventually visited the important cities in those countries, we knew what to look for and could expand our own experience around the groundwork he had given us."[116] Pries offered similar advice and suggestions to almost anyone he heard about who was going to travel in Europe.[117]

Pries was a full participant in the rituals of the school. He was particularly known for attending the Beaux-Arts Ball in extraordinary costumes. One year, in the late 1930s, he arrived in a stunning costume and changed to another halfway through the evening[118] (fig. 7.43). He loved the ceremony surrounding the induction of students into Tau Sigma Delta and never failed to attend in black tie. Many students believed that it was Pries who arranged for the induction ceremonies to take place at a fine restaurant, or at a mansion in Seattle's Capitol Hill neighborhood.[119]

Over the years, Pries collected a variety of art objects, including sculptures, paintings, and artifacts of all kinds. Students thought that his house

Fig. 7.42
Lionel H. Pries,
bookplate for
Robert Ross, on
flyleaf of Jacob
Burckhardt, *The
Civilization of the
Renaissance in
Italy*. This copy of
the book is now
part of the Pries
collection, Univer-
sity of Washington
Libraries, Special
Collections
Division.

was like a museum. Seth Fulcher described it:

> Professor [Pries] was an insatiable collector. He
> had traveled a great deal, but his first love was
> Mexico which he visited each summer . . . he
> acquired many pieces of museum quality from his
> travels. . . . In anybody else's home it would be a
> hodgepodge, but he could sensitively group pieces
> together in fascinating vignettes in fine cases,
> on shelves, walls and his own carefully crafted
> furniture.[120]

Visitors to Pries's house were greeted at the steps by a Chinese figure sculpture, Lao-Tse. Inside, along with several large sculptural pieces—a Buddha and an ancient Egyptian head—Pries had fine paintings, among them one dating to the Renaissance, and smaller cases with Asian objects. On the coffee table were small grotesques—strange figures from different places. There were also things of Pries's own design—several light fixtures with lamp shades that featured his drawings, and a print stand on which he displayed one of his own paintings or drawings. And there were always pillows and a stool for Hamlet. The dining room doubled as the library and included Pries's collection of books in addition to cases with drawers that were filled with postcards of architectural sites.[121] Pries kept his most treasured items in a large carved chest. These he would display one by one, and they included silver jewelry from Taxco and rare textiles from Peru and Mexico. For a time, Pries had a pre-Columbian carving of Quetzacoatl, the feathered serpent.[122]

As soon as Pries moved to the University District, he began welcoming students into his home. In his first years at the university, he held weekly open houses; by the late 1930s, his "soirees," as they came to be called, occurred every few weeks, on a more irregular basis. At Penn, Pries had experienced that school's informal evening gatherings, called "smokers," that introduced students to the traditions of the school and to the wider world of the arts, and this may have been the source of his soirees.[123] Perry Johanson, who began at Washington in 1928, recalled, "Spike had an open house one night a week in those early years. I never willingly missed one. Sometimes the group would end up playing hearts or Russian bank, but always there were his books to pore over and to talk about."[124] Attendees included not only students but also others

who knew Pries in different settings; Lloyd Lovegren, the draftsman at Bain and Pries, recalled:

> I attended countless evening "open house" ses-
> sions in his home to which all those interested
> were invited by the light in the window. Most ses-
> sions were started by our asking questions to
> Spike concerning his vast collection of art objects
> gathered in his annual travels abroad. . . . For the
> pleasure and enlightenment of any visitor, Spike
> had a story to go with every one of the countless
> fabrics, carvings, sculptures, paintings, sketches,
> books, etc., which I never tired of hearing, but
> which eventually I remembered word for word.[125]

Roland Terry had similar recollections from the late 1930s: "For years he had Monday seminars at his

Fig. 7.43
Lionel Pries in costume at Beaux-Arts Ball, ca. 1939–40. Photo courtesy of Robert H. Ross.

house for any and all students wishing to attend after dinner and would regale us all with enticing tales of extensive travel in Mexico and Europe. He had a fantastic architectural library and many fine art objects, particularly of oriental origin."[126] Robert Ross recalled that Pries sometimes greeted visitors at the door wearing a full-length Japanese man's dressing robe of fine material, a signal of the informal nature of the evening.[127]

In the background, Pries always played classical music. Within a few years after he moved to Fifteenth Avenue, he had acquired one of the best record players of the period, a Capehart, which could play a stack of 78 rpm discs one right after another. Pries loved classical music, and he conveyed this love to many of his students. Perry Johanson recalled, "Spike introduced me to the symphony. He had designed a house for Karl Krueger, conductor of the symphony, and he once took me for a visit both to see the house and meet the conductor."[128] Flora Allen Casey offered a similar recollection.

> It was he who introduced many of us to live symphony music. He arranged to reserve a block of seats—I don't remember how many—in the balcony of the Metropolitan Theater. Karl Krueger was the conductor at the time and a friend of Mr. Pries, so "Spike," in tux, sat with Mrs. Krueger and friends in a box, while we were above.[129]

By the mid-1930s, Pries no longer hosted symphony evenings, but he always encouraged students in cultural pursuits—visiting art museums, attending the symphony and ballet, and seeing foreign films.[130]

When Pries moved to an apartment near the university, he began taking in one or two student boarders in the extra bedroom.[131] In the 1930s, the University of Washington had little dormitory space. Students who had family members in Seattle often lived with them. Other options included a fraternity or a sorority (if one was a member) and numerous boarding houses and rental apartments. Because Pries had extra space and no family, he was able to offer lodging to a small number of architecture students, often those from outside Seattle, who had fewer options for housing. After he leased the house on Fifteenth Avenue, Pries had space for as many as six boarders. There were four bedrooms; Pries took one, and the other three were made available to students. Initially the students came from a variety of

majors, but by the mid-1930s the boarders were all architecture students—typically two from a class. All paid room and board. In the early and mid-1930s, Pries had a Swedish cook, Mrs. Nelson, who came every afternoon to prepare dinner.[132] She was followed in the late 1930s by Mrs. Burke. By 1940, Pries had hired a Filipino houseboy, Domingo, who lived in an apartment in the basement; he did the grocery shopping, cooked dinner (according to menus that Pries selected), and kept house.[133] On weekday evenings, the group dined together at 6:00 P.M. Kolb recalled that the multicourse dinners always began with soup; at Pries's insistence, it was hot—so hot that the students could not touch it-but Pries himself would drink it right down. On weekends, the group often piled into Pries's car, a LaSalle, and went to dinner at a local restaurant.[134] Pete Wimberly later recalled, "On Sunday evening, when we were not otherwise occupied with dates, our studies, or working at school, Spike had issued a standing invitation to take any or all of us to dinner at one of the better restaurants in town. He also made it a point to see that we were all served Martinis before dinner. He said that, to be a successful architect, one must be able to withstand and cope with liquor and to understand and be able to order a proper dinner in the fanciest restaurant in town."[135] Riding with Pries to the restaurant was sometimes a source of trepidation, as Pries was regarded as a rather reckless driver, with little regard for posted speed limits.

Those who lived in Pries's house considered it a privilege. Living there meant that they had access to Pries to talk about architecture and about school. They also had free use of his library. And they sometimes got to see his independent professional projects. Of course, some other students were jealous. Kolb recalled:

> The bad part was that others thought that we sort of had a special edge. In some ways, I suppose we did. But in other ways we did not, because we had to maintain a skill and ability, a demand. And we demanded that of ourselves. . . . But there was always this little innuendo: "Oh yeah, you are living with Spike."[136]

Among those who lived with Pries over the years were Palmer D. Koon, Kelly Foss, Harold Foss, Ted Warnecke, Henry and Betty Olschewsky, A. Quincy

Jones, Robert Olwell, John Whitney, Bliss Moore, Pete Wimberly, Julian Willcox, Robert H. Ross, Jay Robinson, Thomas Bell, Roland Terry, Robert Massar, George Thiele, William Paddock, James Klontz, James Cameron, Lewis Crutcher, and Keith Kolb.[137] Pries offered at least one student, Seth Fulcher, whose family was struggling financially because of the Depression, the chance to live at his house rent free so he could quit working and focus on his architectural studies. Fulcher was unable to accept, because he was earning money to help support his parents and siblings as well as himself.[138]

The students who boarded with Pries may not have realized that he saw them almost as family. One evening while they were playing dominoes (a favorite pastime), Robert Ross heard Pries mention "how much he missed his students once they graduated." Ross asked if they didn't visit occasionally; Pries's response, "tinged with sadness," was, according to Ross, "'No, they don't come back.'"[139] Occasionally a former student would stop by, however. Ross remembered how pleased Pries was when Ken Anderson, a graduate of 1935 who had gone to work at Disney, visited and brought some cels from the animated feature *Snow White*.[140]

Pries was interested in talent. He did not treat all students equally. Roland Terry suggested that Pries "had no patience with weak students," although he gave all "sufficient time to prove themselves one way or another." Terry also knew that Pries's unequal treatment of students was sometimes quite deliberate: "I remember him telling me once that if he thought he could make a student better by making him hate him, he would do it."[141] Pries told Kolb that "pushing the best students brought the slower, weaker students up and helped train strong students; helping the weak students did not help strong ones and lowered the general quality of learning."[142] Pries gave the least attention to those who were doing the minimum or just trying to get by, and who did not show the devotion to architecture that Pries thought necessary to success. At any rate, there is no doubt that Pries wished to focus his teaching on the students with talent or promise. In letters written in 1934 to Robert G. Sproul, president of the University of California, Pries lamented the need to carry weak students along, and he argued for the creation of a highly selective architecture school that would push the best architecture students to become "true architectural thinkers."[143] And when Pries

encountered students who displayed talent or promise, he extended himself to support their development. Pries involved Wimberly and Bliss Moore in the decoration of the Willcox residence living room, as already described, and he frequently took Roland Terry along on his Friday afternoon visits to the Willcox residence construction site.[144] Pries also invited selected students to accompany him on his travels in Mexico—Moore and Wimberly went with him on the summer trips recounted earlier—and, as also mentioned earlier, he wrote letters of introduction for others who went to Mexico on their own.[145] But some students felt more comfortable than others with Pries's mannerisms and idiosyncrasies. Some became close enough to call him "Spike," particularly when they were seniors; others were too intimidated and always addressed him as "Professor Pries."[146]

No matter how a student felt about Pries, he or she could not avoid being touched by his influence; as Perry Johanson noted, "Spike's influence pervaded the whole school."[147]

CHANGING TIMES: FROM THE 1930S TO THE 1940S

The years from 1928 to the beginning of World War II were Pries's happiest at the University of Washington.[148] In those years, the architecture faculty—and the local professional community—shared a clear consensus regarding how architecture ought to be taught. The faculty had all been educated within the Beaux-Arts system, and they all believed in continuing that system even as they adapted to new conditions. Members of the faculty worked closely together, and if there were disagreements, most of the time they were over adjustments to the curriculum, or over the handling of individual students, not over fundamental ideas about approaches to design or educational pedagogies.[149]

There was at least one period during the 1930s, however, when Pries was unhappy enough that he sought to return to California. In 1934, Pries contacted Robert Sproul about a position on the University of California faculty. His letter to Sproul dated 26 February 1934 only hints at the source of his dissatisfaction:

The situation at the University of Washington is a rather wretched and hopeless one, redeemed in part by the congeniality within the Architectural Department. This healthful local situation has quite suddenly broken down, with the awkward result that I feel my resignation is imperative if I am to be of any further value as a teacher of architecture. The question moves me deeply, for many loyalties have been developed, and because I also feel, perhaps with too much confidence, that my work has been well done and that the school has received recognition directly because of it.[150]

Pries added that Sproul could contact Ray Childs at Minnesota or Welles Bosworth at Cornell to verify his accomplishments as a teacher. He then asked if there might be a position at the University of California, Berkeley, or possibly in Los Angeles.

His comment about the "wretched" situation at the university was likely a reference to its poor financial condition in the mid-1930s (requiring a reduction in faculty salaries) and perhaps to the poor physical condition of "the Shack," but it may also allude to the unsettled administrative situation of the department. In 1932–33, in a reorganization due to the Depression, the College of Fine Arts was dissolved. The new College of Liberal Arts was formed, including the fine arts, the sciences, business, journalism, and education.[151] Just two years later, the College of Liberal Arts was replaced by the even larger University College. Architecture, which had been one of only a few departments reporting to the dean of the College of Fine Arts, was now just one of more than thirty departments within a much larger and more impersonal unit. Pries also referred to a "break down" within the department, but the nature of this is not known.[152]

Soon after his first letter, Pries wrote a second (undated) letter to Sproul in which he cautioned that his February letter was written "without careful consideration in a moment of considerable stress."[153] Pries then proposed a new type of architecture school that would "boldly maintain a standard beyond that of any architecture school at present existent in this country." Pries argued that architectural education suffered from being "obliged to foster poor and mediocre students at the expense of the promising ones." Therefore, he advocated the creation of a very small and highly selective program in architecture, and he suggested that the University of California at Los Angeles would be the ideal setting for such a program.

Sproul wrote two replies to Pries. In the first, dated 12 March, he called Pries's ideas about architectural education "novel, to say the least."[154] He invited Pries, if he was in the area, to visit him to discuss his ideas further. Five months later, in August 1934, Sproul sent a follow-up on the question of a teaching position in Berkeley.[155] Sproul wrote, "I am convinced that the attitude of the people here is distinctly favorable to you and that they would like to find a place for you." But he added, "However, there are no funds available at the present time and, frankly, there would seem to be no likelihood of any for this purpose in the near future. The only hope I can see lies in deaths or resignations and, as you know, these occur most infrequently in times of depression." Nothing more came of this correspondence. Pries remained at Washington for the rest of his teaching career, although he still occasionally considered moving back to California.[156]

For Pries, the biggest change after he started teaching at Washington occurred when the Bain and Pries partnership dissolved. He had already shown a devotion to teaching, but by 1932 he no longer needed to split his days between the downtown office and the school. Instead, he could work at home and come to school early if necessary. Pries was initially appointed as an instructor, and this appointment perhaps reflected some uncertainty over whether he would ultimately pursue a career in architectural practice or in academia. In the fall of 1932, his position became more permanent when he was named an assistant professor. Six years later, he was promoted to associate professor; as the rank of associate professor typically brings tenure, this promotion officially signaled the permanence of Pries's commitment to teaching.

In 1941, Pries joined the Monday Club. Founded in 1906 and patterned after a similar organization at Harvard, the Monday Club was a "town-gown" association, with members drawn from the faculty and from the leaders of Seattle's business, social, cultural, and religious communities.[157] The group met on the last Monday of every month to have dinner and listen to a lecture by one of the members. It was quite exclusive—one could join only by invitation—and there were just twenty to twenty-five members in that period. The invitation confirmed Pries's acceptance as a prominent member of Seattle's intellectual community.

Toward the end of the 1930s, the architecture school saw three significant changes. First, the department finally got better facilities. In the summer of 1937, the department moved to the second floor and a portion of the first floor of Bagley Hall, the former chemistry building—a building designed by John Galen Howard and used as the Fine Arts Palace for the 1909 Alaska-Yukon-Pacific Exposition (fig. 7.44). The same year, the building was renamed Physiology Hall because the medical school's Physiology Department moved into the basement and part of the first floor.[158] For the rest of Pries's time at the university, this building was the home of the Architecture Department.

The second change was the offering of city planning courses in 1940–41 and the creation of a curriculum in city planning the following year. This probably seemed a minor matter at the time,

Fig. 7.44
Fine Arts Palace, Alaska-Yukon-Pacific Exposition (1907–9), subsequently renamed Bagley Hall (and used as the chemistry building, 1909–37), Physiology Hall (1937–50), Architecture Hall (1950–present); Howard and Galloway, architects. The Architecture Department moved into the second floor and part of the first floor in time for classes in fall 1937. The interior has been significantly remodeled several times. University of Washington Libraries, Special Collections Division, UW5769z.

but it presaged the pedagogical shifts that would overtake the department after 1945. The decision to offer planning reflected the impact of the New Deal. When the federal government established standards for winning grants for low-income housing projects, cities were required to have ongoing planning processes. Universities in Washington had not previously offered planning, but the need for planning professionals was apparent. Further, if architects were to design large public housing projects, they would need knowledge of planning as well. The Department of Architecture had already begun to add new faculty in response to growing numbers of students. Bissell Alderman, who had previously taught at MIT, was appointed in the fall of 1939; William Alexander ["Alec"] MacLaurin, a 1937 Washington graduate, was appointed a year later. Although both taught architecture, they were very interested in planning; under their direction, a city planning curriculum was started in the winter of 1941.[159] Students in city planning took the same program as students in architecture for the first three years (through "Architectural Design Grade II"), but instead of "Architectural Design Grade III," planning students took courses in "City Planning Design."[160] The program was initially small, with only four or five students, but this new arrangement set a precedent for the more diversified and less coherent curriculum that emerged after the war. Further, the pedagogy used in city planning was not that of the Beaux-Arts. For the first time, the Department of Architecture was offering studios on a different model, and this, too, set a new precedent.

The third change of the late 1930s was the gradual transfer of power from Harlan Thomas to Arthur Herrman. When the department had been elevated to the level of a "school," in the late 1930s, Herrman began to play a larger role in administration. About 1941, Thomas became director emeritus; Herrman, who had already taken on day-to-day responsibility for operation of the school, received the title "executive officer."[161] Herrman was the first head of the program who was a full-time faculty member. This change reflected the growing complexity of administration as the school increased in size, and as the new curriculum in city planning was added. Herrman's move into administration was not temporary—he would head the school through the rest of Pries's academic career.

Once the United States had entered World War II, radical change in the architecture school became inevitable, although it began slowly. The curriculum had always included a requirement for two years of physical education and/or two years in the Reserve Officers Training Corps (ROTC); most architecture students elected ROTC. As a result, the men who had already graduated were called to military service immediately, and others departed in 1942. By the fall of 1942, the size of the school had been reduced from one hundred students to eighty. Those who had joined the "enlisted reserve" were called up in the spring of 1943. By the fall of that year, the enrollment had been cut in half. For the next two years, the school regularly saw students depart to join the armed forces. To help students finish their degrees before entering military service, the program was accelerated: Herrman announced a four-year curriculum option in the fall of 1942. The five-year option was retained as well, but it was anticipated that, for the duration of the war, most new students would take the heavier course load in order to complete the program in four years. And the five-year curriculum soon disappeared; the 1944 university catalogue did not even list a fifth year of courses. Moreover, with male students departing, women made up a larger percentage of the very small number of wartime graduates. During the war, Mary Lund sent Alan Liddle, then in military service, a sketch showing the different studio levels: twenty or so freshmen were gathered around a desk for their crit, a dozen students met at the sophomore level, there were only six juniors, and the senior crit included only Mary and Pries[162] (fig. 7.45).

Pries was forty-five years old in 1942, too old for active military service. He continued to teach those students who remained on campus—sophomores in "Design Grade I," and the few upper-level students who were not in the military. But everyone served the war effort in one way or another. Gowen took a leave of absence and served in the Coastal Artillery Corps, designing coastal defenses. Olschewsky taught drawing in the university's "production illustration" program, which was created to train drafters for the war industries, and then he took a leave of absence to design housing for war workers.[163] Pries's initial contribution was to teach camouflage design. Harlan Thomas—in coordination with Pries's former partner, William Bain, now the camouflage officer for the state of Washington—

SOPH CRIT.

JUNIOR CRIT.

SENIOR CRIT.

FROSH CRIT.

Fig. 7.45
Mary Lund (now Mary Lund Davis), sketch of studio critique sent to Alan Liddle, ca. 1944. In the senior studio, Mary Lund is the single student receiving a critique from Professor Lionel Pries. Courtesy of Alan Liddle.

arranged for one of the four West Coast camouflage schools to be located at the University of Washington.[164] Pries was appointed a camouflage instructor in the Office of Civilian Defense and participated in teaching a sixteen-week course in industrial camouflage design to sixty architects, landscape architects, and engineers from October 1942 to February 1943. Pries was particularly involved in the students' actual camouflage projects, as Thomas's report indicates:

> Immediately upon completion of the course of lectures as prescribed by the curriculum, Professor Lionel H. Pries of the School of Architecture, University of Washington, took charge of the preparation of a model of a hypothetical site and conducted this phase of instruction to the end of the course, including supervision of the camouflage of the model by the class and conducting the examination as required by the Headquarters in San Francisco. In connection with all these activities, Professor Pries rendered most efficient and valuable service.[165]

Pries also participated in the training of naval officers. The rapid expansion of the U.S. Navy during the war (and the growth of the Civil Engineering Corps and the Seabees) created a tremendous need for naval officers, who had always been college graduates. In November 1942, the navy inaugurated the V-12 program, which placed potential officer candidates on college campuses; those who completed college-level coursework qualified for officer training schools.[166] To accommodate the program, the university changed to a semester system, with three terms each year. This system lasted for the duration of the war. Beginning in 1943, Pries taught drawing and architectural design to V-12 students in addition to teaching his regular courses for architecture undergraduates. Given the precipitous decline in enrollment in the architecture school, the V-12 students were critical to keeping the school intact; in the fall of 1943, Pries wrote to Keith Kolb that the V-12 students had "saved the school."[167]

The war changed everything. When the architecture program rebounded after 1945, students who had left returned to finish their degrees, and a new cohort, who had served in the war, joined them. Their experiences and their expectations would differ radically from those of the students of the previous decade. To address the demands of these new students, the School of Architecture would change as well. The challenge to Lionel Pries would be to find a way to respond, and to fit into a very different world.

8

MASTER
OF THE ARTS

THE ART INSTITUTE

AND THE COMMUNITY OF ARTISTS

BEFORE WORLD WAR II, STUDENTS IN AMERICAN schools of architecture routinely learned, as necessary skills, drawing and watercolor in addition to the rudiments of sculpture, and they were exposed to the history of art. Although many architects pursued drawing and painting as an avocation, few went much farther. Pries was an exception: an architect who truly excelled as an artist, he was, at least for a time, as much at home in the art community as he was in the architectural profession.[1]

Pries saw art and architecture as one, and he did not accept a distinction between the fine and applied arts. Pries's understanding and abilities were shaped by two traditions: the Beaux-Arts ideal of the artist-architect (or at least the architect as connoisseur), and the ethos of the Arts and Crafts movement, which treasured the decorative as well as the fine arts. Inherent in both traditions was the belief that a building was not complete until it was artistically embellished. In the Beaux-Arts tradition, it was thought that an educated architect should be knowledgeable about and able to advise clients with regard to fine art. Exemplary figures were the architect Charles Platt (1861–1933), who achieved national recognition as an etcher and painter before he became prominent as an architect and landscape architect, and Fiske Kimball (1888–1955), who, after receiving an architecture degree from Harvard, practiced, taught, and wrote about architecture and then, in 1925, accepted an appointment as director of the Pennsylvania Museum of Art, a position he held for thirty years.[2] Pries's understanding was also formed by the spirit of the Arts and Crafts movement; William Morris was the model, with his involvement in interiors and decorative arts, including furniture, painting, stained glass, ceramics, textiles, and book arts. Several leading California Arts and Crafts practitioners had designed not only buildings but also fixtures and furnishings, and most were knowledgeable enough to select such items for their clients.[3] Journals such as *The Craftsman*, which Pries had encountered at Lick–Wilmerding, included articles on etching, pottery, stained glass, textiles, metals, book design, bookplates, and similar topics. From his adolescence, Pries had always seen art as part of everyday life.[4]

At the Art Institute of Seattle

The openness of the Seattle arts community in the late 1920s is reflected in the rapidity with which Pries achieved acceptance and then rose to a position of leadership, as director of the Art Institute of Seattle (later the Seattle Art Museum, after Pries's departure). The institute was the successor to the Seattle Fine Arts Society, which had been organized about 1906 to support "municipal art, pictorial art, plastic art, art in architecture, interior decoration, ceramic art, applied design, landscape gardening, and art in apparel."[5] The society initially provided a venue for traveling shows and offered regular programs of lectures. After 1916, it fostered the development of Northwest artists through annual juried exhibits. Carl F. Gould served as president of the society from 1912 to 1916, and again from 1926 to 1929. In the late 1920s, the society leased the Horace C. Henry residence as its first permanent gallery and, in December 1928, changed its name to the Art Institute of Seattle.[6]

In 1929, the institute appointed John Davis Hatch Jr. executive secretary (he later served as director).[7] Hatch continued the ongoing lecture program and organized an expanded program of exhibits to fill the new galleries. He also initiated art classes for children and adults, including a drawing class for draftsmen and architects.[8] Dudley Pratt of the University of Washington art school was one of the instructors; Pries, who had joined the Fine Arts Society upon his arrival in Seattle, was a critic.[9] Beginning in 1929, Pries was involved in planning for a series of exhibits of Asian art.[10] In 1930, he served as a guest curator, mounting an exhibit of artifacts that he and Richard Pearce had brought back from Mexico.[11]

Richard Fuller, a member of the institute's board and a wealthy collector, was also a University of Washington research faculty member in geology. He had served as vice president of the institute under Gould and became its president in 1930.[12] In October 1931, Fuller and his mother, Margaret MacTavish (Mrs. Eugene) Fuller, announced their gift of $250,000 to build the new Seattle Art Museum in Volunteer Park.[13] About the same time, Hatch resigned his position at the institute to take an extended trip abroad.[14] A few days later, Fuller announced that Pries would be the new director of the Art Institute.[15]

Pries assumed his new position in November 1931. Later that month, Fuller, in a letter to Frederick A. Whiting, president of the American Federation of the Arts, introduced the new director:

> We deserve your congratulations on [Hatch's] successor Lionel H. Pries. He is an architect who had his original training under Mr. Cret at Pennsylvania, where he won the principal award in his class. Mr. Pries can only give us part of his time because he is an architectural critic at the University of Washington. In his three years in his department, the speed and accuracy of his judgment has been highly appreciated by the profession. In that respect, his ability has already been of great value to us in the preliminary plans of the new building. He has an especially broad artistic training and a great aptitude for museum work. Although he has no detailed experience in that regard, he fortunately realizes his short-comings and is very intent on overcoming them. I am sure that he will establish a very essential spirit of cooperation with the staff and with the trustees.[16]

Fuller did not mention that Pries's appointment helped the institute address its financial difficulties. Memberships were the primary source of income. By 1930, the institute had 1,500 members, but the number able to pay the $10 annual dues was falling rapidly in 1931.[17] The institute had to cover staff salaries, rent at the Henry residence, and the costs of programs; although some exhibits were mounted locally, traveling exhibits involved costs for shipping, insurance, and the like. Pries, as a university faculty member, required only a part-time salary; he could work mornings at the institute and afternoons at the university.

Pries's primary role as director was the management of the galleries. He continued exhibits already under way and began planning for 1932 and 1933. Building on Hatch's initial effort, Pries worked to bring the Museum of Modern Art's controversial "International Style" architecture exhibit to Seattle in 1932. Nevertheless, this effort, which was to have been shared by West Coast institutions, failed when several museums in California were unable to raise their portion of the anticipated cost.[18]

Another benefit of Pries's appointment was his architectural expertise. Planning for the new Seattle Art Museum had actually begun before October 1931, when Richard Fuller and his mother had announced their gift. The architectural firm of Bebb and Gould began work that summer, and Gould's early drawings suggested a traditional museum. As the project moved forward, however, the design became more contemporary. At the beginning of October, Bebb and Gould presented the Art Deco/Moderne elevation that became the basis for the building.[19] In December, the artist and critic Kenneth Callahan argued that the museum should "embody the spirit of the modern day"; by then, Gould and Fuller were thinking that way as well.[20] The selection of the Art Deco/Moderne elevation predated Pries's appointment, but the development of the building plans and interiors took place from October 1931 through February 1932, precisely those months when Pries was most influential. In October, Laurence Coleman, director of the American Association of Museums, submitted his report on the program and plan of the new building.[21] Financial constraints led to revisions in November and again in January, when it was determined that only two floors could be afforded. In these months, the design of the lobby and the galleries was explored in a series of schemes. Pries and Gould were both in New York in December 1931, and evidently they had a long discussion about the character of the building. On 16 December, Gould wrote to his wife, "I . . . had a long confab with Pries and found that all my ideas on aesthetics checked. He is an absolute advocate of the modern movement."[22] Although the conversation may have focused on planning, the reference to aesthetics also indicates that it likely dealt with interior spaces and detailing. The term "modern movement" here is a reference to the Art Deco/Moderne, not to the International Style just then emerging from Europe.

In early January, Pries prepared, to scale, a pair of freehand, pencilled floor plans for the museum. His plans show the basement, with administrative, staff, and library spaces, and the first floor, with rooms in each wing arranged around landscaped courtyards—an approach that followed traditional American museum design but resulted in less gallery space.[23] Pries's courtyard scheme was not selected, although his plans may have influenced the layout of some portions of the basement.

Pries may have hoped to play a continuing role in the new museum, but his position as director of the Art Institute was short-lived. At the end of February 1932, the board determined that the worsening defi-

cit necessitated closing the institute's galleries until the new building was complete. Pries had been arranging for exhibits for 1932 and early 1933; now he was faced with the unenviable task of canceling arrangements that he had already made. His letter to the Roerich Museum in New York was typical:

> The Board of Trustees of the . . . Art Institute suddenly decided to close exhibitions completely, retaining only limited office space until the time when our new galleries open at the end of next year. The Board has also decided to dispense with the services of a Director until just before entrance into the new quarters at which time a professionally trained man will probably be brought from the east.[24]

Pries continued to serve as director until the galleries closed, at the end of April. Thereafter, Fuller was in charge. Although planning for the Seattle Art Museum initially had envisioned an experienced director for the new building, in the fall of 1932 the board appointed Fuller to the position; thereafter, he served as both director of the museum and president of the board.[25] The new museum opened in late June 1933. Pries never again held an official role in Seattle's arts community, but he never gave up his wide-ranging interests in the arts.[26]

PAINTING

Pries first exhibited in Seattle in 1928, when three of his watercolors were selected for the Annual Exhibition of Northwest Artists. The jury chose *Hunter's Point, San Francisco* for the thirteenth annual exhibition, held in the spring, and *Watercolor Sketch* and *Shingle Factory* for the fourteenth exhibition, held in the fall.[27]

Pries had learned watercolor as part of his architectural training. Watercolor was routinely included in the curricula of architecture programs, but in this period it was often regarded as a marginal field in American fine arts academies.[28] Still, during the time when Pries was in Philadelphia, the city had two active organizations that sponsored annual watercolor shows, and the Pennsylvania Academy of Fine Arts sometimes exhibited watercolors as well.[29] Pries would have seen paintings by local artists and by leading figures from other eastern cities— John Singer Sargent, for example, was an honorary member of the Philadelphia Water Color Club.[30]

Most Philadelphia artists worked within a traditional framework, but, influenced by Cézanne, Cubism, and other European avant-garde tendencies, a small group had begun exploring new directions.

Pries's artistic career, as distinct from his career as an architect, can be said to have begun with his return from Europe to San Francisco, in 1923. The watercolors that Pries produced during his years in the Bay Area show a freer technique than those he did while in Europe, suggesting that he was beginning to develop his skill as a watercolorist, not just as an architectural delineator (figs. 8.1, 8.2).

When Pries arrived in Seattle, the city's art community was becoming divided between traditional and modern painters and sculptors. In the summer of 1928, a group of artists, unhappy with the jury's selections for the Northwest annual exhibitions, organized the Independent Salon of Northwest Artists, an unjuried, open show with awards voted by the public. In response, the fall 1928 Northwest annual exhibition had two juries—one for traditional works and one for modern works—and offered both jury awards and popular-vote awards.[31] Later Northwest annual exhibitions would have only one jury, but the popular-vote award was retained until World War II. The few published articles on the 1928 exhibitions did not mention Pries's work; had they done so, he would probably have been identified as a traditionalist.

After 1928, it was seven years before Pries again exhibited in Seattle. The delay likely reflects the demands of the Bain and Pries partnership and of teaching at the university. Moreover, during his term as director of the Art Institute of Seattle, it would have been inappropriate for him to submit work for a juried exhibit sponsored by the institute.[32] Pries continued to paint nonetheless. In early 1931, he submitted five watercolors to *Pencil Points*; one of them, *Città Caselli—Piazza San Lorenzo*, appeared in September[33] (fig. 8.3). *Pencil Points* commented favorably on Pries's technique: "The artist has used the white paper effectively and in places has taken advantage of the rough texture to obtain a sparkling effect through use of a fairly dry brush."[34] The paintings that Pries submitted suggest the influence of Sargent; in addition to probably having seen Sargent's paintings in Philadelphia, in 1930 he acquired a book containing plates of Sargent watercolors.[35] With one exception, the paintings Pries submitted to *Pencil Points* were of sites in Europe or North Africa. The exception was *Indian Graveyard, Quattsino*

Sound, Vancouver Island, Pries's earliest identified watercolor of a Northwest site. It shows wet-on-wet technique—watercolor, applied to damp paper, diffused outward and dried without a definite edge—an effective means to represent the misty sky of the Northwest (fig. 8.4). Pries also maintained his San Francisco connections: in December 1932, as an invited exhibitor, he showed *Asilomar Pine* at the First Annual Exhibition of Western Watercolor Painting, held at the California Palace of Fine Arts[36] (fig. 8.5).

Pries's growth as an artist was no doubt enhanced by his interaction with the Seattle arts community. Pries's closest friend among the artists—a friendship that would endure for thirty years—was Raymond ("Ray") Hill (1891–1980), a University of Washington art professor who taught watercolor to the architecture students. Born and raised in Massachusetts, Hill had studied art at the Rhode Island School of Design and went on to teach in Colorado before arriving in Seattle in 1927.[37] Like Pries, he was gay, but he was closeted within the university community. Pries's friend and neighbor Duane Shipman recalled how Pries and Hill met:

> Pries realized that someone was doing a very good job at teaching watercoloring to the architecture students, and so he went over to the School of Art and went into Ray's studio and asked, "Are you Ray Hill?" Of course, this frightened Ray, and he sort of plunged into a closet—a little overwhelmed by Spike. They subsequently became great friends. He was just a little overwhelming to poor Ray, who was a quiet and shy man.[38]

Their individual approaches to watercolor were quite different. Pries rarely revised, accepting the watercolor as it came off his brush; if the result was not acceptable, he would simply begin another painting. Hill typically continued to work on a painting, sponging out and touching up details until he had just the effect he was seeking. Their approaches to teaching also differed; Pries was a perfectionist, while Hill's favorite response to students' efforts was "Just wonderful—that's wonderful—just wonderful."[39] Graduates recalled that the combination of Hill and Pries was particularly effective in developing their interest and skill in watercolor. Pries and Hill often went to dinner and occasionally went on watercoloring trips together. Two paintings from a 1940s trip to eastern Washington suggest

Fig. 8.2
Lionel H. Pries,
untitled water-
front scene, San
Francisco Bay,
ca. 1923–27;
watercolor, 9½

x 15 inches. Pries
collection, Univer-
sity of Washington
Libraries, Special
Collections Divi-
sion, UW23433z.

Fig. 8.1 (*opposite*)
Lionel H. Pries,
untitled interior
view of Temple
Emanu-el,
San Francisco,
ca. 1926–27;
watercolor, 18 x 12
inches. Temple
Enamu-el was one

of Pries's favorite
buildings; he often
described it to his
students. Pries
collection, Univer-
sity of Washington
Libraries, Special
Collections Divi-
sion, UW23501z.

Fig. 8.3
Lionel H. Pries,
Citta Caselli—
Piazza San Lorenzo,
1930–31; water-
color, 9⅝ x 13⅝

inches. Pries col-
lection, University
of Washington
Libraries, Special
Collections Divi-
sion, UW23091z.

Fig. 8.4
Lionel H. Pries,
Indian Graveyard,
Quatsino Sound,
Vancouver Island,
1930–31; water-
color, 9⅛ x 13½
inches. Pries col-
lection, University
of Washington
Libraries, Special
Collections Divi-
sion, 23092z.

Fig. 8.5
Lionel H. Pries,
Asilomar Pine,
1932; watercolor,
13½ x 18½ inches.
Although no title
is found on this
painting, the date
and subject make
it virtually certain

that this is the
painting Pries
exhibited in San
Francisco in 1932.
Color digitally
restored by
Stephen Rock.
Courtesy of
Wendell Lovett.

Fig. 8.6 (*opposite*)
Ray Hill (a) and
Lionel Pries (b),
untitled, unidenti-
fied landscapes in
central Washing-
ton, ca. 1940–46;
watercolors, each

14 x 20 inches.
Damage to each
painting digitally
repaired by
Stephen Rock.
Courtesy of
T. C. Warren.

(a)

(b)

(a)

(b)

Fig. 8.7
Morris Graves
(a), nude of Guy
Anderson, and
Guy Anderson
(b), nude of Morris

Graves, ca.1933–35;
two-sided water-
color, 19½ x 15½
inches. This two-
sided watercolor
was retained by

Pries but given to
his friend Duane
Shipman about
1964. Courtesy
of the estate of
Duane Shipman.

the enjoyment they shared (fig. 8.6). The virtually identical palette suggests that they may have worked out of a single paint box; they likely sat together but looked in different directions.[40] Theirs was a warm friendship, as the inscription on the back of a watercolor that Hill gave Pries suggests: "To Lionel Pries, for his kindness, interest and inspiration in my painting."[41] Yet Pries's watercolor technique shows little of Hill's influence.[42]

Other artists whom Pries met through the university in the 1920s and 1930s were more oriented to new directions coming from Europe. Ambrose Patterson (1877–1962) had studied in Europe and exhibited in Paris and New York; he arrived in Seattle in 1918 to found the university's program in painting and design.[43] In 1922, leadership of the Department of Painting, Sculpture, and Design passed to Walter Isaacs (1886–1964), who had also had training in Europe and exhibited in Paris.[44] Visiting faculty of the late 1930s were drawn from the European avant-garde: Alexander Archipenko in 1936–37, Amédée Ozenfant in 1938, and Johannes Molzahn in 1940.[45]

The other center of Seattle's art community was the Art Institute of Seattle. As director of the Art Institute, Pries had come into direct contact with three of the four younger artists who would later achieve fame as members of the "Northwest School": Kenneth Callahan, Guy Anderson, and Morris Graves.[46] Kenneth Callahan (1905–1986), a self-taught artist, first exhibited in 1926 in San Francisco. In 1929, he began to report on the Seattle art scene, writing columns for the weekly social newspaper *The Town Crier* and, after 1933, for the *Seattle Times*.[47] If Pries did not know Callahan before, they certainly became acquainted during Pries's term as director of the institute.[48] Pries was closer to Guy Anderson (1906–1998) and Morris Graves (1910–2001), both of whom were gay. Anderson was born in Edmonds, Washington, and grew up and studied art in Seattle. From 1933 to 1944, he taught children's art classes and mounted exhibits at the Seattle Art Museum.[49] Graves was born in Oregon but moved to Seattle as a young boy; he started painting in 1932.[50] About 1934, Graves and Anderson shared a studio in Edmonds. Their friendship with Pries also began in the 1930s and was intimate for a brief time. This is reflected in a two-sided watercolor that Pries owned: one side was a nude study of Anderson by Graves, and the other side was a similar study of Graves by

Anderson; Pries, the third person present the night it was painted, retained it for the rest of his life[51] (fig. 8.7).

The 1930s were an experimental period for Seattle artists. The Depression led some to a focus on social realism; the work of the Mexican muralists provided a powerful example. Several Seattle artists, including Callahan, Anderson, and Ambrose and Viola Patterson, visited Mexico early in the decade, but Pries had the deepest and longest interaction with that country.[52] By the summer of 1932, he had begun painting in oils in Mexico. Two of his paintings, both titled *Hacienda da Rocca—Guanajuato*, show the ruins not far from the Valencia mine in the hills above Guanajuato (figs. 8.8, 8.9). The treatment of the landscape, particularly the flattening and compression of the background mountains into layers, suggests Pries's awareness of the New Mexico landscape paintings of Georgia O'Keeffe.[53] The same summer, Pries also painted a more strongly architectural work, *San Andreas—Cholula* (refer to fig. 5.7). In 1934, he again did oils in Cholula and Guanajuato (fig. 8.10).

Three years in a row, Pries entered oils in the Northwest annual exhibitions: *Rockaway* in 1935, *Souvenir of Mazatlán* and *Volcanoland* in 1936, and *The Two Hands* in 1937.[54] *Volcanoland* was the most important of these; it won the 1936 popular-vote award (fig. 8.11). The painting is dramatic, with volcanic cinder cones in deep blue silhouetted against a streaky sky. Pries's approach is much more abstract than in his earlier work and suggests the influence of modernizing tendencies in American art in the 1930s; still, a local newspaper report commented that Pries's picture was one of those "painted in a conservative manner."[55] Pries's choice of title suggests his awareness of the American western painter Maynard Dixon (1875–1946). In the years of Pries's childhood and adolescence, Dixon was a widely published illustrator based in San Francisco. After 1910, Dixon focused on painting and was known for his western landscapes. In the 1920s, his work remained representational but showed the impact of modern tendencies in art.[56] It is likely that the 1927 Dixon painting *Navajoland* inspired the title *Volcanoland*.[57]

Another likely influence on *Volcanoland* was the Canadian painters' collective known as the Group of Seven. The young artists who came together in 1920 to form the Group of Seven specifically sought

Fig. 8.8
Lionel H. Pries,
*Hacienda da
Rocca—Guanajuato,*
no. 1, ca. 1932; oil
on canvas, 20 x 24
inches. Private
collection.

Fig. 8.9
Lionel H. Pries,
*Hacienda da
Rocca—Guanajuato,*
no. 2, ca. 1932; oil
on canvas, 20 x 24
inches. Private
collection.

Fig. 8.10   *Cholula*, 1934;
Lionel H. Pries,   oil on canvas,
Nuestra Senora   18 x 22 inches.
de Guadalupe—   Private collection.

Fig. 8.11
Lionel H. Pries,
Volcanoland, 1936;
oil on canvas, 30
x 36 inches. Lea
family collection.

Fig. 8.12
Lionel H. Pries,
*Hacienda Noria
Alta—Guanajuato,*
1942; oil on canvas,
20 x 24½ inches.
Private collection.

Fig. 8.13
Lionel H. Pries,
untitled, unidenti-
fied Northwest
landscape, ca.
1935–42; oil on
canvas, 24 x 30
inches. Lea family
collection.

to celebrate Canada's diverse landscapes by using innovative pictorial strategies.[58] Initially controversial for the modernity of their paintings, by the late 1920s the members of the group were exhibiting across Canada and occasionally in the United States. Frederick Varley (1881–1969), a founding member, moved to Vancouver in the late 1920s and had solo shows at the Art Institute of Seattle in 1930 and 1931, and he taught on the institute's staff in the summer of 1930.[59] Although the Group of Seven officially dissolved in 1933, the impact of its members was long-lasting, especially in their simplification of form and their bold use of color and light—effects found in *Volcanoland*.

In May 1940, Pries had a solo show of nineteen paintings at the Pacific Gallery, in Seattle. He included his Mexican paintings from 1932 and 1934 but did not include works that had appeared at the Northwest annual exhibitions. The brochure for the show described the work and the artist:

> Pries, with an insatiable desire for travel, has spent three months each year since 1929 in Oriental, European, and Mexican sojourn. Impressed by the architecture, color, and grand history of Mexico, Pries has returned from his various trips to this country with numerous paintings and sketches. The great majority of paintings in his present exhibit are of this group . . . direct, outdoor oils and watercolors, reflecting draftsmanship, solidity and color masterfully handled.[60]

Pries's last known Mexican oil, titled *Hacienda Noria Alta—Guanjuato*, showing an aqueduct and water tower located just outside the city, dates from 1942 (fig. 8.12). Only a single Pries oil of a Northwest scene has been found. This undated canvas shows an unidentified landscape, possibly in the vicinity of Mount Vernon, north of Seattle. The technique is mixed: the foreground recalls the work of such American painters as Grant Wood, while the sky, according to David Martin of Martin-Zambito Fine Art, may reflect the influence of Chinese scroll painting[61] (fig. 8.13).

As a watercolorist, Pries truly excelled. His Mexican watercolors show townscapes and buildings; in the Northwest, his focus was the landscape. Several Mexican watercolors from the mid-1930s show less close rendition of detail, and this feature probably reflects tendencies toward abstraction and simplifi-

cation that were permeating the university's school of art in the period (figs. 8.14, 8.15). But Pries never moved farther than this from representation, and his other paintings of that period were more precise (figs. 8.16, 8.17). An emphasis on crisply delineated geometric form is evident in his watercolor of Taxco seen from above—a painting also unusual for its viewpoint (refer to fig. 5.5). Pries's Mexican watercolors dating from 1942 are all marked by well-defined geometric shapes and bright, saturated colors (fig. 8.18; refer to fig. 5.2). Martin, widely recognized as an authority on Northwest artists of the years after 1900, suggests that the paintings show awareness of the Precisionist school, which includes the work of Z. (Zama) Vanessa Helder (1904–1968), a Northwest painter who had exhibited in Seattle and who was, by the late 1930s, receiving national recognition for her watercolors of Grand Coulee Dam.[62]

Pries's watercolors are particularly effective in capturing different qualities of natural light. His Mexican watercolors usually have saturated colors and white surfaces, indications of bright sunlight. In contrast, his Northwest scenes have skies executed in translucent watercolor washes. Pries explained to Keith Kolb that the bright colors of Mexico could not be used on the Northwest coast because the light is too soft and gray. Pries argued that Northwest Coast Native American colors or Japanese colors work best in western Washington.[63]

Pries's Northwest watercolors are quite varied. *The Derelicts, Mukilteo*, dating from 1939, is in the more abstracted style of his earlier Mexican watercolors (fig. 8.19). *Lenore Lake, Lower Coulee* seems rather gray and presents the quality of light of a late fall day (fig. 8.20). His untitled watercolor of a farm landscape, likely in the vicinity of Puget Sound, captures a misty day in the Northwest—the perspective to the left of center is remarkably effective in this regard, while the finely detailed barbed wire in the foreground pulls the viewer into the scene (fig. 8.21). In *Iceberg Point, Lopez Island*, from 1946–47, the white paper offers an effective rendition of the quality of light reflected from the water's surface (fig. 8.22).

Pries's watercolors demonstrate his mastery of multiple styles and show his knowledge of the leading painters of the period. There is no clear "style of Pries"—rather, his work as a painter reflects the same breadth of interests that shaped other aspects of his

Fig. 8.14
Lionel H. Pries,
*Courtyard Sta
Magdalena*, 1934;
watercolor, 16 x 12
inches. Courtesy
of Robert Winskill.

Fig. 8.15
Lionel H. Pries,
untitled view
of entrance
to courtyard

Sta Magdalena,
1934; watercolor,
15½ x 12 inches.
Courtesy of Robert
Winskill.

Fig. 8.16
Lionel H. Pries,
untitled view of
Mexican village,
ca. 1930s; water-
color on paper,
12¼ x 18¼ inches.

Courtesy of
Dean's Office,
College of
Architecture &
Urban Planning,
University of
Washington.

Fig. 8.17
Lionel H. Pries,
La Pastita,
Guanajuato, 1942;
watercolor, 17 x 20
inches. Courtesy
of Robert Winskill.

Fig. 8.18 (*opposite*)
Lionel H. Pries,
untitled street
scene, probably
Guanajuato, ca.
1938–42; water-
color, 15¼ x 12
inches. Color
digitally restored
by Stephen Rock.
Lea family
collection.

Fig. 8.19
Lionel H. Pries,
The Derelicts,
Mukilteo, 1939;
watercolor, 17 x 21
inches. Courtesy
of Robert Winskill.

Fig. 8.20
Lionel H. Pries,
Lake Lenore, Lower Coulee, ca. 1946;
watercolor, 16⅞ x 20¾ inches.

Seattle Art Museum, Eugene Fuller Memorial Collection, 46.262. Photo by Paul Macapia.

Fig. 8.21
Lionel H. Pries,
untitled Northwest
farm scene,
ca. 1940–46;

watercolor,
17¼ x 21½ inches.
Courtesy of Robert
W. Winskill.

Fig. 8.22
Lionel H. Pries,
Iceberg Point,
Lopez Island,
1946; watercolor

on paper, 16½
x 20⅝ inches.
Courtesy of Keith
Kolb.

Fig. 8.23
Lionel H. Pries,
untitled view
of driftwood,
probably on Lopez
Island, ca. 1946,

16¾ x 20 inches.
Color digitally
restored by
Stephen Rock.
Courtesy of
Georgia Jones.

Fig. 8.24
Lionel H. Pries,
White Horse Creek,
1942; watercolor,
17½ x 21¾ inches.
Courtesy of Robert
Winskill.

Fig. 8.25
Lionel H. Pries,
*Alkalai Meadows,
Lower Coulee,*
1946; watercolor,
17¼ x 21½ inches.
Courtesy of Robert
Winskill.

Fig. 8.26
Lionel H. Pries, *La Bufa—Guanajuato*, 1946; watercolor and tempera, 26¾ x 38 inches. This is one of two large watercolor-and-tempera paintings that Pries probably produced in Seattle for his 1946 Henry Gallery exhibit (for its companion, see Fig. 5.4). Color digitally restored by Stephen Rock. Lea family collection.

life.[64] An untitled painting of driftwood, and two others—*White Horse Creek* and *Alkalai Meadows, Lower Coulee*—all date from the 1940s; without the signatures, one would likely think these three watercolors were by different artists[65] (figs. 8.23, 8.24, 8.25).

In 1946, Pries had a solo show of watercolors at the University of Washington's Henry Art Gallery.[66] Most of these paintings focused on Mexican subjects, and the rest were views of the Northwest (fig. 8.26). T. C. Warren, a student of that period who later practiced both as a watercolorist and as an architect, recalled, "His crisp and direct handling of the scenes left me in silent awe. I have yet to see anyone surpass him. I can say this from experience having been a 'professional-painter-exhibitor.'"[67] David Martin ranks Pries among Seattle's best watercolorists of the twentieth century.[68]

By 1950, Pries had given up painting. His decision may reflect his growing focus on his architectural practice, or it may reflect his disillusionment with the direction of modern art. Pries's attitude is no doubt indicated by "a marvelous story" (perhaps apocryphal) that his friend Duane Shipman recalled hearing from Pries. According to this story, Pries and several professors from the art school "were traveling together around the Olympic Peninsula, and they were at the Pacific Coast, looking out toward the sunset, and one turned to Spike and said, 'Isn't it a pity we can't paint representationally anymore?'"[69]

PRINTMAKING

In the mid-1930s, Pries developed an interest in printmaking, and for a time his output included drypoint prints. Bjarne Olsen, a graduate of the School of Architecture, recalled introducing Pries to printmaking in the basement of the "Shack" about 1935:

> One of the rooms for the architects was used to store an etching press given to the Department by a graduate, name now forgotten. The press was a five-spoke model, top of the line! I had experimented with drypoint and printed small pieces with my mother's hand-operated clothes wringer. A new world opened with the availability of a real press. Pries saw my prints and got me to show how I did it! Then I helped him print the first few copies of his plates.[70]

Printmaking was a growing interest of American artists in the interwar years. Northwest Print Makers began its annual exhibitions in 1929, just one year after the group was formed.[71] In the 1930s, Pries began to purchase books on prints and printmaking.[72] Although he produced some outstanding prints, he never joined the Northwest Print Makers and never exhibited his work.[73] Instead, he seems to have seen printmaking primarily as an avocation and as something he could share with students. John Rohrer, who graduated in 1937, recalled learning to make prints from Pries. According to Rohrer, Pries "had an etching press set up in the basement. . . . Dudley Pratt from the art school used it from time to time, and Spike used it to grind out drypoint prints. He taught us how to use it and showed us how to make a drypoint print. And we used that press in the basement of the Shack quite a bit."[74] Pries also gave his prints to clients and friends.

The term "drypoint" refers both to the printing process and to the kinds of prints that Pries produced. Similar to etchings and engravings, drypoint prints are made from ink that is held by grooves incised in a metal plate. In drypoint, the artist scratches lines directly on the plate (usually copper) with a sharp tool that has a steel or diamond point (Pries used a dentist's pick). The distinguishing feature of drypoint is the metal burr that, when the plate is scratched, is thrown up—on both sides of the groove if the needle is held perpendicularly or on one side if the needle is held at an angle. When the plate is printed, the burr holds ink in addition to the ink held in the groove, and the result is a softer, fuzzy or feathery line. Because the burr wears down under pressure from the press, drypoints are issued in small series—usually no more than fifty prints, and frequently fewer.[75]

Pries created some drypoints that were based on his earlier drawings. For example, the print thought to be Pries's first—a scene of Venice, dating from 1936—is copied from a drawing he had done some years before on the flyleaf of a picture book of Venice[76] (fig. 8.27). In 1943, Pries produced a drypoint of Ronda, Spain; it, too, was a copy, this time of a drawing he had done on his LeBrun Traveling Scholarship tour.

Most of Pries's early drypoints are of Mexican subjects. Two are based on Pries's pair of oils titled *Hacienda da Rocca—Guanajuato* (fig. 8.28; refer to figs. 8.8, 8.9). Others appear to be from the dry

5/9

Fig. 8.27
Lionel H. Pries,
untitled scene in
Venice, ca. 1936;
drypoint print, 8⅛
x 6½ inches. Pries
collection, University of Washington
Libraries, Special
Collections Division, UW23085z.

3/50

Fig. 8.28
Lionel H. Pries,
*Hacienda da Rocca
—Guanajuato,*
ca. 1936; drypoint
print, 5⁷/₈ x 8
inches. Pries
collection, University of Washington
Libraries, Special
Collections Division, UW23089z.

25/40   Lionel H. Pries

Fig. 8.29   ca. 1936–44;
Lionel H. Pries,   drypoint print,
untitled view   5¾ x 8 inches.
of singers and   Private collection.
unidentified town,

Fig. 8.30
Lionel H. Pries,
untitled, unidenti-
fied silver mine,
possibly near
Guanajuato, ca.
1943; partially
completed dry-
point print with
pencil additions,
8 x 5⅞ inches.
Pries collec-
tion, University
of Washington
Libraries, Special
Collections Divi-
sion, UW23082z.

Fig. 8.31
Lionel H. Pries,
untitled view of
cabin belonging to
Harlan Thomas,
1944; drypoint
print, 6 x 8 inches.

Pries collec-
tion, University
of Washington
Libraries, Special
Collections Divi-
sion, UW23083z.

desert areas north of central Mexico, near Guanajuato or perhaps in the area of Jalisco. The buildings have flat roofs, an indication of the dry climate; in groups, the buildings have a blocky, almost abstract character, which was attractive to Mexican artists, particularly Orozco, in the 1930s.[77] In the mid to late 1930s, Pries made a print of a town of this kind. Later he made a second version of this plate, adding a group of singers to the foreground (fig. 8.29). Areas near Guanajuato and Jalisco were locations of silver mines, and Pries made one drypoint of such a mine. A surviving early print shows how Pries developed his images (fig. 8.30). The early partial print showed the mine building, the track, and the tunnel, but most of the landscape features were not yet included; Pries added these in pencil. Once he had achieved the composition and values he wanted, he returned to the copper plate and cut the grooves for these features before making his final prints. Pries often continued to improve his plates: Kolb recalls that after a plate had been printed multiple times, Pries might try to re-elevate the burrs, to enhance the quality of later prints.[78]

After the architecture school moved to Physiology Hall, in 1937, the etching press was placed in storage. About 1941 or 1942, Pries moved the press to his home and started printing again. Pries dried his prints by hanging them from clotheslines in the basement. The last of Pries's nine known drypoint prints, of Harlan Thomas's weekend cabin, is signed and dated 1944, though Kolb recalls Pries making prints as late as 1946[79] (fig. 8.31). When Pries moved to his new house in Laurelhurst, in 1948, his print-making came to an end.

COLLECTING

Although he may have retained a few small things from childhood, Pries began seriously collecting cultural objects in the 1920s.[80] His friend Robert Winskill shared Pries's interest in collecting and has captured this aspect of his life most clearly:

> Spike was an inveterate collector. He bought everything that caught his eye, which was a very good one. At first he collected for his own benefit, rare books for the library, architectural reference works, and things he liked. Later he purchased things that could be incorporated in the houses he designed. And he had an encyclopedic knowledge, which allowed him to recognize the value of things

others might miss. As an example, on a trip to San Francisco, we stopped off at a small shop dealing in Asian, mostly Japanese, goods. He spied what looked like a pile of disassembled wood and bought it for a song. It was a Chinese guardian figure that he reassembled and [it] became part of his living room decor.[81]

In the 1920s, when Pries began collecting, his initial focus was his personal library. In 1922, before departing for Europe, he probably owned no more than thirty to thirty-five books, but by the time of his death, in 1968, his library was close to one thousand volumes.[82] Pries acquired a large number of books in the 1930s, when prices were very low.[83] Although many of his books addressed architecture, drawing, painting, and sculpture, Pries's interests were wide-ranging, and he owned books about etching, typography, textiles, folk art, archaeology, ethnography, religious symbolism, literature, book plates, and book design. And, over time, he acquired more than thirty rare volumes.[84]

Pries's interests as a collector were broad, but from the late 1920s to the 1950s his primary focus was Latin American pre-Columbian and folk arts, Northwest Native American arts and crafts, and occasionally Asian and African art objects. In the 1950s, his collecting shifted primarily to Japanese artifacts of all kinds. When building his personal collection, he not only made purchases but also, like many other collectors, acquired objects through trades. In June 1962, Pries wrote triumphantly to Emma Willits of a recent exchange: "Spratling has for ten years been trying to get me to sell him an Ekoi African sculpture, but this time he brought with him a green quartz Teotihuacan mask of the highest quality for which he got the Ekoi head."[85]

It is unsurprising, given his childhood experience, that some of Pries's earliest collections were Asian. In June 1928, for an exhibit at Seattle's Fine Arts Little Gallery, Pries loaned a selection of Javanese batiks, and students who lived at his house recall some small Asian objects.[86] However, as a result of his travels, his interests expanded to include Mexico and Latin America. In 1939, Pries loaned objects from his collections to the Henry Gallery for an exhibit of "Ancient Mexican Art." The eighty-two religious and secular pre-conquest stone and clay objects, drawn from the Toltec, Maya, Aztec and other cultures, filled five exhibit cases; a sixth case included seven examples of seventeenth-to nineteenth-century Mexican textiles.[87]

Pries was a serious collector of textiles, especially Peruvian pre-Columbian fabrics. [88] Varying from eight hundred to one thousand years old, the roughly fifty-five pieces in Pries's collection came primarily from excavated tombs in the coastal areas of Peru. They showed the extraordinary skills and variety of techniques that the Peruvian weavers had developed. These textiles were the particular favorites of Hope Foote and Grace Denny, University of Washington interior design faculty members who often brought their students to see them.[89] In 1946, Pries exhibited a selection of the fabrics at the Seattle Art Museum.[90] The following year, when he showed them to the Spokane Club, the *Spokesman-Review* reported, "The pre-Inca fabrics Mr. Pries owns, which are not only historically picturesque but remarkable for detail, are the largest and most complete collection in the west. One, of vari-colored feathers, was a gorgeous specimen of a lost art today."[91] In 1948, Pries loaned fifteen pieces for a show at the Henry Art Gallery. The description in the *Seattle Times* began as follows:

> Inside a glass case in the Henry Art Gallery at the University of Washington is an ancient hand-woven wool tapestry, 248 threads to the square inch. It was made by people who never had seen sheep, flax or silk. They had no spinning wheels and their looms, no more than 30 inches across, were hung from tree limbs, tied to tree trunks or pegged in the ground. Yet their expert fingers wove fabrics rivaling the finest ones ever made. The only pieces existing today have come from Peruvian graves and are preserved in a few museums. A privately owned collection of 60 pieces is here in Seattle, the property of Lionel H. Pries. . . . [92]

Pries subsequently exhibited the collection in San Francisco, but in the early 1950s, as his interests changed, he sold the fabrics to a collector who later gave them to the California Academy of Sciences.[93] When the textiles were exhibited again, in 1978, they attracted considerable attention, but by then the link to Pries had been forgotten[94] (figs. 8.32, 8.33).

Pries also had an important collection of baroque Middle American image vestments; these were miniature vestments used to dress church statuary for liturgical holy days and seasons in Catholic churches in southern Mexico and Central America. [95] Kolb recalled these:

> One thing I remember specifically were little pieces of clothes that probably came from cathedrals in Mexico, where they would dress up Jesus and Mary. They had perfect cloth, with finger ironing. They used a kind of starch on linen, and by working with their fingers, they made these little tiny textures, gorgeous textures in cloth, with finger ironing. Spike had collected quite a number of those.[96]

Pries's collections brought him into contact with noted anthropologists and historians. An example was the historian and Pre-Columbian expert Pál Kelemen, who visited Pries in Seattle and gave him copies of his two books. His inscription in the first read "To Lionel Pries, early and discerning pioneer in the pre-Columbian and colonial arts of the Americas," and in the second he wrote, "To Lionel Pries with kindest remembrances of his unique house and rare collection."[97]

In the 1950s, Pries's collecting shifted to Asian, particularly Japanese, antiques. The Japanese economy was slow to recover from World War II, and many objects, formerly in temple storerooms and private collections in Japan, came on the market.[98] Pries worked with the Oceanic Trading Company, a Seattle importer, to build his collection. Oceanic sent him photographs, descriptions, and prices of items that were available, and from these Pries selected those he wished to purchase. His purchases were sometimes for clients; for example, Pries's Richard and Ruth Lea residence, in Seattle, incorporated several Japanese screens, one large figural sculpture, and some carvings. But sometimes Pries fell in love with the objects himself. A March 1955 letter to Oceanic is indicative: "My client is out of town so I will not bother about him after all. If I can possibly swing it, I will keep the figures myself."[99]

Pries's Japanese collections included several dozen Japanese prints representing many of the leading printmakers: Hiroshige, Hokusai, Kunisada, and others.[100] In 1955–56, Pries acquired two large figural sculptures. The first was a painted wood sculpture of the Amida Buddha on a lotus stand; together, the sculpture and the stand measured nearly 54 inches in height. The second was a wood sculpture of Kannon, one of the Buddha's attendants,

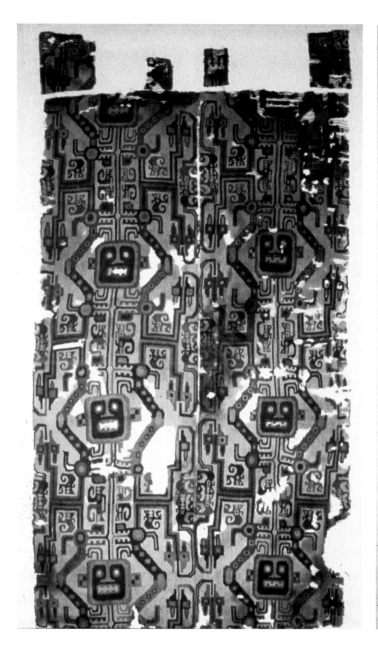

Fig. 8.32
Peruvian archaeo-
logical textile panel,
probably Recuay
style, probably
400 B.C.–500 A.D.
Collected by Lionel

Pries; now in Carl
Rietz Food Tech-
nology Collection,
California Acad-
emy of Sciences,
CAS 389–2368.

Fig. 8.33
Peruvian archaeo-
logical textile panel,
probably north
to central coast,
probably 900 A.D.–
1534 A.D. Collected

by Lionel Pries;
now in Carl Rietz
Food Technology
Collection, Cali-
fornia Academy
of Sciences, CAS
389–2363.

also on a lotus stand, and together this sculpture and its stand measured about 35 inches in height. According to Richard Mellott, former curator at the Asian Art Museum of San Francisco, this Bodhisattva is a notable work likely dating to the fifteenth century[101] (fig. 8.34). In 1956, Pries made one of his most important acquisitions—a pair of six-panel screens, *Bamboo Grove in Spring and Autumn*. Oceanic dated these screens to 1650 C.E. (they are now thought to be older) and credited them (although they are unsigned) to "Sanraku Kano"[102] (fig. 8.35). Pries displayed one of the screens in his living room; in 1964, he sold the other to his friend Duane Shipman. Both screens are now in the collection of the Seattle Art Museum.[103]

Pries collected things that he liked. He was primarily interested in their visual character, not in their art historical significance (although he did sometimes try to find more information about an object once he had acquired it). Nevertheless, he made good choices across a wide variety of cultures, not an easy thing to do.[104] Richard Mellott noted that the objects Pries collected, while not always the very best of their kind, were almost always "pure, straightforward, and beautiful."[105]

Robert Winskill was a beginning collector when he met Pries, in 1949. Soon after their meeting, Winskill had the chance to purchase some Chinese jade pieces. He told Pries that he could not take his eyes off them. Pries responded that this was "just as it should be," adding, "When I buy something, I sleep with it"—meaning, of course, that he, too, was completely enthralled whenever he made a new acquisition.[106]

GRAPHICS

Pries's engagement with the decorative arts is nowhere better demonstrated than in his fascination with fine lettering and its use in books, cards, bookplates, and the like. Pries had a small collection of late-medieval illuminated manuscript pages and several examples of eighteenth-century indentures as well as books about lettering, printing, and book design.[107] His interests, however, extended beyond collecting and appreciation; throughout his life he designed bookplates, Christmas cards, and occasionally announcements or invitations.

Pries was always interested in bookplates, the personal labels found in the fronts of books to indi-

Fig. 8.34 Kannon, attendant to the Buddha, on lotus stand; wood sculpture with gold paint. 35 inches tall. Collection of Robert Winskill. Photo by Kaz Tsuruta, 2005.

Fig. 8.35
Bamboo Grove in Spring and Autumn, 16th century (Muromachi period), one of a pair of six-panel screens; ink, color, and gold on paper, 68½ x 149 inches. Seattle Art Museum, gift of Duane Shipman, 91.235.2. Photo by Susan Cole.

Fig. 8.36
Lionel H. Pries, personal bookplate, ca. 1914–20; 3 x 2¼ inches. Pries collection, University of Washington Libraries, Special Collections Division

cate ownership. A bookplate typically includes a small image, the name of the owner, and sometimes the words "ex libris" or "from the library of." Pries designed his first bookplate in California for his own use, either in high school or in college; it shows two robed female figures sitting in front of a classical exedra in a garden[108] (fig. 8.36). After he moved to Philadelphia, he did not use a printed bookplate; instead, he signed and dated most of his books.

Beginning in the 1920s, Pries made original drawings or watercolors inside some of his books. More than twenty of these illustrations have been found; the earliest with a date was drawn in January 1928, and the latest is from 1939.[109] These images are often related to the content of the book. Opposite the title page of Eberlein's *Villas of Florence and Tuscany* Pries watercolored an unidentified (probably imaginary) villa[110] (fig. 8.37). In Mack and Gibson's *Architectural Details of Northern and Central Spain*, he drew a precisely detailed cathedral interior[111] (fig. 8.38). And, as already mentioned, the source for his first drypoint was a scene that he had drawn in a book about Venice[112] (refer to fig. 8.27). A book on Chinese architecture inspired a two-page watercolor of an imagined Chinese building.[113] And a book on German architecture includes Pries's perspective of the addition to the Krueger residence, the Bain and Pries project of 1930.[114]

Fig. 8.37
Lionel H. Pries,
unknown and
possibly imaginary
villa; watercolor,
10¾ x 7½ inches,
on flyleaf of
H. D. Eberlein,
*Villas of Florence
and Tuscany*. Pries
collection, University of Washington
Libraries, Special
Collections Division, UW23879z.

Fig. 8.38 (opposite) Lionel H. Pries, unknown and possibly imaginary cathedral interior; colored pencil drawing, 13½ x 10 inches, on flyleaf of G. Mack and T. Gibson, *Archi-* *tectural Details of Northern and Central Spain.* Pries collection, University of Washington Libraries, Special Collections Division, UW23876z.

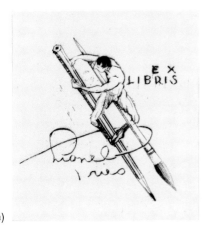

(a)

(b)

(c)

(d)

Fig. 8.39
Lionel H. Pries, personal book-plates, ca. 1935–55;

(a) 2¹/₈ x 2 inches;
(b) 2½ x 2¼ inches;
(c) 2¼ x 3 inches;
(d) 3 x 2⁵/₈ inches.

Pries collection, University of Washington Libraries, Special Collections Division.

Pries's interest in printed bookplates revived in the 1930s.[115] He created several new personal book-plates; four of them he used in parallel over the next two decades. The bookplates are autobiographical; each represents a Pries interest[116] (fig. 8.39). The first shows a small male figure with two large water-color brushes; it was used in books about art and artists.[117] The second, showing a pre-Columbian artifact, is found primarily in books on indigenous art and archaeology. The third shows a reclining fig-ure, apparently an angel; Pries used this plate most often in books on Gothic architecture, religious art, and similar subjects. The last, showing a classical structure with a stairway, was likely intended for architecture books.[118] Pries created his last personal bookplate about 1946; it shows an Asian figure, likely an attendant of the Buddha[119] (fig. 8.40). This, too,

Fig. 8.40
Lionel H. Pries, personal book-plate, ca. 1950–68; 1¾ x 1⁵/₈ inches.

Pries collection, University of Washington Libraries, Special Collections Division.

can be read autobiographically, as it clearly reflects
Pries's growing interest in collecting Asian art; he
used this plate exclusively after the mid-1950s.

Pries also created cards and other graphic works
throughout his life.[120] His 1923 Christmas card
shows a sophisticated use of lettering as well as a
self-portrait as Santa (fig. 8.41). His card for Christmas 1941 is both figural and Modern (fig. 8.42).
His Christmas card of a decade later shows the
entry to his Laurelhurst residence (fig. 8.43). Pries
occasionally designed for others; examples of these
works include an invitation for an AIA event, drawn
in 1930, and a bookplate he created for Blanche
Payne in 1944[121] (figs. 8.44, 8.45).

Fig. 8.42
Lionel H. Pries,
Christmas card,
1941, 5½ x 4½
inches; copy
glued inside
S. B. Tannehill,
*P's and Q's: A Book
on the Art of Letter
Arrangement.* Pries
collection, University of Washington
Libraries, Special
Collections
Division.

Fig. 8.43
Lionel H. Pries,
Christmas card,
1951, 4¼ x 5⅜
inches; copy
glued inside
S. B. Tannehill,
*P's and Q's: A Book
on the Art of Letter
Arrangement.* Pries
collection, University of Washington
Libraries, Special
Collections
Division.

Fig. 8.44
Lionel H. Pries,
invitation to Wash-
ington State AIA
Annual Dinner,
1930, 5 x 7 inches;
copy glued inside
S. B. Tannehill,
*P's and Q's: A Book
on the Art of Letter
Arrangement.* Pries
collection, Univer-
sity of Washington
Libraries, Special
Collections
Division.

Fig. 8.45
Lionel H. Pries,
personal book-
plate for Blanche
Payne, 1944, 2¾ x
2½ inches. Pries
collection, Univer-
sity of Washington
Libraries, Special
Collections Divi-
sion.

Art and Everyday Life

Pries's artistic interests permeated his life. The environment that Pries created in his home was more an echo of Gump's than of his own childhood residence. His books filled the shelves, objects from his collections were displayed or available, and on a print stand he often placed one of his own paintings, changing it every few weeks. There were other objects of Pries's design, such as light fixtures (figs. 8.46, 8.47). Kolb recalled that students who boarded with Pries felt privileged to share what Pries offered, but Kolb also acknowledged that none of them fully realized how extraordinary the home was; all these things were simply part of the world that Pries had created.[122]

Pries's home and collections seemed remarkable to those seeing them for the first time, but only those who had known Pries longer began to realize how deeply sensitive he was to forms, textures, colors, spaces, and the order of things. Kolb recalled accompanying Pries on a visit to a home in Seattle's Capitol Hill neighborhood; when their hostess left the room, Pries rearranged the furniture and reorganized objects on the mantel and the coffee table. It was a better composition, but their hostess was quite upset. Kolb recalled that Pries simply could not help himself—"he just did that instinctively."[123] When Pries had to go to the hospital, in the late 1940s, he brought his own paintings to hang on the walls.[124]

When Pries designed his own house, in 1947–48, he created a seamless environment for his collections. But because the new house had only a single guest room, he no longer took student boarders. Students of the postwar period knew Pries's collections from their occasional visits, but, since Pries had largely given up painting by 1950, few if any knew of Pries's early career as an artist. For Pries, however, fine design was always present as an element of a well-lived life.

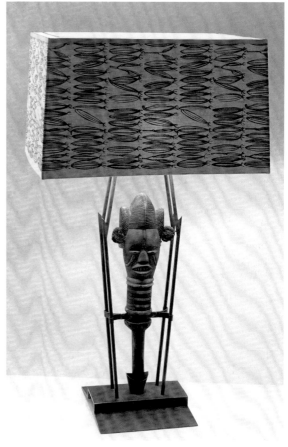

Fig. 8.46 Lionel H. Pries, light fixture (present location unknown). Photo by Charles Pearson. Pries collection, University of Washington Libraries, Special Collections Division, UW 23793z.

Fig. 8.47 Lionel H. Pries, light fixture (present location unknown). Photo by Charles Pearson. Pries collection, University of Washington Libraries, Special Collections Division, UW23794z.

9

IN PRACTICE

ROMANTIC MODERNISM, 1945–1958

AFTER 1945, PRIES ENTERED ONE OF THE MOST productive phases of his professional career. His work drew from his experiences in Mexico, from evolving directions in West Coast architecture, and even from International Style Modernism, but he offered a vision radically different from the dominant tendencies of the postwar years.

Even before the war ended, tendencies that had previously competed with Modernism—Art Deco/ Moderne and a lingering abstract version of classicism—had been completely eclipsed. Mies van der Rohe and Walter Gropius, who had emigrated to the United States from Germany in the late 1930s, emerged as icons of Modernist architectural practice and education and were celebrated as cultural heroes. Although widespread destruction led those in Europe to question the appropriate role of technology, in the United States the postwar period was one of unquestioned technological optimism. Americans understood that their technological prowess had made victory possible. The long years of Depression and war were over; all that was needed was to turn industrial production from war materiel to consumer goods.[1] As early as 1942, American architectural journals began to focus on preparations for the postwar era, trumpeting the design opportunities created by technologies whose development had been accelerated by war.[2] The advertising in professional journals was explicit in this regard, focusing on the war industries that would soon produce new materials for building. The emphasis was not just on technology for its own sake; it was also on the application, through Modern design, of new technologies to everyday life.[3] The new direction was reflected in the West Coast periodical *Arts & Architecture*, which championed residential design featuring new products and technology. The magazine's postwar "Case Study" house program provided multiple examples of suburban houses demonstrating the promise of industrial technology; the early houses showed varying approaches, but modular construction, prefabrication, and skeletal steel-and-glass design had become the focus of the program by the early 1950s.[4]

These directions were not for Pries. He had been shaped too strongly by the culture of the Arts and Crafts movement and the idea of architecture as a fine art. Like American Arts and Crafts architects of an earlier generation, Pries accepted the machine, but only if it remained subservient to human purposes. Pries readily worked with the products of industrial technology—concrete block, steel windows, and the like—but in his projects, technology was always a means, never an end in itself. Similarly, Pries accepted Modernism but rejected the "universalizing" tendencies inherent in the International Style—each of his projects was specifically shaped to its site and to the needs of his clients. Pries never lost his belief that a building should be a place for art; his designs almost always provided a setting for artistic embellishment. Pries sometimes even worked with his clients to fabricate artistic elements specific to their projects. Thus Pries's postwar work demonstrates a vision of a romantic Modernism that was markedly different from the vision of almost all his contemporaries.

PRIES DESIGNS TO 1949

Pries had the opportunity to design a large movie theater in 1945, but the project never went beyond the drafting board. Lloyd Lovegren recalled how this project came about:

> Shortly after V.E. day . . . Benny Priteca [the Seattle architect B. Marcus Priteca] received a commission from the foremost theatre chain in L.A. to come up with a brand new concept of a super Wilshire Blvd. movie theatre to celebrate the end of the long war. Benny stated that his own theatres were now becoming "old hat" and that he had selected Pries to breath new life into long neglected theatre design. Once more I had the privilege of producing a set of presentation drawings with daily crits from Spike Pries. Altho the design was enthusiastically received by the owners in L.A., it did not survive the long drawn out construction curtailment that followed.[5]

After the war, the priority system that controlled the availability of construction materials was only gradually relaxed—this is the "construction curtailment" to which Lovegren referred. Lovegren added that this may have been for the best, "since the 'big movie theatre' was beginning to become obsolete." Still, it is regrettable that Pries never had the opportunity to do a large theater, as such a project might have led to other large commissions-and we are left to imagine how he would have responded to the opportunity to create a romantic, atmospheric, and Modern interior.

Pries's postwar career focused instead on residential projects. The single-family residences that Pries designed beginning in 1946 were clearly Modern, yet they defy easy stylistic classification. The first three of these designs were one-story houses of irregular shape: the Lea residence, on Lopez Island; the Morris residence, in Seattle's Laurelhurst neighborhood; and the Barksdale residence, on Lake Washington, northeast of Seattle.

In the late 1930s, Pries had become friends with Richard Lea Jr., who owned Craftsman Press, a printing company.[6] In 1944, Lea married Ruth ("Sis") Vance.[7] Richard and Ruth Lea became more than clients. Julie Ivarsson, Ruth Lea's daughter by her first marriage, described her parents as "Pries's students" and added, "They just worshiped him." The admiration was mutual; of Richard Lea Jr., Pries later said that he had "exquisite taste."[8]

The Leas had acquired a spectacular site—a large parcel on the south shore of Lopez Island, in the San Juan Island group-where they wished to build a weekend house.[9] With Pries they explored the property, finally siting the house on a rocky promontory facing Davis Bay. Although there were difficulties in obtaining materials, the Leas proceeded with the project in the spring of 1946, and construction was largely complete later that year. In a November letter, Pries described the Lea residence as a "lodge," probably referring to its informal character and its intended use for weekends and vacations.[10]

For the Leas, Pries designed a long, low, one-story residence that serves as a threshold near the water's edge (fig. 9.1). The plan of the house is a shallow, asymmetrical V (fig. 9.2). From the road, the drive passes through a densely wooded area and then arrives at a grassy forecourt to the house. The focus is the entrance, the only element that breaks the horizontal line of the eaves. The entry hall leads to the living-dining room and then to the outside terrace, with stunning views to the water and, across the Strait of Juan de Fuca, to the snow-capped peaks of the Olympic Mountains (fig. 9.3).

Pries's interest in the use of ordinary materials is evident in the walls of concrete block in a running bond; the block was clear-finished on the outside but painted in the interior. The most unusual feature of the Lea residence was the sod roof. *Architectural Record* reported that the roof "never needs trimming since salt spray breaking over it stunts the native grasses and Japanese Iris with which it

Fig. 9.1
Lionel H. Pries,
Richard and Ruth
Lea weekend

residence, Lopez
Island, 1946–47
(altered). Photo
by author, 2002.

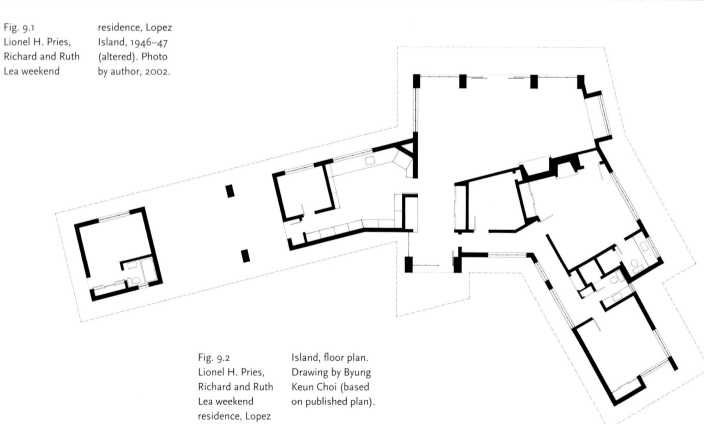

Fig. 9.2
Lionel H. Pries,
Richard and Ruth
Lea weekend
residence, Lopez

Island, floor plan.
Drawing by Byung
Keun Choi (based
on published plan).

Fig. 9.3
Lionel H. Pries,
Richard and Ruth
Lea weekend
residence, Lopez
Island. Photo by
Charles Pearson.
Pries collection,
University of
Washington
Libraries, Special
Collections Divi-
sion, UW18792.

is planted."[11] The continuous horizontal line of
the eaves of the shallow roof weds the house to the
ground and is interrupted only by the canted roof at
the entrance. The importance that Pries placed on
this horizontal line is evident in his extension of the
gutters well beyond the roof, at opposite ends of the
house (fig. 9.4).

The Leas' Lopez Island residence was simply
detailed and furnished to create an atmosphere
appropriate to the informality of a weekend retreat
(figs. 9.5, 9.6). The floor is brown concrete. The
clear-lacquered cedar planks of the ceiling align
with each side of the roughly trapezoidal living-
dining space; their joints match exactly at the center
of the room. Although small, the house has the
feeling of a larger structure.[12] Pries designed most

of the furniture, including a marble dining room
table, built-in benches, and a large sofa and chair.[13]
Pieces of driftwood provided visual accents.[14] A
Native American motif was painted on the under-
side of the entry roof; there was a copper thunderbird sculpture on the chimney.

The Lea residence was the first of Pries's houses
whose plan was composed on Modern, not traditional, principles. This house began an exploration
of complex geometries created by diagonal intersect-
ing walls and volumes, an exploration that Pries
would pursue in many of his succeeding designs.

The Lopez Island house was featured in *Architectural Record* in April 1952, and it was included in the
book *82 Distinctive Houses from Architectural Record*,
published later that year. It fit easily within the

Fig. 9.4
Lionel H. Pries,
Richard and Ruth
Lea weekend
residence, Lopez
Island. To the left

is the residence
by Pries; to the
right is an indoor
swimming pool
designed by
another architect.

Visual Resources
Collection, College
of Architecture &
Urban Planning,
University of
Washington.

Fig. 9.5
Lionel H. Pries,
Richard and Ruth
Lea weekend
residence, Lopez
Island, entrance
hall. Photo by

Charles Pearson.
Pries collection,
University of
Washington
Libraries, Special
Collections Divi-
sion, UW18794.

Fig. 9.6
Lionel H. Pries,
Richard and Ruth
Lea weekend
residence, Lopez
Island, living
room. Photo by

Charles Pearson.
Pries collection,
University of
Washington
Libraries, Special
Collections Divi-
sion, UW18796.

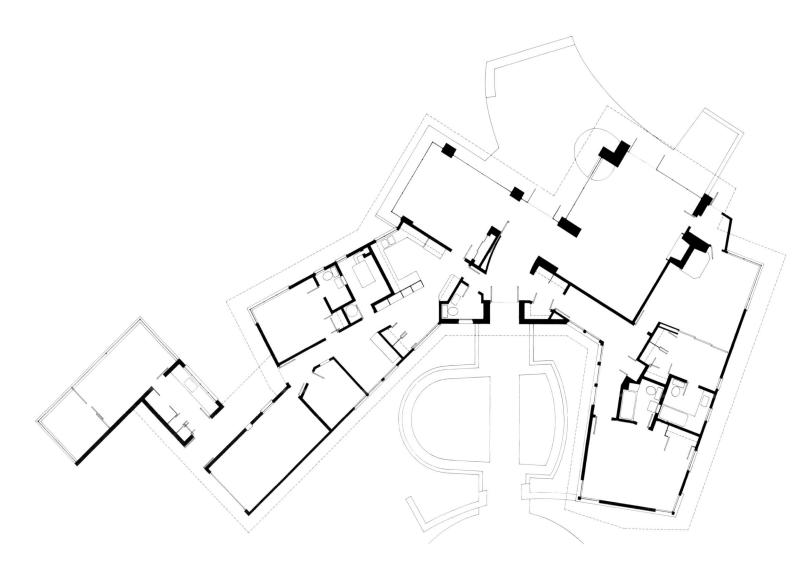

context of other work then being published. *Architectural Record* never mentioned that the Lea residence was nearly six years old.[15] Therefore, readers did not realize how truly prescient the house was: its horizontality, spatially complex composition, and concrete block walls, progressive features in 1946, were not particularly unusual by 1952. Still, the Lopez Island residence stood somewhat apart from the major trends of its time, and it remains a notable project even today. The development of Modern architecture in America in the years after 1945 has sometimes been characterized as a conflict between an orthodox International Style approach in the East and a regionalized Modernism in the West.[16] Pries's design for the Leas fit neither of the dominant paradigms, although it can be considered a precursor of the regional Modernism that was beginning to develop in the Northwest at the time.

The Julia Flett (Mrs. Arthur S.) Morris residence, Seattle (1947–48), is similar in its planning and horizontal form to the Lea residence.[17] Morris's site was extraordinary—a large irregular parcel at the end of

a ridge, at the center of the Laurelhurst peninsula, that offers views to Lake Washington and, in the distance, to Mount Rainier. Morris wanted a small house, but one that took full advantage of the topography. Pries was perfectly matched to the project. He completed the drawings in the fall of 1947; the city issued the permit at the end of December, and the house was finished the following summer.[18]

The Morris residence is a one-story structure of just over 2,700 square feet, with an irregular U-shaped plan (fig. 9.7). A landscaped entry court, inside the U, is separated from the street by a low wall. An unusual aspect of the design, and one that brought constant comment, is the outward curve of the stone gateposts—a detail said to derive from Japanese architecture. The walls facing the entry court have few windows, and most have ribbed glass for privacy. The low wall of the courtyard and the relatively solid north wall of the house emphasize the experience of the building as a series of layers (fig. 9.8). As at the Leas' Lopez Island residence, the Morris residence opens on the opposite side to

Fig. 9.7
Lionel H. Pries, Julia Flett (Mrs. Arthur S.) Morris residence, Seattle, 1947–48 (altered), floor plan. Drawing by Byung Keun Choi (based on blueline print held by owner).

Fig. 9.8
Lionel H. Pries,
Julia Morris
residence, from
above. Photo by
author, 2005.

extraordinary views through floor-to-ceiling glass (fig. 9.9). Although the living and dining rooms are rectangular, these rooms are embedded within an irregular perimeter to create the most geometrically complex plan of Pries's career. This complexity is controlled, however, by simplicity in the third dimension, as the spaces are contained between the horizontals of the floor and the low eaves of the shallow roof.

The primary exterior materials are stone laid up in random ashlar and wood siding. In the living and dining rooms, the walls between the masonry piers are smooth, finished wood; oak veneer was originally called for, but Japanese sen wood was actually used. This provided a background for the display of Julia Morris's collection of early American antiques, Japanese screens, and other artworks.[19] The floor is terrazzo. The windows in the major rooms are covered with sliding Japanese shoji (paper screens on light wood frames), to control light and heat. Detailing provides a strong sense of indoor-outdoor continuity (fig. 9.10).

Pries designed a rug, featuring motifs drawn from Greek mythology, for the entrance hall. Julia Morris, who had experience in weaving, made this rug herself over the next several years; it was completed by early 1951.[20] This collaboration established a pattern that Pries followed with several other residential clients: he designed artistic embellishment that his clients often could fabricate themselves, thereby making the residence truly their own—clear evidence of the continuing influence of Arts and Crafts ideals in Pries's career.

The Morris residence was never published, but it was noticed by the Seattle architectural community. In 1978, Charles Schiff, a Seattle architect, recalled, "Besides his own house, he designed a house for Mrs. Morse [sic] on a promontory nearby which again created a sensation. It is still a very, very handsome house, though built some 25 years ago."[21]

The third house in this group was for Julian and Marajane Barksdale, who wished to expand their small cottage in northeast Seattle, not far from Lake Washington. During the war, Julian Barksdale, a

Fig. 9.9
Lionel H. Pries,
Julia Morris
residence,

south elevation.
Photo by Grant
Hildebrand, 2002.

Fig. 9.10
Lionel H. Pries,
Julia Morris
residence, living

room. Photo by
Grant Hildebrand,
2002.

University of Washington geology professor, served in the Navy with A. Quincy Jones, who recommended Pries for the project. The Barksdales approached him in 1948, Pries became a family friend whom the Barksdales' son, Tucker, remembers calling "Uncle Spike."[22] Although the project was an addition, the older building was totally subsumed within the new house. As at the Lea and Morris residences, Pries designed a spreading one-story building (here with a daylit basement), relatively closed at the front and open to the back. The materials were concrete block and wood (fig. 9.11). The existing cottage dictated that the fundamental geometry of the Barksdale residence would be rectangular, but Pries inserted a diagonal hall, leading from the entrance to the living-dining area, and a zigzag window-wall opening to the east and northeast to views of the lake (fig. 9.12, 9.13). The interiors, finished in richly grained Phillippine mahogany, are particularly striking (fig. 9.14).[23]

Pries's unbuilt design for the Delta Sigma Phi fraternity house likely dates from these years as well[24] (fig. 9.15). The one surviving perspective shows an asymmetrically composed building of brick and stone, articulated by horizontal bands and small areas of carved or cast detail. The steel casement windows are similar to those that were commonly used in Seattle in postwar multifamily residential projects. But by 1947–48, the University of Washington chapter of the fraternity had moved into an existing house, and Pries's project never went forward.

The culminating project of the late 1940s is the house that Pries designed for himself. In 1944, he had renewed the lease on his house on Fifteenth Avenue for three more years, but he anticipated that he would not get another extension.[25] Within a year, Pries had acquired a lot in Laurelhurst and was designing a house for himself. In October 1947, he went ahead with construction[26] (fig. 9.16).

The lot for Pries's house is rectangular, with the west end cut diagonally by the curve of West Laurelhurst Drive.[27] The east (back) half of the lot is about 18 feet above the street. Pries's solution was to place the primary spaces—living, dining, kitchen—on the top floor, opening to a private garden; his bed-

Fig. 9.12
Lionel H. Pries,
Julian and Mara-
jane Barksdale
residence, west
elevation. Photo
by Frank L. Jenkins,
Vista Estate Imag-
ing, 2006.

Fig. 9.13
Lionel H. Pries,
Julian and Mara-
jane Barksdale
residence, floor
plan. Drawing
by Byung Keun
Choi (based on
blueprint held by
owner). In 1954–
55, a bedroom

and office suite,
designed by Pries,
were added in the
location of the
terrace adjacent
to the living room
after a house was
constructed on
the adjacent lot
blocking the view.

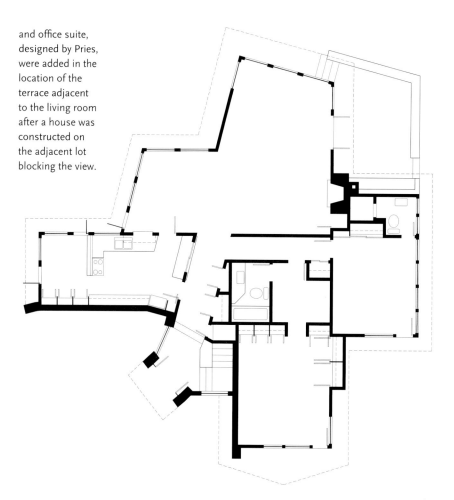

Fig. 9.14
Lionel H. Pries,
Julian and Mara-
jane Barksdale
residence, dining
room and living
room. Photo by
Frank L. Jenkins,
Vista Estate
Imaging, 2006.

Fig. 9.15
Lionel H. Pries,
Delta Sigma Phi
Fraternity House
project, Seattle,
ca. 1946–47
(unbuilt); pencil,
watercolor on

illustration board,
15¾ x 22½ inches.
Pries collection,
University of
Washington
Libraries, Special
Collections Divi-
sion, UW23900z.

room and the guest room are located midlevel on the ground floor. The street-level garage, topped by a wood frame supporting a luxurious growth of wisteria, was pushed into the northwest corner of the site.[28]

The front door is reached via an exterior stair perpendicular to the curve of the street. The small foyer leads in turn to the stair to the main floor. At the top of this stair (which turns to the right), the living room and dining room are to the right, and the yard and garden are to the left. The dining room is an extension of the living room, but the two can be separated by large sliding panels. The west section of the house parallels the sides of the lot, but the east turns at an angle of 20 degrees, an angle that made it possible for Pries to tuck the kitchen and service areas to the north of the primary living areas (fig. 9.18).

The materials of the garage and the ground floor are concrete and concrete block (figs. 9.17, 9.19). The upper floor is wood frame, originally sheathed

in sheets of cement-asbestos board, although concrete block extends up in some places to support the roof cantilevers. The structural capacity of the concrete block allowed Pries to cantilever the upper floor over the lower—the top floor extends 3 feet to the west, sheltering the exterior entrance area; the balcony at the southwest corner of the dining room cantilevers 2½ feet farther. The "butterfly" roof slopes up both to the east and to the west and cantilevers 3 feet to the south, 4 feet to the west, and 7 feet toward the garden. The 8-inch roof rafters taper to only $3^{5}/_{8}$ inches at the end of these cantilevers, emphasizing the lightness and thinness of the roof. These features alone would have made the house a spatial and structural tour de force, well integrated with its site, but they only provided the setting for Pries's incorporation of a variety of artistic elements.

In his own home, Pries finally realized a mix of Modern architecture and fine Arts and Crafts objects that synthesized his lifetime of learning and experience. On the garage door, Pries painted the house

Fig. 9.16
Lionel H. Pries,
Lionel Pries
residence, Seattle,
1945–48 (altered);
watercolor, 8½ x 13
inches. Courtesy
of Jeffrey and Sally
Fiorini.

Fig. 9.17
Lionel H. Pries,
Lionel Pries resi-
dence, view from
street. Photo by
Charles Pearson.
Pries collection,
University of
Washington
Libraries, Special
Collections Divi-
sion, UW18413.

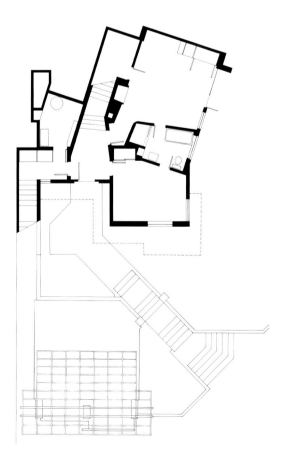

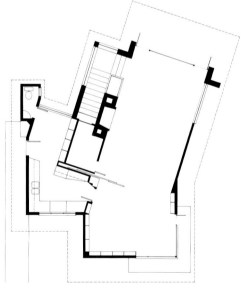

Fig. 9.18
Lionel H. Pries,
Lionel Pries
residence, floor
plans. Drawings
by Byung Keun
Choi (based on
construction

drawings in the
Pries collection,
University of
Washington
Libraries, Special
Collections
Division).

Fig. 9.21
Lionel H. Pries,
Lionel Pries resi-
dence, front door.
Photo by Robert
Mosher.

number and a design based on Northwest Native American motifs (fig. 9.20). He painted similar designs on the wall adjacent to the front entry. The front door and its frame were fabricated from a traditional wood bedstead, originally from Bali[29] (fig. 9.21). The door and decorative features were set against and contrasted with the concrete block walls of the house—a reminder of Pries's willingness to use Modern materials, left unfinished, to create a setting for finely detailed art elements. The roof cantilever facing the garden features a painting by Pries that was based on Northwest Native American traditions (fig. 9.22).

Inside, the house offers a rich mix of colors and textures (figs. 9.24, 9.25). The floors are terrazzo—yellow-ochre for the entry and stair, rose for the main floor. Woodwork throughout is red birch. The ceiling of the living room is surfaced in cork and was originally embellished with Navajo sand paint-ings.[30] At the top of the stairs, a built-in glass case provided display space for some of Pries's small pre-Columbian figures and other objects (fig. 9.23). Japanese stirrups were reused as fireplace andirons. Many of the windows were covered with shoji.

Not all the elements were from indigenous or non-Western cultures. Pries displayed a historical

Fig. 9.22
Lionel H. Pries,
Lionel Pries
residence, roof
cantilever at living
room/garden.
Photo by Charles
Pearson. Pries col-
lection, University
of Washington
Libraries, Special
Collections Divi-
sion, UW18412.

map of Rome in the foyer. The sliding panels that divided the living and dining rooms were faced on one side with a perspective map of Paris. The walls of the dining room were built-in bookcases; Pries inscribed the frieze with a quote from John Ruskin's *Stones of Venice*: "We require of buildings as from men two kinds of goodness: First the doing of prac-

tical duty well and then that they be graceful and pleasant which last is in itself another form of duty."[31] In the center of this room was an expandable dining room table that Pries had brought from his house on Fifteenth Avenue. He decorated the top surface with a floral pattern (in India ink), designed to match no matter how many of the table leaves are

Fig. 9.23
Lionel H. Pries,
Lionel Pries
residence, glass
case at top of
stairs. Photo by
Charles Pearson.
Pries collection,
University
of Washington
Libraries, Special
Collections Divi-
sion, UW23802z.

in place. On the center leaf Pries inscribed a quote from Ruskin's *Modern Painters*: "That virtue of originality that men so strain after is not newness, as they vainly think, it is only genuineness; it all depends on getting to the spring of things and working out from it"[32] (fig. 9.26).

The door to the kitchen is concealed in the dining room bookcases. Pries had encountered a description of a hidden door in *Miss Mapp*, the third volume in the English novelist E. F. Benson's *Make Way for Lucia* series: "There was another cupboard, the best and biggest of all and the most secret and the most discreet. It lay embedded in the wall of the garden room, cloaked and concealed behind the shelves of a false bookcase, which contained no more than the simulacra of books."[33] Pries faced his kitchen (swing) door with wood strips in the pattern of shelves and with the spines of old books, to mimic the built-in

Fig. 9.24
Lionel H. Pries,
Lionel Pries resi-
dence, entry and
stair. Pries collec-
tion, University
of Washington
Libraries, Special
Collections Divi-
sion, UW23796z.

Fig. 9.25
Lionel H. Pries,
Lionel Pries resi-
dence, view of
living room and
dining room. Pries

collection, Univer-
sity of Washington
Libraries, Special
Collections Divi-
sion, UW23795z.

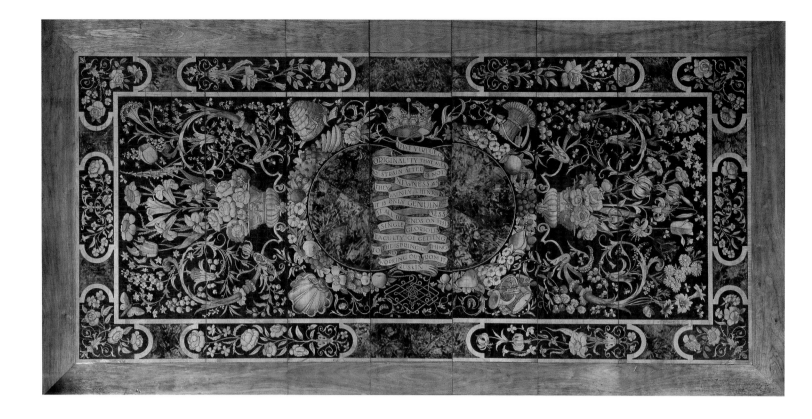

bookcases. Guests often did not initially realize that they were seeing a hidden door. Ed Duthweiler recalled the pleasure Pries took in this feature:

> When he was showing people through the house, he would often come to the dining room and point out something interesting, like the hand-drawn patterns on the dining room table, which he had done himself, and before people could realize it, he had disappeared—he was not in the room; it was one of his little tricks. . . . After a few moments, he would reappear just as suddenly as he had disappeared, and people were just amazed, and he was just delighted.[34]

Everywhere one looked in Pries's house there were new surprises—for example, the carved frogs as door handles on the kitchen cabinets, or the designs Pries painted on the insides of the doors of his record cabinet. The mix was extraordinary; each piece was determined on the basis of its visual and formal characteristics and by the effect of each element in combination with the others.

By keeping the house relatively compact, Pries left space for a series of gardens. The slope at the front of the lot was lushly planted. The bedrooms on the mid level open onto a garden with an existing madrona; the living room opens to a patio

and a lawn, with perimeter garden areas at the back and sides of the lot.[35] Patio furniture includes an irregular concrete table with a mosaic tile top that Pries made himself. From the house on Fifteenth Avenue, Pries brought the figure of Lao-Tse, now placed in the garden. The development of the gardens drew Pries's attention over the rest of his life (fig. 9.27).

The distance between Pries and many other American architects of the period is nowhere more evident than in this house.[36] The Pries residence is almost an exact contemporary of Mies van der Rohe's Farnsworth House, in Plano, Illinois (1946–50). Pries's house is spatially complex, and it is richly and colorfully detailed. In contrast, the house designed by Mies for Dr. Edith Farnsworth is elegantly detailed, but its expressive potential rests in its minimalism, fully embodying Mies's aphorism "Less is more." The Farnsworth House—puritanically austere, with an emphasis on refinement of the minimum elements of structure, transparency, and space—seems far from the formal complexity and layered richness of Pries's best work. The contrast between Pries's home and the austere technological Modernism of the period was also reflected in the reactions of different visitors. When the American Institute of Architects held its national convention in Seattle in 1953, Pries held a reception at his home

Fig. 9.26
Lionel H. Pries, Lionel Pries dining room table, 44½ x 89½ inches. Photo by Kaz Tsuruta, 2005. Collection of Robert Winskill.

for visiting faculty. Kolb recalled that Lawrence B. Anderson, a professor from MIT, "was quite uncomfortable in the lush interior of Spike's home."[37]

The works of the period that were closest in character to the Pries residence are found in Mexico. Buildings at the Ciudad Universitaria (University City), Mexico City (1950–52), are technologically Modern, but they often incorporate murals depicting Mexico's past and present. Best known is the Central Library, by Juan O'Gorman, Gustavo Savvedra, and Juan Martínez de Velasco, but this is only one of several structures with murals. Pries's interiors were echoed in Juan O'Gorman's own residence in El Pedregal, Mexico City (1951; destroyed), where mosaics portrayed pre-Columbian figures, even on the ceiling.[38] Although Pries's residence preceded

the work in Mexico, there is no evidence that Mexican architects were familiar with his design. Rather, the similarities reflect the parallel design thinking of those whose paths had crossed in Mexico in the 1930s.

Many students of the period remember Pries's house as a revelation. They discovered that it was possible to be Modern yet still embrace the arts. The mix of art and architecture captured the attention of the press. When the house appeared in *Town and Country*, in 1952, the headline read, "Early Art in a Contemporary Setting."[39] In 1955, when the Pries residence was included in the Seattle Art Museum's annual architecture tour, the Seattle *Post-Intelligencer* called it "An Artist-Architect's Dream Home."[40]

PRIES DESIGNS IN THE 1950S

Although his pace slowed after he moved into his own house, Pries continued to produce notable projects. Pries never rented outside architectural office space after he split with Bain. He worked at home, on a drafting table set up in his bedroom. He almost always had a project under way; some were realized, and some were not.[41] Pries did not believe in fully detailing a project before it was bid; rather, he would do a set of drawings sufficient to obtain bids and a permit, with the idea that additional details could be supplied as the project went through construction. Kolb recalled, "He knew if the project went ahead, he would make adjustments as it went along. He would always rely on the shop drawings to control all the trades."[42] Pries told Kolb that completely detailed sets of drawings "scared" contractors, and bids would be too high. Thus most Pries projects were constructed from a relatively small number of drawings. Pries's attitudes had been shaped by his background; his belief that the architect and the contractor could work together to craft the project reflects the mind-set of the Arts and Crafts.

Pries occasionally accepted commissions that drew on his skills in the arts. He was responsible for interior features of the Legend Room Restaurant (1950–51; destroyed), at the new Northgate Shopping Center[43] (fig. 9.28). From the earliest plan diagram, Northgate had always included a restaurant for fine dining. The restaurant had initially been called the Haida Room, and Northgate's architects, John Graham and Company, commissioned Pries to carry out this theme.[44] Pries developed the murals on the walls and the ceiling, recommended the colors for the fabrics, and may have consulted on fixtures and furnishings. Although it was a small commission, the Legend Room was one of the few Pries projects that would be seen by the general public. The project also gave Pries a link to the Graham firm—a connection that would prove important a decade later.

Pries did a similar artistic project at the Ginkgo Petrified Forest Museum (now Interpretive Center) on the Columbia River, at Vantage, Washington (1952–53; altered). The architect, Carver ("Charlie") Baker, was a former Pries student and 1947 University of Washington graduate who had gone to work

Fig. 9.28
Lionel H. Pries, Legend Room Restaurant interiors, 1950–51 (destroyed), Northgate Shopping Center, Seattle. Photo courtesy of DLR Group.

Fig. 9.29
Lionel H. Pries, decorative treatment at Ginkgo Petrified Forest Museum (now Interpretive Center), Vantage, Washington, 1952–53 (altered). Pries collection, University of Washington Libraries, Special Collections Division, UW23502z.

Fig. 9.30
Lionel H. Pries, Stephen and Harriette Lea residence, Whidbey Island, Washington, 1949–50, 1951 (altered). Photo courtesy of Stephen Lea Jr. and Judee Lea.

for the Washington State Parks Department. He turned to Pries for decorative features for the front entrance, and possibly in the interior of the museum. Because the state park included not only the petrified trees but also rocks with prehistoric Native American line drawings (or petroglyphs), Pries used these petroglyphs as the basis for his design[45] (fig. 9.29).

Pries took on two smaller residential projects in the early 1950s. The first was the addition and remodeling to the Stephen and Harriette Lea (weekend) residence on Whidbey Island (1949–50, 1951; altered).[46] The Leas acquired the property after the war, and as their family began to grow, they found the two existing cabins on the property increasingly cramped. In 1949, they turned to Pries for a solution. Pries fit an addition, including a new living room, a kitchen, and a utility room (not completed until 1951), between the existing cabins, which were remodeled as bedrooms. The new living room, the heart of the design, measures roughly 25 feet square. The primary structural elements are the masonry piers and the fireplace, constructed of boulders gathered from the site (fig. 9.30). Most of the walls are glazed, providing views to the entry

courtyard and farm and to Admiralty Inlet, the Olympic Peninsula, and the Olympic Mountains. Driftwood logs were used as columns for the passage linking to one of the cabins. The most dramatic features, first seen across the open farm field, are the single-sloped roof and the tall chimney[47] (fig. 9.31).

The second of these two projects, the Charles and Mildred Gates residence, Bellevue, Washington (1950–51; altered), was Pries's smallest design for a completely new house. It is located in the Hilltop, a planned community of single-family residences on large lots that preserved the natural landscape and existing views.[48] The first three houses in the Hilltop were built in 1950; the Gates residence was one of thirteen houses built in 1951.[49] Gates was a professor of history at the university; the family had a very limited budget and could afford only a simple design. Pries proposed a compact house, roughly 26 by 26 feet, with an attached carport; the sloped site allowed outdoor access from the basement and the first floor. The second floor, to have included a living room and deck, could not be afforded initially. (In 1958, the Gates family turned to Bassetti and Morse, who designed a living room that extended the first

floor, so Pries's concept for the house was never actually realized.[50])

At the Alonzo W. and Margaret I. Robertson residence, Bellevue (1955–56), Pries continued his exploration of diagonal geometry.[51] The Robertsons owned a large lot sloping down from Lake Washington Boulevard to Meydenbauer Bay. Pries sited the house on the lower part of the lot, about 55 feet from the water (figs. 9.32, 9.33). Most of the rooms are on a single level; only the recreation room and the guest suite are in a partial basement with direct outside access. The main floor is organized around a courtyard/patio with four bedrooms to the north and east, a garage, an office, a utility room and a kitchen to the south, and a living-dining area to the west (fig. 9.34). This arrangement offers privacy while also fostering indoor-outdoor living. The glazed walls of the living area make it possible to see from the courtyard to the water.

The Robertson courtyard/patio is angled 10 degrees relative to the exterior walls; the resolution of this geometry carries through almost every room of the house. In the living-dining area, the post-and-beam structure is exposed; this kind of expression

Fig. 9.31 Lionel H. Pries, Stephen and Harriette Lea residence. Photo courtesy of Stephen Lea Jr. and Judee Lea.

Fig. 9.32 (opposite, top) Lionel H. Pries, Alonzo and Margaret Robertson residence, Bellevue, 1955–56, view from water. Photo courtesy of Charles and Laurie Lyford.

Fig. 9.33 (opposite) Lionel H. Pries, Alonzo and Margaret Robertson residence, view from drive. Photo by author, 2005.

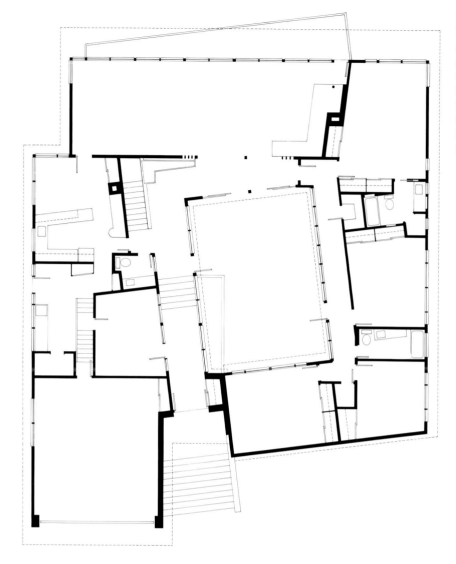

Fig. 9.34
Lionel H. Pries,
Alonzo and Margaret Robertson
residence, primary
floor plan. Drawing
by Byung Keun
Choi (based on
blueline print held
by owner).

was often used by Northwest architects of the period, but Pries added complexity because the structure is turned 10 degrees to the rectangular geometry of the walls. As at the Morris residence in Seattle, the primary materials are stone and wood siding; shoji are used to control light and heat at the glazed walls of the living-dining area (fig. 9.35).

By the time Richard and Ruth Lea commissioned their new Seattle residence, in 1957, Pries's collecting had shifted to the art of Japan. The change in Pries's personal focus was paralleled by national trends, as interest in Japanese art and architecture increased across the United States in the 1950s. The relevance of Japanese architecture to Modern design was suggested by a 1954 exhibit at the Museum of Modern Art, in New York, which included a reconstruction of a traditional Japanese house.[52] In 1960, *House Beautiful* would devote its August and September issues to *shibui*.[53] The popular periodical *Sunset* published occasional articles on how to adapt

Japanese architectural features to American residences.[54] Pries already had a wealth of knowledge about Japanese arts and crafts, so when the Leas turned to him, he drew on Japanese precedents but created a completely original design.[55]

The Leas acquired a large lot facing Lake Washington with a two-story L-shaped house of French (Norman) derivation, dating from the 1920s (fig. 9.36). Pries designed a complete makeover; the permit was approved in May 1957, and the new house was completed about ten months later.[56] Rather than work with the existing vocabulary, Pries designed a radical transformation so that no vestige of the original historical character remained (fig. 9.37). Pries completely reconceived the house as a seamless setting for a collection of Japanese art. Pries enlarged the existing house with a new one-story wing for service spaces (toward the street) and a new two-story wing for an enlarged living room on the first floor and a master suite on the second floor

Fig. 9.35
Lionel H. Pries,
Alonzo and Mar-
garet Robertson
residence, living
room. Photo by
Grant Hildebrand,
2002.

(toward the lake). The result was a roughly Z-shaped plan (fig. 9.38). Although the original had been stucco, the exterior material of the new house is burned cedar.[57]

The Richard and Ruth Lea residence (1957–58, destroyed) is a series of layers that include landscape as well as building. Pries created a space for a Japanese garden as an entry court (fig. 9.39). From the drive, one passes through a gate (which appears to be a door) to a porch formed by the extension of the service wing roof alongside the Japanese garden; at the end of this porch, the front door opens to the entry and stair hall. This hall serves as the circulation core of the house (fig. 9.40). The space was designed around a single figure sculpture that stood on a lacquered shelf that is part of the stair.

The room is paneled in wood, with dark wood bands recalling traditional Japanese framing.

The living space extends through the house from west to east. The west end of the living space looks back to the Japanese garden. This area was designed as a study with built-in bookshelves; there is also a concealed door (similar to the one in Pries's house) that leads to a game room. Near the center of the south wall of the living space is a granite fireplace; the east end is a sitting area for more informal gatherings (fig. 9.41). Windows look across a sill-level lily pond to Lake Washington—Pries was particularly interested in the effect of simultaneously viewing two levels of water.[58] Painted Japanese screens, purchased during the design process, were incorporated along the south wall of the living space (fig. 9.42).

Fig. 9.36
Residence dating
from 1920s, pur-
chased by Richard
and Ruth Lea in
the 1950s; west
elevation prior to
remodeling. State
of Washington
Archives, Puget
Sound Regional
Branch.

Fig. 9.37
Lionel H. Pries,
Richard and Ruth
Lea residence,
Seattle, 1956–57

(destroyed), east
elevation facing
lake Washington.
Photo by author,
2005.

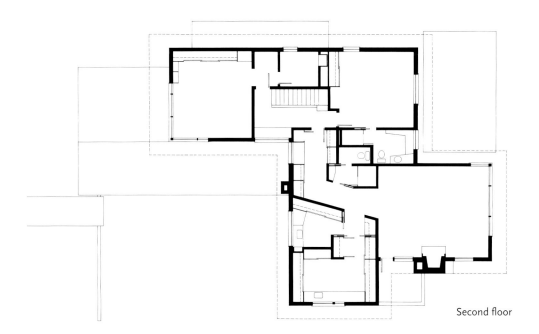

Second floor

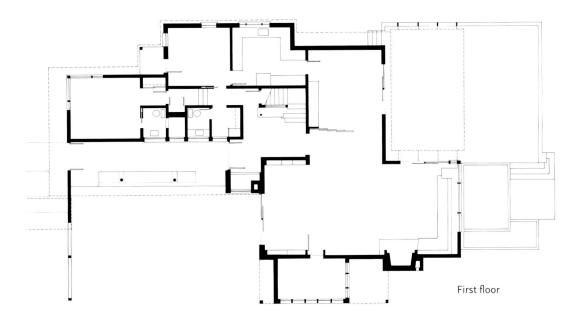

First floor

Fig. 9.38
Lionel H. Pries,
Richard and Ruth
Lea residence,
Seattle, floor

plans. Drawing by
Byung Keun Choi
(based on blueline
prints held by
owner).

Fig. 9.39
Lionel H. Pries,
Richard and Ruth
Lea residence,
Seattle, Japanese
garden court seen
from interior. Art

Hupy photo collec-
tion, University
of Washington
Libraries, Special
Collections
Division.

The living-dining area could be completely separated into a living room and a dining room by sliding panels; the track was topped by Japanese wood
carvings of ocean waves (fig. 9.43). The top of the
dining room table was mosaic tile; Pries drew the
design and helped the Leas do the tilework. Built-in
cabinets and a bar along the west wall incorporated
wood carvings as doorpulls. Sliding doors from the
dining room opened to an east-facing terrace partially
covered by a sloped fiberglass roof. Farther east, steps
led to the lawn sloping down to the lake.

The second floor included three bedrooms. Those
for the Leas' son and daughter included traditional
Japanese shoji over the windows. The master bedroom incorporated another Japanese screen. The
headboard and baseboard of the bed, designed by
Pries, were derived from traditional Japanese wood
forms.

The Lea residence was not a replica of a traditional Japanese house. Rather, it was a Modern
house that incorporated the influence of traditional
Japanese architecture to create a setting for Japanese
art. It reflected Pries's design approach linking

Fig. 9.40
Lionel H. Pries,
Richard and Ruth
Lea residence,
Seattle, entry hall.
Art Hupy photo

collection, University of Washington
Libraries, Special
Collections
Division.

Fig. 9.41
Lionel H. Pries,
Richard and Ruth
Lea residence,
Seattle, living
room, looking
east toward Lake
Washington.
Art Hupy photo
collection, Univer-
sity of Washington
Libraries, Special
Collections
Division.

Fig. 9.42
Lionel H. Pries,
Richard and Ruth
Lea residence,
Seattle, south wall
of living room.
Art Hupy photo
collection, Univer-
sity of Washington
Libraries, Special
Collections
Division.

Fig. 9.43
Lionel H. Pries,
Richard and Ruth
Lea residence,
Seattle, dining
room. Photo by
Tori Williamson,
2001.

Modern architecture with tradition and creating a place for art within an architectural setting. Thus, in April 1959, when the Lea residence was included in the Seattle Art Museum's annual architectural exhibit, an article by Margery R. Phillips, architecture writer for the *Seattle Times*, was headlined "Showplace for Family Treasures."[59]

The Lea residence in Seattle, like the prewar Willcox residence and Pries's own house, reflects Pries's wide-ranging interests in architecture and the arts and his ability to create design syntheses that integrated an extraordinary array of influences and elements. Each of his projects was Modern, yet none is readily classifiable within the popular trends of the time. His work in the postwar years is best understood as the continuation of his search for an American Modernism—a search he began in the 1930s, before the arrival of the European avant-garde.[60] In the postwar period, when American architecture was largely dominated by a technologically driven approach to design, Pries never wavered from his vision of architecture as a fine art.

IO

COLLEAGUES
IN CONFLICT

The University of Washington,
1945–1958

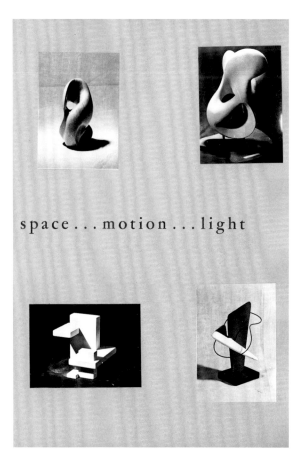

space . . . motion . . . light

In the 1940s and 1950s, Pries enjoyed success as a practicing architect and produced a series of notable designs. The richness of his personal design vision might also have shaped a modern architectural pedagogy. Although Pries never held an administrative position, in the 1930s he had broadly influenced the design education offered at the University of Washington. This might have continued; working with like-minded colleagues, Pries might have found a way to retain what was best from the past while creating a new approach to teaching architecture in the postwar world. But this was not to be. Rapid change within the school of architecture challenged virtually everything in which Pries believed.

The Rush to Modernism, 1945–1951

In August 1945, the war ended. Although some planning for the postwar period at the University of Washington had begun, the 1945–46 academic year saw only gradual change. Demobilization took place slowly—students who had left for military service in midstream were gradually discharged and resumed their schooling.[1] For these students, and for those who began in architecture as late as the fall of 1944, the program seemed largely a continuation of their prewar experience. Although sophomore projects showed an increasingly Modern architectural vocabulary, the traditional pedagogy continued, as reflected in the continuing use of the analytique (figs. 10.1, 10.2). However, these projects and presentations were among the last examples of a waning pedagogy. Beyond the sophomore year, projects were completely Modern and, as such, were a harbinger of the coming transformation of design education, not just at the University of Washington but all over the world (fig. 10.3).

The changes within the school cannot be understood without some consideration of the new intellectual and professional context. Victory in the war and the triumph of International Style Modernism coalesced in a period of unbounded technological optimism. A new generation of architects, energized by the triumph of Modernism, entered practice with the belief that technology could provide the means to improve the lives of ordinary people. The idea that technology should be the primary driver of design was reinforced by the emerging narrative of Modernism. Sigfried Giedion's *Space, Time and Architecture*, published in 1941 and one of the first texts to tell the story of the new architecture, had a profound impact

Fig. 10.1
Doris Treffinger,
"An Observation
Platform Over-
looking a Waterfall
Symbolic of an
Indian Legend,"
sophomore ana-
lytique, 1944–45,
University of
Washington;
pencil, watercolor
on stiff paper,
30¾ x 39¾ inches.
Department of
Architecture
Archives, Univer-
sity of Washington
Libraries, Special
Collections
Division.

Fig. 10.2
Edwin Bryant,
"Entrance to a
Museum of Indian
Art," sophomore
analytique, 1945–
46, University
of Washington;
pencil, watercolor
on stiff paper,
30¾ x 39¾ inches.
Department of
Architecture
Archives, Univer-
sity of Washington
Libraries, Special
Collections
Division.

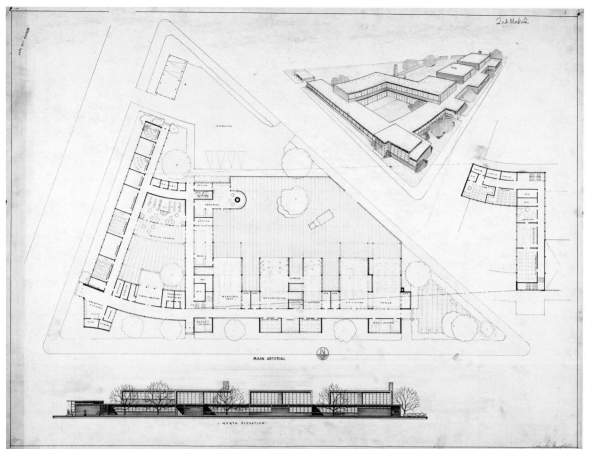

Fig. 10.3
John D. Campbell, "Vocational Arts School," senior project, spring 1947, University of Washington; pencil on illustration board, 30 x 40 inches. Department of Architecture Archives, Architecture Hall.

on postwar discourse.[2] Giedion constructed his history around the promise of "emergent tendencies," many of which he found in nineteenth-century engineering, and he built a unified, linear narrative for International Style Modernism, emphasizing the uniqueness of the new architecture and largely omitting parallel developments, such as Art Deco, and regional variants like those on the West Coast and in Mexico. Giedion's book was as much polemic as history, arguing that a valid architecture must embody the zeitgeist, or spirit of the age. Overall, the emphasis on an architecture of technology became a powerful orthodoxy that shaped the professional and academic discourse of the early postwar years. Technological optimism could not last—in architecture, it would begin to fade by the mid-1950s—but in the first years after the war, the professional and educational emphasis that had previously been on fine art, and on the continuity of culture, shifted to engineering, technology, and experimentation.

At the University of Washington, three other interrelated circumstances led to radical transformation: growth in the number of students, changes in the faculty, and the embrace of the architectural pedagogy of the Bauhaus. Individually, these circumstances might not have resulted in such a radical shift; together, their impact was overwhelming. Similar forces were at work everywhere—no architecture school could resist the impetus for change.

As at all other American universities, enrollment at the University of Washington skyrocketed after the war. The G.I. Bill, which provided financial support to veterans who sought additional education, produced a tidal wave of new students, a small number of whom enrolled in 1945; the fall of 1946 brought an explosion in student numbers. In the years 1938 to 1940, the University of Washington had typically enrolled 10,000 to 11,000 students. Enrollment exceeded 15,000 in 1946 and rose above 16,000 in 1947; veterans made up over half the student body.[3] Until the completion of postwar construction, in 1949 and 1950, the university's facilities were severely overcrowded.[4]

The veterans' focus was often professional education. Engineering, business, prelaw, and premedicine drew the largest numbers. Architecture also saw a flood of new students. In the late 1930s, enrollment in the architecture program had rarely exceeded 100; in June 1948, there were 145 freshmen and 170 sophomores intending to pursue architecture, and there was a total of 420 architecture majors and premajors overall.[5] Close to 90 percent of the architecture students were veterans. By the mid 1950s, enrollment in architecture would stabilize at about 250 to 275 students.

The architecture school was not prepared for such growth. L. Jane Hastings, who entered in January 1946, remembered the severe overcrowding in studios: "There was no way that they could put enough desks in there to take care of the students—a lot of them worked at home. And they would come . . . with their projects and sit on the stairs waiting for their crits because they couldn't work at school because there was no space for them."[6] Sue Harris Alden, who entered in the fall of 1946, noted that some rooms were so full that "you had to walk across the desks to get out to the aisle if you were at the far end."[7] It was difficult, too, to get critiques from faculty because of the number of students. Jane Hastings recalled, "You only saw them [the faculty] about once a week for maybe ten or fifteen minutes, and that's all you got. We learned a lot more from each other than we ever did from critics."[8]

Explosive growth was fundamentally challenging to Pries's elitism. In the mid-1930s, Pries had written to Robert Sproul, president of the University of California, and proposed a program that would focus on a small number of "true architectural thinkers."[9] In 1945, Pries again wrote to Sproul, asking about the rumor of a new architecture school at UCLA and whether he might secure a position there; such a school would likely have been small and selective, at least initially.[10] The rumor proved unfounded, and Pries stayed in Seattle. In the postwar years, the University of Washington, like all other state-supported universities, welcomed the democratization of learning. The architecture school accepted this direction as well. But growth and democratization ran directly counter to Pries's belief that the best architectural education would be achieved by addressing only the most capable students.

Not only did the number of students grow, the new students also had priorities that were especially challenging for someone like Pries. The University of Washington *Daily* questioned whether those who had served in the military would be interested in listening to lectures on antiquity and similar subjects; instead, the veterans were described as "impatient" and preferring "hands-on" training.[11] An editorial in January 1945 suggested that "many of these men will be in a hurry to complete their studies and get into a business or profession."[12] Many veterans were married, and some had children, so they could not focus exclusively on education.

Those veterans who had taken courses from Pries before their military service looked forward to returning; the curriculum was familiar, and they simply wanted to resume their studies. Some who had served in Europe could discuss from personal experience the historical monuments that Pries had described. But those who began in 1945, 1946, or 1947, after serving in the war, were less likely to be impressed by Pries's knowledge, and few were interested in his romantic view of the world. The generation whose adolescence and early adulthood had been shaped by the Depression and the war were more interested in an architecture that addressed practical problems. They tended to see design as driven primarily by new technology and contemporary social needs, and Pries's broad knowledge of architectural history, culture, and the arts seemed to many of them less directly relevant to the future they envisioned. As the headline of a March 1946 *Daily* article indicated, the veterans were a "hard-headed, realistic lot."[13]

In the 1930s, Pries, Lance Gowen, Arthur Herrman, and Henry Olschewsky had handled almost all the design teaching, but after 1945 the school needed many more faculty. As Herrman focused increasingly on administration, he gave up most studio teaching, and, in December 1945, Henry Olschewsky died after a short illness.[14] Only Pries and Gowen were left as regular studio teachers. As a result, throughout the late 1940s there was a constant search for new architecture faculty. In his 1947 report to the president, Herrman noted the difficulty of finding new instructors, given the limited salaries that the university could offer and the many opportunities for professional practice.[15] Nevertheless, the school did find new teachers; in October 1949, the *Daily* reported that that there were nineteen architecture faculty.[16] Usually a new faculty member was appointed as a part-time acting instructor.[17] Some stayed only a few terms; those who proved able to teach, and who wished to stay on, became instructors and eventually began the climb through the professorial ranks. Thus a new

Fig. 10.4
Architecture faculty
and staff, spring
1950; *from left,
front row*:
Robert Hugus,
Omer Mithun,
Wendell Lovett,
Robert Dietz;
second row:
Victor Steinbrueck,
Catherine Wood-
man [secretary],
Roland Wilson,
Lois Sperline
[librarian];
third row:
William Wherette,
Everett DuPen,
Myer ("Mike")
Wolfe,
Arthur Herrman,
Mary ("Connie")
Constant,
George Tsutakawa;
back row:
Lancelot Gowen,
Lionel Pries,
Walter Ross Jr.,
John Rohrer. From
Architecture 1950
(annual), College
of Architecture and
Urban Planning
Library, University
of Washington.

permanent architecture faculty gradually coalesced. Those appointed in the 1940s, who became Pries's colleagues for the rest of his university career, included Victor Steinbrueck (first appointed in 1946), Robert Dietz (1947), Omer Mithun (1947), Donald Radcliffe (1947), Wendell Lovett (1948), John Rohrer (1948), John ("Jack") Sproule (1948), William Wherette (1948), and Myer Wolfe (1949, to teach city planning)[18] (fig. 10.4).

In the 1930s, the four core faculty were a tight-knit group, sharing a pedagogical system and working in concert over the five years of the curriculum. The enlarged postwar faculty was more varied. Inevitably, there were significant disagreements over the curriculum and the direction of the school. Steinbrueck, Dietz, Lovett, Rohrer, and Sproule had all been Pries's students, yet they were members of a younger generation—much more affected by the Depression and the war, optimistic about the application of new technology, and drawn to International Style Modernism, at least initially.[19] Dietz

had worked in the Office of Scientific Research and Development at Princeton during the war; he hoped to apply the methods of science and engineering to architecture and thought students needed to learn in teams.[20] Steinbrueck, later known for his efforts in Seattle preservation and urban design, emphasized architecture's role in addressing social needs and, in the 1940s and 1950s, promoted a strictly functional approach to design.[21] Lovett, who as a child had been fascinated by airplanes, automobiles, and machinery, emphasized experimentation with new structural systems, materials, and technology; his own design work reflected the influence of both Mies van der Rohe and the "Case Study" houses featured in the West Coast periodical *Arts & Architecture*.[22] Thus Pries and Gowen, who hoped that the school's postwar pedagogy would emphasize continuity as well as change, were outnumbered. The new students, too, were impatient with the past. They were more interested in the Bauhaus, in LeCorbusier, Mies, Gropius, and Breuer, and in structure and technology. William Trogdon, who entered the program in 1947, recalled that students saw Pries as "old school"; they had higher regard for the new generation of faculty: "Our real heroes . . . were the younger faculty members advocating the modern International Style, CIAM, and the Bauhaus influence . . . Bob Dietz, Victor Steinbrueck, Wendell Lovett, Omer Mithun, Robert Hugus, Ron Wilson and Bill Wherette."[23] When Arthur Herrman, to keep the school up to date, embraced the new vision, the transformation of the program became inevitable.

The new pedagogy that the University of Washington architecture faculty adopted reflected the influence of Harvard's Graduate School of Design (GSD), which had emerged as the leading American school of architecture by the mid-1940s. Under the leadership of Joseph Hudnut and Walter Gropius, Harvard had adopted not only the language but also the pedagogy of the Bauhaus and International Style Modernism, and Harvard's approach served as a model for architectural education worldwide from the late 1940s to the 1960s.[24]

Harvard's dean, Joseph Hudnut, had received a traditional Beaux-Arts education but, influenced by the city planner Werner Hegemann and by the philosopher, psychologist, and educator John Dewey, had turned to modernism. In the early 1930s, Hudnut became convinced that city planning must become the basis for design, and that architecture and planning needed to address social realities.[25] He also came to believe that education should directly address the community; to do this, architecture students needed to learn more about construction and about sociology and economics. In 1934, Hudnut was appointed dean of the School of Architecture at Columbia University and set about dismantling its Beaux-Arts pedagogy. A year later, he moved to Harvard to become dean of the new GSD, which combined programs in architecture, landscape architecture, and planning. There, too, he dismantled the Beaux-Arts program. In its place, he aimed for an approach that would make design education more practical, scientific, and professional and that would foster collaboration among students and across disciplines. This aim required shifting cultural courses to the undergraduate years so that the professional program could focus on engineering, construction, and design. To implement the new program, however, Hudnut needed a European Modernist who would embody the new direction of

the school. In 1936, he secured Gropius as head of the GSD's Department of Architecture.[26]

Gropius, through a dual career as practitioner and educator, had emerged as one of the key leaders in the Modern Movement in Europe.[27] Even before World War I, Gropius had become known for several forward-looking buildings (done in partnership with Adolf Meyer), among them the Fagus Factory, in Alfed, Germany, and the Model Factory at the Werkbund Exhibition, in Cologne. In 1919, Gropius was appointed head of an arts and crafts school in Weimar, which he transformed into the Staatliches Bauhaus. By the mid-1920s, the school had embraced avant-garde movements in the arts, machine technology, and design for industrial production.[28] Gropius designed a new building for the school in the city of Dessau; completed in 1926, the Bauhaus building is often regarded as the first large structure to embody the design principles of International Style Modernism. Although Gropius resigned as director of the Bauhaus in 1928, he continued to be influential, writing and publishing and pursuing research on the industrialization of housing. In 1934, he moved to England, and in 1937 he arrived at Harvard.[29]

Replacing the previous reliance on precedent, Gropius promoted the abstract design language developed at the Bauhaus. He argued that students should learn a "language of shape" and concepts of "objectively valid visual facts" as a new basis for design.[30] The exploration of this visual language necessitated a course called "Basic Design," which addressed fundamental concepts in space and form and which would be taken before any work in a specific design field. Gropius also emphasized the need for teamwork as learned through group projects. This approach, he believed, would better prepare students for their roles in industrial society and would also lead to the discovery of objective and universal solutions to design problems.[31] By 1945, Harvard had fully implemented this Modernist program.[32] As other American architecture schools groped for an appropriate response to the challenges of the postwar era, Harvard's GSD provided the most powerful example of a fully Modern curriculum.[33]

During the war, the architecture program at the University of Washington had been compressed to four years, largely through reduction in the number of required design studios. The postwar curriculum returned to the five-year structure, but architectural design studios now began only in the third year. As Herrman reported in June 1947, "The new require-

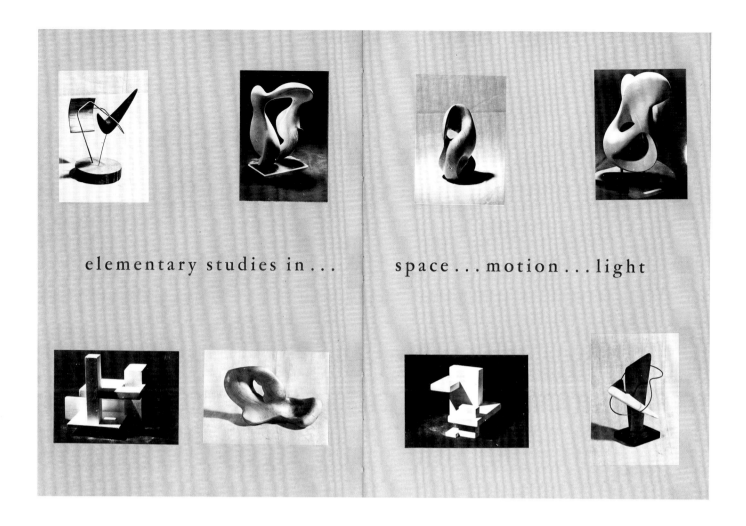

elementary studies in...   space...motion...light

ment includes two years of pre-architecture, under which any deficiencies, all academic subjects and the beginnings of architectural theory and drawing must be completed."[34] The departments of physics, sociology, psychology, and engineering offered "special courses for students in architecture"; the new prearchitecture curriculum also included an introduction to economics.[35] In the fall of 1948, sophomores began taking a new "Basic Design" course sequence, which replaced traditional coursework in architectural drawing and rendering. Initially, the Basic Design sequence was taught by the younger faculty, including Robert Hugus, Roland ("Ron") E. Wilson, John Rohrer, Wendell Lovett, William Wherette, and George Tsutakawa, a member of the art faculty. Although Basic Design still covered the fundamentals of architectural drawing, most of the class time was devoted to problems that addressed the abstract language of Modern design. Early problems were simple (for example, the first problem was a composition using two elements, a dot and a square), but there was a quick progres-

sion to more complex problems in two- and three-dimensional composition (figs. 10.5, 10.6). Toward the end of the sophomore year, assignments in Basic Design included simple architecture and interior or landscape problems, such as a bedroom garden, modular furniture, a motel unit, or a play park.

There was also significant change in the more complex architectural problems, which now began in the third year. The fictitious and sometimes romantic problems of the older program were largely replaced by pragmatic and realistic problems that were not dissimilar to those that the students might encounter in practice. Whereas students had previously been required to imagine or invent a site, the new problems usually included a site plan and were often on sites that the students could actually visit. Problem descriptions included bibliographies of recent research and contemporary examples in professional journals. Herrman even began calling architecture studio projects "research problems."[36] No longer did students prepare esquisses to govern their designs over the course of the project; instead,

Fig. 10.5 Projects for "Basic Design" class, 1948–49, University of Washington. From *Architecture 1949* (annual), College of Architecture and Urban Planning Library, University of Washington.

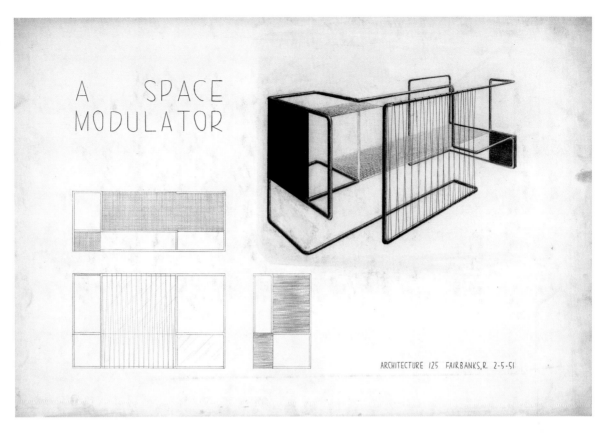

Fig. 10.6
Richard Fairbanks,
"A Space Modu-
lator," project for
"Basic Design"
class, 5 February
1951, University
of Washington;
pencil, colored
pencil on
illustration board,
20 x 30 inches.
Department of
Architecture
Archives,
Architecture Hall.

A SPACE
MODULATOR

ARCHITECTURE 125 FAIRBANKS,R. 2-5-51

they typically spent the first week gathering factual information, which they presented as "research notes" or a "research report." Occasionally they interviewed "real" clients: in the winter of 1949, students in the final year planned a new Washington State cultural museum on the university campus; early in their project, they met with their "clients," the anthropology faculty.[37]

Design and presentation processes were also transformed in important ways. Many studio projects still required a "commitment"—that is, there was still a point in the design process when students "committed" themselves to their designs by submitting preliminary drawings. But, unlike the esquisse, which had been turned in on the first day, the commitment was submitted a week to ten days after the research phase was completed, and for some projects no commitment was required.

The graphic character of presentations also changed. Large watercolor stretches rapidly gave way to drawings on illustration board (figs. 10.7, 10.8). Most presentations were drawn in pencil or ink, and black-and-white graphics predominated, although some color still occasionally appeared. The last studio in which a traditional analytique was required was offered in the winter of 1948; the problem,

conceived by Pries, was "an end wall of a large metropolitan art museum," to include an internationally famous work of art, such as Michelangelo's *David* (fig. 10.9). But Pries could not, by himself, prevent the demise of a waning pedagogy.[38] Whereas Pries and Gowen had previously offered analytique problems in a context where students were already accustomed to watercolor presentations, now the analytique was exceptional, and students were less prepared to handle it. William Trogdon recalled that students of the period regarded the problem with "dread," although he noted that they became fascinated when Pries demonstrated how to apply layers of watercolor wash to develop gradations of tone, shadows, and accents:

Spike invariably would sit down with each of us on the last day to demonstrate and assist with brush in hand and adorn our respective centers of interest with trees, people, light and shade. . . . After catching on to the technique of repeated washes to produce values that made architecture forms read properly with shadows, it became great sport helping and encouraging fellow students to achieve their very best effort.[39]

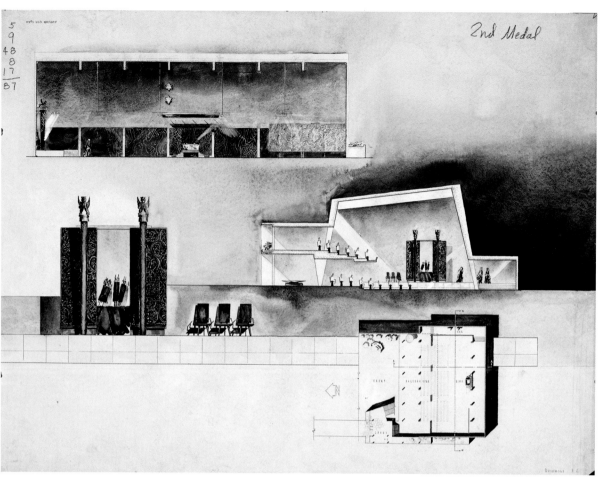

Fig. 10.7
John C. Rushmore, "Interior of an Orthodox Jewish Synagogue," senior/fifth-year project, fall 1948, University of Washington; pencil, watercolor on stiff paper, 29¾ x 39¾ inches. This was one of the last projects of the 1940s presented in watercolor on a traditional stretch. Department of Architecture Archives, University of Washington Libraries, Special Collections Division.

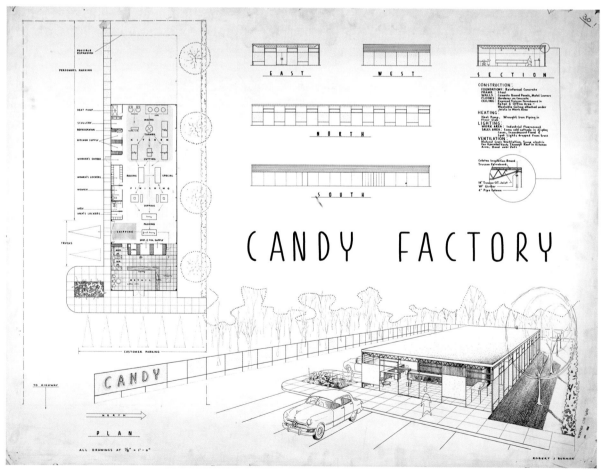

Fig. 10.8
Robert J. Burman, "Candy Factory," junior project, February–March 1950, University of Washington; ink, watercolor on illustration board, 30 x 40 inches. This drawing is representative of the majority of the pen-and-ink on illustration board presentations of the years 1947 to 1952. Department of Architecture Archives, Architecture Hall.

Fig. 10.9
James W. O'Brien,
"End [pavilion] of
an Art Museum,"
with space for
display of
Michaelangelo's
David, sophomore/
junior analytique,
March 1948,
University of
Washington;
pencil, watercolor
on stiff paper,
31 x 39¾ inches.
Department of
Architecture
Archives, Univer-
sity of Washington
Libraries, Special
Collections
Division.

The school also experimented with a more open jury process, but most juries remained closed.[40] Occasionally a jury would be opened so that students could hear the faculty discuss their projects. Very rarely were students allowed to make verbal presentations.[41]

One aspect of the traditional program that was retained was the regular assignment of sketch problems because the faculty still agreed that there was value in students' learning to respond quickly to design challenges—but the term "esquisse-esquisse" was dropped. As in earlier years, sketch problems were assigned at 2 P.M. and due at 10:00 that night. The subjects were as wide-ranging as in the past. The sketch problems at the senior level in 1950–51 are representative: "a bathers' shelter," "a storage unit for a living-dining space," "a roadside display stand," "a diving tower," "a tellers' counter in a bank," "a cabin interior at a tourist court," "a portable bar for a residence," and "a lookout tower"; and, at the fifth year, sketch problems included "a vista shelter," "an executive desk and chair," "a

commemorative postage stamp," "a hermitage," "a master bath and dressing room," "a high altar," "a tennis court shelter," and "an outdoor living and dining area."[42] Solutions were now always in the language of the Modern movement (figs. 10.10, 10.11).

Harvard's emphasis on teamwork was also echoed at the University of Washington. Winter and spring quarters in 1949 saw the school's first collaborative design problem: the design of a new regional shopping center at the north end of Mercer Island.[43] Students from all design studios were combined into seven teams; each team was responsible for developing the full design of the center. The stated purpose of the problem was to teach "coordination and cooperation, use of city planning data, and design of buildings in groups, not in isolation," and the shopping center itself was intended as a "functional, economic and social contribution to better living for modern people."[44] The spring 1950 collaborative design problem, undertaken by eighteen student teams, was the design of new University

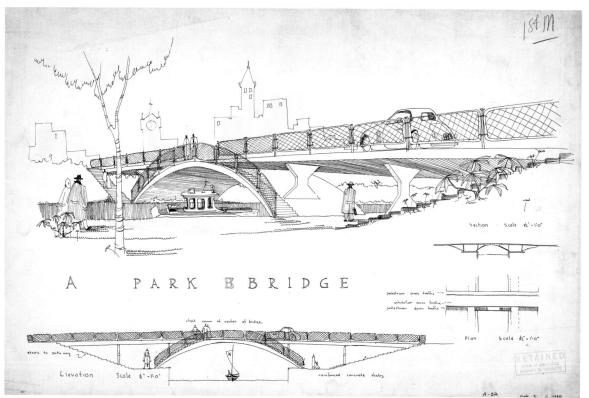

Fig. 10.10
Gordon Varey, "A Bridge in a Park," senior sketch problem, fall 1952, University of Washington; ink on stiff paper, 20 x 30 inches. Department of Architecture Archives, Architecture Hall.

Fig. 10.11
Gerald Pomeroy, "Storefront," senior sketch problem, fall 1952, University of Washington; pencil, watercolor on illustration board, 20 x 30 inches. Department of Architecture Archives, Architecture Hall.

of Washington dormitories (a real program soon to get under way), a new auditorium, and a master plan for the campus extension west of Fifteenth Avenue and south of the new Campus Parkway[45] (fig. 10.12).

Pries and Gowen had little choice but to accept the changes. The younger faculty, in seeking their identity, came to International Style Modernism with the fervor of the newly converted.[46] In the polemical environment of the late 1940s—and in the realpolitik of ending long-standing traditions— the younger faculty argued for a complete break with the past.[47] Pries and Gowen, as gentlemen of the old school, were at a disadvantage in this debate. Furthermore, Pries was suffering from a thyroid condition that lingered for several years, while Gowen had a chronic kidney ailment (diagnosed only after his death, in 1958). Gowen had always been diffident and soft-spoken, but his illness had eroded the energy he had before the war.[48] Pries remained skeptical of any orthodoxy, but skepticism by itself did not offer a clear direction. The influence of Pries and Gowen waned to such an extent that in late 1950 an unnamed student could summarize "the philosophy of the school" as one that required "that all design problems should be solved in the most uncompromising contemporary way."[49] And by the fall of 1950, all students majoring in architecture were products of the new curriculum.[50]

Herrman and the younger faculty were pleased with the new direction of the school. When Herrman returned from the Association of Collegiate Schools of Architecture meeting, at the beginning of April 1949, he proudly proclaimed the University of Washington "a leader in collaborative design."[51] That same month, when architecture schools in the Far West agreed to circulate exhibits of student work, the University of Washington sent a display of student projects from the new course in basic design and planned to follow this display with an exhibit of the first collaborative design projects.[52] Pries saw flaws in the new system, and he voiced his skepticism in faculty meetings, but he and Gowen were outnumbered.[53]

In the spring of 1947, Pries spoke to the Monday Club on present and future developments in architecture. Pries's notes offer one of the few surviving personal statements of his position on architecture and education.[54] Pries framed his concerns about the future of architecture in the larger cultural context, arguing that "golden periods in art" occur only when there is a "healthy and stimulating balance between aesthetics and technology." Decline occurs "when the individual is overwhelmed by the collective, as at the present time." Pries argued that the contemporary crisis in architecture resulted from an "unresolved conflict between the aesthetics of architecture and [its] many-faceted practical aspects." He said that the recent "collapse" of the traditional system of architectural education, a system derived from the example of the Ecole des Beaux-Arts, was merely one symptom of the larger crisis. Another was the "constant use of catchphrases"—for example, the mindless repetition of "form follows function." Among the forces contributing to the architectural crisis, Pries identified the "tremendous development of technology" and "specialization brought about by economic factors." Only if a proper balance was achieved in "the entire cultural field," he said, could architecture move forward in a constructive way. He ended by saying that the artist "must master and direct" the machine "to his own ends."

Pries also expressed his concerns to his friend Robert Winskill, who prefaced his recollections with the "caveat" that he was not educated as an architect:

> The reaction I got from Spike was that they were not teaching the fundamentals. He felt he was the only one there that was teaching, basically, from architectural history. . . . He felt that you had to know the product and the background, the history of the craft, in order to practice it. And that these new teachers were teaching the modern, popular approach to architecture without teaching the background of it. My understanding is that Spike thought of architecture as a developing craft. You don't start it in one place with new thought. It develops out of something else, and my impression was that he felt that this was not being addressed in the later years at the department. In the school of architecture, they were taught that if it was functional—like pipes should be—that it was beautiful, and he thought that was silly because they were always pipes and they were never beautiful.[55]

Pries also worried that the students were not getting what they would need to advance in the profession. He thought that the collaborative problems were a particular concern, as the younger students were not learning as they would have done on individual projects.[56]

The postwar growth led to a new allocation of teaching assignments. As in the 1930s, most faculty taught studio at two levels. Studios met four afternoons each week, on Monday, Tuesday, Thursday,

and Friday. Typically, a faculty member would teach at one level on Monday and Thursday and at another on Tuesday and Friday. However, as the school was larger, there were now multiple faculty at each level. In 1952, Pries taught juniors with Keith Kolb, Sproule, Wherette, Lovett, and Mithun, and he taught fifth-year students with Dietz, Steinbrueck, and Gowen. All the faculty at each studio level taught the same design problems in parallel. Individual faculty members were each responsible for eight to ten students (these changed each quarter). While this arrangement may have seemed to allow each faculty member to teach in his own way, the result could be confusion for students, as different faculty in the same studio sometimes pointed in different directions.[57] Wendell Lovett remembered challenging Pries:

> I felt another point of view, if there was one, should be offered. So when Pries would say something like "Ah, well, this bank that we're doing, this doesn't look like a bank, it doesn't have the character that a bank should have, a bank should look massive"—he would proceed to tell students how banks should look, and I wouldn't—I might say, "Well, I think that maybe we should think about what a bank is in this particular time, this year, and study what it is, what it should do, and then shape the building based on that, and not be concerned with what it has been in the past, because all these institutions change. New forms might emerge." Things like that. Spike wasn't buying this, and I'm sure he didn't like the fact that I was not agreeing with him. He was used to being agreed with, of course, because Lance had always agreed.[58]

Pries was still presenting the Beaux-Arts idea of *caractère,* the idea that design should address issues beyond functional accommodation, and he was continuing the way in which he had been taught. Lovett had come to believe that tradition must be challenged: one must look to an understanding of function as a basis for generating design. This disagreement embodied a conflict not just about design but also about basic understandings of architecture as well as about approaches to teaching. Of course, Lovett also advocated an architecture based on new materials and technology—the very things that Pries questioned.[59] There was no easy way to overcome these differences.

Grades were still given according to a group process: each faculty member in a studio reviewed each project at that level and recommended a grade, and a student's final grade was the average of all these recommendations. Thus Pries's students could be penalized if they followed his lead and did not design in a way that the other faculty in the studio would accept. As Kolb explained, "The difficulty here was that Spike would lead the students along as he always used to do, and the students . . . would get to the [closed] jury . . . [and] be getting low grades because there would be six people on the jury, and four of the six would be saying, 'We don't want to do that today.'"[60] Robert Burman, an architecture student from 1948 to 1951, recalled that he had Pries as a critic for a church problem. In the jury, Pries gave him an A, but the other faculty disagreed, so his final grade on the project was a C-minus.[61] The grading process often served as a way to limit Pries's influence.

The new students were also more outspoken—as Kolb explained, they were often "mature sort of GI's"—and they no longer accepted the directive critiques that had been typical in the 1920s and 1930s, so Pries had difficulties in that area as well. The younger faculty, many of them nearly the same age as the veterans, were fairly informal in their dealings with students. In contrast, Pries, with his sense of hierarchy and formality, often seemed "aloof," "unapproachable," and "temperamental."[62] Yet not everyone felt that way; Robert Patton, a student in Pries's studio in the winter of 1950, was initially intimidated; but, he recalled, "I soon discovered that Pries, as a studio teacher, had a quiet presence about him. He was not adamant in terms of expectations nor was he pontifical when critiquing design. What I remember most about this first encounter was his expression of delight when he made a suggestion that solved a design problem I was having. It made him as happy as it made me."[63]

Still, Pries was clearly frustrated by the changes at the school, which went against so many of his core beliefs, and occasionally that frustration would come to the surface. One such incident occurred in the fall of 1949, soon after Pries had returned to school after treatment for his thyroid problem. Pries was assigned to teach in the junior-level studio. The problem was the design of a truck terminal on a real site adjacent to Spokane Street, in an industrial area in Seattle. Jane Hastings recalled the only critique that Pries ever gave her—it was a disaster:

He wanted me to back my trucks out onto Spokane Street. And I said I couldn't do that. And he said, "Why not?" And I said, "If I may try to explain. Have you ever been to Spokane Street? Do you know what Spokane Street looks like?" And he said, "No." I said, "Well, I live out there. And it's like backing out onto a major highway. No truck"— they were these great big trucks—"could back out there. It's impossible." . . . And so here we were, brand new, in our first quarter of real design, and I was objecting. I think he swore at me, and he threw stuff on my desk and walked away. And never came back.[64]

Pries's anger could hardly have been personal; it more likely reflected his ill health, his general frustration at the changing times, and his particular frustration at being assigned to critique an essentially functional problem, one that made little use of his knowledge and skills and entailed few aspects of which he was a master.

One of Pries's responses to the changes was to curtail his critiques of students' design solutions; instead, he focused primarily on their presentations. Paul Pelland, who graduated in 1949, recalled, "In contrast to the other faculty at the school, he was more interested in artistic presentation or enhancement of architectural features in drawings than in working out structural features."[65] Sidney Cohn, who graduated the following year, noted, "I don't recall much contact with him or help from him in the design phases, but he was of significant assistance when it came to the presentation drawings where he would actually take the brush to revise what I had done."[66] And Pries could still give virtuoso performances; William Phipps recalls Pries's interventions in students' presentation drawings of the first project of the junior year in 1951 (fig. 10.13), a sightseeing shelter:

Spike entered the room, proceeded to the end of the row I was sitting in, and after some looking around at the progress by students, he proceeded to help each student by watercolor painting or scrubbing out the site and repainting the cliffs for them. He was an excellent painter and obviously enjoying himself. The results of his efforts were like an art show. While most of us accepted the help and lesson, there were several students who were excellent artists and did not appreciate the intrusion. It was an interesting event.[67]

Fig. 10.13
Richard Stewart,
"Sight-Seeing
Shelter," junior
problem, October
1951, University
of Washington;
pencil, watercolor
on illustration
board, 30 x 40
inches. Depart-
ment of Archi-
tecture Archives,
Architecture Hall.

The new emphasis of the school doomed Pries's "History of Architectural Ornament" class. The idea of ornament simply did not fit within the framework of the austere and technologically driven Modernism of the late 1940s and early 1950s. Pries's ornament class, which had been so enjoyed by many students in the 1930s, was last taught in 1947–48. Thereafter, Pries incorporated aspects of this material into his teaching of the Byzantine, Romanesque, and Gothic periods in the required sequence on the history of architecture, but now his focus was on the architectural history of these periods, and he could no longer assign such design problems as arabesques, bishops' thrones, and stained-glass windows. This change, as much as the changes in design studio, is emblematic of the shift in the University of Washington's architecture program in the period.

Yet Pries could still influence students by example. In the late 1940s, he continued to hold soirees at his home, and after he moved to Laurelhurst, in 1948, students saw not just his collections but also his house. William Trogdon recalled, "His house in Laurelhurst was unique. . . . The combination of classical design and the modern movement resulted in endless visual delights, focal points, and spaces."[68]

It was a powerful demonstration of a romantic Modernism with a variety of colors, materials, and art objects. Students who, in the context of the school, perceived Pries as old-fashioned or traditional found the house a surprise.

Pries still cared about the students. Whenever he heard that a recent graduate was planning a trip to Europe, he offered suggestions and advice. Jack Crabs recalled that Pries helped him prepare for his trip to Europe in 1954: "He planned our whole journey through Spain."[69] Even Jane Hastings, who never had another critique from Pries after the design problem involving the truck terminal, received a call when she and Connie Ritter were planning to work in Europe: "He called and said, 'You've got to come over and visit with me before you go, because I've got things you have to see.' And so we spent a good deal of time with him, and he told us about all these different things."[70] Pries also gave students other kinds of advice. Robert Burman recalled:

Lionel Pries . . . told me I could never be a good ecclesiastical architect because I couldn't read German. I needed to read a book by Rudolf Schwarz titled *The Church Incarnate,* but it was

not translated into English. In 1958, after I won
my first project in California, I found the English
translation published that year. . . . It was like
reading a 'secret book' of hidden knowledge . . .
on the use of light and space in the arrangement
of people to create sacred spaces.[71]

Burman went on to design a large number of
churches; Schwarz's book became a cornerstone
of his architectural career.

PRIES'S CHANGING LIFE AWAY FROM THE SCHOOL

In the postwar period, Pries's life apart from the
school changed as well. During the war, the number of students boarding at Pries's home dwindled—
Robert Massar and George Thiele remained, but
others departed. When the war ended, Keith Kolb
returned; others who had been residents before the
war moved on.[72] By 1945, when Pries's lease had
only a few years to run, he was already planning his
new Laurelhurst home, where he would have only
a single guest room. With the faculty and students
changing after the war, the increasing separation
between Pries and the school was enhanced by his
move to Laurelhurst; his increasing psychological
distance from the new generation of students was
reflected in his greater physical distance from the
university.

The move to Laurelhurst in 1948 allowed Pries
to develop new personal interests. Most important,
the Laurelhurst lot provided much more space for a
garden, which soon became one of Pries's primary
avocations. Pries did almost all the work himself,
not only selecting, planting, and maintaining the
plants but also casting a concrete table and a Japanese lantern. The garden was both experimental,
in that Pries wanted to try different plant materials,
and aesthetic, as different areas were designed
according to how they would be seen from inside
and outside the house. Robert Winskill recalls that
Pries "had one section which was native plants of
the Northwest and some from California, nicotiana
and what have you, fremontia. That was in a section
outside his bedroom, which was not sprinkled,
because these flowers do not require water. In
another part of the yard he put a small pool in for
lotus to grow. It was an eclectic garden."[73] Pries
devoted a lot of energy to his house and garden,
and he made his house more than just a home; as

Winskill says, "He built himself a social center."[74]

And Pries developed an enhanced social life
apart from the school. Some of his postwar clients,
in particular Richard and Ruth Lea, became very
close friends whom he saw regularly. Other friendships grew around mutual interests. With students
no longer present in his home, Pries was able to
develop an increasing number of friendships in
Seattle's gay community, especially with artists and
collectors. He now began to hold occasional Sunday
afternoon gatherings, and through these he developed a broader network of friends and acquaintances.
Among his new friends was Winskill, who was in
his twenties when he met Pries, in 1948–49:

> I was visiting a friend who was a neighbor of his,
> Rick Brookbank. He took me over on an afternoon
> during the summer. It was just one of those eve-
> nings where we sat outside. Spike had just moved
> into his place, just finished it on Laurelhurst. We
> hit it off. . . . The house was full of Asian things
> and American Indian things, both of which I
> had been collecting, so I recognized some of the
> things that he had, and we were able to talk rela-
> tively intelligently about them, and I think it just
> was good chemistry. I asked him down to have
> dinner at our place in Brown's Point, a suburb
> of Tacoma, about a week later. . . . He came down
> and we just again hit it off, and that became the
> start of our friendship. After that, I spent a lot of
> time in Seattle, and he came down and spent a lot
> of time having dinner or evenings in Tacoma. As
> I got to know him and got to know his library, got
> to know his interests, we were able to share expe-
> riences, and he gave me a very warm and close
> friendship.[75]

Winskill also occasionally helped Pries, putting in
the piping for the sprinkler system in his garden,
or helping him arrange formal portrait photographs
in 1952 (fig. 10.14). Even after Winskill moved to
California, in the mid-1950s, the friendship continued; Winskill later suggested that he may have been
"the son Pries never had."[76] Since Winskill, like
Pries, was gay, Pries could confide in him in a way
that had never been possible with his university
colleagues.

Though he had sought a teaching position in
California in the 1930s, and again after the war, by
the 1950s Pries had come to see himself as a permanent Seattle resident. In the middle to late 1940s, he

had found sympathetic clients and was able to realize his design ideas in buildings, especially his own home. He had a comfortable retreat in which he could feel entirely at ease and where he could focus on his garden, his collections, and his friends.

REVISIONS AND CHANGES: THE SCHOOL OF ARCHITECTURE IN THE 1950S

Pries's position in the school, uncomfortable at the end of the 1940s, changed in the next several years. Although the program would never return to the pedagogy in which he believed, by the mid-1950s the school had reinstituted some elements of the older educational tradition. At the same time, Pries was developing greater flexibility in his interactions with students.

By the 1950s, it was apparent that the crusade for Modernism had been won. But this triumph opened the way to a new debate. Technological optimism was increasingly subject to question. The shift had been prefigured by Joseph Hudnut's 1945 essay "The Post-Modern House," in which the pioneer advocate of Modernism revealed his skepticism about technology as a source of expression: "We have to defend our houses not only against new techniques of construction, but also against the aesthetic forms they engender. We must remember that techniques have no inherent values as elements of expression; their competence lies in the way we use them."[77] Hudnut argued that the house should be a refuge from technology, a place where an owner could stand apart from the "socialized, mechanized, and standardized" world. In 1953, Elizabeth Gordon, editor of *House Beautiful,* authored "The Threat to the Next America," in which she questioned the technological determinism of much of the new architecture and argued that technology should be subservient to humanistic values.[78]

Even as Modernism triumphed, the divisions among Modern architects were increasingly apparent. In 1955, when the architectural historian Wayne Andrews published *Architecture, Ambition and Americans,* a popular history, he described the postwar situation as "the modern muddle" and contrasted two approaches to Modernism: one, based on the (European) International Style, was cold, technologically driven, and site-independent; the other, drawing on the evolution of architecture

Fig. 10.14 Lionel H. Pries, 1952. Photo by Dorothy Conway. Pries collection, University of Washington Libraries, Special Collections Division, UW22200.

in America, was warm, accepting of but not driven by technology, and strongly site-related.[79] Andrews favored the warm, site-related approach. His views resonated in the Northwest; in May 1948, the Portland architect Pietro Belluschi had spoken at the University of Washington, stating that the new architecture should be "modern but not dictated by the machine," and arguing that architecture needed to "express emotional understanding" and "reflect the beauty of its environment."[80]

Belluschi's statements and Andrews's book both indicate the emergence of regionalism as an approach within a more broadly conceived Modernism. In 1932, when Henry-Russell Hitchcock Jr. and Philip Johnson presented European Modern architecture at the Museum of Modern Art, they characterized it as the "International Style" because it seemed to be a universal approach, independent of particularities of place. In asserting a universal design paradigm, early European Modernists were distinguishing themselves from the eclectic architects who had sought historical precedents appropriate to specific locations.[81] The universalizing ideas of the International Style remained ascendant through the mid-1940s, but thereafter the possibility of regional approaches became part of the architectural debate.[82] Lewis Mumford promoted the regionalist approach with his "Skyline" column in the *New Yorker* in

October 1947. Describing modern architecture in the San Francisco Bay Area, he said, "The modern accent is on living not on the machine."[83] Mumford traced the evolution of Bay Area architecture to Bernard Maybeck, John Galen Howard, and others, and noted new work by William Wurster, whose houses did not "resemble factories or museums." In the catalogue for the 1949 exhibit "The Domestic Architecture of the San Francisco Bay Region" (held at the San Francisco Museum of Art), Mumford wrote of the need to "reconcile the universal and the regional, the mechanical and the human, the cosmopolitan and the indigenous."[84]

When the American Institute of Architects held its national convention in Seattle, in 1953, *Architectural Record* devoted its April issue to a discussion of Northwest architecture that continued the debate on regionalism.[85] After an article on the work of Pietro Belluschi, there were short essays on the question "Have We an Indigenous Northwest Architecture?" Seattle practitioners generally favored the idea of regional Northwest design. Paul Thiry noted influences that included the buildings of Northwest Native American tribes, the vernacular architecture of early Northwest mills and sheds, and the post-and-lintel system of Japanese buildings, and then he offered a list of Northwest architects whose work was regional. But the two University of Washington faculty members who wrote essays, Victor Steinbrueck and Robert Dietz, were skeptical. Steinbrueck began by saying, "After due consideration I find myself unsympathetic to the spirit of developing 'regionalism' in architecture . . . our situation is not unique." Dietz said he was "not convinced" that there was a distinctive Northwest architecture; he admitted that the climate and terrain would support a regional architecture, but he argued that it had not yet developed.

By the early to mid-1950s, however, regionalism was widely accepted, and California and the Northwest were recognized as centers of regionalist design. Further, even International Style Modernism was becoming increasingly diverse.[86] LeCorbusier's work of the late 1940s and early 1950s, particularly the Chapel of Notre-Dame-du-Haut, Ronchamp (1950–55), opened the door to sculptural expression within Modern architecture, and a few years later Eero Saarinen emerged as a leader of a new generation of American architects whose work showed a wide range of formal expression.

Student work at the University of Washington reflected these changing ideas. Projects from 1947 to 1951 most often showed regular structural grids, flat roofs, and glass curtain walls, but by the mid-1950s a wider variety of expression was common. Similarly, black-and-white line-drawing presentations, with relatively spare use of color, had predominated in the late 1940s, but by the mid-1950s student work was showing a much greater use of color (fig. 10.15).

Pries clearly benefited from the debates about approaches within Modern architecture. He remained an opponent of technologically determined design, but by the early 1950s his position no longer appeared so unusual, as many of his arguments were echoed in the professional journals. As the Northwest embraced regionalism within Modernism, Pries's own postwar design work came to be seen as both modern and regionally responsive. Pries, of course, would have eschewed any label (such as "regionalist") and would have rejected anything that sounded like a "recipe" for design But he had had an early interest in Native American and Asian arts and crafts, long before these came to be cited as sources for regionalist architecture, and he had always taught an approach to design that emphasized integration with the landscape.[87] Thus his personal design direction no longer seemed exceptional. Pries may also have garnered more respect from colleagues and students in 1952, when his Richard and Ruth Lea residence, on Lopez Island, appeared in *Architectural Record*, demonstrating that his work could draw national recognition.[88]

The School of Architecture also saw changes in the early 1950s that improved Pries's situation. Overcrowding was alleviated both by new facilities and by slackening enrollment. In 1949, with the completion of the first phase of the Health Sciences Building, the Physiology Department moved, and its space was given to the architecture school.[89] The remodeling of old Physiology Hall went forward in the fall of 1949—the basement was converted to architecture studio space, and the main floor housed the library and faculty offices.[90] The new studios had more space and improved lighting. In 1950, the building was renamed Architecture Hall. With 250 to 275 majors in the mid-1950s, there was a much better balance between faculty, students, and the rooms in Architecture Hall.

Changes to the faculty also changed the school.

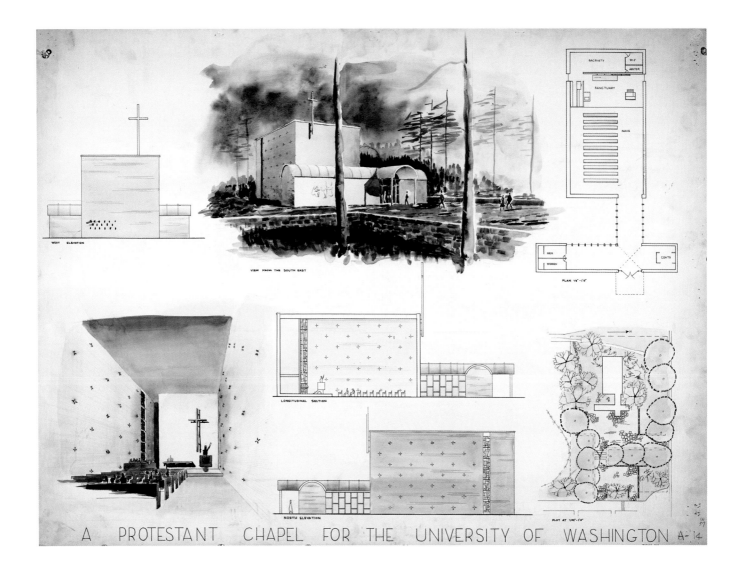

A PROTESTANT CHAPEL FOR THE UNIVERSITY OF WASHINGTON A-14

Robert Hugus and Ron Wilson left; both had been strong advocates of a pedagogy similar to Harvard's. In 1952, Keith Kolb became a member of the faculty. After graduating from the University of Washington in 1947, Kolb had been involved in establishing an architecture program in Montana and then had studied at Harvard under Gropius. Later he had worked in The Architects Collaborative (TAC), the firm that Gropius had established. Kolb had been profoundly affected by his education under both Pries and Gropius; rather than reject one and embrace the other, he sought a way to synthesize their influences.[91] Further, Kolb had been witness to Gropius's evolving attitudes toward architecture; while at TAC, Kolb was particularly impressed by a conversation between Gropius and Ben Thompson, his partner, in which Gropius had lamented the contemporary overemphasis on science and technology and the loss of art and culture in design.[92] And Kolb was skeptical of the teamwork he had seen

at Harvard. He thought that team design worked in professional practice, particularly as he had experienced it at TAC, but he believed that students needed more time to develop their individual skills.[93] Thus Kolb, when he joined the University of Washington faculty, helped bridge the gap between the younger members and Pries and Gowen. Daniel Streissguth would play a somewhat similar role after he joined the faculty in 1955[94] (fig. 10.16).

The school's curriculum also changed in ways that Pries favored. After 1951, the schoolwide collaborative problems were discontinued. A studio project in the fall of 1951 involved architecture students in the design of buildings to fit a community plan for a "phantom city" that planning students had developed the previous spring, but this involved only senior and fifth-year students, and it lasted only seven weeks.[95] Thereafter, such problems were seldom offered; the focus returned to individual students working on individual designs.

Fig. 10.15
Paul Thienes,
"Protestant
Chapel for the
University of
Washington,"
junior problem,
February–March
1957, University of
Washington; pencil, watercolor on
illustration board,
30 x 40 inches.
Department of
Architecture
Archives,
Architecture Hall.

Fig. 10.16 Architecture faculty and staff, spring 1956; *from left, front row*: Betty Austin [librarian],

Maud Hayward [secretary], Clayton Young, Keith Kolb, Wendell Lovett, Myer Wolfe,

Omer Mithun; *middle*: John Rohrer, Victor Steinbrueck, Catherine Woodman [administrative assistant], John

("Jack") Sproule, William Wherette, George Tsutakawa, Arthur Herrman; *back*: Lionel Pries, Gerard Torrence,

Lancelot Gowen, Daniel Streissguth, Alfred Jensen. From *Architecture 55–56* (annual),

College of Architecture and Urban Planning Library, University of Washington.

Beginning in 1952–53, analytiques reappeared as a requirement at the junior year, though they were no longer called by that name. In the fall of 1952, the first problem assigned to juniors had been a shelter for petroglyphs; in the winter of 1953, the first assignment was a "two-dimensional problem," described as a "monochrome presentation[,] using wet media" of each student's design for the shelter for petroglyphs.[96] The reintroduction of the analytique was instigated by Keith Kolb, who argued that it was a good exercise for students and taught necessary composition and presentation skills. Even though there were objections from several colleagues—especially from Kolb's contemporary, Wendell Lovett—enough members of the faculty

agreed, and the analytique became a regular feature at the junior year. Pries and Kolb both routinely taught at this level; so did Jack Sproule, who was widely recognized for his watercolors. The results were outstanding; though the new analytiques were presented traditionally, their designs and compositional strategies were entirely Modern (figs. 10.17, 10.18, 10.19, 10,20). The analytique corresponded to Pries's strengths, and when he was helping students with these presentations, he was in his element. In the 1954–55 academic year, there were three problems at the junior level that required analytiques—an entrance to an art museum for Northwest artists, a stairway to a botanical garden, and the sanctuary of an "Episcopal High Church"—but this was

Fig. 10.17
Emmett Wahlman,
"Shelter for Petro-
glyphs," junior
monochrome
wash presentation
[analytique],
October–November
1952 (design),
23 January 1953
(presentation),
University of
Washington; pencil,
watercolor on stiff
paper, 30¾ x 40½
inches. Department
of Architecture
Archives, Univer-
sity of Washington
Libraries, Special
Collections
Division.

Fig. 10.18
Robert Aujla,
"Entrance to a
Museum of Art,"
junior mono-
chrome wash
presentation
[analytique],
September–
November 1953,
University of
Washington;
pencil, watercolor
on stiff paper,
30 x 39¾ inches.
Department of
Architecture
Archives, Univer-
sity of Washington
Libraries, Special
Collections
Division.

Fig. 10.19
William Thacker,
"Observation
Platform at
Gatty Falls," junior
monochrome
wash presentation
[analytique], Sep-
tember–November
1955, University
of Washington;
pencil, watercolor
on stiff paper,
29¾ x 39½ inches.
Department of
Architecture
Archives, Univer-
sity of Washington
Libraries, Special
Collections
Division.

exceptional; the norm was one analytique in the junior year.

Other changes reflected the softening of the polemics of the late 1940s. Traditional sources occasionally began appearing in the bibliographies included with problem statements. In the winter of 1954, a senior problem for the design of an Episco-pal church (the problem statement was probably written by Gowen, or possibly by Pries) cited tradi-tional churches by Cram, Goodhue, and Ferguson, the American firm of the years 1898–1914.[97] In the same year, the bibliography provided with a junior problem (a small-town library) included Gromort's *L'Architecture classique* and Letarouilly's *Edifices de Rome moderne,* references typically associated with the Beaux-Arts. Most problem statements still cited only contemporary examples and texts, but even this small change meant that students were being exposed to a wider array of design ideas, and that older examples were no longer unacceptable.

In the 1950s, Pries began using a Socratic approach in his critiques, and he became more effective in reaching the students. Gerald Pomeroy, who graduated in 1954, recalled:

He was very good. And I think, when you first started out, you were a little bit fearful of him. You'd sit down: "Well, Mr. Pomeroy, how are you doing and all?" He'd look at what you had there. Then he'd get into it, and he'd begin to talk about it. Of course, when you first had him, before you had any drawing, he'd discuss ways of doing this, and approaches you might take, and sort of dis-cuss the philosophy of whatever the project was.[98]

Douglas Haner, who graduated in 1953, re-membered that Pries asked "leading questions"; he recalled one critique in which Pries questioned his plan:

I had designed a building with a block here, a link, and another block here—a typical Bauhaus connection with an entry in the link in between the two blocks. And I can remember him saying, "But you're entering this building in the least important part, and why are you doing that?" That's almost exactly what he said. I sat there and stared at that, and, you know, he was absolutely right![99]

Fig. 10.20
Alvin Dreyer,
"Sanctuary for
an Episcopal High
Church," junior
monochrome
wash presentation
[analytique];
4 February 1955;
University of
Washington;
pencil, watercolor
on stiff paper,
41 x 31 inches.
Department of
Architecture
Archives, Univer-
sity of Washington
Libraries, Special
Collections
Division.

Pries's questions often stretched students' thinking. Robert Shomler, who graduated in 1959, recalled a studio problem for a single-family residence: "He asked, 'How would you entertain 100 guests in this residence?' Most of us didn't think in those terms, so we had to step back and think a little! Maybe that is what I remember most—that he tried to get a bunch of very young people to think."[100]

Pries adjusted his approach according to the student and the situation. Jon Anders Oien recalled his experience in a final review in March 1958: "I can clearly recall Pries's suggestion for improving my design for 'A Church Sanctuary.' I was very impressed at the time by his genuine enthusiasm for the project. Apart from his suggestion being an extremely good one, his openness and his enthusiastic non-judgmental manner were very encouraging to me as I was then struggling with design and presentation."[101] But Pries could still be critical when he thought criticism the best technique to impart a particular lesson. Gerald Williams recalled, "The common thread that ran through Spike's teaching in 1954–56, when he was my critic on quite a few occasions, was his demand for excellent and creative student performance. He seemed to relish throwing challenges at us. . . . The effect of his sometimes admittedly arbitrary critiques was to make one return to a search for a philosophy of architecture."[102] Pries also believed that criticism helped students develop the character they would need to be successful in their careers. Williams remembered Pries explaining this:

> I remember "Spike" also suggesting after one particularly withering critique that an architect had to be extremely tough in the face of the complexity of the construction process, but also extremely resilient, able to hang on to principles even though the specific details of a design might have to be modified to please a client or satisfy an economic or technical situation. That advice has always served me well.[103]

Students recall that Pries could become quite critical if he perceived that a student was not convinced of his own design decisions. William Phipps remembered:

> He told me he didn't like what I was designing (I have no recollection of the subject). I do recall

that he came on quite strong and I resisted for some time and then conceded to his thoughts and changed what I was doing. The next day, when the project was on the wall and being graded, he scolded me severely and gave me a very low mark. The low mark was for not "sticking to my guns" and designing the project the way I wanted to. This was a sharp lesson, but [it] stuck with me throughout my career.[104]

Most important, however, Pries was always concerned about the character of a building and how it would be experienced. Doug Haner compared Pries's critiques to those he had received as a Harvard graduate student from Eero Saarinen:

> We were doing a church problem, and [Saarinen] came through, and he described his feelings about a church. And he drew this very abstract shape, and then he just scribbled people all across the bottom, and then he said, "That's a church" . . . with this big space and some light coming down through it, and he was right, too. Well, Pries would talk like that—would explain how he felt about a problem, . . . like Eero Saarinen. It was very similar when you would hear those two guys.[105]

To the end of his teaching career, Pries assisted with students' final presentations. Gerhard Olving, who graduated in 1955, recalled witnessing, when he was a junior, Pries helping a senior with his watercolor presentation:

> Close to the door was a fellow with a watercolor that he had slaved over all night, and it looked overworked. The fellow looked up when he saw Pries and asked him what he thought. Pries suggested he clean his [palette] and sponge, and bring some clean water. Pries proceeded to pour the water on his board and sponge off the color (leaving a permanent ink-line drawing). Then Pries worked on it for about twenty minutes (starting with a wet board and gradually drying it off). The result was a beautiful, crisp watercolor. Pries looked at it and said, "That's better," and walked off, leaving the student in a daze.[106]

Pries helped Ron Burke enliven one of his final drawings of "A Dance Pavilion on a Pier" in a

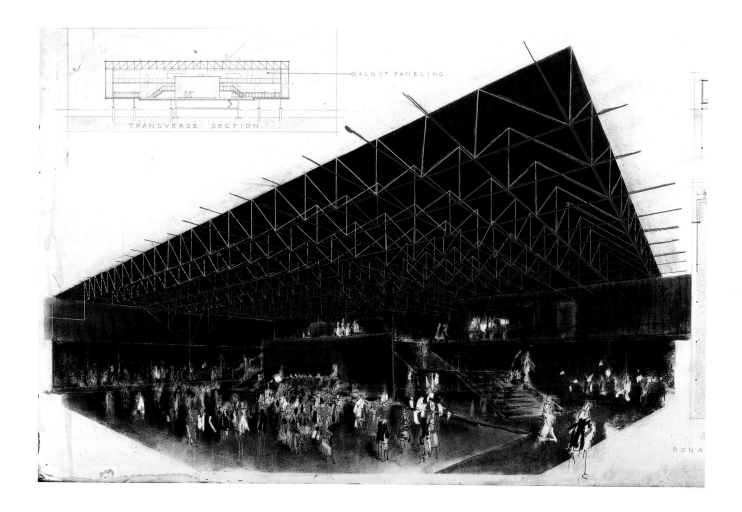

Fig. 10.21
Ron Burke,
"A Dance Pavilion
on a Pier," fifth-year
project, November–
December 1954,
University of Wash-
ington; perspective
(20 x 30 inch
portion of 30 x
40 inch drawing).
Courtesy of Ron
Burke.

November-December 1954 fifth-year studio (fig. 10.21):

Space frames were all the rage at the time, so my scheme had a vast ballroom clear-spanned in both directions. My presentation was on a 30- by 40-inch board with a large interior perspective rendered in pastel chalk. It was supposed to represent a low-light-level scene with the three-dimensional roof trusses highlighted in fluorescent red and blue. There were couples dancing to big-band music in the dim light. Mr. Pries came around a few hours before it was due, frowned and said, "Move over!" Sitting down, he picked up a red chalk and quickly highlighted the tiny band members with bright red jackets. Next he grabbed a yellow chalk and gave them all shining brass instruments, including a sousaphone. The dancers quickly received dabs of black, orange, purple and white chalk. This was all in a period of less than five minutes. "Humph, that's better!" he said and walked off. This, perhaps, would have offended some students, but I was in awe at the transformation. It is one of the highlights of my school memories.

I like to think he felt some partnership in my efforts.[107]

While Pries's position in the school had clearly become more comfortable by the mid-1950s, it would be a mistake to believe that conflict among the faculty had disappeared. The grading of student projects remained contentious.[108] Gerald Pomeroy witnessed a jury in which one of the faculty "gave a student a 5 (the highest grade), and Pries walked up and gave him a 1. One of the professors said, 'What did you gave him that low grade for?' Pries replied, 'That's to make up for that ridiculous grade you gave him!'"[109]

Students in the 1950s were aware that faculty had differing views. Doug Haner recalled the emphases of different faculty: Pries was most concerned about how people perceived and experienced a building; Wendell Lovett was interested in structure and technology; Victor Steinbrueck focused on social issues. Haner valued the differences: "Looking back, . . . I think that that variety—those three people [Pries, Lovett, and Steinbrueck]—was really important to the university at that time."[110] Gerald Pomeroy suggested that the variety of faculty opinions encouraged the students to find their own direction: "If you're listening to the professors, the educators, you get two or three different approaches. It forces you to think. You don't just say, 'Oh, that's the way it's done.'"[111]

In those years, Pries also established a reputation for his course on the history of Byzantine, Romanesque, and Gothic architecture. Robert Patton remembered, "Professor Pries's extensive knowledge of architectural history was displayed in his excellent lecture courses. His classroom was always filled, not only because his lectures were enjoyable but also because his exams were quite demanding, requiring the students to write and sketch clearly."[112] Bryant Milliman noted that Pries had extraordinary visual recall: "In architecture history, he would show a slide in black-and-white taken a number of decades before, and he would speak at length about the colors of the various tiles in the photograph."[113] Ron Burke commented, "His descriptions of the famous gothic cathedrals were so vivid I had a lifelong urge to see some of them in person."[114] However, Pries was much less successful when a curriculum shift forced him to teach the introductory survey course in architectural history to freshmen in 1954–55 and thereafter; no doubt he was unhappy teaching at such a basic level, where students were often not as deeply interested in the material as he was.[115]

In the 1950s, as in the past, Pries followed his students' progress and celebrated their achievements. Graduation was a particularly important milestone, and Pries always participated in the ceremonies. Robert Patton, who graduated in 1957, remembered:

> Professor Pries took the tradition of graduation seriously and always monitored the procession of architectural students. As we waited to enter the stadium, he invited some of us and our families to his home in Laurelhurst for a reception afterward. He had a beautiful garden, which attracted my mother, who was an avid gardener. Her interest earned her some plants and cuttings, which remained in her garden for many years.[116]

Graduates of the 1950s have widely varying recollections of Pries. Some remember him as an excellent teacher and critic, but others found him distant and disengaged, and more than a few recall that

Pries still focused on the best students and offered much less help to others.[117] To many students, Pries was a mystery. Barry Upson, a student from 1952 to 1957, recalled that only a visit to Pries's house really gave him a sense of who Pries was:

> Spike was always a gentleman; good humored; soft spoken; well mannered and cultured. You just knew there was an immense amount of talent, knowledge and experience in the man, but it was hard, at least for me, to glimpse it. One exception was a class visit to his home in Laurelhurst one evening. It was really eye-opening to experience a home that was such a beautiful marriage of structure and native art . . . a "contemporary" home at that.[118]

Robert Patton was a student in 1947–50 and again in 1955–57 because he served in the Korean War. It was only after his time away that he came to appreciate Pries:

> It was sometime later, perhaps when I returned to the university for the second time, that I realized what made Professor Pries special. . . . I assume that his education was, to a large extent, in the classical tradition. What made his teaching unique was that he was able to interrelate the richness of classicism with the discipline inherent in the Modern Movement. To me this is also apparent in two of his projects that I have seen: his own house in Laurelhurst in Seattle, and a house he designed on Lopez Island in the San Juans.[119]

Other students, primarily those with romantic temperaments, found Pries easier to comprehend. Gordon Varey, a strong student who graduated in 1954, reflected the attitudes of those like himself when he recalled, "We looked forward to having Pries. He offered us a window on all the aspects of architecture, like color, texture, materials—the kind of richness we weren't getting from the other professors."[120]

AN UNEXPECTED ENDING

After Lance Gowen died, in February 1958, only Pries and Herrman remained from the program of the 1930s.[121] But Pries and Herrman had never been particularly close, and they became increasingly distant in the postwar years. Pries had never had high regard for Herrman's design abilities, and he had little respect for the choices Herrman had made as head of the architecture program. Herrman, however, believed that he had done what was necessary to protect and enhance the standing of the architecture school in the context of the university in the postwar era, and that Pries, whom he regarded as a prima donna, had failed to recognize this.[122] Pries saw himself as the last representative of his generation—the last member of the faculty who truly understood what design education should be.

There was one brief moment, in the spring of 1958, when Pries's many contributions were acknowledged. Graduates had come from all over the country to exhibit their work and participate in a three-day celebration of the new College of Architecture and Urban Planning. At the banquet on the evening of 16 May, Arthur Herrman, as the new dean of the college, introduced the faculty, one by one. Fred Bassetti recalled:

> For some reason there was a special electric charge in the air when Spike was introduced—everyone rose and cheered and clapped, it appeared forever. It seemed to be a last tribute and we all felt like he, more than anyone else, deserved it. I was very pleased to be there and share in the respect and affection that were shown. He was a great teacher and a great architect.[123]

Pries expected to teach at least until 1962, when he would turn sixty-five. Instead, his teaching career ended abruptly in the fall of 1958. On 31 October, a Friday afternoon, Herrman and Pries met for several hours in Herrman's private office. At the end of the day, when the rest of the faculty went home, Herrman and Pries were still meeting. The following Monday, the other faculty members discovered that Pries had cleaned out his desk and was gone. At a faculty meeting late that afternoon, Herrman announced that Pries was ill, had resigned from the faculty, and had asked that no one try to contact him. Herrman indicated that he thought the illness was probably emotional or mental. When questioned, Herrman would say only that Pries's decision was final.[124] The faculty were stunned. But in the 1950s, people seldom challenged authority, so Pries's resignation remained unexplained. His sudden departure remained a mystery for several decades. In 1984, when Andrew Rocker, then an

architecture graduate student, wrote about Pries, he could say only this:

> In 1958, Pries abruptly and angrily left the teaching position he loved. Friends sensed a large injustice, but neither Pries nor the University were willing to discuss the sudden end to a long and distinguished career. To this day, the circumstances of Pries' departure remain clouded by speculation and accusation, and colleagues from the time are reluctant to be quoted.[125]

Keith Kolb, who was closer to Pries than any other member of the architecture faculty, did contact Pries that Monday evening.[126] Kolb had just seen Pries on Saturday; he knew that Pries was not sick. Pries told Kolb that he could not talk about it then, but that someday he would explain what had happened. He never did. Pries told his story only to Robert Winskill and William Spratling. After Pries's death in 1968, Kolb confronted Arthur Herrman, and Herrman finally related his own version of what had occurred.[127]

In late July or early August of 1958, Pries had been visiting Winskill in Los Angeles. During that trip, Pries was picked up in a vice sting in a city park. At a time when homosexuality was repressed and homosexual acts were criminalized, a man of Pries's generation could find partners only furtively. In Seattle during that period, gay men most often met in one of four locations—private homes, bars, baths, and parks—and Pries sometimes met partners in Seattle's Volunteer Park. What Pries did not realize was that Los Angeles in the 1950s was known for entrapment, especially in its city parks. Pries was never charged with a significant violation, although he may have paid a $200 fine.[128] But at that time there was a law in California that required a report to be sent to a teacher's school if the teacher was arrested on a so-called morals charge, so a report, with either a transcript or a duplicate of the tape recording from the sting, was sent to the University of Washington.

The timing could not have been worse. Charles Odegaard had become president of the university on 1 August 1958. He had been in his position less than two months when he received the police report from Los Angeles. He knew little about the university, even less about individual faculty members and their contributions, and nothing at all about Pries. It was only the previous April that Herrman himself had been appointed permanent dean of the College of Architecture and Urban Planning. His was not the strongest personality, and he had no history of dealing with the new president. It was probably in Herrman's very first meeting with Odegaard that the question came up of what to do about Pries in light of the report from Los Angeles. Odegaard and Herrman are both dead, and no written record was kept, so exactly what was said in their private meeting will never be known. However, when Herrman told the story to Kolb, he said that Odegaard had demanded that he force Pries to resign, citing the "moral turpitude" clause in the university code. Herrman added that he was unsuccessful in his effort to dissuade Odegaard. Herrman also told Kolb that Odegaard had threatened to go public with the tape (or the transcript) unless Pries resigned.[129] Today we wonder why the matter could not simply have been ignored; after all, Pries had taught at the university for thirty years and offered lodgings to architecture students for almost two decades, and there had never been the slightest hint of any kind of impropriety. But in the repressive moral climate of the 1950s, given the stigma then attached to homosexuality, Odegaard apparently decided that Pries had to go.

The timing of Herrman's meeting with Pries was deliberate. Since Pries's forced resignation took place on a Friday afternoon, the weekend passed before anyone discovered that he was gone. Further, the *Daily*, which routinely reported faculty retirements and leaves, was not published on Mondays at that time, and the next day—Tuesday, 4 November—was a national election day. Odegaard's inauguration ceremonies were to begin on Thursday, 6 November. News of the election results and Odegaard's inauguration filled the *Daily* during the week after Pries resigned; his departure went unreported and unnoticed by the university community.[130]

Pries's forced resignation left him shattered. Not only did he leave a position he loved, he also lost his income and insurance, and, just four years short of retirement, he lost thirty years of pension benefits.[131] Although he rarely spoke of it, for the rest of his life Pries was angry and bitter about the way he had been treated. In fact, after he cleaned out his desk on 31 October, he never set foot on the campus again.[132]

II

TRAGEDY

THE LAST YEARS, 1958–1968

THE LOSS OF HIS POSITION DEVASTATED PRIES. In the space of a few hours, his world had collapsed. There was no one in Seattle to whom he could turn. Only to his closest gay friends, far from Seattle, would he reveal the true story.

For the first time in more than three decades, Pries was afraid for the future. What could he do? How would he live? At the age of sixty-one, he was unlikely to find another university position, and any school that might be interested would contact Herrman for information. The only options open to Pries were nonacademic. Perhaps his former students might help. The day after he resigned, he wrote to Robert Mosher, a 1944 University of Washington graduate who had once worked for *House Beautiful* and was now in practice in La Jolla, California:

> Please don't be too startled when you read this note, and also please forgive the directness of its appeal. For many complicated reasons I have resigned from the College of Architecture. To my great embarrassment I find that payments cannot be made to me on my annuity accumulation until I reach the age of seventy, so I must go to work. I couldn't face teaching again, so I must look else-where. I prefer to leave Seattle in order to avoid the constant "whys" and so have put my house up for sale. Most of its contents will have to go as well, for my scale of living will have to be curtailed. My question is whether or not you feel that there is any room for me in the publishing firm where you once took a flyer, and to find out from you whether you could help me there. Also, do you need a drafts-man? I have reached a new level of humility that might make it possible for you to accept me in a subordinate position without embarrassing you. I admit that I have never been a very good drafts-man, but I am still a fair designer. I also have considerable experience in the interior decorating aspects. If you have any ideas that might help me, I very much would appreciate having them. It shames me to write this sort of letter to friends at my age. . . . [1]

Pries departed on a trip to California and Mexico a few days later. In Los Angeles he visited Winskill, with whom he shared the full story. He went on to La Jolla, where he stopped to see Mosher, but Mosher's firm had limited work, and he could not

afford to offer Pries a position.[2] From California, Pries went on to Taxco, where he stayed several weeks with William Spratling at his ranch at Taxco-el-Viejo. Spratling had suffered the loss of his company during the war, seen his efforts to revive the Native crafts of Alaska come to nothing, and suffered financial reverses in the postwar years.[3] He, more than anyone else, could empathize with Pries's situation. To revive Pries's spirits, Spratling engaged him in designing and making two sets of silver goblets[4] (fig. 11.1).

When Pries returned to Seattle, he was still uncertain about his future. He had almost no income, no insurance, and less than $5,000 in savings.

Difficult Years, 1958–1963

By December 1958, Pries had found employment as a draftsman with Durham, Anderson and Freed, a Seattle firm with about twenty employees. The head of the firm was Pries's former student Robert Durham (1912–1998), a 1936 University of Washington graduate.[5]

Pries's life completely changed, but change did not come easily. He had grown accustomed to a university professor's schedule; he now had to work regular hours. As a full professor, he had been a senior member of the faculty; he now had to accept direction from a former student. The situation was particularly demeaning: in Durham's sophomore year,

Pries, concerned about Durham's abilities, had counseled him that he might want to seek a career in a different field.[6] But Pries had no choice but to make the best of a difficult situation. Sue Harris Alden, at that time an employee in the Durham office, recalled that Pries mixed freely with other employees: "Some of us would just go out in the shade and eat lunch—bag lunches—and he would join us, which kind of surprised me—that he would be so informal. He'd talk about his travels and his experiences and so on."[7]

Pries remained with Durham, Anderson and Freed for about a year but was never given complete responsibility for any project. Much of his time was spent adding artistic touches, often to buildings already under way. He designed and may have helped fabricate an 8-foot-tall mosaic figure of the risen Christ for Faith Lutheran Church, Bellingham (1959), and he designed the altar table at Queen Anne Lutheran Church, Seattle (1959)[8] (fig. 11.2). It seems unfortunate that Pries never had the opportunity to design a complete church. He knew the great churches of the world, had studied religious symbolism, and had frequently given church problems to students, yet never in his career did he receive a church commission.[9]

The Durham, Anderson and Freed project for which Pries had greatest responsibility was the International District branch of the Seattle First National Bank, on S. Jackson Street (1958–60; fig.

Fig. 11.2
Lionel H. Pries,
mosaic figure of
risen Christ, 1959,
on the front wall of
the chancel, Faith
Lutheran Church,
Bellingham,
1958–59; Durham,
Anderson, and
Freed, architects.
The figure is now
in storage. Photo
courtesy of Robert
Winskill.

11.3). Although the overall design had been finalized before Pries's arrival, the decorative elements and interiors were largely his work.[10] In 1960, when *Western Architect and Engineer* published the project, the magazine cited Pries's involvement:

> The bank was planned to reflect the character of Pacific Rim nations. The building itself is unpretentious, a rectangle with walls of roman brick, gray metal and glass, but distinction was achieved by making art an essential part of its design. Above the street entrance is a 10 x 40–ft screen designed by Lionel Pries, an unusual and faintly oriental composition of aluminum elements, some gold anodized. U-shaped rectangles are perforated to make a repetitive pattern against a bright vermilion background. Against the rear wall is a second screen of antique gold bearing an abstract map of the Pacific Rim.[11]

Pries was thankful to be employed, but his situation was less than ideal. Ed Duthweiler, who boarded for six months at Pries's house in 1959–60, was surprised when he learned that Pries was working for a firm:

> It wasn't clear to me what Pries was doing at Durham, Anderson and Freed, because he wasn't a project manager or a designer per se; he seemed to be a little vague about it, and a little uncom-fortable. Apparently, as I later learned, he felt underutilized at Durham, Anderson and Freed. I suspect it may have been an arrangement dev-eloped by Bob Durham to help his mentor . . . over a tough time.[12]

Pries joined John Graham and Company by early 1960. This was a better situation, for several reasons. With the success of the Northgate Shopping Center, the Graham firm had achieved international recognition as shopping center designers and had grown to be one of the largest architectural practices in Seattle.[13] Most of the firm's projects were outside Seattle, so Pries was unlikely to encounter clients or consultants who were aware of his previous teaching position. Moreover, the Graham firm, with employees from all over the country, had fewer links to the University of Washington. Thus, at the Graham firm, Pries enjoyed a greater degree of anonymity and faced fewer embarrassing questions. Further, with its large number of projects, the firm could place Pries where his skills would be best utilized.

Pries initially worked on the design of exterior finishes and landscape features for several shopping centers that were already under way. Among these were the Ala Moana Center in Honolulu (1958–60) and the College Grove Shopping Center in San Diego (1959–60). In August 1960 he received a telegram from Marjorie Graham, praising his work: "Your colors, your waterfalls, your effects at College Grove are superb."[14] It is difficult, however, to believe that Pries was particularly enthusiastic about this one-story shopping center. When he talked about the project, he always emphasized the landscape, especially the olive trees that had been moved to the site.[15]

Throughout his time at Graham, Pries was constantly busy. Near the end of June 1961, he wrote to Winskill:

> Wonders never cease in our office. It seems to me that shopping centers must be nearly exhausted, but we have just been given 5 in the English Midlands and 2 in Australia. The Tokyo office bldg. is to go ahead and construction has started on the one in Koala Lumpur [sic], Ilikai in Honolulu (1040 coop apts.!—the world's largest) and the Space Needle here. Retirement homes fill in vacant chinks—the office is again swelling its employment roster![16]

Pries was a member of the project teams for at least two high-rise residential buildings: the twenty-six-story Ilikai in Honolulu (1960–62) and the eleven-story Channing House (retirement home) in Palo Alto (1960–62)[17] (fig. 11.4). He may have worked on one or more office buildings for American International Assurance, as the Graham office did projects for that company in several Asian cities. He also worked on the interior colors and finishes of the

Space Needle, built for Century 21, the 1962 Seattle World's Fair.

By April 1962, Pries was becoming disenchanted with the office. To Winskill he confided, "Work becomes more and more boring, but so far I haven't been fired. Most of the very good men are deserting the ship. Six since the first of the year. Morale is about as low as it could be, but the huge jobs just keep rolling in and designers seem to be expendable."[18] Later that year, he wrote, "For the first time I've been given a design job (because all the good men have to help out in the New York office). It's a relatively unimportant shopping center addition for Calgary, but a welcome change."[19] The project was to expand the Chinook Center, but it never proceeded beyond schematics.

Pries remained with Graham through 1963. By staying as long as he did, he received profit sharing upon his departure.[20] Pries had turned sixty-five in June 1962 and had been working as a full-time practitioner for more than four years. He now qualified for Social Security, so he no longer needed to work to survive financially. Since 1958 he had lived simply, and the balance in his savings account had grown. He had at least one design project in hand and could look forward to others. He hoped to sell some things from his collections, to raise additional funds. Nevertheless, he wrote to Winskill, "The first year after severance here is going to be a very lean one indeed."[21]

LATE DESIGNS

Although Pries had retired, he was still an inventive designer, and he continued to accept design commissions. These helped supplement the limited income he received from Social Security.[22] Most projects were additions or remodelings, but occasionally he took on new designs. The first such commission was Winskill's house, in California. This began as a renovation and addition but grew into a larger project. About 1960, Winskill had acquired a very steep site on a one-lane unpaved road in the hills above Mill Valley, in Marin County. There was already a small house built into the slope, so Pries designed a remodeling to add a new bedroom and a kitchen to accommodate Winskill and his partner, Don Stubbs.[23] The budget was tight, and Winskill served as his own general contractor. When construction began, he found that the existing building had deteriorated and could not be

Fig. 11.4
John Graham and
Company, Ilikai
(apartment build-
ing), Honolulu,
Hawaii, 1960–62.

Lionel Pries was
a member of the
project team.
Photo courtesy
of DLR Group.

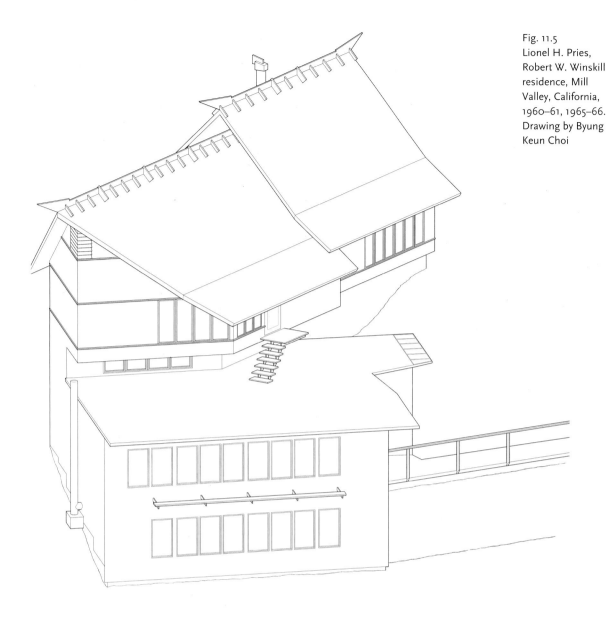

Fig. 11.5
Lionel H. Pries,
Robert W. Winskill
residence, Mill
Valley, California,
1960–61, 1965–66.
Drawing by Byung
Keun Choi

(based on working
drawings in the
Pries collection,
University of
Washington
Libraries, Special
Collections
Division).

reused. Changes were required; thus plywood was used in place of the board-and-batten exterior that Pries had proposed. The Winskill residence (1960–61, altered), as realized, was a compact, flat-roofed house, measuring roughly 26 by 30 feet, of relatively simple materials and details. An adjacent terrace, supported by a dry stone retaining wall, served as an outdoor living area.

In 1965, Winskill and Stubbs returned to Pries for an addition. Pries produced several schemes; in the selected design, a new second floor, with a library, a bedroom, and support spaces, extended up the hill at an angle to the existing house. The addition has a steeply sloping roof, suggesting Asian influence; the flat roof of the older building supports a deck adjacent to the new bedroom. The juxtaposition of the older house and the new addition was unusual, but the interior sequence—from the living and dining

rooms (in the older structure) up the new stair (lit from the side through windows covered with shoji) to the expansive upper-level library, with its high ceiling—reflected Pries's continuing mastery of interior spatial dynamics (fig. 11.5).

Pries designed his last large house, the Max and Helen Gurvich residence in Seattle, in 1964–65. In the late 1950s, the Gurviches had acquired a waterfront lot on Webster Point Road, at the south end of the Laurelhurst peninsula.[24] After briefly considering Taliesin Associates (successors to the practice of Frank Lloyd Wright, who had died in 1959), the Gurviches decided that they would prefer to work with a local architect. At a symphony performance, they mentioned their search for an architect to a friend, who suggested that they seek a recommendation from Pries, who was sitting just a few rows back. Pries recommended himself.[25] Intrigued, the

Fig. 11.6
Lionel H. Pries,
Max and Helen
Gurvich residence,
Seattle, 1964–65;
aerial photo
from the south.
Photo courtesy of
Max and Helen
Gurvich.

Gurviches discussed their project with him; they may also have consulted friends who knew him.[26] Then they gave Pries the commission.

Pries devoted himself to this project. Between the fall of 1964 and February 1965, he produced a fourteen-sheet set of working drawings—the largest he had drawn since the Willcox residence, on Hood Canal. Once construction began, Pries, who lived within walking distance, visited almost every day. The relationship between the Gurviches and Pries was not without occasional disagreements; as Helen Gurvich recalled, Pries considered it "his house," and there were sometimes arguments over Pries's design ideas.[27] Nevertheless, the residence is one of the notable projects of Pries's career (fig. 11.6).

The Gurvich residence is a large two-story house with a complex geometry that responds to its wedge-shaped site. The house opens to the south—to the view of Lake Washington and Mount Rainier—and to the open property to the east (fig. 11.8). The primary floor, at the level of the street and the garage, includes the living room, the dining room, the family room, the kitchen, and the master suite; the lower level includes four bedrooms and a game room (fig. 11.7). As in many Pries residences, a well-designed spatial sequence leads from the front entrance to the primary rooms and the view. Concrete terraces, supported on large columns, provide for indoor-outdoor living. The dining room, the family room, the kitchen, and the master bedroom,

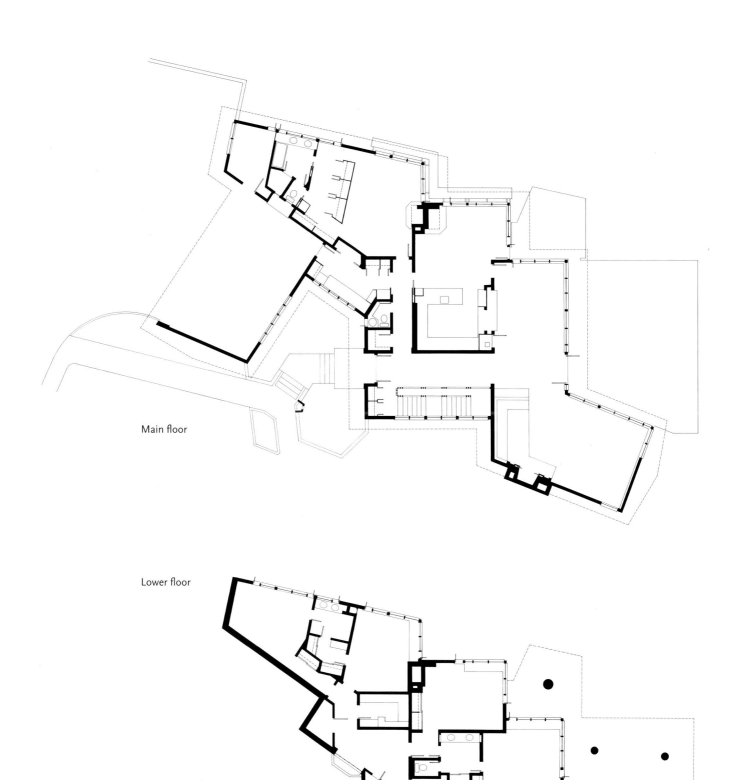

Main floor

Lower floor

Fig. 11.7
Lionel H. Pries,
Max and Helen
Gurvich residence,

floor plans. Draw-
ings by Byung
Keun Choi (based
on blueline prints
held by owner).

with their high ceilings and upper-level fenestration, are spatially dramatic; translucent glazing illuminates the entrance gallery and stair (figs. 11.9, 11.10).

The house is clad in vertical cedar; the exterior colors, particularly the Chinese red soffits and the terra-cotta-color trim, suggest Asian influence. The main floor is a warm rose-brown terrazzo. In the major spaces, Pries had called for "burned and brushed slash-grain" vertical cedar—a treatment similar to the one found in the Lea residence—but the Gurviches found it much too dark; clear cedar stained a light brown was substituted.[28]

Toward the end of the project, Pries made a gift of mosaic tilework as part of the house. Helen Gurvich selected a number of designs from a series of Native American petroglyphs; Max Gurvich asked that the word SHALOM be included.[29] Pries worked all of these elements into the tile design that frames the front door (fig. 11.11).

The Gurvich residence proved especially fine for entertaining. The Gurviches sometimes hosted as many as 150 people, who filled the terraces to watch the boat parade and crew races on the opening day of boating season. In 1972, the Seattle Art Museum included the Gurvich residence in its annual architectural exhibit. In a well-illustrated *Seattle Times* essay, Margery Phillips called attention to the house's fine materials, its changing qualities of light, and its views of Lake Washington, the Cascades, and Mount Rainier.[30] But Pries was no longer alive to read these accolades.

Pries's last projects were alterations and additions.[31] In 1967, he designed alterations to the residence at Graysmarsh, the William G. Reed estate, near Sequim.[32] Early the next year, he did a residential addition for Duane Shipman.[33] Pries's last freestanding building was a "gamekeeper's watching house," a small structure built primarily of logs and driftwood on the beach of the Graysmarsh estate[34] (fig. 11.12).

Fig. 11.9
Lionel H. Pries,
Max and Helen
Gurvich residence,
breakfast room,

ca. 1960.
Photo courtesy
of Max and Helen
Gurvich.

Fig. 11.10
Lionel H. Pries,
Max and Helen
Gurvich residence,
entrance hall and
stair. Photo by
author, 2005.

Fig. 11.11
Lionel H. Pries,
Max and Helen
Gurvich residence,
mosaic at front
entrance. Photo
by author, 2005.

FRIENDSHIPS AND A GAY LIFE

After a period of uncertainly upon leaving the university, Pries recovered and made a life for himself, although his bitterness at how he had been treated never disappeared. Within a few years, he achieved financial stability.[35] Pries isolated himself to a degree, but he still enjoyed an active social life. He retained his excellent symphony seats and frequently attended, often accompanied by one of his women friends. Robert Winskill had become his closest friend, and after Winskill moved away from the Northwest, they maintained frequent contact through correspondence, the telephone, and regular visits. When Winskill moved to California, he became a friend of Pries's friends Emma Willits and Elizabeth Ristine.[36] As Pries grew older, he depended increasingly on Winskill's friendship and advice.

Of his contacts in the university community, only Keith Kolb remained.[37] In 1959–60, Keith, and his wife, Jacques, built a house a few blocks from Pries's

house. They occasionally walked along West Laurelhurst Drive, and, if Pries was home, they would stop in.[38] Keith Kolb also talked regularly with Pries on the phone. His notes of these conversations are one of the best records of Pries's moods in this period. Pries frequently expressed his growing disillusionment with the architecture profession—he felt that it was increasingly dominated by business concerns rather than design. It seems that Pries was most depressed in May 1964: Kolb's notes on a conversation from that period say that Pries "regrets now that he ever decided to be an architect."[39] But in September 1965 he was more upbeat and told Kolb, "I'm just an old teacher with my nose out of joint."[40]

Pries had no contact with architecture students other than Ed Duthweiler, his boarder for a short time. Duthweiler recalled, "Since I had only seen his house once, I thought this would be an interesting opportunity to learn more about what he had learned and what he was like. I knew that he had a large, deep interest in art and architecture that

Fig. 11.12
Lionel H. Pries,
"Gamekeeper's
Watching House,"
William G. Reed
estate ("Grays-
marsh"), Sequim,
Washington, 1967
(destroyed).
Photo courtesy
of Victoria and
Gary Reed.

Fig. 11.13
Reception at
Lionel Pries's
home; *left to right*:
Alfonso Soto
Soria, Ruth Rivera,
William Spratling,
Luis Covarrubias,
Lionel Pries, Wil-
liam McGonagle.
From *Seattle
Post-Intelligencer*,
19 April 1962.
Courtesy of
Keith Kolb.

was never really tapped for classes amongst the
students, so this might be an interesting learning
experience."[41] But during the six months, they did
not spend a great deal of time together:

> Within a short period of time, we evolved into a
> routine that suited us both, I think—it certainly
> suited me—and we didn't spend a great deal of
> time together because he was at work during
> the day, and I was often at the studio at school at
> night. That arrangement worked out fine because,
> frankly, spending much time in his presence got
> to be a strain—he was not an easy conversational-
> ist, didn't engage in small talk, quickly fell into
> the professor-student relationship, and often was
> teaching something about some aspect of archi-
> tecture or allied arts, which sometimes was quite
> intriguing, and other times a bit tedious.[42]

After Duthweiler departed, Pries did not invite
another student to replace him. For the rest of his
life he had little contact with students.

Pries's friendship with William Spratling continued. Pries had visited Spratling at Taxco-el-Viejo in
1958; he went at least twice more in the 1960s.[43]
Spratling also visited Seattle and stayed with Pries.
For the 1962 World's Fair, Mexico had built one
of the most impressive international pavilions.
Spratling, concerned that Mexican dignitaries

visiting Seattle would not receive the attention they
deserved, went to Seattle himself in April 1962.[44]
During Spratling's visit, Pries hosted a reception
for the Mexican delegation. The guests included
Ruth Rivera, secretary of architecture in Mexico
and daughter of Diego Rivera; Luis Covarrubias,
author, muralist, and brother of the late Miguel
Covarrubias; Alfonso Soto Soria, director of the
Museum of the National University of Mexico;
William A. McGonagle, assistant director of the
Honolulu Fine Arts Gallery (he had formerly lived
in Mexico); and Spratling[45] (fig. 11.13). Pries later
helped to arrange an event for a Mexican delegation
at the Lea residence. To Emma Willits, Pries wrote
that the Leas had hosted a "superb cocktail party . . .
that was a sensational success."[46] Pries continued to
trade objects with Spratling; in 1962, Pries traded
an African Ekoi sculpture for a green quartz Teotihuacan mask.[47] The friendship lasted until August
1967, when Spratling was killed in a tragic automobile accident.

During his university years, there had always
been some tension between Pries's personal life
and the public life he was required to live. He now
had the freedom to pursue a more openly gay life.[48]
Over the ten years left to him, and especially after
his retirement from the Graham firm, Pries had an
open and active social life with interesting people.
He built a network of friendships in Seattle's gay

community, as well as with others who were interested in the arts, including John Collins, who headed the University Bookstore; Halsey Jones, a well-known San Francisco interior designer; Harvey Welsh, a Portland architect; and Del McBride, an American Indian expert who had an art gallery (Klee Wyk) in Nisqually.[49]

Pries's tradition of Sunday gatherings was an important part of his social life. The gatherings took place two or three times a month.[50] Duane Shipman, an employee of the Grange Insurance Company, who became a close friend (and an eventual Pries client), was the "social arbiter" of the group. Shipman had many gay friends, and through him Pries met several of the young men he enjoyed entertaining.[51] Richard Proctor began attending the gatherings in 1964, when he was teaching art education and fiber arts at the University of Washington. He remembered, "We gathered in the late afternoon or early evening. . . . Invitations were pretty much open and we called earlier in the week to confirm, regret, or make sure things were 'on'— usually they were."[52] In addition to Shipman and Proctor, those who were "regulars" were Mar Hudson, a University of Washington graduate student in ceramics (and later a faculty member at Everett Community College); Robert Wilkus, a neurologist at the University of Washington Medical School; David Harrington, a medical student (and later a doctor); Robert W. Chittock, a landscape architect; and Gerry Sutter, a hairdresser. The only drinks were "gin martinis straight up"; Proctor's description indicates a congenial group:

> We entertained ourselves with gossip— giddiness—and from time to time Spike would hold forth on some item in his collection, or about a project he was working on. His hidden artifact storeroom was a dependable source of conversation material and he did love to talk about his treasures—primarily Asian, as I recall. He loved books but didn't talk about them much except to locate examples relevant to our conversations in progress. So in spite of all the gin, it wasn't all camping and craziness (only occasionally)—but it wasn't exactly a seminar either. In warm weather a tour of the back garden was usually in order— drinks in hand ("Mind your voices—please!"). His home was small, but open in plan and ideally suited for entertaining a group such as ours.

Dinner conversations often centered around the university community. Spike was eager to know what was going on in the Art Department. What was that mad Howard Kottler up to now? Did I know Ray Hill? Had he told me any stories about Ray? What about Warren Hill, and how does he manage with Hope Foote? Then, inevitably, Ruth Pennington would enter the conversation ("Hopeless" and "Ruthless" in those days). Spike was absolutely silent about his forced resignation.[53]

When Winskill came north to visit his parents, in Tacoma, he would spend time with Pries and was included in the Sunday gatherings as well.[54]

Over these years, Pries had a series of affairs, usually with younger men interested in the arts. None of these relationships was long-lasting.[55] In general, Pries lived a quiet, discreet life—in the 1960s, homosexuality was still not widely accepted in Seattle. Only in November 1967 did *Seattle Magazine* write openly of the city's gay community, and it was not until the 1970s that gays were able to enter freely into the realm of civic activism and the life of the city.[56]

Pries was not particularly introspective, but on his birthday in 1962, he wrote a long letter to Emma Willits (whom he always addressed as "Doctor"), with a few reflections: "sixty five years. This does not seem possible until I remember rather sadly how much has occurred within my memory and experience that counts as ancient history to most of the people I know."[57] Pries discussed the World's Fair: "I wish you could see the exposition here. It is really a very good one. The Federal Science Pavilion designed by Yamasaki of Detroit (a former student) is quite breathtaking. It is disturbing to realize that all the architects involved in the show, excepting those of the foreign pavillions [sic], were once students of mine."[58] Pries's statement was a slight exaggeration: Paul Thiry, principal architect of the fair and designer of the coliseum, had never been Pries's student; he had graduated from the university the spring before Pries started teaching. Otherwise, Pries was correct: it was the generation of architects who had emerged in the 1940s and 1950s who were the primary contributors to Century 21; most of them were his former students.

Fig. 8.22
Lionel H. Pries,
*Iceberg Point,
Lopez Island*,
1946; watercolor
on paper, 16½
x 20⅝ inches.
Courtesy of Keith
Kolb.

Fig. 11.14
Lionel Pries, on
the terrace at his
Laurelhurst home,
ca. 1960s. Photo
courtesy of Robert
Winskill.

Last Days

Pries's health declined in his later years. After his thyroid illness in the late 1940s, he had occasional throat troubles, sometimes severe. In 1962, he was so sick that he missed several weeks of work.[59] In the early 1960s, he was diagnosed as overweight and as having high cholesterol, but by the time he wrote to Emma Willits, in 1962, he had lost twenty-eight pounds and five inches from his waistline.[60] And at some point his reckless driving caught up with him, and he had a bad accident that totaled his Corvette.[61] As the years passed, he was more often tired, and he spent more of his time in his garden (fig. 11.14).

On Sunday, 31 March 1968, while on his way to Duane Shipman's house, then being remodeled to his design, he felt weak and nearly collapsed.[62] The next day, he did collapse—he had suffered a mild heart attack and was hospitalized. At Pries's insistence, Shipman called Winskill, who was then in Pennsylvania. Winskill flew out to Seattle and stayed for a week.[63] Pries improved; Winskill returned to Pennsylvania. On Saturday, 6 April, Pries was alert and talked at length with Keith Kolb. Pries spoke of being tired, of being done with architecture, and of spending time in his garden; he talked about different aspects of his life; he seemed to find special

pleasure in recalling memorable occasions from his rich and rewarding years of teaching.[64]

The next morning, 7 April, a Sunday, Pries died of a second heart attack. Bryant Milliman, a student of the 1950s, recalled visiting Pries a few weeks before his death: "He was radiant and flushed with health—had never (in my memory) looked better. Then suddenly he was gone."[65]

Short obituaries appeared in the two Seattle daily newspapers. Both offered brief summaries of his life; neither gave any details of his teaching, his practice, or his personal life. The *Post-Intelligencer* noted that, at Pries's request, no service was planned, but Richard and Ruth Lea did host a memorial gathering.[66] Nearly one hundred clients, friends, and fellow professionals attended, among them the sisters Constance Willcox and Agnes Britt, Duane Shipman, Robert Winskill, Mary (Mrs. Lancelot) Gowen, Perry Johanson, James Chiarelli, James Fitzgerald, Robert Shields, and Bryant Milliman. Jack Sproule and Keith Kolb were the only architecture faculty invited. Milliman read a poem about Pries, but otherwise, as Kolb later recalled, "We were all standing around having cocktails and telling 'Spike stories.' Everybody had a different story . . . they were wonderful stories."[67]

Robert Winskill carried Pries's ashes back to his native California and buried them at an unmarked site in the Sonoma Mountains.[68]

12

LEGACIES

IN 1978, NEARLY TWO DECADES AFTER PRIES LEFT the university, Victor Steinbrueck solicited recollections from Pries's former students and colleagues. He wrote, "Public recognition of the importance of the contributions of Professor Lionel Henry ('Spike') Pries to architectural education and architecture, to his students, and to a number of clients in Seattle and elsewhere, is long past due."[1] Most who responded shared anecdotes; a few tried to summarize what made Pries such a uniquely gifted teacher. Perry Johanson may have captured this best: "Looking back I realize that his enthusiasm for all of the arts, his great and detailed knowledge, his desire to impart knowledge and to instruct by drawing and illustration as well as by words, created in me an excitement about architecture that knew no bounds."[2]

THE LESSONS OF LIONEL PRIES

Lionel Pries was an inspirational teacher. He brought an extraordinary breadth of knowledge and range of skills. In his practice, his teaching, and his example, he embodied the idea of architecture as a cultural practice. For Pries, architecture was just a part of the larger universe of artistic achievement that he shared with students. He encouraged his students to go to the symphony, to visit art museums, to develop in all ways artistic. His goal was to impart a "sense of design"—to create in the students an inherent awareness of qualities, lines, shapes, textures, colors, rhythms, proportions. Pries understood history as a body of exemplary work and design lessons that could be learned, but he also taught that works of the past were products of specific places and times. He framed his discussions in terms of the broader culture—the literature, art, and music of a period—and showed how a design addressed a particular time and place while incorporating the finest of that time's artistic achievements.

Pries's own design work became a demonstration of what was possible. Few architects, especially in the postwar era, sought the extraordinary merging of art and architecture that Pries achieved in his best works. Pries's best buildings show a sense of richness well beyond functional accommodation; for trusting clients he could weave a romance into their lives through the complete design of enclosure, furnishing, and decorative features. His highest achievement in his search for an architecture that addressed both modernity and tradition was his own home.

To his extraordinary breadth Pries added discipline. He believed that the "sense of design" that students encountered through artistic experience could be fully developed only through practice. Pries taught in an era when faculty believed that struggle and hard work created character. He demanded nothing less than excellence. George ("Pete") Wimberly recalled, "Spike was able to teach us by precept and example that good architecture was not arrived at easily and that any job that we did was worth our best shot."[3] Pries believed that architecture was not an easy calling. By raising the standards as high as he did, Pries taught students how to handle failure—they encountered plenty of that; but, as a result, they learned to work through it and to find within themselves the sources for success. However, Pries also offered demonstrations. He was in full command of the skills he expected his students to develop. His goal always was to help his students understand that they had the ability to do great things. These were lessons for life as well as for architecture—this is why students whose careers were outside architecture still valued Pries.[4] Even those who had once challenged Pries came to appreciate him with time. In 1986, Pries's former student and colleague Wendell Lovett admitted that "as we look back on Spike, his knowledge and teaching with the passing of time, we appreciate him more and more."[5]

Pries was always skeptical of any hint of orthodoxy. He was suspicious of any new theory that promised a solution to every architectural problem. He taught that every design must be addressed on its own terms. Pries's students grew and developed, yet they did so with an unusual degree of independence. There is no "school of Pries"; his students' careers varied widely.[6]

To breadth and discipline, Pries added passion. Through his life and work he showed a complete devotion to architecture that he expected his students to equal. For students who showed aptitude, discipline, and dedication, he was always ready to give more—to share his knowledge, his experience, even his home.

In 1947, Pries told the Monday Club that "the artist must master and direct [the] machine to his own ends."[7] The same year, Pries showed, through the built form of his own house, how this mastery might be achieved. Pries used the products of industrial technology (concrete block, cement-asbestos board, metal windows), but technology was not the

focus. The products of technology provided the setting. The focus was the Native American images and the collection of handcrafted artifacts representing pretechnological cultures; and both the industrial and the handcrafted merged with the gardens that filled the site. Although Pries later turned to Japanese artifacts, these, too, were handmade, products of a handcraft tradition. Pries rarely wrote about architecture, but his own house can be understood as a quiet polemic, embodying his resistance to the dominance of technology and showing how architecture in the modern world might still embody humanity and integration with nature.

LIONEL PRIES AND THE VARIETIES OF AMERICAN MODERNISM

In 1981, the architecture professor Grant Hildebrand, then writing regularly for the *Seattle Times,* devoted a column to Lionel Pries. Hildebrand wrote that, upon arriving in Seattle from Michigan, in the 1960s, he had been surprised by the fine quality of the architecture in the Northwest. In his article, he ascribed this quality to Pries's influence: "The smaller-scale architecture of the Seattle area, which is in considerable degree the architecture of his [Pries'] students, has been a richer, fuller architecture than can be found in most other regions of the country."[8] Hildebrand did not consider the larger implications of his discussion; but, from the perspective of the nearly forty years since Pries's death, it is now possible to suggest how the story of Pries's life and career helps to illuminate the broader development of American architecture in the twentieth century.

In the last two decades we have seen a reconsideration of the Modern Movement in architecture. The pioneering histories of Modernism presented the development of the new architecture in a simplified narrative that emphasized the International Style and overlooked competing directions and regional variations. We now recognize that Modernism was never a single or even a completely unified movement. As William J. R. Curtis has written, "Grand abstractions such as the 'International Style' never did enough to acknowledge the ideological range and regional nuances of Modern architecture in the originating countries; but once instated, they were certainly guilty of overlooking the complexity of a dissemination that gained momentum in the 1930s, and that already witnessed a species of 'cross-fertilization' between certain core concepts of Modernism, and interpretations of diverse national cultures, climates, and traditions."9 Pries's life and work give substance to the American side of this story.

Pries's career reminds us of the complexity of American Modernism, and of the mix of ideas that shaped American architecture in the twentieth century. Pries's work shows the lingering influence of the progressive California Arts and Crafts culture of the years after 1900. Pries represents the generation of architects whose training was shaped by the methods of the Ecole des Beaux-Arts and whose designs initially drew on historic precedent, but who, over the course of their careers, had to come to terms with Modern architecture. Many in Pries's generation were able to survive because the Beaux-Arts had offered a flexible method—it was never just copying, no matter what partisans of Modernism later claimed. Pries also reminds us of the evolution, on the West Coast, of an architecture that was Modern but not European, and he reminds us as well that it was not solely through the northeastern states that Modernism from Europe penetrated the North American continent. Rather, the earliest sustained influence of European Modernism was experienced in Mexico, and the intellectual and artistic interactions between Mexico and the United States in the 1920s and 1930s cannot be ignored in any truly encompassing history of Modern architecture in America. Pries's sojourns in Mexico shaped his understanding; and, through his teaching, some of the lessons he learned in Mexico were passed on to his students. Pries showed that Modernism could be romantic as well as rational, enriched as well as austere, emotional as well as intellectual. Pries's architecture responded to the local and the particular, and it provided a setting for art as well as for function.

The reevaluation of Modernism is not yet complete. New scholarship and publications continue to add to our understanding of the different interpretations of Modernism and of the many ways in which American architects sought to be Modern while also engaging with the particularities of place. The Modern architecture that developed in the Northwest reflects a diverse pedigree: lingering progressive tendencies of the early twentieth century, West Coast regionalism, Mexican Modernism, the European avant-garde, and, in the 1950s, the traditional architecture of Japan all inspired Northwest architects. However inevitable it may seem in retrospect, Northwest Modern architecture was actually the result of an extraordinarily complex interchange —an interchange in which a central figure was Lionel Pries.

NOTES

PREFACE

1. Memo from Kenneth Anderson to Victor Steinbrueck, 11 Feb. 1978.

2. In 1978, Steinbrueck offered a series of lectures on Seattle's architectural history to the UW Alumni Association. To prepare for a lecture on Pries and his influence, Steinbrueck contacted a selection of Pries's students, colleagues and friends. See Victor Steinbrueck, "Collection of Information and Material Regarding Lionel Henry Pries," memo sent to Pries's colleagues, friends, and former students, 9 Jan. 1978 (thanks to Keith Kolb for a copy of this memo). An undated typescript titled "Lionel Pries," probably Steinbrueck's Alumni Association presentation, is found in the Steinbrueck papers, acc. no. 3252–006, Box 4, Folder 26, University of Washington Libraries, Special Collections Division.

Steinbrueck had commented on Pries's significance four years earlier, writing that "almost every architectural student during Pries's years [at the University of Washington] was inspired by his talent and insight into the wonders and delights of architecture. He is easily the most talented architect in this region I have known." See Victor Steinbrueck, "Everyday Architecture in the Puget Sound Area," in *Space, Style, and Structure: Buildings in Northwest America*, vol. 2, ed. Thomas Vaughan and Virginia Guest Ferriday (Portland, OR: Oregon Historical Society, 1974), 502.

3. In response to his memo, Steinbrueck received responses from Kenneth Anderson, Fred Bassetti, Flora Allen Casey, Robert H. Dietz, Perry Johanson, Keith R. Kolb, Lloyd J. Lovegren, Wendell Lovett, Ivan W. Meyer, Robert Ross, Charles H. Schiff, Roland Terry, Gerald Williams, George ("Pete") Wimberly, Robert W. Winskill, and Minoru Yamasaki; thanks to Keith Kolb for copies of these responses. (For background on Ken Anderson, see chap. 12, n. 4). Yamasaki also mentioned Pries's influence in his 1979 autobiography. See Minoru Yamasaki, *A Life in Architecture* (New York: Weatherhill, 1979), 13.

4. Grant Hildebrand, "Richness is found on a small scale," *Seattle Times*, 17 May 1981, F14. Woodbridge and Montgomery had mentioned Pries's influence just a year earlier: "A major educator and member of the University of Washington architecture faculty was Lionel Pries. . . . His influence on the generation of architects who dominated the postwar period was profound." Sally B. Woodbridge and Roger Montgomery, *A Guide to Architecture in Washington State: An Environmental Perspective* (Seattle and London: University of Washington Press, 1980), 21.

5. Andrew Rocker, "Lionel H. Pries: Educator of Architects," *Arcade* 4 (April/May 1984): 1, 8–9; Larry Brown, "Eclectic Architect: Lionel Pries designed things his way," *Seattle Times/Seattle Post-Intelligencer*, 13 Apr. 1986, *Pacific Magazine* section, 22–24.

6. University of Washington architecture graduates and part-time faculty members David Strauss and Kevin Kane were among those responsible for the creation of the Lionel Pries Teaching Award. Strauss indicates that they had heard of Lionel Pries as a legendary teacher

from Professors Victor Steinbrueck and Hermann Pundt. Author discussion with David Strauss, April 2004.

7. The "Roll of Honor" was added to the frieze in Architecture Hall 147 (the auditorium) after the 1986–88 remodeling. The first eight names on the frieze were (in alphabetical order): [Carl] Gould, [Lancelot] Gowen, [Paul] Kirk, [Lionel] Pries, [B. Marcus] Priteca, [Victor] Steinbrueck, [Ellsworth] Storey, [Paul] Thiry. Between 1990 and 1993 two names were added: [Rich] Haag, [Myer] Wolfe. Two more names were added in 2005: [Robert C.] Reamer and [Wendell] Lovett.

8. Drew Rocker, "Lionel H. Pries," in *Shaping Seattle Architecture: A Historical Guide to the Architects*, ed. Jeffrey Karl Ochsner (Seattle and London: University of Washington Press, with AIA Seattle, 1994; rev. paperback 1998), 228–33.

9. In recent years, several biographical monographs have mentioned Pries's influence, but none has provided substantially more information about Pries himself. See Justin Henderson, *Roland Terry: Master Northwest Architect* (Seattle and London: University of Washington Press, 2000), 17; Cory Buckner, *A. Quincy Jones* (London and New York: Phaidon, 2002), 10; Grant Hildebrand and T. William Booth, *A Thriving Modernism: The Houses of Wendell Lovett and Arne Bystrom* (Seattle and London: University of Washington Press, 2004), 11–12.

10. Steinbrueck, "Everyday Architecture in the Puget Sound Area," in *Space, Style, and Structure* 2, 501.

1. INTRODUCTION

1. Keith Kolb, presentation at American Institute of Architects (AIA) Seattle Fellows luncheon, 24 April 2002. Kolb told the same story to the author (author's interview with Keith Kolb, 11 Aug. 1995).

2. Author's interview with Keith Kolb, 11 Aug. 1995.

3. Ibid.

4. The British publication *Architectural Review* stated that Yamasaki "studied at the University of Washington, where the imagination and skill of Lionel Pries inspired all the students, and it is to him, Yamasaki believes, more than any other person, that he owed his first understanding of how exciting architecture could be." See "Genetrix: Personal Contributions to American Architecture—Minoru Yamasaki," *Architectural Review* 121 (May 1957), 366. Reportedly, when students at the University of Washington brought this to Pries's attention, he responded by saying something like "Yamasaki never learned anything I taught him!" Yamasaki also cited Pries in his autobiography; see Minoru Yamasaki, *A Life in Architecture* (New York: Weatherhill, 1979), 13.

5. Cory Buckner, *A. Quincy Jones* (London: Phaidon Press, 2002), 10.

6. Justin Henderson, *Roland Terry: Master Northwest Architect* (Seattle: University of Washington Press, 2000), 17.

7. Author's discussion with Gordon Varey, March 1992.

8. On the Arts and Crafts movement in America, see Robert Judson Clark, ed., *The Arts and Crafts Movement in America, 1876–1916* (Princeton N.J.: Princeton University Press, 1972); Wendy Kaplan, ed., *"The Art That Is Life": The Arts and Crafts Movement in America, 1875–1920* (Boston: Museum of Fine Arts/Little, Brown, 1987); and Eileen Boris, *Art and Labor: Ruskin, Morris, and the Craftsman Ideal in America* (Philadelphia: Temple University Press, 1986). A broader cultural study of the period is T. J. Jackson Lears, *No Place of Grace: Antimodernism and the Transformation of American Culture, 1880–1920* (Chicago: University of Chicago Press, 1983). There were progressive directions in Chicago, but—other than the Carson, Pirie, Scott store by Sullivan—most of the progressive work of Burnham and Root, Adler and Sullivan, and Holabird and Roche dates from the nineteenth century, not the twentieth. The work of Prairie School architects falls within the broader Arts and Crafts movement. Although some Arts and Crafts producers continued in the 1920s, any sense of a coherent movement had faded by 1916.

9. On the origins and character of academic eclecticism, see Richard Longstreth, "Academic Eclecticism in American Architecture," *Winterthur Portfolio* 17/1 (Spring 1982), 55–82; see also Mark Alan Hewitt, *The Architect & the American Country House, 1890–1940* (New Haven, Conn.: Yale University Press, 1990), esp. 31–42.

10. For a well-illustrated, broadly inclusive discussion of Art Deco, see Patricia Bayer, *Art Deco Architecture: Design, Decoration and Detail from the Twenties and Thirties* (London: Thames and Hudson, 1992); see also chap. 6, n. 5, this volume.

11. On the Museum of Modern Art exhibition and its significance, see Terence Riley, *The International Style: Exhibition 15 and The Museum of Modern Art* (New York: Rizzoli/Columbia Books of Architecture, 1992). A short account is found in Franz Schulze, *Philip Johnson: Life and Work* (New York: Knopf, 1994), 70–86. The catalogue was published in two forms, with identical texts: Henry-Russell Hitchcock Jr., Philip Johnson, and Lewis Mumford, *Modern Architecture: International Exhibition* (New York: Museum of Modern Art, 1932), and Alfred H. Barr Jr., Henry-Russell Hitchcock Jr., Philip Johnson, and Lewis Mumford, *Modern Architects* (New York: Norton/Museum of Modern Art, 1932). Published the same year was Henry-Russell Hitchcock Jr. and Philip Johnson, *The International Style: Architecture Since 1922* (New York: Norton, 1932; a paperback edition, with a new foreword and an appendix, "The International Style Twenty Years After," by Henry-Russell Hitchcock Jr., was published by Norton in 1966).

12. For background on Mies, see Franz Schulze, *Mies van der Rohe: A Critical Biography* (Chicago: University of Chicago Press, 1985). For background on Gropius, see chap. 10, n. 27, this volume. Marcel Breuer might also be named here, but he was most influential as a practitioner and less as an educator.

13. The broadest revision of a general text addressing

twentieth-century architecture to appear to date is William J. R. Curtis, *Modern Architecture Since 1900*, 3rd ed. (London: Phaidon Press, 1996).

14. Ibid., 370–91, 490–511. Although the two earlier editions of this book provided inclusive coverage of twentieth-century architecture, the 1996 edition is the only one to address (in the new chap. 21) the wide-raging dissemination of Modern architecture in the 1920s and 1930s.

15. One might also mention the influence of Eliel Saarinen and Cranbrook Academy of Art.

16. The architects of the San Francisco Bay Area are a notable exception to this statement; see Sally Woodbridge, ed., *Bay Area Houses* (New York: Oxford University Press, 1976); see also Robert Winter, ed., *Toward a Simpler Way of Life: The Arts & Crafts Architects of California* (Berkeley: Norfleet Press of University of California Press, 1997). Also see chap. 2, nn. 44–50, this volume.

17. Regionalism as an architectural idea was debated through the course of the twentieth century. Eclectic architects discussed the creation of new designs appropriate to specific sites and locations by drawing upon regionally appropriate historic precedents (for example, the missions in California). Architects who advocated International Style Modernism initially resisted regionalism—after all, the International Style was to be a timeless approach independent of specific local circumstance. Discussion of regionalism within Modernism began in the late 1940s and progressed rapidly in the early 1950s. *Architectural Record* addressed the question of regionalism in the Pacific Northwest when the national AIA convention was held in Seattle in 1953. See "Architecture of the Northwest," *Architectural Record* 113 (Apr. 1953), 134–46. (The debate regarding regionalism within Modernism that took place in the late 1940s and early 1950s is discussed in chap. 10, this volume.) The most developed recent discussion of regionalism is Liane Lefaivre and Alexander Tzonis, eds., *Critical Regionalism: Architecture and Identity in a Globalized World* (Munich: Prestel, 2003). See also Liane Lefaivre and Alexander Tzonis, "Lewis Mumford's Regionalism," *Design Book Review* 19 (Winter 1991), 20–25. (Thanks to Victoria Reed for bringing this review to my attention.)

18. For the pre-World War II history of the four painters most identified with the Northwest School— Mark Tobey, Kenneth Callahan, Morris Graves, and Guy Anderson—see Sheryl Conkelton and Laura Landau, *Northwest Mythologies: The Interactions of Mark Tobey, Morris Graves, Kenneth Callahan, and Guy Anderson* (Tacoma/Seattle: Tacoma Art Museum/University of Washington Press, 2003). A general overview of the 1930s is Martha Kingsbury, *Art of the Thirties: The Pacific Northwest* (Seattle: Henry Art Gallery/University of Washington Press, 1972). Brief biographical summaries of many Seattle artists from the 1920s to the 1950s are found in Sheryl Conkelton, *What It Meant to Be Modern: Seattle Art at Mid-Century* (Seattle: Henry Art Gallery, 1999), 39–44. Information on Seattle artists of

the 1920s and 1930s is also available from David Martin of the gallery Martin-Zambito Fine Art, who has devoted substantial effort to research on Seattle artists of the 1930s. Pries's interaction with Seattle's artistic community is discussed in chap. 8, this volume.

19. The pioneering study of Seattle's gay history is Gary L. Atkins, *Gay Seattle: Stories of Exile and Belonging* (Seattle: University of Washington Press, 2003). However, Atkins does not provide a detailed discussion of the roles played by gays in Seattle's cultural community.

2. Origins

1. See Kevin Starr, *Americans and the California Dream, 1850–1915* (New York: Oxford University Press, 1973).

2. Robert Winter, "Introduction: The Myth of California Expressed in Arts and Crafts Theory," in Robert Winter, ed., *Toward a Simpler Way of Life: The Arts & Crafts Architects of California* (Berkeley: Norfleet Press of University of California Press, 1997), 1. On the broad character of the Arts and Crafts movement in California, see Kenneth R. Trapp, ed., *The Arts and Crafts Movement in California: Living the Good Life* (Oakland, Calif./New York: Oakland Museum/Abbeville Publishers, 1993).

3. University of California president Benjamin Wheeler compared Berkeley to ancient Greece in his 1899 inaugural address. For a discussion of the "new Athens," see Loren W. Partridge, *John Galen Howard and the Berkeley Campus: Beaux-Arts Architecture in the "Athens of the West"* (Berkeley, Calif.: Berkeley Architectural Heritage, 1988).

4. For a broad overview of the influence of Japan, see Lionel Lambourne, *Japonisme: Cultural Crossings between Japan and the West* (London and New York: Phaidon, 2005) and Clay Lancaster, *The Japanese Influence in America*, rev. ed. (New York: Abbeville Publishers, 1983). See also Siegfried Wichmann, *Japonisme: The Japanese Influence on Western Art in the 19th and 20th Centuries* (London/New York: Thames and Hudson/Harmony Books, 1981); Julia Meech and Gabriel P. Weisberg, *Japonisme Comes to America: The Japanese Impact on the Graphic Arts, 1876–1925* (New York: Harry N. Abrams, 1990), exhibition catalogue.

5. David C. Streatfield, *California Gardens: Creating a New Eden* (New York: Abbeville Publishers, 1994), esp. 7–11.

6. According to his baptismal certificate, Lionel Pries was born in San Francisco on 2 June 1897 and baptized at St. Markus Kirke (St. Mark Lutheran Church), San Francisco, on 10 October 1898; the full name on the certificate is Lionel Henry Rathje Joachim Pries (Lionel Pries papers, Special Collections Division, University of Washington Libraries). St. Mark Lutheran Church, a German Lutheran church, survived the earthquake and fire of 1906 but was later destroyed by fire. By the time the research for this book began, none of Pries's close relatives (aunts, uncles, cousins) were still alive. However, Mrs. Robert Spencer, the spouse of a cousin, was

interviewed by the author in 2001. She stated that Rathje and Magdalena Pries had previously had a daughter, who died at the age of four, and that they then adopted an infant boy, whom they named Lionel. The records of the 1890 and 1900 censuses confirm that the Pries family did include another child who had been born after 1890 and died before 1900. No records have been found, however, to indicate that Pries was adopted. Pries never mentioned being adopted to either of his two closest friends, Robert Winskill and Keith Kolb. Pries did say that his birth certificate had been destroyed in the 1906 San Francisco earthquake and fire. The destruction of birth and other records by the 1906 disaster makes it impossible to verify the exact circumstances of Pries's birth.

7. Lionel Pries's mother had arrived in the United States at the age of twenty-one. Census records for 1900 and 1910 may indicate that Magdalena Koepke Pries never became a naturalized citizen; the appropriate spots on the forms are blank rather than filled in. Although she learned to speak English, the family spoke German at home, and she wrote notes to her son in German. One surviving letter, now in the collection of Lionel Pries's papers, has been described as written in "peasant German." Robert Winskill recalls that at least one native German who met Pries stated that Pries was the only American he had ever met who spoke German without an accent (author's interview with Robert Winskill, 26 July 1994).

8. When the Pries family first moved to Oakland, in 1896, their house was on what was then called McKee Street. By 1900, street names in the area had been regularized, and city directories listed the address as 896 61st Street. However, about 1910, when a two-flat was built on the adjacent lot to the west and required two numbers (898 and 896), the Pries' address was changed to 894 61st Street, the address of the property today.

9. The Pries house was built on a lot that measures 50 by 140 feet. The back property line coincides with the boundary between Oakland and Berkeley.

10. Pries's parents were married in San Francisco on 8 July 1882. On the marriage certificate, their names are given as "Roger Pries of New York, New York," and "Helen Koepke of Holstein, Germany" (Lionel Pries papers, Special Collections Division, University of Washington Libraries).

11. Author's interview with Robert Winskill, 26 July 1994.

12. Ibid.

13. Although there was a Southern Pacific passenger station within a few blocks of the Pries house, service was slow, and the commute, including the ferry run, initially took at least an hour in each direction. The situation improved after 26 October 1903, when the San Francisco, Oakland and San Jose Railroad, a network of interurban lines and commuter ferries known as the Key Route (with nearly one hundred scheduled trains a day), initiated service and cut the commuting time in half. The Southern Pacific responded by electrifying its line in 1910 and providing improved service as well; it was at this time that its red vehicles came to be called the Red Trains. For background on the Oakland and Berkeley lines of the Southern Pacific and the Key Route, see Robert S. Ford, *Red Trains Remembered* (Glendale Calif.: Interurban Press, 1980), and Harre W. Demorre, *The Key Route* (Glendale, Calif.: Interurban Press, 1985). After the Key Route began its service, the few remaining empty tracts in the area were rapidly developed, and new houses were also constructed on most vacant lots in the older subdivisions; see North Oakland History file, Oakland History Room of the Main Library, Oakland Public Library.

14. The Bay School, at 62nd Street and San Pablo Avenue, was later renamed the Golden Gate School. The wooden school building, dating from 1892, was replaced by a new building in the 1920s. A photograph of the building can be found in the historical photographs collection, Oakland History Room of the Main Library, Oakland Public Library.

15. Memo to author from Bryant Milliman, 26 Sept. 2003. Kolb recalled that Pries had told him that his father regularly required a drawing (from memory) of one of the blocks they had walked past, including buildings, storefronts, and even items in the store windows (author's discussion with Keith Kolb, 8 Sept. 2004). However, Robert Winskill, Pries's close friend of later life, recalled that Pries had told him that he never had a good relationship with his father; Winskill doubts they went on many long walks together (author's discussion with Robert Winskill, 30 June 2004).

16. Author's interview with Robert Winskill, 26 July 1994.

17. Two recent histories of the San Francisco earthquake and fire are John Castillo Kennedy, *The Great Earthquake and Fire: San Francisco, 1906* (New York: William Morrow, 1963), and Dan Kurzman, *Disaster! The Great San Francisco Earthquake and Fire of 1906* (New York: HarperCollins, 2001).

18. Jack London, "The Story of an Eye-witness," *Collier's* 37 (5 May 1906), 23.

19. Rathje Pries joined Gump's in 1886 as a clerk; by the 1890s, he was identified in city directories as a picture hanger, and at the turn of the century he was identified as a packer. The titles are likely approximations; Rathje Pries no doubt worked in the Gump's store in a wide variety of roles over the course of his life. For the history of Gump's, see Carol Green Wilson, *Gump's Treasure Trade: A Story of San Francisco* (New York: HarperCollins/T. Y. Crowell Company, 1949), and Janet Lynn Roseman and others, *Gump's Since 1861: A San Francisco Legend* (San Francisco: Chronicle Books, 1991).

20. There were many guidebooks and reports published at the time of the Panama-Pacific International Exposition. For a textual account of the art and architecture, see Eugen Neuhaus, *The Art of the Exposition: Personal Impressions of the Architecture, Sculpture, Mural Decorations, Color Scheme & Other Aesthetic Aspects of the Panama-Pacific International Exposition* (San Francisco: Paul Elder and Co., 1915). An exemplary volume of pho-

tographs is *The Great Exposition: The Panama-Pacific International Exposition Illustrated with Two Sumptuous Colored Panoramas and Eighty-Four Pages of Engravings of Its Principal Scenes and Features* (San Francisco: Robert A. Reid, 1915). A recent popular overview is Donna Ewald and Peter Clute, *San Francisco Invites the World: The Panama-Pacific International Exposition of 1915* (San Francisco: Chronicle Books, 1991). See also Burton Benedict, ed., *The Anthropology of World's Fairs: San Francisco's Panama-Pacific International Exposition of 1915* (London: Scolar Press, 1983).

21. Emily Post, *By Motor to the Golden Gate* (New York: Appleton, 1916), 221–24. Gump's reprinted this description in a small brochure; a copy is available at the California Historical Society.

22. Author's interview with Robert Winskill, 26 July 1994.

23. In his will, Jillis Clute Wilmerding (1833–1894), a San Francisco business leader, had provided a bequest to establish the Wilmerding School of Industrial Arts for boys. His idea was that the school should provide an academic education supplemented by training in the practical arts. According to a history published around 1977, the school's first catalogue stated the mission clearly: "Experience has shown that there is no better way to develop solidity of character and the ability of self support than a reasonable amount of academic study combined with thorough training in the handling of tools and building materials"; see Gregory Nelson, *A History of Lick-Wilmerding* (San Francisco: Lick-Wilmerding High School, n.d.).

24. The Wilmerding School opened in 1900 in a building that was just one block from the Lick School, so named because it had been established by a bequest from James Lick (1796–1876), who set up a trust to fund a school "to educate males and females in the practical arts of life." George Merrill, the principal of Lick, became the principal of Wilmerding in 1901. Thereafter, although the two schools did not officially merge their curricula and operations until 1915, there was increasing coordination and sharing of classes. The schools reflected the Arts and Crafts ethos of the period as they offered college-preparatory classes and hands-on technical education. Lux School of Industrial Training, a girls' school founded in 1912, also participated in the 1915 merger. For a time, the merged schools were referred to as Lick-Wilmerding-Lux. The student publication of the three schools was titled *LWL Life*, reflecting the three original names.

25. From 1912 to 1916, Lionel Pries, like his father, would have commuted daily from Oakland to San Francisco; they probably traveled together each morning and may have arrived home together in the evenings as well if Lionel stayed late for school activities or to visit school friends.

26. See *The Wilmerding School of Industrial Arts for Boys, Founded by J. C. Wilmerding, Regents of the University of California Trustees*, circular no. 3 (San Francisco: June 1902), n.p. (copy available at Lick-Wilmerding School library).

27. This summary of architectural problems is based on descriptions in *Wilmerding Life*; see *Wilmerding Life* 11/3 (March 1914), 11/4 (June 1914), 12/3 (March 1915), 12/4 (June 1915).

28. References to Pries's activities are found in *Wilmerding Life* 11/3 (March 1914), 22; *Wilmerding Life* 11/4 (June 1914), 57; *Wilmerding Life* 12/3 (March 1915), 15; *Wilmerding Life* 12/4 (June 1915), 67; and *LWL Life* 1/1 (Oct. 1915), 30. Copies of these issues are held by the Lick-Wilmerding School library; copies of the issues for October and December 1915 are not available.

29. *Wilmerding Life* 11/2 (Dec. 1913), 19. This drawing reappeared in the March 1915 issue.

30. *Wilmerding Life* 11/4 (June 1914), 16, 19; *Wilmerding Life* 12/3 (March 1915), 15; *Wilmerding Life* 12/4 (June 1915), 24; *LWL Life* 1/2 (Dec. 1915), 2; *LWL Life* 1/4 (June 1916), 25. Pries's portrait also appeared each year among those of the art staff, and, in June 1916, his portrait also appeared for his graduation.

31. Each school's student publication devoted an issue to the Panama-Pacific International Exposition: see [*Lick*] *Tiger*, March 1915, and *Wilmerding Life*, June 1915.

32. For Jules Guerin, see F. S. Swales, "Master Draftsmen II: Jules Guerin," *Pencil Points* 5 (May 1924), 63–66, 70. See also obituaries in *Architectural Forum* 85 (Sept. 1946), 148, and *American Institute of Architects Journal* 6 (Sept. 1946), 140.

33. *Wilmerding Life* 12/4 (June 1915), 37–38.

34. Memo to Victor Steinbrueck from Robert H. Ross, undated (ca. Feb. 1978). Pries enjoyed not just the architecture but also the social life that the exposition engendered; the grounds were well lighted in the evening, and the exposition hosted parties and dances that Pries frequently attended (author's interview with Robert Winskill, 26 July 1994).

35. Carlos and Theodore Maas were frequently mentioned in *Wilmerding Life*, and Theodore Maas also appears in *LWL Life*. Both Maas brothers were listed as members of the *Life* staff in *Wilmerding Life* 11/4 (June 1914), 35. The participation of both brothers was sometimes the source of humor; see "A Maas Meeting," *Wilmerding Life* 11/3 (March 1914), 16. Their names, along with that of Pries, frequently appeared in the "Shop Notes" subsection about architecture students.

36. Theodore J. Maas was born in Germany and emigrated to the United States about 1873, settling in Wisconsin. He married Ida Sutter, a descendant of the famous Sutter family of California. Theodore Maas and Ida Sutter Maas had four sons: Donald S. Maas, Carlos J. Maas, Theodore A. Maas, and Henry Bothin Maas. The family moved to California in 1904. Henry Bothin Maas was named after his great uncle, Henry Bothin, an important entrepreneur and real estate developer in San Francisco and Santa Barbara (for background on Henry Bothin, see chap. 3, this volume).

37. Author's interview with Robert Winskill, 26 July 1994; author's discussion with Robert Winskill, 30 June 2004.

38. Pries's Lick-Wilmerding diploma is found in the

Pries papers, Special Collections Division, University of Washington Libraries.

39. For a discussion of these architects and their impact, see Richard Longstreth, *On the Edge of the World: Four Architects in San Francisco at the Turn of the Century* (New York/Cambridge, Mass.: Architectural History Foundation/MIT Press, 1983).

40. Brief essays addressing these architects are found in Robert Winter, ed., *Toward a Simpler Way of Life*. See, for example, Joan Draper, "John Galen Howard," 31–40; Robert Judson Clark, "Louis Christian Mullgardt," 41–50; and Sara Holmes Boutelle, "Julia Morgan," 63–72. A longer study of Morgan is Sara Holmes Boutelle, *Julia Morgan, Architect* (New York: Abbeville Publishers, 1988).

41. On academic eclecticism, see Richard Longstreth, "Academic Eclecticism in American Architecture," *Winterthur Portfolio* 17/1 (Spring 1982), 55–82; an abbreviated version of this discussion is found in Longstreth, *On the Edge of the World*, 9–39. See also Mark Alan Hewitt, *The Architect & the American Country House, 1890–1940* (New Haven, Conn.: Yale University Press, 1990), 31–42.

42. The term "Shingle Style" was created by the architectural historian Vincent Scully; see Vincent J. Scully Jr., *The Shingle Style and the Stick Style: Architectural Theory and Design from Downing to the Origins of Wright*, rev. ed. (New Haven, Conn.: Yale University Press, 1971).

43. Scully's first book on the Shingle Style focused on the mode in the eastern United States. He later wrote the introduction to a book of plates from American architectural journals, showing the national spread of the Shingle Style; see *The Architecture of the American Summer: The Flowering of the Shingle Style* (New York: Rizzoli/Temple Hoyne Buell Center of Columbia University, 1989). Also addressing the Shingle Style, with a set of notable examples from the West as well as from the East, is Leland Roth, *Shingle Styles: Innovation and Tradition in American Architecture, 1874 to 1982* (New York: Henry N. Abrams, 1999). The Shingle Style was called "modernized colonial" in the 1880s, according to Richard Guy Wilson, *The Colonial Revival House* (New York: Harry N. Abrams, 2004), 37.

44. On Burnham's directive and its influence on the California Building at the World's Columbian Exposition, see Longstreth, *On the Edge of the World*, 263–66. The idea of regional expression at the 1893 fair is also discussed in Jeffrey Karl Ochsner, "In Search of Regional Expression: The Washington State Building at the World's Columbian Exposition, Chicago 1893," *Pacific Northwest Quarterly* 86/4 (Fall 1995), 165–77.

45. On the Bay Area Tradition (sometimes called the "Bay Region Tradition"), see Leslie Mandelson Freudenheim and Elizabeth Sacks Sussman, *Building with Nature: Roots of the San Francisco Bay Region Tradition* (Santa Barbara, Calif.: Peregrine Smith, 1974).

46. Charles Keeler, *The Simple Home* (San Francisco: Paul Elder and Co., 1904; rprt. Santa Barbara, Calif: Peregrine Smith, 1979). The influence of Keeler's book is discussed by many authors; see, for example, Winter, ed., *Toward a Simpler Way of Life*, 3–6, 19–21, 52–53, and Longstreth, *On the Edge of the World*, 314–18. *The Craftsman* frequently published buildings by Greene and Greene and other southern California Arts and Crafts architects, but it seldom published work from northern California.

47. *LWL Life* 1/2 (Dec. 1915), 2.

48. For the Mission Revival, see Karen J. Weitze, *California's Mission Revival* (Los Angeles: Hennessey & Ingalls, 1984).

49. For a discussion of downtown San Francisco's development after the 1906 earthquake, see Michael R. Corbett, *Splendid Survivors: San Francisco's Downtown Architectural Heritage* (San Francisco: Foundation for San Francisco's Architectural Heritage/California Living Books, 1979).

50. On Bernard Maybeck, see Kenneth H. Cardwell, *Bernard Maybeck: Artisan, Architect, Artist* (Salt Lake City, Utah: Gibbs M. Smith, 1977), and Sally B. Woodbridge, *Bernard Maybeck: Visionary Architect* (New York: Abbeville Publishers, 1992). See also William H. Jordy, *American Buildings and Their Architects: Progressive and Academic Ideals at the Turn of the Twentieth Century* (New York: Oxford University Press, 1972), 275–313; Longstreth, *On the Edge of the World*, esp. 312–55; Esther McCoy, *Five California Architects* (New York: Reinhold, 1960; rprt. New York: Praeger, 1975), 1–57; and Jeffrey W. Limerick, "Bernard Maybeck," in Winter, ed., *Toward a Simpler Way of Life*, 51–62.

51. "10th Annual Exhibition of the Architectural Association" (8–17 May 1916), *Minute Book of the Architecture Student Association*, 244 (records of the Department of Architecture, University of California, Berkeley; College of Environmental Design Archives, University of California, Berkeley).

52. The school's full name was Ecole Nationale et Spéciale des Beaux-Arts. Reorganized after the French Revolution, the Ecole combined two academies that had been established under Louis XIV: the Academy of Painting and Sculpture (dating from 1648), and the Academy of Architecture (dating from 1671). In 1823, the school promulgated regulations establishing its curriculum, and although these were occasionally amended, its fundamental approach to teaching design, once established, changed little over the next 150 years. My discussion of the educational system of the Ecole is based primarily on Richard Chafee, "The Teaching of Architecture at the Ecole des Beaux-Arts," in Arthur Drexler, ed., *The Architecture of the Ecole des Beaux-Arts* (New York/Cambridge, Mass.: Museum of Modern Art/MIT Press, 1977), 60–109; Neil Levine, "The Competition for the Grand Prix in 1824," in Robin Middleton, ed., *The Beaux Arts and Nineteenth-Century French Architecture* (Cambridge, Mass.: MIT Press, 1982); Joan Draper, "The Ecole des Beaux-Arts and the Architectural Profession in the United States: The Case of John Galen Howard," in Spiro Kostof, ed., *The Architect: Chapters in the History of the Profession* (New York: Oxford University Press, 1977),

209–37; and the entire January 1901 issue of *Architectural Record*.

53. An encompassing study of American architectural education has not been written in the last fifty years. One older study is Arthur Clason Weatherhead, *The History of Collegiate Education in Architecture in the United States* (Los Angeles: 1941, no publisher listed). Comments on the education of American architects in university programs influenced by the Ecole des Beaux Arts are found in Kostof, ed., *The Architect*, chaps. 8 and 9. Only in the 1930s, under the combined impacts of the Depression, new technologies, new aesthetic ideals, and growing social concerns, did the Ecole method begin to be displaced. At the University of Washington, some elements of the tradition endured until the late 1950s.

54. As the French national school, the Ecole had as its fundamental purpose to prepare architects for government service, but students from other countries who were able to pass the entrance exams were accepted on an equal basis. The competition for the highest award, the Grand Prix de Rome, was open only to French students; but by the late nineteenth century, any student who stayed a sufficient time, received the requisite points, completed a thesis, and gained a year's work experience could become *diplômé par le gouvernement*. However, for many students, especially those from abroad, the aim was less to earn the diploma than simply to participate in the Ecole experience, fundamentally the experience of the atelier.

55. John F. Harbeson, *The Study of Architectural Design with Special Reference to the Program of the Beaux-Arts Institute of Design* (New York: Pencil Points Press, 1926), 1 (emphasis in original). This book collects in a single volume a series of articles on the Beaux-Arts method that Harbeson published in *Pencil Points*, beginning in 1921.

56. Although most American architectural schools until the 1940s derived their pedagogy from the Ecole des Beaux-Arts, there were exceptions. In the nineteenth century, German architectural education was much more influential at the University of Illinois under the leadership of Nathan Ricker; see Routa Geraniotis, "The University of Illinois and German Architectural Education," *Journal of Architectural Education* 38 (Summer 1984), 115–21; see also Anthony Alofsin, "Tempering the Ecole: Nathan Ricker at the University of Illinois and Langford Warren at Harvard," in Gwendolyn Wright and Janet Parks, eds., *The History of History in American Schools of Architecture, 1865–1975* (New York: Temple Hoyne Buell Center for the Study of American Architecture/Princeton Architectural Press, 1990), 73–77. A notable West Coast example is the University of Oregon, which broke with the Ecole method in the early 1920s; see Michael Schellenbarger, "Ellis F. Lawrence (1879–1946): A Brief Biography," in Michael Schellenbarger, ed., *Harmony and Diversity: The Architecture and Teaching of Ellis F. Lawrence* (Eugene: University of Oregon, 1987), 8–24.

57. A critical analysis of the Society of Beaux-Arts Architects and the Beaux-Arts Institute of Design has not yet appeared, but a summary of the Society of Beaux-Arts Architects and the BAID is found in Weatherhead, *The History of Collegiate Education in Architecture in the United States*, 76–81. A brief summary of the early history of the Society of Beaux-Arts Architects is "The History and Aims of the Society of Beaux-Arts Architects," *American Architect* 95 (24 Mar. 1909), 101–2. The best source of information on the Society of Beaux-Arts Architects and the BAID are the *Bulletins*, published monthly except in August and September, with design projects, critiques, and illustrations of premiated work. After World War II, as the Beaux-Arts system was eclipsed, the BAID became the National Institute for Architectural Education (NIAE). By the turn of the century, Ecole graduates were heading many American university architecture departments or serving on their faculties. The presence of so many Ecole graduates created more support for the activities of the BAID. After 1910, the number of Americans attending the Ecole actually declined, a development largely attributed to improvement in the education offered by the American schools.

58. For information on John Galen Howard, see Joan Draper, "John Galen Howard and the Beaux-Arts Movement in the United States," unpublished M.A. thesis, University of California, Berkeley, 1972. Shorter essays include Joan Draper, "John Galen Howard," *JAE: Journal of Architectural Education* 33/2 (Nov. 1979), 29–35; Draper, "John Galen Howard," in Winter, ed., *Toward a Simpler Way of Life*, 31–40; Draper, "The Ecole des Beaux-Arts and the Architectural Profession in the United States: The Case of John Galen Howard," in Kostof, ed., *The Architect*, 209–37; and Partridge, *John Galen Howard and the Berkeley Campus*. Howard's papers are in the Bancroft Library, University of California, Berkeley. Howard's drawings are in the College of Environmental Design Archives, University of California, Berkeley.

59. Partridge, *John Galen Howard and the Berkeley Campus*, 61. Woodbridge details the complex sequence of events that led to Howard's moving to Berkeley; see Sally B. Woodbridge, *John Galen Howard and the University of California: The Design of a Great Public University Campus* (Berkeley: University of California Press, 2002), 39–67.

60. This discussion of the Berkeley curriculum is drawn from Draper, "The Ecole des Beaux-Arts and the Architectural Profession in the United States: The Case of John Galen Howard," in Kostof, ed., *The Architect*, 209–37.

61. For a complete discussion of the analytique as understood at the time, see Harbeson, *The Study of Architectural Design*, 7–72. A good retrospective discussion of the analytique as experienced by students is Joseph Esherick, "Architectural Education in the Thirties and the Seventies: A Personal View," in Kostof, ed., *The Architect*, 249–56.

62. Draper suggests that Howard did not use the

BAID programmes; see Draper, "The Ecole des Beaux-Arts and the Architectural Profession in the United States: The Case of John Galen Howard," in Kostof, ed., *The Architect*, 235. However, the collection of studio assignments held by the College of Environmental Design Archives for the years 1916–20 indicates that BAID programmes were occasionally used. Most studio assignments were typed (carbons), a fact suggesting that they were produced by the Berkeley faculty, but a few studio assignments were printed, an indication that they were supplied by the BAID (records of the Department of Architecture, University of California, Berkeley; College of Environmental Design Archives, University of California, Berkeley).

63. This list of guest faculty and critics is found in David Gebhard, *Lutah Maria Riggs: A Woman in Architecture, 1921–1980* (Santa Barbara, Calif.: Capra Press/ Santa Barbara Museum of Art, 1992), 4.

64. For a discussion of the role of John Galen Howard in shaping the Berkeley campus, see Woodbridge, *John Galen Howard and the University of California*. A shorter introduction is Partridge, *John Galen Howard and the Berkeley Campus*. For an overview of the campus history and a discussion of individual buildings to the year 2002, see Harvey Helfand, *The Campus Guide: University of California, Berkeley* (New York: Princeton Architectural Press, 2002).

65. For a discussion of the Ark in the context of the First Bay Tradition, see Draper, "John Galen Howard," in Winter, ed., *Toward a Simpler Way of Life*, 37–39. See also Woodbridge, *John Galen Howard and the University of California*, 91, 93–95.

66. William Wurster, "The Passing of the Ark," *Progressive Architecture* 45 (July 1964), 167. For the history of the Ark, now called North Gate Hall, see Helfand, *The Campus Guide: University of California*, 113–16.

67. Letter to Carl F. Gould from John Galen Howard, 9 Sept. 1914 (Carl F. Gould papers, Special Collections Division, University of Washington Libraries), cited in Norman J. Johnston, *The College of Architecture and Urban Planning: Seventy-Five Years at the University of Washington—A Personal View* (Seattle: University of Washington College of Architecture and Urban Planning, 1991), 8.

68. Two original Pries drawings are found in the documents collection of the College of Environmental Design Archives, University of California, Berkeley. Neither is particularly notable. A set of original Pries drawings of various orders is found in the Pries drawing collection, Special Collections Division, University of Washington Libraries. Pries gave Keith Kolb drawings of three of his senior projects (each stamped with the date it was turned in), "A War Memorial Building" (3 Nov. 1919), "The New Turnbull Inne" (20 Dec. 1919), and "A Memorial Hall" (14 Feb. 1920), and two historical drawings (also date-stamped), "La Cathedrale de Reims" (7 Nov. 1919; a pen-and-ink perspective) and "Santo Spirito, Brunelleschi" (29 Mar. 1920; a pencil and watercolor section). In December 2005, Kolb donated these

drawings to the University of Washington Libraries, Special Collections Division.

69. Records of the University of California architecture program for the years 1916–1920 include multiple scrapbooks containing small blueprints of drawings for students' projects (apparently, for the most part, those that received high marks); a list of senior problems and copies of programs for some of these problems; minute books of the student association; and albums of photographs of students and faculty. All are now held in the College of Environmental Design Archives, University of California, Berkeley.

70. The tile manufactory problem was assigned on 25 March 1920 and was due on 20 April 1920. Unfortunately, the only records of Pries's winning scheme are the blueprints of his drawings in the scrapbooks at the College of Environmental Design Archives. In 1921, the Alumni Prize problem was an automobile service and rest station; the winner was Lancelot Gowen, a student in the master's degree program in architecture. Gowen was to start teaching at the University of Washington in 1924 and would be Pries's faculty colleague from 1928 to 1958.

71. Materials relating to Pries's military service that are now in the collection of Pries's personal papers at the University of Washington include letters and postcards relative to his induction and service in the Coastal Artillery Corps as well as his honorable discharge from the United States Army (Pries papers, Special Collections Division, University of Washington Libraries). There are no surviving records at the National Personnel Records Center in St. Louis of Lionel Pries's military service; Pries's records were very likely among those destroyed by the 12 July 1973 fire at the center. Pries's résumé from the early 1950s includes the notation "Chief of survey party, New Idria power line"; this note suggests that, while serving in the military, he was involved in surveying for a new power line in San Benito County, south of San Francisco, but no records have been found to confirm this activity (Lionel H. Pries, undated résumé, Pries papers, Special Collections Division, University of Washington Libraries).

72. Pries's bench was mentioned in the *Daily Californian*, 21 Jan. 1921; with Pries in Philadelphia, John Galen Howard apparently supervised construction of the bench, since he was quoted with regard to progress in quarrying the travertine and sculpting the two bears. Mora was a well-known sculptor in central California during that period; his plaster model is now in possession of Robert Winskill. The bench was originally placed on the west side of the campanile, facing San Francisco Bay. In 1958, it was moved beneath a new canopy on the north side of the tower, to protect it from falling stone chips. At some point, the bench was rehabilitated and the original carving on the bench supports was shaved off. The bench is briefly discussed, but not illustrated, in Helfand, *The Campus Guide: University of California*, 52–53.

73. Rathje Pries died of prostate cancer on 12 Decem-

ber 1917 (Rathje F. W. Pries's death certificate, Office of Vital Records, Department of Health Services, State of California). According to the death certificate, Rathje Pries had been in the care of a doctor since June 1917. By November, Rathje Pries's illness had progressed sufficiently that his death was anticipated; the family purchased a plot in Sunset View Cemetery, El Cerrito, California, on 1 November 1917.

74. Author's interview with Robert Winskill, 26 July 1994. Kolb also recalled this story; author's conversation with Keith Kolb, 14 Dec. 2004.

75. Magdalena Pries died of pneumonia on 12 May 1919; she may have been a late victim of the worldwide influenza pandemic of 1918–19 (Magdalena Pries's death certificate, Office of Vital Records, Department of Health Services, State of California). Magdalena and Rathje Pries are buried in Sunset View Cemetery, adults section D, plat 1, graves 52 and 53, but there are no markers to identify the graves.

76. *Pencil Points* printed a brief biography of Pries after he won the 1922 LeBrun Traveling Scholarship competition. That biography includes a mention of Pries's previous employment "in the offices of Messrs. John Galen Howard and of Charles K. Sumner in San Francisco." Since Pries left California to go to the University of Pennsylvania at the end of August 1920, he must have been employed by Howard and by Sumner prior to that date, likely in the summer of 1919 or the summer of 1920, or possibly during the school year; see *Pencil Points* 3 (May 1922), 35.

77. The Stephens Memorial Union stands out on the campus because of its unusual Collegiate Gothic style, shown clearly in the photograph of a Pries perspective rendering found in the so-called Pries Scrapbook, 27r; see Pries Scrapbook, Pries drawing collection, Special Collections Division, University of Washington Libraries. The Pries Scrapbook is a three-quarter-bound volume with hand-tooled lettering, SCRAP BOOK, on the spine. This volume was originally seventy-two blank sheets, to which Pries glued sketches, drawings, design studies, and the like, primarily from his California career. Pages are numbered only on the front side. The Stephens Memorial Union drawing is in Pries's personal graphic style.

78. The many late nights in the studio no doubt fostered jokes and pranks, and residents of the neighborhood just across Hearst Avenue complained about late-night noise and profanity, but no specific mention of Pries's involvement survives; see letters from Benjamin I. Wheeler to John Galen Howard, 1916. See University of California Office of the President records (CU-5 ser.2, 1916, 62) and 1921 (CU-5 ser.2, 1921, 88), University Archives, Bancroft Library, University of California, Berkeley.

79. In later years, Pries told the story that his thinness almost prevented him from graduating. The University of California required each student to swim from one end of the university's pool to the other before he or she could graduate. Because Pries was so thin, he had

great difficulty staying afloat. He claimed to have taught himself to hold his breath long enough that, after jumping as far as possible into the pool at one end, he could try to swim until he sank and then walk on the bottom of the pool to reach the other end (author's interview with Robert Winskill, 26 July 1994). Kolb also recalled this story (author's discussion with Keith Kolb, 8 Sept. 2004).

80. Photographs in the Pries collection—without clear labels as to location, unfortunately—show Pries and several of his classmates on various outings. One of these groups includes Pries's classmates Frederick Pearce and Gerald Fitzgerald as well as Lutah Riggs, from the class of 1919. Similar photographs are found in the album of photographs that belonged to Lutah Rriggs, an album now held by the University Art Museum, University of California, Santa Barbara.

81. *Minute Book of the Architecture Student Association*, 11 Dec. 1919, 278–79 (Records of the Department of Architecture, University of California, Berkeley; College of Environmental Design Archives, University of California, Berkeley).

82. Abracadabra had been in existence since about 1895. Sproul, later president of the University of California, Berkeley, had himself been a resident of the Abracadabra house prior to his graduation, in 1913 (memo to author from William Roberts, archivist, University of California, Berkeley, 22 June 1999). In Pries's first three years at the university, however, he had continued to live at home: it was convenient and, more important, less expensive.

83. Helen Earle Sutherland (21 July 1897–30 Oct. 1981) began at the University of California, Berkeley, in 1917 and received her A.B. degree on 17 Dec. 1920.

84. Although Pries was at the University of Pennsylvania in 1920–21, he apparently returned to California in December 1920, probably to spend Christmas with the Maas family. One of the Christmas gifts he received was a book from Helen Sutherland. The friendship continued for several years: the endpaper of his copy of the *1922 Year Book* of the Philadelphia AIA and T-Square Club is inscribed "Lionel H. Pries, Helen Earle Sutherland, 1922." His passport for 1922–23 lists Sutherland's San Francisco address as his own, and during his travels in Europe in 1922–23 Pries regularly received letters from Sutherland. Pries was probably already aware of his sexual orientation, so his relationship with Sutherland may have been significant emotionally but was likely nonsexual; such relationships between gay men and women confidantes were not uncommon in the period (memo to author from Gary Atkins, 12 June 2003). In conversations in the 1930s, he told some students that he had been "jilted," and he told others that, although he planned to marry, he and his fiancée (who remained unnamed) had called it off (author's interview with Kelly Foss, 15 July 2005; author's conversation with Robert H. Ross, 18 July 2005). These stories may have had some truth to them, or they may have been a way for Pries to answer questions about his single status as he remained

deeply closeted in the university community. Pries remained in contact with Helen Sutherland through most of his life. She never married. She practiced for many years as an interior designer: beginning in 1932, the San Francisco city directory lists her as a partner in Schoch, Sutherland and Stanbury; from 1938 to 1961, her firm was Sutherland and Stanbury. In the 1930s, she lived in Sausalito. After 1944, she lived in San Francisco. Her name and address are found in Pries's last address book (compiled in the late 1950s or early 1960s). Kolb recalled that Pries once referred to her as his "lost girl friend" (author's discussion with Keith Kolb, 8 Sept. 2004).

85. Pries's class rank is estimated from the high marks he received on most of his projects (as reflected in the scrapbooks containing small blueprints of drawings held by the College of Environmental Design Archives) and from the fact that no other student placed first as many times. He also won the Alumni Prize with his design for a tile manufactory, and he won the competition for the Class of 1920 Memorial Bench.

86. Lionel Pries no longer owned the Oakland house when he went east to Philadelphia. Proceeds from the sale of the house may have made feasible his enrollment in the graduate program at the University of Pennsylvania.

87. While this discussion emphasizes the role of Paul Cret, a key part was played by Professor Warren Laird. Laird had come to the leadership ranks of the University of Pennsylvania in 1891 with a clear vision for the university's future. In the space of a few years, he raised standards and implemented a curriculum based primarily, but not exclusively, on the Beaux-Arts model. Among his most important policy decisions, however, were those that addressed the composition of the faculty. Laird established a policy of "teaching by experts," and he sought not only faculty with Beaux-Arts classical training but also those who represented a wider range of approaches to design education. By the mid-1890s, the impact of Laird's reforms began to be recognized by the Philadelphia professional community, but the international stature of the school was achieved after Paul Cret became atelier director, in 1903. For Laird's comments on architectural education at the University of Pennsylvania, see Warren P. Laird, "Architectural Design at the University of Pennsylvania," *American Architect* 94 (9 Sept. 1908), 84–85, and Warren P. Laird, "Notes on Architectural Training," *American Architect* 95 (7 Apr. 1909, 115–16; 14 Apr. 1909, 123–24). For a general discussion of the school during the years Pries attended, see George E. Thomas, "The Laird Years," in Ann L. Strong and George E. Thomas, eds., *The Book of the School: 100 Years, the Graduate School of Fine Arts at the University of Pennsylvania* (Philadelphia: GSFA, 1990), 24–39.

88. Elizabeth Greenwell Grossman, *The Civic Architecture of Paul Cret* (Cambridge: Cambridge University Press, 1996), 8.

89. Paul Philippe Cret, "The Training of the Designer," *American Architect* 95 (7 Apr. 1909, 116; 14 Apr. 1909, 128; 21 Apr. 1909, 131–34; 28 Apr. 1909, 138–39). Cret also wrote about the importance of the Ecole; see Paul Philippe Cret, "The Ecole des Beaux-Arts: What Its Architectural Teaching Means," *Architectural Record* 23 (May 1908), 367–71.

90. For a list of designs by Cret and Zanzinger, see Theo B. White, *Paul Philippe Cret: Architect and Teacher* (Philadelphia: Art Alliance Press, 1973), 43–45. Detailed discussion of several of Cret's major competition projects is found in Grossman, *The Civic Architecture of Paul Cret*.

91. White, *Paul Philippe Cret*, 29.

92. Author's discussion with Keith Kolb, 8 Sept. 2004.

93. White, *Paul Philippe Cret*, 27. Cret also argued that the esquisse allowed the studio to emulate the realities of practice, whereas the conditions of the project often do not allow the best design solution to be used.

94. Thomas, "The Laird Years," in Strong and Thomas, eds., *The Book of the School*, 33.

95. White, *Paul Philippe Cret*, 29.

96. Grossman, *The Civic Architecture of Paul Cret*, 100.

97. Pries gave the drawings of the first two of these Penn projects to Keith Kolb in the early 1960s; in December 2005 Kolb gave these drawings to the University of Washington Libraries, Special Collections Division. The elevation of the warehouse project, for which Pries won a BAID First Medal, was published in *American Architect* 120 (20 July 1921), 42. The present location of Pries's gate lodge esquisse-esquisse is unknown; it probably does not survive. It was reproduced in John F. Harbeson, "The Sketch Problem," *Pencil Points*, 4/12 (Dec. 1923), 44; this drawing was reprinted in Harbeson, *The Study of Architectural Design*, 247. Pries also saved one example of a Cret critique, a pencil sketch on yellow tracing paper, now part of the Pries drawing collection, Special Collections Division, University of Washington Libraries.

98. Pries's résumé of the early 1950s states, "Tied for first place, American Academy in Rome competition, 1921" (Lionel H. Pries, undated résumé, Pries papers, Special Collections Division, University of Washington Libraries). The résumé he had submitted when he applied for a teaching position at the University of Washington, in 1928, is clearer: "Placed first in competition for the American Academy in Rome, but eventually given second place because there were already two Penn men in residence at Rome." See Lionel H. Pries, undated résumé attached to letter to David Thomson from Harlan Thomas, 22 June 1928. See University of Washington Office of the President records, acc. no. 71–34, box 113–13, Special Collections Division, University of Washington Libraries. He shared this story with close friends; both Kolb and Winskill mentioned it (author's interview with Keith Kolb, 11 Aug. 1995; author's interview with Robert Winskill, 26 July 1994). Pries's entry in the preliminary Rome Prize competition was among the drawings Winskill donated in 1995 to the Special Collections Division, University of Washington Libraries. Pries gave his drawings for the final Rome Prize competition to

Kolb in the early 1960s. Pries remained disillusioned with the Rome Prize process: when his student Alan Liddle wished to compete for the Rome Prize in the late 1940s, Pries warned him that the selection was "political" and that he stood little chance; nevertheless, Pries did help Liddle submit (author's interview with Alan Liddle, 22 July 1999).

99. The actual medals remain in possession of Pries's heir, Robert Winskill.

100. For a brief mention of the origins of the T-Square Club, see Jeffrey A. Cohen, "Building a Discipline: Early Institutional Settings for Architectural Education in Philadelphia, 1804–1890," *Journal of the Society of Architectural Historians* 53 (June 1994), 181.

101. Cret's involvement with the T-Square atelier is mentioned in White, *Paul Philippe Cret*, 23.

102. Theo White noted that those who studied under Cret regarded him as "a god"; see White, *Paul Philippe Cret*, 29. Pries's personality was described by Norman Johnston, a University of Washington student of the 1930s, as "Olympian"; see Johnston, *The College of Architecture and Urban Planning*, 39. In the late 1920s and early 1930s, Pries even emulated Cret's appearance by growing a moustache and parting his hair in the center.

103. DeArmond, Ashmead and Bickley was initially the partnership of Clarence DeArmond (1880–1953) and Duffield Ashmead Jr. (1883–1952), formed in 1908; they were joined by George H. Bickley (1880–1938) in 1911. According to the *Biographical Dictionary of Philadelphia Architects*, "the work that is documented for the firm represents that mixture often found in early twentieth century Philadelphia firms, consisting primarily of residential commissions with a measure of public buildings"; see Sandra Tatman and Roger Moss, *Biographical Dictionary of Philadelphia Architects, 1700–1930* (Boston: G. K. Hall, 1985), 16, 67–68, 199. DeArmond, Ashmead and Bickley's scheme for the Sesqui-Centennial Exhibition, sited on Wissahickon Creek, in the hilly northwest part of Philadelphia, created a U-shaped arrangement of the principal buildings focusing on the "Court of Pageantry"; see *Report of the Sesqui-Centennial Committee of the Engineers' Club of Philadelphia on Sites* (Philadelphia: Sesqui-Centennial Exhibition Association, 1922), plate 7 (thanks to Sandra Tatman, who brought this to my attention). It was the "Court of Pageantry" that Pries represented in his perspective.

104. John Penn Brock Sinkler (1875–1954), a graduate of the University of Pennsylvania who attended the Ecole des Beaux-Arts, was involved in private practice in Philadelphia after 1902 but served a term as city architect from 1920 to 1924: "His term as City Architect . . . was controversial due to the policy that the City Architect and a few draftsmen would design most of the municipal buildings creating a vast backlog"; see Tatman and Moss, *Biographical Dictionary of Philadelphia Architects*, 727–28.

105. Pries noted, "Position offered tremendous opportunity in the way of office and field experience." Pries's handwritten notes (ca. 1922) are found in the collection of his papers held by the Special Collections Division, University of Washington Libraries.

106. Adam Levine, historical consultant to the Philadelphia Water Department, discovered drawings of the project that clearly show Pries's signature. Levine also found the photograph of the building. Pries may have been involved in other sewage plants as well, and his handwritten résumé indicates that he was involved in restoration work at the "Old Market" and in work at three schools (although schools were not under Sinkler's office, so this indication may be incorrect).

107. *Philadelphia Evening Bulletin*, 29 Sept. 1929. This article was brought to my attention by Adam Levine.

108. Birch Burdette Long, a well-known delineator whose work was often published in *Pencil Points*, provided $250 for prizes for the competition. For a discussion of the winners of the first Birch Burdette Long Sketch Competition, see *Pencil Points* 3 (Jan. 1922), 7; Pries's drawing, captioned "Pencil Sketch of a Bit of Old Philadelphia by Lionel H. Pries, Philadelphia, Winner of a Prize of the Fifth Grade," appeared on page 11. Winners were also published in *American Architect*; see "Awards in Birch Burdette Long Competition," *American Architect* 121 (4 Jan. 1922), 15 (a Pries drawing different from the one in *Pencil Points* appeared with the title *Lionel H. Pries, West Philadelphia, Pa.* on page 20). The locations of the originals of these two drawings are not known; the three other drawings that Pries submitted (and which were never published) are found in the Pries collection, Special Collections Division, University of Washington Libraries.

109. On the regionalist approach of Philadelphia architects, see Hewitt, *The Architect & the American Country House*, 77–82, 197–207.

110. Ibid., 199. Pries retained his membership in the T-Square Club through the early 1930s as he continued to receive its publications and was listed as an out-of-town member.

111. The LeBrun Traveling Scholarship had been established by Pierre LeBrun, a member of the Napoleon LeBrun and Sons architectural firm in New York, after he retired from practice about 1910.

112. Pries's design for the LeBrun competition appeared in *American Architect-Architectural Review* 121 (10 May 1922), 389–90. "Extracts from Competition Program—LeBrun Traveling Scholarship, 1921–1922" appeared in the same issue on page 396. Pries's scheme also appeared in the *Yearbook of the Twenty-fifth Annual Architectural Exhibition* (Philadelphia: Philadelphia AIA and T-Square Club, 1922), n.p.

113. Edgar Viguers Seeler (1867–1929), a native of Philadelphia, graduated from MIT and attended the Ecole des Beaux-Arts. On his return to Philadelphia, he set up his own office, where he did a variety of commercial, institutional, and residential projects; see Tatman and Moss, *Biographical Dictionary of Philadelphia Architects*, 708–9. See also George E. Thomas, "Edgar V. Seeler," in Strong and Thomas, eds., *The Book of the School—100 Years*, 50–51.

114. Pries obtained his passport on 10 April 1922; it includes the notation that he intended to travel in the "British Isles, France, Italy, and Spain." He listed his occupation as draftsman and gave 1043 Clayton Street (the San Francisco address of Helen Sutherland) as his home address, even though he had lived in Philadelphia for nearly two years. At least one later publication has suggested that his itinerary included Greece and North Africa, but his passport includes no stamps for those countries. The passport is in the collection of Pries papers, Special Collections Division, University of Washington Libraries.

115. Pries's travel diary, "My Trip Abroad," is in the collection of Pries material, Special Collections Division, University of Washington Libraries.

116. Pries's itinerary has been assembled from the more than ninety drawings and watercolors held in the Pries drawing collection, supplemented by information in the diary plus three surviving maps of his trip: a *Billete Kilometrico—Tariff 109* (Spanish railway ticket issued to Lionel Henry Pries, 12 May 1922), including the map marked with Pries's route; Karl Baedeker, *Spain and Portugal: Handbook for Travellers*, 4th ed. (Leipsic: Karl Baedeker, 1913), including a map inside the back cover marked with cities visited; and Kurt Hielscher, *Picturesque Italy: Architecture and Landscape* (New York: Brentano's, 1925), including a map on page xiv marked with Pries's route in Italy. The ticket is in the Pries papers and the books are in the Pries book collection, Special Collections Division, University of Washington Libraries.

117. "The Birch Burdette Long Sketch Competition for 1922," *Pencil Points* 3 (Dec. 1922), 12. According to the text, the jury (Cass Gilbert, Alexander Trowbridge, Raymond Hood, Birch Burdette Long, and Eugene Clute) met on 12 November 1922 and selected the winners. Pries's drawing appeared with the caption "Pencil Sketch by Lionel Pries, San Francisco, Cal. Winner of the Second Prize in the Birch Burdette Long Sketch Competition for 1922"; his prize was $50. Pries's drawing was also mentioned in "The Traveling Exhibition of Sketches," *Pencil Points* 4 (May 1923), 66. The original survives in the Pries drawing collection, Special Collections Division, University of Washington Libraries.

118. Information about Pries's *pensione* was provided by Katrina Deines, Rome Center director, University of Washington.

119. Author's conversation with Keith Kolb, Sept. 2003. Pries's drawings of the Pantheon have not been found.

120. "Portfolio of Sketches in France, Italy and Spain by Lionel H. Pries," *Architect and Engineer* 86 (July 1926), 89–97. The nine sketches are *Puente San Martin, Toledo*; *The Vermillion Bridge, Ronda*; *La Tour de Beurre, Rouen, France*; *Sainte Merri, Paris*; *San Andrea de la Frate, Rome*; *Ronda, Seen from House of Marquis de Salviatiera*; *Along the Arno, Florence*; *Garden of Lindaraxa, Alhambra, Granada*; and *Garden of Carmen de Matamoros, Granada*. A copy of Pries's portfolio of reproductions of nine pencil drawings is included in the Pries drawing collection, Special Collections Division, University of Washington Libraries. The drawing names in the portfolio are slight variations on these names.

121. Pries prepared a detailed typescript on places to visit and things to see and made copies available to students and graduates planning trips to Europe. A copy of this undated typescript survives in the Pries papers, Special Collections Division, University of Washington Libraries.

122. Hewitt discusses a strong "regionalist ethos in domestic architecture" that was particularly manifested in Philadelphia, California, the Southwest, and the South. He suggests that the architects in Philadelphia formed a cohesive regional school lasting from the 1880s to the Depression, and that architects in California built on the state's idealized Spanish heritage to create the "most vital" of the regional tendencies; see Hewitt, *The Architect & the American County House*, 197–207 (on Philadelphia), 207–21 (on California).

123. The distinctiveness of his education can best be understood if one contrasts his experience in California and Philadelphia with the experience he would have had if he had moved to New York, which was always the center of the Beaux-Arts movement.

3. Finding His Way

1. The best single source on the Berkeley fire of 17 September 1923 is Susan S. Cerney and Anthony Bruce, eds., *The Berkeley Fire: Memoirs and Mementos* (Berkeley, Calif.: Berkeley Architectural Heritage Association, 1992).

2. Pries took his California architecture registration exam on 28 August 1923; his license (no. 1236) was issued by the State of California on 17 September 1923. The license is in the Pries papers, Special Collections Division, University of Washington Libraries. Pries's having received his architectural license was noted in *Architect and Engineer* 74 (Sept. 1923), 111.

3. A good summary of the state of San Francisco and the local architectural professional community in the 1920s is given in Michael R. Corbett, *Splendid Survivors: San Francisco's Downtown Architectural Heritage* (San Francisco: Foundation for San Francisco's Architectural Heritage/California Living Books, 1979); pages 38–39 discuss San Francisco in the 1920s, and pages 49–53 discuss the evolution of the San Francisco architectural profession.

4. William G. Merchant was a graduate of Wilmerding High School, class of 1906.

5. Pries's involvement in the Medico-Dental Building was recalled by Robert Winskill (author's interview with Robert Winskill, 26 July 1994). Corbett provides a good description of the building: "A handsome medical office building, characteristic in design of Kelham's work. It was noteworthy at the time of its construction for the reliable mechanical systems. According to *Architect and Engineer* this structure was designed as a model of mechanical reliability for all medical office buildings. In composition, it is a two-part vertical block, its top story

functioning as part of the cornice rather than a separate capital section. Ornamentation is attenuated Romanesque with narrow bays culminating in round arches, and a corbeled brick cornice. The existing design is a change from an earlier published sketch which was Renaissance/Baroque in ornamental derivation. The building was constructed by a corporation of tenant stockholders"; see Corbett, *Splendid Survivors*, 156. It is not known whether Pries worked on any other projects for either Kelham or Merchant. It is possible that he was hired only for the Medico-Dental Building; it was not uncommon in that period for firms to hire one or more draftsmen just for the duration of a particular project.

6. Carlos J. Maas, who attended Munson Secretarial College, became president of Judson Manufacturing Company, a steel manufacturer, in 1923, after the death of Henry Bothin. Theodore A. Maas and Donald S. Maas became involved in Bothin real estate ventures. Only the youngest brother, Henry Bothin Maas, seems not to have worked for any Bothin company; he pursued a career as an artist.

7. Henry Ernest Bothin (1853–1923) moved to San Francisco as a young man and, after serving in clerical positions for a few years, founded Bothin, Dallemand & Co., a coffee and spice import and trading company. With his profits from this venture, Bothin began to purchase and develop downtown San Francisco real estate. In the 1880s, he entered the manufacturing field by acquiring control of the Judson Iron Works, in Oakland. He subsequently became involved in insurance through the California Fire Insurance Company, and he was a director of the Pacific Gas and Electric Company, the Natoma Company, and the Sausalito Land and Ferry Company. Although he suffered significant losses in the 1906 earthquake and fire, Bothin retained his properties and rebuilt. After the earthquake, rather than rebuild his personal residence at Jackson Street and Van Ness, in San Francisco, he built a new home in Marin County. The best summary of Henry Bothin's life and career is the obituary that appeared in the publication of the Pacific Gas and Electric Company; see *Pacific Service Magazine* 15 (Oct. 1923), 143. Other obituaries appeared in the *San Francisco Chronicle*, 16 Oct. 1923, 13; the *San Francisco Examiner*, 16 Oct. 1923, 10; and the *Santa Barbara Morning Press*, 16 Oct. 1923, 7. An article discussing the settlement of Henry Bothin's estate appeared in the *San Francisco Examiner*, 26 Sept. 1925, 7.

8. In 1905—at the request of Elizabeth Ashe, one of the founders of San Francisco's Telegraph Hill Neighborhood Association (Settlement House)—Henry Bothin provided the site near Fairfax, in Marin County, that was to be used as a children's summer camp. (On Elizabeth Ashe and Telegraph Hill, see nn. 65, 66, and 67 to this chapter, below.) This property, called Hill Farm, was gradually improved and eventually was incorporated under the name Bothin Convalescent Home. Bothin provided the 35 acres for the Arequipa Tuberculosis Sanitorium for Working Women in 1910. For the history of these properties, see Gunard Solberg, *Hill Farm and Arequipa* (Fairfax,

Calif.: Fairfax Historical Society, 1997). On Arequipa, see also Suzanne Baizerman, Lynn Downey, and John Toki, *Fired by Ideals: Arequipa Pottery and the Arts and Crafts Movement* (Oakland/San Francisco: Oakland Museum of California/Pomegranate Books, 2000). Accounts of the Telegraph Hill Settlement House also often include discussions of Hill Farm and Arequipa. The name of the Bothin Helping Fund was later changed to the Bothin Foundation, the name by which it is known today.

9. On Piranhurst, see Herb Andree, Noel Young, and Patricia Halloran, *Santa Barbara Architecture: From Spanish Colonial to Modern*, 3rd ed. (Santa Barbara, Calif.: Capra Press, 1995), 63.

10. A brief biography of Carlos J. Maas is found in *Men of California, 1924–1925* (San Francisco: Western Press Reporter, 1925), 52. An obituary appeared in the *San Francisco Chronicle*, 13 Apr. 1972, 39.

11. Theodore Maas was less prominent than his brother; no published biographical summary has been found. A brief obituary for Theodore Maas appeared in the *San Francisco Chronicle*, 3 May 1971, 36.

12. Pries did most of his sketches, drawings, and watercolors of design proposals on loose sheets. He then pasted them into a bound book of blank pages —the Pries Scrapbook (see n. 77 to chap. 2, above)— in roughly chronological order. Occasionally he drew directly on the blank pages, but this approach was fairly infrequent. The first designs in the Pries Scrapbook are marked in pencil as a project for Mrs. Maas at Van Ness Avenue and Chestnut Street; a view captioned "living room from entrance lobby," likely an interior of this project, is dated 5 January 1924. A local architectural researcher, Gary Goss, discovered that in 1905 the site at the northeast corner of Van Ness and Chestnut Street had been developed by the Bothin Real Estate Company with five houses. The project for Mrs. Maas was likely a remodeling of one of these houses.

13. The project cost was listed as $15,000. Permit information for the Ida Sutter Maas townhouse was provided by Gary Goss.

14. It is unlikely that all the Maas brothers resided primarily at 1242 Francisco. For example, Theodore Maas married in 1924, and he may simply have given this as his San Francisco address.

15. The building survives today, although a second garage and a partial third floor mar its original character. Two photographs of Pries's apartment were published in R.W. Sexton, *American Apartment Houses of Today* (New York: Architectural Book Publishing, 1926), XXXIII, XLIII.

16. It is possible that Pries did other projects for the Maas family. Several sketches in the Pries Scrapbook show a house adjacent to a stair. The precise location of this project has not been identified, although Gary Goss notes that its location seems similar to that of the Hanford residence, at Vallejo and Taylor, on San Francisco's Russian Hill. The Hanford residence, designed by Houghton Sawyer and completed in 1905, was vacant in 1923–24 and may have been considered for remodeling

by Mrs. Maas (or by another potential client), but nothing came of the project. Thanks to Gary Goss for this information.

17. The Abracadabra permit is mentioned in the (Berkeley) *Daily Gazette*, 25 Sept. 1924, 1, 13, and in the *Daily Californian*, 26 Sept. 1924, 1.

18. A copy of this commentary, "Campus Goes Blind on Seeing New Jail," is pasted inside the front cover of the Pries Scrapbook, next to a copy of the article about Pries that was published in *Pencil Points* when he won the LeBrun Traveling Scholarship. Pries printed in ink, below the article, the caption "Campus razzberry." However, no source for the article has been identified; perhaps this was something a friend of his had printed as a joke, or perhaps it appeared in a campus humor publication.

19. A residence at 3205 Dos Palos Drive, Hollywood, California, is probably a Pries design that dates from this time or earlier. The current owner, Richard Hobbs, was told by a previous owner (who received information from the original owner) that the house had been designed by Lionel H. Pries about the time Pries graduated from architecture school, or soon after. Pries was said to have designed the house for his aunt and his uncle, although they did not build until several years later, which could mean that the house was designed between 1919 and 1922 or in late 1923. Since Pries is not an architect commonly known in the Los Angeles area, this oral history likely has some basis in fact. According to the Los Angeles building permit issued in 1930, the owner of the lot was Baldwin W. Baker, and the contractor was J. H. Thomas & Co. No architect was listed on the permit. If it is assumed that Pries designed the house between 1919 and 1925 and gave the drawings to his relatives, then they most likely built the project without his involvement (especially since Pries was in Seattle after the beginning of 1928). The records of the Los Angeles tax assessor show that the valuation of the property increased in 1931, an indication that the house had been completed. From 1932, the property owners were listed as Eddie and Dolly Nelson. If the oral history is accurate, then the Nelsons were likely related to Pries. The house is Spanish Colonial Revival in design, but it features round, not pointed (Moorish), arches. Pries began routinely using Moorish arches once he moved to Santa Barbara, in mid-1924. Therefore, this house was likely a very early Pries design, perhaps even predating his time in Europe. (Thanks to Anna Smorodinsky, a graduate student in architectural history at the University of California, Los Angeles, who researched local permit and tax records.)

20. The J. M. Johnson residence, at 509 Coleridge, Palo Alto, designed by John White, received a building permit in August 1925.

21. The permit for the Sausalito Land and Ferry Company Building is listed in *Building and Engineering News*, 4 July 1925. The brief description derives from this source.

22. Pries took on work, perhaps on a contract basis, for other architects. His scrapbook includes at least one example, dated 1925: a perspective of a Sacramento residence, by the architect Charles K. Sumner, for Dr. and Mrs. Nathan G. Hale. The location is the southeast corner of 45th and M in Sacramento. Whether the design was by Pries or he only did the rendering is not known. See Pries Scrapbook, 24r, Pries drawing collection, Special Collections Division, University of Washington Libraries. The start of construction of the Hale residence was reported in the *Sacramento Bee*, 28 Nov. 1925, A7; Pries's participation in the project was not mentioned. Thanks to Gary Goss for this citation.

23. *Santa Barbara Morning Press*, 21 July 1925, sec. 2, 1. The paper indicated that the Bothin Helping Fund was independent of the Bothin Real Estate Company but noted that the interests of the two were "allied."

24. Sources for Santa Barbara architectural history include Andree, Young, and Halloran, *Santa Barbara Architecture*; David Gebhard, *Santa Barbara: The Creation of a New Spain in America* (Santa Barbara: University Art Museum, University of California, 1982), exhibition catalogue; David F. Myrick, *Montecito and Santa Barbara*, 2 vols. (Glendale, Calif.: Trans-Anglo Books, 1987, 1991; vol. 1 is *From Farms to Estates*, and vol. 2 is *The Days of the Great Estates*); and Philip H. Staats, *California Architecture in Santa Barbara* (New York: Architectural Book Publishing, 1929; rprt. 1990, with an introduction by David Gebhard).

25. Winsor Soule, "Lessons of the Santa Barbara Earthquake," *American Architect* 128 (5 Oct. 1925), 295–302.

26. *Santa Barbara Morning Press*, 21 July 1925, sec. 2, 1.

27. Andree, Young, and Halloran, *Santa Barbara Architecture*, 87. A more detailed discussion of the Spanish Colonial Revival is David Gebhard, "The Spanish Colonial Revival in Southern California," *Journal of the Society of Architectural Historians* 26 (May 1967), 131–47.

28. The Pries book collection, now held by the University of Washington Libraries, includes a copy of Louis La Beaume and William Booth Papin, *Picturesque Architecture of Mexico* (New York: Architectural Book Publishing/Paul Wenzel and Maurice Krakow, 1915), signed "Lionel H. Pries, Santa Barbara, Aug. 17, 1925." However, given that the permit for the Pries-designed Blake Motor Building was issued on 11 August 1925 (see n. 29 to this chapter, below), Pries was likely in Santa Barbara no later than the end of July. Pries's office was on the second floor of the El Paseo complex, on the east side of the 800 block of State Street.

29. *Santa Barbara Morning Press*, 12 Aug.1925, sec. 2, 1 (permit); *Santa Barbara Morning Press*, 18 Oct. 1925, sec. 2, 5 (completion).

30. Winsor Soule, "The New Santa Barbara," *American Architect* 130 (5 July 1926), 6, 8–10.

31. The Hollingsworth-Overland Agency building was nearly doubled in size in the 1950s, when it was converted to retail use. The garage entry and vertical posts were removed from Pries's arches, which became large store windows. A new entrance under a small gable and

a third arched store window were added to the northwest (left) of Pries's original structure.

32. In October 1925, the city issued a permit for repairs to the Bothin-owned automobile showrooms in the 300 block of State Street (*Santa Barbara Morning Press*, 8 Oct. 1925, sec. 2, 1). The project was fully redesigned in the fall of 1925 because a second permit, for the $35,000 reconstruction, was issued at the end of December (*Santa Barbara Morning Press*, 31 Dec. 1925, sec. 2, 3).

33. After the Seaside Oil Company established its headquarters there, in 1937, it was renamed the Auto Showrooms and Seaside Oil Company Building, the name by which it is known today. Carleton M. Winslow and R. H. Pittman designed the three-arched loggia and its tower, added at the north end of the façade in 1937; see Rebecca Conrad and Christopher H. Nelson, *Santa Barbara: A Guide to El Pueblo Viejo* (Santa Barbara: Capra Press, 1986), 72. The setting of this building was radically altered when State Street was lowered to pass underneath a freeway (highway 101): the slope of State Street necessitated a concrete retaining wall, now topped by planting, directly in front of the building. Although Pries's arcade along the front of the building survives, its original relationship to the sidewalk and street has been lost.

34. Soule, "The New Santa Barbara," 8–10.

35. Conrad and Nelson, *Santa Barbara*, 81.

36. *Santa Barbara Morning Press*, 21 July 1925, sec. 2, 1.

37. Negotiating with existing tenants was one cause of the delay. Another was the need to obtain a special permit for the outside staircase facing the plaza (*Santa Barbara Morning Press*, 2 Apr. 1926, sec. 1, 3; *Santa Barbara Morning Press*, 8 Apr. 1926, sec. 2, 1; *Santa Barbara Morning Press*, 21 Apr. 1926, sec. 2, 1.

38. Another complexity was the structure—a welded steel frame, covered by steel mesh-reinforced concrete (*Santa Barbara Daily News*, 25 Sept. 1926, 15).

39. The McKay Building survives with some minor alterations to the storefronts on State and De la Guerra. Alterations have also been made to the third floor, but these are not readily visible from the street.

40. *Santa Barbara Daily News*, 4 Oct. 1925, sec. 2, 4.

41. In his résumé from the early 1950s, Pries lists work on the Bothin estate in Montecito without specifying what he actually designed (Lionel H. Pries, undated résumé, Pries papers, Special Collections Division, University of Washington Libraries). Robert Winskill recalled that Pries had told him he was responsible for the allée of palm trees on the entry drive, along with other landscape improvements (author's interview with Robert Winskill, 26 July 1994). David Streatfield remarks that the Piranhurst garden was noted for a large outdoor theater that dates from the 1920s. Whether Pries had any part in its design is not known.

42. Although a notice of his relocation to Santa Barbara appeared in *Architect and Engineer* 82 (Sept. 1925), 116, Pries seems never to have regarded the move as permanent. All of Pries's Bothin buildings in Santa Barbara were constructed by the San Francisco contractor Mattock and Feasey. Mattock and Feasey also reconstructed or repaired other Bothin buildings in Santa Barbara that were not of Pries's design. The Bothin Helping Fund's in-house designer handled some less complex projects without requiring Pries's involvement. These included the Ferguson Furniture Company (on W. Cannon; destroyed), the Holland Undertaking establishment (15 E. Sola Street), the Western Machine and Foundry building (400 block of State), the Savoy Hotel (200 block of State), and the Fillmore used-car market (location unknown) and auto salesroom (20 W. Gutierrez). Pries's name appears on the August 1925 permit for the Richelieu Hotel (121 State; altered), a two-story rectangular block of unreinforced masonry. Its utilitarian design with no Spanish Colonial Revival detail is markedly different from all other work by Pries in the city. It may have been built quickly to provide housing for construction workers during the rebuilding of 1925–26. (Thanks to Santa Barbara historian Shelley Bookspan for this information.) Pries was briefly involved in the design of De la Guerra Court (1926), a bungalow court. The September 1926 announcement of its opening credited the project to "A. Toluboff, associated with Lionel H. Pries, Architect" (advertisement in the *Santa Barbara Daily News*, 28 Aug. 1926, 9); Toluboff was an in-house designer for the Bothin Helping Fund. The Moorish arches and other detail features of the eight small units likely reflect Pries's input. In addition, Mattock and Feasey took on non-Bothin jobs in Santa Barbara and may have carried out as many as twenty projects in the city; see *Building and Engineering News*, 1 Aug. 1925, 18.

43. Fletcher is best known for his teaching and writing that were influenced by Japanese art and philosophy. He had begun as director of the Edinburgh College of Art in 1907, and his tenure at the Santa Barbara School of the Arts lasted until he retired, in 1930. Particularly recognized for his prints, he has been characterized as "Great Britain's Arthur Wesley Dow" (after the American woodblock printer who developed an approach to composition based on Japanese woodblock prints).

44. Four blueprints of Pries's construction drawings for the house are now held in the architectural documents collection of the University Art Museum, University of California, Santa Barbara. One blueprint is a floor plan, two others are reproductions of a single sheet of elevations and interior elevations (one of these is incomplete), and the fourth is a sheet of details.

45. A photo album for the 1927 Santa Barbara Better Homes Week (an album now held as part of the Pearl Chase/CDC collection, Special Collections, Davidson Library, University of California, Santa Barbara), includes a description and several photographs of the Fletcher residence. The brief text indicates that the house, at $8,500, exceeded the cost parameters for the competition but was included and given a special award because it was such a notable design. A photograph of the house appeared in the *Santa Barbara Morning Press*,

8 Aug. 1927, 6. Two photographs of the house were published in *California Southland* 97 (March 1928), 26.

46. Pries's return to San Francisco was reported in an article on University of California alumni in *Architect and Engineer* 85 (June 1926), 121. This article also discussed the May 1926 meeting of the Architectural Alumni Association of the University of California; at the meeting, Pries was elected to the executive board of the association for 1926–27.

47. On his return to San Francisco, Pries established his office in the Atlas Building at 604 Mission Street—also the address of the Bothin Real Estate Company. Although this location, and his working with the Bothins' favorite contractor, might have seemed to link him even more closely to the Bothin interests, Pries's clientele began to expand beyond that circle.

48. The permit for the Theodore Maas residence, 144 Miraloma Drive, described as a two-story residence costing $20,000, was listed in *Edwards Abstracts*, 26 Jan. 1926. This house has been destroyed.

49. The permit for the Norris K. Davis residence, 160 Miraloma Drive, described as a two-story house costing $24,000, was listed in *Edwards Abstracts*, 27 Mar. 1926. Norris Davis is listed in the San Francisco city directory as a machinist; no link to the Bothin companies or to Maas or Pries has been discovered.

50. The permit for the Alfred H. and Clarence Feasey residence, 150 Miraloma Drive, described as a two-story house costing $15,000, was listed in *Building and Engineering News*, 10 July 1926.

51. Helen Thompson Hopkins was the widow of Edward W. Hopkins, who died in January 1926. Hopkins was a nephew of Mark Hopkins, one of the founders of the Central Pacific Railroad. Edward Hopkins served as treasurer of the railroad and later as president of the Union Ice Company. His death was noted in the *San Francisco Chronicle*, 20 Jan. 1926, 1.

52. Pries purchased the empty lot (lot 47, between the Feasey and Davis residences) on 28 January 1927 and sold it to Harry F. Sullivan on 11 March 1931. Sullivan sold it to Norris Davis on 14 April 1931. This information was traced by Gary Goss.

53. The Kerrick residence is about three miles from downtown Oakland, in an area planned by the Olmsted Brothers in 1917 and platted as Lakeshore Highlands. Promotional literature in the early 1920s characterized this area as "America's most beautiful residential park." The Kerricks' site was a large parcel where Grosvenor Street crossed the tracks of an interurban line. For Lakeshore Highlands, see Oakland Heritage Alliance, "Lakeshore Commercial District and Lakeshore Highlands: A Brief History," vertical files, Oakland History Room, Oakland Public Library. See also "Lakeshore Highlands: Twenties Residence Park in Trestle Glen," *Oakland Heritage Alliance News* 8/1 (Spring 1988), 1. Little is known about the Kerricks or how they came to select Pries; Oakland city directories identify both husband and wife as Christian Science practitioners.

54. Pries's sketches for two variations on the house's design appeared in *Pacific Coast Architect* 31 (Feb. 1927), 17. The originals of these drawings are found in the Pries Scrapbook.

55. An innovative feature was Pries's use of linoleum, then a new and fashionable material, as the first-floor finish. The custom design—for example, the star pattern of the dining room floor—led the Armstrong Company to feature the house in an advertisement in *Collier's* in August 1928. A proof for the Armstrong Company advertisement is found in the Pries drawing collection, Special Collections Division, University of Washington Libraries.

56. For permits for both buildings, see *Building and Engineering News*, 9 Oct. 1926. The structure at 1521 Hawthorne Terrace was permitted as a $12,000 two-story residence, and 1519 Hawthorne Terrace was permitted as a $6,000 one-story residence.

57. The parcels were later separated; the current address of the Denman studio is 1522 Euclid Avenue. A garage now blocks the view of the studio from Euclid.

58. *Pacific Coast Architect* 31 (Feb. 1927), cover. Yerba Buena Island, today's midspan anchorage of the San Francisco-Oakland Bay Bridge, was formerly known as Goat Island, and Telegraph Hill was once called Goat Hill.

59. That Blanchard was associated with Pries is mentioned in *Architect and Engineer* 85 (June 1926), 121: "Lionel Pries had an office in Santa Barbara for a few months following the earthquake. After completing several commercial structures he moved his offices back to San Francisco and is now in the Atlas Building. Norman Blanchard '11 [*sic*] is associated with him." Norman Kirk Blanchard received a B.A. in 1922 and an M.A. in 1924 and did additional graduate work in 1925. Blanchard was Pries's employee in 1926 and possibly during the first part of 1927. On the blueprints of Pries's construction drawings for the Fletcher residence (drawings now at the University Art Museum of the University of California, Santa Barbara), the title block includes the notations "Drawn by: L.H.P.," and "Traced by: N.K.B." Pries may also have briefly employed William A. Horning; see *California Monthly*, July 1930, 33.

60. *Pacific Coast Architect* 31 (Feb. 1927), cover, 11–21.

61. Drawings by Pries were on the covers of *Pacific Coast Architect* issues for February 1927 and for February, April, May, August, September, and October 1928.

62. Emma K. Willits was born and brought up in western New York. She received her medical degree in 1896 and then went to San Francisco as a resident at Children's Hospital (for women and children). After completing her residency there, she continued in the private practice of surgery and was affiliated with Children's. At first she was on the surgical staff of the hospital's Department of Pediatrics, and then she became chief of the Department of Surgical Diseases of Children; in the early 1920s, she was appointed chair of general surgery. For a summary of Emma K. Willits's life and career, see Muriel Edwards, M.D., "Emma K. Willits, M.D.," *Journal of the American Medical Women's*

Association 5 (Jan. 1950), 42–43. Willits was listed in Josephine S. Lyons, ed., *Who's Who Among the Women of California* (San Francisco: Security Publishing Company, 1922), 566. Other mentions of Willits are found in the *San Francisco Chronicle*, 13 Jan. 1941, 7; the *San Francisco Chronicle*, 16 Jan. 1941, 11; and the *San Francisco Chronicle*, 23 May 1946, 10. Obituaries appeared in the *San Francisco Examiner*, 10 Apr. 1965, 50, and the *San Francisco Chronicle*, 11 Apr. 1965, 22.

63. Author's interview with Robert Winskill, 26 July 1994.

64. The Willits residence permit was listed in *Building and Engineering News*, 16 Apr. 1927. A recent publication on the house, featured in an issue of the *Better Homes and Gardens* Special Interest Publications series, is Gina Covina, "Embrace Color: Want to Jazz Up Your House and Yard? Add a Splash of Bold Color," in *Simply Perfect Garden Rooms* (Des Moines, Iowa: Meredith Corp., 2003), 36–44, 126.

65. For the history of the Telegraph Hill Neighborhood Association, see the *Seventeenth Annual Report of the Telegraph Hill Neighborhood Association*, published in San Francisco, Apr. 1920 (a copy is available at the San Francisco History Center, San Francisco Public Library). A summary of the early history of the Telegraph Hill Neighborhood Association is also found in Solberg, *Hill Farm and Arequipa*, 3–13. For Telegraph Hill during the period, see David F. Myrick, *San Francisco's Telegraph Hill* (Berkeley, Calif.: Howell-North Books, 1972).

66. The chronology of the Telegraph Hill Neighborhood Association in the *Seventeenth Annual Report of the Telegraph Hill Neighborhood Association* includes the construction of the association building (known as the Neighborhood House) in 1907 as well as additions in 1909 (a library) and 1913 (a gymnasium, work rooms, and other spaces).

67. The statement that the Neighborhood House "has done yeoman's service" appeared in Elizabeth H. Ashe, "Report of Board of Directors, April, 1920," in *Seventeenth Annual Report of the Telegraph Hill Neighborhood Association*, 11. Elizabeth Haywood Ashe is profiled in Russell Holmes Fletcher, ed., *Who's Who in California, 1942–43* (Los Angeles: Who's Who Publications, 1941), 29.

68. San Francisco building permit no. 166363 clearly indicates that Lionel H. Pries was the designer of the 1927–28 additions and alterations to the Telegraph Hill Neighborhood House. The sketch plan included in the permit indicates that Pries designed the new building on the north side of the site and altered the existing structures on the south and east sides of the site. Therefore, the form of the courtyard largely reflects Pries's design (thanks to Gary Goss, who obtained a copy of the building permit).

69. About 1962, while conducting research for the book *Here Today: San Francisco's Architectural Heritage*, the Junior League interviewed women, then in their eighties, who had once worked at the association; one of them recalled Pries's statement regarding the 1928

project. The notes prepared by the Junior League in the 1960s, when its members were compiling information for *Here Today*, are now held by the San Francisco Public Library. For Telegraph Hill Settlement House, see "Stockton Street, 1736," in the Junior League of San Francisco *Here Today* files, San Francisco History Center, San Francisco Public Library. See also Roger Olmsted and T. H. Watkins, *Here Today: San Francisco's Architectural Heritage* (San Francisco: Chronicle Books, 1968).

70. For example, Woodbridge lists the 1927–28 addition to the Telegraph Hill Neighborhood House as a Maybeck project; see Sally B. Woodbridge, *Bernard Maybeck: Visionary Architect* (New York: Abbeville Publishers, 1992), 229. In 1954, the Telegraph Hill Neighborhood Association moved to new quarters and sold the older building, which was renovated and is now used for offices and shops.

71. Author's interview with Robert Winskill, 26 July 1994.

72. Ibid.

73. Other Pries projects in 1927 were alterations and repairs at the Bothin Convalescent Home at Hill Farm, the Telegraph Hill Neighborhood Association's rural property in Marin County, and remodeling of the lobby of the Bothin Real Estate Company offices in San Francisco. Pries's résumé from the early 1950s lists the "Hill Farm Convalescent Home," but the precise project Pries may have done there is not known (Lionel H. Pries, undated résumé, Pries papers, Special Collections Division, University of Washington Libraries). The two primary buildings at Hill Farm both predate his involvement: the Woman's Building (now known as the Stone House) was completed in 1919; the Hill Farm building began construction in 1922 or 1923. (The Arequipa Sanatorium building, next door, dates from 1911 and 1913.) It seems likely that Pries was involved in alterations to the main Hill Farm building, but records of this work have not been found, so the extent of his contribution cannot be identified. Pries's design for the remodeling of the lobby of the Bothin Real Estate Company offices, in the Atlas Building, was permitted in May 1927, but the building has since seen several other tenants, and nothing of Pries's work survives. The permit for the Bothin Real Estate office remodeling was listed in *Building and Engineering News*, 14 May 1927; the cost was $2,500.

74. Some of these projects may have come to Pries through recommendations by members of the Maas family. For example, a residence designed for a client named Gerske was to be located in Burlingame Hills, the hometown of Theodore Maas's wife. Another residence was for a client in Hillsborough; both Henry and Donald Maas later lived in that community. Projects in San Mateo, including a residence for a client named Lattin and a building for the San Mateo Polo Club, may have come through recommendations by Carlos Maas; neither project was built.

75. The visit of William J. and Mildred Bain to San

Francisco and the meeting with Pries are noted in William J. Bain and Mildred C. Bain, *Building Together: A Memoir of Our Lives in Seattle* (Seattle: Beckett Publishing Company, 1991), 95. (For a discussion of this book, see nn. 4 and 17 to chap. 4, this volume.)

76. *Architect and Engineer* 92 (March 1928), 107. One other possible reason for Pries's departure from California has been offered. In the early 1990s, David Gebhard, architectural history professor at the University of California, Santa Barbara, told the author that Lutah Riggs had once told him that Pries's decision to leave California came after a sexual indiscretion. With both Riggs and Gebhard no longer alive, there is no way to verify any part of this statement. Pries never mentioned such an incident to Robert Winskill, the person with whom he most openly discussed all aspects of his life.

77. Author's conversation with David Gebhard, ca. 1995.

4. To the Northwest

1. *Seattle Daily Journal of Commerce*, 7 Aug. 1928, 4. The Bain and Pries partnership was initiated in mid-March. However, work then under way was still credited to William J. Bain, and permits listed between March and August 1928 bear only Bain's name. The *Seattle Daily Journal of Commerce* (hereafter abbreviated *DJC*) generally listed Seattle building permits for several days, beginning the day after they were issued. Until the late 1940s, the listings included the name of the owner, a brief legal description, the address, the names of the architect and the builder, and the price. After World War II, the information was abbreviated and is often incomplete. (In the 1940s, listings also began to be carried for buildings in King County, outside the city limits, but this information rarely includes the names of architects and is therefore much less useful to researchers.)

2. In the archives of today's NBBJ (the former Naramore, Bain, Brady and Johanson, which Bain joined in the mid-1940s) are records of William J. Bain's practice, including his various partnerships. Although many records of the firm have not survived, projects that reached the stage where construction drawings (working drawings) were produced are known because those drawings were later recorded on microfiche. From available records, it is evident that Bain assigned a number to a project after initial contact with the client. Some projects never proceeded to the design stage, others went through design but did not end in construction, and many projects actually were built. Therefore, the construction drawings (including incomplete sets of construction drawings) recorded on microfiche, although they form the best surviving record, provide an incomplete record of the firm's clients and potential clients. To judge from assigned project numbers, the Bain and Pries office interacted with 150 to 170 clients over its four years of practice. This number is inexact because there is no way to determine just how many projects

were already under way in March 1928, when the partnership was formed. On the basis of available records, it is possible to say that approximately sixty projects were constructed that can be fully attributed to Bain and Pries. A list of these projects is found in the appendix to this volume.

3. Available records do not indicate the exact terms of the partnership agreement between Bain and Pries. It is possible that Bain controlled a larger portion of the revenue, at least initially, since Pries joined his firm after it was established.

4. For a short summary of the architectural career of William J. Bain, see Duane A. Dietz, "William J. Bain, Sr.," in Jeffrey Karl Ochsner, ed., *Shaping Seattle Architecture: A Historical Guide to the Architects* (Seattle: University of Washington Press/AIA Seattle, 1994), 216–21. Other important accounts addressing the career of William J. Bain are "Work of William J. Bain," *Architect and Engineer* 146 (Aug. 1941), 16–37, and "William Bain: A Half Century of Seattle Architecture," *DJC*, 3 Dec. 1980, 7. Bain's obituary appeared in the *Seattle Post-Intelligencer*, 23 Jan. 1985, D2. The memoir *Building Together*, co-authored by William and Mildred Bain, presents personal recollections as well as career information. William and Mildred Bain individually authored many of the chapters, giving their own independent points of view. Because William Bain died in 1985, the final version of the book, published six years later, was edited by Mildred Bain. See William J. Bain and Mildred C. Bain, *Building Together: A Memoir of Our Lives in Seattle* (Seattle: Beckett Publishing Company, 1991).

5. For Willcox and Sayward, see Norman J. Johnston, "W. R. B. Willcox," in Ochsner, ed., *Shaping Seattle Architecture*, 138–43.

6. Bain and Bain, *Building Together*, 22–24.

7. Ibid., 44–48.

8. Ibid., 53–57, 85–86.

9. Throughout his life, Bain's interest in residential work never wavered. After becoming a partner in Naramore, Bain, Brady and Johanson, Bain formed a separate partnership, Bain, Overturf and Turner (later Bain and Overturf), so that he could continue to carry out residential commissions. See Dietz, "William J. Bain, Sr.," 219; Bain and Bain, *Building Together*, 125.

10. Essays addressing these designers are found in Ochsner, ed., *Shaping Seattle Architecture*. See, for example, Thomas Veith, "Arthur Loveless," 150–55; Duane A. Dietz, "J. Lister Holmes," 204–9; "Ivey, Edwin J.," 345–46; and S. Sian Roberts and Mary Shaughnessy, "Elizabeth Ayer," 210–15.

11. See David A. Rash, "Schack, Young & Myers," in Ochsner, ed., *Shaping Seattle Architecture*, 156–61. For Bebb and Gould, see T. William Booth and William H. Wilson, *Carl F. Gould: A Life in Architecture and the Arts* (Seattle: University of Washington Press, 1995); T. William Booth and William H. Wilson, "Bebb & Gould," in Ochsner, ed., *Shaping Seattle Architecture*, 174–79.

12. For a brief discussion of 1920s eclecticism in Seattle, see Jeffrey Karl Ochsner, "Introduction: A His-

torical Overview of Architecture in Seattle," in Ochsner, ed., *Shaping Seattle Architecture*, xxvii-xxx.

13. The project for Oriental Lodge no. 72, F. & A. M., is mentioned in *DJC*, 18 Apr. 1924, 1. The article describes a planned two-story structure at 2000–2006 Market Street for $40,000, to include the Masonic Hall and retail space, but no further mention was made of the project in subsequent issues of *DJC*. This was the only project by William J. Bain mentioned in *DJC* in 1924. However, projects costing less than $1,000, such as small remodelings, were not reported in *DJC*. For 1924, the surviving records for Bain's firm found in the NBBJ archives (microfiche of working drawings, with incomplete sets of working drawings) include projects numbered 107–12; earlier client contacts (numbers 101–6) did not progress to working drawings and are therefore unknown.

14. Bain and Bain, *Building Together*, 85.

15. Notable large residences were the $50,000 William D. Comer residence, at 902 37th Avenue N. (now 1002 37th Avenue E., reported in *DJC*, 16 Aug. 1927, 1; *DJC*, 25 Aug. 1927, 4 [permit]; and *DJC*, 31 Aug. 1927, 1), and the $25,000 Prescott K. Smith residence, in the exclusive community on Puget Sound known as The Highlands (reported in *DJC*, 7 Sept. 1927, 1; *DJC*, 13 Sept. 1927, 1; and *DJC*, 14 Oct. 1927, 1).

16. For Bain's AIA awards, see Arthur L. Loveless, "Honor Awards Washington State Chapter A.I.A.," *Architect and Engineer* 19 (Dec. 1927), 35–37, 48, 52–53, 73, 77; see also "Seattle Honor Awards, Washington State Chapter, A.I.A.," *American Architect* 133 (5 Feb. 1928), 185–90. (A photo caption in Ochsner, ed., *Shaping Seattle Architecture*, 216, erroneously states that Bain and Pries made an addition to the Shoremont in 1930–31, but the building is entirely Bain's work.) The *Seattle Daily Journal of Commerce* first discussed the Shoremont Apartments in 1925. See *DJC*, 12 Mar. 1925, 1; the permit for the project was listed in *DJC*, 28 Mar. 1925, 4. The building was completed in 1926.

17. In *Building Together*, William Bain never mentions Pries's participation in the firm. Mildred Bain discusses Pries's participation very briefly and suggests that his joining the firm was the result of a misunderstanding. The story she tells—that Pries gave up his California practice and moved to Seattle without a real agreement with William Bain—seems somewhat implausible; see Bain and Bain, *Building Together*, 95. The notice that Pries had moved to Seattle to join a firm called Bain and Pries appeared in the March 1928 issue of *Architect and Engineer*. (Given the typical time lag between the date when information was submitted to a professional journal and the date when it appeared—at least a month, often longer—the decision to create the partnership must have been made no later than the end of January. But Pries was still in San Francisco in early February, as book purchases he made at that time are clearly signed with the location "San Francisco." Thus the announcement of the firm Bain and Pries must have been made before Pries completed his move from San Francisco.)

Mildred Bain was deeply loyal to her husband, and it is undoubtedly correct that she was not entirely happy when Pries joined the firm. She writes, "He was a very fine man and a wonderful designer," and she describes him as "brilliant" but adds that he "was not very tactful" and claims that his lack of tact lost the firm several large jobs. (Given the ready wit that Pries displayed as a teacher, it would not be surprising to learn that some clients found him difficult.) In *Building Together*, Mildred Bain routinely refers to William J. Bain's practice as if she were a full participant, although she was not an architect. To cite just two examples, writing about the 1928–29 period, she states, "We were busy working on a number of large residences" (Bain and Bain, *Building Together*, 94), and, summarizing the breakup of Bain and Pries, she writes, "We had to eliminate a partner" (95). Thus she evidently saw herself as a full partner and seems to have been less accepting of Pries. *Building Together* never mentions that Bain and Pries renewed their partnership in 1941, or that Pries worked with Bain in the camouflage office during the World War II. Indeed, Pries himself told Robert Winskill that he believed Mildred Bain never fully accepted his joining William Bain's firm (author's interview with Robert Winskill, 26 July 1994).

18. Lionel H. Pries, undated résumé attached to letter to David Thomson from Harlan Thomas, 22 June 1928. See University of Washington Office of the President records, acc. no. 71–34, box 113–13, Special Collections Division, University of Washington Libraries.

19. Memo to Victor Steinbrueck from Ivan W. Meyer, 10 Jan. 1978.

20. Memo to Victor Steinbrueck from Lloyd Lovegren, 13 Jan. 1978.

21. Memo to Victor Steinbrueck from Ivan W. Meyer, 10 Jan. 1978.

22. Bain and Pries projects that may have provided limited opportunities for Pries's design input included industrial buildings and other, similar structures, such as the Furniture Specialty Company plant (1929), 1122 W. 54th Street (now 1122 N.W. 54th); an addition to the Stewart Lumber Company store (1930), 1761 Rainier Avenue; and an addition to the City Ice & Cold Storage warehouse (1930), 4750–56 Shilshole Avenue. Among the apartment projects by Bain and Pries that were Bain family investments were the Lombardy Court, Bel-Roy, Waverly, Consulate, Envoy, Embassy, and Viceroy apartment buildings. Pries may have had limited involvement in some of these, but the decorative treatment at the Bel-Roy likely reflects his creative contribution. For Bain family ownership of various apartment buildings, see Bain and Bain, *Building Together*, 95–97.

23. Memo to Victor Steinbrueck from Lloyd Lovegren, 13 Jan. 1978.

24. Memo to Victor Steinbrueck from Ivan W. Meyer, 10 Jan. 1978.

25. The original drawing for the Woodway Park brochure is found in the Pries drawing collection, Special Collections Division, University of Washington Libraries.

This drawing was included as fig. 2 in Andrew Rocker, "Lionel H. Pries," in Ochsner, ed., *Shaping Seattle Architecture*, 229, but at that time it was unidentified. The drawing has since been matched to the illustration in the Woodway Park brochure. Arthur Loveless, Edwin Ivey, and J. Lister Holmes also drew speculative homes for the brochure, several copies of which are held in private collections.

26. "Home for Normandy Park," *Seattle Post-Intelligencer*, 12 Aug. 1928, 23. Thanks to David Rash for bringing this article to my attention.

27. A color slide of a perspective by Pries of a proposed Spanish Colonial design for the St. Clair residence is found in the slide collection at the University of Washington College of Washington College of Architecture and Urban Planning. The location of the original drawing is unknown; no source is identified on the slide. The records in the NBBJ archives include only the working drawings for the St. Clair residence as actually built.

28. Mark Alan Hewitt, *The Architect & the American Country House, 1890–1940* (New Haven, Conn.: Yale University Press, 1990), 104–17, 197–221.

29. On Batchelder's life and career, see Robert Winter, *Batchelder—Tilemaker* (Los Angeles: Balcony Press, 1999). For tiles produced by the Batchelder Tile Company, see Norman Karlson, *American Art Tile, 1876–1941* (New York: Rizzoli, 1998), 157–61, esp. p. 160, which features an image of the hexagonal tiles used in the entry hall to the Stewart residence.

30. *DJC*, 12 Dec. 1930, 1; the description was repeated in *DJC*, 8 Jan. 1931, 1.

31. "A Home of Western Woods for Normandy Park, Seattle," *Pacific Builder and Engineer* 36 (21 June 1930), 15. The article specifically credits the design to "William J. Bain of Bain and Pries." As part of the publicity for the "Prudence Penny Budget Home," the *Seattle Post-Intelligencer* published a series of drawings by Bain and Pries as well as a landscape plan by Butler Sturtevant; see *Seattle Post-Intelligencer*, 2 Mar. 1930, 16 (exterior perspective); *Seattle Post-Intelligencer*, 9 Mar. 1930, 10 (floor plan); *Seattle Post-Intelligencer*, 16 Mar. 1930, 6 (interior perspective); *Seattle Post-Intelligencer*, 6 Apr. 1930, 16 (kitchen cabinets); and *Seattle Post-Intelligencer*, 27 Apr. 1930, 10 (landscape plan). The house, at 17954 Brittany Drive S.W., was open for public inspection on 25 May 1930. Thanks to David Rash for this information.

32. Howard H. Riley, "The Story of Red Cedar and Its Uses for Building Purposes," *Architect and Engineer* 137/3 (June 1939), 23. At the top of page 23 is an illustration captioned "Residence of Lyman Bunting, Yakima, Washington, William J. Bain and Lionel H. Pries, architects." The caption notes that the house features an exterior of "untreated cedar left to weather in natural lines."

33. George and Harry F. Reifel were sons of Henry Reifel, a brewer, distiller, and notorious bootlegger (during American prohibition). Both brothers built Spanish Colonial Revival houses on large estates overlooking the mouth of the Fraser River. Neither house was by Bain and Pries. Rio Vista, the Harry Reifel house (2170 SW Marine Drive), built in 1930–31, was designed by Bernard Palmer; Casa Mia, the George Reifel house (1920 SW Marine Drive), built in 1932, was designed by Ross A. Lort (information provided by Don Luxton and Hal Kalman, 2 Nov. 1999). A color slide of a perspective by Pries of a proposed Spanish Colonial design for the George Reifel residence is found in the slide collection at the University of Washington College of Architecture and Urban Planning. The location of the original drawing is unknown; no source is identified on the slide. The records in the NBBJ archives include no mention of the Reifel residence.

34. Author's interview with Wendell Lovett, 17 Aug. 1999.

35. Ibid.

36. The Convalescent Home was intended to provide care for recovering children who no longer needed hospitalization at Children's Orthopedic Hospital. The Bucks, a branch of the Washington State Elks Association, provided the funding and obtained the site. The Junior League outfitted the building and managed its operation and finances. The Junior League effectively served as the client; William Bain was the primary contact with the Junior League (information provided by Christine Carr and Monica Wooten, who researched the history of the Convalescent Home to prepare a City of Seattle Landmark nomination in 2001). For the history of Children's Orthopedic Hospital, see Emilie B. Schwabacher, *A Place for the Children: A Personal History of Children's Orthopedic Hospital and Medical Center* (Seattle: Children's Orthopedic Hospital and Medical Center, 1977; rprt. 1992).

37. Memo to Victor Steinbrueck from Lloyd Lovegren, 13 Jan. 1978. The Y-shaped plan of the Convalescent Home allowed for a logical division of spaces: the boys' and girls' wards were located in the two arms of the Y, and the entrance and shared spaces were in the stem. At the base of the Y was a larger block, with a sewing room, a dining room, a kitchen, and a living room with a large central fireplace.

38. "City Hospital: New Hospital Home Opens Sunday," *Seattle Times*, 30 Oct. 1930, cited in a report titled *City of Seattle Landmark Nomination* (Sept. 2001; copy provided by Christine Carr).

39. Peter Staten, introduction to Bain and Bain, *Building Together*, xiii. Unfortunately, the building no longer stands. In 2001, the Seattle Landmarks Preservation Board chose not to designate the building as a landmark. It was subsequently demolished, and the site is now a residential development.

40. Ibid., xi.

41. Memo to Victor Steinbrueck from Ivan Meyer, 10 Jan. 1978.

42. For Karl Krueger's tenure at the Seattle Symphony Orchestra, see Esther W. Campbell, *Bagpipes in the Woodwind Section: A History of the Seattle Symphony Orchestra and Its Women's Association* (Seattle: Seattle Symphony Women's Association, 1978), 14–20. Karl Krueger's reappointment is mentioned in *Town Crier*, 17 Dec. 1930, 50.

For Krueger's resignation and the difficulties the orchestra faced in 1931, see *The Argus* 38 (7 Nov. 1931, 6; 14 Nov. 1931, 3; 28 Nov. 1931, 6; 12 Dec. 1931, 4).

43. Memo to Victor Steinbrueck from Ivan Meyer, 10 Jan. 1978.

44. Kolb recalled that Emita Krueger became confined to a wheelchair after she was accidentally shot during an altercation between a servant and a paramour (author's conversation with Keith Kolb, 8 Sept. 2004).

45. Memo to Victor Steinbrueck from Ivan Meyer, 10 Jan. 1978.

46. Wilson Eyre's work had been featured in *The Craftsman*, a fact that suggests another link to the Arts and Crafts.

47. *Seattle Times*, 18 May 1930, rotogravure pictorial section, 6. See also "New Hamrick Home Cleverly Blends Age and Modernity," *Seattle Post-Intelligencer*, 4 May 1930, 8. (Thanks to David Rash for pointing out this article.) The *Seattle Post-Intelligencer* article gave design credit to John Hamrick and C. W. Hamrick (John Hamrick's brother, the contractor for the house). Pries may have worked so closely with the Hamricks that they felt as if they were responsible for the design.

48. Notices of the Christopher Columbus Memorial Lighthouse Competition appeared in architectural journals in early 1928; see, for example, "The Pan-American Union Monument Competition," *Western Architect* 37 (Feb. 1928), 26. The results of the first (open) competition were also widely reported; see "Competition for the Columbus Memorial Lighthouse," *Pencil Points* 10 (June 1929), 423–24, which quotes from a letter by competition advisor Albert Kelsey that includes the report of the jury.

49. Pries's copy of the competition book—Albert Kelsey, ed., *Rules and Program for the Competition for the Selection of an Architect for the Monumental Lighthouse, Which the Nations of the World Will Erect in the Dominican Republic to the Memory of Christopher Columbus* (Washington, D.C.: Pan American Union, 1928)—is now part of the Pries collection, Special Collections Division, University of Washington Libraries. It is signed and dated 22 Oct. 1928; also included are typescripts of three "bulletins," which provide answers to questions submitted by the competition. Three Pries sketches, which formed the basis of his design, are pasted on an inside page.

50. Six loose typescript pages, which appear to be two slightly different versions of Pries's text for his competition design, were found inside Pries's copy of the *Rules and Program for the Competition*. Pries's final text may not have matched exactly the wording of either of these drafts, but it was likely close to them.

51. The jury review is described in the second book issued for the competition; see "An Introductory Statement and the Report of the International Jury," in Albert Kelsey, ed., *Program and Rules of the Second Competition for the Selection of an Architect for the Monumental Lighthouse, Which the Nations of the World Will Erect in the Dominican Republic to the Memory of Christopher Columbus—Together with the Report of the International*

Jury, the Premiated, and Many Other Designs Submitted in the First Contest (Washington, D.C.: Pan American Union, 1930), 3–9 (copy found in Pries collection, Special Collections Division, University of Washington Libraries). The ten first-stage winners were Will Rice Amon (New York); Louis Berthin, Georges Doyon, and Georges Nesteroff (Paris); Douglas D. Ellington (Asheville, North Carolina); Joseph Lea Gleave (Nottingham, England); Helmle, Corbett and Harrison, Robert P. Rogers and Alfred E. Poor, and W. K. Oltar-Jevsky (New York); Theo Lescher, Paul Andrieu, Georges Défontaine, and Maurice Gauthier (Paris); Pippo Medori, Vincenso Palleri, and Aldo Vercelloni (Rome); Donald Nelson and Edgar Lynch (Paris and Chicago); Joaquin Vaquero Palacios and Luis Moya Blanco (Madrid); and Josef Wentzler (Dortmund, Germany).

52. Kelsey, ed., *Program and Rules of the Second Competition*, 142. Three drawings from Pries's scheme are included on pages 142 and 143; Pries's site plan is the very last foldout page at the back of the book. Pries's copy of this volume is now part of the Pries collection, Special Collections Division, University of Washington Libraries.

53. It may have been fortunate that Pries had no further involvement with this competition. Although the second stage proceeded in 1930–31, the project was doomed by the Depression and World War II. The year after the war ended, the winning but still unbuilt scheme by Joseph Lea Gleave was illustrated in a single-page article; see "War Memorial: Columbus Memorial Lighthouse Project," *Architect and Engineer* 165 (May 1946), 13.

54. Three Bain and Pries projects were mentioned in *DJC* in 1931. The Sigma Phi Epsilon fraternity house project was described as "delayed" in *DJC*, 28 Apr. 1931, 1. The Chelan Hotel project, Chelan, Washington, was described as a Georgian design projected to cost $100,000; according to *DJC*, 17 June 1931, 1, it was to proceed whenever funds were available. The Lionel H. Pries residence project (to have been built at 3655 50th Avenue N.E. at a cost of $5,000), was "to start at once," according to *DJC*, 24 Aug. 1931, 1; however, no permit was ever issued, and Pries moved to 4546 15th Avenue N.E. by late 1931 or early 1932 (that was his address in the 1932 city directory). Records in the NBBJ archives indicate that Bain and Pries did have several other commissions in 1931, and two or three of these proceeded to construction, but they were small structures or additions.

55. Pries's drawing for the Bain and Pries scheme for the Theta Chi fraternity house is in the Pries drawing collection, Special Collections Division, University of Washington Libraries. The building, actually constructed in 1931, was designed by the architect Walter Lund; see *DJC*, 27 Apr. 1931, 4 (permit), and *DJC*, 28 Apr. 31, 1.

56. Bain and Bain, *Building Together*, 94.

57. Pries's academic career is the subject of chapters 7 and 10 in this volume. How Pries became director of the Art Institute of Seattle is discussed in chapter 8.

5. Seeking a New Synthesis

1. For a discussion of Art Deco, see chapter 6, n. 5, this volume.

2. Elizabeth Greenwell Grossman, *The Civic Architecture of Paul Cret* (Cambridge: Cambridge University Press, 1996), 140–211.

3. The issues of the journal that Pries retained from vol. 1 (1931) were nos. 2 (Jan.), 4 (March), 5 (Apr.), and 8 (July). The March issue focused on Modernism and, in addition to featuring Howe and Lescaze's PSFS design, included an editorial titled "The Modernist," with excerpts from Howe's address to the May 1930 AIA convention, and an essay on "the New Architecture," with illustrations of new European buildings. (Copies of the *T-Square Club Journal* of Philadelphia are in Pries book collection, Special Collections Division, University of Washington Libraries).

4. On the 1932 International Style exhibition and its significance, see chapter 1, n. 11, this volume.

5. On Pries at the Art Institute and the failed attempt to bring the International Style exhibition to the West Coast, see chapter 8, this volume.

6. William J. R. Curtis, "'The General and the Local': Enrique del Moral's Own House, Calle Francisco Ramírez 5, Mexico City, 1948," in Edward R. Burian, ed., *Modernity and the Architecture of Mexico* (Austin: University of Texas Press, 1997), 115.

7. Ibid., 115–18. See also William J. R. Curtis, *Modern Architecture Since 1900*, 3rd ed. (London: Phaidon Press, 1996), 12–16, 690–91.

8. Curtis, *Modern Architecture Since 1900*, 390.

9. As this chapter deals with Pries's experience of Mexico, the treatment of the artistic development of Mexico in the period is necessarily simplified. In particular, I have omitted the relationship between politics and visual art, since Pries seems to have had little interest in political questions. On the complexity of the visual arts in Mexico, see Karen Cordero Reiman, "Constructing a Modern Mexican Art, 1910–1940," in James Oles, ed., *South of the Border: Mexico in the American Imagination, 1914–1947* (Washington, D.C.: Smithsonian Institution Press and Yale University Art Gallery, 1993), 10–47.

10. Pries's résumé of the early 1950s indicates that he had spent fourteen summers in Mexico (Lionel H. Pries, undated résumé, Pries papers, Special Collections Division, University of Washington Libraries). However, the brochure for Pries's solo show of his paintings, at the Pacific Gallery in Seattle, in May 1940, includes the following sentence: "Pries, with an insatiable desire for travel, has spent three months each year since 1929 in Oriental, European, and Mexican sojourn" (copy of brochure available in the Fine Arts Department, Seattle Public Library, Central Branch). If Pries visited every year from 1929 through 1942 except 1933 (the year he went to Europe), then the total number of his summers in Mexico would be thirteen. He may have gone again between 1947 and 1950, but no documents indicate such trips, nor does Robert Winskill recall any trips by Pries

to Mexico between the time they met, in 1949, and the mid-1950s. If Pries started traveling to Mexico in 1928, then he could have made fourteen trips before World War II; however, it seems less likely that he went in 1928, his first year with Bain. If all fourteen trips took place before the war, and if Pries skipped 1928 as well as 1933, then his first visit to Mexico would have taken place in 1927. Pries's last visit was in the summer of 1942. Seth Fulcher thought Pries had not traveled to Mexico in 1941 because he became seriously ill with dysentery during his trip in 1940 (author's interview with Seth Fulcher, 28 July 1999), but Keith Kolb believed that Pries was in Mexico in both 1941 and 1942 (author's discussion with Kolb, 8 Sept. 2004). Pries renewed his partnership with Bain in 1941, and that year their practice was quite busy from March through September. If Pries did go to Mexico in 1941, his trip may have been relatively brief.

11. T. Philip Terry, *Terry's Guide to Mexico: The New Standard Guidebook* (Boston: Houghton Mifflin, 1930). The foldout map included in Pries's copy of this guide is marked with lines to indicate routes and circles around the chief cities and towns visited (copy in Pries collection, Special Collections Division, University of Washington Libraries).

12. This conclusion is based on surviving paintings and photographs. Pries's paintings from Guanajuato are dated 1932, 1934, 1942, and 1946. An aerial photograph of Guanajuato is found in the Pries photograph collection; the back is marked with a notation showing where Pries stayed. It is the only such photograph in the collection. Pries's paintings from Cholula are dated 1932, 1934, and 1938. One of Pries's paintings of Taxco is dated 1938; most of his Taxco paintings are undated. The Taxco painting by Pries's student Bliss Moore is dated 1935. There are no Pries paintings from Puebla; however, Puebla is well represented in Pries's two albums of documentary photographs of Mexican buildings. (The two 1946 paintings from Guanajuato are identical views to two oils that Pries had painted while visiting Guanajuato in 1932; it seems likely that the 1946 paintings were actually painted in Seattle, with Pries working from the earlier views. These two later paintings were likely produced in winter and spring, before Pries's May 1946 exhibit at the Henry Gallery.)

13. Pries and a fellow faculty member, Richard Pearce, traveled together in the summer of 1930 and exhibited tapestries, wood carvings, and other artifacts from their Mexican trip at the Art Institute of Seattle, Nov. 1930–Jan. 1931; see *The Daily* (student newspaper of the University of Washington), 26 Nov. 1930, 1. Another year, Pries and his department head, Harlan Thomas, apparently went to Mexico together by train (author's discussion with Keith Kolb, 8 Sept. 2004). Pries took Ted Warnecke, a student, to Mexico in 1932 (author's interview with Kelly Foss, 15 July 2005). Pries took Bliss Moore to Mexico in 1935; in 1938, he took Bliss Moore and Pete Wimberly. A watercolor of Taxco by

Moore, dated 1935, is now held by Robert Winskill. Wimberly, in a memo to Victor Steinbrueck dated 15 Feb. 1978, noted that he and Moore had traveled to Mexico with Pries in 1938.

14. Not only are there no available written records of these trips, none of the faculty members or students known to have traveled with Pries to Mexico is alive to share recollections (a few of Wimberly's letters to his future wife survive from the 1938 trip, but they are relatively brief), nor do the letters of introduction survive that Pries wrote to William Spratling, Fred Davis, Diego Rivera, and others on behalf of his students Robert Shields, Roland Terry, and Robert Massar when they traveled to Mexico about 1940 (author's conversation with Robert Shields, 10 Feb. 2004).

15. David Gebhard has noted that the Santa Barbara architects George Washington Smith and Lutah Riggs traveled in Mexico from December 1922 to January 1923, sketching, taking photographs, and making measured drawings of various details. Over the course of a month, they visited more than a dozen cities and towns, including Cuernavaca, Puebla, Guadalajara, Guanajuato, and Mexico City; see David Gebhard, *Lutah Maria Riggs: A Woman in Architecture, 1921–1980* (Santa Barbara, Calif.: Capra Press/Santa Barbara Museum of Art, 1992), 10.

16. For the most complete overview of American interest in Mexico during the period, see Helen Delpar, *The Enormous Vogue of Things Mexican: Cultural Relations between the United States and Mexico, 1920–1935* (Tuscaloosa: University of Alabama Press, 1992). For the visual arts, see Oles, ed., *South of the Border.*

17. Mary Ann Miller and James Oles, introduction to Oles, ed., *South of the Border,* 3.

18. Delpar, *The Enormous Vogue of Things Mexican,* 10. Delpar adds that Mexico appealed to lingering "romantic primitivism," an attitude that had informed the Arts and Crafts movement—another aspect that would have appealed to Pries.

19. Miller and Oles, introduction to Oles, ed., *South of the Border,* 5.

20. Delpar, *The Enormous Vogue of Things Mexican,* 34, 61–81, 157–64, 177–80; Oles, ed., *South of the Border,* 49–213. On Modotti and Weston in Mexico, see Sarah M. Lowe, Tina Modotti, and Edward Weston, *The Mexico Years* (London/New York: Barbican Art Gallery/Merrell Publishers, 2004).

21. Laura Landau, "Points of Intersection: Chronicling the Interactions of Tobey, Graves, Callahan, and Anderson," and Sheryl Conkelton, "Pantheons of Dreams," in Sheryl Conkelton and Laura Landau, *Northwest Mythologies: The Interactions of Mark Tobey, Morris Graves, Kenneth Callahan, and Guy Anderson* (Tacoma/Seattle: Tacoma Art Museum/University of Washington Press, 2003), 16, 18, 43–44.

22. Delpar, *The Enormous Vogue of Things Mexican,* 199.

23. Ibid., 10.

24. The Pries oil *San Andreas, Cholula* bears the date 1932. No paintings of Mexican sites have been found

with earlier dates, although Robert Winskill retains four undated oils that appear to be very early, possibly before 1932. Multiple Pries watercolors are dated 1942. The two Pries paintings (tempera and watercolor) of Guanajuato dating from 1946 may have been painted in Seattle (see n. 12, above). On the development of Pries's painting, see chapter 8, this volume.

25. Terry, *Terry's Guide to Mexico,* 138.

26. Everett Gee Jackson, *Burros and Paintbrushes: A Mexican Adventure* (College Station: Texas A&M University Press, 1985), 43.

27. Ibid., 50.

28. Memo to the author from Robert Winskill, 12 Mar. 2004. The painting shows significant fading. It is also mounted on highly acidic cardboard, which has caused the watercolor paper to turn brown. The illustration shown in fig. 5.4 has been digitally "restored" (color-corrected).

29. Letter to Henriette Harris from Witter Bynner, 19 Dec. 1931, in Bynner, *Selected Letters,* ed. James Kraft (New York: Farrar, Straus, and Giroux, 1981), 136–37, quoted in Delpar, *The Enormous Vogue of Things Mexican,* 67–68.

30. Undated letter (summer 1938) to Janice Brebner from Pete Wimberly, courtesy of Janice B. Wimberly.

31. In the 1920s and 1930s, in the wake of the Mexican Revolution, Mexican artists and intellectuals emphasized the continuing contributions of the indigenous people. See Reiman, "Constructing a Modern Mexican Art," in Oles, ed., *South of the Border.* More recent scholarship has argued that pre-Columbian traditions were largely extinguished within a few decades after the Spanish conquest; see George Kubler, "On the Colonial Extinction of Motifs in Pre-Columbian Art," in Thomas F. Reese, ed., *Studies in Ancient American and European Art: The Collected Essays of George Kubler* (New Haven, Conn.: Yale University Press, 1985), 66–74. See also George Kubler, *Mexican Architecture of the Sixteenth Century* (New Haven, Conn.: Yale University Press, 1948), 116–86, 361–416.

32. The best sources of information on William Spratling are two recent biographies. Joan Mark, *The Silver Gringo: William Spratling and Taxco* (Albuquerque: University of New Mexico Press, 2000) proves to be an overview of Spratling's complete life and work; Taylor D. Littleton, *The Color of Silver: William Spratling, His Life and Art* (Baton Rouge: Louisiana State University Press, 2000) offers more detail on Spratling's early life and less on his businesses. Both biographies correct errors in William Spratling, *File on Spratling: An Autobiography* (Boston: Little, Brown, 1967). A well-illustrated account of Spratling's activities as a designer and producer of silver is Penny C. Morrill, *William Spratling and the Mexican Silver Renaissance: Maestros de Plata* (New York/San Antonio: Harry N. Abrams/San Antonio Museum of Art, 2002). Spratling's activities in Mexico are also explored and illustrated in Penny Chittim Morrill and Carole A. Berk, *Mexican Silver: 20th Century Hand-wrought Jewelry & Metalwork* (Atglen, Penn.: Schiffer

Publishing, 1994), 13–21, 31–97; many of Spratling's apprentices, who later went on to their own careers in the silver crafts, are profiled in this book. For additional biographical information, along with a guide to Spratling's designs, see Phyllis M. Goddard, *Spratling Silver: A Field Guide* (Altadena, Calif.: Keenan Tyler Paine, 2003). A short account of Spratling's years at Tulane is found in Bernard Lemann, Malcolm Heard Jr., and John P. Klingman, eds., *Talk About Architecture: A Century of Architectural Education at Tulane* (New Orleans: Tulane University School of Architecture, 1993), 61–80.

33. See William P. Spratling and Lyle Saxon, *Picturesque New Orleans: Ten Drawings of the French Quarter* (New Orleans: Tulane University, 1923), and William P. Spratling, *The Art of Pencil Drawing* (New Orleans: Searcy and Pfaff, 1923).

34. Spratling and Faulkner collaborated on a small book; see William P. Spratling and William Faulkner, *Sherwood Anderson and Other Famous Creoles* (New Orleans: Pelican Bookshop Press, 1926; rprt. *Texas Quarterly* 9 [Spring 1966]).

35. In the mid-1920s, Frans Blom and Oliver LaFarge, faculty members at Tulane's Middle American Research Institute, emerged as leaders in the study of pre-Columbian Mexico, and their work sparked Spratling's interest; see Delpar, *The Enormous Vogue of Things Mexican*, 106–9.

36. William Spratling, "Some Impressions of Mexico," *Architectural Forum* 47/1 and 2 (July 1927, 1–8; Aug. 1927, 161–68); the citation is from page 1 of the July issue.

37. William Spratling, "Indo-Hispanic Mexico: Some Notes on the Manner in Which Indian Form and Impulse Has Persisted and Continued through an Imposed Culture," *Architecture* 59/2 and 3 (Feb. 1929, 75–80; Mar. 1929, 139–44); the citation is from page 140 of the March issue. Spratling's sketches of Mexico were also published in *Pencil Points*; see William Spratling, "The Expressive Pencil," *Pencil Points* 10 (June 1929), 364–72.

38. Author's conversation with Keith Kolb, 23 Sept. 2003.

39. On the foreign summer schools and seminars, see Delpar, *The Enormous Vogue of Things Mexican*, 18–19, 48–50, 72–74.

40. The circle around the summer schools is mentioned in ibid., 72–73, and in Morrill and Berk, *Mexican Silver*, 18–19.

41. William P. Spratling, "Figures in a Mexican Renaissance: Being Various Encounters Among the Intelligentsia Mexicana," *Scribner's Magazine* 85 (Jan. 1929), 14–21; the citation is from page 21.

42. The reason for Spratling's move to Mexico has been the subject of some debate. See Mark, *The Silver Gringo*, 15–17, and Littleton, *The Color of Silver*, 84–86. Spratling's move to Mexico was partially financed by an advance for a book, published in 1932 as *Little Mexico* and intended "to picture normal life in a small Mexican village"; isolated Taxco seemed the perfect setting. See William P. Spratling, *Little Mexico* (New York: Jonathan Cape and Harrison Smith, 1932), reissued as William P. Spratling, *A Small Mexican World* (Boston: Little, Brown, 1964).

43. The ease with which American and Mexican artists and intellectuals interacted is demonstrated by Spratling's circle of friends. Among the most important were Dwight W. Morrow, the American ambassador, and Elizabeth Cutter Morrow, his wife. They asked Spratling to help purchase pottery and other artifacts to furnish their Cuernavaca residence. Elizabeth Morrow also commissioned Spratling to design and illustrate *Casa Mañana*, the book the Morrows published about their Mexican home; see Elizabeth Cutter Morrow, *Casa Mañana* (Croton Falls, N.Y.: Spiral Press, 1932). In turn, in 1929, Spratling convinced the Morrows to commission Diego Rivera to paint a mural in the Cortes Palace in Cuernavaca; see Littleton, *The Color of Silver*, 146–53, and Delpar, *The Enormous Vogue of Things Mexican*, 67.

44. Author's interview with Robert Winskill, 26 July 1994. This may have been as early as 1927 and was certainly no later than 1929. Given the lifelong friendship that developed between Pries and Spratling, it may be that they had become acquainted with each other when Spratling was still at Tulane, or at least that Pries was aware of Spratling because of his publications.

45. Undated letter (summer 1938) to Janice Brebner from Pete Wimberly, courtesy of Janice B. Wimberly.

46. Five albums of photographs are found in the Pries collection, Special Collections Division, University of Washington Libraries. Three of these albums include snapshots from his travels; almost all the snapshots are small (often 1 by 1 inch) and unlabeled. Two albums include 3–by–5–inch photographs of buildings in Mexico, each with a typewritten label.

47. Pries's preliminary measured drawings of details of Mexican buildings fill fifty-eight sheets measuring roughly 11 by 14 inches; the drawings are freehand pencil on stiff paper. Only one example of a finished ink drawing based on this material survives; it may be that Pries prepared one ink drawing as a sample to show potential publishers. The drawings are included in the Pries drawing collection, Special Collections Division, University of Washington Libraries. Pries's résumé of the early 1950s states, "Have measured and drawn for publication details and plans of many Mexican monuments. This book would be of major architectural importance. No publisher available due to lack of interest in Spanish Colonial Architectural antiquities. (Pál Kelemen is of decided different opinion so resubmission might be possible)" (Lionel H. Pries, undated résumé, Pries papers, Special Collections Division, University of Washington Libraries). Kelemen, a noted Hungarian historian and a leading authority on the pre-Columbian art and civilization of the cultures of Latin America, visited Pries in the early 1950s (see chapter 8, this volume); nonetheless, the book was never completed or published.

48. "Biographical Data: Lionel H. Pries," memo to Victor Steinbrueck from Keith Kolb, 6 Feb. 1978.

49. Memo to Victor Steinbrueck from Pete Wimberly,

15 Feb. 1978. On Spratling's involvement with illegal trade in pre-Columbian artifacts, see Mark, *The Silver Gringo*, 93–112.

50. Memo to Victor Steinbrueck from Lloyd Lovegren, 13 Jan. 1978.

51. The interconnections are quite complex. What was then called "primitive" art (the art of Africa, Oceania, pre-Columbian America, and other non-Western cultures) is thought to have been a source of inspiration for Modern art (the work of Braque, Picasso, and, indirectly, LeCorbusier). Subsequently, the dissemination of the ideas of LeCorbusier and other Modern architects was inflected by local conditions, nationalism, and an interest in integrating local site and organizational typologies as well as local decorative arts into works of architecture; certainly this approach influenced Mexican architects, including Juan O'Gorman, Barragan, Del Moral, and others. All these architects were influenced by Mexican artists— and LeCorbusier would himself produce a series of Mediterranean "vernacular" houses (memo to author from Edward R. Burian, 16 Jan. 2005).

52. José de la Borda, who arrived in Taxco from Spain in 1716, had discovered the silver and developed the mines in the mountains around Taxco. With his new wealth, de la Borda commissioned the construction of the Church of Santa Prisca, completed in 1758, a remarkable late Baroque structure, which, with its tall towers, still dominates the community. But Taxco's prosperity was relatively short lived. After de la Borda departed, in the 1760s, silver mining entered a long, slow decline.

53. On Spratling's opening of his silver workshop, see Mark, *The Silver Gringo*, 47–64; Littleton, *The Color of Silver*, 223–56; and Spratling, *File on Spratling*, 67–87.

54. Oles, ed., *South of the Border*, 133. For a description of Spratling's designs, see Goddard, *Spratling Silver*, and Morrill and Berk, *Mexican Silver*. Two other recent discussions of Spratling's designs in silver are Sandraline Cedarwall and Hal Riney, *Spratling Silver* (San Francisco: Chronicle Books, 1990), and Lucia García-Noriega Nieto, "Mexican Silver: William Spratling and the Taxco Style," *Journal of Decorative and Propaganda Arts* 10 (Fall 1988), 42–53. For a general history of jewelry making in Mexico, see Mary L. Davis and Greta Pack, *Mexican Jewelry* (Austin: University of Texas Press, 1963).

55. Jean Charlot, *The Mexican Mural Renaissance, 1920–1925* (New Haven, Conn.: Yale University Press, 1963), 1–39.

56. According to the art historian Jacinto Quirarte, "The nationalistic tendencies in Mexico combined with the new orientation of the art world aroused interest in Indian arts and crafts, pre-Columbian art, and the work of earlier 'authentic' Mexican talents. . . . Ultimately the aim of the new Mexican artists was to create an art based on Mexican reality and experience"; see Jacinto Quirarte, "Mexican and Mexican American Artists: 1920–1970," in *The Latin American Spirit: Art and Artists in the United States, 1920–1970* (New York: Bronx Museum/Harry N. Abrams, 1988), 14.

57. Author's interview with Robert Winskill, 26 July

1994. Frederick W. Davis (ca. 1880–1961), a native of Illinois, had gone to Mexico before 1910 and worked initially for the Sonora News Company, selling newspapers, guidebooks, and souvenirs on the Southern Pacific Railway line south from Nogales, Arizona. Davis began traveling to different parts of Mexico, buying folk art and learning about the artistic traditions of different regions. When the Sonora News Company opened a showroom in Mexico City for Mexican arts and crafts, Davis became its manager. During the turbulent years of the Mexican Revolution (1910–1917), a large number of Mexican antiques came on the market. Because few other collectors were initially interested in folk art, Davis was gradually able to build up a notable collection of pre-Columbian and contemporary arts and crafts. When stability returned to Mexico, after 1920, Davis's shop became a routine stop for American collectors as well as for other visitors to the country. His showroom also carried Spratling's early designs. In 1933, Davis left the Sonora News Company and entered a partnership with Frank Sanborn, who owned several stores serving the tourist trade. For the next two decades, Davis headed Sanborn's department of antiques and fine crafts in the Mexico City store, and he continued to encourage and support Mexican artists and craftsmen and to display and sell their work. Information about Frederick W. Davis is limited. The most complete account is found in Morrill and Berk, *Mexican Silver*, 22–29. Various short accounts are included in Oles, ed., *South of the Border*, 123–27; Delpar, *The Enormous Vogue of Things Mexican*, 5–6, 65–66; Davis and Pack, *Mexican Jewelry*, 160–57; and Erna Fergusson, *Mexico Revisited* (New York: Knopf, 1955), 305–13. See also Patricia Fent Ross, "To Market, To Market! Craft and Commerce in a Changing Economic Scene," *Craft Horizons* 15 (July/Aug. 1955), 26–27.

58. Geoffrey T. Hellman, "Profiles: Imperturbable Noble," *New Yorker* 35 (7 May 1960), 60. The importance of the circle surrounding Frederick Davis's shop is also noted in Morrill and Berk, *Mexican Silver*, 25–16, and in W. Jackson Rushing, "Marketing the Affinity of the Primitive and the Modern: René d'Harnoncourt and 'Indian Art of the United States,'" in Janet Catherine Berlo, ed., *The Early Years of Native American Art History: The Politics of Scholarship and Collecting* (Seattle: University of Washington Press, 1992), 196.

59. On Covarrubias and the circle around Davis's shop, see Adriana Williams, *Covarrubias* (Austin: University of Texas Press, 1994), 53–132.

60. Oles, ed., *South of the Border*, 127.

61. René d'Harnoncourt was born to an aristocratic family in Austria. Although he showed an interest in art as a child, he received a technical education. In 1924, after his family suffered severe financial losses, he moved to Paris, and he went to Mexico in 1926. D'Harnoncourt initially eked out a minimal living as a commercial artist but quickly acquired a reputation for his knowledgeable advice to American antique collectors. For background on d'Harnoncourt, see Robert Fay Schrader, *The Indian Arts & Crafts Board: An Aspect of New Deal Indian*

Policy (Albuquerque: University of New Mexico Press, 1983), 124–28; Russell Lynes, *Good Old Modern: An Intimate Portrait of the Museum of Modern Art* (New York: Athenaeum, 1973), 264–83; and Hellman, "Profiles: Imperturbable Noble," 49–112. Short accounts are found in Morrill and Berk, *Mexican Silver*, 25–28; Fergusson, *Mexico Revisited*, 307–9; and Oles, ed., *South of the Border*, 124–33. Like Davis and Spratling, d'Harnoncourt became a friend of the Morrows, and he later did drawings to illustrate Elizabeth Morrow's book on Mexico; see Elizabeth Cutter Morrow, *The Painted Pig* (New York: Knopf, 1930).

62. Rivera is particularly important in this regard, since he spent the years of the Mexican Revolution in Paris as part of the circle of Braque and Picasso. See Pete Hamill, *Diego Rivera* (New York: Harry N. Abrams, 1999), 46–79.

63. On the relationship of politics and theory to Mexican art and architecture, see "Mexico, Modernity, and Architecture: An Interview with Alberto Pérez-Gómez," in Burian, ed., *Modernity and the Architecture of Mexico*, 24–44.

64. The participation of O'Gorman in the circle around Davis's shop is not mentioned in many accounts. However, O'Gorman is included in a descriptive letter by Lesley Simpson, quoted at length in William Spratling's autobiography; see Spratling, *File on Spratling*, 59.

65. Edward R. Burian, "The Architecture of Juan O'Gorman: Dichotomy and Drift," in Burian, ed., *Modernity and the Architecture of Mexico*, 127. See also Edward R. Burian, "Modernity and Nationalism: Juan O'Gorman and Post-Revolutionary Architecture in Mexico, 1920–1960," in Jean-François LeJeune, ed., *Cruelty & Utopia: Cities and Landscapes of Latin America* (New York: Princeton Architectural Press, 2005), 210–23.

66. Burian, "The Architecture of Juan O'Gorman," in Burian ed., *Modernity and the Architecture of Mexico*, 127.

67. For the role and influence of José Villagrán García, see Antonio E. Méndez-Vigatá, "Politics and Architectural Language: Post-Revolutionary Regimes and Their Influence on Mexican Public Architecture, 1920–1952," in Burian ed., *Modernity and the Architecture of Mexico*, 74–81.

68. Burian, "The Architecture of Juan O'Gorman," in Burian ed., *Modernity and the Architecture of Mexico*, 129.

69. Ibid., 135–37.

70. Ibid., 136. O'Gorman's client Frances Toor exemplifies the interconnectedness of the Mexican and American intelligentsia. Toor was an American who first visited Mexico in 1922 and then moved there permanently. From 1925 to 1937 she published the bilingual *Mexican Folkways*, which introduced Mexican arts and crafts to a wide American audience. *Mexican Folkways* commissioned illustrations from such Mexican artists as Rivera, Siqueiros, Roberto Montenegro, and Carlos Mérida, and it frequently described new archaeological discoveries as well as living traditions in folk art. See Delpar, *The Enormous Vogue of Things Mexican*, 36,

62, 93, and Oles, ed., *South of the Border*, 121.

71. Ibid., 136–39. See also Burian, "Modernity and Nationalism," in LeJeune, ed., *Cruelty & Utopia*, 216–19.

72. The Pries drawing collection includes twelve prints of drawings by Juan O'Gorman. Ten blueline prints, measuring approximately 16 by 13 inches, show drawings (dated 1925) of details of Spanish Colonial buildings: five are titled *Casa del Bachiller Don Manual Marco d'Ibarra en San Juanico, Tacuba, D.F*; three are titled *Casa de Moneda de la Ciudad de Tlalpan, D.F.*; and two are titled *Casa de Vecindad en la Calle de Mesones, Mexico, D.F.* All ten have original signatures in ink by O'Gorman. There is also one blueprint, 32 1/2 by 25 inches, titled *Portada Pral de la Iglesia de Sn Geronimo en Sn Angel, D.F.*, and there is one brownline print, 41 by 25 inches, titled *Portada de la Casa de Humboldt, Tasco, GRO.* The two larger prints are unsigned. In addition, there are seven brownline prints, roughly 16 by 13 inches, of drawings of other Spanish colonial structures. These are by several different drafters; on the back of each is the ink stamp of Carlos Obregón Santacilia, with the date 17 March 1925. All are found in the Pries drawing collection, Special Collections Division, University of Washington Libraries.

73. Burian, "The Architecture of Juan O'Gorman," in Burian ed., *Modernity and the Architecture of Mexico*, 139–48. In 1940, Juan O'Gorman married the sculptor Helen Fowler (who sometimes exhibited under the name Helen Lanpher). She had briefly studied art at the University of Washington, in Seattle—another possible connection between O'Gorman and Pries.

74. Author's interview with Robert Winskill, 26 July 1994; confirmed by memo to author from Robert Winskill, 12 Mar. 2003. Winskill notes that Fogarty inscribed a translation of *Don Quixote* to Pries. Sergio Palleroni, formerly a professor of architecture at the University of Washington, was in Mexico in February 1996 and visited a former member of Cementos Tolteca, who recalled Pries and remembered his nickname, "Spike," of which Palleroni had been unaware.

75. Anita Brenner, *Your Mexican Holiday: A Modern Guide* (New York: Putnam's, 1935), 265.

76. Ibid., 53, quoted in the pioneering study of Mexican Modern architecture by Esther Born, *The New Architecture in Mexico* (New York: Architectural Record/ William Morrow, 1937), 12. Oles has discussed Fogarty's activities as well, particularly the influence of the company magazine, with its Modern graphics and images emphasizing the aesthetic possibilities of Modern architecture; see James Oles, "La nueva fotografía y cementos Tolteca: una alianza utópica," in *Mexicana: Fotografía Moderna en México, 1923–1940* (Valencia: Institut Valencià d'Art Modern, 1998), 139–51. Burian notes that numerous other companies also became advocates for the Modern architecture that appeared in such journals as *Arquitectura*; in the 1940s, for example, Cementos Portland Monterrey produced its own magazine advocating Modern architecture (memo to author from Edward R. Burian, 16 Jan. 2005).

77. Central to almost all of Pries's encounters in Mexico (except, perhaps, his interaction with Fogarty) was a linkage between Modernism and indigenous as well as folk (*mestizo*) arts and crafts. Of the years after 1920, Delpar writes: "During these years Mexican art in its various manifestations—preconquest art, folk art, and contemporary muralism—stirred extraordinary enthusiasm in the United States and contributed immensely to the Mexican vogue of the era. Mexican art spoke eloquently to the many Americans who were questioning European dominance in the arts and expressing the desire for an auchthonous art based on national culture and traditions"; see Delpar, *The Enormous Vogue of Things Mexican*, 164. On Mexican Modern architects and these artistic traditions, see the following contributions to Burian, ed., *Modernity and the Architecture of Mexico*: "Mexico, Modernity, and Architecture: An Interview with Alberto Pérez-Gómez," 30–32, 40–44; Antonio E. Méndez-Vigatá, "Politics and Architectural Language: Post-Revolutionary Regimes in Mexico and Their Influence on Mexican Public Architecture," 72–78; and Burian, "Architecture of Juan O'Gorman," 127–149.

78. Oles, ed., *South of the Border*, 127–33. The exhibition catalogue, compiled by René d'Harnoncourt, emphasizes that these are works of art that are specifically Mexican in character, not just created within the geographical boundaries of Mexico; see *Mexican Arts: Catalogue of an Exhibition Organized for and Circulated by the American Federation of Arts, 1930–31* (New York: American Federation of Arts, 1930). In 1933, d'Harnoncourt left Davis, moved to the United States, and became director of a radio program, *Art in America*.

79. Rushing, "Marketing the Affinity of the Primitive and the Modern," in Berlo, ed., *The Early Years of Native American Art History*, 198. For the detailed history of the IACB, see Schrader, *The Indian Arts & Crafts Board*. Delpar notes that, as a result of experience in Mexico, "many artists and intellectuals in the United States reassessed the culture of Native Americans"; see Delpar, *The Enormous Vogue of Things Mexican*, 193.

80. A summary of the exhibition is found in Lynes, *Good Old Modern*, 268–73. A detailed interpretation is Rushing, "Marketing the Affinity of the Primitive and the Modern," in Berlo, ed., *The Early Years of Native American Art History*, 191–236. The exhibition is also addressed in W. Jackson Rushing, *Native American Art and the New York Avant-Garde: A History of Cultural Primitivism* (Austin: University of Texas Press, 1995), 104–20. Pries owned a copy of the catalogue produced for the exhibition; see Frederic Douglas and René d'Harnoncourt, *Indian Art of the United States* (New York: Museum of Modern Art, 1941).

81. The phrase "the affinity of the primitive and the modern" derives from Rushing's essay in Berlo, ed., *The Early Years of Native American Art History*. The essay incorporates this phrase both in its title and in a subsection titled "Merchandising the Affinity of the Primitive and the Modern."

82. The 1941 show was not the first exhibit of non-Western art at MOMA; previous MOMA shows of non-Western art had included "American Sources of Modern Art" (1933), "African Negro Art" (1935), "Prehistoric Rock Pictures in Europe and Africa" (1937), and "Twenty Centuries of Mexican Art" (1940). However, d'Harnoncourt's "Indian Art of the United States" has been recognized as establishing a new standard for the exhibition and aestheticization of such work and is thought to have changed the public perception of non-Western art more radically than any show before or since. See Rushing, "Marketing the Affinity of the Primitive and the Modern," in Berlo, ed., *The Early Years of Native American Art History*, 199–200, 205, 208, 216–25.

83. The totem pole was carved by the Haida artist John Wallace in 1939; see Rushing, "Marketing the Affinity of the Primitive and the Modern," in Berlo, ed., *The Early Years of Native American Art History*, 207.

84. In 1937, some University of Washington students, responding to a studio problem for the design of a museum of northwest Native American arts, juxtaposed totem poles with relatively simple (almost Modern) building forms.

85. Ludwig Goldscheider, *Art Without Epoch: Works of Distant Times Which Still Appeal to Modern Taste* (New York: Oxford University Press, n.d. [ca. 1937]). Pries acquired this volume in 1938.

86. René d'Harnoncourt, *Modern Art Old and New: A Portfolio Based on the Exhibition 'Timeless Aspects of Modern Art' Held at the Museum of Modern Art in New York*, Teaching Portfolio no. 3 (New York: Museum of Modern Art, 1950). It should be recognized that the kinds of cultural connections that today are considered so important, as one considers the arts and crafts of any cultural group, were regarded as less significant from the 1930s to the 1960s.

6. In Practice

1. It is likely that there are Pries design projects, especially unbuilt projects, that have not been discovered. The projects that are discussed in this chapter were identified from a variety of sources. It is believed that the projects discussed here are most if not all of Pries's important projects of these years.

2. Knowledge of Pries's route in the summer of 1933 is based on multiple sources. The books that Pries purchased in Sweden, Germany, and Austria are often signed with date and location. Pries's route in Germany is marked in his copy of Karl Baedeker, *Southern Germany (Baden, Black Forest, Wurtemberg, and Bavaria): Handbook for Travellers*, 13th ed. (Leipzig/London/New York: Karl Baedeker/George Allen and Unwin/Charles Scribner's Sons, 1929), map inside back cover (copy in Pries book collection, Special Collections Division, University of Washington Libraries). One of Pries's photo albums includes unlabeled photographs from his 1933 trip; these make it possible to identify buildings that Pries saw.

3. Because Pries understood architectural development as evolutionary, his photographs often focus on

buildings that suggest new directions but do not represent a complete break with the past. The Art Nouveau sources for Olbrich's Secession Building (Vienna) are well known; the building clearly embraces the new even as it retains traditional planning strategies, such as bilateral symmetry. Hitchcock classified such works as the Grundtvig Church (Copenhagen) and the Stockholm Town Hall as "traditional" and called them "Medievalizing," even as he noted their superb siting and theatricality, and pointed to the relationship of the Grundtvig Church to Expressionism; see Henry-Russell Hitchcock Jr., *Architecture: Nineteenth and Twentieth Centuries* (Baltimore: Penguin, 1968), 396–97. More recently, Frampton has suggested that the Stockholm Town Hall was a "seminal work in Scandinavian architecture, without which the whole of Asplund's and Aalto's achievement would have been very different," and he wrote of the Grundtvig Church, "The undeniable power of these forms seems to derive from a deeply felt spirituality," even as he pointed to its sources in the stepped-gable tradition of southern Sweden; see Kenneth Frampton, *Modern Architecture, 1851–1945* (New York: Rizzoli, 1983), 143, 218. This transformation of traditional sources to achieve spiritual space would have interested Pries.

4. The Century of Progress Exposition was open from 27 May to 1 November 1933, and the entire issue of *Architectural Forum* 59 (July 1933) was devoted to it. For the history of the Century of Progress Exposition, see John E. Findling, *Chicago's Great World's Fairs* (Manchester, England: Manchester University Press, 1994), 43–155. A summary of the exposition's architecture and construction is Carl W. Condit, *Chicago, 1930–70: Building, Planning, and Urban Technology* (Chicago: University of Chicago Press, 1974), esp. chap. 1, "The Century of Progress Exposition," 3–22. A good collection of images of the Century of Progress buildings is *The Official Pictures of A Century of Progress Exposition, Chicago 1933* (Chicago: Reuben H. Donnelley, 1933). A contemporary essay on the exposition's architecture is Franklin Booth, *The Buildings: Their Architectural Meaning* (Winnetka, Ill.: Book and Print Guild, 1934). A recent critical analysis that places this exposition in the cultural context of other fairs of the interwar years is Robert W. Rydell, *World of Fairs: The Century of Progress Expositions* (Chicago: University of Chicago Press, 1993).

5. The term "Art Deco" is derived from the Exposition Internationale des Arts Décoratifs et Industriels Modernes that took place in Paris in 1925. The Art Deco mode sought modernity and embraced the Machine Age. While the style consciously rejected historical vocabularies in search of newness, it retained much of the planning approach of traditional architecture. "Art Deco" as a general term includes architecture of the 1920s and early 1930s with low-relief geometrical designs, zigzags, chevrons, and stylized floral motifs as well as the streamlined, curvilinear forms that emerged in the 1930s. However, some historians use the term "Art Deco" only for the first phase and use the term

"Art Moderne" or "Streamline Moderne" to describe the streamlined architecture of the second phase. For a short discussion of Art Deco in the generic sense, see John C. Poppeliers, S. Allen Chambers Jr., and Nancy B. Schwartz, *What Style Is It? A Guide to American Architecture* (Washington D.C.: Preservation Press, 1983), 88–91. A general guide that differentiates between Art Deco and Art Moderne, classifying them as two forms of architecture called "Modernistic,": Virginia and Lee McAlester, *A Field Guide to American Houses* (New York: Knopf, 1984), 464–67. A well illustrated and broadly inclusive publication is Patricia Bayer, *Art Deco Architecture: Design, Decoration and Detail from the Twenties and Thirties* (London: Thames and Hudson, 1992).

6. See Meredith Clausen, interview with Paul Thiry, 15–16 Sept. 1983, Smithsonian Archives of American Art, http://artarchives.si.edu/oralhist/thiry83.htm.

7. No one who knew Pries in the 1930s recalls any buildings of his design that were constructed after the breakup of Bain and Pries, until the Willcox residence. Review of the permit listings in the *DJC* from 1932 to 1940 did not turn up any Pries projects.

8. After this plan went unbuilt, the Buschmann family did not turn to a different architect. Instead, the family continued to live at 1104 Minor Avenue through the end of the 1930s, and this fact suggests that the project died because of the Depression.

9. Borgendale's office was on University Way just north of N.E. 45th Street, roughly one block from Pries's own house; Borgendale may have been Pries's dentist.

10. Pries's monogram with the 1936 date is found in the landscape at the right end of the house. The scale of the project seems rather odd—the proportions and detailing of the fenestration suggest a one-story building rather than a building with two stories.

11. The drawings of this project are undated; however, the Kruegers were listed in the Los Angeles city directory in 1937, a fact that suggests the 1936–37 project date.

12. Two versions of this project survive. The scheme shown was the first that Pries designed. The second is of a similar scale and organization, but it shifts some of the spaces to address functional concerns and reduces the total size of the project in an attempt to limit its cost.

13. Julian P. Willcox served in the Marines from 1905 to 1935 and from 1942 to 1944. He served primarily in the United States and aboard various ships but was also sent to Haiti (1915–16), Cuba (1916–17), the Philippines (1926–28), and Shanghai, China (1934–35). Willcox served at the Puget Sound Navy Yard in the late 1920s and early 1930s. He was recalled to service for two years during World War II.

14. As was not uncommon among the wealthy in the early twentieth century, Constance and her younger sister, Agnes, spent much of their early lives in Europe, and both spoke German as well as English.

15. The surviving construction documents for the Willcox residence are now in possession of Philip and Cecilia Hughes, the house's current owners (2006). The documents include a partial set of blueprints of working

drawings for the house (sheets 4, 7, 9–11, 13, and 16–17; sheet 4 is dated 10 August 1936, and sheet 17 is dated 9 March 1937), an original typewritten set of specifications (undated), a mimeographed set of mechanical specifications (prepared by Lincoln Bouillon, mechanical engineer, and dated September 1936), two blueprints of window-shop drawings prepared by Fentron Steel Works of Seattle (with November 1936 dates), a hardware schedule for 117 doors, a hand-lettered list of rooms with dimensions and areas (on Pries's letterhead), a blueline print of a landscape plan (dated 20 October 1937), and a survey of the property (undated).

16. Pries's drawings show even the abstract detail of a dolphin (about 1 inch in height) cut in the glass at the front entrance, and in the mirrored top of the built-in dressing table in the women's powder room. The last sheet, number 17, dated 9 March, shows details of the bar and game room and is marked to indicate that all shop drawings require the architect's approval.

17. A surviving blueline print of the landscape plan shows all the site features planned by Pries, including the lily pool, the saltwater swimming pool, a trout pond, and a Japanese landscape.

18. The main block of the house, facing southwest, measures 90 feet long by 30 feet wide; the service and guest wing is 60 feet long. The two wings form an L around the circular entrance drive. The service wing had the kitchen, the maids' rooms, and the garage on the first floor and guest bedrooms and the chauffeur's apartment on the second floor.

19. Why Constance Willcox wanted simulated stone rather than real stone is not known; perhaps cost was an issue. The current owners have covered the simulated stone with white cloth.

20. Unfortunately, the saltwater swimming pool was destroyed in February 1999 when the house was threatened by landslides caused by heavy rain and underground streams. It was necessary to fill the pool so that trucks and earthmoving equipment could move across the property to save the house. See *Seattle Times*, 6 Feb. 1999, D8; *Seattle Post-Intelligencer*, 8 Feb. 1999, A1, A4.

21. Both exterior totem poles were removed by a later owner.

22. The interior totem poles were also removed by a later owner.

23. Wimberly wrote (unpublished manuscript, ca. 1990), "Spike had designed a beautiful living room which was about 20 by 40 feet. It had a very high ceiling and, in order to set off all the furniture and artifacts, he designed or rather had us copy a textile Indian design in a rather large scale for the ceiling. Bliss Moore and I were taken over to the Hood Canal site (I believe it was during the summer as it was very fine weather) and the acoustic material for the ceiling which was in 2–by–4–foot pieces was laid out on the floor of the barn. We proceeded to paint the design, using brilliant primary colors. . . . Both Bliss and I had a marvelous time; the Colonel and his wife were magnificent as host and hostess. . . . It was a wonderful experience for a couple

of young, embryo architects as we were there for nearly three weeks and actually saw the construction of the house proceed while we were doing the ceiling mural. It also gave us a first hand illustration of the relationship between a good architect, a good contractor and a client as we were in the middle of all of this while we were there." When the current owners, Philip and Cecilia Hughes, renovated the property to convert it to a bed-and-breakfast inn, they removed the ceiling paintings (which were painted on fabric), both because they found the design overwhelming and because they thought it made the living room rather dark. They saved the fabric panels so that they could be reinstalled by a future owner.

24. For a detailed discussion of the effort by American architects to reconcile Modern architecture and the tradition of the American country house, see Hewitt, *The Architect and the American Country House*, 241–57. My discussion largely derives from Hewitt.

25. F. R. S. Yorke, *The Modern House* (London: Architectural Press, 1934). The first book to focus on American Modern houses was James Ford and Catherine Morrow Ford, *The Modern House in America* (New York: Architectural Book Publishing, 1940). The only firms in the Northwest included in this book were the Portland architects A. E. Doyle and Associate (Pietro Belluschi, design architect) and the Seattle architects Paul Thiry and Alban Shay.

26. For the Mandel residence, see "Residence of Richard Mandel, Mount Kisco, N.Y.," *Architectural Forum* 60 (March 1934), 185–86; "House of Richard Mandel, Mt. Kisco, New York," *Architectural Forum* 63 (Aug. 1935), 78–89.

27. For publication of "Square Shadows," see *Fortune* 12 (Oct. 1935), 28; "Square Shadows, Whitemarsh, Pa. . . . Dictated by the Necessities of Plan, Executed in Local Materials, Blending and Fitting Into Its American Background. Modern, but Not European," *Architectural Forum* 62 (March 1935), 192–205.

28. Hewitt called "Square Shadows" "the most important transitional American country house" because it occupies a "middle ground" in drawing upon both tradition and modernity; it seems also a regionally appropriate solution in its use of brick and stone; see Hewitt, *The Architect & the American Country House*, 252.

29. In 1926–28, Julian Willcox had been on detached military duty at MGM Studios, Culver City, California, where he met Gable, Flynn, and other emerging film stars.

30. For the participation of Moore and Wimberly, see n. 23, above. Sources for visits by other students to the Willcox residence are the author's interviews with William Svensson, 14 Sept. 1994, and Roland Terry, 16 Aug. 1999.

31. Pries sought no broader publicity for his achievement: the Depression lingered, and he was aware that some architects believed it was unfair that he was not only receiving his state-supported faculty salary but had also secured the Willcox project, perhaps the largest residential commission in the region in the mid-1930s.

There was no mention of the Willcox project in local papers or in the *DJC*. Given the scale of the project in the depressed economy of the 1930s, the absence of any mention in the press suggests an effort to keep the project out of public view. Pries did arrange for Phyllis Dearborn to photograph the Willcox residence; however, Dearborn and Pries did not get along, and she made only four photographs of the house (and two of the gatehouse that was built in 1939). These photographs are now part of the Dearborn-Massar collection, Special Collections Division, University of Washington Libraries.

32. Pries had by now become a good friend of the Willcoxes. He drew their 1936 Christmas card, which featured a map of Puget Sound with the house location and a drawing of the elevation. (A photocopy of the Christmas card is in possession of the current owners of the Willcox residence, Philip and Cecilia Hughes.) In 1968, the Willcox sisters attended the gathering in Seattle that followed Pries's death (see chap. 11, this volume).

33. No drawings for the gatehouse have been discovered. A letter to Julian Willcox from the plumbing contractor, B. B. Lents, with recommendations for plumbing for the gatehouse, is dated 25 March 1939.

34. The gatehouse survives, but the logs of the arch were partially cut in February 1999 to allow passage of the earthmoving equipment needed to save the Willcox residence.

35. Ernest R. Gayler served as a construction engineer in the U.S. Navy from the 1900s to the 1930s. He was primarily responsible for construction projects at naval stations and naval yards in the United States but was also sent to Haiti (1916–20). Gayler served at the Puget Sound Navy Yard in 1920–24, 1927–30, and 1936–38. He was recalled to service for four years during World War II.

36. Anne Roberts Gayler, "One Hundred Years," unpublished manuscript, ca. 1982. The manuscript of Anne Gayler's memoirs, completed soon after her one hundredth birthday, is the best available source of information for the Gaylers' life, and for the design and construction of their home on Hood Canal. A copy of Mrs. Gayler's memoirs, duplicated from the copy held by William and Judy Matchett, is in possession of the author.

37. Gayler, "One Hundred Years," 214–18. Mrs. Gayler's account has been supplemented by observations made on site and by discussions with the current owners of the house, William and Judy Matchett. Other than one landscape plan, none of Pries's drawings have been discovered.

38. Anne Gayler implies that she and her husband made the change from the four-sided courtyard to the atrium without consulting Pries. It seems more likely that Pries prepared a schematic proposal with a courtyard that the Gaylers rejected, and that Pries then prepared drawings for the U-shaped house that was built. Pries's landscape plan for the site shows the U-shaped plan.

39. The new fireplace on one side, and two new exterior concrete buttresses on the other, compensated for the instability created by removal of the ceiling joists.

40. The Gaylers' willingness to rough it is reflected in the fact that once their house had been constructed, it was still several years before they had either electricity or phone service (Gayler, "One Hundred Years," 214–18, 240).

41. Anne Gayler credits her husband with the circular stairway to the garage, but the intense blue color of the stair's ceiling is clearly something only Pries would have proposed. Similarly, the inside corner window facing the courtyard is related to corner windows at Pries's Willcox residence and at his Gardner residence of a few years later. Thus the final design was likely resolved by the Gaylers working together with Pries.

42. Gayler, "One Hundred Years," 240. Pries's landscape drawing for the site survives in possession of one of the Gaylers' granddaughters.

43. This wing wall was not initially constructed. It is impossible to determine whether this wall was Pries's idea or the result of a decision made independently by the Gaylers, without Pries's involvement. As already noted, there was a Pries-designed "moon gate" at the Willcox residence, but whether this may have influenced the Gaylers is not known.

44. For Pries's appointment as director of the Art Institute of Seattle, see chap. 8, this volume.

45. Pries's drawings for the Hoggson residence have not been found. Duane Shipman recalled visiting Janet Hoggson with Pries, and talking about the design of the house (author's interview with Duane Shipman, 3 Aug. 1994). Keith Kolb also recalled that Pries had designed a French-influenced residence in The Highlands (author's interview with Keith Kolb, 11 Aug. 1995). The Hoggson drawing collection includes eleven sheets for the Hoggson residence, but almost all relate to Hoggson's landscape designs; see Hoggson collection (M148, folder 9), Special Collections Division, University of Washington Libraries.

46. Yesler Terrace was first mentioned on page 1 of *DJC* on 3 Oct. 1939. The client was the Seattle Housing Authority. The architects whose firms were involved in the design of the project were listed in this article: J. Lister Holmes, William J. Bain, William Aitken, George W. Stoddard, and John T. Jacobsen. Another article appeared on page 1 of *DJC* on 5 Dec. 1939. The project proceeded slowly: it was not until August 1940 that site clearing began; a construction contract was not signed until early 1941.

47. Jeffrey Karl Ochsner, ed., *Shaping Seattle Architecture: A Historical Guide to the Architects* (Seattle: University of Washington Press/AIA Seattle, 1994), 217, erroneously gives the date for the Pi Beta Phi Sorority House as 1932–35; that date was based on the assumption that the signed drawing by Pries had been prepared during the Bain and Pries partnership years, 1928–32. The project is mentioned in *DJC*, 10 Oct. 1940, 1; *DJC*, 4 Feb. 1941, 1; *DJC*, 12 Feb. 1941, 1; and *DJC*, 26 Mar. 1941, 1. The permit was issued on 10 Apr. 1941 (*DJC*, 11 Apr.

1941, 3). The construction drawings on microfiche in the archives of NBBJ (the former Naramore, Bain, Brady and Johanson) are dated 20 Jan. 1941. The original perspective drawing by Lionel Pries has been lost. The perspective is known from its publication in "Work of William J. Bain," *Architect and Engineer* 146 (Aug. 1941), 16–37. A color slide of the perspective is found in the Visual Resources Collection of the College of Architecture and Urban Planning, University of Washington.

48. A colored pencil perspective of the proposed Julius and Jean Weber residence, Seattle, labeled as the work of "William J. Bain and Lionel H. Pries," includes Pries's monogram, with the date January 1941 (Pries drawing collection, Special Collections Division, University of Washington Libraries).

49. The construction drawings produced by the 1941 Bain and Pries partnership are labeled "William J. Bain and Lionel H. Pries, Architects, Edwin T. Turner, Associate." The earliest drawing set with both names, dated 18 February 1941, is for the unbuilt Milton and Helen Joseph residence, Seattle. However, not all projects in late February and March 1941 include Pries's name; projects labeled only "William J. Bain" are likely those that were under way before the partnership was formed. Bain's simultaneous involvement in 1940–41 in the large joint venture that was responsible for the Yesler Terrace Housing Project, and his separate partnership with Pries that carried out smaller residential projects, established the pattern that Bain followed for the rest of his architectural career. After 1945, Bain was a partner in Naramore, Bain, Brady and Johanson (NBBJ), a firm that carried out large projects, and simultaneously he was a partner in Bain, Overturf and Turner (later Bain and Overturf), a firm that continued to do single-family residences and other small commissions.

50. The lowest project number on any Bain and Pries project in 1941 is 700 (the unbuilt Joseph residence, dated 18 Feb. 1941); the highest is 741 (the Harry and Lenore Gilbert residence project, Mercer Island, dated 22 Oct. 1941). (There is a drawing for a proposed scheme for the James Scripps residence project in project file 747, but that early scheme never went forward, and the Scripps family only built a guest house, which is the project to which the number 747 was actually assigned.) However, not all projects between number 700 and number 741 are labeled "William J. Bain and Lionel H. Pries"; a few are labeled only "William J. Bain." Thus it appears that approximately thirty-five projects can be credited to "Bain and Pries"; of these, about two dozen were constructed.

51. The issuing of permits was reported for the Stiffler residence (*DJC*, 25 Apr. 1941, 3), the Wasson residence (*DJC*, 25 July 1941, 3), and the Guffler residence (*DJC*, 23 Aug. 1941, 3). The architects are listed as "W. J. Bain and L. H. Pries" on the permits. Other Bain and Pries projects permitted in Seattle in 1941 had both partners' names on the working drawings but were listed in *DJC* with only Bain's name; why Pries's name was omitted is not known.

52. Some elements—for example, the bay windows of many of these designs—are identical to features of houses that Bain's office had designed before the new partnership with Pries; see, for example, the Albert Brygger residence, Port Madison (1937–38), pictured in "Work of William J. Bain."

53. Only two perspectives of projects from the 1941 partnership are known: the perspective of the proposed Julius and Jean Weber residence, Seattle, and the perspective of the proposed J. W. Gilbert residence, Mercer Island, illustrated in fig. 6.23. Both are found in the Pries drawing collection, Special Collections Division, University of Washington Libraries.

54. Kolb, who visited the house shortly after its completion, understood it to be Pries's project (author's conversation with Keith Kolb, 10 June 2004). Kolb added that he met Ray Gardner Jr., the son of Ray and Martha Gardner, in Europe in 1945, when both were serving in the military; one of the subjects of their conversation was Lionel Pries and the Gardners' house.

55. The windows at the Willcox and Gardner residences were fabricated by the Fentron Steel Works of Seattle. The Gardner windows have fewer and larger panes than the Willcox windows; but, with the exception of the outward slope of the windows on the second floor at the Willcox house, the detailing of the windows at both houses is similar.

56. A tall narrow window projecting from the stair through the front of the house anticipates a similar feature in Pries's unbuilt design for the Delta Sigma Phi Fraternity House (see chap. 9, this volume).

57. Some of the projects of the Bain office after September 1941 likely began as Bain and Pries projects. However, the dissolution of the partnership in mid-September apparently included an agreement that Bain would continue those projects under his own name. Thus there is no way to determine whether Pries made significant design contributions to any of the projects completed under Bain's name in late 1941.

58. Lionel H. Pries, undated résumé, Pries papers, Special Collections Division, University of Washington Libraries.

59. The Pries collection includes nine photos (measuring 3 by 5 7/8 inches) of a house under construction in a location that may be Phoenix, Arizona. The back of one photo is dated 3 December 1941; the eight others are dated 10 December 1941 (Pries photograph collection, folder 563/3/6, Special Collections Division, University of Washington Libraries).

60. For the teaching of camouflage at the University of Washington, see chap. 7, this volume. The camouflage at Boeing is routinely credited to William J. Bain, camouflage director for Washington State; see Duane A. Dietz, "William J. Bain, Sr.," in Ochsner, ed., *Shaping Seattle Architecture*, 219, 220. However, Keith Kolb recalled that Pries was involved in the Boeing camouflage project as a designer under Bain's direction (author's conversation with Keith Kolb, 15 April 2004). Pries also told Winskill about his involvement in the design of the

camouflage at Boeing (memo to the author from Robert Winskill, 20 Sept. 2004).

7. EDUCATOR OF ARCHITECTS

1. Surviving correspondence between Pries and the University of Washington dates from June 1928. William Bain may have recommended Pries for the position at the University of Washington. However, no correspondence between Bain and the university is known. Pries later told Keith Kolb that Mildred Bain had negotiated the teaching position without his knowledge, but this seems improbable; see William J. Bain and Mildred C. Bain, *Building Together: A Memoir of Our Lives in Seattle* (Seattle: Beckett Publishing Company, 1991), 95.

2. Letter to David Thomson from Harlan Thomas, 22 June 1928; letter to Lionel Pries from David Thomson, 24 June 1928 (University of Washington Office of the President records, acc. no. 71–34, box 113–13, Special Collections Division, University of Washington Libraries).

3. This episode is discussed in detail later in this chapter.

4. The best history of the conversion of Harvard to Modernism, one that also includes a brief mention of the situation at Columbia, is Anthony Alofsin, *The Struggle for Modernism: Architecture, Landscape Architecture, and City Planning at Harvard* (New York: Norton, 2002). See also Jill Pearlman, "Joseph Hudnut's Other Modernism at the 'Harvard Bauhaus,'" *Journal of the Society of Architectural Historians* 56 (Dec. 1997), 452–63. The changes at Harvard, and their influence on other American architecture schools, including the architecture school at the University of Washington, are discussed in detail in chap. 10, this volume.

5. For the revolt against the Beaux-Arts system at the University of California, see William Littmann, "Assault on the Ecole: Student Campaigns against the Beaux Arts, 1925–1950," *JAE: Journal of Architectural Education* 53 (Feb. 2000), 159–66. There were student revolts at other schools, such as the Architectural Association, London (1936) and the School of Architecture at McGill University, Montreal (1938); see Rhodri Windsor Liscombe, *The New Spirit: Modern Architecture in Vancouver, 1938–1963* (Montreal/Vancouver: Canadian Centre for Architecture/Douglas & McIntyre, 1997), 31.

6. Oien's statement appears in notes titled "From an Account of His Life by Anders Oien, 1907–2000," provided to the author by Jon Anders Oien, 24 June 2001.

7. For general background on Carl F. Gould, see T. William Booth and William H. Wilson, *Carl F. Gould: A Life in Architecture and the Arts* (Seattle: University of Washington Press, 1995). A short summary of Gould's career is T. William Booth and William H. Wilson, "Bebb & Gould," in Jeffrey Karl Ochsner, ed., *Shaping Seattle Architecture: A Historical Guide to the Architects* (Seattle: University of Washington Press/AIA Seattle, 1994), 174–79. For Gould's role in planning and design for the University of Washington campus, see Norman J.

Johnston, *The Fountain and the Mountain: 100 Years of Architecture at the University of Washington* (Woodinville, Wash.: Documentary Book Publishers), 1995. The latter book has also appeared in a second edition; see Norman J. Johnston, *The Fountain and the Mountain: The University of Washington Campus in Seattle* (Seattle: Documentary Media/University of Washington), 2003.

8. Norman J. Johnston, *The College of Architecture and Urban Planning: Seventy-Five Years at the University of Washington—A Personal View* (Seattle: College of Architecture and Urban Planning, University of Washington, 1991), esp. chap. 1, "The Gould Years: 1914–1926," 3–32, which presents a detailed summary of the early history of the department, and which revises and expands Norman J. Johnston, *Architectural Education at the University of Washington: The Gould Years* (Seattle: College of Architecture and Urban Planning, University of Washington, 1987). My discussion of the early history of the department derives largely from Johnston.

9. Gould's models were said to be Columbia and Harvard, and in the early years he corresponded with Warren Laird and Paul Cret at Penn, John Galen Howard at California, and Ellis Lawrence at Oregon, seeking advice and course materials. For correspondence with regard to the Department of Architecture at the University of Washington, see Gould Family papers, acc. no. 3516–5, box 19, Special Collections Division, University of Washington Libraries. Correspondence with John Galen Howard, Ellis Lawrence, and others is cited in Johnston, *The College of Architecture and Urban Planning*, 7–9.

10. Quoted in Keith R. Kolb, "1958 Celebration: College History Text," unpublished manuscript, 2. This nine-page chronology was prepared by Keith Kolb as part of the celebration in May 1958 of the creation of the College of Architecture and Urban Planning.

11. By 1915–16, the first full year of the program, Washington was affiliated with the Beaux-Arts Institute of Design, and students were receiving BAID problems in studio. In a February 1916 letter to the university president's office, Gould noted that students had already "received a fair number of mentions." The school assigned BAID programmes throughout Gould's tenure, but at times there was concern about the responses received from New York. In 1924, Gould wrote to BAID: "We use the programmes to the fullest extent, but the boys are a bit dissatisfied in not getting their drawings back more promptly and in not receiving by mail slips giving results. Fuller criticism would be appreciated if it were possible." Gould, like Howard at California, supplemented the BAID studio problems with projects that were locally or regionally based. In the 1916–17 academic year, one of the second-year projects was a summer resort along the Columbia River, and one of the third-year problems was a bridge over the Lake Washington canal; a two-week problem given the same year was the design of a decorative flagpole base on the university campus. See Johnston, *The College of Architecture and Urban Planning*, 15–16.

12. Early enrollment figures are difficult to ascertain exactly. The numbers cited here are based on the list in Johnston, *The College of Architecture and Urban Planning,* 29. In the first years, Gould often recommended that the better students complete their education in the East; he felt that the facilities and equipment at Washington were limited, and he believed that the students needed exposure to a wider array of architectural achievement than could be found in Seattle. Because students often finished elsewhere, the department produced few graduates—only twenty architecture degrees were awarded during Gould's tenure. (Johnston and Kolb differ slightly in reporting the number of graduates; the total of twenty is based on Kolb, "College History Text," 3–4.) One student who completed his degree in the East was Samuel Chamberlain, who had entered the University of Washington in 1914. Chamberlain graduated from MIT and became well known as an architectural illustrator. Many of his drawings appeared in *Pencil Points* in the 1920s. By the mid-1920s, the situation was improving: a description of the school, written for the tenth anniversary, listed a library with 650 volumes, 3,000 plates and photographs, 1,750 lantern slides, and 72 architectural casts as well as access to additional materials in other departments.

13. Up to the beginning of the 1940s, the spaces occupied by the Department of Architecture continued to be called "the Shack" even though the department moved three times. The name appears to have died out later in the 1940s, probably because of the discontinuity that resulted from World War II and the extraordinarily rapid growth of the department after 1946.

14. See Booth and Wilson, *Carl F. Gould,* 60–130.

15. Johnston, *The College of Architecture and Urban Planning,* 20–21.

16. Local professional architects who taught courses in the department in its early years include David J. Myers and Arrigo M. Young. A variety of faculty in other departments taught courses required for architecture students. Most important in this regard were faculty in art and faculty in engineering.

17. Letter to Lionel Pries from Carl Gould, 2 Aug. 1923, Gould Family papers, box 19 (Carl F. Gould, Washington University Architecture Department, General Correspondence), cited in Johnston, *The College of Architecture and Urban Planning,* 21, but incorrectly dated 12 Aug. 1923.

18. Johnston, *The College of Architecture and Urban Planning,* 22.

19. Arthur P. Herrman (3 Dec. 1898–17 Mar. 1993) was born and raised in Milwaukee. He received his B.A. in architecture from Carnegie Institute of Technology in 1921. He was apprenticed to Alden & Harlow, in Pittsburgh, from 1921 until 1923, when he was appointed to the faculty at the University of Washington as an instructor. He became an assistant professor in 1925, an associate professor in 1929, and a professor in 1937. He became executive officer of the School of Architecture about 1940, when Harlan Thomas became director emeritus. Herrman became dean of the newly formed College of Architecture and Urban Planning in 1958, where he served until 1962. He continued to teach until his retirement in 1968. After retiring, he moved to California. He died in La Verne, California, in 1993.

20. In April 1925, Gould wrote an assessment of Herrman's performance: "Mr. Arthur Herrman has shown marked ability in his instruction work in his different courses, particularly those pertaining to the technical side of Architecture and Architectural Design. He has commanded the attention of the students and has retained it throughout the year more successfully than we have been able to do heretofore. His courses are well laid out in advance and he understands the technique of instruction in the field of Architecture. His ability has improved much over last year, and he seems interested in his work. He has a certain diffidence and lack of initiative, but I find him, nevertheless, a very useful man"; see confidential report to University of Washington President Henry Suzzallo from Carl Gould, Gould Family papers, box 19 (Carl F. Gould, Washington University Architecture Department, General Correspondence), cited in Johnston, *The College of Architecture and Urban Planning,* 23.

21. Lancelot Gowen (16 Dec. 1894–10 Feb. 1958) was born and raised in Seattle. He received his B.A. in architecture from the University of California, Berkeley, in 1916 and then worked in Seattle for John Graham and for Augustus W. Gould and Edouard F. Champney. He served as an infantry officer in the United States army from 1917 to 1919. After a year in New York with Starrett and Van Vleck, he returned to the University of California, where he earned two more degrees—an M.A. in architecture (1921) and the degree of "graduate" in architecture (1922)—and where he worked for John Galen Howard. Appointed an American Field Service fellow, he studied at the Ecole des Beaux-Arts, in Paris, and traveled in Europe until arriving at the University of Washington, in the fall of 1924. He was appointed instructor in 1924, assistant professor in 1925, associate professor in 1929, and professor in 1937. During World War II, he served as a coast artillery officer. He died unexpectedly in Seattle in 1958 (see chap. 10, this volume).

22. Report to Carl Gould from John Galen Howard, 8 Apr. 1924, cited in Johnston, *The College of Architecture and Urban Planning,* 24.

23. Confidential report to President Henry Suzzallo from Carl Gould, Apr. 1925; see Gould Family papers, box 19 (Carl F. Gould, Washington University Architecture Department, General Correspondence), cited in Johnston, *The College of Architecture and Urban Planning,* 25.

24. As both head of the architecture school and campus architect, Gould was linked to President Suzzallo and thus became a target when Governor Hartley moved against Suzzallo. After Hartley had appointed a majority of the Board of Regents, they ruled that an architect should not receive both a state-supported salary and state-supported architectural fees, so Gould was forced to choose between designing projects for the

campus and heading the architecture school. For Gould's resignation, see Johnston, *The College of Architecture and Urban Planning*, 29–32.

25. For background on Harlan Thomas (1870–1953), see Norman J. Johnston, "Harlan Thomas," in Ochsner, ed., *Shaping Seattle Architecture*, 126–31.

26. Richard James Pearce (2 Oct. 1903–20 Feb. 1932) was born and raised in Denver. He graduated from the University of Washington in architecture in 1926 and subsequently studied at Harvard, receiving his M.Arch. in 1928.

27. For Pearce's death, see "Slide Buries U. Teacher on Rainier," *Seattle Times*, 21 Feb. 1932, 1; "Body of Teacher Killed in Slide brought to City," *Seattle Times*, 22 Feb. 1932, 4; "Snow Slide Kills Instructor on Moonlight Trip: Richard Pearce, Instructor of Architecture, Buried in Avalanche," *The Daily*, 23 Feb. 1932, 1. Pearce's death certificate indicates that the information about Pearce was provided by Pries. Pearce's replacement, Henry J. Olschewsky (17 Apr. 1907–16 Dec. 1945) was born and raised in Seattle. He won the 1930 University of Washington architecture traveling fellowship and graduated with "high scholarship" from the department in 1931.

28. Johnston, *The College of Architecture and Urban Planning*, 24.

29. The 1929–30 university catalogue made this clear: "A knowledge of design is the most essential subject in a course preparing students for the profession of architecture. The program of studies is so arranged, therefore, that most weight is given to these subjects. The student gives the greater part of his afternoons to work in the drafting room. This work consists largely of problems in architectural design presented as far as possible to develop technical skill without hindering individuality of expression. After the freshman year, problems will be judged by a committee of practicing architects and faculty appointed by the head of the Department"; see *Annual Catalogue of the University of Washington for 1929–1930* (Seattle: University of Washington Press, 1929), 171–72. The last year in which this statement appeared in the University of Washington catalogue was 1932–33. After that year, when the College of Fine Arts was dissolved because of the financial impact of the Depression, the catalogue text was shortened. Thereafter, the separately published *Bulletin of the Department of Architecture* repeated the same statement, at least until the early 1940s.

30. The University of Washington never appointed a "director of design" modeled after the *patron* of the Ecole ateliers. Because Harlan Thomas's appointment was only half-time, responsibility for establishing the spirit of the program fell primarily to the full-time faculty. Although Pries was junior to Herrman and Gowen, Herrman was regarded by the students as somewhat colorless and as a not particularly strong designer, and Gowen was diffident and notoriously absentminded. Herrman, Gowen, and Olschewsky were married, moreover, and had families; Pries was single, and by 1930 he

lived near campus, so he became a presence in the evenings and on weekends. Pries was involved in every aspect of the school, so his dominant personality meant that he influenced everything that went on in the school. Pries taught in Grade I and Grade III studios. Grade I was equivalent to the sophomore year, but after 1928, when the University of Washington, following the national trend, extended the Bachelor of Architecture program to five years, Grades II and III were not exactly equivalent to the junior and senior years. Most students continued to do Grade II problems in at least the first quarter of their fourth year (although superior students might accumulate enough points to enter Grade III sooner), and students in the fifth year, called "graduating seniors" or "fifth-year seniors," continued to do Grade III studio problems. After World War II, when the architecture program changed dramatically, the terms "Grade I," "Grade II" and "Grade III" took on new meanings; see chap. 10, this volume.

31. Although tuition was only $32.50 in the fall quarter and $27.50 in the winter and spring quarters, even this amount was difficult for many families. Taking time off from school to earn money was a common experience. For example, Bjarne Olsen, Seth Fulcher, Bill Svensson, and Alan Liddle were all known to have taken a year or more away from the program in the 1930s and early 1940s, to earn enough money to stay in school. Others, who have not been identified, likely did the same.

32. This summary is drawn from Seth M. Fulcher, "Jealous Mistress: The Profile of a Profession," unpublished manuscript, n.d., 8. In the late 1990s, Fulcher shared with the author this unpublished roman à clef about his years in the architecture program at the University of Washington. Fulcher changed names (for example, Henry Sirkorsky instead of Henry Olschewsky, and Leonidas Pope instead of Lionel Pries), but otherwise faithfully recorded his recollections of his time in the school of architecture.

33. The process of making a stretch is described in Johnston, *The College of Architecture and Urban Planning*, 36. Another description of the process is found in Joseph Esherick, "Architectural Education in the Thirties and the Seventies: A Personal View," in Spiro Kostof, ed., *The Architect: Chapters in the History of the Profession* (New York: Oxford University Press, 1977), 246.

34. The first year also included one quarter of modeling and sculpture and two quarters of freehand drawing, primarily in charcoal, all based on plaster casts of architectural ornament, and all taught by an art professor, Dudley Pratt. Students who had had some exposure to art or to mechanical drawing in high school found the courses challenging but manageable; those who had never taken these subjects were usually hard pressed to keep up.

35. Because this is a general description, it may not be completely accurate for every year during the 1930s. For example, some students from the early 1930s did not recall the process of the esquisse being introduced until the sophomore year (author's interview with John Rohrer,

9 Sept. 1999). Keith Kolb also recalled that the esquisse was not introduced in the 1940–41 freshman year (author's conversation with Keith Kolb, 18 Aug. 2005).

36. Graduates recall that Herrman had the "gift of gab"; many of them learned only later that Herrman had not actually visited many of the buildings and monuments he described so well. He made his first trip to Europe in the late 1940s (author's interview with William Svensson, 14 Sept. 1994). First-year architecture students also took "Elements of Building Construction," an introduction to basic principles of structures, taught most years by Sergius Sergev, professor of engineering.

37. From the 1900s to the 1940s, the term in common use in American schools of architecture to describe lower-level students working on the presentation drawings of upper-level students was, unfortunately, "niggering." The term is used in the definitive text on the Beaux-Arts method in American schools of architecture; see John F. Harbeson, *The Study of Architectural Design with Special Reference to the Program of the Beaux-Arts Institute of Design* (New York: Pencil Points Press, 1926), 3. Because the book collects Harbeson's articles on the Beaux-Arts method that were published in *Pencil Points* from 1921 on, the term was already in wide use by the time the book was published. Use of the term at the University of Pennsylvania is cited by Esherick, "Architectural Education in the Thirties and the Seventies," in Kostof, ed., *The Architect*, 243, and at the University of Washington by Johnston, *The College of Architecture and Urban Planning*, 37. Given the extreme negative connotations of this term, I have eschewed its use in this book.

38. The ceremonies surrounding induction into Atelier were sometimes reported in the student newspaper. See *The Daily*, 27 Jan. 1931, 1; *The Daily*, 18 Jan. 1932, 2; *The Daily*, 15 Jan. 1935, 1; *The Daily*, 10 Jan. 1936, 1; and *The Daily*, 25 Jan. 1938, 1.

39. In 1932, architecture projects were included with painting and sculpture projects in *PSD*, the annual publication by Lambda Rho (the art student organization) and Atelier. Beginning in 1933, Atelier began publishing the *Department of Architecture Annual* (often abbreviated as the *Annual*), which showed work produced by students in the department. The *Annual*, published yearly through 1942, was suspended during World War II, started again in 1946, and then published through 1961. This publication provides one of the best overviews of the kinds of work produced by students during that period and of the changes in design influences on their work.

40. On the importance of pageantry in Beaux-Arts education, see the 1924 essay by Warren P. Laird, "Pageantry as a Factor in Education," in Ann L. Strong and George E. Thomas, eds., *The Book of the School: 100 Years, the Graduate School of Fine Arts at the University of Pennsylvania* (Philadelphia: GSFA, 1990), 40–41. The University of Washington Beaux-Arts Balls were frequently reported in the campus newspaper. See *The Daily*, 15 Feb. 1935, 3; *The Daily*, 24 Apr. 1936, 2; *The Daily*, 14 May 1937, 1, 4; and *The Daily*, 8 Apr. 1938, 1, 2. For a discussion of the controversy surrounding risqué

advertising for the 1938 ball, see Johnston, *The College of Architecture and Urban Planning*, 41–43.

41. The murals were retained in the school archives until sometime in the 1960s, when they were apparently destroyed. Johnston indicates that at least one mural survived until the 1980s, but none of the murals are known to remain today. Photographs of a few of the murals may exist in private collections. See Johnston, *The College of Architecture and Urban Planning*, 41.

42. Author's interviews with William Svensson, 14 Sept. 1994; Alan Liddle, 22 July 1999; and Roland Terry, 16 Aug. 1999.

43. The only other required architecture course in the sophomore year was a three-quarter sequence in history, taught for many years by Harlan Thomas. Nonarchitecture classes taken in the second year usually included mathematics and a foreign language, typically French. In addition, freshmen and sophomores were required to take physical education or to enroll in the Reserve Officer Training Corps (ROTC).

44. This list of problems is based on those represented by student projects included in the *Annual* in the 1930s.

45. Author's interview with Keith Kolb, 11 Aug. 1995.

46. Ibid.

47. Memo to Victor Steinbrueck from Robert H. Dietz, 13 Nov. 1977.

48. Memo to Victor Steinbrueck from Roland Terry, 17 Feb. 1978.

49. Memo to Victor Steinbrueck from Fred Bassetti, 23 Jan. 1978.

50. Author's interview with Keith Kolb, 11 Aug. 1995.

51. Memo to Victor Steinbrueck from Minoru Yamasaki, 3 Feb. 1978.

52. Esherick, "Architectural Education in the Thirties and the Seventies," in Kostof, ed., *The Architect*, 255.

53. Memo to Victor Steinbrueck from Flora Allen Casey, 18 Jan. 1978.

54. Letter to Bjarne Dahl from Julia Morgan, 29 May 1931, quoted in Sara Holmes Boutelle, *Julia Morgan, Architect* (New York: Abbeville Publishers, 1988), 245–46.

55. Memo to Victor Steinbrueck from Roland Terry, 17 Feb. 1978.

56. Memo to Victor Steinbrueck from Robert Hugh Ross, ca. 1978.

57. Memo to Victor Steinbrueck from Robert H. Dietz, 13 Nov. 1977.

58. Author's interview with William Svensson, 14 Sept. 1994. However, Alan Liddle recalls that Pries once did knock over a bottle of India ink on a student's drawing (memo to the author from Alan Liddle, 19 March 2003).

59. Memo to Victor Steinbrueck from Wendell Lovett, ca. 1978.

60. Author's interview with John Rohrer, 9 Sept. 1999.

61. The literal meaning of the French word *charrette* is "cart," and the term initially described the cart that

was wheeled through the ateliers at the Ecole to collect student projects for judgment. Sometimes students would put their boards on the cart but ride along, putting on finishing touches. Over time, the term came to mean the final rush to complete the drawings, and it is still used this way in architecture schools today.

62. Harbeson, *The Study of Architectural Design*, 280.

63. After war was declared, in December 1941, this became more difficult—blackout shades were required, and campus buildings were officially closed at night. Still, architecture students found a way to get into the studios via a fire escape and a roof access hatch—a practice officially frowned upon, unofficially condoned.

64. The Department of Architecture Archives includes an extraordinary collection of work representing the years from the 1910s to the 1970s. Over the years, unfortunately, some projects were removed and not returned, so the collection does not now include all "retained" work. In the 1980s, students won a legal case that determined that they owned their own work, and those years are much less well represented.

Prior to the 2006–7 remodeling of Architecture Hall, the Architecture Archives were divided. Drawings on watercolor paper, including all drawings from the 1910s to 1946 and a small number of drawings from 1946 to 1960, were transferred in early 2006 to the Special Collections Division, University of Washington Libraries. Drawings on illustration board (the bulk of the collection after 1946) were retained by the Department of Architecture and continue to be stored in Architecture Hall. These drawings may be transferred to the Special Collections Division, University of Washington Libraries, at a future date.

65. Author's interview with John Rohrer, 9 Sept. 1999.

66. Esherick, "Architectural Education in the Thirties and the Seventies," in Kostof, ed., *The Architect*, 256. Esherick has also pointed out the complexity of the analytique as well as the multiple lessons it embodied: "The analytique as a teaching device was, at its best, rich, complex, and composed of a wide range of interlocking objectives. Emphasis could be placed in a variety of ways, but generally the problem was one of the assembly of elements . . . in some orderly and pleasing fashion— in short a study in composition. Proportion was important, as was scale. Good proportions were generally those similar to the accepted great monuments; scale was always more vaguely defined and was generally taken to be something beyond mere technical feasibility or reasonableness."

67. Author's interview with Keith Kolb, 11 Aug. 1995. In the 1990s, several of the graduates of that period, interviewed as part of the research for this book, pointed to analytiques that they had done while in school; these had been framed and were still on display in their homes. About 1980, when Professor Astra Zarina was seeking student work to display in the new University of Washington Rome Center, she selected several analytiques from the Department of Architecture archives. (Most

of these are smaller analytiques—measuring about 16 by 24 inches or 20 by 30 inches—of classical character that students completed toward the end of the freshman year.) Those whose work is on display in the Rome Center include Elizabeth Ayer, Erling H. Bugge, Robert Durham, Perry Johanson, Paul Kirk, Wendell Lovett, Jerry Nevius, John Rohrer, and Roland Terry. (Thanks to Trina Deines, director of the Rome Center, for this list.)

68. This list of Grade I sketch problems for 1938–39 is based on the set of handouts retained by George Graham, which he allowed the author to copy.

69. Author's interview with John Rohrer, 9 Sept. 1999.

70. Ibid.

71. This list of problems is based on those represented by student projects included in the *Annual* in the 1930s.

72. Memo to Victor Steinbrueck from Fred Bassetti, 23 Jan. 1978.

73. Memo to Victor Steinbrueck from Robert H. Ross, ca. 1978.

74. Author's interview with Alan Liddle, 22 July 1999. Alexander Archipenko (1887–1964) was active in Paris at the beginning of the twentieth century. He exhibited with the Cubists in 1910 and at the Salon d'Automne in 1911–13.

75. Author's interview with Daniel Streissguth, 10 Sept. 1999. David Roberts (1796–1864) was a painter and engraver known for his picturesque paintings of topography and architecture, especially in Spain and in Palestine; these were published as lithographs in the 1830s and 1840s.

76. For example, in the spring of 1939, Guy Ardilouze, a visiting instructor from France, taught with Herrman in Grade II, but his appointment lasted only one quarter.

77. This list of problems is based on those represented by student projects included in the *Annual* in the 1930s.

78. For information on Raymond Hill, see chap. 8, this volume. Topics of other third-year classes included working drawings (Olschewsky), Renaissance and Baroque architectural history (Herrman), structures and construction (Sergev), and mechanical systems (heating, plumbing, and electrical, taught by Professor Merlin Hahn of the Department of Engineering). The list of required junior-year courses derives from the lists in the University of Washington catalogues of the period; see, for example, *University of Washington Bulletin: Catalogue Number for the 1936–1937 Session* (Seattle: University of Washington Press, 1936), 159–60.

79. Some students who had completed other requirements, or who juggled their schedules, took this class as juniors, but most waited until the senior year. Lance Gowen had created a one-quarter course in the history of architectural ornament in the mid-1920s; when Pries took it over, about 1929, he extended it to three full quarters.

80. Harbeson, *The Study of Architectural Design*, 225.

81. Memo to Victor Steinbrueck from Robert H. Dietz, 13 Nov. 1977.

82. Fulcher, "Jealous Mistress," 29–30.

83. Author's interview with John Rohrer, 9 Sept. 1999.

84. The course load in addition to studio was somewhat lighter—one quarter of architectural theory (Gowen), one quarter of specifications and office practice (Charles Alden), one quarter of advanced structures (Sergev), two quarters of life drawing (Professor Walter Isaacs or Professor Ambrose Patterson of the Department of Art), and some electives—so the students' primary focus could be on studio. See, for example, *University of Washington Bulletin: Catalogue Number for the 1936–1937 Session* (Seattle: University of Washington Press, 1936), 159–60. For information on Walter Isaacs and Ambrose Patterson, see chap. 8, this volume.

85. Project titles and descriptions from the *Annual*, 1933.

86. Project titles and descriptions from the *Annual*, 1936.

87. Project titles and descriptions from the *Annual*, 1940.

88. This list of Grade III design problems for 1941–42 is based on the set of handouts retained by George Graham, which he allowed the author to copy.

89. Ibid.

90. Memo to Victor Steinbrueck from Robert H. Ross, ca. 1978.

91. Ibid.

92. Ibid.

93. For background on Art Deco, see chap. 6, n. 5; for the Century of Progress Exposition, see chap. 6, n. 4.

94. *DJC*, 24 May 1934, 1–2.

95. *The Daily*, 12 Dec. 1933, 1. In the *DJC* article on the exhibit of student work, architecture students referred to some of the architecture at the Chicago exposition as "bizarre."

96. Author's interview with George Hazen, 21 July 1999. On Wright's visit to Seattle in 1931, see Donald Leslie Johnson, "Frank Lloyd Wright in the Northwest: The Show, 1931," *Pacific Northwest Quarterly* 78 (July 1987), 104.

97. Students' awareness of Neutra was mentioned by John Rohrer, Seth Fulcher, and Roland Terry; students' awareness of Aalto was mentioned by George Hazen and Seth Fulcher (author's interviews with George Hazen, 21 July 1999; Seth Fulcher, 28 July 1999; Roland Terry, 16 Aug. 1999; and John Rohrer, 9 Sept. 1999).

98. The LeCorbusier exhibit at the Henry Gallery (30 March–14 Apr. 1936) was mentioned in *The Daily*, 30 Mar. 1936, 1. The Aalto exhibit at the Henry Gallery (1–15 May 1940) was briefly described in *DJC*, 6 May 1940, 1, 5. Both were traveling exhibits from the Museum of Modern Art, in New York.

99. However, some students remembered that he left school early on Friday afternoons while the Willcox residence was under construction (author's interview with William Svensson, 14 Sept. 1994).

100. Pietro Belluschi's H. M. Myers residence, 1670 Magnolia Boulevard (Seattle permit no. 340086) was mentioned in *DJC*, 11 Sept. 1940, 4. A photograph of the house as it was before alteration is included in Victor Steinbrueck, *A Guide to Seattle Architecture, 1850–1953* (New York: Reinhold, 1953), 34.

101. Marco Frascari, "The Tell-the-tale Detail," *Via* 7 (1984), 24.

102. Author's interview with William Svensson, 14 Sept. 1994. Other students of the period have similar recollections.

103. Author's interview with Daniel Streissguth, 10 Sept. 1999.

104. *Annual*, 1937.

105. Memo to Victor Steinbrueck from Fred Bassetti, 23 Jan. 1978.

106. Those who worked with Pries at Bain and Pries also recalled Pries's skepticism and his belief that the solution should be responsive to the problem, not preconceived according to a singular design ideology (memo to Victor Steinbrueck from Ivan W. Meyer, 10 Jan. 1978).

107. The closest thing to a student revolt occurred in 1932, and it was not related to changing architectural vocabularies. Perry Johanson recalled (memo to Victor Steinbrueck, 23 Jan. 1978), "During my senior year an event occurred which saddened me. We were doing an esquisse for a project, the program seemed ambiguous and late in the evening the entire class boiled over in frustration. In rebellion most of us decided not to turn in the esquisse." This kind of overt refusal to do the assignment seems never to have occurred again.

The decision of the Architecture Department in 1931–32 to discontinue its affiliation with the BAID may also have allowed the Department to accommodate changing architectural vocabularies more easily thereafter.

108. City directories listed Pries's addresses as follows: 1743 Boylston Avenue (1928); 720 Seneca (1929); 4002 Brooklyn, Apt. B (1930–31); 4546 Fifteenth Avenue N.E. (1932–48).

109. Memo to Victor Steinbrueck from Flora Allen Casey, 18 Jan. 1978.

110. Memo to Victor Steinbrueck from Minoru Yamasaki, 3 Feb. 1978.

111. Memo to Victor Steinbrueck from Perry Johanson, 23 Jan. 1978.

112. Memo to Victor Steinbrueck from Robert H. Ross, ca. 1978. This incident is also described in Johnston, *The College of Architecture and Urban Planning*, 39. This copy of Burckhardt's *Civilization of the Renaissance in Italy* was later donated by Ross to the Architecture and Urban Planning Library at the University of Washington. It is now part of the Pries book collection, Special Collections Division, University of Washington Libraries.

113. This quotation is from the author's interview with Keith Kolb, 11 Aug. 1995; a radio incident was also recounted in the author's interview with John Rohrer, 9 Sept. 1999, and in the memo to Victor Steinbrueck from

Robert H. Ross, ca. 1978. Since these students were in school in different years, Pries may have thrown students' radios out the window more than once.

114. Memo to the author from Alan Liddle, 19 March 2003.

115. For the quotation ("He told my parents . . ."), see the memo to Victor Steinbrueck from Robert H. Ross, ca. 1978; the recollection is from the author's conversation with Robert H. Ross, 18 July 2005.

116. Memo to Victor Steinbrueck from Perry Johanson, 23 Jan. 1978.

117. Memo to Victor Steinbrueck from Charles H. Schiff, 13 Feb. 1978.

118. Fulcher, "Jealous Mistress," 93–100; author's interview with Seth Fulcher, 28 July 1999.

119. Author's interview with William Svensson, 14 Sept. 1994.

120. Fulcher, "Jealous Mistress," 57–58.

121. Author's interview with Keith Kolb, 11 Aug. 1995.

122. Fulcher, "Jealous Mistress," 58–59.

123. Esherick, "Architectural Education in the Thirties and the Seventies," in Kostof, ed., *The Architect*, 248.

124. Memo to Victor Steinbrueck from Perry Johanson, 23 Jan. 1978.

125. Memo to Victor Steinbrueck from Lloyd Lovegren, 13 Jan. 1978.

126. Memo to Victor Steinbrueck from Roland Terry, 17 Feb. 1978. In the late 1930s, some students misunderstood and thought they needed an invitation to attend. Seth Fulcher characterized those students who were invited as a "preferred list" (Fulcher, "Jealous Mistress," 57). Keith Kolb and Robert H. Ross both recall that all students were welcome. In fact, Pries sometimes wondered why more students did not come; perhaps he did not realize that students thought they needed an invitation (author's discussion with Keith Kolb, 8 Sept. 2004; memo to the author from Robert H. Ross, 18 July 2005).

127. Memo to the author from Robert H. Ross, 18 July 2005.

128. Memo to Victor Steinbrueck from Perry Johanson, 23 Jan. 1978.

129. Memo to Victor Steinbrueck from Flora Allen Casey, 18 Jan. 1978.

130. Memo to Victor Steinbrueck from Robert H. Ross, ca. 1978.

131. Palmer D. Koon was one of the very first students to board with Pries (author's interview with Palmer D. Koon, 7 Oct. 2003).

132. Author's interview with Kelly Foss, 15 July 2005; unpublished manuscript by George ("Pete") Wimberly, ca. 1990. According to Foss, Mrs. Nelson was a widow who arrived in midafternoon six days a week, prepared dinner, and kept house. Wimberly wrote that in his years, students helped clean the house.

133. Author's interview with Keith Kolb, 11 Aug. 1995.

134. Author's interviews with Keith Kolb, 11 Aug. 1995; Roland Terry 16 Aug. 1999; and James Klontz, 18 Aug. 1999.

135. Unpublished manuscript by George ("Pete") Wimberly, ca. 1990.

136. Author's interview with Keith Kolb, 11 Aug. 1995.

137. List provided by Keith Kolb, supplemented by information from Palmer D. Koon, Kelly Foss, Roland Terry, and James Klontz. Harold Foss was one of the first students to board at Pries's house on Fifteenth Avenue. From 1932 to 1934, his younger brother Kelly also boarded at the house. Roland Terry was there only one year. Lew Crutcher and James Cameron may have lived at Pries's house for only one or two terms. Others who may have lived at Pries's house include Burr Richards and Herbert Gallagher.

138. Author's interview with Seth Fulcher, 28 July 1999.

139. Memo to the author from Robert H. Ross, 18 July 2005.

140. Anderson gave Pries several cels from Disney animated features, which Pries retained for the rest of his life. These are now held by his heir, Robert Winskill.

141. Memo to Victor Steinbrueck from Roland Terry, 23 Jan. 1978.

142. Author's discussion with Keith Kolb, 12 Sept. 2003.

143. Letter to Robert G. Sproul from Lionel Pries, 26 Feb. 1934; letter to Robert G. Sproul from Lionel Pries, n.d. (ca. early March 1934). See University of California Office of the President records (CU-5 ser.2, 1934, 25), University Archives, Bancroft Library, University of California, Berkeley. These letters are discussed in detail later in this chapter.

144. Unpublished manuscript by George ("Pete") Wimberly, ca. 1990; author's interview with Roland Terry, 16 Aug. 1999.

145. Memo to Victor Steinbrueck from George ("Pete") Wimberley, 15 Feb. 1978; author's interview with Keith Kolb, 11 Aug. 1995; letters to Janice Brebner from Pete Wimberley, n.d. (summer 1938), courtesy of Janice B. Wimberly. Pries wrote letters of introduction to William Spratling, Fred Davis, Diego Rivera, and others for his students Robert Shields, Roland Terry, and Robert Massar when they traveled to Mexico about 1940 (author's conversation with Robert Shields, 10 Feb. 2004). Pries took Ted Warnecke to Mexico in 1932, but this trip had been arranged by Warnecke's father (author's interview with Kelly Foss, 15 July 2005).

146. Author's interview with William Svensson, 14 Sept. 1994.

147. Memo to Victor Steinbrueck from Perry Johanson, 23 Jan. 1978.

148. Author's interview with Robert Winskill, 26 July 1994.

149. Author's interview with Keith Kolb, 11 Aug. 1995.

150. Letter from Lionel Pries to Robert G. Sproul, 26 Feb. 1934. See University of California Office of the President records (CU-5 ser.2, 1934, 25), University Archives, Bancroft Library, University of California, Berkeley.

151. In July 1932, Harlan Thomas wrote to the university president that architecture should be considered a fine art, not a technology program, and that it should therefore be grouped with the other fine arts and not with engineering. A year later, Thomas submitted a lengthy report arguing that the Department of Architecture should be an autonomous unit. See letters to M. Lyle Spencer from Harlan Thomas, 27 July 1932 and 2 Aug. 1933 (University of Washington Office of the President records, acc. no. 71–34, box 113, folder 13, Special Collections Division, University of Washington Libraries).

152. To judge from the information in Pries's subsequent letter, the issue may have had to do with the need to teach weaker students as well as strong ones. The incident in which a senior class refused to do an esquisse (see n. 107, above) took place in 1932, and the students involved had graduated by 1934, so that incident was not the immediate cause of Pries's decision to seek a way of leaving Washington.

153. Letter to Robert G. Sproul from Lionel Pries, n.d. (ca. early March 1934). See University of California Office of the President records (CU-5 ser.2, 1934, 25), University Archives, Bancroft Library, University of California, Berkeley.

154. Letter to Lionel Pries from Robert G. Sproul, 12 March 1934. See University of California Office of the President records (CU-5 ser.2, 1934, 25), University Archives, Bancroft Library, University of California, Berkeley.

155. Letter to Lionel Pries from Robert G. Sproul, 20 Aug. 1934. See University of California Office of the President records (CU-5 ser.2, 1934, 25), University Archives, Bancroft Library, University of California, Berkeley.

156. Author's interview with Robert Winskill, 26 July 1994.

157. Monday Club materials, acc. no. 1641, 1497, Special Collections Division, University of Washington Libraries. An incomplete list of the papers Pries presented to the club includes "Art of Pre-conquest Mexico" (26 Oct. 1942), "A Nation Turns to Greece" (27 Nov. 1950), "Gothic Cathedrals of Europe" (28 Apr. 1952), "Baron Haussman/Paris" (26 Apr. 1954), and "St. Peter's in Rome" (Nov. 1956). Pries's texts for his addresses on Gothic cathedrals, Baron Haussman, and St. Peter's are included in the Pries papers, Special Collections Division, University of Washington Libraries. The text for a critical analysis of Modern architecture also survives, but the date on which that paper was presented is not known.

158. "Bagley Hall Odor Vanishes: Restless Architects Move In," *The Daily*, 13 Oct. 1937, 4. For articles discussing the problems with mice in the previous location of the Department of Architecture, see *The Daily*, 11 Dec. 1936, 1, and *The Daily*, 8 June 1937, 1. The new quarters were a physical improvement over the wood-frame "Shack," but architecture students were now occasionally assailed by the odor of the formaldehyde used to preserve carcasses for dissection in the basement of Physiology Hall.

159. Harlan Thomas, "Biennial Report for the Period 1939–41," manuscript, 29 May 1940 (Department of Architecture records, acc. no. 70–37, Special Collections Division, University of Washington Libraries).

160. *Bulletin: University of Washington Catalogue, 1940–1941* (Seattle: University of Washington, 1940), 82–83; the new course requirements in city planning are titled "Curriculum in City Planning Leading to the Degree of Bachelor of Architecture in City Planning." The catalogue for 1941–1942 presents the same information.

161. The 1940–41 university catalogue lists Harlan Thomas as director emeritus and Arthur Herrman as executive officer. Although Herrman was responsible for day-to-day administration after 1940, Thomas remained involved in the school at least through 1943. In the fall of 1942, it was Herrman who announced the new four-year architecture curriculum, but a camouflage class report produced in 1943 was credited to Harlan Thomas as director of the department. By the end of the war, Herrman was fully in charge of the program. In 1946–47 and 1947–48, he authored various reports to the university president's office. Thomas was still listed as director emeritus in the 1946–47 university catalogue but was no longer included in the 1947–48 catalogue.

162. Letter to the author from Alan Liddle, 27 July 1999. Mary Lund (later Mary Davis) graduated in 1945.

163. Olschewsky's leave to undertake production illustration was reported in *The Daily*, 7 Jan. 1943, 1.

164. For the camouflage class, see *The Daily*, 6 Oct. 1942, 1.

165. Harlan Thomas, "Report to the Camouflage Division, Office of Civilian Defense, Ninth Civilian Defense Region, San Francisco, California," in Washington State Defense Council, *Camouflage Report* ([Seattle]: Washington State Defense Council, [1943?]), 1–2 (copy in Architecture and Urban Planning Library, University of Washington). This document consists of several brief reports in addition to the one by Thomas. Each is individually paginated, and the reports are followed by a summary of the complete lecture program of the fifteen-week camouflage school. Thomas's report constitutes the second section of this document; the first is William J. Bain, "Fifteen Week School" (including a mention of Pries), and the third is Lionel H. Pries, "Summary of Procedure, O.C.D. Camouflage School, University of Washington" (dealing primarily with students' work on building a model of a camouflage installation). For an article summarizing contemporary thinking on camouflage design, see "Industrial Plan Protection," *Architectural Forum* 77 (Aug. 1942), 49–59.

166. Those who successfully completed their college courses qualified for naval midshipman school or Marine Corps Officer Candidate School, which led to commissions as navy ensigns or Marine Corps second lieutenants. Those selected for the program attended regular college classes on the campuses of 131 colleges

and universities. About sixty thousand participants completed the curriculum and went on to receive commissions; see the Web site of the U.S. Navy Memorial Foundation, http://www.lonesailor.org/v12history.php.

167. Letter to Keith Kolb from Lionel Pries, undated (but Kolb, on receiving the letter, added the date "Sept. '43"). Pries noted that the program had ended faculty vacations and travel, since the university had converted to a year-round schedule.

8. Master of the Arts

1. Pries's entry in the 1941 *Who's Who in Northwest Art* reads as follows: "PRIES, Lionel H., 4546 15th Ave. N.E., Seattle, Wash. Architect; Painter (watercolor, oil); Printmaker (drypoint); Teacher—Born San Francisco, Calif., June 2, 1897. Pupil of Univ. of Calif., Berkeley; Univ. of Pennsylvania; Lick and Wilmerding Schools, San Francisco. Exhibitor at Bohemian Club, San Francisco, 1922; Architectural League, New York, 1923; Seattle Art Mus. Associate professor of architecture, Univ. of Wash., Seattle"; see Marion Brymer Appleton, ed., *Who's Who in Northwest Art: A Biographical Directory of Persons in the Pacific Northwest Working in the Media of Painting, Sculpture, Graphic Arts, Illustration, Design, and the Handicrafts* (Seattle: Frank McCaffrey, 1941), 57.

2. See Keith Morgan, *Charles A. Platt: The Artist as Architect* (New York/Cambridge, Mass.: Architectural History Foundation/MIT Press, 1985); Lauren Weiss Bricker, "The Writings of Fiske Kimball: A Synthesis of Architectural History and Practice," in Elisabeth Blair MacDougall, ed., *The Architectural Historian in America: A Symposium in Celebration of the Fiftieth Anniversary of the Founding of the Society of Architectural Historians* (Washington, D.C./Hanover, N.H.: National Gallery of Art/University Press of New England, 1990), 215–35. The Pennsylvania Museum of Art was later renamed the Philadelphia Museum of Art.

3. California Arts and Crafts architects such as Greene and Greene have become widely known for their commissions in the first decade of the twentieth century that incorporated furniture, stained glass, fixtures, and rugs of their own design. In northern California, Julia Morgan was directly involved in the design of many elements of her commissions for the Hearst family, and other architects sometimes designed selected interior elements or were involved in the selection of furnishings for their clients.

4. Multiple dimensions of the Arts and Crafts movement were represented in *The Craftsman*. Articles on selected topics appeared as follows: bookplates (May 1903, March 1904, April 1904); etchings (Oct. 1906, Oct. 1907, Feb. 1909, Jan. 1913, Oct. 1916); Japanese prints (Oct. 1903, May 1916); and Japanese screens (Oct. 1911). As this chapter shows, Pries designed multiple bookplates, and he collected Japanese objects. Pries also made intaglio prints, although he did drypoints, not etchings. Over its history, *The Craftsman* carried more than twenty articles on Native American design and

more than forty articles on Japanese design and its influence. Pries may not have read these articles, but the breadth of the Arts and Crafts movement clearly shaped his architectural and artistic pursuits.

5. Quoted in T. William Booth and William H. Wilson, *Carl F. Gould: A Life in Architecture and the Arts* (Seattle: University of Washington Press, 1995), 55.

6. Seattle Art Museum papers, box 31, folder 1 ("History"), acc. no. 2636, Special Collections Division, University of Washington Libraries; *Town Crier*, 22 Dec. 1928, 7.

7. In the early 1980s, Hatch prepared a summary of recollections of his time at the Art Institute. Hatch had been trained as a landscape architect. He was initially asked to serve a three-month term as executive secretary of the Fine Arts Society; after three months, the position was extended, and Hatch was given funds to travel to various institutions in the East to learn more about running an art museum. See John Davis Hatch Jr., "The Transition Years 1928 to 1932: The Fine Arts Society—to the Seattle Art Institute—to the Seattle Art Museum," unpublished manuscript, July 1984. Hatch gave copies of the manuscript to several friends, including Alan Liddle, from whom the author received his copy.

8. Seattle Art Museum papers, box 31, folder 1 ("History"), acc. no. 2636, Special Collections Division, University of Washington Libraries.

9. T. William Booth, "The Man, the Moment and the Museum," *Seattle Weekly*, 20–26 Nov. 1985, 31. See also Seattle Art Museum papers, box 31, folder 1 ("History"), acc. no. 2636, Special Collections Division, University of Washington Libraries. John Davis Hatch had apparently been a member of Abracadabra when he was a student at Berkeley. He refers to Pries as "a California fraternity brother I had early met when first in Seattle"; see Hatch, "Transition Years," 2.

10. Hatch recounts a meeting with "the China Club, the Far East Society, the Japanese Society and the Oriental Department of the University of Washington" that was attended by Richard Fuller, Pries, and himself; see Hatch, "Transition Years," 7.

11. It was reported in the spring of 1930 that Pries and Pearce planned to travel together in Mexico; see *The Daily*, 4 June 1930, 3. A report that Pries and Pearce would exhibit Mexican novelties, tapestries, and wood carvings at the Art Institute appeared in *The Daily*, 26 Nov. 1930, 1.

12. Booth and Wilson, *Carl F. Gould*, 142. See also Seattle Art Museum papers, box 31, folder 1 ("History"), acc. no. 2636, Special Collections Division, University of Washington Libraries.

13. Although the Fullers began planning in 1930 to give funds for a new building, the Depression delayed the gift. In October 1930, Richard Fuller wrote to Gould of the shrinkage of his father's estate and the need to delay announcing the gift of funds to build the art museum (letter to Carl F. Gould from Richard Fuller, 18 Oct. 1930, Gould Family papers, box 14, acc. no. 3516–5, Special Collections Division, University of

Washington Libraries). The gift was finally announced in October 1931.

14. Board meeting minutes, Art Institute of Seattle, Seattle Art Museum papers, box 31, folder 28, Special Collections Division, University of Washington Libraries. Hatch later wrote that he had resigned because his advice regarding the design of the new art museum was being ignored by Carl Gould. He did not believe that he could, at the age of twenty-four, be effective in shaping the project; see Hatch, "Transition Years," 9.

15. For the announcement of Pries's appointment, see "Pries to Fill Institute Post," *The Daily*, 28 Oct. 1931, 1.

16. Letter to Frederick A. Whiting, President, American Federation of the Arts, from Richard Fuller, 23 Nov. 1931, Seattle Art Museum papers, box 31, folder 30, Special Collections Division, University of Washington Libraries.

17. The Art Institute of Seattle received numerous letters of resignation from members who were unable to pay their dues (Seattle Art Museum papers, box 31, folder 52, Special Collections Division, University of Washington Libraries).

18. See Seattle Art Museum papers, box 31, folder 58, Special Collections Division, University of Washington Libraries.

19. On the development of the art museum design by Bebb and Gould, see Booth, "The Man, the Moment and the Museum," 30–35, 38–41; Booth and Wilson, *Carl F. Gould*, 153–161.

20. Callahan wrote, "Everything about the museum— its architecture, those conducting the organization— everything should embody the spirit of the modern day and modern life. Art and architecture have depended too much upon the past"; see Kenneth Callahan, "Future Museum," *Town Crier*, 5 Dec. 1931, 34–35.

21. Laurence Coleman visited Seattle between 30 September and 1 October 1931; his report took the form of a twenty-four-page letter sent in late October (letter to Richard Fuller from Laurence Coleman, 29 Oct. 1931, Seattle Art Museum papers, box 31, folder 29, Special Collections Division, University of Washington Libraries).

22. Letter to Dorothy Gould from Carl F. Gould, 16 Dec. 1931, Gould Family papers, box 22 ("Gould, Dorothy Fay, Incoming Letters"), Special Collections Division, University of Washington Libraries. Kenneth Callahan was simultaneously advocating a modern approach; see Callahan, "Future Museum," 54–55.

23. Pries's two pencilled floor plans, one for the basement and the other for the first floor, show his proposed layout of the art museum (Bebb and Gould drawings for the museum, Seattle Art Museum papers, Special Collections Division, University of Washington Libraries).

24. Letter to Louis Horch, Roerich Museum, New York, from Lionel H. Pries, 10 March 1932, Seattle Art Museum papers, box 33, folder 12, Special Collections Division, University of Washington Libraries.

25. Fuller wrote in May 1932 to Frederick A. Whiting, president of the American Federation of the Arts, about the need for an experienced museum director when the new building opened; five months later, he wrote that he would take on the position of director in addition to remaining president of the board when the new building opened (letters to Frederick A. Whiting from Richard Fuller, 17 May 1932 and 17 Oct. 1932, Seattle Art Museum papers, box 33, folder 7, Special Collections Division, University of Washington Libraries).

26. Pries's relationship with Richard Fuller was publicly cordial, but privately Pries sometimes referred to "Dickie" Fuller. Pries felt that he had been forced out so that Fuller could consolidate his personal control over the museum.

27. In 1928, the Art Institute of Seattle switched its Annual Exhibition of Northwest Artists from spring to fall. Rather than leave eighteen months between exhibitions, the Art Institute held two in 1928. The Thirteenth Annual Exhibition took place 1–30 April, and the Fourteenth Annual Exhibition took place 29 September– 25 October. Brochures for all the exhibitions are found in the Seattle Art Museum papers, Special Collections Division, University of Washington Libraries. David Martin of Martin-Zambito Fine Art, in Seattle, brought Pries's inclusion in the annual exhibitions to my attention. Unfortunately, none of the paintings that Pries exhibited in 1928 have been discovered. The discussion that follows in this chapter is based on known Pries paintings produced after 1923 that were not connected to architectural projects. Twelve Pries oils and nearly forty Pries watercolors were discovered during the research that led to this book. As many as twenty additional paintings by Pries may have been shown in various exhibitions (there is no list of paintings that Pries exhibited in his 1946 solo show), but they have not been found. Pries no doubt produced additional paintings that he never exhibited.

28. Carol Troyen, "A War Waged on Paper: Watercolor and Modern Art in America," in Sue Welsh Reed and Carol Troyen, eds., *Awash in Color: Homer, Sargent, and the Great American Watercolor* (Boston/London: Museum of Fine Arts/Bulfinch Press/Little, Brown, 1993), xxxvi, lvi-lvii.

29. Philadelphia's two organizations were the Art Club of Philadelphia and the Philadelphia Water Color Club; see Troyen, "A War Waged on Paper," in Reed and Troyen, eds., *Awash in Color*, liv-lvi.

30. In the spring of 1920, the Pennsylvania Academy of Fine Arts presented "Painting and Drawings by Representative Modern Masters," including 256 works by French artists of the late nineteenth and early twentieth centuries. However, it seems likely that Pries arrived in Philadelphia in middle to late summer, after the show closed. The next year, the academy hosted its "Exhibition of Paintings Showing the Later Tendencies in Art," with 280 modern works by American artists; Pries definitely would have seen this exhibit. Pries may also have seen an exhibit of contemporary European work at the academy in the spring of 1923. See Carolyn Diskant, "Modernism at the Pennsylvania Academy, 1910–1940," in *In This*

Academy: The Pennsylvania Academy of Fine Arts, 1805–1976 (Philadelphia: Pennsylvania Academy of Fine Arts, 1976), 206–7.

31. *Town Crier,* 7 Apr. 1928, 14; *Town Crier,* 28 July 1928, 6; *Town Crier,* 4 Aug. 1928, 6; *Town Crier,* 29 Sept. 1928, 8.

32. According to Bjarne Olsen, a University of Washington student of the 1930s, Pries may actually have exhibited in 1932, 1933, or 1934 under an alias, but this possibility cannot be definitively ascertained (memo to the author from Bjarne Olsen, 28 Sept. 2003).

33. *Pencil Points* 12 (Sept. 1931). Marco Frascari identified *Città Caselli—Piazza San Lorenzo* as a square in Città di Castello, a town in Umbria; he noted that the two women near the well are wearing the typical dress of the region. In addition to *Città Caselli—Piazza San Lorenzo,* Pries prepared four other paintings of similar technique, with similar mats and lists of colors: *Comaras—Court of the Elephants; Eda—The Mosque of Ali; Souk-al-Hafiz;* and *Indian Graveyard, Quatsino Sound, Vancouver Island.* All except *Souk-al-Hafiz* are found in the Pries collection, Special Collections Division, University of Washington Libraries; Pries gave *Souk-al-Hafiz* to Keith Kolb in the 1960s. Pries did not finish a matching sixth watercolor; although matted, it lacks any title or list of colors, an indication that he chose not to submit it to *Pencil Points.* This unnamed painting is also held by Keith Kolb.

34. Drybrush is a technique in which the artist controls the amount of color on the brush so that when the brush is "dragged across a somewhat rough surface, color will be deposited on the high points of the surface, skipping over the low points"; see Roy Perkinson and Annette Manick, "Notes on Media and Papers," in Reed and Troyen, eds., *Awash in Color,* lxxx. The full text on the back of the *Pencil Points* plate reads, "This water color sketch by Lionel H. Pries was made on a fairly rough water color paper. The colors used were all transparent and included Alizarin Crimson, Cadmium Pale, Yellow Ochre, Raw Sienna, Burnt Sienna, Cerulean Blue, French Blue, and Emerald Green. The original sketch measures 13½ by 9½ inches. The artist has used the white paper effectively and in places has taken advantage of the rough texture to obtain a sparkling effect through use of a fairly dry brush."

35. In September 2003, David Martin noted the likely influence of Sargent on Pries's 1931 paintings. Pries would have known Sargent's work from his years in Philadelphia, but a more direct influence may have been the book on Sargent's watercolors that Pries acquired at Christmas 1930: *Famous Water-colour Painters,* vol. 7: *J. S. Sargent* (London/New York: The Studio/William Edwin Rudge, 1930). For watercolors by John Singer Sargent, see Carl Little, *The Watercolors of John Singer Sargent* (Berkeley: University of California Press, 1998).

36. Brochure for First Annual Exhibition of Western Watercolor Painting at the California Palace of Fine Arts, San Francisco 5 December 1932–8 January 1933; copy in possession of David Martin.

37. There is no published biography of Raymond ("Ray") Hill. A brief summary of his career is found in Sheryl Conkelton, *What It Meant to Be Modern: Seattle Art at Mid-Century* (Seattle: Henry Art Gallery, 1999), 41.

38. Author's interview with Duane Shipman, 3 Aug. 1994.

39. Author's discussion with Keith Kolb, 22 Sept. 2003.

40. Ray Hill delivered these two watercolors to T. C. Warren as a wedding gift from Pries and himself in June 1947.

41. Inscribed on the Ray Hill painting *From Gold to Grey,* which once belonged to Lionel Pries; now in the collection of Keith Kolb.

42. A point noted by David Martin, 13 July 2004.

43. Ambrose Patterson's wife, Viola, was also a practicing artist. Brief sketches of the careers of Ambrose and Viola Patterson are found in Conkelton, *What It Meant to Be Modern,* 43. The Pattersons built one of the first International Style houses in Seattle. Their residence at 3927 Belvoir Place N.E. was first discussed in the *DJC* in February 1934. Although the permit was in the name of Harlan Thomas, the younger Jack Sproule has traditionally been credited with the design. The Pattersons would have been familiar, from their years in Europe, with the developing architectural direction of the International Style.

44. A brief biographical sketch of Walter Isaacs is found in Conkelton, *What It Meant to Be Modern,* 41.

45. The visits of Archipenko, Ozenfant, and Molzahn are mentioned in Martha Kingsbury, *Art of the Thirties: The Pacific Northwest* (Seattle: Henry Art Gallery/University of Washington Press, 1972), 15.

46. Mark Tobey was the fourth member of this group. Tobey seems to have had little or no connection to Pries, having spent most of the 1930s in England. Like Ambrose Patterson, and unlike others who were still searching for direction, Tobey was already a mature artist when he arrived in Seattle. For Mark Tobey's career in the 1930s, see Sheryl Conkelton and Laura Landau, *Northwest Mythologies: The Interactions of Mark Tobey, Morris Graves, Kenneth Callahan, and Guy Anderson* (Tacoma/Seattle: Tacoma Art Museum/University of Washington Press, 2003).

47. There are numerous publications that address the work and life of Kenneth Callahan; for a general overview of his career, see Thomas Orton and Patricia Grieve Watkinson, *Kenneth Callahan* (La Conner, Wash./Seattle: Museum of Northwest Art/University of Washington Press, 2000). For a detailed examination of Callahan's career in the 1930s, see Conkelton and Landau, *Northwest Mythologies.*

48. Callahan became part-time curator and later assistant director of the Seattle Art Museum, beginning in 1935.

49. There are numerous publications that address the work and life of Guy Anderson; for his career in the 1930s, see especially Conkelton and Landau, *Northwest Mythologies.*

50. There are numerous publications that address the work and life of Morris Graves; for his career in the 1930s, see Theodore F. Wolff, *Morris Graves: The Early Works* (La Conner, Wash. Museum of Northwest Art, 1998); Conkelton and Landau, *Northwest Mythologies*.

51. This painting was in the estate of Duane Shipman, who received it as a gift from Lionel Pries about 1965. Pries told Shipman the story of his evening with Anderson and Graves, and Shipman in turn told it to his nephew, Lincoln Bartley. In 2005, the two-sided watercolor was for sale on consignment at Martin-Zambito Fine Art, Seattle.

52. Callahan lived in Mexico for several months in 1932. On his return to Seattle, he began a large mural project, *Logging in the Northwest*; in 1935, he received a commission to paint murals in Seattle's new Marine Hospital. In 1934, Graves and Anderson traveled together to Los Angeles, and Anderson went on alone to Texas and Mexico; see Conkelton and Landau, *Northwest Mythologies*, 16–18, 29n6, 44. In 1934, the Pattersons went to Mexico, where they painted with the muralist Pablo O'Higgins; see Kingsbury, *Art of the Thirties*, 16–17.

53. There are numerous publications that address the work and life of Georgia O'Keeffe. For a discussion of O'Keeffe's move to New Mexico, with illustrations of some of her New Mexico landscape paintings, see Lisa Mintz Messenger, *Georgia O'Keeffe* (New York: Thames & Hudson, 2001), 104–48. In the caption to *Black Mesa Landscape, New Mexico/Out Back of Marie's II*, a painting dated 1930 (fig. 75 in Messenger's book), Messenger explains that in order to "capture the enormity of the New Mexico landscape," O'Keeffe had compressed "the receding space into a series of stacked layers." (The comparison of Pries's paintings to O'Keeffe's landscapes was suggested independently by Grant Hildebrand and Sergio Palleroni.)

54. The Twenty-first Annual Exhibition of Northwest Artists took place 2 October–3 November 1935; the Twenty-second Annual Exhibition of Northwest Artists took place 30 September–31 October 1936; the Twenty-third Annual Exhibition of Northwest Artists took place 29 September–31 October 1937. Brochures for all the annual Northwest exhibitions are found in the Seattle Art Museum papers, Special Collections Division, University of Washington Libraries.

55. The quotation is from a newspaper clipping titled "Lionel Pries' 'Volcanoland' Wins Award," which Pries pasted in his scrapbook (Pries Scrapbook, 64v, Pries drawing collection, Special Collections Division, University of Washington Libraries). The source of the clipping has not been identified.

56. For the life and career of Maynard Dixon, see Donald J. Hagerty, *Desert Dreams: The Art and Life of Maynard Dixon* (Layton Utah: Peregrine Smith, 1993; rev. ed. 1998).

57. Maynard Dixon's *Navajoland* is now in a private collection. The Thunderbird Foundation for the Arts will be allowed to exhibit *Navajoland* at the Maynard Dixon Museum when it is completed, in 2008 or 2009.

58. For the Group of Seven, see Charles C. Hill, *The Group of Seven: Art for a Nation* (Ottawa: National Gallery of Canada, 1995).

59. For Frederick Varley and the Group of Seven in western Canada and the United States, see Robert Stacey, "Heaven and Hell: Frederick Varley in Vancouver," in Catherine M. Mastin, ed., *The Group of Seven in Western Canada* (Calgary/Toronto: Glenbow Museum/Key Porter Books, 2002), 63–87. John Davis Hatch recalled that Emily Carr's work was also exhibited at the Art Institute of Seattle during his term as director; see Hatch, "Transition Years," 5.

60. The Pacific Gallery was at 1106 Pine Street, Seattle. A copy of the brochure for Pries's show there is held by the Art Department of the Central Branch, Seattle Public Library.

61. Comments by David Martin, 16 March 2004.

62. Precisionism was an American tendency of the 1920s and 1930s that responded to European Cubism. Sometimes called "Cubist Realism," Precisionism was an approach to representation in which urban and architectural subjects were rendered realistically but with an emphasis on geometrical form. Z. (Zama) Vanessa Helder (1904–1968) exhibited at the Seattle Art Museum in 1939, where Pries no doubt saw her work. For a brief introduction to Helder's work, see Larry Schoonover, "Vanessa Helder and Grand Coulee Dam," *Columbia* 4/2 (Summer 1990): 34–35.

63. Author's discussion with Keith Kolb, 8 Sept. 2004.

64. Pries does seem to have had continuing awareness of certain American artists. Pries's treatment of the mountains in the background of his pair of *Hacienda da Rocca* oil paintings, dating from the 1930s, may suggest the work of Georgia O'Keeffe. Similarly, the untitled driftwood painting of the mid-1940s may indicate the continuing influence of O'Keeffe. In 1930–31, O'Keeffe began painting the bleached bones found in the New Mexico desert. Initially she painted skulls; in the 1940s, she also painted pelvises. She usually placed these above desert landscapes so that the bones appeared to float in the foreground, with the landscape receding in the distance. See Messenger, *Georgia O'Keeffe*, 122–39. Gnarled driftwood on the Pacific coast is probably the closest Northwest equivalent to bleached bones in the Southwest. However, Pries's driftwood does not float above the landscape but is situated in the foreground with a scene of water in the background. (Unfortunately, Pries's driftwood watercolor was displayed in a sunny room in Hawaii for more than fifty years. As a result, the background scene—probably beach and water extending to a horizon—has largely faded.)

65. David Martin suggests that *Alkalai Meadows, Lower Coulee* shows Pries's awareness of the works of the American watercolorist Charles E. Burchfield (1893–1967).

66. Although Pries exhibited a few watercolors in 1940, and over thirty watercolors in 1946, he did not join or exhibit with the Northwest Watercolor Society, a group formed in 1940. In contrast, Ray Hill was a

member and sometimes exhibited with the society (information provided by David Martin).

67. Letter to the author from T. C. Warren, 12 July 2003. For reports of Pries's exhibit, see "Professor Pries shows Paintings," *The Daily*, 7 May 1946, 4; "University of Washington News: Henry Art Gallery Has Display of Watercolors by L. H. Pries," *Seattle Star*, 8 May 1946, 7.

68. "Pries was one of the most talented watercolorists ever active in the Northwest . . .," David Martin, "Classic Modern Art in the Northwest," *http:/www.360modern. com/home/?s=articles&aid=10*. Author conversation with David Martin, 25 May 2004.

69. Author's interview with Duane Shipman, 3 Aug. 1994.

70. Memo to the author from Bjarne Olsen, 28 Sept. 2003.

71. Kingsbury, *Art of the Thirties*, 10.

72. Pries's library included several books on etching and printmaking; for example, Levon West, *Making an Etching* (London and New York: The Studio, 1932), 6–8, includes a good description of the drypoint process. Pries was no doubt aware of the work of the Northwest Print Makers even though he did not exhibit with them. Pries also would have been familiar with the work of Thomas Hanforth, then living in Tacoma, who did drypoint prints. Hanforth exhibited at the Art Institute of Seattle between 1928 and 1931; see Hatch, "Transition Years," 5.

73. Information provided by David Martin, who has a complete run of the exhibit brochures for the Northwest Print Makers.

74. Author's interview with John Rohrer, 9 Sept. 1999.

75. Drypoint differs from etching in that acid is not used. It differs from engraving because the tool that an engraver uses cuts a deep-shaped line, which removes the metal burr completely and results in a crisp line. Drypoint is a deceptively difficult process. While it appears little different from drawing, the artist must control the force used as well as the depth and angle of the tool as it cuts into the metal; this also controls the height and configuration of the burr. A skilled drypoint artist will manipulate the cutting tool to shape the burr for maximum effect. The artist can also use different tools that produce lines of varying width and cross-section, and some artists even use metal brushes to produce tonal effects.

76. The original drawing is found on the flyleaf of M. da Cimbro, *Venedig* (Zurich: Amalthea-Verlag, c. 1929). This book was a gift from Pries's clients Karl and Emita Krueger. Pries's signature is dated July 1931 (copy in Pries book collection, Special Collections Division, University of Washington Libraries).

77. Analysis provided by Sergio Palleroni, 3 Sept. 2003. Orozco's work was exhibited at the Art Institute of Seattle between 1928 and 1931; see Hatch, "Transition Years," 6.

78. Author's interview with Keith Kolb, 11 Aug. 1995.

79. Kolb identified this as the cabin owned by Profes-

sor Harlan Thomas; the site was near what is now Stillaguamish Country Club (author's conversation with Keith Kolb, 5 Oct. 2003).

80. Winskill, who inherited Pries's collections, notes that Pries did retain a few items from his childhood collecting, including some coins and medals from world's fairs (among them the Pan American Exposition, Buffalo, 1901; the Alaska-Yukon-Pacific Exposition, Seattle, 1909; and the Panama-Pacific International Exposition, San Francisco, 1915). Winskill also retains a small Japanese chest of drawers that Pries used to hold small items, many less than 1 inch in size. These include Japanese, Chinese, African, Mexican, and Native American objects. Some may be items that Pries kept from childhood.

81. Memo to the author from Robert Winskill, 1 March 2004.

82. Pries's library does not survive intact. In 1995, Pries's heir, Robert Winskill, gave the bulk of Pries's collection—close to nine hundred books and periodicals— to the Special Collections Division, University of Washington Libraries. (These were initially inventoried in 1996–97; they were reorganized and reinventoried by the author in 2003–4.) Winskill retained roughly one hundred rare items, which he sold in 1996. In 2004, Winskill still retained twenty to thirty books that once belonged to Pries.

83. Many students in the University of Washington architecture program before World War II regarded Pries's library as superior to the school's (author's interview with Keith Kolb, 11 Aug. 1995).

84. George H. Tweney, "Library Appraisal: Estate of Lionel Pries, Deceased," unpublished manuscript, June 1968. The original manuscript is in the possession of Pries's heir, Robert Winskill, who gave a copy to the author.

85. Letter to Emma Willits from Lionel Pries, 2 June 1962.

86. For Pries's loan of Javanese batiks, see *Town Crier*, 9 June 1928, 7; 16 June 1928, 7; 23 June 1928, 7; 30 June 1928, 11. Batiks are fabrics with colored designs produced by covering the material with wax in a pattern, dyeing the exposed parts, and removing the wax; the process is repeated for multiple colors and complex designs.

87. Pries's handwritten list of objects in the exhibit is found in the Records of the Henry Art Gallery, Box 10, Folder 14, Accession No. 75-006, University of Washington Libraries, Special Collections Division. Pries listed the culture of origin and a general location where each object was acquired. Unfortunately, his description of each object is brief, often only one or two words ("jade head," "jade figure," "monkey mask," "malachite frog," "obsidian discs"), providing little about its specific characteristics.

88. Kolb understood that Pries made his initial acquisitions from a Peruvian student, who had brought the textiles to the United States to sell as a way to pay for his education (author's interview with Keith Kolb, 11 Aug. 1995).

89. Author's interview with Keith Kolb, 11 Aug. 1995.

90. "Peru Textiles at Art Museum," *Seattle Post-Intelligencer*, 3 Feb. 1946, 10.

91. "Inca Fabrics Interest Club," *Spokesman Review*, 28 Mar. 1947, 12.

92. Lucile MacDonald, "Ancient Tapestries from Peru at U. of W.," *Seattle Times*, 23 May 1948, *Pacific Parade* magazine section, 2.

93. Carl Rietz, the collector who bought the textiles, apparently saw them when they were exhibited in San Francisco and purchased the collection after the exhibit closed. Pries's 1950s résumé indicated that he thought these textiles had become the "property of Mills College Museum," but this was incorrect. Rietz exhibited the textiles at Mills College but retained ownership. He subsequently gave the textiles to the California Academy of Sciences (CAS). Because the number of items donated was greater than one hundred, it is clear that Rietz had obtained Peruvian textiles from sources in addition to Pries. Russell Hartmann, curator at CAS, notes that some smaller pieces, mostly fragments, were later given by CAS to the C. E. Smith Museum of Anthropology at California State University, Hayward. The rest of the textiles are now part of the Carl Rietz Food Technology Collection at CAS.

In 1946–47, Pries had offered his collection to the noted collectors Walter and Louise Arensberg, but they chose not to purchase any of his pieces. See Arensberg Archives, Correspondence, Box 15, Folder 29, Philadelphia Museum of Art.

94. The Rietz Collection of pre-Columbian Peruvian textiles was exhibited by the California Academy of Sciences (CAS) in 1978. CAS published a catalogue and slide set that helped bring the collection to the attention of textile scholars; see *Peruvian Archaeological Textiles— A Weaver's Art: Slide Catalog* (San Francisco: California Academy of Sciences, n.d. [1978]). According to Ann P. Rowe, curator at the Textile Museum, Washington, D.C., several of the pieces drew widespread interest, such as one in the Recuay style; that piece was "something of a sensation when it was first exhibited, since Recuay textiles are not common and this one is so large and with fancy iconography." When contacted by the author, Rowe recognized the textiles illustrated in the 1948 *Seattle Times* article (see MacDonald, "Ancient Tapestries from Peru at U. of W.") and informed the author that the Pries textiles were at CAS.

95. The miniature vestments are mentioned in a résumé from the early 1950s (Lionel H. Pries, undated résumé, Pries papers, Special Collections Division, University of Washington Libraries).

96. Author's interview with Keith Kolb, 11 Aug. 1995. Unfortunately, the present location of this collection is unknown. The locations of several other Pries collections are also unknown. Pries's heir, Robert Winskill, donated some items to the Smithsonian after Pries's death, but these have not been identified. Pries's small collection of Northwest Native American artifacts was loaned by Winskill to the Washington State Capital Museum in Olympia until the mid-1980s but was then sold to a private collector.

97. Pál Kelemen, *Medieval American Art: A Survey in Two Volumes* (New York: Macmillan, 1944); Pál Kelemen, *Baroque and Rococo in Latin America* (New York: Macmillan, 1951). Both books, with Kelemen's original inscriptions, are in the Pries book collection, Special Collections Division, University of Washington Libraries.

98. Author's discussion with Richard Mellott and Robert Winskill, 29 June 2004.

99. Letter to Mr. Krupp of Oceanic Trading Company, Seattle, from Lionel Pries, 20 March 1955 (retained by Robert Winskill).

100. Author's discussion with Richard Mellott and Robert Winskill, 30 June 2004. This print collection was inherited by Winskill, and most of the prints were later sold. Winskill retains a Japanese scroll from Pries's collections.

101. Photographs and descriptions from Oceanic Trading Company, March and Apr. 1955; invoice from Oceanic Trading Company, 3 Jan. 1956 (retained by Robert Winskill); author's discussion with Richard Mellott, 29 June 2004.

102. Photographs, descriptions, and invoices from Oceanic Trading Company, 15 June 1956 (retained by Robert Winskill). Scholarship regarding Japanese screens has progressed considerably since 1956. Kawai Masatomo, professor at Keio University, Japan, and Yukiko Shirahara, associate curator of Asian Art, Seattle Art Museum, indicate that the exact date and authorship of the screens are difficult to verify, especially since the screens are unsigned, and some sections have more than one layer of paint (an indication of early repairs). On the basis of their research, the screens are now thought to date from the sixteenth century, during the Muromachi period (1392–1573), and not from the seventeenth century, during the Edo period, as Oceanic had indicated to Pries. Funding has recently been provided by the Sumitomo Foundation for repair and conservation of the screens, a project completed in 2007. The screens may be the subject of additional scholarly study and publication in the future.

103. The screen that Pries retained was bequeathed to Duane Shipman upon Pries's death (1968), with the proviso that upon Shipman's death both screens would pass to the Seattle Art Museum. Shipman arranged to give the screens to the museum in 1991, but he retained a life estate, and so the museum gained possession only in 2000, after Shipman's death. (The Seattle Art Museum accession numbers are 91.235.1 and 91.235.2.) In the early 1990s, the museum moved from its Volunteer Park building to a new building downtown. The Volunteer Park building was then renovated to house the museum's Asian collections. The Volunteer Park building is now called the Seattle Asian Art Museum.

104. According to Richard Mellott, it is not unusual to be able to recognize high-quality objects within a limited field or within a group of related cultures, but

Pries's ability to make good choices across a wide range of cultures was quite unusual, and it reflected a strong artistic sensibility.

105. Author's discussion with Richard Mellott and Robert Winskill, 30 June 2004.

106. Ibid.

107. Pries's collection of illuminated manuscript leaves includes an Italian gospel dictionary leaf (ca. 1150), a French Bible leaf (ca. 1310), two French breviary leaves (ca. 1260 and 1350), an English psalter leaf from the Book of Hours (ca. 1350), and five miscellaneous undated leaves. Pries also owned five manuscript indentures on vellum, including one signed by Charles I (1641), George II (n.d.), George III (1769), in addition to other miscellaneous prints and papers. These items remain in the possession of Robert Winskill. This descriptive information is from George H. Tweney, "Library Appraisal: Estate of Lionel Pries, Deceased," unpublished manuscript, June 1968.

108. Twelve books in Pries's surviving library have this bookplate. The last one is a University of California yearbook, *Blue and Gold 1919: Being a Record of the College Year 1917–1918*.

109. Pries painted two watercolors inside Kurt Heilscher, *Picturesque Germany* (New York: Brentano, c. 1924). The watercolor opposite page vii is dated 26 Jan. 1928. Pries's drawing of an Italian villa on the flyleaf of volume 3 of Paul Letarouilly, *Édifices de Rome moderne* (London: John Tiranti, n.d.) is labeled "Villa for Cardinals, Junior Problem 1939"; clearly identified as a junior design studio problem for that year, it is the only one of these drawings and paintings that bears a label. A copy of this volume is in the Pries book collection, Special Collections Division, University of Washington Libraries. Pries usually did not do these illustrations when he acquired the books; rather, he added them at a later date—sometimes several years later.

110. Harold Donaldson Eberlein, *Villas of Florence and Tuscany* (Philadelphia/ New York: J. B. Lippincott/ Architectural Record Company, 1925) (Pries book collection, Special Collections Division, University of Washington Libraries).

111. Gerstle Mack and Thomas Gibson, *Architectural Details of Northern and Central Spain* (New York: William Helburn, 1930) (Pries book collection, Special Collections Division, University of Washington Libraries).

112. da Cimbro, *Venedig*.

113. Ernst Boerschmann, *Chinesische Architektur*, vol. 2 (Berlin: Verlag Ernst Wasmuth, 1925) (Pries book collection, Special Collections Division, University of Washington Libraries).

114. Julius Baum, *Die schoene deutsche Stadt Sud-deutschland* (Munich: R. Piper & Company, 1925) (copy in Pries book collection, Special Collections Division, University of Washington Libraries). For information about the Krueger residence, see chap. 4, this volume.

115. In December 1923, Pries acquired Sallie Belle Tannahill, *P's and Q's: A Book on the Art of Letter Arrangement* (Garden City, N.Y.: Doubleday, Page & Company, 1923),

which addressed bookplate design (55–56). In 1927, Pries acquired Richard Braungart, *Das moderne deutsche Gebrauchs-exlibris . . .* (Munich: F. Hanfstaengl, 1922), a book on contemporary German bookplates. Into this book Pries glued samples of bookplates—his own, and those he designed for friends (Pries book collection, Special Collections Division, University of Washington Libraries).

116. Pries appears to have designed at least five different personal bookplates in the mid-1930s. In addition to the four described in this chapter, he created a bookplate of a much more traditional character, a figure planting a tree; however, he used this in only two volumes, and apparently he abandoned it almost immediately in favor of the four bookplates he used from the mid-1930s to the mid-1950s. The original copper plate for this bookplate is retained by Robert Winskill.

117. Pries apparently designed this bookplate for Henry Olschewsky but then decided to keep it for himself. A large pencil sketch of this design (with Olschewsky's name) survives in the Pries drawing collection, Special Collections Division, University of Washington Libraries.

118. Pries likely intended to use these different bookplates for specific categories of books. However, he was not completely consistent in their use. For example, each of the four appears in at least one book about architecture.

119. Richard Mellott identified the figure as an attendant of the Buddha. When Pries decided to create a new bookplate, in the mid-1940s, he apparently studied many alternatives. For these alternatives, and for versions of earlier Pries bookplates that were never used, see his scrapbook (Pries Scrapbook, 53v–54r, Pries drawing collection, Special Collections Division, University of Washington Libraries). Pries retroactively applied this bookplate to many books that he had acquired decades earlier. One might be led to think that he had developed this bookplate earlier, but it is the only one of his bookplates to dispense with the traditional phrase "Ex Libris . . ." using instead "From the Library of. . . ." Further, it was not until the mid-1940s or even the 1950s that Pries's self-portrait would have been framed in an Asian character, a reflection of his new focus on collecting Asian artifacts.

120. This discussion is based on the selection of cards held in the Pries collection, Special Collections Division, University of Washington Libraries. Several cards are glued into Pries's copy of Tannahill, *P's and Q's*. The earliest surviving example is his birthday card for his mother (1918). Additional cards are in the possession of Keith Kolb.

121. Blanche Payne (1897–1972) taught historic costume and apparel design in the School of Home Economics at the University of Washington from 1927 to 1966. She engaged in intensive research on clothing and historic costume and developed a significant textile-based costume research collection; see Blanche Payne, *The History of Costume, from the Ancient Egyptians to the*

Twentieth Century (New York: Harper & Row, 1965).

122. Author's conversation with Keith Kolb, 17 Jan. 2004.

123. Author's interview with Keith Kolb, 11 Aug. 1995.

124. Memo to the author from Keith Kolb, 7 Dec. 2004.

9. IN PRACTICE

1. Alfonso Pérez-Méndez has written, "Since in postwar USA faith in technological progress was not questioned, for many Modern architects the machine remained a metaphorical model for architecture. A period of unbounded optimism began; all that was needed was to steer the structures of production from war equipment to consumer goods"; see Alfonso Pérez-Méndez, *Craig Ellwood: In the Spirit of the Time* (Barcelona: Editorial Gustavo Gili, 2002), 12.

2. *Architectural Forum* used several issues to present architects' proposals for postwar construction. "The New House of 194X," *Architectural Forum* 77 (Sept. 1942), was devoted to thirty-three new single-family residential project proposals. The introduction to that issue emphasized the use of prefabrication, the increase in production brought about by the war, and the availability of new materials. The featured projects, called "pilot proposals," included designs with packaged bathrooms, prefabricated kitchens, and modular elements as well as houses built primarily from such new materials as lightweight metal and molded plastic. The proposal by Seattle's Paul Thiry (pp. 82–83), a house built of prefabricated elements, had photovoltaicly controlled lighting, an advanced HVAC system, and a circular core enclosing an elevator. "New Buildings for 194X," *Architectural Forum* 78 (May 1943), included a hospital, an office building, an apartment block, a shopping center, a theater, and other buildings, and all the designs displayed the vocabulary of the International Style. From December 1942 to June 1943, the journal also ran a series of articles on prefabrication and industrial processes applied to building. These articles addressed prefabrication techniques for various materials (concrete, wood, steel) as well as applications to repetitive building types, such as housing. See, for example, "Building's Postwar Pattern," *Architectural Forum* 77 (Oct. and Nov. 1942), which addressed rationalization of the construction industry.

3. Wartime advertising routinely emphasized products for better living. *Architectural Forum* 77 (Nov. 1942), 16, to cite just a single example, showed a General Electric ad titled "What Do Gun Turrets and 'Garbage Grinders' Have in Common?" The text explained that the gun turret was the "operating equipment" of an airplane and then stated, "In tomorrow's homes, the 'garbage disposal,' and other 'operating equipment,' which in large measure determine how a house *functions*, will assume new importance" (emphasis in original). The ad focused on the need for the "right kind of operating equipment" in airplanes and in "After Victory homes." It cleverly combined ideas of General Electric's contributions to the war effort, its production of consumer products, and functionalism.

4. See Esther McCoy, *Modern California Homes: Case Study Houses, 1945–1962* (New York: Reinhold, 1962; 2nd. ed. Los Angeles: Hennessey and Ingalls, 1977); Elizabeth T. Smith, ed., *Blueprints for Modern Living: History and Legacy of the Case Study Houses* (Los Angeles/Cambridge, Mass.: Museum of Contemporary Art/MIT Press, 1989). During the war, John Entenza changed the name of his periodical from *California Arts & Architecture* to *Arts & Architecture*, to reflect its new international perspective.

5. Memo to Victor Steinbrueck from Lloyd Lovegren, 13 Jan. 1978.

6. Pries evidently met Richard Lea through Lea's mother, for whom Pries may have designed a small remodeling (author's discussion with Keith Kolb, 8 Sept. 2004).

7. Ruth Lea's first husband, Lloyd Vance, died in the early 1940s. Sometime thereafter, Ruth Vance met Richard Lea Jr., who was serving as a naval supply officer in the Pacific. The Leas married in 1944, when Richard Lea was on leave in Seattle (author's discussions with Joseph Vance, son of Ruth and Lloyd Vance, 31 Mar. 2000 and 22 Mar. 2001; author's discussion with Julie Vance Ivarsson, daughter of Ruth and Lloyd Vance, 12 June 2003).

8. Author's interview with Julie Ivarsson, 13 June 2003. There is general agreement that the Leas followed Pries's lead in the designs for both their houses (author's interview with Robert Winskill, 26 July 1994; author's discussion with Joseph Vance, 31 Mar. 2000). Winskill recalled Pries's comment regarding Richard Lea's "exquisite taste."

9. Richard Lea Jr. had owned a weekend house on Whidbey Island, but this was taken during the war for the expansion of the naval air station (author's discussion with Joseph Vance, 31 March 2000).

10. The first paragraph of a letter dated 6 Nov. 1946, from Pries to an unidentified person named "Harry" at 8527 West 3rd Street, Los Angeles, California, included the following sentence: "The architectural picture is certainly a dismal one, although much to my surprise, I managed to get under way with fair hope of completion, a $35,000 sod-roofed lodge up in the San Juan Islands." The rest of the letter dealt with Pries's offer to sell his collection of Peruvian pre-Columbian fabrics (Pries papers, Special Collections Division, University of Washington Libraries).

11. "Island Week-end House for All-Year Use: Country House for Mr. Richard Lea, Lopez Island, San Juan Group, Washington, Lionel H. Pries, Architect," *Architectural Record* 111 (Apr. 1952), 178–80. This article was reprinted in *82 Distinctive Houses from Architectural Record* (New York: F. W. Dodge Corporation, 1952), 66–68, a volume that went through three printings. Only a few other Northwest architects initially followed Pries's use of sod as roofing. For example, Roland Terry, Pries's

student in the 1930s, used a sod roof on his own Lopez Island house, begun in 1965; see Justin Henderson, *Roland Terry: Master Northwest Architect* (Seattle: University of Washington Press, 2000), 110–15. However, "green roofs" have become more popular since 1995, as part of a growing environmental consciousness.

12. Joseph Vance recalled that, with rolling cots in the living room and on the front patio, a large group could stay at the house (author's discussion with Joseph Vance, 22 March 2001).

13. Ibid. Many of these pieces remain in the house today.

14. Keith Kolb noted that Pries sometimes brought pieces of driftwood from Lopez Island back to Seattle and turned them into sculptures (author's interview with Keith Kolb, 21 March 2001).

15. The only article that actually mentioned the age of the house was "The Sod Roof . . . Cool, Green, and Alive," *Sunset: The Magazine of Western Living* 123 (Aug. 1964), 68. *Sunset* had also published the house more than a decade earlier; see "Sod Roof Takes All of Puget Sound's Weather," *Sunset: The Magazine of Western Living* 110 (March 1953), 52–53. A photograph of the house appeared in the Sunset Book *Cabins and Vacation Houses* (Menlo Park, Calif.: Lane Book Co., 1960), 9. This book went through more than a dozen printings between 1960 and 1975.

In the late 1940s or early 1950s, Pries designed the remodeling of the offices of Richard Lea's Craftsman Press at Fairview Avenue North and Valley Street (author's conversation with Keith Kolb, 16 Aug. 1005).

16. The argument that the East Coast and the Far West responded differently to the international Modern movement that had originated in Europe was advanced by Harwell Hamilton Harris in his address to the 1954 AIA Northwest Regional Council in Eugene, Oregon. More than a decade later, the text of his address was included in a student publication; see Harwell Hamilton Harris, "Regionalism and Nationalism," in *Harwell Hamilton Harris: A Collection of His Writings and Buildings* (Raleigh: School of Design, North Carolina State College of the University of North Carolina, 1965), 25–33. A longer discussion of the controversy regarding regionalism and Modernism is found in chap. 10, this volume.

17. Julia Morris had commissioned a house from William J. Bain in 1937, but a decade later, when she decided to build a new Seattle residence, she turned to Lionel Pries. The residence that Bain designed for Morris is mentioned in *DJC*, 4 Nov. 1937, 1; *DJC*, 13 Nov. 1937, 1; and *DJC*, 15 Nov. 1937, 4 (permit). Bain's house for Morris, at 3707 47th Place N.E., stands just to the west of the Pries-designed Morris residence.

18. The Morris residence drawings are dated 15 Sept. 1947, and the permit was issued at the end of the year; see *DJC*, 31 Dec. 1947, 3 (permit).

19. Author's conversation with Susan Morris, daughter-in-law of Julia Morris, 12 Aug. 2003.

20. Ibid.

21. Memo to Victor Steinbrueck from Charles H. Schiff, 13 Feb. 1978. Schiff misstated the interval between the building of the house and the date of his memo: it was thirty years, not twenty-five.

22. Julian Barksdale was a professor in the Department of Geology at the University of Washington. Pries's former student A. Q. Jones had served with Barksdale in the U.S. Navy during World War II. Jones recommended Pries to Barksdale (author's discussion with Tucker Barksdale, son of Julian and Marajane Barksdale, 19 May 2005). The construction drawings are dated 4 July 1949.

23. In 1954–55, Pries designed two small additions for the Barksdales: a suite with a guest bedroom and study, and a carport (unbuilt). Drawings for the additions are dated 23 Feb. 1954 and 25 June 1955.

24. The Delta Sigma Phi Fraternity had struggled financially in the late 1930s, and there was no active chapter at the University of Washington from 1940 to 1947. When the chapter was reorganized, in 1946–47, Pries may have prepared this design proposal.

25. Letter to Keith Kolb from Lionel Pries, undated (but Kolb, on receiving the letter, added the date "Sept. '43"). The adjacent church owned Pries's house and wished to expand. Soon after Pries moved out, the house on Fifteenth Avenue was demolished as the church constructed new facilities. Pries's design for his Laurelhurst house was influenced by the changes he experienced during the war. By 1943–44, the architecture student boarders who had lived with Pries had nearly all departed for military service, as had Domingo, Pries's longtime cook and housekeeper (author's interview with Keith Kolb, 11 Aug. 1995).

26. The Pries residence is mentioned in *DJC*, 24 Sept. 1947, 3 (authorization for A. W. Peterson to proceed with construction), and in *DJC*, 2 Oct. 1947, 3 (permit no. 383171, issued 1 Oct. 1947; the cost listed on the permit was $16,000).

27. The lot measures 60 feet wide; it is 142 feet along the north side but only 88 feet along the south side.

28. A watercolor dated 1945 shows a scheme in which the residence rises above the garage, but this scheme proved too expensive; in the built design, the house is set back from the street. The location of the original watercolor of Pries's first design for the Laurelhurst residence is unknown; a photographic copy is in the Pries drawing collection, Special Collections Division, University of Washington Libraries. Kolb recalled seeing plans for the initial design, and he remembered that it had proved more expensive than Pries could afford (author's conversation with Keith Kolb, 20 Feb. 2004). A fully enclosed stair runs from the garage up to the lower floor; the top of the stair passageway is a steep ramp from the street, up 18 feet to the back door of the kitchen (on the upper floor). Pries designed a little cart (tram) that could be used to bring up heavy loads; a motor in a small shed pulled a cable that attached to the tram to bring loads up to the kitchen door. When not in use, the cart was stored in the shed.

29. Rocker identified the door as Burmese; see Andrew

Rocker, "Lionel H. Pries," in Jeffrey Karl Ochsner, ed., *Shaping Seattle Architecture: A Historical Guide to the Architects* (Seattle: University of Washington Press/AIA Seattle, 1994), 232. However, Robert Winskill has corrected this identification (personal communication to the author from Robert Winskill, March 1999).

30. Winskill has identified the source of the sand paintings as Jeff King, *Where the Two Came to Their Father: A Navajo War Ceremonial* (New York: Pantheon, 1943; 2nd ed. Princeton, N.J.: Princeton University Press, 1969), a book featuring text and paintings by Maud Oakes and commentary by Joseph Campbell (memo to the author from Robert Winskill, 1 Mar. 2004).

31. Pries's inscription is a slightly edited version of a statement from *Stones of Venice*, vol. 1, chap. 2, para. 1: "We require from buildings as from men two kinds of goodness: First the doing their practical duty well; then that they be graceful and pleasing in doing it; which last is itself another form of duty."

32. The quotation at the center of the table is abridged and slightly edited from Ruskin, *Modern Painters*, part 3, sec. 2, chap. 3, para. 6: "And that virtue of originality that men so strain after, is not newness, as they vainly think, (there is nothing new,) it is only genuineness; it all depends on this single glorious faculty getting to the spring of things and working out from that; it is coolness, and clearness, and deliciousness of the water fresh from the fountain head, opposed to the thick, hot, unrefreshing drainage from other men's meadows."

33. E. F. Benson, *Make Way for Lucia*, vol. 3: *Miss Mapp* (London: 1922, 1923; rprt. New York: Harper & Row, 1977), 87–88. (This source for Pries's concealed door was pointed out by Richard Frahm.)

34. Comments recorded by Edward (Ludwig) Duthweiler, 30 Nov. 2003.

35. To Pries's disappointment, the madrona did not survive. He later learned that watering it during the summer may have killed it. He replaced it with a pine (memo to the author from Robert Winskill, 20 Sept. 2004).

36. That Pries had created a showplace did not prevent him from tinkering. Winskill recalled, "When I first met Spike in 1950, his house was predominately [*sic*] decorated with American Indian motifs—not exclusively, he had Chinese vases and African sculptures on display here and there. . . . But he was constantly changing things around, taking objects out of his 'secret room' behind the fireplace, putting them on display for awhile. . . . [Several years later] he decided to get rid of the paintings on the ceiling. I came over to see him on a Sunday and they were gone, washed off. This was when he began collecting Japanese antiques" (memo to the author from Robert Winskill, 1 March 2004). Perhaps the first evidence of Pries's growing interest in Japanese artifacts appeared about 1950, when he hung Japanese lanterns with his own monogram (his "mon," as he called it) just inside the living room window/door.

37. Author's interview with Keith Kolb, 11 Aug. 1995.

38. For photographs of O'Gorman's residence and several of his buildings with large mosaics, see Clive Bamford Smith, *Builders in the Sun: Five Mexican Architects* (New York: Architectural Book Publishing, 1967), 15–42.

39. "Northwest Architectural Trends: Early Art in a Contemporary Setting," *Town and Country* 106 (Aug. 1952), 77.

40. "An Artist-Architect's Dream Home," *Seattle Post-Intelligencer*, 24 Apr. 1955, sec. 2, 27–28; a week earlier, the house had been included in the article "Tour of Homes to Aid Art Museum," *Seattle Post-Intelligencer*, 17 Apr. 1955, sec. 4, 1. The house was vertically expanded by subsequent owners. After Pries's death, University of Washington faculty member Myer Wolfe purchased the house from the Pries estate. He added a small room one level above the main living floor. Later owners added a complete second-floor master suite.

41. Kolb retains an undated blueprint of a Pries design for Dr. L. L. Foote's office (unbuilt). This small project is just one of many that Pries may have designed that did not go ahead, and for which no records survive.

42. Author's discussion with Keith Kolb, 8 Jan. 2004.

43. For Northgate Shopping Center, see Meredith Clausen, "Northgate Regional Shopping Center: Paradigm from the Provinces," *Journal of the Society of Architectural Historians* 43 (May 1984), 128–39.

44. Blueline prints of drawings for the murals are in the Pries drawing collection, Special Collections Division, University of Washington Libraries. Photos of the Legend Room interior are held by the Seattle office of the DLR Group (successors to the John Graham firm).

45. Pries's paintings were later removed. Pries may also have contributed to the interiors, but any work he did there was lost in subsequent redesign of the exhibits.

46. Like his brother Richard, Stephen Lea was involved in the printing business as owner of Sterling Engraving, in Seattle. After World War II, and soon after Richard Lea had acquired his Lopez Island property, Richard advised his brother to purchase a Whidbey Island farm that had just come on the market. With the property came a barn and two shingled cabins—one measuring roughly 15 by 30 feet, the other about 15 feet square—about 48 feet apart on the bluff overlooking Admiralty Inlet (author's discussions with Julie Ivarsson, 13 June 2003, and Stephen Lea Jr. and Judee Lea, 12 July 2003). Pries probably designed alterations to the barn about 1947–48 (author's discussion with Keith Kolb, 8 Sept. 2004).

47. Pries returned twice more to the Stephen and Harriette Lea residence. In 1953, he designed a caretaker's residence. This was a simple rectangular structure with a gabled roof. The building was later destroyed by fire. In 1963, Pries designed an enlargement of the kitchen. The roof of the residence was later extended to form a shed and garage, an alteration that somewhat obscures Pries's design.

48. For general background on the Hilltop commu-

nity, see Victor B. Scheffer, *Hilltop: A Collaborative Community* (Bellevue Wash.: Bellevue Historical Society, 1994). The houses of the Hilltop community have been described as "archetypal 1950s, informal, imaginative, and intended for comfortable living, not display." Many of the houses were by Pries's former students, including Paul Kirk, Perry Johanson, Fred Bassetti, Wendell Lovett, and others. See Sally B. Woodbridge and Roger Montgomery, *A Guide to Architecture in Washington State: An Environmental Perspective* (Seattle and London: University of Washington Press, c. 1980), 240.

49. The family of Charles and Mildred Gates was one of the eighteen "founders," the group of families that first contributed funds to bring the planned community from concept to reality; see Scheffer, *Hilltop*, 82.

50. Scheffer illustrates the Gates residence and credits Lionel Pries with the design (see Scheffer, *Hilltop*, 76, fig. 30). However, the photo actually illustrates the house as it was in the early 1990s, and it includes the Bassetti and Morse living room addition, dating from 1958, as well as a substantial remodeling and addition of the 1980s. Very little evidence of Pries's original design actually survives.

51. Alonzo Robertson was a contractor who had built residences and institutional structures in the Seattle suburbs, and he was the contractor for his own house. How the Robertsons selected Pries is not known.

52. For a discussion of the influence of Japanese architecture and photographs of the Japanese house as presented at the Museum of Modern Art, see "The Japanese Had Some of Our Best Ideas—300 Years Ago," *House & Home* 5/6 (June 1954), 136–41.

53. *House Beautiful* devoted its August 1960 issue to design in Japan; the September 1960 issue focused on the influence of Japanese design in the United States. Both issues addressed architecture, furnishings, and gardens. The August issue characterized *shibui* as "the grammar of beauty"; the cover of the September issue included the caption "How to be *shibui* with American things." See *House Beautiful* 102 (Aug. and Sept. 1960).

54. Often these articles did not credit Japanese sources for the ideas presented; for example, see "How Sliding Screens Divide Space," *Sunset: The Magazine of Western Living* 124 (March 1960), 101.

55. In the late 1940s and early 1950s, the Lea family lived on Capitol Hill and actually began planning a new house on Lakeside Drive. They had intended to rent the house at 230 40th Avenue N. (now E.), in the Denny Blaine neighborhood of Seattle, during construction, but they were so taken with the site facing Lake Washington that they acquired the property on 1 March 1957 (author's discussion with Joseph Vance, 31 Mar. 2000).

56. The property is identified as tract 1 in the Denny Blaine-Lake Park Addition. Records indicate that a 1,740-square-foot house was built on the site in 1923 (permit no. 292301). The building was slightly remodeled in 1927 and then completely remodeled to Pries's design in 1957–58 (permit no. 454907). (Charles D. Choo researched the permit history of the property.)

57. The Leas and several employees of Craftsman Press worked together with blowtorches and wire brushes to achieve the burned-cedar effect (author's discussion with Keith Kolb, 7 Apr. 2000). About this time, Pries also designed a fine conference room for the Craftsman Press offices, featuring shoji screens and Japanese paintings (author's conversation with Keith Kolb, 16 Aug. 2005).

58. Both Joseph Vance and Keith Kolb noted Pries's interest in creating a pond at sill level and in establishing a perspective that encompassed two levels of water as a viewer looked toward Lake Washington (author's discussions with Joseph Vance, 31 Mar. 2000, and Keith Kolb, 7 Apr. 2000).

59. Margery R. Phillips, "Showplace for Family Treasures," *Seattle Times*, 19 Apr. 1959, Sunday pictorial section, 18, 20, 22–23, 25. Although *House Beautiful* considered publishing the Lea residence, apparently Pries did not pursue publication. On 22 August 1960, Pries wrote to the magazine's editor, Elizabeth Gordon, congratulating her on the upcoming month's issue; he included a P.S.: "Your beautiful September issue would indicate you do not really need pictures of the Lea house" (Elizabeth Gordon papers, Freer Gallery of Art and Arthur M. Sackler Gallery Archives, Smithsonian Institution, Washington, D.C.; gift of Elizabeth Gordon, 1988). After Ruth Lea's death, in 2004, the Japanese screens and the figure sculpture were removed from the house before it was sold and subsequently demolished.

60. Pries's use of industrial materials and the sophistication of his projects, particularly their incorporation of fine art, set him apart as well from the "woodsy" regionalist design direction that had emerged on the West Coast.

10. COLLEAGUES IN CONFLICT

1. Many students experienced an education interrupted by World War II. Most students in the class that included Keith Kolb, Alan Liddle, and Wendell Lovett, who had entered the University of Washington in the fall of 1940, were in their junior year when they went into military service. Most students in their class returned in 1945 or 1946 and graduated in 1947 or 1948 (author's interviews with Keith Kolb, 11 Aug. 1995; Alan Liddle, 22 July 1999; and Wendell Lovett, 19 June 2000). Many students who entered in the fall of 1941, such as Dan Streissguth, left in spring quarter of their sophomore year. They typically returned in 1946 and graduated in 1948 (author's interview with Daniel Streissguth, 10 Sept. 1999). A very small number of students, who were assigned to military units involved in construction and who therefore had access to drafting equipment, were able to complete some assignments and mail them to the school (author's interview with T. C. Warren, 30 March 2004).

2. Sigfried Giedion, *Space, Time and Architecture: The Growth of a New Tradition* (Cambridge, Mass.: Harvard

University Press, 1941; 5th ed. 1967). A brief commentary on the way in which Giedion framed his narrative is found in William J. R. Curtis, *Modern Architecture Since 1900*, 3rd ed. (London: Phaidon Press, 1996), 12–14, 690.

3. *The Daily*, 22 Aug. 1946, 1 (18,000 students expected, including 12,000 veterans); *The Daily*, 3 Oct. 1946, 1 (enrollment 15,400); *The Daily*, 14 Jan. 1947, 1 ("now 15,778 enrolled"); *The Daily*, 1 Oct. 1947, 1 (enrollment expected to "skyrocket" to 17,000); *The Daily*, 2 Oct. 1947, 1 (estimated enrollment 16,541); *The Daily*, 7 Oct. 1948, 1 (enrollment 16,560).

4. Food lines, crowded housing, and inadequate classrooms are all described in *The Daily*, 2 Oct. 1946, 1.

5. Arthur Herrman, "University of Washington School of Architecture: President's Annual Report, Academic Year 1947–48," manuscript, 10 June 1948 (Department of Architecture records, acc. no. 70–37, Special Collections Division, University of Washington Libraries).

6. Author's interview with L. Jane Hastings and Sue Harris Alden, 13 Aug. 2003.

7. Ibid.

8. Ibid.

9. Letter to Robert G. Sproul from Lionel Pries, n.d. (ca. early March 1934). See University of California Office of the President records (CU-5 ser.2, 1934, 25), University Archives, Bancroft Library, University of California, Berkeley.

10. Letter to Robert G. Sproul from Lionel Pries, 17 July 1945; letter to Lionel Pries from Robert G. Sproul, 30 Aug. 1945. See University of California Office of the President Records (CU-5 ser.2, 1945, 72), University Archives, Bancroft Library, University of California, Berkeley.

11. *The Daily*, 4 Feb. 1944, 1.

12. *The Daily*, 19 Jan. 1945, 1.

13. *The Daily*, 21 March 1946, 4.

14. The death of Henry Olschewsky was reported in *The Daily*, 18 Dec. 1945, 1. He had suddenly become ill on 11 December 1945, and he died five days later, on 16 December. According to his death certificate, Olschewsky died of a "cerebral hemorrhage, meningitis and encephalitis." Because of a printers' strike, there were no Seattle newspapers published in December 1945, and so there was no obituary other than in *The Daily*.

15. Arthur Herrman, "University of Washington School of Architecture: President's Annual Report, Academic Year 1946–47," manuscript, 6 June 1947 (Department of Architecture records, acc. no. 70–37, Special Collections Division, University of Washington Libraries).

16. *The Daily*, 13 Oct. 1949, 6.

17. Part-time faculty in the late 1940s included Barney Grevstad, Bjarne Olsen, John Morse, Marvin Patterson, and Lawrence Waldron.

18. Norman J. Johnston, *The College of Architecture and Urban Planning: Seventy-Five Years at the University of Washington—A Personal View* (Seattle: University of Washington College of Architecture and Urban Planning, 1991), 57.

19. The following new faculty of the late 1940s who were University of Washington graduates had received their bachelor of architecture degrees in the years indicated: Jack Sproule (1934), John Rohrer (1937), Victor Steinbrueck (1940), Robert Dietz (1941), and Wendell Lovett (1947).

20. Author's interview with Keith Kolb, 11 Aug. 1995. Kolb suggested that Dietz wanted architecture education to be modeled on the education given in an engineering school.

21. Author's interview with Robert Winskill, 26 July 1994. Winskill recalled that Pries described Steinbrueck in the postwar years as "a proponent of 'form follows function' design."

22. Author's interviews with Wendell Lovett, 19 June 2000, and L. Jane Hastings and Sue Harris Alden, 13 Aug. 2003.

23. Memos to the author from William Trogdon, 15 July 2003 and 16 July 2003. CIAM is the acronym for les Congrès internationaux d'architecture moderne, founded in 1928 by Hélène de Mandrot, Sigfried Giedion, and Le Corbusier and dedicated to redirecting architecture toward Modernism.

24. The best history of the emergence of Harvard as the leading architecture program in the postwar era is Anthony Alofsin, *The Struggle for Modernism: Architecture, Landscape Architecture, and City Planning at Harvard* (New York: Norton, 2002). A good contemporary description of the program at its peak is the entire issue of *L'Architecture d'aujourd'hui* 20 (Feb. 1950), which was devoted to Walter Gropius and his influence. See especially Walter Gropius, "Plan pour un enseignement de l'architecture" (translated as "Blueprint for an Architect's Training"), *L'Architecture d'aujourd'hui* 20 (Feb. 1950), 69–75; see also, in the same issue, examples of Harvard student work (76–89).

25. For background on Hudnut, see Alofsin, *The Struggle for Modernism*, 116–21. See also Jill Pearlman, "Joseph Hudnut's Other Modernism at the 'Harvard Bauhaus,'" *Journal of the Society of Architectural Historians* 56 (Dec. 1997), 452–63.

26. On Hudnut and the appointment of Gropius, see Alofsin, *The Stuggle for Modernism*, 130–35; Jill Pearlman, "Joseph Hudnut's Other Modernism," 463–66.

27. There are many biographies of Walter Gropius. A standard English-language source, written at the peak of Gropius's influence, is James M. Fitch, *Walter Gropius* (New York: George Braziller, 1960). A somewhat more critical presentation is Winfried Nerdinger, ed., *The Walter Gropius Archive: An Illustrated Catalogue of the Drawings, Prints, and Photographs in the Walter Gropius Archive at the Busch-Reisinger Museum, Harvard University* (New York/Cambridge, Mass.: Garland/Harvard University Art Museums, 1990–91).

28. There are numerous works on the Bauhaus. A good English-language source is Marcel Franciscono, *Walter Gropius and the Creation of the Bauhaus in Weimar: The Ideals and Artistic Theories of Its Founding Years* (Urbana: University of Illinois Press, 1971). See also

Hans Maria Wingler, *The Bauhaus: Wiemar, Dessau, Berlin, Chicago* (Cambridge, Mass.: MIT Press, 1979); Gillian Naylor, *The Bauhaus Reassessed: Sources and Design Theory* (London: Herbert Press, 1985).

29. Gropius became particularly influential because he both taught and practiced; see Alofsin, *The Struggle for Modernism*, 164–71.

30. For Gropius's description of his approach to education, see Walter Gropius, "Education toward Creative Design," *American Architect* 150 (May 1937), 26–30; see also Walter Gropius, "Architecture at Harvard University," *Architectural Record* 81 (May 1937), 8–11.

31. Bernard M. Boyle, "Architectural Practice in America, 1865–1965: Ideal and Reality," in Spiro Kostof, ed., *The Architect: Chapters in the History of the Profession* (New York: Oxford University Press, 1977), 324.

32. Alofsin, *The Struggle for Modernism*, 171–75, 176–227 passim.

33. Hudnut and Gropius were not only influential teachers, they were also prolific writers, and from the late 1930s both actively promoted Modern architecture in the profession and in the academy; see Alofsin, *The Stuggle for Modernism*, 154–56, 164–66. Alofsin notes the part that Hudnut played in seeking to bring Modern architecture to the Mall in Washington, D.C., through the competition for the Smithsonian Gallery of Art. Hudnut prepared the program and included Gropius on the jury. For details of this competition, see Elizabeth Greenwell Grossman, *The Civic Architecture of Paul Cret* (Cambridge, England: Cambridge University Press, 1996), 200–211; Travis C. McDonald Jr., "The Smithsonian Institution Competition for a Gallery of Art," in James D. Kornwolf, ed., *Modernism in America, 1937–1941: A Catalog and Exhibition of Four Architectural Competitions* (Williamsburg, Va.: Joseph and Margaret Muscarelle Museum of Art, College of William and Mary, 1985), 176–223. For international acclaim of the Harvard Graduate School of Design in the 1940s and 1950s, see Alofsin, *The Struggle for Modernism*, 215–27.

34. Herrman, "President's Annual Report, 1946–47."

35. The freshman and sophomore pre-architecture curriculum listed in University of Washington catalogues for 1947–48 and 1948–49 included (in addition to art and architecture courses) physics, economics (survey for nonmajors), sociology (survey and "American housing problems"), and psychology (social psychology addressing the "psychology of institutions"). See *Bulletin: University of Washington, Catalogue Issue, 1947–1948* (Seattle: University of Washington, 1947), 73; *Bulletin: University of Washington, Catalogue Issue, 1948–1949* (Seattle: University of Washington, 1948), 91.

36. Herrman, "President's Annual Report, 1946–47."

37. *The Daily*, 4 Feb. 1949, 1.

38. Students in the first class to be enrolled in the new curriculum entered as freshmen in the fall of 1946 and graduated five years later, in the spring of 1951. But many changes were implemented even before they progressed all the way through the program. Thus, for example, the problem for the spring 1947 alumni prize (assigned to

seniors) was public restrooms and associated facilities at a site in downtown Seattle, and, in 1948, students developed proposals for a new building for the architecture school at a site on the university campus. Solutions were all completely Modern. When the five-year curriculum was reinstated, in 1946, the levels were renumbered: Grade I referred to the junior-year design studio, Grade II referred to the senior-year design studio, and Grade III referred to the fifth-year design studio. The first two years, including "Basic Design," did not have grade numbers. However, beginning in the fall of 1952, the numbering changed; thereafter, Grade I referred to the sophomore-year studio ("Basic Design"), Grade II referred to the junior-year design studio, Grade III referred to the senior-year design studio, and Grade IV referred to the fifth-year design studio. Because these numbers can be confusing, they are generally avoided here.

39. Memos to the author from William Trogdon, 15 July 2003 and 16 July 2003.

40. *The Daily*, 3 Nov. 1948, 1.

41. Author's interview with L. Jane Hastings and Sue Harris Alden, 13 Aug. 2003.

42. This list of sketch problems is taken from the department's list of possible sketch problems retained by Keith Kolb.

43. A copy of the Mercer Island project program (Feb.–June 1949) is found in "Design Probs 1948/49–1952/53," one of several three-ring binders of studio programs from the late 1940s to the 1960s, previously held by the Architecture and Urban Planning Library but transferred in 2004 to the Special Collections Division, University of Washington Libraries.

44. *The Daily*, 25 Feb. 1949, 1; *The Daily*, 12 Apr. 1949, 1; *The Daily*, 1 June 1949, 2.

45. *The Daily*, 16 June 1950, 2; author's interview with L. Jane Hastings and Sue Harris Alden, 13 Aug. 2003.

46. As Alofsin has noted, "This was an era when fervor mattered"; Anthony Alofsin, "Modernist Responses: The Ups and Downs of Architectural History at Harvard's Graduate School of Design," paper presented at the 56th annual meeting of the Society of Architectural Historians, Denver, Colo., Apr. 2003.

47. The term "realpolitik" is borrowed from Alofsin, who wrote, "The realpolitik of the modernist curriculum required the defamation of the preceding generation, which consisted largely of the claim that the Beaux-Arts had nothing to offer the modern design professions"; see Alofsin, *The Struggle for Modernism*, 154.

48. Author's discussion with Patricia Gowen Aitken, 17 Feb. 2004. Gowen's death certificate indicates that heart failure was the immediate cause of death, but kidney disease was a significant contributing factor.

49. *The Daily*, 3 Nov. 1950, 4. The writer also observed that the students' projects were "striking in common simplicity of line and openness of structure."

50. Design problems in the fall of 1950 included a children's play park (in the third-year design studios), a bowling alley and restaurant (fourth year), and a new neighborhood branch library (in the Ballard neighbor-

hood) for the Seattle Public Library system (fifth year); see "Design Probs 1948/49–1952/53," Special Collections Division, University of Washington Libraries.

51. *The Daily*, 1 Apr. 1949, 4.

52. *The Daily*, 5 Apr. 1949, 2.

53. There was seldom open strife. The Northwest has always had a tradition of politeness and civility, and it carried over into faculty deliberations. In the late 1940s, because space was so tight, the school's faculty meetings routinely took place at a smorgasbord restaurant in the University District; the atmosphere helped to smooth over disagreements. See *The Daily*, 17 Feb. 1949, 2.

54. Kolb typed Pries's notes for his talk and retained a copy (Kolb's notes, Pries talk for Monday Club, spring 1947).

55. Author's interview with Robert Winskill, 26 July 1994.

56. Ibid.

57. Alan Liddle recalled such confusion from the period when he taught, in 1953–54 (author's interview with Alan Liddle, 22 July 1999).

58. Author's interview with Wendell Lovett, 19 June 2000.

59. Students remember that when Lovett began teaching, he had specific ideas of what a building should be like (author's interview with L. Jane Hastings and Sue Harris Alden, 13 Aug. 2003). For example, as Jane Hastings recalled, "When Wendell started, if you didn't do a glass box with a core in the center of it—forget it!"

60. Author's interview with Keith Kolb, 11 Aug. 1995.

61. Memo to the author from Robert Burman, 17 July 2003.

62. Memos to the author from Sidney Cohn, 23 July 2003, and Paul Pelland, 19 Aug. 2003.

63. Memo to the author from Robert Patton, 22 October 2003.

64. Author's interview with L. Jane Hastings and Sue Harris Alden, 13 Aug. 2003.

65. Memo to the author from Paul Pelland, 19 Aug. 2003.

66. Memo to the author from Sidney Cohn, 23 July 2003.

67. Memo to the author from William Phipps, 18 July 2003. The newer faculty were not always sympathetic to Pries's painting on students' projects. In March 1950, Pries helped Jack Crabs with the rendering of his design for a candy factory by adding a large tree to the perspective (author's interview with L. Jane Hastings and Sue Harris Alden, 13 Aug. 2003). Jane Hastings recalled, "When they were jurying the project, everybody said, 'Well, there's nothing wrong with this building, but that awful tree!'" Pries's role in adding the tree is confirmed by Jack Crabs, although he did not recall the critique (memo to the author from Jack Crabs, 30 Dec. 2003).

68. Memo to the author from William Trogdon, 15 July 2003. This, students recall, was the one time Pries showed an interest in current events. Trogdon noted that Pries "invited students and others to join him Tuesday evenings for informal discussions of art, architecture, drama, current politics, etc., and to admire his home. The Canwell investigations of communistic activities on campus, particularly within the Drama Department, was a deep concern at the time, in the late '40s, following World War II. We listened to the hearings on the radio and discussions followed."

69. Letter to the author from Jack Crabs, 25 June 2005.

70. Author's interview with L. Jane Hastings and Sue Harris Alden, 13 Aug. 2003.

71. Memo to the author from Robert Burman, 17 July 2003. *The Church Incarnate*, Burman noted, has a foreword by Mies Van der Rohe, "who said he read it over and over again"; see Rudolf Schwarz, *The Church Incarnate: The Sacred Function of Christian Architecture*, trans. Cynthia Harris (Chicago: Regnery, 1958).

72. There were several new boarders—for example, Lewis Crutcher—but the house never completely filled up (author's interview with Keith Kolb, 11 Aug. 1995).

73. Author's interview with Robert Winskill, 26 July 1994.

74. Ibid.

75. Ibid. Richard Link Brookbank, who introduced Winskill to Pries, was responsible for the University of Washington Lectures and Concert Program from 1952 to 1956.

76. Memo to the author from Robert Winskill, 2 Apr. 2004.

77. Joseph Hudnut, "The Post-Modern House," *Architectural Record* 97 (May 1945), 70–75.

78. Elizabeth Gordon, "The Threat to the Next America," *House Beautiful* 95 (Apr. 1953), 126–30, 250.

79. See Wayne Andrew, *Architecture, Ambition and Americans: A Social History of Architecture* (New York: Harper and Brothers, 1955), esp. chap. 7, "The Modern Muddle," where Andrews contrasted the "Veblenites" (described as "cool," "impersonal," "anti-individualistic," "dogmatic," "absolutist," "worshippers of the machine," "spellbound by modern materials such as steel and glass," "experts at factories, sanitariums, and other impersonal buildings," and "willing to disregard the site") with the "Jacobites" (described as "warm," "personal," "individualistic," "casual," "pragmatic," "willing to take the machine for granted," "much more concerned with the texture of materials than with their modernity," "at their best in domestic work," and "haunted by the site"). Andrews admitted his own sympathies, identifying himself as a "frantic Jacobite."

80. *The Daily*, 14 May 1948, 4.

81. Allen R. Kramer, "Letters: Is Regionalism Dying?" *Pencil Points* 22 (June 1941), 14. Kramer, a professor at Cornell, argued that the International Style was anti-regional in that, being "international," it did not recognize any place-related differences but advocated one style everywhere.

82. Although the emergence of regional architecture in Texas and California had been discussed in *Pencil Points* by Talbot Hamlin in 1939 and 1941, the celebration

of architecture based on technology seemed to make such discussions of regional design irrelevant. See Talbot Hamlin, "What Makes It American? Architecture in the Southwest and West," *Pencil Points* 20 (Dec. 1939), 763–76; Talbot Hamlin, "Architecture in California: Whys and Wherefores," *Pencil Points* 22 (May 1941), 339–44. Among other articles that discussed regionalism was the series "The Architect and the House," which appeared in *Pencil Points* from the late 1930s to the early 1940s; particularly notable are articles on the California architect William Wurster (Aug. 1938) and the Texas architects O'Neil Ford (Apr. 1940) and John Staub (Jan. 1942). In his article on Staub, James Chillman offered the following: "Regionalism in architecture is but a respectful consideration of the limits imposed by climate, topography, and a people's way of life. Grant this and any architectural form, no matter what its derivation, will become one with the environment"; see James Chillman, "John Staub of Houston," *Pencil Points* 23 (Jan. 1942), 15–26. (Thanks to Stephen Fox for pointing out this quotation.) The interest in regionalism in architecture in the late 1930s and early 1940s was related to the broader explorations of regionalism in the American culture of the period. For a short summary of regionalism in the 1930s and 1940s, see Richard M. Brown, "The Great Raincoast of North America: Toward a New Regional History of the Pacific Northwest," in David H. Stratton and George A. Frykman, eds., *The Changing Pacific Northwest: Interpreting its Past* (Pullman: Washington State University Press, 1988), 41–53. One discussion of American regionalism as it was seen at midcentury is Merrill Jensen, *Regionalism in America* (Madison: University of Wisconsin Press, 1951).

83. Lewis Mumford, "The Skyline: Status Quo," *The New Yorker* 23 (11 Oct. 1947), 104–6, 109–10. Mumford wrote, "People like Bernard Maybeck and William Wilson Wurster, in California, . . . took good care that their houses did not look like factories or museums" and "I look for the continued spread of that native and humane form of modernism which we might call the Bay Region style, a free yet unobtrusive expression of the terrain, the climate, and the way of life on the Coast." Mumford's argument generated an immediate reaction from Alfred Barr and Henry-Russell Hitchcock Jr., who organized a debate titled "What Is Happening to Modern Architecture?" The debate was held at the Museum of Modern Art on 11 February 1948. It was structured largely as a critique of Mumford and of the regionalism that was emerging in California. For a discussion of Mumford's position and of the development of the postwar controversy about regionalism, see Liane Lefaivre and Alexander Tzonis, "Lewis Mumford's Regionalism," *Design Book Review* 19 (Winter 1991), 20–25. See also Liane Lefaivre, "Critical Regionalism: A Facet of Modern Architecture Since 1945," in Liane Lefaivre and Alexander Tzonis, eds., *Critical Regionalism: Architecture and Identity in a Globalized World* (Munich: Prestel, 2003), 24–28.

84. Lewis Mumford, "The Architecture of the Bay Region," in *Domestic Architecture of the San Francisco Bay Region* (San Francisco: San Francisco Museum of Art, 1949), n.p., exhibition catalogue. See also "Domestic Architecture of the San Francisco Bay Area—Exhibition of the San Francisco Museum of Art," *Architectural Record* 106/3 (Sept. 1949), 119–26 (the Western edition of this issue of *Architectural Record* included "Domestic Architecture of the Bay Region—A Guide," 32-1–32-4).

85. "Architecture of the Northwest," *Architectural Record* 113 (Apr. 1953), 134–46. The independent direction of architects in the American West from the 1930s to the 1950s was also discussed by Harwell Hamilton Harris; see chap. 9, n. 16, this volume.

86. Walter Gropius, "Eight Steps toward a Solid Architecture," *Architectural Forum* 100 (Feb. 1954), 156–57ff. By 1954, Sigfried Giedion, the Modern polemicist, had written approvingly of regionalism as well; see Sigfried Giedion, "The State of Contemporary Architecture: I. The Regionalist Approach," *Architectural Record* 115 (Jan. 1954), 132–37. Belluschi, then serving as dean at MIT, also wrote in favor of regionalism; see Pietro Belluschi, "The Meaning of Regionalism in Architecture," *Architectural Record* 118 (Dec. 1955), 131–39.

87. After reading an early draft of the manuscript for this book, Seth Fulcher, who graduated in 1942, emphasized that Pries had always taught that the design of architecture and landscape should be seen as one thing, not as separate or distinct (author's conversation with Seth Fulcher, Sept. 2003).

88. "Island Week-end House for All-Year Use: Country House for Mr. Richard Lea, Lopez Island, San Juan Group, Washington, Lionel H. Pries, Architect," *Architectural Record* 111 (Apr. 1952), 178–80.

89. *The Daily*, 29 Apr. 1949, 1; *The Daily*, 13 Oct. 1949, 6; *The Daily*, 11 Jan. 1950, 2.

90. Although there was only one private office (for Arthur Herrman), space was provided for fourteen desks for individual faculty.

91. Author's interview with Keith Kolb, 11 Aug. 1995.

92. Kolb kept a record of Gropius's comments: "I just don't know what we are coming to, where we are going. . . . I keep insisting we must have some culture. What's happened to culture, like the old European culture? How are they going to learn? Where are they going to find this culture? . . . Only the artist can grasp and integrate all the truths. It's always the artist, the poet who can do this! Our only hope is the artist" ("Conversation between Ben Thompson and [Walter] Gropius, overheard by Keith," manuscript, 18 May 1951; copy provided to the author by Keith Kolb, 8 Jan. 2004).

93. Author's discussion with Keith Kolb, 8 Jan. 2004.

94. New faculty who joined the Department of Architecture in the 1950s included Keith R. Kolb (1952), Gerard R. Torrence (1954), Daniel M. Streissguth (1955), Richard M. Stern (1955, in building sciences), Carl L. Timpe (1957, in building sciences), and Ibsen A. Nelsen (1958). This list is based on Johnston, *The College of Architecture and Urban Planning*, 57.

95. The autumn 1951 program at Grades II and III

(senior and fifth-year students), "A Neighborhood Unit in 'Phantom City,'" is found in "Design Probs 1948/49–1952/53," Special Collections Division, University of Washington Libraries.

96. "A Shelter for Petroglyphs" was assigned on 27 Oct. 1952 and was due on 14 Nov. 1952. The problem required that the shelter cover six petroglyphs. Three totem poles were also to be included, although they did not require shelter. The project bibliography included multiple references for petroglyphs and totem poles, but none for contemporary architecture. The analytique assignment, titled "Two Dimensional Problem," was given on 5 Jan. 1953 and was due on 23 Jan. 1953. The assignment required an elevation at 1/4 inch = 1 foot, 0 inches, and three elements at 1 1/2 inch = 1 foot, 0 inches. The problem statement included the following directions: "Scale and proportion, detailed consideration of parts, sheet composition and presentation are of paramount importance" and, in the next paragraph, "The final presentation will be done on a stretch in a monochrome wet medium"; see "Design Probs 1948/49–1952/53," Special Collections Division, University of Washington Libraries.

97. The senior problem (Grade III), titled "A Parish Church," was assigned on 8 Feb. 1954 and was due on 12 March 1954; the program described the project as an "Episcopal High Church." Although most of the bibliographic references were to recent books on modern churches, also included was *American Churches: A Series of Authoritative Articles on Designing, Planning, Heating, Ventilating, Lighting and General Equipment of Churches as Demonstrated by the Best Practice in the United States, with an Introduction by Ralph Adams Cram* (New York: American Architect, 1915). This book includes traditional buildings by such architects as Henry Vaughan; Cram, Goodhue and Ferguson; Howells and Stokes; Elmer Grey; and many others.

98. Author's interview with Gerald Pomeroy, 3 Sept. 2003.

99. Author's interview with Doug Haner, 22 Aug. 2003.

100. Memo to the author from Robert Shomler, 24 Nov. 2003.

101. Memo to the author from Jon Anders Oien, 19 Sept. 2003.

102. Memo to Victor Steinbrueck from Gerald Williams, Jan. 1978.

103. Ibid.

104. Memo to the author from William Phipps, 18 July 2003. Douglas Haner recalled witnessing a similar sequence of events (author's interview with Douglas Haner, 22 Aug. 2003).

105. Author's interview with Douglas Haner, 22 Aug. 2003. Haner, a student at Harvard's Graduate School of Design, was enrolled in a studio at MIT when he encountered Eero Saarinen as a critic. His perception of parallels in the thinking of Pries and Saarinen reflects Saarinen's increasing focus on the expression of "character" in his buildings, a point noted by Alan Colquhoun,

Modern Architecture (New York: Oxford University Press, 2002), 247.

106. Memo to the author from Gerhard Olving, 26 October 2003.

107. Memo to the author from Ronald R. Burke, 24 July 2003.

108. Pries, Lovett, and Kolb were all teaching at the junior level in the winter of 1953; the problem was the shelter for petroglyphs, with totem poles also to be included in the design. Kolb recalled, "Wendell [Lovett], with his students, ignored the totem poles completely. . . . Wendell spent all of his time with his students talking about materials and different kinds of plywood—forms with plywood to make shelters for the petroglyphs. . . . Wendell was interested in forms and plywood shapes, connections, and things. And, of course, he was stimulating the students that way. And Spike, of course, was working with the romantic, with the relationship of the totem pole, what was the totem pole worth, what is the difference between a real totem pole and a fake totem pole, what is a real petroglyph, and what does it look like, how do you draw it, and what kind of a shelter is appropriate to a petroglyph, and how do people come around into a space to see things like that? Wendell wasn't doing any of that. . . . Well, we got to the jury, and Wendell is looking at Spike's [students'] things and giving them all D's because they aren't being innovative—they are just doing all of this old stuff—and Spike is giving Wendell's students D's because they weren't doing the problem. And I was doing the same thing, because I was thinking 'Well, they have a composition they have to deal with here.' It was really unfair to the students, of course, because it wasn't the students' fault. It was really this friction going on between differing points of view at the time." Kolb added that he and Lovett were then and are still good friends, but in those years they often argued about the best way to teach design (author's interview with Keith Kolb, 11 Aug. 1995).

109. Memo to the author from Gerald Pomeroy, 3 Sept. 2003.

110. Author's interview with Douglas Haner, 22 Aug. 2003.

111. Author's interview with Gerald Pomeroy, 3 Sept. 2003.

112. Memo to the author from Robert Patton, 22 Oct. 2003.

113. Memo to the author from Bryant Milliman, 26 Sept. 2003.

114. Memo to the author from Ronald R. Burke, 24 July 2003.

115. Comments recorded by Edward (Ludwig) Duthweiler, 30 Nov. 2003.

116. Memo to the author from Robert Patton, 22 Oct. 2003.

117. Comments recorded by Edward (Ludwig) Duthweiler, 30 Nov. 2003. Donald Leslie Johnson, who graduated in 1957, recalled that many students did not consider Pries an effective design teacher, adding that Pries "was known (rather mystically) to have been better

in the past and something special; why, we never knew" (letter to the author from Donald Leslie Johnson, 18 June 2005).

118. Memo to the author from Barry Upson, 23 July 2003.

119. Memo to the author from Robert Patton, 22 Oct. 2003.

120. Author's discussion with Gordon Varey, March 1992.

121. Jeffrey Karl Ochsner, ed., *Shaping Seattle Architecture: A Historical Guide to the Architects* (Seattle: University of Washington Press/AIA Seattle, 1994) erroneously gives the date of Gowen's death as 3 March 1958. According to his death certificate, Lancelot Gowen died on 10 February 1958 of heart disease and heart failure, with kidney disease and kidney failure also contributing. For obituaries, see *Seattle Times*, 11 Feb. 1958, 41; *DJC*, 12 Feb. 1958, 2. Gowen's funeral was held at St. Mark's Cathedral on 14 February 1958.

122. Author's interview with Keith Kolb, 11 Aug. 1995.

123. Memo to Victor Steinbrueck from Fred Bassetti, 23 Jan. 1978. Kolb recalled that Pries "received a spontaneous and long, long standing ovation from all the former students. It was a very precious and truly heartfelt and warm ovation of gratitude and admiration" (memo to the author from Keith Kolb, 7 Sept. 2004).

124. Author's interviews with Keith Kolb, 11 Aug. 1995; Wendell Lovett, 19 June 2000; Daniel Streissguth, 10 Sept. 1999; and John Rohrer, 9 Sept. 1999. Kolb recorded the events of the day: "4:00—faculty meeting. Mr. Herrman said he had some very sad news. Mr. Pries had resigned from this faculty late Friday afternoon for reasons of ill health to be effective immediately. His health problem was probably emotional or mental. The action was final and decided" (notes by Keith Kolb, written Monday evening, 3 Nov. 1958). Kolb's notes indicate that there was discussion among a small group about what might have happened; after all, if it was truly a health problem, Pries could take a leave of absence. Steinbrueck, according to Kolb's notes, speculated that there might have been outside pressure due to Pries's homosexuality.

125. Andrew Rocker, "Lionel H. Pries: Educator of Architects," *Arcade* 4 (Apr./May 1984), 9.

126. Kolb was Pries's friend, and he was responsible for coordinating the junior year (Grade II), a level at which Pries was teaching; thus Kolb had a basis for contacting Pries (author's interview with Keith Kolb, 11 Aug. 1995; author's discussions with Keith Kolb, 10 June 2003 and 8 Jan. 2004). After the phone conversation, Kolb recorded the following: "I called Spike as soon as I got home at 6:00. I asked if I could come see him— he said, 'No, Keith, I'd rather not discuss it'—he was too emotionally involved—it would be upsetting" (notes by Keith Kolb, written Monday evening, 3 Nov. 1958).

127. Author's interviews with Keith Kolb, 11 Aug. 1995, and Robert Winskill, 26 July 1994. The discussion that follows is based on independent interviews with Keith Kolb and Robert Winskill. Winskill heard the story directly from Pries. Kolb received his information from Herrman. Kolb and Winskill agree on the essential aspects of the story. Where they differ is on the degree of culpability to be ascribed to Arthur Herrman.

128. In May 2004, officials of the Los Angeles Police Department indicated that they no longer had records of vice arrests going back to July or August 1958. Thus no legal record survives of Pries's arrest and fine. Herrman told Kolb that Pries had paid a $200 fine.

129. Notes provided to the author by Keith Kolb, 27 Apr. 2004. There is no way to verify the truth of Herrman's account, which places all blame on Charles Odegaard. Kolb believes that Herrman's account is correct, and that Odegaard forced the issue. Kolb adds that Herrman was "really very saddened by these events." Neither the Odegaard papers nor the University of Washington Office of the President records from the Odegaard years, both in the Special Collections Division, University of Washington Libraries, includes any written materials related to Pries's forced resignation.

130. In the month of November 1958 there was no mention of the resignation of Lionel Pries in any issue of the *Daily*.

131. Pries received a token stipend, $60 per month, until he qualified for Social Security.

132. The students were not given any reason for Pries's sudden departure. Robert Shomler recalled, "Pries was my critic early in my last year. Just a few weeks into the design project he left the University very abruptly. I don't think there was any explanation to the students from the rest of the faculty. I just remember it being very odd. Also, the students who had him for a critic on that project were left adrift and didn't fare very well when it came time for judging" (memo to the author from Robert Shomler, 24 Nov. 2003).

11. TRAGEDY

1. Letter from Lionel Pries to Robert Mosher, 1 Nov. 1958, courtesy of Robert Mosher.

2. During this visit, Pries critiqued one of Mosher's design projects, as Mosher recalled: "I was in the process of designing a legitimate theatre for The Actors Company, a Hollywood Group composed of Dorothy McGuire, Mel Ferrer, Joseph Cotton and Gregory Peck. It was a great project and Spike really got into the spirit of it. He gave me insights that proved extraordinarily helpful. He had the ability to analyze a developing *parti*, seeing through the often-confused beginning and aiming one towards a valid solution. He not only pointed out what turned out to be flaws in the scheme which I had ignored in my enthusiasm for my ideas, but he gave me confidence in my approach to the design character of the project as a whole. He demonstrated to me, once again, after some fourteen years['] absence from my life, that he could both critically guide and positively encourage a student, a quality I had long ago come to recognize and admire." Mosher went on to say, "Unfortunately, the theater was never built and The Actors Company was

dissolved" (memo to the author from Robert Mosher, 16 Sept. 2003).

3. On Spratling's disappointments of the postwar period, see Joan Mark, *The Silver Gringo: William Spratling and Taxco* (Albuquerque: University of New Mexico Press, 2000), 65–92; see also Penny Chittim Morrill and Carole A. Berk, *Mexican Silver: 20th Century Handwrought Jewelry & Metalwork* (Atglen, Penn.: Schiffer Publishing, 1994), 54–55, 62–67.

4. A valid question is the degree to which Pries played a role in the design of these silver goblets. Spratling produced other objects with silver beads and twisted wire supports. Candlesticks with these features (although of a different design)—illustrated in Penny C. Morrill, *William Spratling and the Mexican Silver Renaissance: Maestros de Plata* (New York/San Antonio: Harry N. Abrams/San Antonio Museum of Art, 2002), 249, fig. 387—have a hallmark that Spratling did not use after 1956; thus he was already thinking in this direction. However, most Spratling objects with twisted wire supports and beads appear to date from 1959 or later. Pries had a strong aesthetic sense but no known prior experience as a silver designer. Spratling likely took the lead, but likely also involved Pries in the design (and possibly in the fabrication process), to help raise Pries's spirits.

5. After finishing school, Durham had worked for the Seattle architect B. Dudley Stuart and had then taken a position with the Federal Housing Authority. In 1942, he rejoined Stuart in the partnership Stuart and Durham, and for the next few years the firm prospered, primarily designing housing. After the war, their practice range expanded to include institutional and commercial work. When Stuart retired, in 1954, the firm was reorganized by Durham and two new partners, David Anderson and Aaron Freed, as Durham, Anderson and Freed.

6. In later years when Durham talked about hiring Pries, he often mentioned that Pries had once advised him to consider another career (author's interview with Keith Kolb, 11 Aug. 1995).

7. Author's interview with L. Jane Hastings and Sue Harris Alden, 13 Aug. 2003.

8. The mosaic of the risen Christ fits into the sequence of Pries's other mosaics—the mosaic dining room tabletop at the Lea residence in Seattle (described in chap. 9, this volume) and the mosaic at the entrance to the Gurvich residence in Seattle (discussed later in this chapter). In the early 1980s, unfortunately, the mosaic tiles began falling off the Christ figure at Faith Lutheran Church. It was removed from the chancel and is now in storage at the church. The interior of Queen Anne Lutheran Church, including Pries's altar table, remains intact. An illustration of the interior was published in Marion P. Ireland, *Textile Art in the Church Today* (New York: Abingdon Press, 1977), 177. (Thanks to Dennis Andersen for this citation.)

9. Kolb and Winskill commented independently on how sad it was that Pries never had the opportunity to design a church (author's interviews with Keith Kolb, 11 Aug. 1995, and Robert Winskill, 26 July 1994).

10. A rendering and brief description of the bank appeared in the *Seattle Times*, 12 Aug. 1958, 14. The caption explained that bids would be called in about forty-five days; thus the project was just beginning construction when Pries joined Durham, Anderson and Freed. The decorative screen designed by Pries required a separate building permit that was issued on 16 November 1959; the city may have requested the separate permit because of concern about the structural attachment of the screen. (Thanks to David Rash for sharing his research on this building.)

11. "Art Adds Distinction to a Small Branch Bank in a Reviving Neighborhood," *Western Architect and Engineer* 219 (March 1960), 34.

12. Comments recorded by Edward (Ludwig) Duthweiler, 30 Nov. 2003.

13. On John Graham Jr., see Meredith Clausen, "John Graham, Jr.," in Jeffrey Karl Ochsner, ed., *Shaping Seattle Architecture: A Historical Guide to the Architects* (Seattle: University of Washington Press/AIA Seattle, 1994), 258–63. Pries's previous consulting on the Legend Room interiors at Northgate probably gave him credibility with the Graham firm (see chap. 9, this volume).

14. Telegram to Lionel Pries from Marjorie Graham, 25 Aug. 1960 (copy in possession of Robert Winskill).

15. Author's interview with Keith Kolb, 11 Aug. 1995.

16. Letter to Robert Winskill from Lionel Pries, undated (ca. June 1961, according to references in the letter).

17. Two letters to Robert Winskill from Lionel Pries, undated (ca. June 1961; the second letter cannot be dated).

18. Letter to Robert Winskill from Lionel Pries, undated (ca. April 1962, according to a reference to a visit by William Spratling).

19. Letter to Robert Winskill from Lionel Pries, undated (summer or fall 1962).

20. Letter to Robert Winskill from Lionel Pries, undated (ca. fall 1963, according to a reference to Pries's anticipated departure from the Graham office). It was previously thought that Pries had left the Graham office in 1962, after he turned sixty-five, but Keith Kolb's written notes from his telephone conversations with Pries indicate that Pries was still at the Graham office in August 1963. Pries mentioned to Kolb in an August 1963 telephone conversation that he had paid off his mortgage. It may be that Pries remained at Graham until the mortgage was paid off.

21. Ibid.

22. Some were continuations of earlier projects. In 1963, for example, Pries designed the kitchen addition to the Stephen and Harriette Lea residence on Whidbey Island (discussed in chap. 9, this volume).

23. Author's interview with Robert Winskill, 26 July 1994; memo to the author from Robert Winskill, late 2003. Drawings for the Winskill residence are in the Pries drawing collection, Special Collections Division, University of Washington Libraries.

24. Max Gurvich was a prominent Seattle business

leader who sold industrial chemicals. The Gurviches paid $45,000 for the lot—then a record amount for undeveloped property in Seattle. However, just a year or two later, another lot on Webster Point Road sold for $70,000 (author's discussion with Helen Gurvich, 19 Aug. 2003).

25. Ibid.

26. Max Gurvich apparently asked Lloyd Lovegren about Pries. Although Lovegren believed that he was the one who steered Gurvich to Pries, it seems more likely that Lovegren was merely asked to provide a reference. In 1978, Lovegren wrote to Steinbrueck, "When he [Max Gurvich] stated the impressive ideals he hoped to achieve and the magnitude of the project, it left no doubt in my mind that my recommendation had to be Spike Pries, and that was who Max selected, I was pleased to learn later. About two years later I ran across Max Gurvitch [sic] again at which time he thanked me enthusiastically for steering him to Spike who had produced a house beyond Max's highest expectations" (memo to Victor Steinbrueck from Lloyd Lovegren, 13 Jan. 1978).

27. Author's discussion with Helen Gurvich, 19 Aug. 2003.

28. Ibid. Attention to detail is apparent throughout the house. An example is the use of a thin walnut bead, routed in at the interior corners, to protect the softer cedar used on the walls. Pries also fully detailed the wood cabinetwork and the stone fireplaces.

29. Author's discussion with Max and Helen Gurvich, 19 Aug. 2003.

30. Margery Phillips, "The Lake Is Their Backyard," *Seattle Times*, 7 May 1972, Sunday pictorial section, 38, 40–45.

31. In April 1966, Pries told Kolb that William Bain, his former partner, had offered him a position as a consulting architect at "the Combine" (Naramore, Bain, Brady & Johanson). His role would have been that of design critic. But they could not reach an agreement, and nothing came of the offer (Keith Kolb's notes of telephone conversation with Lionel Pries, 25 Apr. 1966).

32. The Graysmarsh residence, originally known as the Anderson house, was designed by Bebb and Mendel and was built in 1909–10. William G. Reed acquired the house in 1941. He had alterations made to the residence several times; George W. Stoddard was the architect for alterations made in 1945. Several small alterations were made in the early 1960s. In 1967, Reed hired Pries to design the enlargement of the master suite and the addition of two guest bathrooms (William G. Reed, unpublished manuscript of memoirs, provided by Gary and Victoria Reed, Aug. 2003).

33. The Shipman residence had previously been the home of Henry Olschewsky, Pries's former student as well as his colleague and friend.

34. "Another project by Pries was his extraordinary and interesting design of the gamekeeper's watching house built on the beach of logs and driftwood" (William G. Reed, unpublished manuscript of memoirs, provided by Gary and Victoria Reed, Aug. 2003).

35. Some who knew Pries perceived his difficult financial condition but did not realize the cause. Theodore Foss, whose father, Harold Byron Foss, had been a Pries student of the early 1930s and had kept in touch with Pries, recalled, "As a little kid I remember Spike coming to our house in Palo Alto sometime around 1959 to 1963 and asking my parents if they would be interested in buying a Qing dynasty chair that he had. My dad said: 'I think that Spike needs money, but what would we do with a Chinese antique chair?' My father was completely unaware of Spike's dismissal from UW; if he had only known, he would have been eager to help for he held his mentor in such high regard" (memo to the author from Theodore N. Foss, 13 Jan. 2003). Ross Edman, who worked at the Seattle Art Museum and saw Pries occasionally between 1959 and 1961, remembered that Pries may have been trying to make some money selling Japanese artifacts. He wrote about "one evening at Duane's when Spike had a bunch of photographs of Japanese art Spike was prepared to order from a Japanese source. . . . He could not have been making a lot of money from the project. I paid $17.00 for a 13–inch gift lacquered Buddha (24 inches overall with intricate lotus pedestal and aureole)" (letter to the author from Ross Edman, 4 Oct. 2003).

36. Author's interview with Robert Winskill, 26 July 1994.

37. Unfortunately, Pries's thirty-year friendship with Ray Hill was effectively terminated when Pries departed—Hill was no doubt fearful about his own situation (author's conversation with Robert Winskill, 18 June 2003).

38. Author's conversation with Keith Kolb, 16 Sept. 2003.

39. Keith Kolb's notes of telephone conversation with Lionel Pries, 13 May 1964.

40. Keith Kolb's notes of telephone conversation with Lionel Pries, 25 Sept. 1965.

41. Comments recorded by Edward (Ludwig) Duthweiler, 30 Nov. 2003.

42. Ibid.

43. Pries visited Mexico at least three times after he left the University of Washington. His visit in November 1958, after the loss of his position, has already been discussed (author's interview with Robert Winskill, 26 July 1994). Ed Duthweiler recalled a Pries visit to Mexico while he was staying at the house in 1959–60 (comments recorded by Edward (Ludwig) Duthweiler, 30 Nov. 2003). This visit is confirmed by Pries's letter dated 22 August 1960 to Elizabeth Gordon, in which he mentions "a stay at Bill Spratling's Taxco [-el-] Viejo" (Elizabeth Gordon papers, Freer Gallery of Art and Arthur M. Sackler Gallery Archives, Smithsonian Institution, Washington, D.C.; gift of Elizabeth Gordon, 1988). Pries's friend Richard Frahm recalled a Pries visit to Mexico during which Frahm cared for the house. This was most likely between 1962 and 1964 (author's discussion with Richard Frahm, 16 July 2003).

44. Author's interview with Keith Kolb, 11 Aug. 1995.

45. Pries's event was briefly described in the caption to the published photograph: "A group of the republic of Mexico's leading citizens are in Seattle this week to assist with the installation of the Mexican Pavilion at Seattle World's Fair. Photographed Tuesday afternoon at a cocktail party given by Mr. Lionel Pries, well known Seattle architect, at his home on West Laurelhurst Drive are (left to right) Mr. Alfonso Soto Soria, director of the Museum of the National University in Mexico; Miss Ruth Rivera, Secretary of Architecture in Mexico, and daughter of Diego Rivera, famous Mexican muralist; Mr. William Spratling, the gentleman who was instrumental in reviving the silver industry in Taxco; Mr. Luis Covarrubias, well known author and muralist, and brother of the late Miguel Covarrubias, noted painter; Mr. Pries, and William A. McGonagle, assistant director of the Honolulu Fine Arts Gallery" (*Seattle Post-Intelligencer*, 19 Apr. 1962, WS2). Pries had also invited Keith and Jacques Kolb, whom he introduced to Spratling and the others. Spratling gave Kolb a signed English-language copy of his book *More Human than Divine* (Mexico City: Universidad Autónoma de México, 1960).

46. Letter to Emma Willits from Lionel Pries, undated (probably 2 June 1962, according to a reference to Pries's turning sixty-five; copy in possession of Robert Winskill).

47. Ibid.

48. Author's interview with Robert Winskill, 26 July 1994.

49. Memo to the author from Robert Winskill, 14 Apr. 2004. For McBride and Klee Wyk, see Maria Pascualy, "Klee Wyk: Artists on the Nisqually Flats," *Columbia* 12/4 (Winter 1998–99): 12–15.

50. Author's interview with Duane Shipman, 3 Aug. 1994.

51. Memo to the author from Robert Winskill, 20 Apr. 2004.

52. Memo to the author from Richard Proctor, 19 Jan. 2004.

53. Ibid.

54. Pries had a Japanese paper banner representing a fish that he hung on a bamboo pole when Robert Winskill came. Pries told Winskill that it was "to welcome his son—a Japanese tradition" (memo to the author from Robert Winskill, 14 Apr. 2004).

55. Only one time did Pries allow a partner to move into his home. This arrangement lasted less than two months. Pries would not have been an easy person to live with (author's discussion with Robert Winskill, 30 June 2004).

56. Gary L. Atkins, *Gay Seattle: Stories of Exile and Belonging* (Seattle: University of Washington Press, 2003), 105–257 passim.

57. Letter to Emma Willits from Lionel Pries, undated (probably 2 June 1962, according to a reference to Pries's turning sixty-five; copy in possession of Robert Winskill).

58. Ibid.

59. Letter to Robert Winskill from Lionel Pries, 1962 (precise date unknown).

60. Letter to Emma Willets from Lionel Pries, undated (probably 2 June 1962, according to a reference to Pries's turning sixty-five; copy in possession of Robert W. Winskill).

61. Author's discussion with Keith Kolb, 8 Sept. 2004.

62. Author's interviews with Duane Shipman, 3 Aug. 1994, and Keith Kolb, 11 Aug. 1995.

63. Author's interview with Robert Winskill, 26 July 1994.

64. Author's interview with Keith Kolb, 11 Aug. 1995; Keith Kolb's notes of last meeting with Lionel Pries, 6 Apr. 1968. Kolb also recorded that Pries said, "You know, I have always had kind of a way with the students, but Lance [Gowen] really knew far more about architecture than I did."

65. Memo to the author from Bryant Milliman, 26 Sept. 2003. Richard Proctor had an identical reaction to the suddenness of Pries's death: "Duane called one day to say Spike was in the hospital. . . . Then he was gone" (memo to the author from Richard Proctor, 19 Jan. 2004).

66. For Pries's obituaries, see *Seattle Times*, 10 Apr. 1968, 77; *Seattle Post-Intelligencer*, 11 Apr. 1968, 40; *University District Herald*, 17 Apr. 1968, 6. The Leas' gathering took place on 9 April 1968; for a brief description, see Alf Collins, "Odd Parcels," *Seattle Times*, 14 Apr. 1968, C5.

67. Author's interview with Keith Kolb, 11 Aug. 1995.

68. Author's interview with Robert Winskill, 26 July 1994.

12. LEGACIES

1. Victor Steinbrueck, "Collection of Information and Material Regarding Lionel Henry Pries," memo sent to Pries's colleagues, friends, and former students, 9 Jan. 1978.

2. Memo to Victor Steinbrueck from Perry Johanson, 23 Jan. 1978.

3. Memo to Victor Steinbrueck from George ("Pete") Wimberly, 15 Feb. 1978.

4. Kenneth Anderson may be the best example of a student who valued Pries, though he never became a practicing architect. After graduating in 1934, Anderson went on to a forty-four-year career with the Walt Disney Company, where he played a wide variety of roles in the creation of numerous animated films, including *Snow White and the Seven Dwarfs, Fantasia, Alice in Wonderland,* and *101 Dalmatians,* and also worked on the development of Disneyland. The animator and historian John Canemaker devoted a chapter to Anderson in *Before the Animation Begins: The Art and Lives of Disney Inspirational Sketch Artists* (New York: Hyperion, 1996), 168–82. A brief biographical note that mentions Pries's influence is found in Robin Allan, *Walt Disney and Europe: European Influences on the Animated Feature Films of Walt Disney* (Bloomington and Indianapolis: Indiana University Press, 1999), 248 n. 26. When he

wrote to Steinbrueck in 1978, Anderson described Pries as "the greatest single influence on my life" (memo from Kenneth Anderson to Victor Steinbrueck, 11 Feb. 1978).

5. Lovett's full statement: "He was a little strange, aloof, almost a loner, but as we look back on Spike, his knowledge and teaching with the passing of time, we appreciate him more and more"; see Larry Brown, "Eclectic Architect: Lionel Pries Designed Things His Way," *Seattle Times/Seattle Post-Intelligencer*, 13 Apr. 1986, *Pacific Magazine* section, 24.

6. It is unknown whether Pries recognized the degree to which the students of the years 1928 to 1946 treasured his influence. A few—Minoru Yamasaki is the notable example—acknowledged their debts to Pries in public statements. Others may have thanked him privately. In 1957, when A. Quincy Jones sent Pries a copy of his new book, *Builders' Homes for Better Living*, he signed it with the inscription "None of your students could feel stronger about your contributions to architecture than I do." In a letter accompanying the book, Jones wrote: "Spike, I don't quite know how to say this, but it is my ever increasing belief that you have done more in architecture than anyone I know or know of. Your contribution to the philosophy and technical abilities of my contemporaries has been present for many years, and with each successive year, the proof is even more evident"; see A. Quincy Jones and Frederick E. Emmons, with John L. Chapman, associate, *Builders' Homes for Better Living* (New York: Reinhold, 1957). The copy of the book inscribed from Jones to Pries, and the accompanying letter, are in possession of Robert Winskill.

7. Keith Kolb's notes, Pries's talk to the Monday Club, spring 1947.

8. Grant Hildebrand, "Richness Is Found on a Small Scale," *Seattle Times*, 17 May 1981, F14.

9. William J. R. Curtis, "'The General and the Local': Enrique del Moral's Own House, Calle Francisco Ramírez 5, Mexico City, 1948," in Edward R. Burian, ed., *Modernity and the Architecture of Mexico* (Austin: University of Texas Press, 1997), 115.

BUILDINGS
AND PROJECTS

KNOWN BUILDINGS, PROJECTS, AND COMPETITION entries by Lionel H. Pries are listed here in order, by date, as compiled from available evidence. Because no complete listing of Pries's projects has been discovered, this list has been assembled from a wide variety of sources. Pries's personal résumés provide a very incomplete record of his design projects. The Pries Scrapbook provided leads to projects in California; a more complete list was developed from *Building and Engineering News* and *Edwards Abstracts,* supplemented by local newspaper accounts. The *Seattle Daily Journal of Commerce*'s daily posting of Seattle building permits provided the initial basis for a list of Bain and Pries projects in Seattle. Research in the NBBJ archives' microfiche of William J. Bain drawings significantly expanded the Bain and Pries project list. The list of Pries's own buildings and projects after 1932 was developed from surviving drawings and photographs and was supplemented by interviews and by additional research using the *Daily Journal of Commerce,* Seattle permit records, and similar sources. Some projects were discovered simply by word of mouth. Because this list drew on such a variety of sources, some Pries projects undoubtedly have been missed. Interview subjects vaguely recalled projects by Pries in or near San Diego/Chula Vista, California; Phoenix, Arizona; and Madison, Wisconsin. None of these projects has been discovered. There is also a gap in the list for the early 1950s, suggesting that Pries may have had one or two more projects in that period. The list of projects on which Pries worked as an employee is no doubt incomplete as well.

Building names are as indicated in contemporary accounts, with later names added in parentheses. Addresses are based on historical locations and street names (with current locations in parentheses). Dating is based on contemporary accounts; the date of a project is indicated from the earliest report of the commission to the completion of construction. Approximate dates, where exact evidence is not available, are indicated by the use of "ca." Not all projects by Bain and Pries were verified: projects identified from the drawings in the NBBJ archives, but not verified from other sources or in the field, are labeled "unverified." Additional clarifications are provided, as appropriate, throughout the list.

The projects in this appendix are primarily single-family, privately owned residences. The privacy of owners must be recognized. Inclusion in this list does not signify any right of access to any property.

DESIGNER

Class of 1920 Memorial Bench, 1920–21
University of California campus (adjacent to Sather
 Tower, known as the Campanile)
Berkeley
Slightly altered
"Weeping Bear" figures by Joseph Jacinto ("Jo") Mora

DRAFTSMAN, OFFICE OF CHARLES K. SUMNER, SAN FRANCISCO, CALIFORNIA, CA. 1920

No projects identified

DRAFTSMAN, OFFICE OF JOHN GALEN HOWARD, BERKELEY, CALIFORNIA, 1920

Stephens Memorial Union, 1920–1923
University of California campus
Berkeley
Altered
Pries worked on design drawings

DRAFTSMAN, OFFICE OF DEARMOND, ASHMEAD AND BICKLEY, PHILADELPHIA, PENNSYLVANIA, 1921

Sesqui-Centennial Exhibition proposal, 1921–22
Wissahickon Creek site
Unbuilt
Pries worked on design drawings

DRAFTSMAN, OFFICE OF JOHN P. B. SINKLER (CITY ARCHITECT), PHILADELPHIA, PENNSYLVANIA, 1921–22

Southwest Sewage Treatment Works, 1921–22
Philadelphia
Altered
Pries was project architect

HEAD DRAFTSMAN, OFFICE OF EDGAR V. SEELER, PHILADELPHIA, PENNSYLVANIA, 1922

No projects identified

DRAFTSMAN, OFFICE OF GEORGE KELHAM, WILLIAM G. MERCHANT (ASSOCIATED ARCHITECT), SAN FRANCISCO, CALIFORNIA, 1923–24

Medico-Dental Building, 1923–25
470 (490) Post Street
San Francisco
*Pries worked on construction documents, possibly on lobby
 design*

ARCHITECT, SAN FRANCISCO, CALIFORNIA, 1923–25

Mrs. Ida Sutter Maas townhouse project, 1923–24
Van Ness Avenue (northeast corner of Van Ness and
 Chestnut)
San Francisco
Unbuilt

Mrs. Ida Sutter Maas apartment house, 1924
1242 Francisco Street
San Francisco
Altered

Abracadabra House, 1924–25
Ridge Road
Berkeley
Destroyed (1950s)

J. M. Johnson residence project, ca. 1924–25
509 Coleridge
Palo Alto
Unbuilt

Sausalito Land and Ferry Company Building project,
 1925
Sausalito
Unbuilt

Eddie and Dolly Nelson residence, ca. 1919–25(?),
 1930–31
3205 Dos Palos Drive
Hollywood
Altered
*Pries probably did drawings; residence constructed
 without his participation*

CONTRACT DRAFTSMAN, OFFICE OF CHARLES K. SUMNER, SAN FRANCISCO, CALIFORNIA, 1925

Dr. and Mrs. Nathan G. Hale residence, ca. 1925
Southeast corner of 45th and M
Sacramento

ARCHITECT, SANTA BARBARA, CALIFORNIA, 1925–26

Blake Motor Car Company, 1925–26
1330 State Street (at Sola)
Santa Barbara
Destroyed

Richelieu Hotel
121 State Street
Santa Barbara
Altered

Overland Willeys Knight Building, 1925–26
404–406 State Street
Santa Barbara
Altered

Bothin Building, 1925–26
903–911 State Street
Santa Barbara

El Camino Real Garage (Auto Showrooms and
    Seaside Oil Company Building), 1926
318–330 State Street
Santa Barbara
Altered

McKay Building (LaPlacita Building), 1925–26
746 State Street (at De la Guerra)
Santa Barbara
Minor alterations

A. B. Watkins real estate office project, 1925–26
6 E. Carrillo
Santa Barbara
Unbuilt

De la Guerra Court, 1926
221 W. De la Guerra
Santa Barbara
A. Toluboff, associated with Lionel H. Pries

Bothin estate (Piranhurst) landscape design,
    ca. 1925–26
Montecito
Extent of Pries's design is unknown

Frank Morley Fletcher house/studio, 1926–27
2626 Puesta Del Sol
Santa Barbara
Minor alterations

ARCHITECT, SAN FRANCISCO, CALIFORNIA, 1926–28

Theodore A. Maas residence, 1926
144 Miraloma Drive
San Francisco
Destroyed

Norris K. Davis residence (1926)
160 Miraloma Drive
San Francisco
Interior alterations

Alfred H. Feasey residence (1926)
150 Miraloma Drive
San Francisco

Mrs. Edward W. (Helen Thompson) Hopkins
    residence project, ca. 1926
Miraloma Drive
San Francisco
Unbuilt

Fred B. and Cleo A. Kerrick residence, 1926–27
953 Grosvenor
Oakland

Dr. Clair H. Denman residence, 1926–27
1521 Hawthorne Terrace
Berkeley

Dr. Clair H. Denman studio, 1926–27
1519 Hawthorne Terrace (now 1522 Euclid Avenue)
Berkeley
Altered

Bay Bridge preliminary scheme, 1926
San Francisco-Oakland
Pries served as architect

A. Gerske residence project, ca. 1926–27
2891 Hillside
Burlingame Hills
Unbuilt

Dr. Emma K. Willits residence, 1926–27
1155 Waverly
Palo Alto
Altered

Telegraph Hill Settlement House reconstruction and
    addition, 1927–28
(Telegraph Hill Neighborhood Association)
1736 Stockton Street
San Francisco
Altered for commercial office use

Bothin Real Estate Company offices, interior remodel-
    ing, 1927
Atlas Building
604 Mission Street
San Francisco
Destroyed

Residence project, 1927
Jackson Street near Spruce Street
San Francisco
Unbuilt

Bothin Station Manor Sanitarium remodeling (Hill
    Farm Convalescent-Orthopedic), ca. 1927
Bothin Station
Kentfield (Marin County)
Pries's specific project is unidentified

R. H. Louden residence project, ca. 1928
Hillsborough
Unbuilt

UNDATED, UNBUILT CALIFORNIA PROJECTS
FOR WHICH DRAWINGS SURVIVE

Polo Club project
San Mateo

Lattin residence project
San Mateo

Robert McCulloch cottage
Alameda

Residence project
Beverly Hills

James J. Lee residence project
San Francisco (probably)

ARCHITECT (PARTNER), WITH WILLIAM J. BAIN,
BAIN AND PRIES, SEATTLE, CA. 1928–32

Watson and Grace Visser residence project, 1928
Seattle
Unbuilt

Emily L. Taggart residence, 1928–29
2453 43rd Avenue W.
Seattle

Peter and Edyth Andrae residence, 1928–29
2304 Broadmoor Drive E.
Seattle
Minor alterations

Maud B. Morse residence project, 1928–30
Seattle
Unbuilt

Francis and Mildred Powell residence, 1928–29
4404 52nd Avenue N.E.
Seattle

Walter and Edith Johnson residence, 1928–30
2530 W. Viewmont Way W.
Seattle

Viceroy Apartments, 1928–30
505 Boylston Avenue N. (now Boylston Avenue E.)
Seattle

Richard and Jean Frayn residence, 1928–29
938 34th Avenue N. (now 34th Avenue E.)
Seattle
Minor alterations

Gilpin M. Moore residence project, 1928–29
39th Avenue W. and Elinor Drive
Seattle
Unbuilt

Arthur and Louise Symons summer residence, 1928
Union City
Unverified

Rodney and Marno Shelton residence, 1928
1929 Sunset Avenue S.W.
Seattle

Karl and Emita Krueger residence, 1928–29, 1930
14301 Third Avenue N.W.
Seattle
Minor alterations

Alpha Tau Omega Fraternity House (now Delta
    Kappa Epsilon), 1928–30
1800 E. 47th Street (now N.E. 47th Street)
Seattle

Millard and Alice May residence project, 1928–29
1619 Shenandoah Drive E.
Seattle
Unbuilt (constructed house by Fred Anhalt)

Shingle display room for Pacific Specialty Company,
    1928
4711 Ballard Avenue
Seattle
Destroyed

Roy and Jean Turner residence project, 1928
Seattle
Unbuilt

Exhibit for Robinson Tile & Marble Company, 1928
Seattle
Destroyed

Arthur and Hazel Coffin residence, 1928–29
Terrace Heights
Yakima
Likely altered

Henry and Hazel Coffin residence project, 1928
Yakima
Unbuilt

Lyman and Mary Bunting residence, 1928–29
Terrace Heights
Yakima
Altered

Edward and Elizabeth Hanley residence alterations,
    1928–29
2609 Broadway N. (now Broadway E.)
Seattle
Unverified

Lombardy Court (apartments), 1928–29
421 Summit Avenue N. (now Summit Avenue E.)
Seattle
Altered

Furniture Specialty Company factory, 1928–29
1122 W. 54th Street (now N.W. 54th Street)
Seattle
Altered

Gunnar B. Thorlakson residence, 1928–29
3032 W. 69th Street (now N.W. 69th Street)
Seattle

William H. and Winnie St. Clair residence, 1929
1666 Shenandoah Drive E.
Seattle
Minor alterations

William V. Tanner residence, 1929
1219 Parkside Drive E.
Seattle
Altered

B. T. Cottle Store Building project, 1929
Seattle
Unbuilt

Raymond Cottle residence, 1929
Union City
Unverified

Lizzie F. Fischer residence, 1929
3702 E. Prospect Street
Seattle

Stanton and Virginia Frederick residence, 1929
504 McGilvra Boulevard E.
Seattle
Destroyed

Envoy Apartments, 1929
821 Ninth Avenue
Seattle

Carleton I. Sears residence, 1929
Olympia
Unverified

Lynn and Lucy Vaughn residence project, 1929
Seattle
Unbuilt

George and Anne Harroun residence project,
    1929–30
Broadmoor
Seattle
Unbuilt

Kappa Delta Sorority House, 1929–30
4524 17th Avenue N.E.
Seattle
Altered

Gilbert and Winifred Skinner residence project, 1929
Seattle
Unbuilt

Gilbert and Winifred Skinner residence alterations,
    1929
3001 W. Laurelhurst Drive N.E.
Seattle
Unverified

Norman and Evelyn Abrams residence, 1929–30
321 W. Highland Drive
Seattle
Minor alterations

Robert and Nellie Moody residence, 1929–30
317 W. Highland Drive
Seattle
Altered

John and Fannie Hamrick residence, 1929–30
1932 Blenheim Drive E.
Seattle
Altered

Helen Ardelle Candy Company shop (interior), 1929
Fifth Avenue Building
Seattle
Destroyed

H. R. Davis residence project, 1929–30
Seattle
Unbuilt

David W. Baldwin, Inc. store interior, 1929–30
Fifth Avenue Building
Seattle
Destroyed

Malmo & Company Nursery office, 1929–30
6620 Ellis Avenue (Georgetown)
Seattle
Destroyed(?)

City Ice & Cold Storage warehouse addition, 1929–30
4750–4756 Shilshole Avenue N.W.
Seattle
Likely altered

Stewart Lumber Company store addition, 1929–30
1761 Rainier Avenue
Seattle
Likely altered

Convalescent Home for Crippled Children (Magnolia
    Health Center), 1929–30
4646 36th Avenue W.
Seattle
Destroyed

Summit Investment apartment building, 1929–30
West side of Yale Avenue, between Olive and Howell
Seattle
Unbuilt

Arthur and Marjorie Anrud residence, 1930
4326 53rd Avenue N.E.
Seattle
Altered

G. Irving and Coramae Gavett residence project, 1930
Seattle
Unbuilt

Irving and J. Marie Dix residence, 1930
4544 55th Avenue N.E.
Seattle
Altered

"Prudence Penny Budget Home," 1930
17954 Brittany Drive S.W.
Normandy Park
William J. Bain project

United Pacific Realty Corporation office (interior),
   1930
215 Pine Street
Seattle
Destroyed

Northwest Washing Machine Company Building
   project, 1930
W. 51st Street at 11th Avenue W.
Seattle
Unbuilt

Bel-Roy Apartments, 1930–31
300 E. Roy (now 703 Bellevue Avenue E.)
Seattle

Horace and Anne Peyton residence, 1930–31
212 Waverly Way E.
Seattle
Altered

Housing Corporation apartment building, 1930
1715 Yale Avenue
Seattle
Destroyed

George and Eleanor Dickenson summer residence,
   1930
Port Madison
Unverified

R. H. Bunn store and apartment buildings, 1930
4108–4112 E. Madison Street: stores
1815 41st Avenue N. (now 41st Avenue E.): apartments
Seattle
Altered

Jackson residence alterations, 1930
Lakota Beach
Unverified

Francis Brown apartment building, 1930–31
6202 Carleton Avenue
Seattle
Minor alterations

John and Blossom McCracken residence, 1930
3425 47th Avenue W. (now Perkins Lane N.W.)
Seattle
Altered

Eldin and Irma Lynn residence alterations project,
   1930
3863 50th Avenue N.E.
Seattle
Probably unbuilt

William J. and Mildred Bain residence project, 1930
Broadmoor
Seattle
Unbuilt

Eric Nelson residence addition, 1930
4326 Maynard Avenue
Seattle
Unverified

Donald and J. Marcella McDermott residence
   addition, 1930–31
522 McGilvra Boulevard E.
Seattle
Unverified

Elam and Vera Hack residence (Minimichi), 1930–31
Mercer Island
Unverified

Mrs. R. K. McCausland residence project, 1930
Seattle
Unbuilt

Virginia Mann residence project, 1930
Broadmoor
Seattle
Unbuilt

Seattle Trust Company residence, 1930–31
2500 W. Viewmont Way W.
Seattle
Altered

Ralph E. and Evelyn Stewart residence, 1930–31
10455 Maplewood Place S.W.
Seattle
Minor alterations

Sigma Phi Epsilon Fraternity House project, 1930–31
4504 16th Avenue N.E.
Seattle
Unbuilt

Callison residence addition project, ca. 1930–31
Seattle
Unbuilt

Aaron and Beulah Evans residence project, 1930–31
Seattle
Unbuilt (project resumed by William J. Bain, 1936)

C. Groome and Grace Gamble residence, 1930–31
Park Road and Wachusett Road (Woodway Park)
Edmonds
Unverified

James Bridge cottage, 1930–31
Burton, Vashon Island
Unverified

Eugen and Evelyn Dight residence project, 1930–31
Seattle
Unbuilt

Harry and Isabel Ives residence project, 1930–31
Woodway Park
Edmonds
Unbuilt

Theta Chi Sorority House project, 1930–31
4535 17th Avenue N.E.
Seattle
Unbuilt (constructed building designed by Walter Lund)

Mrs. Holister T. Sprague residence addition, 1931
Three Tree Point
Burien
Unverified

Chelan Hotel project, 1931
Chelan
Unbuilt

Mutual Laundry & Dry Cleaning Building project,
    1931
Mercer Street
Seattle
Unbuilt

Lionel H. Pries residence project, 1931
3655 50th Avenue N.E.
Seattle
Unbuilt

Walter and Alice McDonald residence alterations,
    1931
2200 13th Avenue N.W.
Seattle
Unverified

UNDATED, UNBUILT BAIN AND PRIES PROJECTS
FOR WHICH DRAWINGS (OR PHOTOS OR SLIDES OF
DRAWINGS) SURVIVE

Alpha Omicron Pi Sorority House project
University District
Seattle

Brubaker and Esther Hutchinson residence project
Broadmoor
Seattle

George C. Reifel residence project
Vancouver, British Columbia

George W. Weatherly residence project
Portland, Oregon

NOTE
The George Youell residence (1928–29) at 550
36th Avenue N. (now E.) in Seattle has routinely
been credited to Bain and Pries. The building permit
indicates that the Youell residence was designed by
Dean and Dean, a partnership based in Sacramento,
California. How the Youell residence came to be
associated with Bain and Pries is unknown; it is
possible that Bain and Pries served as local supervising architects for the project, although no documentary evidence has been found to substantiate
their involvement.

ARCHITECT, SEATTLE, 1932–42

Trygve W. and Katherine Buschmann residence
    project, ca. 1932–34
Unidentified site facing Lake Washington
Seattle
Unbuilt

Paramount Securities alterations project, 1935
932 13th Avenue
Seattle
Unbuilt

Glenn and Helen Borgendale residence project, 1936
Broadmoor (unidentified site)
Seattle
Unbuilt

Karl and Emita Krueger residence project, 1936–37
Greendale and North Faring Road
Los Angeles, California
Unbuilt

Julian and Constance Willcox residence, 1936–37
Tekiu Point (on Hood Canal)
Seabeck
Site alterations/Native American elements removed

Ernest and Anne Gayler residence, 1937–41, 1945–46
Nellita Point (on Hood Canal)
Seabeck
Enlarged/minor alterations

Noble and Janet Hoggson residence, 1937–38
The Highlands
Addition/minor alterations

Julian and Constance Willcox residence gatehouse,
    1939
Tekiu Point (on Hood Canal)
Seabeck

Unidentified residence(s), 1941–42
Phoenix, Arizona (probably)
Unverified

ARCHITECT (PARTNER), WITH WILLIAM J. BAIN,
BAIN AND PRIES, SEATTLE, 1941

Milton and Helen Joseph residence project, 1941
W. Howe Street
Seattle
Unbuilt

George W. Coplen apartment complex project, 1941
Norman Street and Lakeside Avenue
Seattle
Unbuilt

James and Marion Scripps residence project, 1941
Seattle (Windermere)
Unbuilt

C. O. Browne residence project, 1941
Location unknown
Unbuilt

Ethel B. (Mrs. M. B.) Hevly residence, 1941
2647 40th Avenue W.
Seattle
Altered

Lester H. and Rita Stiffler residence, 1941
5143 Laurelcrest Lane N.E.
Seattle
Minor alterations

Elizabeth G. (Mrs. John H.) Powell residence, 1941
1232 38th Avenue N. (now 38th Avenue E.)
Seattle

Joseph and Bernadine Bittner residence, 1941
Voltaire Avenue
Yakima
Unverified

Wilber and Elizabeth Coleman residence, 1941
Redmond
Unverified

Raymond and Martha Gardner residence, 1941–42
6575 Windermere Road N.E.
Seattle
Minor alterations

Randolph and Elizabeth Cunningham residence, 1941
Englewood Heights
Yakima
Unverified

Frank and Irene Judd residence, 1941–42
3440 E. Laurelhurst Drive N.E. (now 4939 Laurelcrest
    Lane N.E.)
Seattle
Altered

Clarence and Leah Terry residence, 1941–42
3850 51st Avenue N.E.
Seattle

Mr. and Mrs. J. R. Cunningham residence, 1941
Enumclaw
Unverified

Grace E. (Mrs. Julius C.) Lang residence alterations,
    1941
1100 22nd Avenue N. (now 22nd Avenue E.)
Seattle
Unverified

Harold and Beulah Nichols residence, kitchen
    alterations, 1941
4827 Beach Drive
Seattle
Unverified

National Grocery Company warehouse building,
    1941–42
Anchorage, Alaska
Unverified

Frank H. Jr. and Alice Hogue residence, 1941–42
3949 Surber Drive
Seattle
Altered

George and Mary Waterman residence, 1941–42
2233 Sunset Avenue S.W.
Seattle

Harold K. and Evelyn Wasson residence, 1941–42
3646 42nd Avenue W.
Seattle

L. N. Reichmann residence, 1941–42
Mukilteo
Unverified

Otto B. and Myrtle Gufler residence, 1941–42
1931 Blenheim Drive E.
Seattle
Altered

Tradewell Modern Food Stores (store building for D. R. Bain), 1941–42
104th Avenue N.E.
Bellevue
Destroyed

Morris and Wyoma Moulton residence, 1941–42
Mercer Island, Washington
Unverified

Wellwood and Jean Beall residence, 1941–42
Medina
Unverified

Herbert and Dorothy Bryant residence, 1941–42
1304 Lexington Way E.
Seattle

George Francis Store Building addition, 1941–42
Pacific Avenue at 4th Street
Bremerton
Unverified

Joe D. Green residence project, 1941–42
Windermere Road N.E.
Seattle
Unbuilt

Josephine A. Troxell residence project, 1941–42
Bayard Avenue
Seattle
Unbuilt

Charles and Margaret Callahan residence, 1941–42
Maplewild Avenue
Burien, Washington
Unverified

Ann E. Murphy residence, 1941–42
Hunt's Point, Washington
Unverified

Robert and Constance Wilson residence alterations (fire repair), 1941–42
4315 Semple Street
Seattle
Unverified

Mr. and Mrs. Donn F. Lawwill residence, 1941–42
Bel-Aire Avenue
Aberdeen
Unverified

Harry W. and Lenore Gilbert residence project, 1941–42
Mercer Island
Unbuilt

Julius and Jean Weber residence project, 1941
Seattle
Unbuilt

UNDATED, UNBUILT BAIN AND PRIES PROJECTS FOR WHICH DRAWINGS (OR SLIDES OF DRAWINGS) SURVIVE

Taxi Office
8th Avenue
Seattle

Chester R. and Irma Storaasli residence alterations project
Mercer Island

Cecil and Leona Jenks residence project, ca. 1941
4305 E. 38th Street
Seattle

S. L. Savidge Company (auto dealers) offices, 1941
1401 Broadway
Seattle

ARCHITECT, SEATTLE, 1942–58

Movie theater project, ca. 1945–46
Los Angeles
Unbuilt
Pries served as design architect for B. Marcus Priteca

Richard Jr. and Ruth Lea weekend residence, 1945–46
2200 Davis Bay Road
Lopez Island
Minor alterations

Delta Sigma Phi Fraternity House project, ca. 1946
Seattle
Unbuilt

Mrs. Arthur (Julia Flett) Morris residence, 1947–48
3704 48th Avenue N.E.
Seattle
Minor alterations

Lionel H. Pries residence, 1947–48
3132 W. Laurelhurst Drive N.E.
Seattle
Altered

Julian and Marajane Barksdale residence, 1948–49,
    1954–55
13226 42nd Avenue N.E.
Seattle

Stephen and Harriette Lea weekend residence,
    1949–51, 1963
29807 Highway 525
Coupeville
Altered

Craftsman Press office interiors, ca. 1946–52
2030 Westlake Avenue
Seattle
Destroyed

Charles and Mildred Gates residence, 1950–51
5315 148th Avenue S.E. (Hilltop community)
Bellevue
Altered

Legend Room (restaurant), 1950–51
Northgate Shopping Center
Seattle
Destroyed
*Pries served as design architect for John Graham and
    Company*

Ginkgo Petrified Forest Museum, 1952–53
Ginkgo State Park
Vantage
Altered
*Pries was responsible for exterior and interior decorative
    features (destroyed)*

Stephen and Harriette Lea caretaker residence, 1953
29807 Highway 525
Coupeville
Destroyed

Alonzo W. and Margaret I. Robertson residence,
    1955–56
9529 Lake Washington Boulevard
Bellevue
Minor alterations

Richard Jr. and Ruth Lea residence remodeling/
    addition, 1957–58
230 40th Avenue E.
Seattle
Destroyed

Craftsman Press conference room, ca. 1957–58
2030 Westlake Avenue
Seattle
Destroyed

DRAFTSMAN, OFFICE OF DURHAM, ANDERSON AND
FREED, SEATTLE, 1958–59

Faith Lutheran Church, 1958–59
2750 McLeod Road
Bellingham
*Pries designed interior features, including mosaic figure
    of risen Christ, now in storage*

Queen Anne Lutheran Church, 1958–59
2400 8th Avenue W.
Seattle
*Pries designed details and interior elements, including
    altar table*

Seattle First National Bank, International Branch,
    1958–60
525 S. Jackson Street
Seattle
Pries designed metal screen and other decorative features

DRAFTSMAN, OFFICE OF JOHN GRAHAM
AND COMPANY, SEATTLE, 1959–63

Ala Moana Center (shopping center), 1958–60
Honolulu, Hawaii
Altered
Pries worked on finishes and landscape design

College Grove Shopping Center, 1959–60
San Diego, California
Altered
Pries worked on landscape design and exterior features

Ilikai (co-op apartments), 1960–62
Honolulu, Hawaii
Altered
Pries was a member of the project team

Channing House (retirement home), 1960–62
850 Webster Street
Palo Alto, California
Pries was a member of the project team

Washington Junior High School (now Washington
    Middle School), 1960–63
2101 S. Jackson Street
Seattle
Pries was a member of the project team

Space Needle, 1960–62
Century 21 (Seattle World's Fair)
Seattle
Altered
Pries worked on interior finishes and colors

Chinook Center addition project (shopping center),
    1961–62
Calgary, Alberta
Unbuilt
Pries served as project architect

ARCHITECT, SEATTLE, 1960–68

Robert Winskill residence, 1960–61, 1965
50 Madrone Park Circle
Mill Valley, California
Altered

Henry and Marjorie Anderson residence remodeling,
    ca. 1960–66
1115 N. I Street
Aberdeen, Washington
Altered

Max and Helen Gurvich residence, 1964–65
3006 Webster Point Road N.E.
Seattle

William G. Reed residence (Graysmarsh) alterations,
    1967
Reed estate, near Sequim

Gamekeeper's watching residence, 1967–68
Reed estate, near Sequim
Destroyed

Duane Shipman residence addition and alterations,
    1968
4011 45th Avenue N.E.
Seattle
Altered

MAJOR ARCHIVAL SOURCES

THE REPOSITORIES LISTED BELOW HOLD SIGNIFICANT collections of original materials related to Lionel Pries. A few Pries letters are held in other locations as indicated in the Notes in the present volume.

PRIES COLLECTION, SPECIAL COLLECTIONS DIVISION, UNIVERSITY OF WASHINGTON LIBRARIES, SEATTLE

The primary collection of material related to Lionel Pries, found at the Special Collections Division, University of Washington Libraries, includes materials gathered by Victor Steinbrueck about 1978, a large number of items donated by Robert Winskill in the mid-1990s, and a selection of Pries's student work donated by Keith Kolb about 2005. The Pries Collection holds four types of documents:

(1) personal papers (baptismal certificate, diplomas, military papers, and passports; personal resumes; travel diary from his 1922–23 European trip; typescript of suggestions for those intending to travel in Europe; typescripts of Monday Club lectures);

(2) drawings and paintings (a selection of Pries's student projects; about ninety drawings and paintings from his 1922–23 European trip; the "Pries scrapbook," primarily including sketches and watercolors for architectural projects from 1923 to 1928; a small number of loose sketches and watercolors from 1923 to the late 1930s; measured drawings made in Mexico; a selection of drypoint prints; a few drawings and renderings from his professional practice; and working drawings for the Pries residence and the Winskill residence);

(3) photographs (a small selection of personal photographs; photographs of some of his architectural works; and five small photo albums, primarily photos taken in Mexico and in Europe);

(4) selected books from Pries's library (more than twenty with original Pries paintings or drawings).

As of mid-2007, the Pries Collection had not been completely catalogued so was not yet readily available to visiting scholars.

ARCHITECTURE DEPARTMENT ARCHIVES, SPECIAL COLLECTIONS DIVISION, UNIVERSITY OF WASHINGTON LIBRARIES, SEATTLE; AND ARCHITECTURE DEPARTMENT ARCHIVES, DEPARTMENT OF ARCHITECTURE, UNIVERSITY OF WASHINGTON, SEATTLE

Drawings by students in the Department of Architecture, including many projects from classes taught by Lionel Pries in the years 1928 to 1958, are housed at the Special Collections Division, University of Washington Libraries, and at the University of Washington Department of Architecture. Roughly 1,000 drawings, including all surviving student projects from 1914 to 1947 and watercolor projects on paper from 1947 to 1960, were transferred to the Special Collections Division of the University of Washington Libraries between January and March 2006. This collection includes studio projects, sketch problems, and a selection of projects from Pries's "History of Architectural Ornament" class. In mid-2006, staff at Special Collections began conserving and cataloging the drawings; the Architecture Archives Collection will likely be available for limited access in 2008. Drawings by students in the Department of Architecture from the years after 1947 (primarily drawings on illustration board for the years 1947 to 1980), are housed in the Department's archives room in Architecture Hall. As this collection is not staffed, access is very limited at the present time.

COLLEGE OF ENVIRONMENTAL DESIGN ARCHIVES, UNIVERSITY OF CALIFORNIA, BERKELEY

Records of the University of California architecture program in the years 1916–20 (when Pries was enrolled) include multiple scrapbooks of small blueprints of drawings of student projects, a list of senior problems and programs for some of these problems, minute books of the student association, albums of photographs of students and faculty, and two original drawings by Pries.

NBBJ ARCHIVES, NBBJ, SEATTLE

Microfiche of construction drawings (working drawings) for projects of William J. Bain's professional practice, including his partnerships with Lionel Pries in 1928–31 and 1941, are retained in the NBBJ Archives.

SEATTLE ART MUSEUM, SEATTLE

The Museum collection includes three Pries drypoint prints and one Pries watercolor. The Museum also owns two six-panel screens that were once part of Pries's collection of Japanese art objects.

CALIFORNIA ACADEMY OF SCIENCES, SAN FRANCISCO

The Carl Rietz Food Technology Collection at CAS includes many of the Peruvian pre-Columbian textiles that once belonged to Pries.

VARIOUS COLLECTIONS OF PAPERS, SPECIAL COLLECTIONS DIVISION, UNIVERSITY OF WASHINGTON LIBRARIES, UNIVERSITY OF WASHINGTON, SEATTLE

Additional records of Pries's career can be found at Special Collections Division, University of Washington Libraries, in the records of the UW Department of Architecture and the College of Architecture and Urban Planning, the records of the UW President's Office, the Gould family papers, the Victor Steinbrueck papers, and the Seattle Art Museum papers (which include records of the Art Institute of Seattle).

GENERAL BACKGROUND READING

Alofsin, Anthony. 2002. *The Struggle for Modernism: Architecture, Landscape Architecture, and City Planning at Harvard.* New York: W. W. Norton and Company.

Atkins, Gary L. 2003. *Gay Seattle: Stories of Exile and Belonging.* Seattle: University of Washington Press.

Andree, Herb, Noel Young, and Patricia Halloran. 1995. *Santa Barbara Architecture: From Spanish Colonial to Modern.* 3d ed. Santa Barbara: Capra Press.

Bain, William J., and Mildred C. Bain. 1991. *Building Together: A Memoir of Our Lives in Seattle.* Seattle: Beckett Publishing Company.

Booth, T. William, and William H. Wilson. 1995. *Carl F. Gould: A Life in Architecture and the Arts.* Seattle and London: University of Washington Press.

Born, Esther. 1937. *The New Architecture in Mexico.* New York: Architectural Record/William Morrow and Company.

Buckner, Cory, A. 2002. *Quincy Jones.* London and New York: Phaidon.

Burian, Edward R., ed. 1997. *Modernity and the Architecture of Mexico.* Austin: University of Texas Press.

Charlot, Jean. 1963. *The Mexican Mural Renaissance, 1920–1925.* New Haven and London: Yale University Press.

Conkelton, Sheryl. 1999. *What It Meant to be Modern: Seattle Art at Mid-Century.* Seattle: Henry Art Gallery.

———, and Laura Landau. 2003. *Northwest Mythologies: The Interactions of Mark Tobey, Morris Graves, Kenneth Callahan, and Guy Anderson.* Tacoma: Tacoma Art Museum; Seattle and London: University of Washington Press.

Delpar, Helen. 1992. *The Enormous Vogue of Things Mexican: Cultural Relations between the United States and Mexico, 1920-1935.* Tuscaloosa and London: University of Alabama Press.

Freudenheim, Leslie Mandelson, and Elizabeth Sacks Sussman. 1974. *Building with Nature: Roots of the San Francisco Bay Region Tradition.* Santa Barbara and Salt Lake City: Peregrine Smith.

Gebhard, David. 1992. *Lutah Maria Riggs: A Woman in Architecture, 1921–1980.* Santa Barbara: Capra Press and Santa Barbara Museum of Art.

Harbeson, John F. 1926. *The Study of Architectural Design with Special Reference to the Program of the Beaux-Arts Institute of Design.* New York: Pencil Points Press.

Henderson, Justen. 2000. *Roland Terry: Master Northwest Architect.* Seattle: University of Washington Press.

Hildebrand, Grant, and T. William Booth. 2004. *A Thriving Modernism: The Houses of Wendell Lovett and Arne Bystrom*. Seattle: University of Washington Press.

Johnston, Norman J. 1991. *The College of Architecture and Urban Planning, Seventy-Five Years at the University of Washington: A Personal View*. Seattle: University of Washington College of Architecture and Urban Planning.

——. 1995. *The Fountain and the Mountain: The University of Washington Campus 1895–1995*. Woodinville, Wash.: Documentary Book Publishers. (2d ed. Seattle: University of Washington, 2003).

Kingsbury, Martha. 1972. *Art of the Thirties: The Pacific Northwest*. Seattle: University of Washington Press for the Henry Art Gallery.

Kostof, Spiro, ed. 1977. *The Architect: Chapters in the History of the Profession*. New York: Oxford University Press.

Littleton, Taylor D. 2000. *The Color of Silver: William Spratling, His Life and Art*. Baton Rouge: Louisiana State University Press.

Mark, Joan. 2000. *The Silver Gringo: William Spratling and Taxco*. Albuquerque: University of New Mexico Press.

Morrill, Penny C. 2002. *William Spratling and the Mexican Silver Renaissance: Maestros de Plata*. New York: Harry N. Abrams; San Antonio: San Antonio Museum of Art.

Ochsner, Jeffrey Karl, ed. 1994. *Shaping Seattle Architecture: A Historical Guide to the Architects*. Seattle: University of Washington Press, with AIA Seattle. (Rev. paperback ed. 1998).

Oles, James, ed. 1993. *South of the Border: Mexico in the American Imagination 1914–1947*. Washington, D.C.: Smithsonian Institution Press; New Haven: Yale University Art Gallery.

Roseman, Janet Lynn, et al. 1991. *Gump's since 1861: A San Francisco Legend*. San Francisco: Chronicle Books.

Smith, Clive Bamford. 1967. *Builders in the Sun: Five Mexican Architects*. New York: Architectural Book Publishing.

Spratling, William. 1967. *File on Spratling: An Autobiography*. Boston: Little, Brown and Company.

Starr, Kevin. 1973. *Americans and the California Dream, 1850-1915*. New York: Oxford University Press.

Streatfield, David C. 1994. *California Gardens: Creating a New Eden*. New York: Abbeville Publishers.

Trapp, Kenneth R., ed. 1993. *The Arts and Crafts Movement in California: Living the Good Life*. Oakland: Oakland Museum; New York: Abbeville Publishers.

White, Theo B., 1973. *Paul Philippe Cret: Architect and Teacher*. Philadelphia: Art Alliance Press.

Wilson, Carol Green. 1949. *Gump's Treasure Trade: A Story of San Francisco*. New York: HarperCollins/ T. Y. Crowell Company.

Winter, Robert, ed. 1997. *Toward a Simpler Way of Life: The Arts and Crafts Architects of California*. Berkeley: Norfleet Press of University of California Press.

Woodbridge, Sally B., and Roger Montgomery. 1980. *A Guide to Architecture in Washington State: An Environmental Perspective*. Seattle: University of Washington Press.

Yamasaki, Minoru. 1979. *A Life in Architecture*. New York: Weatherhill.

INDEX

Note: Page numbers in boldface indicate illustrations. (Illustrations that fall on pages with related text are not indexed separately from the text.) Projects listed under Pries's various architectural practices and under Bain and Pries are generally those addressed in the text; for a complete list of Pries projects, see "Buildings and Projects," pp. 369–79.

Architectural works are in Seattle unless otherwise noted. Buildings and projects by Lionel Pries (or by Bain and Pries) located outside Seattle are indexed by location as well as by name.

The author and publisher gratefully acknowledge
the following individuals and organizations for
generously supporting publication of *Lionel H. Pries,
Architect, Artist, Educator.*

N. Sue Alden

Dennis A. Andersen

Fred Bassetti

Ronald R. Burke

Ronald D. Childers and Richard M. Proctor

Edward Duthweiler

The C. R. Foss Living Trust

The Graham Foundation for Advanced Studies
    in the Fine Arts

The Max and Helen Gurvich Advised Fund
    at The Seattle Foundation

Nanhee and William Hahn

Norman Johnston and Jane Hastings

Johnston-Hastings Endowment,
    College of Architecture and Urban Planning,
    University of Washington

Keith R. Kolb

Alan Liddle

Bryant Milliman

Margaret Morrison

Robert Mosher

Jon A. Oien

Victoria Reed

University of Washington Architecture Publications
    Fund

Barry and Louise Upson